D1084319

Manuel de Falla

His Life and Music

Nancy Lee Harper

The Scarecrow Press, Inc.
Lanham, Maryland, and Oxford
2005

SCARECROW PRESS, INC.

Published in the United States of America
by Scarecrow Press, Inc.
A wholly owned subsidiary of
The Rowman & Littlefield Publishing Group, Inc.
4501 Forbes Boulevard, Suite 200, Lanham, Maryland 20706
www.scarecrowpress.com

PO Box 317
Oxford
OX2 9RU, UK

Copyright © 2005 by Nancy Lee Harper

British Library Cataloguing in Publication Information Available

Library of Congress Cataloging-in-Publication Data

Harper, Nancy Lee.
  Manuel de Falla : his life and music / Nancy Lee Harper.
    p. cm.
  Includes bibliographical references and index.
  ISBN 0-8108-5417-1 (hardcover : alk. paper)
  1. Falla, Manuel de, 1876–1946. 2. Composers—Spain—Biography. I. Title.

ML410.F215H33 2005
780'.92—dc22

2004024260

♾™ The paper used in this publication meets the minimum requirements of
American National Statndard for Information Sciences—Permanence of
Paper for Printed Library Materials, ANSI/NISO Z39.48-1992.
Manufactured in the United States of America.

To Barry

Contents

v

Credits

All photographs, with the exception of Pablo Picasso's sketch of the set design for *The Three-Cornered Hat*, © 2001 Estate of Pablo Picasso/ Artist Rights Society (ARS), New York, belong to the Archivo Manuel de Falla (AMF), Granada, Spain, and have been used with their kind permission.

All printed musical examples have also been used with the kind permission of the AMF, Granada; Chester Music Edition; and Manuel de Falla Editions (MFE).

Gratitude is extended to the AMF for providing some unpublished correspondence, from which some excerpts appear.

Portions of chapter 15 were used with authorization of the University of Melbourne's (Australia) musicological magazine, *Context*.

All quotes from *On Music and Musicians* are also used with the very generous authorization of Marion Boyars Publishers.

David Dubal, professor of piano literature at the Juilliard School in New York, also granted permission to quote from George Copeland's unpublished autobiography.

Musical Examples and Tables

Chapter 12: From Folksong to Plainchant: Musical Borrowings and the Transformation of Manuel de Falla's Musical Nationalism in the 1920s

Chapter 15: Manuel de Falla's Personal Library and Insights into the Composer's Annotations

Chapter 16: Youthful Period (1896–1904)

Titles of Musical Works

(Spanish-French-Latin-English)

This list is ordered by genre and according to the catalogue numbers given in the *Catalogo de obras de Manuel de Falla* (Catalogue of Works by Manuel de Falla) by Antonio Gallego, Ministerio de Cultura, Dirección General de Bellas Artes y Archivos (Madrid, 1987). The official Catalogue number appears as a Roman numeral, with more than one number appearing when Falla made a substantial revision or transcription of the work. Only the modern Spanish or French titles have been translated, leaving the Latin or old Spanish in their original form. Not all works were completed by Falla, nor are extant. Not all are cataloged. Some incomplete projects are not included.

THEATRICAL WORKS

1. *El conde de Villamediana* (I)—The Count of Villamediana.
2. *La Juana y la Petra, o La casa de Tócame Roque* (XVII)—Joana and Petra or the House of Tócame Roque.
3. *Los amores de la Inés* (XXVI)—The Loves of Inés.
4. *Limosna de amor* (XXVII)—Alms of Love.
5. *El cornetín de ordenes* (XXXI)—The Cornet of Orders.
6. *La cruz de Malta* (XXXII)—The Cross of Malta.
7. *Prisionero de guerra* (XXXIII)—Prisoner of War.
8. *La vida breve* (XXXV, XXXIX)—The Short Life.
9. *El amor brujo* (XLIV, XLV, XLVIII, LI, LXVIII, LXIX)—Love Bewitched.

10. *El corregidor y la molinera* (L) (revised as *El sombrero de tres picos*) (LIII, LVIII, LIX, LX)—The Magistrate and the Miller's Wife.
11. *Fuego fatuo* (LII)—Foolish Fire.
12. *El retablo de Maese Pedro* (LXV)—Master Peter's Puppet Theater.
13. *Atlántida* (CII)—Atlantis.

SYMPHONIC WORKS

14. *Noches en los jardines de España* (XLIX)—Nights in the Gardens of Spain.
15. *Homenajes, Suite* (LXXXVI)—Homages, Suite.

VOCAL WORKS

16. *Preludios ("Madre, todas las noches")* (XVI)—Preludes ("Mother, every night").
17. *Rima ("Olas gigantes")* (XIX)—Rhyme—("Giant Waves").
18. *¡Dios mío, qué solos se quedan los muertos!* (XX)—My God, how alone remain the dead!
19. *Tus ojillos negros, canción andaluza* (XXVIII)—Your Little Black Eyes, Andalusian Song.
20. *Cantares de Nochebuena* (XXXIV)—Christmas Eve Song Cycle.
21. *Con afectos de jubilo y gozo* (XXXVI)—With Affects of Joy and Enjoyment.
22. *Trois mélodies* (XXXVIII)—Three Melodies.
23. *Siete canciones populares españolas* (XL)—Seven Popular Spanish Songs.
24. *Oración de las madres que tienen a sus hijos en brazos* (XLII)—Prayer of the Mothers Who Hold Their Children in Their Arms.
25. *El pan de Ronda que sabe a verdad* (XLVII)—The Bread of Ronda That Knows the Truth.
26. *Psyché* (LXVII)—Psyché.
27. *Soneto a Córdoba de Luis de Góngora* (LXXII)—Sonnet to Córdoba of Luis de Góngora.
28. *Jesus ait* (LXXVII).
29. *Balada de Mallorca* (LXXVIII)—Ballade of Mallorca.
30. *Invocatio ad individuam Trinitatem* (LXXXII).

CHAMBER MUSIC AND INSTRUMENTAL WORKS

31. *Melodía para violonchelo y piano* (IV)—Melody for Violoncello and Piano.
32. *Romanza para violonchelo y piano* (VI)—Romance for Violoncello and Piano.
33. *[Pieza para violonchelo y piano en do mayor]* (VII)—Piece for Violoncello and Piano in C Major.
34. *Cuarteto en sol* (VIII)—Quartet in G.
35. *Mireya (poema) "Canto V"* (IX, X)—Mireya, 5th Song.
36. *Serenata andaluza* (violino y piano) (XII)—Andalusian Serenade (violin and piano).
37. *Movimento para cuarteto de cordas* (XXX)—Movement for String Quartet.
38. *Homenaje, Pièce de guitare écrite pour "Le tombeau de Claude Debussy"* (LVI, LVII)—Homage, Guitar Piece Written for "The Tomb of Claude Debussy."
39. *Fanfare pour une fête* (LXI)—Fanfare for a Festival.
40. *Concerto per clavicembalo (o pianoforte), flauto, oboe, clarineto, violino e violoncello* (LXXI)—Concerto for Harpsichord (or Piano), Flute, Oboe, Clarinet, Violin and Violoncello.
41. *Fanfare sobre el nombre de Arbós* (LXXX)—Fanfare on the Name of Arbós.

WORKS FOR PIANO

42. *Gavotte et Musette* (II)—Gavotte and Musette.
43. *Nocturno* (III)—Nocturne.
44. *Scherzo (en do menor)* (V)—Scherzo.
45. *Mazurca en do menor* (XI)—Mazurka.
46. *Serenata andaluza* (XIII)—Andalusian Serenade.
47. *Pascale Torero* (XVIII)—Pascale Torero.
48. *Canción* (XIV)—Song.
49. *Vals capricho* (XV)—Capricious Waltz.
50. *Cortejo de gnomos* (XXI)—Procession of the Gnomes.
51. *Serenata* (XXII)—Serenade.
52. *Segunda serenata andaluza* (XXIII)—Second Andalusian Serenade.
53. *Suite fantástica* (XXIV)—Fantastic Suite.
54. *[Pieza para piano en mi mayor]* (XXV)—Piano Piece in E Major.
55. *Allegro de concierto* (XXIX)—Concert Allegro.

56. *Pièces espagnoles, Cuatro piezas españolas* (XXXVII)—Spanish Pieces, Four Spanish Pieces.
57. *Fantasía bætica* (LV)—Betic Fantasy.
58. *Canto de los remeros del Volga (del cancionero musical ruso)* (LXII)—Song of the Volga Boatmen (from the Russian Musical Songbook).
59. *Pour le tombeau de Paul Dukas* (LXXXIII)—For the Tomb of Paul Dukas.

INCIDENTAL MUSIC

60. *Soleá* (XLI).
61. *Amanacer* (XLIII)—Daybreak.
62. *Otelo [tragedia de una noche de verano?]* (XLVI)—Otello [A Summer Night's Tragedy?].
63. *El corazón ciego* (LIV)—The Blind Heart.
64. *Españoleta* (LXIII)—Ancient Spanish Dance.
65. *Misterio de los reyes magos* (LXIV)—Mystery of the Wise Men.
66. *El gran teatro del mundo* (LXXIII)—The Great Theater of the World.
67. *La vuelta de Egipto* (LXXXI)—The Flight from Egypt.
68. *Comedia famosa de la Moça de Cántaro*—(possible collaboration of Falla). Famous Comedy of the Girl from Cántaro.

ARRANGEMENTS OR ORCHESTRATIONS OF WORKS BY OTHER COMPOSERS

69. *Obertura de "El barbero de Sevilla"* (Rossini) (LXX)—Overture from "The Barber of Seville" (Rossini).
70. *Prélude à l'après-midi d'un faune* (Debussy) (Not listed in AMF Catalogue, considered here as CIII)—Prelude to the Afternoon of a Faune.
71. *Dos Preludios—Preludio, no.1* (Adolfo Salazar) (LXVI)—Two Preludes—Prelude, no. 1 (Adolfo Salazar).
72. *Himno marcial* (Pedrell) (LXXXV)—Military Hymn (Pedrell).
73. *Canción de la Estrella* (*Los Pirenos* de Pedrell) (CI)—Song of the Star (*The Pyrenees* by Pedrell).
74. "La morte de Giovana" (*Los Pirenos* de Pedrell)—Giovana's Death (*The Pyrenees* by Pedrell).

75. "I Guinocchi" (*Los Pirenos* de Pedrell).
76. *Romance de Don Joan y Don Ramón* (Pedrell) (C)—Ballad of Don Joan and Don Ramón (Pedrell).
77. *Glosa* (Pedrell).

EXPRESSIVE VERSIONS

78. *Duo seraphim clamabant (in festo S. S. Trinitatis)* (*Tomás Luis de Victoria*) (LXXIV).
79. *Sanctus* (T. L. de Victoria) (LXXV).
80. *Ave María* (Tomás Luis de Victoria) (LXXVI).
81. *L'Amfiparnaso* (Horatio Vecchi) (LXXIX).
82. *Officium hebdomadae sanctae,* (T. L. de Victoria) (LXXXIV).
83. *Emendemus in melius* (C. de Morales) (LXXXVII).
84. *Madrigal: Prado verde y florid* (F. Guerrero) (LXXXVIII)— Madrigal: Green and Flowered Meadow.
85. *Romance de Granada (Qué es de ti, desconsolado)* (J. del Encina) (LXXXIX).
86. *Tan buen ganadico* (J. del Encina) (XC).
87. *¡Ora, sus!* (Escobar) (XCI).
88. *O magnum mysterium (In circuncisione Domine)* (T. L. de Victoria) (XCII).
89. *Tenebrae factae sunt (Responsorium V)* (T. L. de Victoria) (XCIII).
90. *Miserere mei Deus, Salmo 50* (T. L. de Victoria) (XCIV).
91. *Vexilla regis* (T. L. de Victoria) (XCV).
92. *In festo Sancti Jacobi (O lux et decus hispaniae)* (T. L. Victoria) (XCVI).
93. *Benedictus* (de la Misa *"Vidi Speciosam"* de T. L. de Victoria) (XCVII).
94. *Gloria* (de la Misa *"Vidi Speciosam"* de T. L. de Victoria) (XCVIII).
95. *Glorya al Senyor* (Pedrell) (XCIX)—Glory to the Father (Pedrell).

Abbreviations and Useful Addresses

ABBREVIATIONS

A	Alto (voice)
A.B.C.	Madrid newspaper, founded in 1905 by Torcuato Luca de Tena
Accomp.	Accompaniment
AMF	Manuel de Falla Archive (Archivo Manuel de Falla)
Ant.	Anticipation
Ap.	April
Appog.	Appoggiatura
Art. Cit.	Article cited
Aug.	August
Autogr.	Autograph
AV	Audiovisual
B	Bass (voice)
B. Cl.	Bass clarinet
Bib.	Bibliography
Bull.	Bulletin
BWV	*Bach Werke Verzeichnis* (Catalogue of J. S. Bach's Works)
©	Copyright
C.A.	Cor anglais (English horn)
Ca	*circa*
Cast.	Castanets

Cb.	Contra-bass
CD	Compact Disc
Cel.	Celesta
Cfg.	Contra-fagot (Bass bassoon)
CH	Chester Music
Chap.	Chapter
Choregr.	Choreography
Cie	Cie. (Company—theatre)
Clarinet	
Coll.	Collection
CSIC	Consejo Superior de Investigaciones Cientificas
	(Superior Council of Scientific Investigation)
Cymb.	Cymbals
D	Discography
D	Éditions Durand
Dec.	December
Dict.	Dictionary
Dir.	Direction
Distr.	Distribution
Doc.	Document(s)
Éch.	Échappée
Ed.	Edition
EMF	Éditions Manuel de Falla (MdF Editions) or MFE
Ens.	Ensemble
Env.	Environ
Ex.	Example
Facs.	Facsimile
FAMF	Fundación del Archivo Manuel de Falla
	(Foundation of the Manuel de Falla Archive)
Feb.	February
Fg.	Fagot (bassoon)
Fig.	Figure
Fl.	Flute
Fn.	Footnote
FPS	Fondation Paul Sacher (Paul Sacher Foundation in Basel)
Fr.	French

Glock.	Glockenspiel
Guit.	Guitar
Hpsd.	Harpsichord
Ibid.	*Ibidem*
Id.	*Idem*
IDEA	Instituto de Estudios Asturianos (Asturian Studies Institute)
Ill.	Illustrated
INAEM	Instituto Nacional de las Artes Escenicas y de la Música (National Scenic Arts and Music Institute)
Instr.	Instrument
Intro.	Introduction
Jan.	January
J.-C.	Jesus Christ
Lat.	Latin
L.D.	Laser Disk
Lyr.	Lyric
M.	Monsieur
Maj.	Major
Mar.	March
ME	Éditions Max Eschig
MGG	*Die Musik in Geschichte und Gegenwart*
Min.	Minor
Mme.	Madame
Mov.	Movement
MQ	*The Musical Quarterly*
M.Sop.	Mezzo Soprano
Ms.	Measure
Mss.	Manuscript
Mus.	Music
N.	Note
N.D.	No Date
N.L.	No Label
Nov.	November

Ob.	Oboe
OBC	Orquesta Bética de Cámara
Oct.	October
Op.	*Opus* (work)
Op. cit.	*Opus citatum* (work cited)
Orch.	Orchestra
OSP	Orchestre Symphonique de Paris (Paris Symphony Orchestra)
OSR	Orchestre de la Suisse Romande

p	*Piano* (dynamic)
p.	Page no.
pp.	Number of pages
pp	*Pianissimo*
Ped.	Pedal
Perc.	Percussion
Picc.	Piccolo
Pno.	Piano (instrument)
Polyph.	Polyphonic
Pta.	Peseta(s)
Pub.	Publisher
PUF	Presses Universitaires de France (University Presses of France)

R	G. Ricordi & Co.
Reprod.	Reproduced
Ret.	*Retard*
Rhy.	Rhythm
RIMF	*Revue Internationale de Musique Française*
RM	*La Revue Musicale*
RM	Real Musical
RTVE	Radio-Television España (Spanish Radio-TV)

S	Soprano (voice)
SAL	Éditions Salabert
SACEM	Société des Auteurs, Compositeurs et Éditeurs de Musique (Society of Authors, Composers, and Publishers of Music)
SAE	Sociedad de Autores Españoles (Society of Spanish Authors)

SATB	Soprano, Alto, Tenor, Bass
SCH	Schott Publishers
Sept.	September
SGAE	Sociedad General de Autores Españoles
SMI	Société de Musique Indépendante
	(Society of Independent Music)
SNI	Société Nationale Indépendante
	(National Independent Society)
Sop.	Soprano
St.	Saint
St.	Strings
Suppl.	Supplement
Symph.	Symphony, symphonic

T	Tenor (voice)
T.T.	Tam tam
Tabl.	Tableau
Tamb.	Tambour
Tb.	Tuba
Tb.B.	Bass tuba
Timb.	Timbale
Trans.	Translator, translation, translated
Transcr.	Transcribed, transcription
Trb.	Trombone
Trpt.	Trumpet

UME	Unión Musical Española
Univ.	University

Ver.	Version
Vib.	Vibraphone
Vla.	Viola
Vlc.	Violoncello
Vol.	Volume

Xyl.	Xylophone

W	Work

ADDRESSES

Archives

Archivo Manuel de Falla (AMF)
Centro Cultural Manuel de Falla
Paseo de los Martires s/n
18009 Granada, Spain
Telephone: +34 958 228 318
Fax: + 34 958 215 955
E-mail: archivo.falla@grx.servicom.es

Fundación Archivo Manuel de Falla (FAMF)
Bretón de los Herreros, 55, Bajo F
28003 Madrid, Spain
Tel: +34 91 442 6035
Fax: +34 91 442 6096

Publishers of Falla's Music

Chester Music (CH)
8/9 Frith Street
London W1 V 5TZ, England
www.musicsales.co.uk; music@musicsales.com

Editions Durand (D)
4-6, Place de la Bouise
75002 Paris, France
E-mail: durand-eschig@bmgintl.com

Editions Max Eschig (ME)
4-6, Place de la Bouise
75002 Paris, France
E-mail: durand-eschig@bmgintl.com

Editions Salabert (SAL)
4-6, Place de la Bouise
75002 Paris, France
E-mail: salabert@bmgintl.com

Manuel de Falla Ediciones, SL (MFE)
Bréton de los Herreros, 56—Bajo F
28003 Madrid, Spain
www.manueldefallaediciones.es;
info@manueldefallaediciones.es

Real Musical (RM)
Apartado de Correos, 27
28670 Villaviciosa de Odon
Madrid, Spain

G. Ricordi & Co. (R)
Via Berchet, 2
20121 Milano, Italy
www.ricordi.com; ricordi@ricordi.it

Schott (SCH)
Weihergarten, 5
D-55116 Mainz, Germany

Unión Musical Española, SL (UME)
Marqués de la Ensenada, 14-3°
28004 Madrid, Spain

Acknowledgments

With current musicological research into the life and works of Manuel de Falla now facilitated through the creation of the Archivo Manuel de Falla (AMF) located in Granada, Spain, various questions regarding this twentieth-century composer may be studied in more depth than ever before possible. The need for a more up-to-date and comprehensive study in English of Falla's life and works is long overdue. Falla's early biographers, such as J. B. Trend, Alexis Roland-Manuel, and Jaime Pahissa, made important contributions in their time and often with Falla's guiding hand. Also, not to be overlooked is Suzanne Demarquez's insightful biography, mostly based on Pahissa, and translated into English from the original French. And while Federico Sopeña's "definitive" Spanish biography contains numerous errors, its style of writing is oriented towards nonneophytes. Many doctoral studies too on Falla—in English, French, Spanish, German, and Italian—have been recently undertaken, such as those by Andrew Budwig, Michael Christoforidis, Yvan Nommick, Carol A. Hess, Christopher Guy Collins, Elizabeth Seitz, Anna Rita Addessi, Eckhard Weber, and Elena Torres, to list a few.[1] The high quality and results of these works have enhanced and changed existing opinions on various aspects concerning Falla. *Fallaphiles* will indeed welcome this literature.

I came to Falla through one of the members of the "Grupo de Ocho," Rodolfo Halffter. His invaluable help and materials given during my doctoral studies on his piano sonatas led me to explore the fascinating subject of Falla. Too, as a professional musician in Córdoba, Argentina, living in the suburb of Unquillo, I was not far from Falla's residence of

"Los Espinillos." These aspects doubtless have contributed to my reflection about Falla.

There can be many approaches to biographical studies. I have preferred to draw on recent studies, new editions of works, unpublished and published correspondence, catalogues from expositions, concert programs, amongst other sources, most of which are housed at the AMF. Because of specific studies on varying aspects about Falla, I decided not to present only a "life and works" type of biography, but to add yet another section. Due to Falla's intensity and multifaceted personality, I made the decision to show several aspects more in depth. Thus, this book is divided into three sections: biography, facets of Falla's life and works, and works.

The first section is ordered according to Falla's geographical stays. The second section deals with such subjects as religion, pedagogy, various influences in Falla's world, his relations with his colleagues, his musical borrowings, and his personal library, amongst others. The last section is based on Yvan Nommick's stylistic classifications from his doctoral thesis in an attempt to clarify Falla's evolutionary process. It is the first time this classification appears in a Falla biography.

Grateful appreciation goes to all of the staff at the AMF: to Yvan Nommick, musical director and marvelous researcher; to Elena García de Paredes ("Coco"), the great-niece of the composer and general director; to Concepción ("Concha") Chinchilla Puertas, immaculate archivist and assistant; to José Manuel Sanchez Pradas, for his infinite patience in scanning musical examples and photographs; and to Mariano Cano Aravaca, Antonio Bernardo Espinosa Ramírez, and María Victoria Rojas Ramos. Special thanks is given to Ana García de Paredes at the Fundación AMF in Madrid for her quick and able assistance in reproducing the photographic materials.

Appreciation is also extended to those at Scarecrow Press: to Bruce Phillips, Melissa Ray, Jessica McCleary, Jeff Wolf, Sam Grammer, and Rhonda Baker, and JCG, Robbin Gabriel, and Jessee Carter, for their invaluable assistance and patience.

Grateful thanks is also given to those magnificent authors who contributed so brilliantly and generously to the book: Michael Christoforidis, Louis Jambou, and Chris Collins. Without the help of Chris Collins and Louis Jambou, the proofing would have been much more tedious. Patrícia Lopes Bastos was of immense help in facilitating the translation of chapter 14. Other translations were done by the author, especially of the many letters that appear in *Poesía: Número monográico dedicado a Manuel de Falla, no. 36 and 37*, ed. Jorge de Perisa (Madrid:

Ministerio de Cultura, 1991) or are as yet unpublished and were provided by the AMF. I take responsibility for the inevitable errors. Generous support has also been given by Catheryn Kilgarriff at Marion Boyars Publishers, Ltd., to quote from the English translation of Falla's writings, *On Music and Musicians*, while although not complete, is the most accessible source for English language readers. This book would have been much the poorer without this rich source.

Grateful appreciation is also extended to the editors of the University of Melbourne publication, *Context,* for which much of Michael Christoforidis's article about Falla's personal library is derived, and for which I was a referee. The same heartfelt appreciation is extended to those at the *Journal of the Royal Musical Association* for the opportunity to draw upon the article, "Manuel de Falla, *L'acoustique nouvelle* and Natural Resonance: A Myth Exposed," by Chris Collins, that was published in May 2003.

Kind acknowledgment is extended to David Dubal, professor of piano literature at Juilliard School of Music, for inclusion of portions of an unpublished autobiography of pianist George Copeland.

Attention to the unpublished correspondence of Francisco Lacerda to Falla, regarding the *Atlántida* project, was drawn to me by José Bettencourt da Câmara of Lisbon.

Abbreviations should help the uninitiated reader into the musical world, while Spanish titles have received their English equivalent in parenthesis at their first appearance. All titles of Falla's works follow Antonio Gallego's official Catalogue, *Católogo de obras de Manuel de Falla* (Madrid: Ministerio de Cultura, 1987).

Beyond the sketch material at the AMF, Falla's works were consulted in various editions. These do not appear, unless in facsimile, in the bibliography.

Appreciation must also be extended to the Universidade de Aveiro, Portugal, and the research unit (UnICA) headed by Armando Jorge Oliveira and Fernando Ramos for financial support of some of this project. Tânia Costa too was indispensable in her technological assistance, as was Rosemary Smith Mountain.

Last and certainly not least goes a loving "thank you" to my writer-husband, Barron, who, in spite of his difficult illness, gave me immense support and help with many details and in so many ways.

NOTE

1. See the bibliography.

Chronology

1876 (Cádiz)
Manuel de Falla born on 23 November, at Plaza de Mina, no. 3, in Cádiz.

1878 (Cádiz)
"La Morilla's" stories, songs, and dances are impacted upon Falla's memory. Brother "Pepito" is born.

1882 (Cádiz)
Sister María del Carmen is born.

1885 (Cádiz)
Piano studies with Eloísa Galluzo, having first begun with his mother. Death of brother, "Pepito."

1886 (Cádiz)
Serious interest in music begins. Attends musical evenings at Viniegra's house. Receives his first communion of the Roman Catholic Church on 26 June. First trip to Seville.

1889 (Cádiz)
Continue his musical studies in piano with Alejandro Odero and Harmony and counterpoint with Enrique Broca. With some of his friends he creates and publishes the literary magazine, *El Burlón*. Birth of twin brothers, Servando and Germán. Death of Servando.

1890 (Cádiz)

Shows especial interest in the theater, literature, and painting. Creates another magazine, *El Cascabel*, in which he is collaborator and later director.

1894 (Cádiz)

His true vocation to become a composer is determined.

1896 (Cádiz)

Makes regular trips to Madrid in order to study piano with José Tragó at the National School of Music and Declamation (Madrid Conservatory). His family experiences serious financial trouble.

1897 (Cádiz, Madrid)

Finishes *Melodía* for 'cello and piano on 19 June, dedicated to Salvador Viniegra, whose house was the setting for many musical soirees. Falla family moves to Madrid.

1898 (Madrid)

As a "free" student of the National School of Music and Declamation in Madrid, he completes first three years of solfège and five years of piano. He composes *Scherzo* in c minor dated 9 September 1898.

1899 (Madrid)

Finishes "with honors," by unanimous decision of the jury, the seven-year course in two years at the National School of Music and Declamation in Madrid. Premières of his *Romanza* for 'cello and piano were held at the Viniegra house on 14 July 1899, followed by *Melodía* for 'cello and piano, *Cuarteto en sol, Serenata andaluza* for violin and piano, *Nocturno* at Salón-Quirell in Cádiz on 16 August. On 10 September the debut of *Mireya*, subtitled *El Ródano*, takes place at the Teatro Cómico in Cádiz.

1900 (Madrid)

Finishes *Canción* on 2 April. On 6 May debuts *Serenata andaluza*, *Vals capricho*, and *Mireya* (transcription) at the Ateneo of Madrid. In order to help the financial situation of his family he begins to give piano lessons and to compose *zarzuelas* (*La Juana y la Petra, o La casa de Tócame Roque*).

1901 (Madrid)

Finishes two piano pieces, *Cortejo de gnomos* on 4 March and *Serenata* on April 2. Works on the *zarzuelas Los amores de la Inés* and *Limosna de amor.* Meets Felipe Pedrell and begins his studies with him.

1902 (Madrid)

Debut of *Los amores de la Inés* at Madrid's Teatro Cómico on 12 April. Meets Joaquín Turina and Federico Chueca, *zarzuela* composer. The Sociedad de Autores (Society of Authors) publishes two works, *Vals capricho* and *Serenata andaluza.*

1903 (Madrid)

Composes and presents his *Allegro de concierto* to the Madrid Conservatory competition, which Enrique Granados ultimately won. The Society of Authors publishes *Tus ojillos negros* and *Nocturno.* He begins his collaboration with Amadeo Vives in three *zarzuelas, Prisionero de guerra, El cornetín de órdenes,* and *La cruz de Malta.* Revises *La casa de tócame Roque.*

1904 (Madrid)

The Royal Academy of Fine Arts of San Fernando announces a competition for a one-act Spanish opera. Falla begins work on *La vida breve* with Carlos Fernández Shaw, asking for details of Granada, the city where the plot take place and which Falla does not know, from his friend Antonio Arango. Still under Pedrell's tutelage, he also writes *Cantares de Nochebuena.* Romance is in the air when he falls in love with María Prieto Ledesma, his cousin.

1905 (Madrid)

A double prize winner, Falla takes the Ortiz Cussó prize as pianist, premiering his *Allegro de concierto* at the Madrid Ateneo on 15 May and the Academy Prize on 13 November for *La vida breve.* Father Fedriani counsels Falla in the affairs of the heart.

1906 (Madrid)

Work is begun on *Cuatro piezas españolas.* Attempts to stage *La vida breve* bear no fruit.

1907 (Madrid, Paris)

Gives concert with violinist Paul Kochansky in Bilbão on 11 January. Makes a tour of France, Germany, Belgium, and Switzerland as pianist in a pantomime company that performs A. Wormser's *L'enfant prodigue*. Encouraged by Turina, moves to Paris during the summer. Meets Ricardo Viñes on 29 September and has a decisive meeting with Albéniz at the Salón in Paris on 3 October. Also meets Dukas, Debussy, Ravel, Roland-Manuel, Florent Schmitt, and Joaquín Nin. Moves from Hotel Kleber, where Turina lived, to a pensión in the Avenida Bois de Bologne.

1908 (Paris)

Thanks to the intervention of Albéniz, Falla receives a grant from the Spanish Crown that permits him to continue living in Paris and finish his *Cuatro piezas españolas*. He makes a concert tour in Spain in Bilbao and Oviedo with violinist Antonio Fernández Bordás and cellist Víctor Mirecki. He completes *Con afectos de júbilo y gozo* on 23 March. Paul Milliet translates the libretto of *La vida breve* into French in hopes of a French debut. Falla moves back to the Hotel Kleber.

1909 (Paris)

Cuatro piezas españolas premiered by Ricardo Viñes in Paris, Salle Erard, on 27 March and published by Jacaues Durand (Durand & Fils) upon the recommendation of Dukas, Debussy, and Ravel. He begins work on *Noches en los jardines de España* and substantially revises the orchestration of *La vida breve*.

1910 (Paris)

Debut of *Trois mélodies*, on texts by Théophile Gautier, by the composer and soprano Ada Adiny-Milliet at a Paris concert of the Societé Nationale Indépendante on 4 May. *Trois mélodies* is published by Rouart, Lerolle et Cie. in Paris. Meets Georges Jean-Aubry, Joaquín Nin, Wanda Landowska, and Ignacio Zuloaga. Meets Stravinsky at Cipa Godebski's house in Paris.

1911 (Paris)

On 24 March travels to London for the first time, where he plays *Cuatro piezas españolas* and *Trois mélodies*. Receives counsels from Debussy regarding *La vida breve* in October.

1912 (Paris)

Travels to Switzerland and Italy. In Milan, he negotiates the publication of *La vida breve* with Tito Ricordi. Contends with illnesses and "religious crises." Meets Melchor Fernández Almagro de San Martín in January. Debut of *Cuatro piezas españolas* on 30 November at the sociedad Filarmónica in Madrid by Ricardo Viñes.

1913 (Paris)

Debut of *La vida breve* on 1 April at the Municipal Casino in Niza. Max Eschig in Paris publishes the score and becomes Falla's publisher. Meets the Martínez Sierra couple. On 30 December a general rehearsal of *La vida breve* is held at the Théâtre National de l'Opéra-Comique (Comic Opera) to public and critical acclaim.

1914 (Paris, Madrid)

Official debut of *La vida breve* at the Comic Opera in Paris on 7 January. He composes *Siete canciones populares españolas*. With the threat of World War I, Falla returns to live in Madrid. Debut of *La vida breve* at Madrid's Teatro de la Zarauela on 14 November. Opera project conceived on *La devoción de la cruz*. *Oración de las madres que tienen a sus hijos en brazos* dates from December 1914.

1915 (Madrid, Barcelona)

Homage concert to Falla and Turina at Madrid's Ateneo on 15 January, at which the debut of *Siete canciones populares españolas* is performed by soprano Luisa Vela and Falla at the piano. Debut of *Oración de las madres que tienen a sus hijos en brazos* on 8 February at the Ritz in Madrid with soprano Josefina Revillo and Falla in a concert of the Sociedad Nacional de Música (National Society of Music). Debut of *El amor brujo* (one-act Gypsy ballet) at Madrid's Teatro Lara on 15 April with Pastora Imperio as Candelas and conductor José Moreno Ballesteros, and Father Federico Moreno Torroba, who plays the piano part. Meets Azaña. At the end of March and beginning of April, Falla travels with María Lejárraga (Martínez Sierra) to Granada, staying at the Pensión Alhambra, and subsequently visiting Ronda, Algeciras, and Cádiz. Travels to Barcelona with the Martínez Sierras and stays there almost six months. Because he complained of the noise, Santiago Rusiñol invites him to stay at Cau Ferrat de Sitges, where Falla works intensively on Nights in the Gardens of Spain. On 23 September, Falla's sextet version of *El amor brujo* is premiered in Portugal by the José Media Villa Sextet. Finishes *El pan de*

Ronda que sabe a verdad on 18 December in Barcelona on a text of María Lejárraga and writes incidental music for *Otelo*.

1916 (Madrid)
   The concert version of *El amor brujo* is premiered at the Hotel Ritz in Madrid at a concert of the Sociedad Nacional de Música with Enrique Fernández Arbós and the Orquesta Sinfónica de Madrid on 28 March. *Noches en los jardines de España* is premiered at the Teatro Real (Madrid) on 9 April with pianist José Cubiles and conductor Enrique Fernández Arbós and the Orquesta Sinfónica de Madrid. Some of Falla's writings are published: (1) Tribute to Granados, "Enrique Granados, Evocación de su obra" (Enrique Granados, Evocation to His Work) published in *Revista Musical Hispano-Americana* in April; (2) "Introducción al estudio de la música nueva" (Introduction to New Music) in December, both in *Revista Musical Hispanoamericana*; and (3) "El gran músico de nuestro tiempo: Igor Stravinsky" (The Great Musician of Our Time, Igor Stravinsky) in the newspaper *La Tribuna* on 5 June. Published "El gran músico de nuestro tiempo: Igor" in *La Tribuna* on 5 June. Wrote the prologue to Jean-Aubry's *La música francesa contemporánea* (Contemporary French Music). Possible stay in a sanatorium in Córdoba, but not verified. Falla works on the pantomime The Magistrate and the Miller's Wife (based on the novel *The Three-Cornered Hat* of Pedro Antonio de Alarcón) with the Martínez Sierras. Makes contact with Sergei Diaghilev and the Ballets Russes, as well as Igor Stravinsky in Madrid. Travels with Diaghilev, the Ballets Russes, and dancer Leonid Massine to the south of Spain. Plays concerts in Sevilla, Cádiz, and Granada, as well as his own Nights in the Gardens of Spain on 26 June in Granada at the Palacio de Carlos V with the Sinfónica de Madrid (Madrid Symphony) under Arturo Saco del Valle.

1917 (Madrid)
   Première of *El corregidor y la molinera* at Madrid's Teatro Eslava on 7 April, with an orchestra formed by professors of the Filarmónica de Madrid (Madrid Philharmonic) conducted by Turina. On 29 April, a concert version for small orchestra of *El amor brujo* is performed by the Orquesta Sinfónica de Madrid (Madrid Symphonic Orchestra) conducted by E. Fernández Arbós in the Teatro Real (Royal Theater). Wrote the prologue to Turina's *Enciclopedia abreviada de la música* (Abbreviated Encyclopedia of Music). Published " Nuestra Música" (Our Music) in the magazine *Música* in June. During June made another trip with

Diaghilev and Massine. Attended the inauguration of a monument to Francisco de Goya at Fuendetodos on 8 October. Made a concert tour of northern Spain with soprano Aga Lahowska.

1918 (Madrid)
Busy collaborating with librettist María Martínez Sierra on the comic opera (operetta) *Fuego fatuo* (Foolish Fire). Turned down Diaghilev's offer to compose *Pulcinella*; given to Stravinsky instead (ca. 1919). On 27 April gives a lecture entitled "El arte profundo de Claude Debussy" (The Profound Art of Claude Debussy) at an homage to Debussy at the Ateneo in Madrid. The Princesse de Polignac in Paris commissions a work to be premiered in her Paris salon and Falla conceives the idea of *El retablo de maese Pedro* (Master Peter's Puppet Theater).

1919 (Madrid)
Both parents died: father on 12 February, mother on 22 July. A partial debut of the concert version of *El sombrero de tres picos* at Teatro Eslava by the Orquesta Filarmónica de Madrid and conductor Pérez Casas on 17 June. Debut of ballet *El sombrero de tres picos* on 22 July, Alhambra Theater, London, with ballerinas Massine and Karsavina and sets and costumes by Picasso. Falla's last virtuoso solo piano work is composed, the *Fantasía bœtica*, commissioned by pianist Artur Rubinstein. Opera project conceived on *La Gloria de D. Ramiro*. Visit to Granada with sister María del Carmen and the Vazquez Díaz couple for the homage given to Falla at the Centro Artístico (Artistic Center) on 15 September.

1920 (Madrid, Granada)
Debut of *Noches en los jardines de España* in Paris on 4 January with pianist J. Nin and conductor Fernández Arbós. Also in January *El sombrero de tres picos* with the Ballets Russes at the Paris Opera is a huge success. *Fantasía bœtica* is premiered in February by A. Rubinstein in New York. Through the encouragement of guitarist Ángel Barrios, Falla moves to Granada in mid-September, having made several visits during the summer in order to find a house and residing at the Pensión Carmona before settling into the house at Santa Engracia, Calle Real de la Alhambra, no. 40. *Homenaje pour le tombeau de Claude Debussy* is composed, dated 20 August, Granada. Homage concert in Cádiz in December with Falla both playing and conducting. Published his article "Claude Debussy et l'Espagne" in *La revue musicale* in December.

1921 (Granada)

Began to formulate the *Cante jondo* competition. Debut of *Homenaje a Debussy* in Paris on 24 January by Mme. M. L. Henri Casadesus, harp-lute, with the guitar debut by Miguel Llobet in a Spanish tour slightly later (AMF earliest concert program dated 13 February in Burgos). Meets important cultural and political figures such as Fernando de los Ríos, Miguel Cerón, Hermenegildo Lanz, Manuel Ángeles Ortiz, and Federico García Lorca. Travels to Paris and London in May where he performs the solo part of *Noches en los jardines de España* in London at Queen's Hall. J. & W. Chester published *El amor brujo* and *El sombrero de tres picos*. Break with the Martínez Sierras after a disagreement over the project *Don Juan de España*. Makes arrangements of two suites from *El sombrero de tres picos*. Composes *Fanfare pour une fête*, published in the first issue of *Fanfare* magazine in London in August.

1922 (Granada)

At the beginning of January, moves to his permanent Granadine house, Carmen de la Antequeruela Alta, no. 11. *Suite* no. 2 from *El sombrero de tres picos* is premiered by Pérez Casas in Madrid on 13 January. Commissioned by his diplomatic friend, Ricardo Baeza in aid of Russian refugees, composes *Canto de los remeros del Volga*. Publishes the announcement of the *Cante jondo* competition in *El Defensor de Granada*, in collaboration with Miguel Cerón and Federico García Lorca. Debut of *Homenaje a Debussy* in Paris on 2 December by E. Pujol. Eschig published *Siete canciones populares españolas* and *Noches en los jardines de España*, while Chester publishes *Fantasía bœtica*. Meets Segismundo Romero and Eduardo Torres in Sevilla during Holy Week, future collaborators in the Orquesta Bética de Cámara. Meets Wanda Landowska, who performed in concerts on 23 and 25 November, organized by the Sociedad Filarmónica at the Hotel Alhambra Palace. More illness. Pedrell dies.

1923 (Granada)

On 6 January, Falla, Hermenegildo Lanz and Federico García Lorca organize a program at Lorca's house in Granada for the Títeres de Cachiporra, giving premières of: *Misterio de los reyes magos*, (13th-century *auto scaramental)*; *Los dos habladores* (Miguel de Cervantes) and *La niña que reiga la albahaca y el príncipe preguntón* (Federico García Lorca) to Falla's arrangement of incidental music. Published "Wanda Landowska en Granada" and "Felipe Pedrell" in *La revue musicale* in

February. A concert version of *El retablo de Maese Pedro*, conducted by Falla is presented at the Teatro San Fernando, Seville, 23–24 March with the scenic version of *El retablo*, conducted by Vladimir Golschmann, in the Princesse de Polignac's salon in Paris on 25 June (costumes by Manuel Ángeles Ortiz, puppets by Hermenegildo Lanz). Tour of several European capitals in France, Belgium, Italy. Meets Ernesto Halffter in Madrid. Landowska commissions the *Concerto per clavicembalo*. Falla and Ángel Barrios are proposed for admission into the Real Academia de Bellas Artes de Granada.

1924 (Granada)

On 21 February Falla and Ángel Barrios are unanimously elected into the Real Academia de Bellas Artes de Granada. Completes *Psyché* (text by Georges Jean-Aubry). On 7 April is named Honored Academic into the Real Academia Hispano-Americana de Ciencias y Artes de Cádiz (Hispanic-American Royal Academy of Sciences and Arts). Chester publishes *El retablo de Maese Pedro*; Madrid debut is given on 28 March. The Manifest of the Orquesta Bética de Cámara is drawn up in May and its first concert takes place on 11 June at the Sevillian Teatro Llorens. Falla makes an arrangement of Debussy's *Prélude à l'après-midi d'un faune* for it, which is performed on 10 December at the Sevillian Teatro San Fernando under the baton of Ernesto Halffter.

1925 (Granada)

Psyché is premiered in Barcelona (9 February with members of the OBC at the Palau de la Música), directed by Falla, and in Paris with Mme. Alvar and Lili Laskin. Falla accepts the position as Honored Academic into the Real Academia Hispano-Americana de Ciencias y Artes de Cádiz. On 22 May the definitive version of *El amor brujo* is debuted at the Trianon-Lyrique in Paris, with dancers "La Argentina" and Vicente Escudero, scenery and costumes by Gustavo Bacarisas, and Falla as musical director. Arrangement of the *Obertura de "El barbero de Sevilla"* for the OBC made and performed on 20 November, E. Halffter conducting. On 29 November *El retablo* is given by the New York Philharmonic Symphony Orchestra with Wanda Landowska and Willem Mengelberg, conductor. Falla is named as member of the Hispanic Society of America.

1926 (Granada)

Falla participates in the homage to Luis Bagaría at the Granada Artistic Center. *El retablo de Maese Pedro* (Luis Buñuel, scenic director) is

performed in Amsterdam on 26 April with William Mengelberg conducting, and at the Festival of SIMC in Zurich on 20 June. Première of
the *Concerto* with Landowska and Falla in Barcelona on 5 November at
the Palau de la Música. For his fiftieth birthday, he receives tributes in
Seville (20 March, "Adopted Son") and Cádiz ("Favored Son"). The
idea of *Atlántida* begins to take shape.

1927 (Granada)
   8–9 February concerts of the OBC, conducted by E. Halffter and Falla
at the Coliseo Olympia in Granada. Named "adopted son" of Guadix on
28 February. Falla Festival in Barcelona on 17 March, with Falla present as well as at the Ateneo of Granada (homage to Beethoven) in April.
Debut of *Concerto* at Salle Pleyel in Paris with Falla at the piano and the
Soneto a Córdoba (written for Luís de Góngora's third centenary) with
Mme. Greslé and Wurmser-Delcourt on 14 May; London debut of *El
retablo* on 22 June in a concert dedicated to Falla, who also played the
Concerto. 27 June (postponed from 18 June due to technical problems)
debuts Falla's incidental music for Calderón de la Barca's *auto scar-
mental* entitled *El gran teatro del mundo*, organized by Ateneo of
Granada and the Junta de Damas de Honor y Mérito and presented in the
Plaza de los Aljibes of the Alhambra with Antonio Gallego Burín (artistic director), Hermenegildo Lanz (set designer), and Ángel Barrios (conductor). Falla Festival in Madrid on 5 November with debut of *Concerto*
played by Falla; homage by the city of Madrid. Chester publishes *Psyché*. Plays a homage recital of fourteen sonatas of Domenico Scarlatti on
11 December at the Ateneo in Granada.

1928 (Granada)
   Falla assumes his academic position at the Academia de Bellas Artes
in Granada. In February Federico García Lorca's magazine, *Gallo, Revista de Granada*, appears in which it is announced that a *Cancionero
popular de Granada*, under Falla's direction, will be published, but
never was. In March Falla travels to Paris to supervise a production of
El amor brujo (dancer "La Argentina; sets/costumes by Bacarisas). The
Comic Opera in Paris debuts a production of *El retablo* underwritten by
Ignacio Zuloaga. On 14 March Falla is named to the French Legion of
Honor (l'Ordre National de la Légion d'honneur). Presentations of *El
sombrero* and *El amor brujo* in Bilbao. Travels with Juan Gisbert Padró
to Italy for a concert of SIMC in Siena, where composer played his *Con-
certo* on 12 September. Eschig in Paris publishes *Concerto per clav-*

icembalo. On 29 October he is designated member of the Kungl Svenska Musikaliska Akademien Vágnar of Stockholm. Invitation to go to Buenos Aires refused; invitation extended to collaborate with the Argentine magazine *Criterio.* Health problems with iritis. Receives a visit from Ravel.

1929 (Granada)

On 9 February Falla writes to Federico García Lorca of his displeasure in the way that the poet has treated the theme of his work, *Oda al Santísimo Sacramento del Altar* (dedicated to Falla) as published in the December 1928 issue of *Revista de Occidente.* Falla refuses proposal to be admitted to the Academy of Fine Arts of San Fernando (to take Manuel Manrique de Lara's place) because of Conrado del Campo's exclusion, yet was unanimously admitted on 13 May. He never read his inaugural address. In New York, John Brande Trend publishes the first monograph about Falla. Proposed project with José María Sert to compose a pantomime (*Atlántida*) for the Universal Exposition in Seville or Barcelona.

1930 (Granada)

At the end of January, he receives a visit from Alfredo Casella, who was in Granada to give some concerts with the Trio Italiano. In June, he records the *Concerto*, as well as some songs with María Barrientos. In December he travels to Cádiz to conduct a concerto in the theater that bore his name, later visiting Sancti Petri, the site of the Pillars of Hercules, inspiration for *Atlántida.*

1931 (Granada)

Makes his last trip to London, to conduct *El retablo* for a BBC broadcast. On 14 April the Second Republic is declared in Spain. On 14 May Falla sends a telegram to the president of the Republic, Niceto Alcalá Zamora and to his friend Fernando de los Ríos (Justice Minister) asking them to take measures against the burning and looting of the churches, a "dis-evangelizing" of Spain. Voting member of the Junta Nacional de Música. Nervous state continues.

1932 (Granada)

Makes his first will in February. Conducts concert in San Sebastián on 3 September with *El retablo* and Falla's "expressive interpretations" of T. L. de Victoria. Travels to Venice with P. Segura and Andrés Segovia through Paris and Geneva. Venetian debut of a new production of *El retablo*, conducted by Falla at SIMC Festival. Returns via Barcelona where a Falla Festival is organized by the Associació de Música "da Camera" at the Palau (December 13). Oxford University Press publishes *Soneto a Córdoba*.

1933 (Palma de Mallorca, Granada)

In order to calm his frayed nerves, Falla and his sister leave for a stay in Mallorca (28 February–26 or 27 June). He composes *Balada de Mallorca* (choral piece on text by Jacint Verdaguer and music by Chopin), which the Capella Clásica debuts in Valldemosa on 21 May. Published "Notas sobre Wagner en su cincuentenario" in *Cruz y Raya* in September. Friction with his publisher, Chester, over author's rights. On 19 November votes for the first time in his life in elections in Granada. Travels to Barcelona in order to conduct his works at the Liceo. Returns to Palma de Mallorca at the beginning of December.

1934 (Palma de Mallorca, Granada)

Remains in Mallorca until 18 June. Makes a revision of *Balada de Mallorca*. Composes *Fanfare sobre el nombre de Arbós* premiered at homage concert to Fernández Arbós on 28 March at Madrid's Teatro Calderón with the Symphonic Orchestra of Madrid. Makes his expressive interpretations of *L'Amfiparnaso* (Horatio Vecchi). Initiated as a member of the French Institute. Granadine artist, José María Rodríguez-Acosta, with two of his brothers, created the Foundation Rodríguez-Acosta in memory of their parents, naming Falla, with José Ortega y Gasset, Fernando de los Ríos, José Segura Soriano, Emilio García Gómez, Alfonso García-Valdecasas, and Ramón Pérez de Roda as patrons; yet the project never was completed.

1935 (Granada)

On 10 January Falla is designated member of the music section of the Belgium Académie Royale des Sciences, des Lettres et des Beaux-Arts. On 26 January, as proposed by Paul Dukas, Falla is elected member of the musical composition section of the French Institute's Académie des Beaux-Arts, thereby occupying the seat left vacant by Edward Elgar. Break with José Bergamín on 16 February over editorial differences of the *Cruz y Raya*. Wrote the prologue to Pujol's *Escuela razonada de la guitarra*. Addendum to will made on 9 August. Composed incidental music for the *auto sacramental* of Lope de Vega's *La vuelta de Egipto* that was performed on 9 June, organized by the Universidad de Granada for the third centenary of the writer's death with collaboration of Antonio Gallego Burín (artistic director), Valentín Ruiz-Aznar (musical direction), and Hermenegildo Lanz (scenic director). Rests a few days in Lanjrón. Nervous illnesses continue. Commissioned by *La Revue Musicale* he composes *Pour le tombeau de Paul Dukas*, who died in May.

1936 (Granada)

On 28 April, pianist Joaquín Nin-Culmell debuts in Paris *Pour le tombeau de Paul Dukas*, published in *La Revue Musicale* in the May–June issue. Drafted the second part of his will, dated 4 August. García Lorca assassinated on August 19. Illness and reclusion. In November tries to help his friend Hermenegildo Lanz, after his first political detention.

1937 (Granada)

Falla's health remains delicate. The unexpected death of his friend, Pepe Segura, leads him to create a foundation to aid his widow and children. Collaborates with José María Pemán in the work *Himno marcial* for the national forces. For this, Falla arranges and adapts Pedrell's "Canto de los Almogávares" from the opera *Los Pirineos*, to Pemán's words.

1938 (Granada)

Without his prior knowledge, and by a decree given in Burgos on 1 January, Falla is named president of the Instituto de España (Spanish Institute), created by this same decree. Falla did not accept. He projected the orchestral suite, *Homenajes*, based on earlier works.

1939 (Granada, Buenos Aires)

Published "Notas sobre Ravel" in *La Revue Musicale* in March. Because of an invitation from the Fernández Montes family, Falla left for the "Huerta Grande" de la Zubia, where he spent the summer with his brother Germán and family. He worked on his expressive interpretations and the *Homenajes*. With his sister, Falla left Granada on 28 September, traveled to Barcelona, and sailed on 2 October for Buenos Aires, Argentina (a neutral country during World War II) arriving on 18 October on the boat *Neptunia* and staying a few days at the Plaza Hotel. Accompanied by Juan José Castro, conducts concerts (4, 11, 18, and 23 November) in the Teatro Colón in the Argentine capital on the twenty-fifth anniversary of the Institución Cultural Española. Debut of his suite *Homenajes*, same locale, on 18 November. Homage to Falla on 20 November at the Wagnerian

Association of Buenos Aires. In an attempt to secure his return to Spain, the French government offered him a substantial pension. Falla refused.

1940 (Villa Carlos Paz, Villa del Lago, Argentina)
   Takes up residence in a suburb of Córdoba, first in Villa Carlos Paz, then in Villa del Lago. On 30 May, conducts a concert with the Symphonic Orchestra of Córdoba in a benefit for flood victims in the capital city. Receives the Gran Cruz de la Orden Civil de Alfonso X el Sabio (Great Cross of the Civil Order of Alfonso X the Wise) on 13 July. On 8 and 15 December conducts concerts for radio "El Mundo," leaving the only recorded examples of his voice. Begins to work on expressive arrangements of works by T. L. de Victoria in anticipation of a memorial concert. Economic worries ensue from author's rights not arriving because of World War II.

1941 (Villa del Lago, Argentina)
   Health seriously deteriorates. The San Miguel studios propose a film version of several of his works. Falla envisions the possibility of *El retablo* and *La vida breve*. Revises the orchestration of several of Pedrell's works (*Canço de l'Estrella, Glorya al Senyor, Romanç de don Joan i don Ramon*) with the upcoming centenary of Pedrell's birth in mind that the Wagner Association was considering producing. Work on *Atlántida* continues.

1942 (Córdoba, Argentina)
   In November moves to his last house, "Los Espinillos," in the Alta Gracia district of Córdoba. In December travels for the last time to Buenos Aires to conduct some concerts for Radio "El Mundo."

1943 (Córdoba, Argentina)
   Work on *Atlántida* continues, in spite of health problems, especially iritis, that does not allow him to travel for several months. A proposal to publish some of his expressive interpretations of Victoria is made to Ricordi Americana, even though the project is never finalized. In November, Metro Goldwyn Mayer proposes to stage and film a two-piano version of the "Ritual Fire Dance" with pianists José and Amparo Iturbi. Falla accepts this offer some months later.

1944 (Córdoba, Argentina)
   Considers the possibility of giving a concert version of parts of *Atlántida*. Jaime Pahissa, Catalan composer exiled in Buenos Aires, visits Falla

several times for the purpose of collecting data for his future book, *Vida y obra de Manuel de Falla* (Life and Works of Manuel de Falla). Falla works on the preliminary scenes of the the film version of *El retablo*.

1945 (Córdoba, Argentina)
At the beginning of the year is nominated to the advisory council of the CSIC. Rafael Alberti visits Falla in October. On 10 October Falla is named corresponding academic for the Academia Nacional de Ballas Artes de Argentina (Argentine National Academy of Fine Arts). "Falla" concerts given at the Teatro Rivera Indarte in Córdoba on 27 and 28 October. Meets Sergio de Castro. Continues to have health problems, but continues to work on *Atlántida*, beginning to transcribe the definitive version of some sections.

1946 (Córdoba, Argentina)
Continues to work on *Atlántida*, copying out the final version of the prologue in June. The last manuscript is dated 8 July. Dies of cardiac arrest in his sleep at his home in Alta Gracia on during the night of 13–14 November, nine days before his seventieth birthday. Funeral in the Córdoba Cathedral on 19 November. On 22 December his remains leave for Spain with his sister, María del Carmen.

1947 (Cádiz, Spain)
Falla's remains arrive in Cádiz on 9 January where they are laid to rest in the Cádiz Cathedral. Debut in Barcelona of *Homenajes* on 26 February.

The information contained in this chronology is based on information from several biographies, from *Poesía*, from Yvan Nommick's doctoral thesis, *Manuel de Falla: Œuvre et Évolution du langage musical*, and Concha Chinchilla's chronology in *Manuel de Falla en Granada*. For complete bibliographical references, see the bibliography.

Introduction

The extraordinary life and work of the supreme Spanish composer of the 20th century, Manuel de Falla, bear witness to a fascinating man and musician. The renovation of Spanish music in the first half of that century is unthinkable without his presence. Indeed Spain may well have remained on the periphery of European musical thought had it not been for Falla. Thus, he is quite justly considered by many to be the most outstanding Spanish composer since Spain's golden age of polyphony as represented by Tomás Luis de Victoria.

A converging point for the consolidation of nationalistic tendencies and a turning point for modernism in the Iberian peninsula, Falla was both conservative and radical—conservative in the sense that he was hugely bound to his country and to his religious beliefs; radical in that he deliberately pushed those bonds to the limit, without breaking them. In his mature life, he found himself both the object and the victim of international attention: cheered abroad, criticized at home. Politically unable to align himself with either the left (Socialists, Communists, anarchists) or the right (Carlists, Fascists, Catholics, monarchists, militarists), Falla, along with some of his fellow countrymen, intentionally or unintentionally, established loyalty to a Third Spain.[1]

The public and private images of Falla differ greatly. Artistically inclined in his youth, Falla abandoned his early literary vocational bent in favor of music. Though he was fond of saying that he felt a strong, compelling force to be a composer when he was seventeen, nevertheless, for the first time, we learn that he confessed to his piano mentor in Madrid, José Tragó, that he was considering returning to Cádiz in order to become a professor of piano.[2] And though composition did become his lifelong endeavor, Falla continued concertizing as a pianist throughout much of his adult life. His literary bent was fulfilled through his writings on music and the more than 20,000 pieces of correspondence with musicians and other leading figures, pieces with which he often took painstaking measures in order to realize their proper expression. Never in the history of Western music do we find a composer with such a prolific epistolary opus.

A life at the edge, a life of paradoxes and contradictions, Falla was ascetic by choice and did not seem to want much from the world. Yet he became the most famous Spanish composer in the 20th century. Too, his shy and sensitive nature did not keep him from seeking and enjoying the company of the world's leading composers—Debussy, Dukas, Ravel, Stravinsky, Milhaud, Albéniz, Granados, for example, and of the world's leading artists and political leaders, such as Picasso, Diaghilev and the Ballets Russes, José Ortega y Gasset, Miguel de Unamuno, Fernando de los Ríos, Federico García Lorca, Artur Rubinstein, Wanda Landowska, Andrés Segovia, the Martínez Sierras, Luis Buñuel, and Salvador Dalí, amongst others.

Falla was an unlikely hero, slight of build, modest, unpretentious, balding in his middle years, anorexic-like, generous beyond belief to others but self-effacing and self-denying in his modest personal life, loquacious on many subjects but maddeningly silent about his own creative processes. Although expressing very direct opinions about many composers and musical trends, he often remained ambiguous about his own style, preferring to leave clues for others to unravel. One such example was his denial of having incorporated literal folksongs in his compositions, leading others to think that he composed the melodies himself. However, his sketch material of the popular works is often replete with specific references to the printed sources used, including the exact page numbers. He became obsessed with the idea of renewal—the necessity to re-create and refine a work into perfection. This obsession eventually became a vicious circle from which he could not or did not want to extricate himself in order to finish his last work.

He was enormously well read and studied the latest currents of thought, often making current his latest interest. His ability to distill the essence of a style was remarkable, to the point that few suspected the great intellectual depth, thought and transformation that were behind his expressive and passionate music. His fascination with the exotic led him to explore various tonal and modal systems of expression from Moroccan scales to Indian ragas, from Gypsy chanting to oriental musings.

His deep religious beliefs led him to the mystical and mysterious. He wrote passionate, earthy music, and he wrote for the gods, his God. There was often a fine line between religion and superstition, as evidenced in his studies of the 12th century St. John of the Cross (one of the influences in *Nights in the Gardens in Spain*), or readings in the realm of magic and the supernatural (inspiration for *El amor brujo*), or by his visit to the Pillars of Hercules at Sancti Petri in search of the lost Atlantis, (taking into account Plato's reference, which some interpret today to be situated in the New World of the Bolivian altiplano), his *Atlántida*.

Falla could have been a wealthy man—indeed he was born into wealth—but he preferred to give his money and his time to others, not falling into the obliging trap that his popular works brought to him. Always true to his high principles, he once remarked that he could have written twenty *Amor brujos*,[3] yet he did not occupy himself in going after easy financial remuneration. He was not interested in composing for monetary compensation after his youthful excursions into *zarzuelas* and salon pieces. Rather, each beginning became as a new link in the evolutionary chain. If a composer such as Beethoven had insisted on similar development, his thirty-two piano sonatas might have been reduced to three.

Nor did Falla seem to have any interest in promoting a school of composition. After all, according to him, there was only one Maestro, God the Creator. Yet more than one generation felt his definite influence. Eight composers, the "Grupo de los Ocho,"[4] banded together adhering to the new aesthetic path that Falla had opened. According to Rodolfo Halffter, they never considered Falla to be an Impressionist composer even though it is well documented that he was strongly influenced by Debussy and the French school.[5]

Falla inspired the "Generación del '27" (of which the "Grupo de los Ocho" was a part)—the Gongorists—whose membership included the Spanish cultural and artistic elite. Its mission was to renew a nationalist Spanish expression by venerating Spain's golden age as epitomized by the Cordobese poet Luis de Góngora (1561–1627). Falla became its "spiritual leader." Music, he humbly acknowledged, was the medium that God had given him to make himself useful to his fellow creatures.[6] The creative energies unleashed by Generación del '27, the like of which was never repeated in the 20th century, formed the cornerstone of the movement that began with the end of the Spanish-American War (1898) and lasted until the outbreak of the Spanish Civil War (1936), a movement now referred to as Spain's silver age.

Falla was a forceful figure. To hear his voice (the only recorded example extant and taken from the "El Mundo," an Argentine radio recording in 1940)[7] is to understand his passion, strength of will and character, and unqualified devotion to a cause. As a child, he was strong-willed; as an adult he became a leader in spite of himself. The inner struggle and personal demons were known to only a few.

Shrewd regarding human nature, he was tight-lipped when it came to his own compositions. Yet he did not hesitate to vocalize his differences of opinion over artistic, religious, or political matters (for example, to García Lorca, José Bergamín, Manuel Azaña), nor to intervene on behalf of his friends or his country during the horrible injustices heaped upon them prior to the Civil War. He was devastated by their losses, his losses. Used as a political front, Falla abhorred and cried out about it. His famous scruples did not allow him to compromise. He suffered greatly, opting to leave his homeland for the New World.

After attaining worldwide acclaim—so glowing, colorful, archetypal almost—he became astonishingly (yet understandably) paralyzed with fear over the possible failure of *Atlántida*, unable or unwilling to finish this last work. Revered and visited by many important persons during his last years in Argentina, he nevertheless missed the contact with his native soil. Only in death did he return, buried in the Cádiz Cathedral, the city of his birth.

In spite of his relatively small musical output, Falla's example and musical invention remain his greatest legacies. Twentieth-century Spanish music would be unthinkably impoverished without the masterpieces of *El sombrero de tres picos, El amor brujo, Noches en los Jardines de España, Siete canciones populares españolas, El retablo de Maese Pedro, and Concerto,* at least. Fortunately for posterity, the miracle and complexity of Falla's passionate musical personality continues to be deciphered in the twenty-first century.

NOTES

1. Paul Preston, *Las tres Españas del 36* (Barcelona: Plaza & James) referred to by Carol A. Hess in the introduction of her book, *Manuel de Falla and Modernism in Spain, 1898–1936* (Chicago and London: The University of Chicago Press, 2001, 5).

2. For more details, see chapter 9.

3. Otto Mayer-Serra, "Falla's Musical Nationalism" in *The Musical Quarterly*, vol. XXIX, no. 1, January, 1943, 6, fn. 3.

4. Rodolfo and Ernesto Halffter, Salvador Bacarisse, Gustavo Pittaluga, Julián Bautista, Fernando Remacha, Juan José Mantecón, and the only female member, Rosa García Ascot.

5. "... De Falla nunca fue considerado por nuestro Grupo como un compositor impresionista." Cited by Rodolfo Halffter in *Rodolfo Halffter* (1990) by Xochiquetzal Ruiz Ortiz. México, D.F.: CENIDIM, 49.

6. "La música, dice De Falla, es el medio que Dios me há dado para hacerme útil a mis semejantes." Cited by Rodolfo Halffter in Ruiz Ortiz, *op. cit.*, 55.

7. Now available on CD-ROM, *Manuel de Falla, Colección Música en los Jardines de España*/Music in the Spanish Gardens, Ministerio de Educación y Cultura, 1997.

Part I

BIOGRAPHY

Chapter 1

Cádiz (1876–1897)

An outstanding and remarkable figure of 20th-century music, Manuel de Falla is quite rightly considered as the greatest native Spanish composer since the Renaissance polyphonist Tomás Luis de Victoria. . . .[1]

Probably the key to the miracle *[of Falla]* is not aesthetic but moral, residing not so much in the genius of the musician as in his humility, his loving self-surrender, the unassailable candour of the man.[2]

BEGINNINGS

Manuel María de los Dolores Clemente Ramón del Sagrado Corazón de Jesús de Falla y Matheu was born into a well-to-do merchant family at the port city of Cádiz, Spain, on 23 November 1876.[3] His early morning arrival, at 6 a.m., in the family home on no. 3, Plaza de Espoz y Mina street, would solidify the dawning of a new era in the renovation of Spanish music.[4] In an era when Italian as well as other European and Russian music dominated cultural circles, this timely renovation, like Falla's career, would experience a difficult birth.

The firstborn in a family of five children, Manuel united several influences through his parentage. His father, José María Falla Franco (1849–1919), hailed from Valencia in the east, while his mother, María Jesús Matheu Zabala (1850–1919), came from Catalonia in the north. From his paternal ancestry, Falla's fascination with the city of Sevilla (whose cathedral reportedly holds the remains of Christopher Columbus) and the region of Andalusia may have germinated. From the maternal side, Falla had a connection to the New World, specifically Guatemala, where

3

some of his ancestors were born. His inherited musical and lyrical ability, also from his mother's side of the family, showed definite Italian influence.

The marriage was strongly opposed by Falla's maternal grandfather, Manuel Matheu Parodi (1819–1884), a wealthy industrialist, who did not feel the couple was suited to each other, and so did not wish his daughter to marry José María Falla. With opposition from the young people and through the realization that he could not stop the romance, Manuel Matheu gave not only his consent to the marriage, but also a substantial dowry to the couple in the amount of 400,000 pesetas (approximately 80,000 U.S. dollars). Later, another sum of 2,000,000 pesetas was bequeathed upon the couple at his death. Thus, married life for the Falla couple began in luxury, but unfortunately it did not end so. Young Manuel would become very attached to this generous maternal grandfather, whose dual love for music and for tobacco he would later share.

José María Falla, Manuel's father, developed an export shipping trade, but through unwise decisions was not able to keep it afloat over the years. He invested badly in the stock market and overspent his capital, losing most of the family's fortune. His lavish way of life was cause for more than one person to complain. Nevertheless, he did encourage the education of his children. Supposedly, like Manuel Matheu, he loved Italian opera.[5] To his credit, he did not oppose the music lessons of Manuel and his sister María del Carmen.[6]

Manuel's mother, María Jesús Matheu, was a gifted pianist, who had considerable accomplishments. She would be the motivating force behind her son's emerging talent, shaping and directing it into protective channels. Her role in Manuel's spiritual and musical education was primary and permanent. From her influence his young life would be given the impetus it needed to express itself artistically and humanely. His first contact with the piano came from her.

CÁDIZ

The Cádiz of Falla's birth was certainly different, perhaps more lustrous, than that of today. This beautiful, enchanting seaport city had a checkered past, partially shrouded in myth and partially shaped by its historical conquerors. Not far from the Pillars of Hercules where Africa and Europe meld and where the mountains of Morroco may be seen, Cádiz—formerly the ancient city of Gadir—was said to be linked to the legend of Atlantis through Gadeirus, one of its kings who was the son of the god Poseidon and the mortal Cleito. After the Atlanteans (who may have been the Tartesians) came the Phoenicians, the Carthagenians, the Romans, the Visigoths, the Berbers (whose chief Jebel Tarik "took the rock that thereafter was to bear a corruption of his name"—Gibraltar), the Muslims, and then the Christians led by Alfonso the Wise in 1262.[7] Important for its strategic position in trade routes to Spain's many American colonies and the Pacific, as well as to the Far East before the Suez Canal was opened, Cádiz was a Piscean jewel, uniting both the masculine and the feminine, the stormy and cold Atlantic Ocean with the calm and warm Mediterranean Sea. It was a colonial city and a cosmopolitan city, where traders from Italy, England, Germany, Denmark, and various regions within Spain itself settled. Cádiz, projecting "like a swollen sickle into the sea near the southern-most point of Spain,"[8] bustled with life.

The French poet, Théophile Gautier, whom Falla would later set in his work *Trois mélodies* (1909–1910), told of his arrival in the city—"a narrow island linked to the continent by a slender thread of earth"—in 1840. He described it:

> There are no colors or tints on the painter's or writer's palette that are bright or luminous enough to convey the striking impression that Cádiz made. . . . Two unique tints of blue and white catch your eye; the blue is as vivid as turquoise, sapphire, cobalt, or whatever you can imagine as being extravagantly azure, and the white is as pure as silver, milk, snow, marble, and the best crystallized sugar of the islands! The blue was the sky, mirrored by the sea; the white was the city itself.[9]

Young Falla must have been enthralled by this atmosphere, one that stimulated his already active imagination, one that must have lured him to the Atlantis legend and his future work *Atlántida*.

"La Morilla"

Another stimulus in the development of Manuel's imagination occurred in the daily routine. Family life in well-to-do households included care by a *nodriza* or nursemaid. In this case, it was a Moorish nanny, "La Morilla" (the little lady Moor), who endeared herself to Manuel.

> The rich boy has a poor nursemaid who gives him her savage milk and infuses him with the essence of his people. These nurses, along with the

cleaning women and other humble servants, have for a long time carried
out the important task of transmitting ballads, songs, and stories to the
houses of aristocrats and the middle-class.[10]

Falla commented upon the magic that his nanny wove "[. . .] in my
early infancy, when I only was two or three [years old]. It was then that
the songs, the dances, and the stories of la Morilla opened the doors of
a marvelous world to me."[11] These tales, "worthy of inclusion in *The
Arabian Nights,*" became Falla's inspiration and the "bewitching Fla-
menco-Moorish combination took root—a combination which would
fire his singular and moving music more than any other abundant sensual source."[12] La Morilla's charm too may have had a part in developing "his compassion for the poor, his suspicion of civil authority, and his
Andalusian superstitiousness about drafts, flies, and evil omens."[13]

HOME SCHOOLING

In addition to being cared for by nursemaids, children of upper-class European families usually did not attend school like the other children.
They were tutored at home. This long-standing tradition was the basis of
academic life for the Falla children, one of whom died in infancy and another who died in childhood: Manuel (1876–1946), José María "Pepito"
(1878–ca.1885), María del Carmen (1882–1971), and the twins Servando (b. and d.1889) and Germán (1889–1959).

Instruction in French as a second language was given using the Ollendorff method.[14] The task of teaching reading and writing to young
Manuel fell to Clemente Parodi. This tall, strong man must have made
an impression upon the youth with his top hat, frock coat, black moustache, and hairy hands.[15] Of Italian origin, Parodi may have been related
to the Falla family. It is speculated that one of Falla's names came from
him. Early on he signed himself *Manuel Falla*, but owing to confusion
with yet another person of the same name, he took to signing as *Manuel
de Falla*. Photographs of the young lad dressed in Carnival costumes
show him first as serious "bullfighter" and then as a pensive "Don Juan."

MUSICAL STUDIES

The young Manuel was not a child prodigy, nor was he particularly
precocious. Yet, early on, his mother recognized his talent. It is said

that from Parodi he learned his first letters, from his mother his first musical notes. The young boy heard his mother play such works as the Beethoven *Moonlight* and *Pathétique* sonatas, as well trendy opera transcriptions and works by Chopin. She assisted him in playing duets. And he would joyfully improvise on his maternal grandfather's old harmonium, whose keys were yellowed by the stains of the tobacco he used. At some point Falla's mother decided that her young son needed another influence in the instruction of piano.[16] One of the best teachers in Cádiz was brought in to teach him for a few years until she entered a convent, Sisters of Charity,[17] to become a nun. Eloisa Galluzzo, an excellent pianist and friend of Manuel's mother, undertook the development of his musical instincts beyond the improvisation on his grandfather's harmonium. To discipline his wandering fingers, he received raps on the knuckles with a baton. Yet in spite of it all, he was quite fond of this teacher, who instructed him for two or three years. After that, her teacher, Alejandro Odero, a former Paris Conservatory pupil, continued his lessons.

Manuel's studies with Odero also included solfeggio and harmony at the Academia de Santa Cecilia, where he had entered the course of *bachillerato* with average grades.[18] Manuel's father was so proud of him that he invited him to celebrate the occasion with a cool drink made of green grapes. Apparently he also attended the Instituto Columela in Cádiz, as records of his studies have been found.[19]

After Odero's death, Manuel then studied harmony and counterpoint with Enrico Broca. This teacher may very well have been the one who started him on his legendary way of analyzing anything he could in order to discover the secrets of the great composers. He showed a special affinity for Wagner.

As for the musical scene in Cádiz, Italian operas and *zarzuelas* (a type of Spanish opera or operetta) were all the rage. Symphonic and chamber music concerts as well as solo recitals were also staples. Preeminent amongst the repertoire, Falla heard "heavenly Bellini," Gounod's *Faust*, works of Mozart, Beethoven, and Grieg, who was in vogue.

On the evening that young "Manolo," as he was affectionately called, was to attend his first opera performance with his parents— that of *Faust*—a last-minute change of program featured *Lucia di Lammermoor*. This incident instilled a lifelong dislike in the budding composer for Donizetti. A few days later *Faust* was announced again. Young Manuel was enthralled—he could not yet have been eight years old, for his grandfather was still alive—but his parents, sensing the late hour for such a tender age, took him home before the final act, in spite of his protests.[20]

An early public performance occurred when he played a duo version of Haydn's *The Seven Last Words of Our Saviour* (published as *The Seven Words of Jesus Christ* by Henry Litolff and used by Falla) with his mother at the San Franciscan Church where he had been baptized.[21] This work had a Good Friday tradition in Cádiz, having been commissioned in 1773 from Franz Joseph Haydn by the Chapel-master of the Cádiz cathedral, Francisco de Paula Miconi. It was first conceived as an instrumental oratorio for string quartet. Later it passed through various transformations until it found its definitive version for four voices and orchestra. The work was first published in 1785 in its orchestral version and later in 1891 for voices and orchestra using a German text. The orchestral version may have been the model for choosing the instrumental makeup of Falla's project, the Orquesta Bética de Cámara.[22] This would be: "[violin], viola, violoncello, contrabass, two flutes, two oboes, two French horns, two trumpets, tympani, plus harpsichord or piano."[23] However, in Falla's personal copy of Wanda Landowska's *Musique ancienne* (1921), he notes the section that refers to the 18th century ideal orchestra as having winds and strings in equal proportions.

From the age of ten, Manuel would attend the chamber music evenings at the home of Salvador Viniegra, a famous painter, accomplished amateur cellist, and friend of Saint-Saëns. The latter always passed by Viniegra's home en route to his stays in the Canary Islands. In this way Falla came to know the great French composer and later visited him abroad. Customarily polite, Falla, in order to avoid a potentially embarrassing problem, spoke French with him. However, Saint-Saëns, who naturally wanted to practice, responded in Spanish.

The musical setting at the Viniegra home would later become the venue for the debut of Falla's first solo piano performance, around the age of twelve.[24] Viniegra's son, Juan, recalled the incident.

> We lived then at the Plaza de la Candelaria, no. 4, and its beautiful drawing room was converted into a concert hall. I still remember it, even though many years have passed by, for those first impressions of life are not easily forgotten. At the back was a grand piano; in the center, a magnificent Erard harp, and on the left, a harmonium; it was perfectly decorated, and on its walls hung some paintings from the House of the Marquises of Ureña, ancestors of our family. The sofa, the armchairs, and chairs were of black wood with red upholstery.

There, in that drawing room, Manuelo played the piano for the first time before a select audience, which was the kind that came to the concerts held in our house. He never forgot those first performances of his.[25]

The enthusiasm generated from these musical evenings also inspired Manuel to compose several works for cello and piano, such as *Melodía* for cello and piano, dedicated to Salvador Viniegra. The proud senior, who resembled a taller Richard Wagner, told Manuel, "You are going to be a great composer!"[26]

Another businessman with a foreign name, Manuel Quirell, offered a hall in his large piano store for musical *soirées*. It was there that Falla first performed a program dedicated to his own works, playing the piano part in them. These included: a Melody for 'cello and piano; an Andante and Scherzo for piano quartet; and a "fantasy" quintet for violin, viola, 'cello, flute, and piano based on Frédéric Mistral's poem *Mireya*, which had captivated Falla from childhood. Upon hearing this latter work, a lady on the front row exclaimed, "Oh, one would think that one were at the opera."[27] Formal invitations and printed programs had been issued. The success of this private concert led to a public one the following year. The programmatic *Mireya* had several movements: "The Rhone"; "The Night of St. Médard"; "The Procession of the Drowned Along the River Banks"; "The Sinking of Elzear's Boat"; "Dance of the Ghosts on the Bridge of Trinquetaille." Many years later on a return journey from Italy, Falla would see this old wooden bridge before it was replaced with a modern stone one.

Still another youthful work probably written during the Cádiz years was a nocturne for piano in a Chopinesque idiom. Falla says it was written "when I was still a child" between seventeen and twenty years of age.[28] It was first performed by the composer on 16 August 1899, in Salon Quirell.

Two portraits of the young Manuel are given by Juan Viniegra, his boyhood friend in Cádiz, and María Martínez Sierra, later Falla's collaborator in various projects. The former described the young lad as "normal."

In general, geniuses, artists and saints are presented to us as exceptional beings from their childhoods; but in all truthfulness, I can't say that Manolito ("little Manuel") stood out from the other children of his age.

During the first period of his life, he was a normal child, who played and had a good time like the others, and enthusiastically attended the children's parties he was invited to.[29]

María Martínez Sierra, later one of his collaborators and who did not know Falla in his youth, described him:

> He spent his childhood and youth until the age of 20 nonchalantly aware that he didn't need to think about making a living at all. He was a 'young Andalusian gentleman' redeemed from the frivolity of others like him because of his love for music and his desire to make his mark on the divine art.[30]

RELIGIOUS INSTRUCTION

In addition to academic and musical instruction, Manuel was dutifully provided religious guidance. He took his first communion in 1896. Chiefly brought up in an era of Marian thought, of which feminine influence was predominant, the Falla family made sure that Manuel also had a strong masculine role model. Thus, the ancient Oriental saying—"From your mother, you learn the love of God; from your father, you learn the fear of God"—applied to him. The fear of God was amply learned not from his own father but from the very authoritative figure of Father Francisco de Paula Fedriani, who pertained to the secular, not Jesuit, clergy.[31] This spiritual guide held rein over Falla for many years. Unfortunately, Falla's letters to Fedriani were destroyed by this priest. Only Fedriani's responses remain in the Archivo Manuel de Falla today. The strict devotion which Fedriani espoused is shown in his spiritual guidance given during Falla's teenage years dated 8 December 1892.

> You shall devote the days of the week to the following purposes:
>   Sunday to the Holy Trinity.
>   Monday to the Holy Sacrament.
>   Tuesday to the Holy Virgin.
>   Wednesday to Saint Joseph.
>   Thursday to all the Angels and Saints.
>   Friday to the Lord's Passion.
>   Saturday to the Holy Virgin.
>   All the works of charity and religion and all your good acts will be dedicated in penance for your sins and in demonstration of your love of God and his Holy Mother; and they will be dedicated also to the benefit of the members of your family and friends, devoting one or more days of the week for each one or to various people, and when you wish to receive some favor from the Lord, you will dedicate one or various days of the week towards this purpose according to the permission of your Spiritual Guide who Blesses you.[32]

Fedriani also involved himself in the Falla family affairs. Having personally paid, in good faith, 800 reales for alms on the part of Falla's father, Fedriani tried repeatedly for several months to collect this debt owed to him. Bitter letters blaming José María Falla of squandering money, of spending for the pleasures of Carnival, of living as he had always lived in spite of the economic downturn passed between the two men in 1896. Fedriani suggested that so far José María's wife or son had not been told, for Manuel would suffer horribly with the news.

> The little warmth and consideration that you have, for a son to whom God loves so for his purity and virtue, and the hate with which you look at me, who knows if they would be the principal causes of the heap of disgust that weighs upon you.[33]

Fedriani ended his plea by encouraging José María to find ways to correct the situation, adding that he had nothing to lose by doing so.

This shocking and cruel correspondence perhaps reflects a bit about the character of both men, leaving Manuel in the middle of the dispute. His sensitive nature undoubtedly would have perceived the tension that abounded. On the one hand, José María might be perceived as irresponsible, Fedriani as dictatorial, and Manuel as the helpless victim. Fedriani was much more involved in Manuel's life than just his religious instruction. This included advice about his lessons with José Tragó and Felipe Pedrell in Madrid and his decision not to marry his cousin, María Prieto Ledesma. Whatever Manuel might have felt for Fedriani is not known through his writings. If there had been negative or ill feelings toward his spiritual adviser, these feelings were later resolved in life, for Falla remembered Fedriani in his will. To Manuel's father's credit, he was very aware of daily expenditures, for, at one point, he noted: "cod fish = 1.50 pesetas (pta.); sugar = .25 pta.; bread = .10 pta.; meat = 1.00 pta.; eggs = .25 pta.; total = 3.90 pta."[34] Certainly, given the sinking economic fortune of the Falla family, there would have been considerable tension.

Falla's relationship with his father is generally not a subject of great depth in the biographies. As one biographer described it: "Falla's feelings for his father, like those of Beethoven for his, were ambiguous, for both composers far surpassed their fathers in accomplishment and, as a result, found it difficult to respect them."[35] It is true that Manuel's maternal side of the family played a larger role in his life. On the paternal side, he never knew his grandmother, María Dolores Franco Noche, who died in 1869. His paternal grandfather, Francisco de Paula de Falla Álvarez, died when Manuel was an adolescent and little is known about him.

TRAGEDIES

Spiritual health was not only a concern for the young Falla, so was physical health. As a child Manuel apparently contracted pulmonary tuberculosis, complications of which he would allegedly suffer much of his life. His fear of contagious diseases and subsequent obsession with cleanliness probably dates from this time. His fastidious adherence to daily physical and spiritual ablutions soon thereafter developed into a strict and, at times, excessive regimen. Later, in Paris, he vowed silence and refused to speak to anyone before 1 p.m. And during those years, according to Francisco García Lorca, Federico's brother, Falla spent a full hour brushing his teeth each morning. Later, in 1919, just a week after his mother's death, he inquired about prices and conditions of inexpensive flats near the Alhambra in Granada, further qualifying his query with the words: "Is there any typhus there? I suppose from what I read that until now it is only a false alarm."[36]

Given the tragedies in the impressionable lad's life, it is easy to understand Manuel's later exaggerated behavior. The middle years of the 1880's were turning points in the boy's childhood. His beloved grandfather, Manuel Matheu, passed away in 1884, before the boy's eighth birthday. The following year a devastating and virulent strain of cholera swept through Cádiz, taking Manuel's aunt Magdalena and 553 other victims. When the doctor arrived and confirmed that this dearly loved aunt had succumbed to the illness, out came Manuel's father and cried from the steps of the first floor to those who were with the children on the ground floor, "Cholera! It's gotten to the children!"[37] The Falla family retreated to El Puerto (the same as in *Iberia* of Albéniz) nearby. Manuel's little brother and playmate, "Pepito," died in 1885, although it is not stated from what cause. Yet another brother would pass four years later, Servando, Germán's twin. Manuel's first encounters with death must have deeply affected his sensitive soul and certainly left their indelible marks.

SEVILLA AND COLÓN (SEVILLE AND COLUMBUS)

In the spring of the next year, the Falla family visited Sevilla, the birthplace of Manuel's paternal grandfather. Here Falla's love for the piano blossomed. He practiced so vigorously that the neighbors at the Fonda de Madrid, where the family was staying, complained loudly. The ceremonies surrounding the birth (17 May 1886) in Madrid of the future Alfonso XIII, heir to the Spanish throne, also made a lasting impression on the young Falla at that time. Awaiting this birth, the Spanish people would be advised by the type of the flag hoisted as to the sex of the child—the Spanish flag, if a boy, or a white flag, if a girl. Falla was so enamored of Sevilla that he begged his parents to move there.

The disappointment in not being able to live in Sevilla, coupled with the earlier presence of death and illness that so intimately affected young Manuel in Cádiz, must have contributed greatly to the need for solitude and self-expression. From the ages of nine to fifteen, a boyhood fascination of "Eden" (Manuel's secret chamber where a mystical city called *Colón* was created) was privy only to his sister.[38] *Colón* was populated, governed, and defended, as any self-respecting city should be. It contained a town council, newspapers, academics, administrators (including tax collectors), a theater ("in which plays, characters, and sets were conceived, written, composed, painted, and fashioned by little Manuel himself"[39]), and, of course, musicians, of which he was the magnificent Maestro, the "applauded composer and irresistible conductor of the successful *El Conde de Villamediana, ópera séria.*"[40]

Literary (and artistic) pursuits were realized in *Colón* through the juvenile "publications," illustrated by the author, of *El Més Colombino* (The Columbus Monthly), *El Burlón* (The Buffoon), and *El Cascabel* (The Rattle-Brain), with its series explaining how students could avoid the terrors of examination time. Apparently Manuel possessed the key, for he successfully passed his entrance exams for *bachillerato* (Bachelor's degree)[41] at the Cádiz Academy of Music of St. Cecilia. Some of these home magazines in which Manuel both contributed articles, served as editor, and sold, are preserved in the AMF (*El Burlón* from 1889 and *El Cascabel* from 1891). While the childish drawings that illustrated Manuel's home magazines do not convey a developed artistic talent, a beautiful watercolor copy of *Madonna and Child* by the pre-Raphaelite artist, Nicolai Baralbino,[42] is impressive. Manuel supposedly painted it when he was only eleven years old. Today it hangs in the Casa-Museo in Granada and clearly shows the talent of the child-artist.

At a time when aviation and automobiles were unknown, Manuel created fantastic vehicles for his *Colón*, vehicles that could immediately transmit messages.[43] Elections and revolutions were other events created to stimulate life there, giving vent to the boy's love of Spanish history, as did his *Don Quijote* plays created and produced there. Even though the parents had bought him a fancy marionette theater, he was simply not interested in it, preferring instead his own secret creations. This "laboratory" of self-apprenticeship became the germinating factor for his greatest works—*Atlántida* (1927–1946) and *El retablo de Maese Pedro* (begun in the year of the death of his parents, 1919 and completed in 1923) as well as those of *Españoleta* and *Misterio de los reyes magos*, produced in 1922 with Federico García Lorca.

That young Manuel was able to conceal his adventures for the extended period of six years is a testimony to his ingenuity. He preferred his imaginary world to the real world. During one Carnival, he showed no interest in watching the parade of masks passing beneath the windows of his house. It was the day in which the administrators were to collect the taxes in *Colón*. One day, however, his imaginary world came crashing to an end when his parents entered his dark room, full of books, and discovered the incriminating papers and receipts. No one had suspected anything, neither the parents, nor Odero, nor Broca with whom Manuel was studying. Frightened that such fantasy was close to delusional, the parents consulted a doctor, who told them to remove Manuel from this situation before it turned into madness.[44]

TO BE A COMPOSER

The chilling impact of the removal of his pastime sobered Manuel and caused his creativity to take a different road. It was around this time (c. 1892) that he wrote his first real composition (*Gavotte and Musette*),[45] a piano work inspired by a piece by Bach that had been published in an insert of a Paris fashion magazine, *Journal des demoiselles*, to which his mother subscribed. He wrote it at first secretly (a trait that followed him into adulthood) during his recreation times, being too shy to show it to anyone. Eventually he mustered the courage to work on it openly as he gained confidence.

All the qualities later manifest in Falla as a mature composer were doubtless nurtured from childhood and youth: his keen imagination, his creativity, his sensitivity, his seriousness, his perseverance and determination, his penchant for detail, his strong sense of orchestral color, his secretiveness and inherent shyness, his deep religious sentiment, his strong passions, his obsessive superstitions, and last but not least, his great love of native Andalusian folk music. He was perhaps a difficult child at times, pensive and taciturn. Yet his strong and rich inner life caused him to develop a firm and marked mature artistic and spiritual personality.

According to biographer Roland-Manuel, "Manuel loved to date his true profession to the day of his seventeenth year where he heard for the first time an orchestra in the great hall of the museum of Cádiz."[46] There, amongst the Zurbaran paintings, he heard works by Beethoven and Grieg, which inspired his profound conviction, at the age of seventeen-eighteen, to become a composer.[47]

> That calling was so strong . . . that it even made me feel afraid; the illusions it filled me with were far beyond what I believed myself capable of doing. I do not mean from a purely technical point of view, for I knew that with time and work the technique could be acquired by any slightly gifted musician; but it is the INSPIRATION, in the truest and highest sense of the word—that mysterious force without which we all know too well that it is impossible to realize anything truly useful—of which I believed myself incapable. So, without the supporting aid of my religious convictions, I would never have had the courage to follow such a path in which darkness fills the greatest part. Curious thing, in my first vocation (literature), fear was always absent, without a doubt because it was simply a question of a childish whim.[48]

Falla, however, would have some doubts still. As will be seen later, Falla even considered returning to Cádiz to become a piano teacher after he had finished his studies under Prof. José Tragó at the Madrid Conservatory. Thus, this statement does not reflect the entire situation. Uncertainty and economic worries also entered into the picture, reflecting that Falla, in his twenties, was still unsure of himself. Only by taking the daring leap to go to Paris would his destiny as a composer become solidified.

NOTES

1. Yvan Nommick, *Manuel de Falla: Œuvre et Évolution du Language Musical*, Université de Paris-Sorbonne (Paris IV), 1998–1999, I, abstract of doctoral thesis.

2. Fedele d'Amico quoted in Ronald Crichton's *Falla*, London: BBC Music Guides, 1982, 102–103.

3. Gilbert Chase and Andrew Budwig, *Manuel de Falla, A Bibliography and Research Guide*, New York: Garland Publishing, 1986, 5. Falla's baptism took place in the parish Catholic church of Nuestra Señora del Rosario on the day of his birth. His baptismal certificate reads: "In the city of Cádiz, capital of its province and bishopric, on 26 November 1876, I Don Manuel Marañón, the

godfather, by the authority of this parish, solemnly baptize Manuel, María de los Dolores, Clemente, Ramón del Sagrado Corazón de Jesús, who was born the 23rd day of this month at six in the morning of Don José María Falla and Doña María Jesusa Matheu, natives of Cádiz, married in [the parish of] of San Antonio: paternal grandparents of Don Francisco de Falla and Doña María Dolores Franco, natives of Cádiz; maternal grandparents, Don Manuel [Matheu y Parodi], native of Cádiz, and Doña María Jesusa García, native of Guatemala; godparents, the maternal grandfather and [the maternal aunt] Doña Magdalena Parodi, advised of their obligations. Witnessed by Don Francisco Falla and Doña Jesusa Matheu. And signed so that it be put in effect, ut supra. (signed) Manuel Pérez Marañón." Falla's birth occurred one day after St. Cecilia day, the martyr-patron saint of music.

4. Suzanne Demarquez, *Manuel de Falla,* translated from the French by Salvator Attansaio, New York: Da Capo Press, 1983, 5, and *Manuel de Falla: His Life and Works*, Poesía, ed. Gonzalo Armero and Jorge de Persia, Madrid: Ministerio de Cultura, 1996, 18. Originally named after a hero of the Peninsular War; this street is now called Plaza del Generalissimo Franco and the house number has been changed to no. 37. This street was commonly referred to as *Calle Ancha*—"Broad Street," or the best street in town, even though this was not its official name. It was then Plaza de Mina, no. 3. A bronze plaque marks Falla's birthplace—a multistory house, where Falla's parents had a first floor apartment with large windows, glass-enclosed balconies, interior marble, and tiled patio. The congenial palm-lined plaza must have been an agreeable spot for children to play. Later the Fallas would move to Fonda de Cádiz in the Plaza de San Antonio. *Fonda* was tantamount to "hotel" and this particular one also housed the Consul of Denmark who befriended the young Manuel.

5. Luis Campodónico, *Falla* (translated by F. Ávila), 2nd ed. Barcelona: Edicions 62, 1991, 5.

6. Manuel Orozco, *Manuel de Falla, Historia de una derrota*, Barcelona: Ediciones Destino, S. A., 1985, 31.

7. Demarquez, 2–3.

8. Crichton, *Falla,* 9.

9. Demarquez, 4.

10. Chase-Budwig, 6.

11. Letter Falla-Roland-Manuel, dated 30 December 1928, from Granada (draft in AMF 7520; photocopy of the original typewritten letter in AMF 7521), cited in Nommick, Thesis, III, 566: "[. . .] dans ma toute première enfance, quand je n'en comptais que deux ou trois [ans]. C'est alors que les chants, les danses et les histoires de la Morilla m'ouvrirent les portes d'un monde merveilleux."

12. *Poesía,* 20.

13. Chase-Budwig, 6.

14. Orozco, 32.

15. Letter to Roland-Manuel cited in *Poesía,* 19.

16. Amongst Manuel's books of study are included: *The Art of the Piano* by Robert Schumann, *The Seven Words of Jesus Christ* by Haydn, the Symphonies of Beethoven for four hands, etc.

17. Roland-Manuel, *Manuel de Falla*, Paris: Editions d'aujourd'hui, 1977 (based on the text of 1930 edition), 15.

18. Letter to Roland-Manuel, cited in *Poesia*, 21.

19. Orozco, 23. A chronicle of the relationship of several local musical institutions may be found in *La Historia del Conservatorio de Cádiz en sus documentos* by Diego Navarro Mota, with prologue by José María Péman. Cádiz: Instituto de Estudios Gaditanos, Excma. Diputación Provincial, 1976.

20. Antonio Gallego, "Reflexiones sobre El año Falla 1996" in *Manuel de Falla, latinité et Universalité*, ed. Louis Jambou, *Actes du colloque International tenu en Sorbonne 18–21 Novembre 1996*, *Musique/Écritures, série Études*, Paris: Presses de l'Université de Paris-Sorbonne, 1999, 545.

21. Jaime Pahissa, *Vida y obra de Manuel de Falla,* 2nd revised and enlarged edition, Buenos Aires: Ricordi americana, 1956, 22.

22. Pahissa, 23. (most biographers give his age as eleven, although Pahissa records this event at the age of nine, which would have coincided with the 100th anniversary of the composition of the piece). Roland-Manuel says that Falla was not older than eleven when he made this debut (R-M, 16).

23. Orozco, 29–30.

24. Campodónico, 6.

25. Juan J. Viniegra y Lasso de la Vega, in collaboration with Carmen and Carlos Martel Viniegra, *Vida Íntima de Manuel de Falla,* Cádiz: Diputación Provincial y Ayntamiento-Caja de Ahorros y Monte de Piedad-Cámara oficial de Comercio, Industria y Navegación, 1966, 47.

Vivíamos, entonces, en la Plaza de la Candelaria, número 4, y su hermosos salón, se convertía en sala de conciertos. Aún lo recuerdo, a pesar de que han transcurrido muchos años; pero, esas primeras impresiones de la vida, no se olvidan fácilmente. Al fondo, había un gran piano de cola; en el centro, una magnífica arpa Erard y, a la izquierda, un armonium; estaba perfectamente decorado, y de sus paredes pendían algunos cuadros, procedentes de la Casa de los Marqueses de Ureña, antecesores de nuestra familia. El sofá, las butacas y las sillas, eran de madera negra y forrados de rojo.

Allí, en aquel salón, tocó Manolo por vez primera el piano ante un selecto público, que era el que acudía a los conciertos que se celebraban en nuestra casa. Aquellas primeras actuaciones suyas, no las olvidó él nunca.

26. Viniegra-Veja, 62. "Tú vas a ser un gran compositor."

27. Demarquez, 9.

28. Antonio Gallego, *Catalogo de obras de Manuel de Falla*, Madrid: Ministerio de Cultura, Dirección General de Bellas Artes y Archivos, 1987, 13.

29. Viniegra-Veja, 41.

30. Michael Christoforidis, "Las respresentaciones y el representado, Manuel

de Falla y las imagenes del artista/Representations and the Represented, Manuel de Falla and the Images of the Artis, bilingual text in *Iconografía Manuel de Falla, 1876–1946, La imagen de un músico/The Image of a Musician*, 2nd ed. Javier Suárez Pajares, ed., Madrid: Sociedad General de Autores y Editores, 1996, 22.

31. Federico Sopeña "La Espiritualidad de Manuel de Falla" in *Manuel de Falla tra la Spagna e l'Europa, Atti del convegno Internazionale di Studi*, Paolo Pinamonti, ed. (Venice, 15–17 maggio 1987). Quaderno della Rivista Italiana di Musicologia, no. 21, Firenze: Leo S. Oslchki, ed., 1989, 73.

32. Letter Fedriani-Falla, 8 December 1892, AMF 6962.

> Dedicarás los dias de la Semana a las seguinetes intenciones
>   Domingo a la Santa Trinidad
>   Lunes al Santo Sacramento
>   Martes a la Santa Virgen
>   Miercoles a S[anto]. José.
>   Jueves a todos los Angeles santos y santas.
>   Viernes a la *Pasión* del Senior
>   Sabado a la Santa Virgen
>   Todas las obras de piedad y religion y todo lo bueno que hagas lo aplicarás en penitencia de tus pedaos y manifestaren al amor a Dios y a su Santa Madre además lo aplicara tambien en benficia al las personas de tu familia y amistad dedicando uno ó mas días de la semana para cada una ó mas personas y cuando deseas receber del Señor algun beneficio aplicaras ser esta intencion uno o varios dias a la semana segun te permita tu Director Espiritual que le Bendice.
>   Dia 8 de Diciembre de 1892

33. Orozco, 22–23. "El poco cariño y consideración que tiene Vd. a un hijo a quien Dios tanto ama por su pureza y virtud, y el odio con que a mí Vd. Me mira, quién sabe si podrían ser las principales causas del cúmulo de disgustos que sobre Vd. pesan."

34. Federico Sopeña, *Vida y obra de Falla*, Madrid: Turner Libros, S.A., 1988, 32, fn. 11, referring to cite in Pérez Galdós's book *Misericordia* of 1896, O.C.T., 1.

35. Chase-Budwig, 7.

36. Letter to Ángel Barrios in Granada from Falla in Madrid, dated 4 August 1919, published in *Atlántida, Introducción a Manuel de Falla* (1962) by Federico Sopeña. Madrid: Taurus Ediciones, p. 61. "¿Qué hay del tifus? Supongo, por lo que leo, que hasta ahora sólo se trata de una falsa alarma."

37. Pahissa, 24. "¡Cólera! ¡Que se lleven a los niños!"

38. *Poesía*, 23.

39. Demarquez, 2.

40. Roland-Manuel, 16. "Dont le maestro Manuel de Falla est à la fois le compositeur applaudi et le chef d'orchestre irrésistible."

41. This was not the highest level of study, nor equivalent today to a Bachelor's degree in an American university nor to a three-year "Bachelor's" degree in a European university. Falla's higher level of music training would later be done in Madrid at the National Conservatory of Music and Declaration.

42. Chase-Budwig, 33; Orozco, 23.

43. Demarquez, 2.

44. Pahissa, 25–26.

45. Actually there is only one piece and more correctly entitled *Gavotte* or *Musette*. For more details, see the Works section.

46. Roland-Manuel, 19fn1. "Manuel de Falla aime à dater as vocation véritable du jour de as dix-septième année où il entendit pour la première fois un orchestre, dans la grande salle du musée de Cadix."

47. *Ibid.*

48. Nommick, Thesis, III, 569. Yvan Nommick points out that from concert programs archived in the AMF, Falla was respectively seventeen and eighteen years old at the time that he heard orchestral concerts in Cádiz that would be the determining factor in his choice of music as a profession. The first concert is dated 7 October 1894, by the Pequeña Sociedad de Concertos [Little Concert Society] under the direction of Manuel Martínez. This program included Beethoven's First Symphony and Grieg's *Peer Gynt Suite,* no. 1. The concert is dated about six weeks later, 25 November 1894, by the same organization and director, but this time in Beethoven's Second Symphony and Grieg's *Peer Gynt Suite,* no. 2.

> Cette vocation est devenue si forte . . . que j'en ai même eu peur; les illusions qu'elle éveillait en moi étant trop au-dessus de ce que je me croyais capable de faire. Je ne dis pas cela au point de vue technique, car je savais qu'avec le temps et le travail la technique peut être acquise par n'importe quel musicien moyennement doué; mais c'est "l'inspiration," dans le vrai et le plus haut sens du mot—cette force mystérieuse sans laquelle, nous le savons trop, on ne peut rien réaliser de vraiment utile—dont je me croyais incapable. Or, sans l'aide puissante de mes convictions réligieuses, je n'aurais jamais eu le courage de poursuivre un chemin dont les ténèbres emplissaient la plus grande partie. Chose curieuse: de ma première vocation (la littérature) la crainte était toujours absente; sans doute parce qu'il s'agissait simplement d'un caprice d'enfant.

Chapter 2

Madrid (1897–1907)

It was Joaquín Turina who introduced me to Falla in Madrid the afternoon of the burial of Ruperto Chapí, who died some days after his opera
"Margarita la Tornera" had been premiered at the Teatro Real. At that
time Manuel de Falla had a bushy moustache and wore a bowler hat. He
was in a period of black misery . . . he charged two pesetas an hour for
piano lessons, and, if the potential student haggled, he lowered the tu-
ition to six reales.[1]

CONSERVATORY STUDIES

With the Falla family business in shambles, young Manuel's life was
radically changing. From 1896 he made frequent trips to Madrid to
further his piano studies.[2] Carrying a letter of recommendation from
the Viniegra family, he was able to began piano studies with José
Tragó at the Conservatório Nacionale de Música y Declamación.[3]
Professor Tragó had been a pupil of George Mathias, who had been a
pupil of Chopin.[4] Falla would possess a predilection for Chopin all of
his life, so to study with a teacher of that illustrious lineage surely
must have been a dream fulfilled for the youth. Tragó too was pleased
with his young student and claimed he "is a very studious, very conscientious boy; with a very good artistic temperament. A very rosy future surely awaits him in our difficult art form."[5]

In 1897 Falla officially enrolled as a "free student" at the Conservatory. His purpose was to complete the course as fast as possible so that
he could earn a living and then proceed to Paris for further studies. This

ambition drove him to complete the seven-year course in just two, taking his final exams against Tragó's wishes. He passed the equivalent of three years of solfège and seven years of piano study with high grades. In 1899 he was unanimously awarded the First Prize of Piano at the Madrid Conservatory.

These early years in Madrid leave some doubt as to specific dates of certain events. Accounts vary as to exactly when he and his family moved to Madrid.[6] Biographer Orozco also notes that his obsession with the number seven took hold "from around 1897."[7] And sometime around 1900, he began to add the "de" before his last name.[8]

Financial Survival

Falla periodically returned to his home town of Cádiz to give professional solo piano recitals on 28 March 1898, 10 September 1899, and 16 September 1900. He charged three pesetas (about eighty cents) for a box and one peseta for the balcony.[9] His repertoire included Romantic works, such as Chopin, Schumann, Grieg, and others, as well as his own compositions.

After 1900 he began to give piano lessons to help support his family of five, a family that had been accustomed to the best that wealth could buy. It was an awesome responsibility and challenge that any struggling musician could hardly match. Too, his meager income of concertizing was supplemented by the small royalties of his piano pieces *Mazurka en do menor* (Mazurka in c minor), *Serenata andaluza*, (Andalusian Serenade) and *Vals capricho* (Capricious Waltz).

Reality was a harsh teacher. Falla's hopes for Paris were dashed when no funds were forthcoming from Count de Morphy, to whom he had once again presented a letter of introduction from his old friend Salvador Viniegra. The Count had been responsible for introducing the Catalan cellist, Pablo Casals, to Queen Maria Cristina. She financially patronized his studies at the Paris Conservatory.[10] The same benefactor had made it possible for Albéniz to study piano in Brussels.[11] Unfortunately, Falla was not so lucky. Falla's teacher, Tragó, advised him to compose, for the only way a Spanish musician could solve this dilemma and secure a financial future was through the composition of *zarzuelas*. This advice was well-taken, but not with the desired results.

ZARZUELAS

The *zarzuela* tradition is peculiar to Spain, and particularly (although not exclusively) Madrid, although other countries have produced their own forms of opera and operetta. Originally *zarzuela* was the typical "Spanish form of musical comedy untainted by opera until the end of the 17th century, when it succumbed to Italianate styles."[12] Taken from the Spanish word *zarza* ("bramble bush" or the common European blackberry bush that grows wild), the *genre* has its origins as far back as 1615 when a popular fifteenth century form, *pastourelle* (ca. 1420), was incorporated into *Baile de la Zarzuela* (Dance of the Zarzuela). From the theme of that early rustic musical comedy the entertaining nature of the *zarzuela* can be discerned. Roaming the hills around the old Zarzuela Inn, a wayfarer is subsequently invited to spend the night in the flirtatious shepherdess's hut.

King Philip IV had much to do with the development of the *zarzuela* when, in 1634, he ordered his son to rebuild a royal hunting place in the forested, overgrown grounds of the Prado. This place became known as "La Zarzuela" ("The Zarzuela"). Some early examples of this aristocratic pastime were written by Lope Félix de Vega Carpio's *La Selva sin amor* (The Forest without Love) in 1629 and Pedro Calderón de la Barca *Ni amor se libra de Amor* (Neither Love is freed from Love) around 1640. *Fiestas de Zarzuela* (Festivals of Zarzuela) were distinguished from those theatrical productions at another Madrid theater, the Buen Retiro. *Los cielos hacen estrellas* (The Heavens make Stars) by Juan Hidalgo and Juan Vélez is the "earliest play with enough of the original music surviving to give an adequate idea of a 17th-century *zarzuela*."[13] The work, possibly produced as early as 1644[14] or as late as 1672,[15] uses recitatives as well as madrigal-like choruses. The aspect of spoken dialogue interspersed with singing (found in later forms such as *Singspiele* and comic opera) is a characteristic of the *zarzuela*. Dancing too occurred in both the *zarzuela* itself, as well as the interludes between the acts. Popular songs could also be used between the acts, but were not generally found as an integral component of the *zarzuela* structure. Double choruses increased the dramatic aspect. While no orchestral scores as such have survived, it is thought that stringed instruments such as the violin, guitar, harp, or keyboard would complement percussion instruments.

After 1700, Italian influence dominated the *zarzuela* during the Bourbon rule. Even Greek mythological subjects became fodder for them. Thus began a decline of the *zarzuela*, as well as Spanish drama. An attempt at a revival around 1770 by Ramón de la Cruz with composer Rodríguez de Hita was only moderately successful. Ramón de la Cruz's two act *sainetes* ("farce"), along with those *genres* of Antonio Soler and Blas de Laserna, actually propelled the popular reaction against the *zarzuela* and gave rise to the *tonadilla*, whose short scenic, comic interludes were performed between the acts of a play, later became independent pieces. Popular songs and dances, such as the *seguidilla* or *jotas*, as well as vocal quartets and choruses could also be found in these predecessors of the modern *zarzuela chica* ("little *zarzuela*"). Italian composers living in Spain, such as Boccherini and Brunetti, also collaborated with Ramón de la Cruz. Some Italian operas were actually converted into *zarzuelas*. However, after his death in the second half of the 18th century, the Italian influence was too strong to permit the Spanish flavor to continue.

In 1830, Queen Maria Cristina (the consort of King Ferdinand VII and an Italian who hailed from Naples) created the Madrid Music Conservatory. Even the Spanish language gave way to Italian as the official language of instruction. After two years, Spanish resistance took over. This push-pull attitude was reflected in a satire attacking Italian opera, written by Spanish Manuel Bretón de los Herreros and Italian Basilio Basisli in 1839, called *El novio y el concierto* (The *Fiancé* and the Concert) and was to be credited as being the first "zarzuela-comedy" since Ramón de la Cruz. A surge followed and the *zarzuela* became the favorite populist form of entertainment with as a distinctly national character as the English Gilbert and Sullivan operettas. Some examples are found in the works of Francisco Barbieri (1823–1894), Ruperto Chapí y Lorente (1851–1909), Tomás Bretón y Hernández (1850–1923), and Amadeo Vives (1871–1932).

The modern multiact *grande zarzuela*, usually in three acts, became distinguished from the *zarzuelito* or *zarzuela chica* of one act. This was the tradition that Falla would come to know well. His contact with Bretón and Vives in Madrid would be more than casual. The battle for a Spanish identity continued. Even in 1917, the year that Falla's article on "Our Music" appeared in the Madrid periodical *Música*, cosmopolitan ingredients were still a fundamental part of the *zarzuela*'s makeup.

> . . . an exceedingly curious and interesting phenomenon is now taking place in Spanish music. Spanish composers have never shown before so deep a conviction of national values, yet never before have the critics (some at least) accused them, as they do now, of betraying those values.

But what is still more worth mentioning is that the models such accusers invite us to revere are—save for very rare exceptions—the result of the most obvious foreign imitation to be found in the whole history of European art. I, or rather, "they," refer to our so-called "zarzuela grande" which, as anyone can establish with very little effort, is nothing but an echo of the Italian opera in vogue at the time of their composition. In a certain sense this is not wrong, for the dramas providing the plots for comic operas or "zarzuelas" could not possibly have a national character, most of them being only simple adaptations of foreign works.

Barbieri, wishing to "hispanisize" our music, broke with that way of proceeding, as "El barberillo de Lavapiés" and "Pan y toros" so nobly demonstrate. But even in these sincerely national compositions, musical techniques very seldom remain uninfluenced by the Italians.

Only some time later, when Felipe Pedrell showed us through his works what the national way should be—a direct consequence of our popular music—did some honest thinking men propose following in the path opened by the distinguished master.

Please do not believe I am trying to reject everything composed during the period I have just been dealing with. Not only was it not my intention, but I have always expressed my admiration for a number of "zarzuelas," be they "grandes" or "chicas," which have been our chief musical activity for so long a period. Many of them will honourably survive in Spanish art, and the gracefulness of their melodies will hardly be surpassed by present or future composers. But between this fact and the declaration that the seasoning, as it were, with which these works are dressed, is purely national, there "is" a gap. Included in "zarzuelas" are songs written in a major or minor key (the "jota" or "seguidilla," for example) that of course keep all their national characteristics. But surely our national treasure does not only consist of "jotas" or "seguidillas"? And besides, who will convince me that the rhythms of the "chotis," of the waltz, or of the mazurka, with which those works are so generously supplied, are Spanish? I hesitate to criticize, and all I have just said is not intended to censure, but to be a statement.[16]

Although *zarzuela* music was generally pleasing to the audience— "graceful, brilliant, and enjoyable" as Pahissa put it[17]—the truth of the matter was any serious composer would not be judged by a musical form whose content was often technically weak, without artistic caliber, trivial, sometimes shallow, and often vulgar. In spite of all these derogatory characterizations, the *zarzuela* could be the way to immediate financial security—a great necessity for Falla at that time.

Before composing *zarzuelas*,[18] Falla had only written small forms, such as piano pieces and chamber music, although his *Mireya* was his first attempt at large-scale theatrical, albeit programmatic, music. Around

1900 he tried his hand at *La Juana y la Petra, o La casa de Tócame Roque* (Joana and Petra, or the House of Tócame Roque), a *zarzuela* in one act and two scenes with chorus, spoken dialogue, fifteen characters (ten of them singers and yet others who do not), guitar, tambourine, and other instrumentation. The libretto was by Javier Santero, and was based on the farce of the same title by Ramón de la Cruz. While the manuscript of the work has not been located, Falla's notebook, *Apuntes de harmonía* (notes on harmony),[19] indicates five musical numbers. According to Pahissa, this was the only one of his *zarzuelas* that Falla felt worthy of his efforts. From it, some of the prelude with its Scarlattian second theme found its way into the "Danza del corregidor" in *El sombrero de tres picos* (The Three-Cornered Hat). He hoped one day to rework the Prelude. Some discussion of revising the work is mentioned in a letter from Padre Fedriani in 1902, who urges Falla not to spend too much time on the matter, rather to be practical.

Falla was a friend of Ruperto Chueca, the successful *zarzuela* composer who admired Falla. In order to help Falla get a performance of *La casa de Tócame Roque*, he let it be known that he had collaborated with him. However, the rumor backfired and circulated that Falla had "orchestrated" some of Chueca's works.[20]

In *Los amores de la Inés* (The Loves of Inés)[21] was the only *zarzuela* by Falla that saw the light of day in a theater, that of Teatro Cómico in Madrid on 12 April 1902. It contains *seguidillas*, an instrumental interlude, chorus, and eight characters. It was apparently published by Faustino Fuentes and Falla notes his royalties from 1903. The action takes places in Madrid in an inn owned by "Lucas," who throws a party to celebrate. In the second part, two marriages are consummated, those of Inés and Juan, and that of Fatigas and Felipe.

The reviews were generally more favorable to the composer than to the librettist, with the subject matter being too hackneyed and excessive for good taste. The critic of *La Correspondencia de España* said, "In his first work for the theater the composer of the music, Señor Falla, reveals an exceptional talent for composition, and there is reason to believe that these happy faculties will have an important development in his subsequent works."[22] His orchestrational aptitude was also praised, as well as the "admirably sung" Juan's Ballade by Señor Rodondo. Another critic commented on the refined performance of the artists which contributed to its success.[23]

Of the six numbers, two are for orchestra. The principal theme suggests a *zarzuela* by Albéniz, *San Antonio de la Florida*, performed eight years earlier.[24] The second number in which Juan (just released from prison) and the chorus sing is "very banal and weak."[25] A passionate love duet between Inés and Juan uses alternating binary and ternary meters, as found in the Andalusian *petenera* (dance characterized by the alternation of 3/4 and 3/8) and as later incorporated into *El sombrero de tres picos* and *Noches en los jardines de España*. After the duo, a shoe dance" follows—the rousing *zapateado* with heel clicking and stamping. After the subsequent instrumental interlude, the work ends with an ensemble, including chorus.

The work received about twenty performances in all and was performed by the troupe of the famous Loreto Padro and Enrique Chicote Company. The orchestra was weak, with only one violist, no oboe, and a bass player who preferred the corner bar to the music.

Limosna de amor with librettist José Jackson Veyán was written around 1901–1902. In one act, the work had five numbers: "Pablo," "Romanza de Elena," "Dúo de Elena y Pablo," "Elena," and a final chorus of sopranos, tenors, and basses. The manuscript of the piano-vocal score is extant in the AMF. The orchestration includes strings, winds, tympani, and percussion. Falla was more fastidious than some *zarzuela* composers, for he made several notes in his *Apuntes de Harmonía* notebook about his inspirational sources.[26] For example,

"Bacanal"—*La Tosca*, p. 77. Take this air. "*La Gioconda*" has a chorus with the same air (6/8). See the chords in the Treatise of Richter, p. 23. See the Waltz, p. 90 V. 1st, Schumann in order to use this rhythm. "La Bacanal" is referred to in no. 1. The Waltz in no. 2.[27]

A delay in starting work on this piece occurred. Jackson had asked Falla to compose the music for a *zarzuela* based on a text by Arregui, but the librettist insisted that the music must be done by a "well-known" composer. Jackson, writing to Falla on 4 December 1901, had tried to arrange several librettos for Falla, but with no luck from his friends, saying that he is not to blame for what has happened. He then promised to write one himself for Falla at a later date, complaining that he is overwhelmed with rehearsals on *La Cariñosa* and must write "six librettos" in March upon departure for Mexico. He implores Falla to be patient and to meanwhile begin composing some light polkas, waltzes, and other pieces which "we" can use later.[28]

A debut was planned for *Limosna de amor*, but it seems not to have taken place. From a letter to José J. Rodríguez y Fernández, dated

22 May 1902, Falla notes that he has sent him his two published piano works and that he has been extremely busy preparing for the debut of his *zarzuela* with libretto by Jackson at the Comic Theater in Madrid in the next week, not even having time for the festivities at this time of year. He also noted that there was no scarcity of good music in Madrid, but since the Madrid public did not appreciate the quality of the operas at the Lyric Theater and since the Lyric would not likely be able to give all of the works announced for that season, Falla predicted that the future for Spanish national opera would continue to be a "pipe dream."[30]

In 1903–1904 three other *zarzuelas* followed—some biographers list a total of five—that were composed with Amadeo Vives on texts by unknown librettists: *El cornetín de ordenes* (The Cornet of Orders), *La cruz de Malta* (The Cross of Malta) and *Prisionero de guerra* (Prisoner of War). *El cornetín de ordenes* was commissioned by a commercial business. It was the first *zarzuela* of the "grande" form and contained three acts. A letter from Vives to Falla reveals the fate of this unperformed *zarzuela*. He writes to "Faya" in 1904, mentioning that the season only lasts until Epiphany and that the producer, Borges, "doubts that he will be able to present all the works he has engaged. In view of this I consider our efforts are in vain and that we can save ourselves the trouble of visiting him today."[31]

Falla paid his dues. Once again this experience of trying his hand at composing *zarzuelas* served Falla as a laboratory or testing ground. Some experiments were successful, some were not. But the process was the important ingredient, as he himself acknowledged when he commented years later about Pedrell's failure to become acknowledged as a composer, noting that there is no substitution for practical experience. The experience Falla gained was invaluable and would later pay big dividends, literally and figuratively. Yet the disappointment of so many foiled attempts to have his *zarzuelas* performed must have been great. He himself confessed that this was only a means to an end, the means being financial and the end being study in Paris. He admitted that composing *zarzuelas* went against his musical vein and was not done to make himself popular in Madrid.

However, it proved that his music was good enough for an orchestra, at a time before he studied instrumentation with Felipe Pedrell (from 1901–1904). It was also fortunate that his *zarzuelas*, in general, were not successful. This failure became yet another challenge and one that became a turning point in his career.

PEDRELL

In 1901, during the "*zarzuela* years," Falla met and soon afterwards began his studies with composer-musicologist Felipe Pedrell (1841–1922). Pedrell was professor of music history and aesthetics at the Madrid Conservatory of Music and at the Athenaeum. He was voted a member of the prestigious Real Academia de Bellas Artes. Falla studied privately with him, his lessons being paid for by his rich friend Melquiades Almagro de San Martín.[32]

Pedrell led the way for creating a new Spanish nationalistic musical language. He was in line with the "Generación del '98"[33] (Generation of 1898), amongst whose writers such as Miguel de Unamuno or Antonio Machado directed the way to a new Spanish nationalistic expression. Pedrell's manifesto, *Por Nuestra Música*,[34] (1 September 1891) called for a return to "Spanish roots." He proposed this through the rediscovery of: (1) Spain's masterpieces—its great polyphonic tradition, taken as far back as the 13th century; and (2) the nation's wealth of folklore. According to Falla, "His theories are based on an axiom enunciated by Father Antonio Eximeno at the end of the eighteenth century, and according to which 'each nation must build its musical system on the popular song of its country.'"[35] Pedrell also propounded, "the character of a really national music is to be found not only in popular song and in the instinctive expression of primitive ages, but also in the great masterpieces."[36]

Pedrell's vast erudition can be seen in the multivolume *Hispaniae scholae musica*,[37] his four-volume *Cancionero popular español* (Spanish Popular Folksong Book),[38] his operatic trilogy *Los Pirineos* (The Pyrénées)—accepted by the Teatro Real but never staged in spite of having been "previously approved"[39] by the prestigious Real Academia de Bellas Artes—and other works. Pedrell's disappointing failure as a composer was commented upon by Falla in 1923. ". . . Pedrell lacked the experience that can be acquired only through practical artistic activity, through performance, the stage and the public. Nothing can replace this."[40]

Pedrell taught some of the leading young composers of the day—Isaac Albéniz, Enrique Granados, Luis Millet, Amadeu Vives, Bartolomé Pérez Casas, and Roberto Gerhard. Falla described his inspirational lesson. ". . . with what joy he informed us of the discovery of one of those old manuscripts that revealed the eternal character of our art, and how his eyes shone as he explained those qualities, tracing with his finger the curves of a musical line ideally sketched in space!"[41] He further commented, "Pedrell was a TEACHER in the highest sense of the word; through his doctrine, and with his example, he led Spanish musicians towards a profoundly national and noble art, a path that at the beginning of last century was already considered to be hopelessly closed."[42]

Falla's contact with Pedrell influenced him for the rest of his life, claiming that it was to Pedrell's teaching that he owed "the clearest and strongest direction of my work."[43]

> The mere comparison of some of the songs transcribed and harmonized by Pedrell with the transcription and the harmonization of the same songs appearing in preceding collections, will show us how a song that we hardly noticed before becomes singularly significant in his hands. The reason is that the very peculiar modal character of some of those songs is reduced in the older collections to the invariable tonal sentiment of the major and minor scales, whereas Pedrell extracted from them their true modal and harmonic essence."[44]

Falla would come to understand all too well the lack of appreciation Pedrell felt in Madrid and in Spain in general. Madrid did not receive Falla easily, nor warmly. His appeals for some kind of work at the Conservatory later were heartrending and not forthcoming. So in his article published in the *Revue Musical Paris* in February 1923, Falla commiserated in an attempt to keep such things from recurring in his native country.

> For Pedrell was in his country a victim, not only of general indifference and lack of appreciation but also of the ill will of many. When in 1904 he moved from Madrid to Barcelona because of his health, the Real Academia de Bellas Artes that some years before had felt honoured to receive him as a member, hastened to declare vacant his academic seat.[45]

While it has been said that Pedrell did not appreciate Falla's talents, Falla always acknowledged his gratitude to his mentor. This is obvious from the "expressive arrangements" that Falla continued to make in his later years as well as the closure on his letters of "your grateful student." Upon the première of *La vida breve*, Pedrell acknowledged Falla as a "modest, ever humble, but remarkable composer."[46] Some years later, on the occasion of the *Cante jondo* Competition organized by Falla and Federico García Lorca in 1922, Pedrell, at the age of eighty-one and just two months before his death, sent a message saying, "Tell your friends that

I'm now singing *cante jondo* inwardly; if I'm not among you, I'll always be with you, and with all my heart."[47]

COMPOSITIONS

In the years just prior to and during Falla's studies with Pedrell, he composed several works other than his *zarzuelas.* These included the piano pieces *Canción* (Song) (1900),[48] *Serenata andaluza* (Andalusian Serenade) (1900) (not to be confused with the piece by the same title for violin and piano), *Vals capricho* (Capricious Waltz) (1900), *Pasacale torero* (1900), *Cortejo de gnomos* (Procession of the Gnomes) (1901), *Serenata* (Serenade) (1901), *Segunda serenata andaluza* (Second Andalusian Serenade) (1901), an untitled work referred to as *Pieza para piano en mí mayor* (Work for Piano in E Major) (1901), *Suite fantástica* (Fantastic Suite) (1901), and *Allegro de concierto* (Concert Allegro) (1903–1904), which won an "honorable mention" at the Madrid Conservatory with Enrique Granados taking the first prize with a composition by the same name. Not all are complete, nor extant.

Vocal works, other than the *zarzuelas,* included *Preludios, ("Madre, todas las noches")* (Preludes) (1900), based on a poem by Antonio Trueba; *Rima: ("Olas gigantes")*—Rhyme—("Giant Waves") (1900), on a text by G. A. Bécquer; *¡Dios mío, qué solos se quedan los muertos!* (My God, how alone remain the dead!) (1900), text by G. A. Bécquer; *Tus ojillos negros, canción andaluza* (Your Little Black Eyes, Andalusian song) (1902–1903), on a poem by Cristóbal de Castro; *Cantares de Nochebuena* (Christmas Eve Song Cycle) (1903–1904), and nine songs for voice, guitar, and percussion. A partial Scherzo movement with *da capo* remains from an intended quartet (1903).

It is interesting to note that one song with strong Andalusian characteristics, *Tus ojillos negros* (Your Little Black Eyes) had success in America, was recorded by Hipólito Lázaro, and was arranged for violin and piano, unbeknownst to the composer. Falla's collection of Christmas Eve songs, *Cantares de Nochebuena,* show Pedrell's indubitable influence and Falla's handling of several *Cancioneros* (Spanish folksong books), those of Inzenga, Hurtado, Olmeda, and Dámaso Ledesma Hernández. One of these songs, "Un pastor lleva un pavo," has the same melody, though in a minor mode, of the "Canción" used in Falla's *Siete canciones populares españolas* (found as "Canto de Granada" in José Inzenga's *Ecos de España*) (Echos of Spain) many years later.

Falla would disown his youthful compositions, saying that whatever he had written before 1904 was worthless nonsense, even though some early works were published during his lifetime. Yet another time he contradicted himself. When asked about these early musical works, he allegedly answered, "After all, they weren't so bad."[49]

Falla normally exerted careful control over his works, especially in his mature years. Yet, in 1940, Unión Musical Española of Madrid republished, without Falla's consent, some of the youthful works: *Serenata andaluza*, *Vals capricho*, *Nocturno*, and *Tus ojillos negros*.[51]

LOUIS LUCAS

Sometime during the early 1900s (Falla told Roland-Manuel that it was during the time he was composing his opera *La vida breve*—The Short Life—begun in 1904), Falla chanced upon a book that would radically alter his life. In an outdoor secondhand bookstore in the Cuesta Moyano near the Botanical Gardens of Madrid he happened upon Louis Lucas's *L'Acoustique nouvelle, ou Essai d'application d'une méthode philosophique aux questions élevées de l'acoustique, de la musique et de la composition musicale* (The New Acoustics, an Attempt to Apply a Philosophical Theory to Music—Preceded by a Preface by Théodore de Banville and Followed by a Treatise by Euclid and by Plutarch's Dialogue on Music. Paris, published by the author, 1854). An earlier edition was published in 1849 by Paulin et Lechevalier (Paris), but with poor, or no, sales.

Among the many ideas discussed by Lucas is one that no doubt appealed to Falla, in harmony with the Spanish tradition of folk music, *cante jondo* and constant need for renewal. Lucas supported the idea that by adhering only to major and minor modes we build "an impassable barrier between ourselves and the entire Orient and many other peoples too numerous to list."[52] As a solution, he suggested the use of micro divisions of the tone and espoused *enharmony* in the ancient Greek and folksinger's use of it. He noted that "in the mobile, voluntary division of tone, in this infinite decomposition of sound, the application of the phenomenon of attraction (is) pushed to its extreme limits. . . . Nature has placed therein the most complete force for expressing our instincts and passions."[53]

Falla studied this book in depth and annotated his personal copy, at least two-thirds of it. Like strict adherence to his religious beliefs and to his faith in God, Falla also regarded the "eternal law of tonality"[54] as infallible. Loyalty to his country also fell into the same category. Thus, Lucas's book presented him with a way to stay on the straight path but to go far afield without fear of negating the basic precept of tonality. It also provided him with a different way to view Spanish musical idioms. The use of various modes was also in line with Pedrell's thinking. Falla did not go so far as to use quarter tones that Lucas purported, unless the *cante jondo* undulations be counted as such. However, the creation of harmony from melody or melodic scales became one of Falla's working processes. Hence, his interest in modes and scales from a multitude of sources is clearly understandable.

Biographer Roland-Manuel claimed Falla gained the idea from Lucas of "the arrangement of internal rhythm . . . of the harmony born of the dynamic equilibrium of phrases, depends on the judicious placement of related sounds."[55] Falla developed an enormously rich and complex system of harmonic superpositions, referred to by Rodolfo Halffter as "a theory of resonance."[56] Yet whether Falla developed a "theory of resonance" or not, he began developing these ideas before leaving for Paris (for example, "Montañesa" in *Cuatro piezas españolas*, begun in 1906).

Years later, in his article "Notes on Richard Wagner on the Fiftieth Anniversary of His Death," published in *Cruz y Raya*, in Madrid, September 1933, Falla hints at Lucas. Falla spoke of the "internal union of rhythm and tonality" and alluded to his system of chord generation.

> Let us not forget that music develops in time and in space. To perceive effectively time and space, it is essential to determine their limits, to establish the initial, central and final points, or the points of departure and suspense, linked by a close internal relation. Sometimes this relation apparently blurs the tonal sense established by its limits; but it is only for a short time and with the intention of underlining that very tonal value, which becomes more intense when it reappears after having been eclipsed. We should not forget either, that it is necessary to be fully convinced of the fundamental truth offered by the natural acoustic scale in order to establish the harmonic—and therefore contrapuntal—basis of the music, as well as to give a tonal structure to a series of melodic periods which, being generated by the same resonances which integrate that scale, have to move at different levels. What I mean is that the intervals forming that column of sounds are the only real possibility for the constitution of the chord, as well as an infallible norm for the tonal-melodic construction of those periods that, limited by cadential movements, compose every musical work.[57]

Doubtless, Falla's working out his personal philosophy of composition owes much to the discovery of the Lucas book.[58]

TWO COMPETITIONS—TWO FIRST PRIZES

Falla's serious attitude toward composition was paying off. He was developing technical prowess coupled with his own unique individuality. In 1904 the Academia de Bellas Artes de San Fernando (San Fernando Academy of Fine Arts) announced a competition for a one-act opera, as well as for a symphonic work. The deadline was 31 March "before sunset" to turn in the competing scores. The first prize was to be a performance of the work at the Teatro Real and 2,500 pesetas. Falla was immediately attracted. He searched for a libretto and found one in Carlos Fernández-Shaw's *La vida breve*. Fernández-Shaw (Cádiz 1865–Madrid 1911) was a poet and libretto writer for *zarzuela* composers, which might explain the nature of the plot of the opera. It involves a gypsy girl, Salud, who lives with her grandfather and her aunt in the Albaïcin district of Granada. She is seduced by Paco, the hero, and they subsequently plan to marry. They both pledge eternal love, but Paco quickly becomes enamored of the rich Carmela. At the wedding Salud reproaches Paco, then falls dead at his feet—an unlikely story, but one that Falla worked on wholeheartedly.

Yet another competition had been announced—the Ortiz y Cussó Prize for Piano. The first prize was a grand piano, compliments of the Ortiz y Cussó piano firm. Falla decided to enter, thinking he had nothing to lose, but not expecting to win. He had little time to practice, for his work on *La vida breve* absorbed him. His teacher, José Tragó, supported him in this endeavor.

March 30 arrived and Falla still lacked the final touches on his opera. Working most of the night to finish, Falla needed additional assistance. Ingeniously he asked his brother Germán to write the words of the arias under the musical notes. Unfortunately Germán, not having any musical training, wrote many words under the musical rests. When Falla discovered this error, it was too late to do anything about it. His father hurriedly went to turn in the score just before the deadline of sunset on 31 March, with Falla's note saying that, due to the shortness of time, he had used a copyist who erroneously misplaced the words in some places and that this error was in no way a reflection of the composer.

The next day began the Ortiz y Cussó competition. Falla was to play in last place, amongst the thirty-three entrants. This was luck, for it gave him yet another two weeks to practice. The jury members consisted of Tomas Bretón as chairperson; Joaquín Malats, the famous Catalan pianist; José Pellicer, professor at the Municipal School of Music in Barcelona; María Cervantes of the firm Ortiz y Cussó; and professors Pilar Mora and José Tragó, Falla's mentor, from the Madrid Conservatory.[59]

One of the competitors, the famous and brilliant Frank Marshall (Granados's favorite pupil), was expected to win. Indeed when he played the hall was full, the applause convincing. Falla congratulated him.

When it came time for Falla to play, there were hardly any people in the audience. However, he put forth great effort and emotion, playing sensitively works of Bach, Scarlatti, Beethoven, Chopin, Schumann, Liszt, Saint-Saëns, and his own *Allegro de concierto*. His emotional communication moved the jury. Pilar Mora cried. They unanimously voted him first prize and took him to lunch as a sign of respect. When it came time for him to play his winning recital, he was unable to maintain the emotional intensity that he had achieved earlier. Technically less proficient than Marshall, Falla's performance was almost a deception. He simply did not have the nervous constitution for a solo concert career. He himself admitted,

> As far as my pianistic virtuosity goes, in reality it has never existed, because my assiduousness and patience in "purely musical" studies have at no time been shared by instrumental ones.[60]

LOVE

During the heat of the two competitions, Falla was tortured by his feelings for his cousin, María Prieto Ledesma, his mother's sister's daughter. He was now approaching his thirtieth year, no longer a youth, but without a stable income to support a wife. He was plainly timid and uncertain of himself, not knowing if she shared his feelings. He vacillated in revealing his love to her. Padre Fedriani once again stepped in and advised him, telling him to either declare his intention once and for all or else to desist completely. He also advised that if God wanted this to be then it would be, and if not, it would be for Falla's own good.[61] The last reference to the affair is dated 14 November 1905. Fedriani encourages Falla to make a stand one way or the other, to stop the ". . . foolishness, suppositions, inquiries, conjectures, excuses, and moreover, the same ridiculous and idiotic constraints. . . ."[62] In the end Falla never married.

TOWARDS PARIS

Despite the successes in Madrid, Falla became ever more disillusioned with his life there. He applied for official financial aid from the state and was rejected. He played a series of concerts, hoping to raise money for his trip. His one-act opera *La vida breve* still had not been performed. His dream of going to Paris still burned brightly.

In 1906 Falla had his first communication with France's chief composer. He wrote to Debussy asking his advice about performance indications in his *Danse sacrée et danse profane* (1904),[63] the harp part of which he was to perform on the piano on 4 February 1907 with Bretón conducting. Debussy's response, dated 13 January 1907 from Avenue 64 Bois du Boulogne in Paris, is illuminating.

> Sir, I found your kind letter last night on returning from Brussels and I beg you to forgive the tardiness of my reply. . . . Moreover what you ask me is quite difficult to answer! One cannot demonstrate the exact value of a rhythm just as one cannot explain the dreamy expression of a phrase! The best thing, in my opinion, is to refer it to one's own feelings. . . . For me, the color of the two dances is clearly contrasted. You must find some way of connecting the "seriousness" of the first with the "humor" of the second. For a musician like yourself it should not be difficult, and I believe that I can surrender myself to your judgement with complete confidence.
>
> Accept sir, my sincere artistic cordiality and my best wishes. Claude Debussy.[64]

Falla's ever-present desire to go to Paris doubtless was further enhanced by Debussy's response. Yet another incident fueled the fire to hasten Falla's final step towards the French capital. On 11 January 1907, the secretary of the Bilbao Philharmonic, Juan Carlos Gortazar, was visiting Madrid and took it upon himself to organize a concert for the composer. However, when Falla arrived in Bilbao, he was told he was to accompany the violinist Paul Kochansky. After the concert the duo had supper with the violinist's impresario from Paris who offered to organize a series of concerts for him during the following summer. The concerts were not immediately forthcoming. Falla wrote again and suggested some dates, receiving word from the impresario that he would meet him at the station. So, on that promise he left for Paris in the summer of 1907 with "enough enthusiasm for a lifetime, [and] in his purse enough money for a few days."[65]

NOTES

1. Mario Verdaguer, *Medio siglo de vida barcelonesa*. Barcelona, 1957, 181; description of his meeting with Falla in 1909.

Fue Joaquín Turina quien me presentó a Falla en Madrid la tarde del entierro de Ruperto Chapí, que murió unos días después de haber sido estrenada en el Teatro Real su ópera "Margarita la Tornera." En aquella época Manuel de Falla usaba poblados bigotes y llevaba sombrero hongo. Atravesaba una época de miseria negra. Y era cuando le salían lecciones de piano a dos pesetas la hora y si el solicitante regateaba rebajaba el aleccionamiento hasta seis reales.

2. Concha Chinchilla, "Cronología de manuel de falla" in *manuel de falla En Granada*, Granada: AMF, 2001, 155.
3. Hereafter referred to as the Madrid Conservatory.
4. For a further Chopin-Bach link, see chapter 10.
5. Letter to Salvador Viniegra (17 December 1899) from José Tragó, Christoforidis-Iconografía, 23.
6. Andrew Budwig claims that until his immediate family joined him in 1900, he lived with his aunt Emilia and her husband, José Ledesma (Chase-Budwig, 8). Pahissa says that when Falla was twenty his family decided to move to Madrid and that from the age of fifteen he began to study with Tragó (Pahissa, 31). Orozco says that Falla made his first trip to Madrid in 1890 to enroll in the Conservatory (Orozco, 36).
7. Orozco, 36–37. Falla was born in the '70s, he traveled to Sevilla in 1887, moved to Madrid in 1897. He later would go to Paris in 1907 and stay for seven years. Subsequently he would die just before his seventieth birthday.
8. Chinchilla, 155.
9. Chase-Budwig, 8.
10. Pahissa, 31.
11. Demarquez, 12.
12. Jack Sage in "Zarzuela," *The New Grove Dictionary of Music and Musicians*, 1980, vol. 20, 649.
13. Sage, 649.
14. *Harvard Dictionary of Music*, ed. Wili Apel, 2nd ed./8th printing. Cambridge, Mass.: The Belknap Press of Harvard University Press, 1974, 932.
15. Sage, 650.
16. Falla in "Our Music," '*Música,*' Number 2, Madrid, June 1917, published in *On Music and Musicians*, 30–31 (hereafter as OMM).

17. Pahissa, 32.
18. Pahissa counts Falla's output as five, although Falla says in an interview with F. Martín Caballero in Madrid and published in the *Noticiero sevillano* in November 1914, that he had written six theatrical works in his youth. These *zarzuelas* would be:

1. *La Juana y la Petra, o la casa de Tócame Roque* (J. Santero)—c. 1900;
2. *Los amores de la Inés* (Emilio Dugi, alias Manuel Osorio y Bertrand)— c. 1901–1902 (debut on 12 April 1902, at Teatro Cómico in Madrid (published by Unión Musical Española in 1903);
3. *Limosna de amor* (José Jackson Veyán)—1901–1902;
4. *El cornetín de ordenes* with composer Amadeo Vives (librettist unknown)—1903;
5. *La cruz de Malta* with composer Amadeo Vives (librettist unknown)— 1903;
6. *Prisionero de guerra* with composer Amadeo Vives (librettist unknown)— 1903–1904.

19. *Manuel de Falla. Apuntes de Harmonía. Dietario de Paris [1908]*, facsimile edition of the daily professional life of the composer between 1901–1908. Granada: Publicaciones del Archivo Manuel de Falla, colección "Facsimiles," serie "Documentos," no. 1, edited by Francesc Bonastre and Yvan Nommick, at press. *Manuel de Falla. Apuntes de Harmonía. Dietario de Paris (1908)*. Edición facsimilar, limitada y numerada, de un cuaderno de apuntes y de un dietario que documentan la vida profesional y diaria de Falla entre 1901 y 1908. Edición y estudios musicológicos a cargo de Francesc Bonastre e Yvan Nommick. Publicaciones del Archivo Manuel de Falla, colección "Facsímiles," serie "Documentos," no. 1 (2001).
20. Pahissa, 33.
21. The work has one act and two scenes with libretto by Emilio Dugi, alias Manuel Osorio y Bertrand.
22. Demarquez, 16.
23. Diário de Cádiz, 17 April 1902, AMF 6408/40.
24. Demarquez, 16.
25. Demarquez, 16.
26. Various pages from Falla's *Apuntes de Harmonía. Dietario de Paris* (1908).
27. *Apuntes de harmonía*, 128, referred to in AGC, 51.
28. Letter José Jackson Veyán-Falla, ("Amigo Falla"), dated 4 December 1901, from Arrieta, 11, entresuelo derecho, Madrid, AMF 7144.
29. *Poesía*, 35.
30. *Poesía*, 35.
31. *Poesía*, 36.
32. Sopeña, 26.
33. Campodónico, 25.

34. *For Our Music* or could be translated as *Through Our Music*, sometimes referred to as *Por Nuestra Música.*

35. Falla, OMM, 55.

36. Falla, OMM, 55.

37. Falla, OMM, 57. "Thanks to that publication, the works of Cabezón, Victoria, Morales and Guerrero could be extensively studied and commented on by musicologists from all over the world. . . . "

38. Falla, OMM, 60. "A fundamental work that is like a synthesis of all his artistic creation. In it, a Spanish musician will find more than the manifold modal and harmonic values that emerge from the rhythmic-melodic substance of that music."

39. Falla, OMM, 61.

40. Falla, OMM, 58.

41. *Poesía*, 41.

42. Falla, *La Revue Musicale Paris*, February 1923 (OMM 54).

43. Demarquez, 22.

44. Falla, OMM, 60.

45. Falla, OMM, 61.

46. *Poesía*, 61.

47. Falla, OMM, 61.

48. Dates given here are based on those attributed by musicologist Antonio Gallego in the Archivo Manuel de Falla's *Catálogo de obras de Manuel de Falla* (1987) Madrid: Ministerio de Cultura, Dirección General de Bellas Artes y Archivos (hereafter AGC).

49. Epistolary, AMF.

50. Demarquez, 9.

51. Demarquez, 17.

52. Demarquez, 20.

53. Demarquez, 20.

54. Nancy Lee Harper, "Rodolfo Halffter and the Superposiciones of Manuel de Falla." *ex tempore*, Summer, 1996, 58–94.

55. Demarquez, 20–21.

56. Harper, *ex tempore*, 59.

57. OMM, 83–84.

58. For a more detailed discussion, see chapter 11.

59. Orozco, 37–38.

60. *Poesía*, 43.

61. Letter Fedriani-Falla, 5 April 1905 ". . . Tu estáte muy tranquilo y déjate de majaderías y tonterías que si está de Dios y cuando esté de Dios será y si no sucede para tu bien será. De modo que tranquilidad y absoluta indiferencia." AMF 6962.

62. Letter Fedriani-Falla dated 14 November 1905. ". . . tonterías, suposiciones, averiguaciones, conjeturas, cavilaciones y demás del mismo jaez ridículo y necio. . . ." AMF 6962.

63. Debussy also made a two-piano version of the piece in the same year, 1904.

64. Letter Debussy-Falla, Sunday, 13 January 1907, from 80, Avenue du Bois de Boulogne (*Dimanche, 13 janv 07*), AMF 6898. Grateful appreciation is given to Chris Collins for the use of his transcription of Debussy's letter which appears in his doctoral thesis (U. Bangor, Wales) as appendix 3A.

Monsieur,

Revenu depuis hier soir d'un voyage a Bruxelles, je trouve votre aimable lettre et vous prie de m'excuser d'y répondre aussi tardivement. Ce que vous me demandez est d'ailleurs assez difficile à résoudre! On me peut démontrer la valeur exacte d'un rhythme, pas plus qu'on explique l'expression diverse d'une phrase!

Le meilleur, à mon avis, et que vous en remettiez à votre sentiment personnel. La couleur des deux danses me paraît nettement tranchée. Il y a quelque chose à trouver dans l'enchaînement de la "gravité" de la première à la "grâce" de la seconde, pour un musicien tel que vous, ce ne peut être un difficulté, et je crois pouvoir m'abondonner à votre gout en toute confiance.

Croyez, Monsieur[,] à ma sincère cordialité artistique et à mes meilleurs sentiments.

Claude Debussy

65. Demarquez, 35.

Chapter 3

Paris (1907–1914)

Without Paris, I would have remained buried in Madrid, done for and forgotten, laboriously leading an obscure existence, living miserably and keeping my first prize, like in a family album, with the score of my opera in a cupboard. To be published in Spain is worse than being published at all. It's like throwing the music into a well.[1]

While the long-term reality of this statement was positive, the short-term effect was certainly precarious. The risk Falla took by leaving Madrid and his family and professional circle of friends—not to mention the ten years of building relationships in his budding career—might have seemed foolish for anyone without Falla's inner fortitude and discipline. Madrid had looked more promising to him after having won two prestigious first prizes. His disappointment in not having his opera, *La vida breve*, staged at the Teatro Real as stipulated in the Academia de Bellas Artes competition propaganda (a similar situation of Pedrell and *Los Pirineos*) may have given him the impetus to take the decisive step. This step initially—Paris—was a bit of a step down. Although work was forthcoming, years of deprivation continued. Falla, in spite of his meager income and financial resources, strove to send some money to his family in Spain. He clipped newspaper coupons in order to obtain free food samples. From extant diaries, his arithmetic calculations show him to be fastidious in budgeting on a mere pittance. His health would eventually pay the price, although perseverance would also pay him the professional dividends for which he yearned.

ARRIVAL

Luck, or destiny, was with Falla. He had arrived in the French capital when Spain and Spanish culture were trendy, with Debussy having written *Lindaraja* (1901), "La soirée dans Granade" from the suite *Estampes* (1903), and *Iberia* (1905–1908); and Ravel having composed his *Rapsodie espagnole* (1907–1908) and *L'Heure espagnole* (1907–1909).

The Polish pianist, Artur Rubinstein, for whom Falla would later write his *Fantasía bætica*, described the scene.

> . . . the obelisk in the center of this unique square *[Place de la Concorde]* from where you see the four most beautiful perspectives in the world: to the right, the Madeleine, the church where Chopin's funeral took place; to the left, the Chambre des Députés, both built in a pure Greek style; before me, the majestic Champs-Élysées, at the end of which the Arc de Triomphe, bathed in a pink and red sunset, soars in to the air; and behind me, the charming, terraced Tuileries Garden leading to the large and venerable buildings of the Louvre.
>
> I was so overwhelmed by the beauty of it all that my voice broke . . . I couldn't utter a word, but I made silently, there and then, a sacred vow never to live anywhere in the world but in this divine city! . . .
>
> This was 1904; the boulevards were still the heart of Paris. The big theaters, the best restaurants and cafés, were concentrated on these historical blocks.
>
> The sidewalks were crowded. I was intrigued by some of the fast-walking, vivacious Parisiennes who would raise slightly one side of their floor-length skirts with three finger tips; their faces were covered by "Voilettes," and they wore large, ornate picture hats on top of their hair. Probably they were on their way to some romantic rendezvous. Young couples would stroll by in close embrace; "flaneurs," the Paris version of our "city slickers," were looking for adventure; nobody seemed to be in a hurry. Buses, carriages, cabs, driven by horses, were dashing up and down the street; trees were beginning to shed their golden leaves. The air, filled with the aroma of perfume mixed with a strong scent of horses, was brought to one's nostrils by a mild autumnal breeze.
>
> This was my first encounter with the Parisian street scene, and its fascination has prevailed to this day [ca. 1973] as I write these lines.[2]

Falla arrived in Paris at the height of the summer, although the exact date is speculated. A tour of France, Belgium, Germany, and Switzerland, was forthcoming.[3] He served as pianist and director of a small orchestra for a company of pantomime artists in André Wormser's *L'enfant prodigue* (an unknown Prix de Rome composer, who was "exceedingly demanding and inspired terror").[4] In the first letter to his family (Paris, 16 August 1907), he mentions the heat in Geneva and the impressiveness of Switzerland. He adds that a second tour was begun on the 21st or 22nd (July?), and that yet another "more artistic" tour was planned for October.[5] His conducting debut was apparently made in Luxembourg on Monday, 23 December 1907.[6]

In between tours Falla took up lodging at the Hôtel Kléber, on Belloy Street, where his old friend Joaquín Turina also lived. But this stay was short-lived, because of other musicians' daily practice becoming too noisy. Falla moved to another more modest hotel on the Avenue de Bois de Boulogne.[7] Always very frugal, he was then paying one franc per day for lodging, surviving on a daily total of five francs, and taking his meals at "the Restaurant Chartier on the Avenue de la Grande-Armée."[8] Piano and harmonium lessons drew ten francs each.[9] In 1908 he returned to the Hôtel Kléber,[10] where he remained until 1914. The oft-quoted remark of Claude Debussy, that Falla "moved more often than Beethoven" hardly seems exact, but indicates their contact with each other.[11]

INFLUENTIAL FRIENDS AND COLLEAGUES[12]

Slightly built, dark-complexioned, nervous, with a penetrating look and piercing eyes under a resolute forehead, an Andalusian face that showed Arab traces, a face in which Spain was strongly reflected, while his brief and rare utterances, from the beginning, gave me the feeling of a man who was simultaneously passionate and meditative. . . . His artistic life is an example of meticulous choice and firm will, of considered prudence and prompt resolution[13]—(Jean-Aubry upon meeting Falla in Paris).

Soon after his arrival in Paris, Falla met Paul Dukas, who was responsible for introducing him to Isaac Albéniz (3 October 1907, at the Salón) and Claude Debussy, to whom he had previous correspondence. Falla had initially planned to enter the Schola Cantorum to further his studies, but Dukas advised him against this course, encouraging him to work on his own instead.

With a letter of recommendation, Falla met the distinguished Catalan pianist, Ricardo Viñes on 29 September. Viñes, who was an excellent sight-reader, played many of the premières of Debussy's, Ravel's, and later Falla's works. Falla describes his first experiences with the French compositional elite to his librettist, Carlos Fernández-Shaw.

My first big satisfaction in Paris, I had shortly after my arrival when I went to visit [Paul] Dukas. (Debussy was then absent.) During that first visit I explained to Dukas the reasons which brought me to Paris: to work and to study in order to become acquainted with the technical methods of the modern French school, as I found them applicable to my manner of perceiving music. He asked me to let him hear some of my work to see which direction would be best for me to follow: I played for him *"La vida breve,"* and I will never forget the kindness and the interest with which he listened to my reading. Until then he had been reserved (naturally so, because not only was this the first time that he had spoken to me, but also I went to see him without even a presentation card); but when he had heard my work everything changed, and his words filled me with such encouragement that, as I told him, I had the impression of waking from a bad dream. With insistence, he advised me to take great care not to change my personal feeling for music and to continue working alone, as I then did. With great precision he indicated the plan that I should follow, placing himself at my disposal for any questions I might have, and was prepared to examine all that I continue to write. He introduced me to Albéniz, who welcomed me in a truly magnificent fashion. . . . This animated me immensely, he presented me to many of his friends, and under all concepts, acted with me as a great and loyal friend. He was, as you will remember, the person who presented me to Paul Milliet, and this is one of the greatest favors that I owe him,[. . .].

Later, when I heard that Debussy was back in Paris, I went to see him, because I had to recite what we could call a litany of gratitude, as I owed him so much for the interest he had taken in my work and for the artistic protection which, like Dukas, he had had the goodness to grant me, guiding me, like that, in my work, getting it published and encouraging me constantly to press on with my plans and projects. At the same time I went to visit Ricardo Viñes, the great Spanish pianist, and through him I met Maurice Ravel, Florent Schmitt, [Michel Dmitri] Calvocoressi, etc., and to all of them I have nothing more than motives of gratitude.[14]

It was through Viñes too that Falla was inducted into the circle of young progressive musicians called the "Club des Apaches," with members other than Ravel, such as Charles Koechlin, Florent Schmitt, Maurice Delage, Calvocoressi, Joaquín Nin, and others. Delage hosted the group every Saturday night at his hotel on Rue de Civry in Auteuil. Stravinsky would later become a member. Through Falla's friendship with fellow Spaniard, Joaquín Turina, he was able to keep ties to musicians at the Schola Cantorum. Through Viñes, he also met Roland-Manuel and Gustave Samazeuilh, and eventually entered the Godebski circle on Rue d'Athènes, where all French or foreign artistic elite met on Sundays.

Some of the large group of Spanish artists who lived in Paris at this time became known to Falla through Viñes and Albéniz. He became good friends with guitarists Miguel Llobet, whom he had heard play in Madrid, and Ángel Barrios, who was part of the Trio Iberia that enjoyed a certain degree of success in Europe.[15] He also had cordial relations with Catalan artists such as Pablo Casals, Enrique Granados, and conductor Fernández-Arbós. It seems contact with Picasso would come at a later date. Also, he met José María Sert, with whom he would form a close friendship and professional association in the *Atlántida* project. Towards the end of his Paris sojourn, he would meet Gregorio and María Martínez Sierra in 1913, with whom he would soon collaborate in several works.

Through the *soirées* at Cipa Godebski's, Falla would also meet Wanda Landowska, Ignacio Zuloaga, and Igor Stravinsky in 1910. Stravinsky tells of their first encounter.

> Sometime in 1910, at Cipa Godebski's, I was introduced to a man even smaller than myself, and as modest and withdrawn as an oyster. I took him, Manuel de Falla, for an "homme sérieux"; in fact his nature was the most unpityingly religious I have ever known—and the least sensible to mani-festations of humour. I have never seen anyone as shy.[16]

Concert tours, piano lessons to children of the well-off Hispanic-American families, and occasional disagreeable bar performances helped to supplement the precarious and meager income. If the income was erratic, the adventure must have compensated. Falla took advantage of the rich musical life there, hearing such works as Debussy's *Pelléas et Mélisande* (three times in one week!—on 17, 19, and 21 June 1908)[17] and Mussorgsky's *Boris Godunov*, which impressed him deeply. He also attended the Concerts Colonne series, as well as many symphony concerts, chamber music recitals, and new music concerts, hearing Richard Strauss conduct his own music.

When Falla met Debussy in the autumn of 1907, he failed to recognize the French composer at first because Debussy looked more like a sailor than the famous musician. "Cést moi, cést moi-même" ("It's I, it's I myself"), Debussy uttered. Falla very awkwardly tried to converse with his idol, saying that he had always liked French music, to which Debussy retorted, "Well, I haven't." Having been previously advised by Dukas that "un petit espagnol tout noir" (a little Spaniard all in black) had been to see him, Debussy then asked Falla to play his opera for him. He heard it to the end, giving it praise. Many doors would open because of these contacts.[18]

Some thirteen years later, in homage to Debussy, Falla wrote an article that was published in the *Revue Musicale* in Paris in December 1920.

> Without knowing Spain, or without having set foot on Spanish ground, Claude Debussy has written Spanish music. He came to know Spain through books and paintings, through songs and dances performed by native Spaniards. . . . Debussy . . . spontaneously, I dare say unconsciously, created such Spanish music as was to arouse the envy of many who knew her only too well. He crossed the border only once, and stayed for a few hours in San Sebastián to attend a bullfight: little enough experience indeed. However, he kept a vivid memory of the unique light in the bullring, of the astonishing contrast between that side flooded by sunlight and the one in shadow. . . . We might say that, up to a certain point, Debussy has taken to new lengths our knowledge of the modal possibilities in our music already revealed by our teacher Felipe Pedrell. But while the Spanish composer to a large extent uses in his music the authentic popular material, the French master avoids them and creates a music of his own, borrowing only the essence of its fundamental elements. This working method, always praiseworthy among native composers . . . acquires still greater value when practised by those who write music which is, as it were, alien. There is still another interesting fact regarding certain harmonic phenomenon which occur in the particular texture of Debussy's music. In Andalusia they are produced on the guitar in the most spontaneous way. It is curious that Spanish composers have neglected, even despised as barbaric those effects, or they have adapted them to the old musical procedures. Debussy has taught the way to use them . . . if Claude Debussy has found in Spain a source of one of the most beautiful facets in his work, he has paid us back so generously that it is Spain who is today his debtor.[19]

COMPOSITIONS

At the end of January of 1908, Falla earned some money from another tour of Bilbao and Oviedo playing six trios with violinist Antonio Fernández Bordás (the future director of the Madrid Conservatory) and cellist Victor Mirecki. Through Albéniz in 1908, additional assistance was forthcoming from the King of Spain, as a result of the intervention of the Marquis de Borja. This compensation allowed Falla to dedicate time to composition.

Within the sketch material for "Andaluza" and "Aragonesa" from Falla's *Cuatro piezas españolas* is found a work not cited in biographies, called *Con afectos de júbilo y gozo* (With Expression of Jubilation and Enjoyment) for soprano, female chorus, and piano on an unknown text.

The work is dated 23 March 1908. The circumstances of its composition are not known. However, the subject matter is about young school girls greeting their Mother Superior.

On 30 June 1908, he played his *Pièces espagnoles* or *Cuatro piezas españolas* before Debussy, the sketches of which he brought with him from Madrid.[20] In 1909, he finished them, dedicating them in gratitude to Albéniz. On the recommendation of Dukas, Debussy, and Ravel, they were published the same year by Durand, who paid him three hundred francs. The story goes:

> Debussy exclaimed, "So, they've paid you 50 francs more than they gave me for my Quartet." "And the same amount that they gave me for The Sorcerer's Apprentice," Dukas said, joining in. "Well, they didn't give me anything for my composition, Catalonia," added Albéniz. "They didn't even want my Quartet given away free," finished Ravel.[21]

The première of *Cuatro piezas españolas* was played by Viñes on 27 March in an Societé Nationale Indépendante (SNI) at the Salle Erard. Falla was fortunate to have such a pianist, for he undoubtedly attracted more attention than if the composer had played them himself. Viñes's playing has been described by Joaquín Nin-Culmell, the son of Cuban pianist Joaquín Nin, present at the time.

> What makes his performances different from other performances? . . . They weren't performances. . . . They were the inner sharing of a discovery he had made on his own, but in which nothing of his own self remained. He "was" the "Pictures" [Pictures at an Exhibition by Mussorgsky], he "was" the "Nights in the Gardens of Spain," he "was" the "Gallo Mañanero" of Joaquín Rodrigo. Viñes never played Viñes the way Segovia plays Segovia. It was almost a mystical approach to the art of interpretation. Disappear and the composition will come to life. Forget about yourself and Debussy or Ravel or Poulenc [another of his pupils] will speak out. He was self-effacing to the point of obliteration, but never quite. Viñes was always there, but always in good company. Chatterbox as he was, he never interrupted the music with personal gestures, or professional tics, or technical excesses, or limitation. His technique was there but only to be hidden. It was perfect in that it was never brought up.[22]

Between 1909–1910, Falla composed his *Trois mélodies* for voice and piano, based on poems by Théophile Gautier, who had visited Cádiz almost seventy years earlier. They contain: (1) "Les Colombes," dedicated to Mme. Ada Adiny-Milliet; (2) "Chinoiserie," dedicated to Mme. R.

Brooks; and (3) "Séguidille," which was dedicated to Mme. Claude Debussy. Dukas arranged to have the work published by the Paris firm of Rouart-Lerolle in 1910, although there was some intervention by Debussy with Durand, as confirmed in a letter to Falla on 23 October 1909.[23] The debut of the work took place at Salle Gaveau on 4 May 1910, by Mme. Adiny-Milliet with the composer at the piano at the second concert of the newly-formed Societé Nationale Indépendante. The SNI, through the efforts of Ravel and Fauré, with Falla's assistance, was a series dedicated to contemporary music.

Debussy's influence in *Trois mélodies* is noted by biographer Jaime Pahissa.

> When he had completed the "Trois Mélodies" he took them to Debussy, who liked and praised them. However, in "Chinoiserie" he felt that the introduction, or rather the vocal part preceding "la machine chinoise," as he called it with its whimsical air, was not in keeping with the song proper in this kind of music. Falla, reluctant to revise a work which he thought he had finished, asked what was to be done about it.
>
> "I don't know," Debussy replied. "You will find out. 'Seek and ye shall find,' as Jesus said." Falla went home and set himself to find the trouble. He eventually saw that the heavy piano part which underlay the vocal section was unnecessary. Once it had been removed, to leave only the melodic line with an introductory chord and a transitional chord leading to "la machine chinoise," everything was all right. When this had been done Debussy thought that the piece was very good.[24]

From 1909, urged on by Albéniz and Viñes, Falla also began a series of piano pieces, called *Nocturnos* (Nocturnes). Three of these four pieces would eventually become the famous *Noches en los jardines de España* (Nights in the Gardens of Spain), completed later, after eliminating the one dedicated to Cádiz.

If Cádiz had served as his childhood "laboratory" for developing a rich and vivid imagination and Madrid as an apprenticeship for spawning large-scale compositions, especially the large-scale theatrical *zarzuelas*, then Paris was Falla's workshop for developing orchestrational perfection. Advised by Debussy and Dukas with regard to these revisions necessary to enhance *La vida breve*, Falla seriously undertook this task in 1909, although he had been sporadically reworking it since 1905.[25] With the objective to make the necessary alterations for the French version, as translated by Paul Milliet, who had been Massenet's librettist and was the secretary for the French Society of Authors, the one-act opera would now have two. The first dance especially would undergo great orchestral transformation from February to April 1908.[26] Falla's and Milliet's objective was to persuade Albert Carré, of the Parisian Opéra Comique, to produce it. A reading of the work took place before Carré on 3 July 1908.[27] As might be expected, there was only a limited number of foreign works allowed each season.

Notes taken by Falla after a meeting with Debussy on 10 October 1911, reflect the extent to which Debussy intervened in the revision of *La vida breve* and give suggestions for his next opera, in which he says "Two parallel actions, dramatically and musically well directed, can produce an effect of great novelty."[28] The suggestion of alternation between sung and spoken dialogue was also emphasized. Falla would incorporate these suggestions later in his masterpiece *El retablo de Maese Pedro*. Falla was obviously concerned with strengthening the ending of *La vida breve* by tightening its action and dramatic flow. A second document with specific orchestrational suggestions, although undated, untitled, and unauthored, may also have emanated from this same meeting with Debussy. Suggestions about the use of the harp, for respecting the effects of the acoustical vibrations of instrumental groupings, for obtaining the specific effects desired, for being objective in the orchestrational approach, etc., are included.[29]

Other operatic projects were undertaken in Paris. He began work on another "garden-inspired" idea based on *Le Jardinier de la Pompadour* (The Pompadour's Gardener) by Eugène Demoldier, with the libretto by Michel-Dimitri Calvocoressi. Other considerations were a sequel to *Carmen* and a new version of *Il barbiere di Siviglia* (The Barber of Seville), the latter which Debussy called a "magnificent" idea. Pahissa reported, "Debussy thought the idea a superb one and encouraged him to carry it out. When he heard that someone had advised Falla not to attempt such a thing he asked who had been such a fool, not knowing that it had been his friend Dukas."[30] Unfortunately no musical sketches of these works survive. Only those sketches of *Las flores* by the Álvarez Quintero brothers are extant. It seems that only Falla was interested in seeing this project through, not the brothers.[31] It is curious that during a trip to Italy in 1912, Tito Ricordi, of the famous Milanese publishing house, offered Falla the libretto of another of the authors' works, *Anima allegra*, a libretto rejected by Puccini. Ricordi was not interested in publishing *La vida breve*, nor Falla in Ricordi's offer. Before Falla left Paris to return to Madrid because of the First World War, he was enthused about developing a project—a lyric drama—based on Calderon de la Barca's *Devoción a la Cruz* (Devotion to the Cross), "a splendid piece."[32]

RELIGIOUS CRISIS

On the initiative of Georges Jean-Aubry, Falla was invited to perform in London, on 24 May 1911, playing his *Cuatro piezas españolas*. He also performed the Debussy-André Caplet two-piano version of *Iberia* with pianist-organist Franz Liebich.[33] Apparently, in order to make the trip, Falla needed funds and asked his cousin, Pedro de Matheu, on 17 May for a loan of 100 francs for five or six days, saying that his friend Turina could only advance him thirty francs until the end of the month.[34] His music was being performed now in wider circles, thanks to Henri Collet, Jean-Aubry, Émile Vuillermoz, Jean-Pierre Altermann, and above all, Joaquín Nin.[35]

Apparently, periods of bad health afflicted Falla upon his return to Paris. The winters of 1910 and 1911 were particularly hard on him, as he noted in a letter to his parents dated 9 September 1912. "I hope I can spend winter outside Paris. . . . Moreover, I have not forgotten the damage the last two winters caused me."[36] Earlier he had written to Pedrell on 6 June 1911: "My health wasn't very good either last winter. It rained terribly and consequently the humidity did me a lot of damage. As soon as I am able, I am going to divide my time between Paris and Andalusia; but I don't envisage this happening for some time yet."[37]

Biographer Luis Campodónico mentions hospitalization in 1912.[38] And it seems that Falla underwent some kind of religious crisis, in the positive sense that he both hungered for and feared God.[39] In perhaps an otherwise celibate life, Campodónico suggested that Falla suffered from syphilis. In an attempt to set the record straight, Falla's niece, María Isabel de Falla, corresponded and personally visited several Parisian hospitals in order to obtain records. She found nothing.[40] After Falla's death, medical doctor and biographer Manuel Orozco was able to scrutinize many analyses and documents preserved amongst Falla's belongings. He concluded that there was no evidence of syphilis. Having examined Falla's cadaver, Dr. Orozco contended that he died a virgin.[41]

In like manner, homosexuality accusations were denied by biographer Federico Sopeña in his investigation.[42] Two personal books were scrutinized, Falla's French edition of the catechisms of *San Pío V*, used in daily meditation, and his annotated and highlighted personal edition of *San Juan de la Cruz.* In the former is found a theological index of ascetic scruples, which, Sopeña concedes, few saints could emulate. And from the latter, Sopeña cites from the section of imperfections one must overcome in order to attain mystical ascendancy: ". . . we see Falla doesn't underline lust, ire, gluttony" but rather marks a "yes" to "envy with regard to being opposed to charity" and clearly marks "to avoid impatience." Taken together, "I believe that we have the decisive portrait."[43]

Whatever the crisis, the result was an increased religious fervor. And Falla was joined in this shared sentiment by Viñes, Léon Bloy, Jean-Pierre Altermann, and the Bishop Léonce Petit, all linked through the Apaches.

Melchor de Almagro de San Martín described the young Falla, around 1912, as looking like the "poor man of Assisi" reincarnated.[44] His poverty was quite apparent yet he maintained his dignity by wearing an impeccable, but threadbare, black suit. He told of his preference for French composers to German ones and of his dream to live in Granada one day. A small but meaningful gesture of his compassionate nature was shown by his daily distribution of breadcrumbs to the birds shivering in the snow outside, that caused, according to Melchor, his impassive face to break into "an indescribably radiant smile,"[45] reflecting a saintly "sweetness."[46] "And in a few years this saint was to be revealed as one of the greatest composers of the world."[47]

EXOTICISM AND REVIVAL OF THE PAST

The French taste for exotic music, especially after the World Expositions of 1889 and 1900, stimulated Falla, with his already open and curious mind. Even before arriving in Paris, he knew the works of Bourgault-Ducoudray, which would have an influence in his "Chinoiserie" of *Trois mélodies.* Another member of the Apaches, Maurice Delage, brought his love of Chinese music to the group as a result of his many travels. Charles Koechlin went so far as to write pieces for Javanese *gamelan* ensemble performed in a Société Nationale Indépendante concert. And Falla experimented with harmonizing a Greek song based on its melodic range.[48] Falla's fascination of exotic scales, originally stimulated in Madrid through Pedrell and Lucas, was further enhanced in Paris.

Indeed Falla's first encounter with Ravel opened his ears and confirmed his thinking about these technical procedures.

I met Ravel a few days after my arrival in Paris, in the summer of 1907; this was the begnning of a heartfelt friendship. . . . He welcomed me most warmly; attracted by his prestige this flattered me as a Spaniard. I did not suspect then that I would soon owe so much to his art and to his strong friendship.

He [Ravel] and Viñes played a sight reading of "Rhapsodie espagnole" which Ravel had just published in its original version for four hands, and which would first be performed at a concert at the "Nationale." The "Rhapsodie," apart from musically confirming my impression of the "Sonatine," surprised me with its Spanish character. That character, coinciding with my own aims—unlike what Rimsky had done in his "Caprice"—was not attained by simply arrangement of folklore material but rather, except for the "jota" of the Foire, through a free use of rhythmic, modal-melodic and ornamental elements of our people's song; and these elements did not alter the composer's own manner, although they were applied to a melodic language so different from that of the "Sonatine." Certain objections raised by Viñes as to practical difficulties, prompted Ravel to orchestrate the original version—a plan soon and splendidly carried out. Thus he began the admirable series of transportations of piano works for orchestra that show unsurpassed talent and virtuosity.[49]

Another musical trend taking place in Paris was the inspiration drawn from music written before the nineteenth century, such as in by Ravel for Couperin, Debussy for Rameau, and Dukas and Nín for Domenico Scarlatti. Nín especially underlined the Spanish character of Scarlatti's keyboard sonatas. Falla too was attracted to this wave, attending concerts at the Schola Cantorum and of those performers who presented this music, such as Wanda Landowska, Alfredo Casella, and the Casadesus family.[50]

BALLETS RUSSES

Falla became a great admirer of the Ballets Russes after having seen Serge Diaghilev's production of *Boris Godunov* in 1908. In 1909 the troupe began its permanent Parisian season. Russian music had been an attraction earlier for the Apaches. In 1897 Viñes and Ravel took a special interest in Balakirev, Glazunov, and Rimsky-Korsakov when they embarked on a sight-reading binge.[51] Falla too was smitten by Stravinsky's *Petrouchka* and *Le Sacré du printemps*, which would play an important part in his future artistic creation, as did operas of Rimsky-Korsakov.

Some of the greatest talent of the times would become closely associated with Falla—Massine, Karsarvina, Picasso, amongst others. The seeds for this collaboration were sewn during these Paris years.

Première of *La vida breve*

Having undertaken several revisions (1905, 1908, 1911), Falla and Paul Milliet, the French translator of *La vie brève* (*La vida breve*), renewed their efforts to produce the opera. So far there had been no success in Madrid, Paris, Brussels, London, and Milan.[52] Finally, on 1 April 1913, the opera was premiered as "A Lyrical Drama in Two Acts and Four Scenes" at the Municipal Casino in Nice. Falla's moment of triumph was sweet. The opera enjoyed several performances.

Unable to share the joy with the opera's librettist, Falla wrote immediately to his widow, Celia de Yturralde. In a letter dated 4 April 1913, he describes the event.

> At last, the first night arrived. Its success was greater than I could have hoped, and even greater at the public première than at the Figaro party, which was considerable. Outstanding interpretations, Mlle. Lillian Grenville made an absolutely glorious "Salud." She is going to study her role in Spanish now, because I am determined that if *La vida breve* is performed in Madrid it should be sung by her. . . .[53]

Some months later, the Paris debut was given on 30 December 1913 at the Opéra Comique, with the "official" debut taking place there a week later on 7 January 1914. Albert Carré, before retiring from the management of the Opéra Comique, was responsible for the staging of the work, casting his wife Marguerite as Salud. Amadeo Vives recounts, "The success which greeted *La vida breve* in Paris is more resounding and enthusiastic than that which met it at its première in Nice last spring. It is a great honour, not often granted to foreigners, unless they are among the world's most famous composers, to receive a first night at the Paris Comic Opera. . . ."[54]

It was around this time that Falla, through Turina, met the couple Gregorio and María Martínez Sierra. They would exert a strong influence on him over the next several years. María de la O Lejárraga, alias María Martínez Sierra, describes the meeting and the life as it was at that time.

> I met Manuel de Falla in Paris, in 1913, a few months before the First World War. Joaquín Turina, our friend and later our collaborator, had spoken to us about him, and thanks to him we met. He lived then in one of those sad, sordid and disgusting hotels—as Cervantes would have said, "there is room for all discomfort"—in which Paris has sheltered such artistic dreams and hopes for future glories.[55]

The only luxury Falla allowed himself was a rented upright piano that sounded more like scrap metal than a musical instrument, according to María, during this period of "forced asceticism."

> Forced? Not completely. Manuel de Falla, if he had wished, could have condescended, like many, to come down to earth once in a while to easily earn the necessary francs. . . . [He could have] given lessons, written an ingratiating song for his publishers, an ordinarily jolly waltz, that little piece for piano which sounds like all the others, but without too many technical difficulties so that romantic girls can play it without ruining it. The market was open. . . . [He] showed a rare loyalty to his Muse, and preferred hunger to abandoning his principles: yes hunger . . . he was often obliged to resort to the "food trials" which food manufacturers advertised, and thus, filling in and cutting the coupons out of newspapers he would receive, now and again, a sample of powdered cocoa, canned food, or a packet of lacteous flour. And when, at times, invited to supper at a rich acquaintance's house, he managed to eat normally, he was so accustomed to not eating that he was ill the next day.[56]

When María met Falla for the first time, through Turina, she knew nothing of his music. He received them courteously, but refused to play any of his own music for his visitors. He was then deciphering Stravinsky's *Rite of Spring* and preferred to show this to his guests.

> As I already said, Manuel de Falla was nearly always a bundle of nerves. But he delighted us for more than an hour—he was a prodigious pianist— with a formidable interpretation at the piano of the score which he had been savouring alone when we rang at his door.[57]

María turned pages for Falla, sensing something not quite natural, when she observed that the composer sported a "toupée."

> The falseness which had bothered me was not, fortunately, in Falla's soul, but in his toupée. Which, moreover, soon disappeared. When war broke out in August 1914, Falla escaped France as quickly as possible. In his hurry to catch a train he lost his toupée. And thus, he arrived in his homeland once more parading, with complete frankness, the copious ivory patch, which heightened his ascetic appearance.[58]

With all the successes behind him, Falla had decided to settle in Paris permanently. He had chosen a house on the outskirts of the city and was inviting his parents to come to live with him. However, shortly before signing the lease on his house, the First World War broke out. Florent

Schmitt and Ravel left Paris. Turina had already returned to Madrid before the war began. Falla followed suit. In his single suitcase he returned
to Madrid with the scores of the *Siete canciones populares españolas*
and some of *Noches en los jardines de España*.

NOTES

1. Elaine Brody, *Paris: The Musical Kaleidoscope* ("The Spaniards Living
in Paris"), 188.
2. Rubinstein, *My Young Years,* 122–23.
3. For more details, see chapter 13, Chris Collins's "Falla in Europe: Relations with His Contemporaries."
4. Demarquez, 36.
5. *Poesía*, 51.
6. Letter to Viniegra in *Poesía*, 52.
7. Sopeña, 272.
8. Demarquez, 36.
9. *Poesía*, 52.
10. Sopeña, 272.
11. Budwig, 16.
12. This aspect is given in more detail in chapter 13 by Chris Collins.
13. Demarquez, v.
14. Letter to Carlos Fernández-Shaw from Paris dated 31 May 1910, cited in
appendix 4 of Yvan Nommick's "Manuel de Falla: de *La vida breve* de 1905 à *La
vie breve* de 1913" in *Mélanges de la Casa de Velázquez, École des hautes Études
Hispaniques, Separata, tome XXX-3*, Madrid, 1994, 91. A partial French translation may also be found on p. 78. The original letter is found in the Fernández-
Shaw Archive (no. CFS-AE 6-246) housed at the Juan March Foundation in
Madrid. Also a transcription by Pilar Lozano may be found in Guillermo Fernández-Shaw's *Larga historia de "La vida breve,"* 2nd ed., Madrid: Ediciones de la
Revista de Occidente, S. A., 1972, 96–101.

Mi primera gran satisfacción en Paris, la tuve poco después de mi llegada, cuando
visité a Dukas. (Debussy estaba entonces ausente). En aquella primera visita hice ver
a Dukas los propósitos que me traían a Paris: trabajar y estudiar por conocer los procedimientos técnicos de la escuela moderna francesa, por ser los que encontraba
aplicables a mi manera de sentir en música. Me pidió que le hiciera conocer algún
trabajor p.ª saber el camino que me convenía seguir; le hice oír *La vida breve*, y
jamás olvidaré la bondad y el interés con que atendió a mi lectura. Hasta entonces
habia estado reservado (cosa muy natural, pues no solo era aquella la vez primera
que me hablaba, sino que fui a verle sin llevar siquiera una tarjeta de presentación;
pero desde que oyó mis trabajos todo varió, y tales ánimos me dieron sus palabras
que, como le dije, me parecia que despertaba de un mal sueño. Me recomendó con

insistencia que cuidase much en no cambiar mi sentimiento personal en música y que siguiese trabajando particularmente, como entonces hacía. Me indicó con gran precisión el plan que debía seguir, ofreciéndoseme para cuantas consultas quisiera hacerle, como también para examinar cuanto siguiese escribiendo. Me presentó a Albéniz, quien me acogió de un modo verdaderamente magnífico [. . .]. Este me animó enormemente, me presentó a muchas personas de su amistad y, bajo todos conceptos, se portó conmigo como un grande y leal amigo. El fue como Vd. Recordará, quien me presentó a Paul Milliet, y éste es uno de los mayores favores que le debo, [. . .].

Después, en cuanto supe que Debussy estaba de regreso en París, fui a verle, porque he de seguir lo que podríamos llamar *letanía* de gratitudes, siendo tantas las que le debo por el interés que se há tomado en mis trabajos y por la protección artística que, como Dukas, há tenido la bondad de concederme, guiándome, como aquel, en mis trabajos, haciéndolos publicar y animándome continuamente a proseguir mis planes y proyectos. Al mismo tiempo fui a visitar a Ricardo Viñes, el gran pianista español, y por él conocí a Maurice Ravel, a Florent Schmitt, a Calvocoressi, etc. y de todos no tengo más que motivos de gratitud.

15. Michael Christoforidis, "Manuel de Falla" in *Diccionario de la música española e hispanoamericana*, ed. Emilio Casares, 897. Madrid: ICCMU, 2000.

16. *Stravinsky in Conversation with Robert Craft,* London: Penguin Books, 1962, 211.

17. Michael Christoforidis, "Manuel de Falla, Debussy and *La vida breve*" in *Musicology Australia*, XVIII, 3–10, 1995, 4.

18. Pahissa, 51–52.

19. OMM, 41–45.

20. Christoforidis, *Musicology Australia*, 4.

21. Pahissa, 55.

Al oírlo, Debussy le dice: —Pues le han dado 50 francos más que a mí me dieron por el "Quarteto."—Y lo mismo que me pagaron a mí por *L'apprenti sorcier*— agrega Dukas.—Pues a mí, nada me dieron por la partitura de "Catalonia"— añade Albéniz.—Y a mí, ni regalado me quisieron el "Cuarteto"—termina Ravel.

22. Brody, 185–186.

23. Christoforidis, *Musicology Australia*, 4.

24. Christoforidis, *Musicology Australia*, 4.

25. Christoforidis, *Musicology Australia*, 8.

26. Christoforidis, *Musicology Australia*, 8.

27. Christoforidis, *Musicology Australia*, 4.

28. Christoforidis, *Musicology Australia*, 5.

29. For more details, see Christoforidis, *Musicology Australia*.

30. Pahissa, 110, and Christoforidis, *Musicology Australia*, 11.

31. See Antonio Iglesias, *Manuel de Falla (su obra para piano)*, 308–9. This reference is given in chapter 4 ("Back to Madrid") when discussing Nights in the Gardens of Spain.

32. *Poesía*, 77.

33. Orozco, 75.

34. Sopeña, 54.

35. Christoforidis, *Enciclopedia*, 897.

36. *Poesía*, 76.

37. Letter dated 6 June 1911 cited in Christoforidis, *Iconografia*, 24–25.

38. Campodónico, 82–83.

39. Sopeña, 57.

40. Sopeña, 58.

41. Sopeña, 204.

42. Sopeña, 135. Sopeña also deals with the homosexual accusation between Falla and Federico García Lorca made by Francisco Umbral. He says, "I have spoken with all those who were intimate friends of Falla—[Antonio] Gallego Burín, [Alfonso] García Valdecasas, [Emilio] García Gómez, and many whom I knew before his death—and neither directly nor indirectly has this sense been affirmed. Granted, the paternal vocation is inseparable with authentic bachelors and more so with religious men. . . ." ". . . in the case of Ernesto [Halffter] the affection is intense, but Ernesto is in Madrid and probably (in) the illusion of Falla (was) for the Orquesta Bética of Seville . . . which in those years continues stealing time from his work—in this, was the possible closeness to Ernesto." Translated in Nancy Lee Harper, *Manuel de Falla: A Bio-Bibliography*. Greenwood Press, 1998, 22.

43. Sopeña, 135–46.

44. Demarquez, 36–37. *A.B.C.* of Madrid (6 August 1929).

45. Demarquez, 37.

46. Demarquez, 37.

47. Demarquez, 37.

48. Christoforidis, *Enciclopedia*, 897.

49. OMM, 93–94.

50. Christoforidis, *Enciclopedia*, 897.

51. Brody, 184.

52. Chase-Budwig, 16.

53. *Poesía*, 60.

54. *Poesía*, 61.

55. María Martínez Sierra, *Gregorio y yo, Medio siglo de colaboracion*, México, D. F., Biografias Gandesa, 1953, 120.

Conocí a Manuel de Falla en París, en 1913, pocos meses antes de la primera guerra mundial. Joaquín Turina, nuestro amigo y después nuestro colaborador, nos había hablado de él, y gracias a él le encontramos. Vivía a la sazón en uno de esos tristes, sórdidos, repelentes hoteles en los cuales, como hubiese dicho Cervantes "toda incomodidad tiene su asiento," en los que París há cobijado tanto sueño de arte y tanta esperanzada ilusión de futura gloria.

56. María Martínez Sierra, *Gregorio y yo*, 120–121.

¿Forzado? No del todo. Manuel de Falla, si hubiera, como tantos, condescendido a bajar del ensueño de cuando en cuando, habría podido ganar holgadamente los francos necesarios . . ., dar lecciones, escribir para los editores tal cancioncilla insinuante, tal vals corrientemente sensual, tal piececilla para piano con melodía evocadora de otras y sin demasiadas dificultades de ejecución que las niñas románticas pudieran destrozar en el piano. El mercado estaba abierto . . . fué como muy pocos fiel a su musa, y prefirió el hambre a la claudicación: el hambre, sí, . . . se vió no pocas veces obligado para comer a recurrir a las "primas" que ofrecían en sus anuncios las fábricas de productos alimenticios, y así, llenando y recortando "bonos" en los periódicos, obtenía devez en cuando una muestra de cacao soluble, una lata de conservas, un paquete de harina lacteada. Si, a días, invitado en casa de un amigo rico, alcanzaba a cenar normalmente, era ya tal su costumbre de no comer, que al día siguiente estaba enfermo.

57. María Martínez Sierra, *Gregorio y yo*, 123.

Ya he dicho que Manuel de Falla tenía casi siempre una legión de diablos dentro del cuerpo. Pero nos deleitó—era prodigioso pianista—durante más de una hora con la formidable intrpretación pianística de aquella partitura que estaba saboreando a solas cuando llamamos a su puerta.

58. María Martínez Sierra, *Gregorio y yo*, 125.

La falsedad que así me inquietaba no estaba, afortunadamente, en el alma de Falla, sino en su bisoñé. Que, por otra parte, bien pronto desapareció. Al estallar la guerra en agosto de 1914, Falla escapó de Francia a toda prisa. En su precipitación, al tomar un tren por asalto, perdió el bisoñé. Y así, entró de nuevo en su patria ostentando con toda franqueza la marfileña y espaciosa calva, la cual acentuaba el carácter ascético de su dueño.

Chapter 4

Back to Madrid (1914–1920)

It is difficult to imagine a man like Manuel de Falla, Spain's greatest composer, in the midst of a noisy café. Nevertheless, sometimes Falla goes to a café.

But whilst the customers shout, gesticulate, cough, growl and expectorate, he sits back thoughtfully in his chair, waiting perhaps for an opportune moment of silence to secure a melody in his mind. But it is not easy to find silence in modern Madrid.—Walter Starkie[1]

SPANISH PREMIÈRE OF
LA VIDA BREVE (THE SHORT LIFE)

After experiencing professional success in New York with his song *Tus ojillos negros* early in his career and subsequently the Niza and Parisian ovations given to his opera *La vida breve*, Falla's return to Madrid would not be the disappointing experience of his previous residency in the Spanish capital. Through hard work, he had achieved technical perfection. He had overcome the negative connotation of his name.[2] He took a flat at no. 24, Calle Ponzano.[3]

On 14 November 1914, the first Madrid performance of *La vida breve* at the Teatro de la Zarzuela was an enormous success. Luisa Vela sang the role of Salud. The opera had twenty-six performances. Max Eschig in Paris had earlier published the work in 1913.

María Martínez Sierra reveals the situation at the time.

There remained, however, another prejudice to break: that which considered Spanish folk music as "vulgar" and solely suitable for common peoples' revels and for avid tourists on the look out for anything "picturesque." This prejudice had . . . distanced another great Spanish musician Isaac Albéniz from Spain—and ironically brought him success in the rest of the world.[4]

As the music and subject matter of *La vida breve* were Andalusian in nature, María Martínez Sierra says she and Falla felt the necessity to publish an article before its debut at the Zarzuela Theater in Madrid to inform the audience and "perhaps the critics" that such

> "popular and vulgar" subjects were what, in Germany, Beethoven had extolled and sublimated in his "Pastoral Symphony." Falla was doing something similar with the folk rhythms of *La vida breve*, but in a Spanish context. The fact is that the respectable audience liked every last one.[5]

The article, "The Magic Guitars," appeared the day before the opening in one of Madrid's largest selling newspapers.

Falla's success caused his name to be one everyone's lips, with some of the "loudest bells" ringing his praises.[6] Yet the support of his parents and sister still preoccupied him. María conceded that he should have taken advantage of his good fortune and written a few more zarzuelas to ease the financial pain. However, she said, "this was like asking an elm tree to bear pears."[7]

According to Falla, he had four aims in composing *La vida breve*.

> 1) To make a Spanish opera in dramatic form, something which I could find no example of in the entire history of Spanish lyrical theatre; 2) To compose the music from a series of popular songs and dances; 3) To try, above and beyond all else, to evoke the feelings of fear and joy, of hope and torment, of life and death, or exultation and depression, all linked to certain personal images of places, moments, landscapes, etc.; 4) To notch up some money in order to carry on working.[8]

Antonio Gallego reports how Falla tried to secure work at his former *alma mater*, the Madrid Conservatory. In August of 1914, Falla wrote to José Tragó, his former piano professor there, and almost pleaded, "I am disposed to work in whatever, something so that I and my family can live."[9] But nothing was forthcoming for him, in spite of his fame and lavish praise of the critics, who, in a fickle manner, bemoaned the fact that he first found success abroad.

THE MARTÍNEZ SIERRAS

Meanwhile, Falla's friendship with playwrights Gregorio and María Martínez Sierra, whom he had met in Paris, was strengthening. Falla lived with the couple for over a year while he was composing *El amor brujo*, amongst other works. They began collaboration on *La Pasión*, produced on 30 November 1914, in which Falla composed a *Soleá* for voice and guitar. A song set to Gregorio Martínez Sierra's text, *Oración de las Madres que tienen a sus hijos en brazos*, followed in December of 1914. It was premiered at the Sociedad Nacional de Música de Madrid on 8 February 1915 with Josefina Revillo and the composer.

Several other projects would result, some remaining uncompleted.[10] The relationship finally broke in 1919. María spoke of Falla's "hypersensitive and self-tormented" personality, describing him as a late sleeper, slow to dress, obsessed with his morning routine, which included the obligatory gymnastic exercises, and above, ardently religious.[11]

SIETE CANCIONES POPULARES ESPAÑOLAS (SEVEN POPULAR SPANISH SONGS)

In the midst of all this activity the music of Falla and his longtime friend Turina was presented in an "homage" concert at the Madrid Ateneo on 14 January 1915. There, Falla and Luisa Vela premiered the *Siete canciones populares españolas*, a work that would have enormous success and be trasncribed many times for various musical mediums. These songs were begun after Falla harmonized a Greek folksong according to the ideas of "natural resonance" that he gleaned from Lucas's *L'Acoustique nouvelle* and from Felipe Pedrell, who had stated in the preface of the third volume of his *Cancionero* that the folksong should be based on ancient modes and not simply subject to the laws of major and minor modes. He advocated, not unlike Lucas, a return to "natural música" as sung on the strings of the lyre since antiquity.

The seven songs—"El paño moruno," "Seguidilla murciana," "Asturiana," "Jota," "Nana," "Canción," and "Polo"—come from various folksong collections of José Inzenga, José Hurtado, and Eduardo Ocón, as well as a melody from the play *Las flores* (2nd ed., 1906) by Serafín and Joaquín Alvarez Quintero.[13] Falla's work was completed in July of 1914, but not published until 1922, by Max Eschig of Paris. The Paris première took place in May of 1920 in a concert sponsored by the Société National de Musique (SNM) at the Conservatoire.

In *Siete canciones* Falla used a synthesis of folksongs from published sources. He would seemed to have broken his own rules when he declared the following statement.

In popular song I think the "spirit" is more important than the "letter." Rhythm, tonality, and melodic intervals, which determine undulations and cadences, are the essential constituents of these songs. The people prove it themselves by infinitely varying the purely melodic lines of their songs. The rhythmic or melodic accompaniment is as important as the song itself. Inspiration, therefore, is to be found directly in the people, and those who do not see it so will only achieve a more or less ingenious imitation of what they originally set out to do.[14]

In spite of the numerous recordings made of *Siete canciones populares españolas* and in many transcriptions, Falla did not profit monetarily from them. María Martínez Sierra remarked, perhaps somewhat exaggeratedly, that in fifteen years Falla didn't earn enough to buy even a bottle of champagne.[15]

Falla's *Siete canciones* and *Oración de las Madres que tienen a sus hijos en brazos*, along with chamber works of Turina and Granados, opened the newly formed Sociedad Nacional de Música of Madrid at the Hotel Ritz on 8 February 1915. At the beginning of the year, Falla wrote incidental music for Gregorio Martínez Sierra's comedy, *Amanacer*. The year 1915 was stellar in other ways: it saw the creation of *El amor brujo* for the gypsy dancer Pastora Imperio and the realization of Falla's initial trip to the city of his fantasies and of *La vida breve*—Granada. The "Granada syndrome"—the rampant romantic notions that surrounded the Moorish city—was somewhat ameliorated when Falla visited the sites there with María Martínez Sierra. The trip, which took place during March and April, also included stops at Ronda, Algeciras, and Cádiz. Work was subsequently begun on *Pascua florida*, a series of songs of which only *El pan de Ronda que sabe a verdad* remains. María left a description of the thrill of Falla's visit to the Alhambra with her in April, describing his joy upon seeing its beauty for the first time. "I believe that that moment of complete happiness—his shout left no doubt—was one of the raptures which compensated for the torments of his existence surrounded by so much meanness and, at times, dullness."[16]

EL AMOR BRUJO (LOVE BEWITCHED)

The origin of the work is found in the Gypsy ballerina's (Pastora Imperio) expressed desire to have a "song and a dance" written by Martínez Sierra and Falla. She came from a family steeped in a rich tradition of Andalusian music and a mother, Rosario la Mejorana, who was a great dancer. From hearing the latter weave her magic by telling the ancient fables and legends to Martínez Sierra and chanting s*oleares, siguiriyas, polos,* and *martinetes* to Falla, the plot of the sung Gypsy ballet came to take shape.

Slightly reminiscent of some aspects of *Carmen*, the story takes place in Granada, in the Gypsies' home, where Candelas is awaiting her fiancé, who has been neglecting her. She consults the cards for her future. The answer bodes evil, as intensified by the sound of the sea. Despairing, she throws incense on the fire and dances the "Ritual Fire Dance."

There follows an interlude to the second scene, which takes place in the cave of a witch. Candelas is terrified of the night birds and dances the *Dance of the Tarantula* to exorcise the evil spirits. Her incantations succeed in bringing back her lover. She disguises herself with a veil and seduces him. Dawn breaks and the ringing of the morning bells signifies the lovers' reconciliation.

Pastora Imperio's entire family took a part in the production: Pastora played the part of Candelas; her brother, Vito Rojas, played Carmelo, the lover; a sister-in-law, Perlita Negra, played the part of the beautiful, elegant Agustina; her daughter (María Imperio), later to become the famous María del Albaïcin, had the role of a "Gitanilla"; and the old Gypsy Woman was played by Rosa Canto. The organist Moreno Ballesteros conducted.

El amor brujo was premiered at the Teatro Lara on 15 April 1915, amidst varied response—less attractive from the critics, enthusiastic from the gypsy world. Some critics disliked the orchestration, while another encouraged Falla to give up these "Minor Essays" and dedicate his energies to "a great work." Gregorio Martínez Sierra wrote in *El Imparcial* that the music was "savage, cruel and sweet, harsh and vibrant, heart-rending, desolate, at once Moorish and mystical!"[17]

The *Heraldo de Madrid* championed Falla as another upholder of the new Spanish musical renaissance. The right-wing *ABC* praised Falla's orchestration and stated that he had succeeded in stamping his strong musical personality through French technique. Madrid was not yet ready to champion a minority. Only the Gypsy community rallied around

Falla. Singer Paco Meana prophesied that "this music will soon become world famous." The Parisian première, ten years later, at the Théâtre Bériza with Antonia Mercé ("La Argentina") and Vincente Escudero was enormous. Falla reportedly replied, "I could have written twenty *Amor brujos*."[18]

Pedrell commented after the first performance in Madrid, "Bravo Manuel, now you can see with such attention and interest I follow your author's feats, because I have *always* recognized you to be a sincere, high-minded composer, a faithful, honorable man and an ever dignified, all-deserving . . . artist. . . ."[19]

Pianist Artur Rubinstein recounts how he asked Falla for a copy of "that" dance (i.e., the "Ritual Fire Dance") and wished to make an arrangement of it.

> Manuel de Falla and I became very friendly. One night he took me to see Pastora Imperio, the famous gypsy singer and dancer, perform his ballet called "El amor brujo." It was given late at night in a theater after the regular play. The ballet was about a girl fallen under the spell of witchcraft cast on her by a man (a fine dancer). The music was performed by five or six players, the usual ensemble one hears at nightclubs; the pianist played on an upright piano. But the music fascinated me, especially a dance called the "Fire Dance," magnificently performed by Pastora Imperio. "Could you lend me the score of this dance?" I asked the composer. "I would love to arrange it for the piano and play it in a concert." He laughed. "Of course I will let you have it," he said, "but I doubt if it would make any effect." I did arrange it, just picking it up from the primitive score. When I played it as an encore at my next concert, the public went wild. I "had" to repeat it three times.[20]

Many revisions would be undertaken. Antonio Gallego presents a detailed study of the multitudinal changes which Falla submitted. During 1915 Falla prepared a new orchestration for *El amor brujo*. He also wrote the incidental music for Gregorio's adaptation of Shakespeare's *Othello*, which had its debut in October of 1915 at the Teatro Novedades in Barcelona, the home to his old friend-rival, Frank Marshall, and his mentor, Pedrell.

On 28 March 1916, Falla's revised concert version of *El amor brujo* was presented at the Hotel Ritz in the Sociedad Nacional de Música series with the Orquesta Sinfónica de Madrid, Enrique Fernández Arbós conducting (instead of the Orquesta Filarmónica with Bartolomé Pérez-Casas conducting, as is sometimes reported). This revised concert version had, by now, practically the definitive orchestration of the other revisions yet to come.[21]

On 29 April 1917, the concert version of *El amor brujo* for small orchestra was premiered at the Teatro Real in Madrid with the Orquesta Sinfónica conducted by Enrique Fernández Arbós. During the following months, Turina would conduct the work on more than seventy occasions in various places in Spain.[22]

NOCHES EN LOS JARDINES DE ESPAÑA[23]
(NIGHTS IN THE GARDENS OF SPAIN)

Another work completed in Madrid but begun in Paris was *Noches en los jardines de España*, subtitled by Falla *Impresiones sinfónicas para piano y orquesta* (Symphonic Impressions for Piano and Orchestra). According to Ann Livermore, the work was to have been dedicated to the Martínez Sierra couple, but owing to the cooling relationhip, Falla dedicated the work instead to Ricardo Viñes.[24] In spite of attempts by the Martínez Sierras and Diaghilev himself, Falla refused to turn this work into a ballet. It was commissioned by Enrique Arbós, who conducted its première on 9 April 1916, at Madrid's Royal Theater with the Symphonic Orchestra and Cádiz pianist, José Cubiles, playing. Artur Rubinstein was present, but it seems that the work did not have a great effect, for it is reported that he said nothing about the performance to the musicians, preferring to chat and drink his chocolate.[25] Rubinstein himself later said that it was because Cubiles did not play the work from memory, which caused the work to lose some of "its bite."[26] Repeat performances were soon given in several cities and by various interpreters. Apparently, Rubinstein became very enthusiastic about the work after hearing Viñes play it later that year.[27]

Falla had begun work on the piece in Paris after his *Quatro piezas españolas* were published. He intended the work to be four piano pieces, but Albéniz advised him: "Nothing of 'sweet cakes' [i.e., salon music]. Paintings! Paintings!"[28] Thus, Falla projected four piano pieces with orchestra,[29] two of which were to be entitled Nocturne of Seville and Nocturne of Cádiz.[30] However, parts of the Nocturne of Cádiz became integrated into *Amor brujo* (into the 7/8 *tanguillo* of *Pantomima*) and into *Atlántida* (announcement of the arrival of Hercules at Cádiz). The definitive movements eventually became known as: "En el Generalife" (In the Generalife), "Danza lejana" (A Distant Dance), and "En los jardines de la Sierra de Córdoba" (In the Gardens of the Sierra of Córdoba).

Falla himself allegedly said,

Bear in mind that the music of these nocturnes does not pretend to be descriptive, but simply expressive, and that something more than rumors of festivals and dances has inspired these sonorous evocations, that in them pain and mystery also have their part.[31]

Yvan Nommick writes of the genesis of the work, noting that the first reference to the project appears in a letter from Falla to his family in Madrid dated 13 January 1909, when he asks for the book, *Jardins d'Espanya,* by the Catalán artist Santiago Rusiñol, to be sent to him in Paris.[32] Other sources mentioned by various authors include: (1) *Granada (Guía emocional)* by Gregorio Martínez Sierra;[33] (2) *Tierras Solares* (1904) by Nicaraguan Rubén Darío,[34] heavily annotated by Falla in the chapter dedicated to Seville;[35] (3) three *Nocturnos* (Nocturnes) by Darío ("deeply moving . . . meditations on death and . . . life . . .") as found in the series *Poema del Otoño* (Madrid, 1910);[36] and (4) *Cinq poèmes de Francis Jammes*[37] by French musicologist-composer Henri Collet (five songs for voice and piano dated June 1909–May 1910[38]). In the piano part of the third song, "Ce sont de grandes lignes paisibles," may possibly be found the musical inspiration derived from the folksong "Pregón de pescaderas de la Rábita," and collected by pianist Francisco Garcia Carrillo.[39]

During the summer of 1915 Falla traveled with the Martínez Sierra couple to Cataluña, stopping briefly at the village of Sitges before proceeding to Barcelona. Falla stayed at the hotel Subur in Sitges, "whose patio inspired Rosiñol's painting *El pati blau*."[40] The Martínez Sierras and Falla stayed in Sitges from 28 June until 21 July, arriving in Barcelona on 22 July 1915.[41] Nommick says that Falla probably worked there on the first concert version of *El amor brujo* (debut on 28 March 1916), as well as on *Noches*, not completing the latter until 27 March 1916.[42]

The seven years that it took Falla to complete *Noches* reveals both his immersion in other projects—such as *La vida breve, Trois mélodies, El amor brujo*, and *Siete canciones populares españolas*—and his striving for perfection. The extraordinary transformation that his mature works underwent was normally prodigious. The works of the Paris years, years of Falla's final maturation as a composer, are well reflected by Henri Collet: "Such was his genius for transformation that I would have never perceived [the connection], had he not told me. . . ."[43]

Noches has been described as communicating "in Spanish tones a muffled anguish which is heard throughout the three movements."[44] Falla's reference to the "pain and mystery" contained in *Noches* may have something to do with religious mysticism.[45] António Iglesias, in his analysis of the piano works of Falla, mentions that he was given an annotated manuscript of Gerardo Diego with notes about the genesis and development of *Noches*.[46] A reference is made to "The Martyrs" being associated with the entire theme of the second movement. Falla was closely connected with the Carmelite Order for all of his life,[47] even eventually going to live nearby during his Granada years. The third movement, according to Ann Livermore, is closely allied to Darío's third poem or Nocturne, in which is heard "a muffled density of pain out of which rise sighs of grief at death's nearness, life's awareness of lost opportunities. . . ."[48] This certainly would be in line with Pahissa's denial that this movement has anything to do with a "Gypsy festival" (*zambra gitana*), as stated by J. B. Trend and Gilbert Chase, nor a Gypsy song, the "polo."[49]

Falla gave *Noches* and other works to Max Eschig to publish in an attempt to help him reestablish his firm after his release from a concentration camp during the war.[50]

EL CORREGIDOR Y LA MOLINERA
(THE MAGISTRATE AND THE MILLER'S WIFE)

On the heels of the gypsy ballet version of *El amor brujo* came ideas for other projects between the Martínez Sierras and Falla. In a letter dated 1 June 1915, María Lejárraga (Greogorio Martínez Sierra's wife's maiden name) wrote to Falla proposing to "plan for you an optimistic and happy work that knows the earth, bread, and apple blossoms, and that will be nonsensical, as Maestro Turina would say."[51]

In 1916, work was begun with the Martínez Sierras on *El corregidor y la molinera* (The Magistrate and the Miller's Wife[52]) based on the text by Pedro de Alarcón. Gregorio Martínez Sierra produced the script within a fortnight, following Alarcón's novel very closely.[53] Falla began writing the music in February of the same year, having moved back to live with his family in Madrid.

Because of wartime difficulties, a mimed version (*El corregidor y la molinera)* of the story was first presented, followed by a ballet version, *El sombrero de tres picos* (The Three-Cornered Hat). In the former, it contained clever references to some familiar popular tunes and even references to Beethoven, whose importance and caricature would have been immediately understood. In the latter, extensively revised, rescored, and produced by Diaghilev in London in 1919, with sets by Picasso, it was a resounding success.

The simplified story is of a humpbacked (only in the pantomime version, but not in the ballet),[54] ugly, but clever miller, who eventually outwits a lecherous magistrate in his attempt to win the pretty and vivacious miller's wife. Teasing and flirting, set to regional musical references, add to the charm. A bit of "El paño moruno" is heard to indicate the miller coming from Murcia, in the south. His wife, a northerner from Navarre, is characterized by a *jota*. A provocative *fandango* is danced. The opening motive of the 1st movement and 3rd movement of Beethoven's 5th Symphony (greatly reduced in the ballet version), as well as the beginning of the last movement of Beethoven's 1st Symphony (completely omitted in the ballet) is also heard in the mimed version.[55] Falla also quotes himself (only in the mimed version), when the Magistrate makes gestures towards the Miller's wife for the second time, at which time Falla underscores this moment with the love duo from the first act of *La vida breve* of Paco singing the *gitanilla* "For you I scorn the glories of the world."[56] The neighbors are celebrating the St. John's summer festivities with a *seguidilla*, while the miller entertains them by dancing the fiery *farruca* (a last-minute addition by Falla for Leonide Massine). Truth triumphs and general rejoicing is heard by all.

On 7 April 1917, the première of *El corregidor* (pantomime in two acts) was premiered at Madrid's Teatro Eslava with the Martínez Sierra's company, with Turina conducting. It was written for seven actors and approximately twelve instrumentalists. In Europe, pantomime was just as progressive as ballet. However, in Spain, there was a general lack of pantomime artists on a par with the rest of Europe, which accounted for the need for foreign artists or would limit the number of performances. Antonio Gallego concludes that Falla maintained the validity of this version all along.[57] Falla's British publisher, Chester, refused to publish it for many years. Diaghilev heard of the pantomime's success from Italy and "leaked rumors to the press about his plans to mount the work as a ballet in order to undermine Falla's production."[58]

Falla also began work in 1917 on a new version of *El corregidor*, which would eventually become *El sombrero de tres picos* for the large Russian corps de ballets and with a full orchestra. The choreography by Leonide Massine with sets by Picasso "brought Falla greater recognition than anything else he ever did."[59] Earlier in 1916 Massine had specifically studied traditional Spanish dancers in order to prepare for this work. "I was fascinated by their instinctive sense of rhythm, their natural elegance, and the intensity of their movements. They seemed to combine perfect physical control with flawless timing and innate dignity, something I had never seen before in any native folk dancing."[60]

The opening was delayed due to financial problems with Diaghilev's Ballets Russes. It would turn out to be the most successful of the company's season. Falla subsequently refused Diaghilev's proposed contract to adapt *Noches* for his ballet troupe, instead agreeing to one for *El corregidor*. However, all was not roses between Diaghilev and Falla. Economic difficulties tried Falla's patience. He wrote to María Martínez Sierra, "Diaghilev is paying, but at an exasperating rate . . . so far I've received 750 pesetas . . . I'm exhausted from this economic battle with the Muscovite theater."[61]

Artur Rubinstein told of the difficult financial times the troupe had, but replied how the dancers never lost their boisterous spirits in spite of going days without proper food, unpaid hotel bills, and no money. They would not let their hardships interfere with their work, nor did Diaghilev with his indomitable spirit. Without Falla's music, the project would not have been a success.

> Manuel de Falla I found to be an unusual personality. He looked like an ascetic monk in civilian clothes. Always dressed in black, there was something melancholy about his bald head, his penetrating black eyes and bushy eyebrows; even his smile was sad. But his music betrayed a passion so intense that it seemed a complete contrast to the man. Shy and self-conscious about doing a ballet score, he put some old-fashioned minuets and gavottes into the music, but Diaghilev had no use for them.
>
> "I want it all Spanish and none of this outlandish trash," Diaghilev shouted. The next day poor de Falla brought a short sketch of a jota, the classical Spanish dance. "This is just what we need," said Diaghilev, and Massine nodded approvingly, "and we want much more of it." So, from day to day, de Falla's jota developed into a long passionate dance for the finale, to the delight of his tormentor. The result was stunning; "The Three-Cornered Hat" became one of the most successful ballets of the repertoire.[62]

The Barcelona première of the pantomime took place on 28 June 1917. A new finale for the ballet, then in preparation, was never used in the pantomime. This finale used the blanket-tossing of the effigy figure, or *pelele*, in order for the audience to enjoy a well-known image from a Goya painting that offset Picasso's startling drop-curtain used during the introduction. María Martínez Sierra lamented the fact that it would be used in the Barcelona première and said, "I like very much the modifications you've made on *El corregidor y la molinera*. . . . The Finale as

it was before always struck me as being too short. . . ."[63] Musicologist
Andrew Budwig agreed.

> The very brief finale of *El corregidor y la molinera* not only fails to con-
> clude or summarize the story but is also unsatisfactory from a musical
> point of view. The Finale of the "ballet" . . . is essential to the dramatic and
> musical unit of the work and is its climatic point as well.[64]

Budwig has paralleled the texts of both *El corregidor* and *El sombrero
de tres picos* in his article, "The Evolution of Manuel de Falla's *The Three-
Cornered Hat* (1916–1920).[65] He quotes Falla's letter (21 July 1941) to
Floro Manuel Ugarte, director of the Teatro Colón in Buenos Aires.

> The choreography of the first part of the "ballet" has a converse relation-
> ship to the lighting. That is to say only a very few dancers are used, and
> even in the cortège of the Corregidor and Corregidora, the only scene
> which allows for an augmentation of forces, the number of dancers should
> be kept to a minimum. In the other scenes of the first part only the "real"
> characters should be present. Only by these means may an equilibrium be-
> tween the action and the music be reached, given that the size of the en-
> semble in this part of the "ballet" has been intentionally limited to that of
> a chamber orchestra. Later, on the contrary, from the beginning of the sec-
> ond part, the choreographic and orchestral elements gradually increase,
> culminating in the final Dance.[66]

EL SOMBRERO DE TRES PICOS
(THE THREE-CORNERED HAT)

Sergei Diaghilev's production of The Three-Cornered Hat, as has been
mentioned, combined some of the greatest talents of the time: scenery
by Pablo Picasso, choreography by Leonide Massine, music by Falla,
and of course the dancing by the Ballets Russes featuring Tamara
Karsavina and Leonide Massine as the principal dancers.

A concert version in the Teatro Eslava in Madrid organized by the
Sociedad Nacional de Música and played by the Orquesta Filarmónica
de Madrid with Barolomé Pérez Casas conducting, preceded the ballet
debut on 17 June 1919. The London première took place on 22 July
1919, at the Alhambra Theater, to clamorous praise. The French première took place on 23 January 1920, at the Théâtre National de la
Opéra, receiving enthusiastic press. The general consensus conveyed
the "universal appeal of Spanish music, of which they considered The

Three-Cornered Hat a perfect example."[67] "Falla was congratulated for embodying 'for the first time in Spanish music an [essentially Spanish] sense of humor' and for incorporating both 'a Spanish outlook on [folklore] and a Spanish outlook on music in general.'"[68] The London *Times* reported that the choreography "left one helpless with amusement and excitement" and that the musical score was "a wonderful maze of rhythmical dexterities."[69] However, Ernest Newman found ballerina Karsavina to be miscast, like "a racehorse being set to take a coster's cart to the Derby."[70] However, almost everyone agreed that Massine "went beyond anything he has yet done"[71] and that he was "the greatest actor whom we have in London."[72] Later, Edward Dent would find Falla's orchestration not always "felicitous," but then went on to compare him with Stravinsky. Falla was the intellectual, in contrast to Stravinsky's "barbaric style."[73]

The Madrid debut at the Teatro Real on 5 April 1921, however, "provoked shrill controversy."[74]

Some reviewers hailed *The Three-Cornered Hat* as a liberating influence on their nation's art; among these were theater historian and librettist Matilde Muñoz and art critic Juan de la Encina. Others, like composer Julio Gómez and musicologist Adolfo Salazar, admired many aspects of the ballet, but doubted it would win favor with the Madrid public. Some reviewers questioned the compatibility of modernist stylization with the Spanish literary tradition, while others countered that the work's unsentimental stance was in fact the "ideal" depiction of Spanish character.

Yet another group of critics found the ironic score, flamboyant choreography, and "cubist" set a travesty of the national image. With epithets like "misguided," "arbitrary," "grotesque," and "untrue to the Spanish soul," they attacked the ballet on both artistic and philosophical grounds. All members of this latter contingent were employed by right-wing newspapers, that is, publications espousing views congenial to various traditionalist factions within Spanish political life. Attracting a conservative readership, the right-wing press furnished a mouthpiece for many monarchists, authoritarian Catholics, supporters of the military, Carlists, and members of those political parties that anticipated the ideals of Spanish fascism.[75]

The push-pull tug-of-war between the political right and left, one espousing a traditional Spain protected against foreign influences and the other, as propounded by philosopher José Ortega y Gasset, encouraged a more open policy with a broader European perspective. In Spanish music, the *zarzuela* would be the embodiment of conservative nationalism.

Falla's Three-Cornered Hat, rather than being a prime example of his "nationalistic" or "Andalusian" period

> . . . can now be seen as an affront to the traditionalist view of the national image and the españolista mentality in general. That this occurred despite Falla's lifelong reluctance to associate himself with political or aesthetic factionalism merely reflects "The Three-cornered Hat's" potential for political appropriation and the extent to which music critics, like their political counterparts in the press, inclined towards propaganda.[76]

The French première of *Le tricorne* (The Three-Cornered Hat) observed "long ovations greeted each of the *entrées*."[77] However, the reaction of the intellectual press was mixed, due to their "presumed simplicity of the Ballets Russes prewar Russian soul" and what they regarded as the loss of the Ballets Russes identity.[78] Massine, for one critic, was almost an "hallucination of Nijinsky," but he found not the depth in him nor in his choreography as the former legend.[79] The qualities of innocence and absence of "narcissistic individualism" had given the Ballets Russes "a sort of automatic access to spiritual truth."[80]

The overall production was seen as "trendy" with the latest kind of decor that could be seen in the local art gallery with its primitivism being called a bit superficial. Falla's score was seen by one critic as "narrow nationalism" and to be "forcing himself into a collective 'folk' mode," which resulted in "banality."[81] Clearly, the production caught everyone's attention in this period now referred to as the silver age.[82]

FALLA, THE WRITER

Falla was also engaged in other activities at this time—a series of concerts organized by Segismundo Romero in Seville, Cádiz, and Granada. Too, his former mentor, Felipe Pedrell, had recommended Falla teach the talented young Rosa García Ascot. A gifted budding pianist, she would also compose.

It was during 1916 and 1917 that Falla wrote a series of articles to express his views on music. These were published in *Revista Musical Hispano-Americana*, *La Tribuna*, *Música*, and as the preface to Turina's *Enciclopedia Abreviada de Música*. Others remained in manuscript, such as those that speak about the creation of a class of musical technique in the conservatory studies and the study of orchestration and the creation of a National Lyrical Theater.[83] In the published works he made reference to Spanish music in "Nuestra Música" (1917); contemporary music in "Introducción de la música nueva" (1916) and in the prologue to the Spanish translation of Jean-Aubry's *La música francesa contemporánea* (1916); paid homage to Granados and Stravinsky (1916); and gave sound pedagogical advice. The Madrid artistic elite would deem Falla as the musical leader of his generation, with Adolfo Salazar becoming his greatest defender. Abroad, Jean-Aubry would publish the first comprehensive study on Falla's work (1917).

Falla's prologue to Turina's short music encyclopedia gives illuminating advice to young composers and, at the same time, sheds light on Falla's working processes.

> But I wonder how this book will be used by those aspiring to benefit from its teachings. Light can prove blinding for many who, having lived for a long time in darkness, now enjoy it for the first time. I firmly believe that art should aim only at generating emotion in all its aspects, and I fear therefore that somebody using the means as an end, will transform art into artifice, and think he is fulfilling his duty as an artist by treating sounds as a kind of chess problem, a hieroglyph, or some other innocent and useless pastime. . . . I ask them to look towards the past—though without losing the ground others have conquered—to consider the admirable and constantly growing progress of this art since it was born; to admire, full of gratitude, those artists who, instead of following in the beaten track of their predecessors, have opened new ones; and to decide to imitate their example.
>
> It is my humble opinion that the classical forms of our art should only be studied to learn order, equilibrium and an often exemplary technique. Their help should consist in stimulating the creation of new forms in which those same qualities appear, never in being copied (unless some other special formula is pursued), like a cooking recipe. To be fair, I must confess that in this book, not only the tendencies, but also the fruits of the new music are judged from a particular point of view that is not always mine. I believe that, nowadays, the main use of craft is to help us to make music sound so natural that it somehow seems an improvisation; but, at the same time, so balanced and logical, that the work as a whole, as well as in its details, reveals a higher perfection than that we admire in classical compositions presented to us until now as infallible models.[84]

Falla was all too aware of the sometimes provincial attitude of Madrid's musical tastes. In his article "Igor Stravinsky, The Great Musician of Our Time," he questions the ability of the Madrid public—

"anonymous mass"—to understand the importance of Stravinsky's works (*The Firebird* and *Petroushka*) being premiered in the Spanish capital.

> Does Madrid know that one of Europe's greatest artists is its guest? Will the city be able to reject the opinions of those who say that this composer's works will confuse the listener rather than lead him towards the truth? This, more than anything else, is what I would like people to know. Because Stravinsky's work is imbued with sincerity; the kind of brave, unbowed sincerity of one who says what he thinks fearless of what those who do not think or feel like him might say.[85]

Falla describes Stravinsky's music as

> . . . like a poster shouting defiance at timid people who will only follow a track that has been worn by several generations. . . . Let us not forget, too, that Russian composers—Glinka and Rimsky-Korsakov among others—were the first to write Spanish symphonic music, and let us show Stravinsky the gratitude that we owe to the nation he so brilliantly represents by awarding him the admiration and the high artistic respect which his own work inspires in us.[86]

The sensitive and moving account Falla evoked after the death of Granados is another testimony of Falla's deep and passionate nature.

> I start writing in deep emotion after experiencing the music of Enrique Granados, music that so many times conjured up things and beings from times past, and now helps me to evoke the great artist who composed it. Those of us who have had the good fortune to hear him perform his own works will never forget the strong aesthetic impression we experienced.
>
> Therefore now, while playing those of his piano works I most prefer, I unconsciously repeated the rhythmic accents, the nuances, the inflexions which he used to impress on his music. And, in doing so, it seemed to me that the soul of Granados was present in the tremulous sonorities he wrote down for us, as if it were his testament.
>
> I shall never forget his reading of the first part of his opera "Goyescas" which he gave us in Paris, at Joaquín Nín's house. The extremely brilliant dance of Pelele which begins the work; the "tonadilla"-like phases exquisitely set, the elegance of certain melodic turns, sometimes full of unaffected melancholy, sometimes full of uninhibited spontaneity, always refined and, above all, evocative, as though expressing the artist's inner visions, all this I have just recaptured in playing his music.
>
> But how differently!

Then we were confident that success was near; the work was to have its première next winter at the Paris Opéra; nobody suspected that a cruel and unjust war would be sparked off a few weeks later by a neighbouring state which still described itself as a friend.

Now our wishes, our hopes, have been partly fulfilled. The opera has had its première, the success was great, but Paris did not witness it, and its composer—the victim of those who at that moment were still hidden enemies—could not share it with his relatives and friends in his country.

We who have been honoured by the composer's friendship and have admired his exceptional talent, must demand proper retribution for those who have wrenched away from us an artist who so brilliantly represented Spain abroad. And after fulfilling that duty, both humanitarian and patriotic, we must unite to praise and to preserve as a treasure the heritage Enrique Granados left us when he died, the loftiest heritage a man can leave to his country: the product of his intelligence and his will.[87]

Granados's tragic death may have been the final contribution to break in Falla's health. A possible stay at a sanatorium in Córdoba sometime in 1916 is cited in Campodónico's biography (second edition) by Sopeña. However, there is scant evidence to support either the theory or the timing of the alleged occurrence after the debut of *Noches*.[88]

DEBUSSY'S DEMISE

Upon Debussy's death in 1918 Falla participated in a concert at the Madrid Ateneo in his memory in which Falla read his lecture about the French composer-colleague's "profound art." Aga Lahowska, Artur Rubinstein, and the Orquesta Filarmónica also participated. Falla's written tribute to Debussy included these words:

During the last World Fair at the Champ de Mars two young French musicians were to be seen going about together listening to exotic music from more or less distant countries. Unobtrusively mixing with the crowd, they absorbed the magic of sound and rhythm the strange music contained. New unexpected emotions arose in them. These young musicians later on became two of the most famous names in contemporary music—Paul Dukas and Claude Debussy.

This story explains the origin of many facets of Debussy's music: the vast horizons of sound unfolding before him, encompassing Chinese and Spanish music, made him glimpse possibilities that were to be realized in fine compositions. "I have always been an observer," he used to say, "and profited from these observations for my work." This way he understood as well as expressed the very essence of Spanish music shows how true this was. . . .

We know how much contemporary music owes to Debussy, from this point of view as well as from many others. Let us be quite clear: I am not referring to the servile imitators of his music, I am referring to the direct and indirect consequences of his work, to the feeling of emulation it has stirred up, to the unfortunate prejudices it has destroyed once and for all.[89]

SEPARATION FROM FAMILY AND FRIENDS

The year 1919 was a year of highs and lows. Great personal grief came on the heels of Debussy's passing when Falla lost both parents within a few months. His father died in February and his mother in July. He had gone to London for the première of his completed ballet *El sombrero de tres picos* with Diaghilev at the Alhambra Theatre at which time he learned of his mother's serious condition. Returning urgently to Madrid, he heard of the news of her death, which had occurred on the exact day of the *Sombrero* debut.

María del Carmen tells of her brother's reaction.

He could not bring himself to enter (his home), and remained in the vestibule, completely disheartened. Sitting on a chair, without uttering a single word, he burst into tears like a child. Never had I seen him cry, so I was incredulous, thinking him too strong for tears.[90]

Change was in the air. Falla and María del Carmen visited Granada in September, staying a few days with the Vázquez Díaz family. Falla spent time with the guitarist Ángel Barrios and his father "El polinario." Englishman J. B. Trend also encountered the Fallas in Granada. New life was on the horizon, while the old was drawing to an end, for it was later in the year that the final rupture with the Martínez Sierras occurred. He composed two songs for the fourth act of Gregorio Martínez Sierra's *El corazón ciego* (The Blind Heart), which was premiered in November of 1919 in San Sebastián and later in Madrid. This was probably their last collaboration.

FANTASÍA BÆTICA (BETIC FANTASY)

The only [work] written by me with "purely pianistic" intentions, to that which its instrumental technique is referred. Another thing: the title of

"Baética" does not have any "especially Sevillan" significance.[91] With it I have only attempted to render homage to our Latin-Andalusian race.[92]

The origin of Falla's last virtuosic solo piano piece is an interesting one. On 10 March 1918, Ernest Ansermet wrote to Falla from Lausanne, in Switzerland, about Stravinsky's dire financial straits because of the closure of his publishing house in Russia due to the 1917 Russian revolution.[93] Ansermet asked Falla to inform Artur Rubinstein, then in Madrid, of the situation, to see if he could do something for Stravinsky. The first thought was that Rubinstein would buy[94] the manuscript of Stravinsky's *L'Oiseau de feu* (The Firebird). However, Rubinstein had "a better" idea—to commission a work, perhaps a concerto, from him instead.[95] The commission resulted in Stravinsky composing his *Piano-Rag Music*. With details of the financial agreement finally worked out (5,000 francs), Rubinstein, always generous, also commissioned a work from Falla—the *Fantasía bætica*.

Falla wrote the work rather quickly, in three or four months,[96] in order to have it ready for Rubinstein's return from a concert tour. However, the pianist did not have time to prepare it for his upcoming Barcelona concerts. He did give the première in New York on 20 February 1920, in a concert sponsored by the Society of the Friends of Music, along with works by Albéniz, Szymanowski, Poulenc, Ravel, and his own transcription of *L'Oiseau de feu*.[97] From 1922–1926 Rubinstein played the work only a handful of times in such cities as London, Madrid, Barcelona, Malaga, and Cádiz,[98] eventually abandoning it, claiming that it was too long. He found it to possess too many technical problems with its *flamenco* idioms imitative of the guitar, or too many glissandis, and so on.[99] Falla told him of his idea of transcribing the work for piano and orchestra, to which Rubinstein reacted positively. This never happened.

The technical-musical difficulties found in *Fantasía bætica* may account for its little accessibility and few performances during its early years. According to Pahissa, Falla thought that perhaps the work was either too long or too excessive. Falla's director at the publishing firm of Max Eschig in Paris commented that his daughter was studying the work and did not find it excessively long.[100] Not all pianists agreed, for pianist Emile Bosquet (Honorary Professor of the Royal Conservatory of Brussels), in his 1953 book *La Musique de Clavier* (Brussels: Les Amis de la Musique) wrote to take cuts on page seventeen, after the fourth stave to page eighteen, second measure; from page eighteen, fourth measure to page eighteen, fourth stave, second measure; and from the finale on page twenty to page twenty-two, second stave, second measure.[101]

From the historical usage of the term "fantasy" is seen the improvisatory type from harpsichord-organ tradition of Frescobaldi, Louis Couperin to those of Bach, Haydn, or Mozart. Contrasting this type with later romantic forms—as found in the piano works of Schubert, Chopin, and Schumann—we find Falla's work to fall more into the second category.[102] The term *bætica* was the name for the ancient Roman province that is essentially Andalusía, or southern Spain, parts of Extremadura, and Portugal, today.[103] In a letter dated 2 March 1922, from Harry Kling, director of J. W. Chester publishing firm in England, Falla was asked to consider an adjective that would better describe his *Fantasía*, its original title. By the end of April the definitive title, *Fantasía bætica*, was decided on with the archaic spelling using the dipthong *æ* instead of the separate letters. Falla was adamant about this spelling.[104]

Fantasía bætica has been described as an Andalusian fantasy[105] but not a historical evocation.[106] It has close ties to *El amor brujo* and the *Siete canciones populares españolas* from just a few years prior. The Andalusian qualities would be experienced in a different guise in 1922 when Falla organized, with García Lorca, the first *Cante jondo* Competition in Granada.[107] Many *flamenco* (Andalusian songs and dances by trained performers) elements are found in Falla's piano work, which may include some, but not all, of the following: the *cante jondo* (deep song or group of Andalusian songs); the *toque jondo* (deep touch); the *baile jondo* (deep dance); the *taconeo* (heel stamping such as found in the dance of the *zapatedo*); associations with the guitar such as the *punteado* (plucking) or *rasgueado* (strumming); *falsetas* (guitar solos that introduce and/or play in between the vocal part of the *cantaor/ra* or singer); chords formed from the notes of the guitar strings (EADGBE); the various songs and dances, such as the *polo* (dance in triple time)*, guarija* (Spanish dance of Cuban origin with alternating meters of 6/8 to 3/4)*, and *buleria* (lively *flamenco* song and dance in triple time); *martinete* (improvised Gypsy lament, using only the representational beat of the hammer to denote the ancestral link)*, siguiriya* (the most tragic of the Gypsy chant), *soleá* (free, yet profound and solemn chant on themes of jealousy or love, that, with the *siguiriya,* make up the two basic branches of *flamenco*), and *saeta* (chant used in religious processionals); *zambra* (group of dances in which the Gypsies draw upon more Andalusian characteristics); *fandango* (old Spanish dance with marked triple meter, sometimes with elongated second beat much in the way of the Sarabande and with forms from different regions such as Malaga, Granada, Múrcia, and Ronda); *carcelera* (Gypsy prison song); *malagueña* (song and dance from Málaga, derived from the strongly-marked triple-metered *fandango*); *habanera* (dance from Havana, although it may have originated in Spain and returned there from Cuba and is similar to the *tango*); *jota* (fast dance with many variations throughout Spain, such as the *jota aragonesa* characterized with its triplet figures); *seguidilla* (very popular quick song and dance in triple time, one type of which is found from Seville); *bolero* (dance in triplet time with triplet figure on the weak part of the first beat of the measure and is more deliberate than the *seguidilla*; *rondeña* (*fandango* from the region of Ronda); and *copla* (basic poetical form of the popular Spanish chant on varying themes, can also be used as interludes or stanzas between other verses).[108] The melodic range of a sixth is usual, while the employment of many modes is typical, especially the phrygian used with its descending A-G-F-E Andalusian pattern.

From amongst Falla's personal holdings are found several guitar works or manuals. Especially interesting are those volumes by Rafael Marin, published as early as 1902 and annotated by Falla, and containing such categories as *siguirillas gitanas, soleares, tangos, malagueñas,* and *rondeñas,* amongst others.[109] Yvan Nommick in his analysis of *Fantasía bætica* shows many interesting parallels.[110] He also points out the multiple modal usage, which includes—apart from the expected phrygian (including Andalusian tetrachord), aeolian, and dorian modes—the mixolydian and lydian modes all woven into a rich harmonic tapestry. Resultant chordal formations are also inspired from the string tunings of the guitar mentioned above and "an attempt at utilizing the Hindu" *Sriraga* (G-A̲-B-C-D̲-E̲-F)[111] mode, the result of which occurs in the opening chord of the piece and which has striking similarities to the chord derived from the guitar's string tunings.[112] Nommick also finds usage of the *soleares, buleria, siguiriya, quejío* with its cry of *ay,* amongst others, using the *flamenco* techniques of *cante jondo, cante toque, cante baile, falsetas, coplas, tocaneo* and *tacaneo redoble* (with drum figure), and of the *cantaor.* But perhaps the most interesting, less obvious, example is the *guajira* in the Intermezzo, with its alternating two-measure patterns of 6/8 and 3/4. Falla does not indicate this metric change, leaving the section in a constant 3/8.

Returning to the letter that Falla received from Ansermet on 10 March 1918, just two weeks later Falla's great mentor and model, Claude Debussy, would die on 25 March. It is this author's premise that *Fantasía bætica*, in spite of its obvious Andalusian character, is Falla's tribute to Debussy on the piano, even though he wrote another in 1920 as a transcription from the guitar work, *Homenaje, Pièce de guitare écrite pour "Le tombeau de Claude Debussy."* Debussy's Spanish-inspired works were always marvels for Falla, for Debussy managed to capture its essence without ever having visited that country. In spite of its strong marked *flamenco* idioms, *Fantasía bætica* also possesses a subtle French character underneath. Several passages are reminiscent of Debussy or Falla's own works: (1) in ms. 56–57 a passage similar to Debussy's "Jardins sous la pluie" from *Estampes* reveals a pianistic treatment not outwardly Andalusian; (2) another passage, ms. 97–98 (and the parallel section) have commonalties with Debussy's quartet; (3) the vacillating two-note motive in thirty-second notes, which García Poliz likens to Ravel (see below) in measures 36+ and 306+, also have a melodic parallel to Golaud's leitmotif in *Pelleas*, with the alternating D-E in various non-Spanish rhythmic patterns; (4) Falla's own *Noches*, whose work was begun in Paris, is recalled in ms. 369–380, especially measures 378 and 380, which are reminiscent also of "Jardins sous la pluie"; (5) in terms of execution, the piece is best (and perhaps more easily) executed from a French school conception of execution with its high finger articulation, closer to the idea of plucked strings of the guitar. It is noteworthy that the French school comes from a long line of harpsichord tradition, whereas the Russian school, strongly based on the use of arm and body weight, does not have the harpsichord tradition. The recording of Mark Hambourg (a Leschetitsky[113] student), whom Falla probably heard in Paris, given the program housed at the AMF (NFE-032 on 5 April 1911, at Salle Gaveau), must be the shortest on record and is executed in about half the time as other pianists—eight minutes. Hambourg's approach is very Debussyian. Also, it is allegedly reported that Frank Pelleg recorded the work on harpsichord.[114] Possessing such a pedal-harpsichord designed for contemporary music, this author has experimented with the idea, agreeing that Falla's aesthetic and sonorous conception are very viable on the harpsichord in spite of the lack of a sustaining pedal. Because of the lightness of the action of the keys, the technical difficulties are not so great. The harpsichord realization is also more closely allied to that of the guitar, even though Falla had not written any works yet for harpsichord. He would soon embark on *Retablo* and the *Concerto*, both of which have prominent harpsichord parts. Naturally, of course, the timbric colors possible with the pedals of the piano give a different perspective of the work; (6) the opening of Falla's work is characterized by Nommick as a nontraditional *bulerias*, which does not correspond to the normal rhythmical pattern of 1 2 3̲ |4 5 6̲ | 7 8̲ 9 | 10̲ 11 12̲, but is a "free evocation."[115] Yet the return always to the same pattern gives it an underlying ostinato effect. It is interesting to note its rhythmical similarities to the *bolero*. Instead of the *bolero*'s characteristic triplets, Falla uses four thirty-second notes instead. The obvious French example is Ravel's *Bolero* (1928). Lest it not be forgotten Falla embarked around the same time on another project closely allied to France—the ill-fated *Fuego fatuo*.

Another author finds some similar and different evidence from that presented above. Susana García Poliz in her article "*Cante jondo y vanguardia europea en la Fantasía bætica*"[116] says the opening of the piece is considered to be akin to the danceable *bolero (bolerías)*, possibly the etymological ancestor of the *bulerías*. The author attributes characteristics of the *seguidillas andaluzas* or *sevillanas* to the beginning of the Giocoso (molto ritmico) section, as well as a *fandango* ("*seguidillas afandangadas*") in its second part. From measure 150 the primitive rhythmic repetition is closely allied to the *Rite of Spring* of Stravinsky (1913) and *Allegro Bárbaro* (1911) of Bartók. The triplet rhythmic figure in measure 184 is typical of the *taconeo* of the *bailaor.* García Poliz also notes the typical features of "interruption of the discourse" as being closely associated with the *cante jondo* style. The undulating thirty-second-notes (ms. 36+) are likened to those found in works of Ravel, particularly *Sonatine* (1905), "Ondine" from *Gaspard de la Nuit* (1908), and *Valses Nobles y sentimentales* (1911), while melodic features from "Une barque sur l'océan" from *Miroirs* are found in measures 87–90. García Poliz agrees with many authors that the normal melodic range in this type of music is generally a sixth and that the phyrgian or andalusian mode is preferred. She also identifies the *falsetas* (ms. 114+) as setting up the entrance of the voice and alternating with it in the Lento sections (ms. 120+) or in its "jipio" expression (broken voice) in measure 134+ and parallel sections. Like Nommick, she identifies the rhythmic nature of the Intermezzo as a *guajira*, and further theorizes that Falla shaped it ("el zorongo") from similar ones found in *Flores de España* of Isidoro Hernández (1884) and *Ecos de España* of José Inzenga (1874) and also used in some of his other works. *Acciacaturas* bear a Scarlattian influence. Further Ravelian influence is taken from "Alborada del gracioso" (*Miroirs*) in the Spanish flavor of the repeated notes; and (7) Faure's *Ballade* is felt in ms. 97–103, 317–320. Falla was termed a "Frenchified" composer by the Madrid press after his return from Paris. His close association with Debussy, Dukas, and Ravel threatened the idea of a Spanish national identity, replacing the former "Wagnerism." Falla was thus viewed as a *compositor afrancesado* and no doubt was sensitive to this criticism.

(See Carol Hess's *Manuel de Falla and Modernism in Spain, 1898–1936*, Chicago: The University of Chicago Press, 2001.)

Falla's personal copy of *Albéniz et Granados* by Henri Collet (1926) is heavily annotated in the parts that refer to the popular elements in *Iberia*. It perhaps sheds more light on the fascinating subject of how Falla incorporated and transformed these elements into his own works, the most abstract perhaps being *Fantasía bœtica*.

FUEGO FATUO
(FOOLISH FIRE)

In 1918 a new project, *El fuego fatuo*, a comic opera[117] in three acts based on pieces of Chopin and orchestrations of Falla, was begun with the composer and María Martínez Sierra as librettist. This work was not premiered during Falla's lifetime, as there was little interest in Spain, or abroad, for this type of project. Falla's Spanish music was much preferred to his orchestrations of Chopin, in spite of the popularity that Tommasini's Scarlatti enjoyed, thanks to the Ballets Russes.[118]

The plot of *Fuego fatuo*, succinctly summarized, takes place in 19th-century Naples; in act II, specifically in a palace of Princess Lisa. The action involves a composer (Leonardo) and his love (Clara), as well as Lord Tristan and the Princess Lisa, one of Lord Tristan's former lovers. Lord Tristan helps the Princess to seduce the composer, who falls madly in love with her. However, the Princess quickly tires of him. This causes him to become ill and to eventually reestablish his relationship with Clara, who, like a saint, has waited patiently for him. In conformity with all happy endings, Princess Lisa discovers that it is really Lord Tristan whom she has loved all along.[119]

Falla uses almost all types of musical forms in this "compilation," except for the concerto, the impromptu, the nocturne, the polonaise, the prelude, the sonata, and the variation form.[120] For example:[121]

Act	Number	Chopin Work
I	1	Ab Waltz, op. 64/3;
		Scherzo, no. 2, op. 31
	2	Scherzo no. 4, op. 54
	3	Mazurka in C, op. 24/2
	4	Bolero, op. 19
	5	Mazurka in b, op. 33/4
	6	Scherzo, no. 2

Act	Number	Chopin Work
II	1	Polish Song, op. 74/2
	2	Étude, op. 10/3
	3	Ab Mazurka, op. 7/4
	4	Ballade, no.1, op. 23
	5	Ab Waltz, op. 42
		Mazurka in a, op. post.
	6	Étude, op. 10/12
III	1	Tarantella, op. 43
	2	Polish Song, op. 74/1
	3	Berceuse, op. 57
	4	Ballade, no. 4, op. 52
	5	Barcarolle, op. 60

The big question has remained: why would Falla undertake such a project: a) his love for Chopin? b) normal performance practice of the time? c) his desire to maintain his close relationship with the Martínez Sierras, especially María? d) other. Looking at each of these possibilities sheds some light on the matter.

Falla's love for Chopin is well-known and well-documented, from his studies with José Tragó, a former pupil of a pupil of Chopin,[122] to his compositions inspired by Chopin, such as his *Mazurka, Nocturno,* parts of *Allegro de concierto, Fuego fatuo,* and his *Balada de Mallorca.* Falla often performed works of Chopin in his recitals, either as soloist or by accompanying singers, such the Polish Aga Lahowska.[123]

The performance practice around Chopin at the beginning of the 20th century had multiple influences, some of which were still carried over from the preceding century.[124] "Chopin in France" would have been remembered in various settings, such as the Ballets Russes's production of *Les Sylphides* (debut in Paris at the Théâtre du Châtelet on 2 June 1909, with choreography by Michel Fokine and sets/costumes by Alexandre Benois, in which Stravinsky had orchestrated Chopin's Ab Nocturne, op. 32/2 and the Eb Waltz, op. 18);[125] Debussy's piano studies dedicated to Chopin (*Études,* first edition of 1915);[126] or the French mezzo-soprano of Spanish origin, Pauline Viardot's interpolations into the Chopin mazurkas, transcriptions which Chopin himself admired.[127] The practice of putting words to instrumental music may, at first, seem strange, but upon closer investigation into both Chopin's and Falla's music, the affinity with and the use of folk music in their erudite works is very great. Vocal transcrip-

tions or interpolations would thus be a natural possibility. Falla himself refers to Viardot's role in spreading the song form, the *habanera*,
amongst the best composers in Paris.[128] Liszt too was amongst the
first to make transcriptions of Polish songs, such as the well-known
Chopin melody, "Mädchens Wunsch," op. 74/1. Bizet, Thalberg, and
others followed in this "singing pianist" or "pianist singing" tradition.
Falla in Paris was also privy to hearing some of the best Chopin interpreters of the time, such as Cortot and Rubinstein, amongst others.

Falla's relationship with the Martínez Sierra couple began in Paris in
1913 and deepened considerably upon their return to Spain in 1914.
Subsequent collaborations on *El amor brujo*; the incidental music for *La
pasión* (*Soleá*), *Amanecer*, and *Otelo*; the songs *El pan de Ronda que
sabe a verdad* and "Oración de las madres que tienen a sus hijos en brazos; *El corregidor y la molinera* and *El sombrero de tres picos*; and *El
corazón ciego* would take place in one of the most intensive, creative periods of the composer's life—a period which lasted five years at the
most. Falla collaborated with both Gregorio and his wife María de la O
Lejárraga (her maiden name). However, from documents that came to be
housed in the AMF (as yet undetermined how)—eight folders of theater
pieces, librettos, articles, poetry, etc.—it is clear that the majority of the
works signed by Gregorio were actually written by María.[129]

Other possible reasons for Falla's embarking on such a project may be
found in Paolo Pinamonti's reasoning when he comes to four "provisional conclusions": (1) as a "slow consciousness on the part of Falla of
that posture of neo-classic elegance that characterizes French music of
the last decades of the 19th century and the first years of the 20th century . . . a posture whose maturation is not beyond the acceptance, im-
minently French, of Chopin"; (2) "This opera is also proof of the great
passion for Chopin, that . . . the Spanish composer took almost to an
expressive identification of the Polish musician. . . ."; (3) ". . . it cannot
be spoken of *Fuego fatuo* as a neo-classic opera, in [the] first place because there doesn't exist a unique [uniform] acceptation of musical neoclassicism. . . . In second place, because there is expressly lacking in
Falla this disenchanted distance, when not also unembarrassed, that we
find again in other operations analogous in the European panorama in
those years"; and (4) Perhaps this work, which accompanied him during
the hot summer of 1918, without which never got to be staged but towards which Falla felt a great emotion, favored the maturation of this
particular compositional elegance and sobriety that we find in the years
of the '20s. In other words, *Fuego fatuo* is his personal tribute to that

"call to order," to that "return to order" that, however, will never be in sync with Falla because of its expressive coldness; and this is perhaps the reason that the enigmatic *Fuego fatuo* cannot more than be redirected to the narrative experience of theatrical vocal expression."[130]

María Martínez Sierra gives her account of the genesis of the work, while biographer Jaime Pahissa, whose work was read and approved by Falla, gives another. According to María,

> Falla, great admirer of Chopin, formed the project of orchestrating some of his best pages—ballades, nocturnes, mazurkas, studies—with the proposi-tion of linking them in a stageable dramatic action, according to him and to me, with hopes for indubitable success. [. . .] He imagined a "plot" with all the romanticism corresponding to the music and to the epoch in which it would be written.[131]

Pahissa says that it was Gregorio Martínez Sierra's idea to do the proj-ect. Falla told him that he would not embark on such a task without guar-antee that it would be staged. Gregorio had then rented the Teatro Eslava in Madrid, which he had given to another composer for the 1919 season, on the condition that the new work would be staged there.[132]

Falla worked very hard on the project, up to ten hours daily. María complained that the work was much more difficult for her than for Falla.

> I have never known a task more grueling than that of inserting or adding words to a melody composed beforehand, conserving rhythms, accents and until definite articulations could be sung without insurmountable difficulty, while at the same time is intended to say with clarity and feeling common to that which the plot and logic required. At times, in this ungrateful task, I was at the point of losing, if not the patience, the sense. . . . [. . .] I was not used to this absurd method of work.[133]

Gregorio sent the title of the work to Falla in a telegram dated 25 Au-gust 1918. Falla was still working at fever-pitch in mid-September to ready the work for the upcoming season. However, the debut was not forthcoming at the Eslava Theater, nor at the Victoria Theater, nor in Barcelona through the assistance of Aga Lahowska, nor at the Ópera Comique (Comic Opera) in Paris, the latter of which specifically indi-cated that they preferred Falla's original music to his adaptations.[134]

María gives yet another viewpoint. As the dramatic conflict was in-evitably about love, Falla's famous scruples came forward. And as the li-brettist was a woman, and the "sought-after" was a composer pursued by two women, instead of vice versa, Falla's shyness and natural gallantry could in no way lower the ideal of the "woman eternal." "Even though it killed me to explain to him that between two angels confirmed in grace there could be no conflict, and that if the three were saints, the respectable public would die of boredom, there was no way to convince him."[135]

Perhaps Falla found the plot of *Fuego fatuo* could be interpreted as somewhat autobiographical.[136] Yet, he supports Pahissa's version when he said to his relative, Pedro de Matheu Montalvo, that he had been given assurance that the work would be staged. As since it was not forthcoming, and since the work would need a large revision in order to make it possible, he was not able to do this as he was busy working on *Atlántida*.[137] It is important to note that he never disavowed the work either.[138]

Work on *El fuego fatuo* and another uncompleted project, *Don Juan*, in 1918, with the Martínez Sierras led to the eventual break with the couple. The composer and María had exchanged letters almost daily from 1915–1918. The fiasco of the ill-fated *El fuego* project would deter Falla from accepting another, more prestigious, offer from Diaghilev. That would go instead to Stravinsky, becoming his *Pulcinella*.

Other events in 1918 also occupied Falla's time. On 3 June Falla performed a shortened two-piano version of *Noches* at the Société National Indépendante in Paris with his piano pupil, Rosa García Ascot. Shortly afterwards, on 9 June, Picasso finished his famous drawing of the composer. Falla also embarked on a tour with singer Aga Lahowska, going from Madrid to the northern part of Spain, performing five times with her in at least one song from *Fuego fatuo*, the first Polish Song, what would be used for the second number of act III.

NOTES

1. Walter Starkie, *Aventuras de un irlandés en España,* Madrid: Espasa Calpe, 1958, 226.

2. Velázquez, 333. (In nautical terms, Falla means = "defect; deficiency"; in geological terms, "fault.")

3. Falla's Madrid addresses were: Serrano 70 (1901–1907); Ponzano 24 (1914–1918); and Lagasca, 119 (1918–1919). Sopeña, 114.

4. María Martínez Sierra, *Gregorio y yo*, 126. "Quedaba, sin embargo, outro prejuicio por destruir: el consideraba cosa "vulgar" y propia únicamente para juergas entre gente ordinaria o ante turistas ávidos de lo "pintoresco" la música popular española. Esse prejuicio había . . . alejado de España—y hecho triunfar en el rest ode Europa—a outra gran músico español, Isaac Albéniz."

5. María Martínez Sierra, *Gregorio y yo*, 126–27. . . . *de que tan "populares y vulgares" eran en alemania los temas que Beethoven magnificara y sublimara en su "Sinfonía pastoral" como pudieran serlo en España las seguidillas de "La vida breve." Las cuales gustaron, en efecto, al respetable público franca y totalmente.*

6. María Martínez Sierra, *Gregorio y yo*, 127.

7. María Martínez Sierra, *Gregorio y yo*, 127.

8. *Poesía*, 63.

9. Antonio Gallego, "Manuel de Falla y el Conservatorio" in *Cuatro Lecciones magistrales*. Madrid: 1992, 37–38, translated in Nancy Lee Harper *Bio-Bibliography*, 90.

10. Evidence found in the AMF points to the fact that María was the chief playwright, signing for her husband. See fn 129 below.

11. *Poesía*, 87.

12. Demarquez, 68.

13. Michael Christoforidis, "Folksong Models and their Sources in Manuel de Falla's *Siete canciones populares españolas*" in *Context 9*, 1995, 12–21; 14–18.

14. OMM, 31–32.

15. *Poesía*, 69.

16. María Martínez Sierra, *Gregorio y yo*, 135. "Pienso que esse momento de total felicidad—su grito no dejaba lugar a duda—fué uno de los éxtasis que compensaron el tormento de su existencia roída por tanto mezquino y, a veces, innecesario sin sabor."

17. Demarquez, 67.

18. Otto Mayer Serra, "Falla's Musical Nationalism" in *The Musical Quarterly*, XXIX, January 1943, 1–17.

19. Letter Pedrell-Falla dated 6 May 1915. AMF 7389. "Bravo, Manuel, ya pueda V. figurar con mucha atención e´[y] interesse sigo su progreso de autor, porque en V. *siempre* he reconocido el compositor sincero y de altas intensiones y al hombre leal y honorado, siempre Digno, siempre artista . . . y merecedor de todo. . . ." On the reverse side are notes by Falla, referring to Enrique Gorrá, "El mundo," etc.

20. Rubinstein, 472.

21. Antonio Gallego, *El amor brujo*, Madrid: Alianza Música, 1990, 126.

22. Christoforidis, *Enciclopedia,* 898.

23. For a detailed description regarding the origin of interpretation, related works and manuscripts, see AMF Exposition book (30 October–30 January, 1997) *Jardines de España de Santiago Rusiñol a Manuel de Falla* (1996). Madrid: V.E.G.A.P. copyright Santiago Rusiñol, 8. (Hereafter referred to as Nommick-Noches).

24. Ann Livermore, *A Short History of Spanish Music*. London: Gerald Duckworth, 1972, 194.

25. Pahissa, 101.

26. Rubinstein, 477.

27. Pahissa, 101.

28. Antonio Iglesias Álvarez (2001) *Manuel de Falla (su obra para piano) 2º ediition y "Noches en los jardines de España"* Madrid: coedition Manuel de Falla Ediciones and Editorial Alpuerto, S. A., 309. . . . Isaac Albéniz exclamó: "Nada de tablillas. ¡Cuadros! ¡Cuadros!"

29. It was Ricardo Viñes who suggested them to be for piano and orchestra. Iglesias, 309.

30. AMF XLIX, A1, h. [3]. And AMF XLIV A4, 1, p. 2, viewed in Nommick, Noches, 8.

31. Program notes at the debut in 1916 at Madrid's Royal Theater cited in Nommick, Noches, 3, 18 with three programs preserved at AMF (FN 1916-006, 007, and 010). "Téngase presente que la música de estos nocturnos no pretende ser descriptiva, sino simplemente expresiva, y que algo más que rumores de fiestas y de danzas há inspirado estas evocaciones sonoras, en las que el dolor y el misterio tienen también su parte."

32. Nommick, Noches, 7. (Letter in AMF folder 7808). Rusiñol's book dates from 1903 and contains twenty-nine pages with forty reproductions of his paintings with texts by various authors (AMF 3967 and 3968).

33. París Barnier, 1910, 339 pp (AMF 2131).

34. Rubén Darío and Falla apparently knew each other in Madrid and in Paris. Both left the latter city in 1914, with Darío going to Guatemala where he would die in February of 1916, just a few weeks before the debut of Falla's *noches*. See Livermore, 194.

35. In the AMF are three Darío books: *Tierras solares* (1904) Madrid: Leonardo Williams (AMF 2786); *Canto a la Argentina y otros poemas* (1914) Madrid: Biblioteca Corona (AMF 2783); and *Antología Poética* (1927) Madrid: Renaciemiento (AMF 3786). For more details, see Nommick, Noches, 13.

36. Livermore, 194.

37. AMF 291, referred to in Nommick, Noches, 14.

38. Nommick, Noches, 15.

39. Published in *Manuel de Falla y Granada* (1963), Rafael Jofré García (ed.) in a homage edition by the Centro Artístico, Literario y Científico of Granada.

40. Letter Falla-Pedrell, 2 July 1915 (AMF 7389), Nommick-Noches, 9.

41. See Nommick, Noches, 10, for more details.

42. Nommick, -Noches, 10. Letter to María Martínez Sierra dated 27 March 1916 (photocopy in AMF 7252).

43. Henri Collett in *La Revue Musicale*, January 1947 cited in Demarquez, 86.

44. Livermore, 194.

45. Falla's personal copy of *Santa Teresa de Jesús's las Moradas Obras de San Juan de la Cruz* (Madrid: Apostolado de la Presnsa, 1926) found in the AMF (no. 2931) is heavily annotated. Important works associated with the "Carmen de los Mártires," then the "Convento de los Santos Mártires de Carmelitas Descalzos de Granada" (Convent of the Holy Martyrs of the Barefoot Carmelites of Granada)—written by its head from 1582–1588, St. John of

the Cross, and by St. Teresa of Jesus—were studied in great detail by Falla in his Granada years. See also Christoforidis's article on Falla's personal library in chapter 15.
	46. Iglesias, 308.

> Versión primitiva de *"Noches"*—Los amigos le regalan los *Jardines de España* de Rusiñol. Se entusiasma. Compone el de Tarragona. Cantera com cipreses. Brolladores del Generalife. Los Mártires. (Danza lejana: todo el tema). Cementerio de Montserrat = 'último jardín.' Quiso componer Las Flores, pero los Quintero no. El Buscón y?

From these jottings, it would seem that one of the Nocturnes was influenced by region of Tarragon and that the influence of "Los Mártires" (the Martyrs) was to be present in the entire theme of the second movement. There is also a comment about the Cemetery of Montserrat (during his Catalonia stay?) being used in the "last garden" (last movement?). What is interesting also is the reference to the unrealized opera project between Falla and the Quintero brothers, the former who wanted it and the latter who did not.
	47. Nommick, Noches, 16.
	48. Livermore, 195.
	49. Pahissa, 103.
	50. Pahissa, 104.
	51. Antonio Gallego "Evolción de *El corregidor y la molinera* a *El sombrero de tres picos* in *Los Ballets Russes de Diaghilev y España*, ed. Yvan Nommick and Antonio Álvarez Cañibano, Granada: Fundación Manuel de Falla and Centro de Documentación de Música y Danza-INAEM, 2000. 65–72, 67, known herewith as BR (or AG-BR). Letter housed in AMF.
	52. Pedro Antonio de Alarcón (1833–1891), whose novel also was the basis for Hugo Wolf's opera *Der Corregidor* (1896). Andrew Budwig, "The Evolution of Manuel de Falla's *The Three-Cornered Hat* (1916–1920) in *Journal of Musicological Research*, V, Spring, 1984, 191–212, 193, hereafter known as Budwig-3picos.
	53. Budwig-3picos, 193.
	54. Budwig-3picos, 194.
	55. AG-BR, 71.
	56. AG-BR, 72. "Por ti yo desprecio las galas del mundo."
	57. AG-BR, 72.
	58. Budwig-3picos, 196.
	59. Budwig-3picos, 202–3.
	60. Budwig-3picos, 191.
	61. Chase-Budwig, 22.
	62. Rubinstein, 469–70.
	63. Letter from MMS-Falla dated 22 June 1917, AMF.
	64. Budwig-3picos, 200.
	65. See fn. 52.
	66. Budwig-3picos, 195.

67. Carol A. Hess, "Manuel de Falla's *The Three-Cornered Hat* and the Right-Wing Press in Pre-Civil War Spain" in *Journal of Musicological Research*, vol. 15, 55–84, 1995; 5, known hereafter as Hess-1995.
68. Hess-1995, 55.
69. Joan Acocella, "The Critical Reception of *Le Tricorne* in *Los Ballets Russes de Diaghilev y España*, ed. Yvan Nommick and Antonio Álvarez Cañibano, Granada: Fundación Manuel de Falla and Centro de Documentación de Música y Danza-INAEM, 2000, 105–13; 106, herewith known as Joan Acocella-BR.
70. Joan Acocella-BR, 106.
71. Joan-Acocella-BR, 106.
72. Joan Acocella-BR, 107.
73. Joan Acocella-BR, 108.
74. Hess-1995, 55.
75. Hess-1995, 55–56.
76. Hess-1995, 59.
77. Joan Acocella-BR, 109.
78. Joan Acocella-BR, 109.
79. Joan Acocella-BR, 110.
80. Joan Acocella-BR, 109.
81. Joan Acocella-BR, 110.
82. Carol Hess draws attention to this term in her article "Un alarde de modernismo y dislocación: Los Ballets Russes en España, 1916–1921" in *Los Ballets Russes de Diaghilev y España*, edición Yvan Nommick and Antonio Álvarez Cañibano, 2000, Granada: AMF, Centro de Documentación de Música y Danza INAEM, 215–27. See further José-Carlos Mainer, *La Edad de Plata (1902–1939)*. Madrid, Cátedra, 4th ed. 1987.
83. Christiforidis, *Enciclopedia*, 899.
84. OMM, 27–28.
85. OMM, 11.
86. OMM, 9–10.
87. OMM, 7–8.
88. Sopeña, 89, 102.
89. OMM, 41,44–45.
90. Chase-Budwig, 23.
91. Demarquez, 109, who says the term *bética* comes from Bétis, or the poetic name for the Guadalquiver river of Seville.
92. Gallego, *Catalogo*, 170. Falla's words to José Ma Gálvez, when the work was included in the homage to him at the Real Academia Filarmónica de Santa Cecilia in Cádiz in 1926:

Es "la única [obra] escrita por mí con intenciones *'puramente pianísticas'* en lo que a su técnica instrumental se refiere. Otra cosa: el título de Bætica no tiene ninguna especificación *'especialmente sevillana':* Con él sólo he pretendido rendir homenaje a nuestra raza latino-andaluza."

93. Specific details are given in Nommick-thesis I, 168–69; general details are found in Pahissa, 114–16; Sopeña, 113–15; Orozco, 114–15; Demarquez, 109–11; Iglesias, 205–8, 317–18, to name a few sources.

94. Nommick, Thesis, 169, fn. 9. The money was transferred from Credit Lyonnais to Geneva.

95. Nommick, Thesis, 169, fn. 8: "Mais le mieux serait qu'Arthur lui commande une œuvre de piano, un concerto par exemple."

96. Pahissa, 115.

97. Nommick, Thesis, I, 169, fn. 11.

98. Sopeña, 115.

99. Artur Rubinstein, *My Long Years*, II, New York: Alfred A. Knopf, 1980, 131.

100. Pahissa, 115

101. Iglesias, 317.

102. Sopeña, 113. Sopeña does not include the Haydn or Frescobaldi and Couperin examples.

103. Nommick, Thesis, I, 172.

104. Letters Falla-Kling in AMF 9133. See Nommick, Tutti, Nov. 1997, 12–13.

105. Glibert Chase, *The Music of Spain* 2nd revised edition. New York: Dover, 1941. "Falla's music for piano solo, 45–46.

106. Nommick, Thesis, I, 172.

107. Particularly interesting is the recording from this event: *I concurso de Cante Jondo, Colección Manuel de Falla, Granda Corpus de 1922; Colección Federico García Lorca, Discografía flamenca utilizada por el poeta* (1997) Sonifolk 20106.

108. Definitions derived from Linton Powell's *A History of Spanish Piano Music*. Bloomington: Indiana University Press, 1980, and *Diccionario Enciclopédico-Ilustrado de Flamenco*.

109. For a more complete study of Falla and the guitar, see Michael Christoforidis's articles: "Manuel de Falla y la guitarra flamenca" in *Concerto 5*, February–March 1995, 19–26; "Manuel de Falla, Debussy e la chitarra" in *Il Fronimo 90*, January 1995, 29–35; "La chitarra flamenca nell'opera e nel pensiero di Manuel de Falla" in *Guitart, I*, 1996, 35–40.

110. Nommick, Thesis, I, 174–75.

111. Nommick, Thesis, I, 189. The underlined notes are the fixed notes, while the others are the moveable notes of the mode. The tunings are not given, but are probably adjusted to their respective functions.

112. Falla makes a clear distinction between the Moorish guitar (similar to lute and bandurria)—whose strings were plucked and whose function was melodic—and to the Andalusian Spanish-Latin guitar, whose function is harmonic and whose strings are strummed and which results in "a marvellous revelation of unsuspected possibilities of sounds." Falla, OMM 111.

113. Theodore Leschetitsky (1830–1915), along with Liszt, was the main piano pedagogue of the second half of the 19th century. His class of students included

Paderewski (in spite of their off-on relationship), Ignaz Friedman, Artur Schnabel, and Annette Essipoff, to mention a few.

114. Piero Rattalino, "Dal pianoforte al clavicembalo" in *Manuel de Falla tra La Spagna e L'Europa, atti del convegno internazionale di studi (Venezaia, 15–17 maggio 1987), a cura di Paolo Pinamonti*: Firenze: Leo S. Olschki Editore, 1989, 177.

115. Nommick-thesis, I, 176 and 176, fn 39.

116. Susanna García Poliz, "*Cante jondo* y vanguardia europea en la *Fantasía baética*" in *Manuel de Falla, Latinité et Universalité*, ed. Louis Jambou, Actes du Colloque International tenu en Sorbonne 18–21 Novembre 1996, *Musiques/Écritures, Série Études*, Presses de l'Université de Paris-Sorbonne, Paris, 1999, 239–250.

117. Falla himself categorizes *Fuego fatuo* as a comic opera, when he includes it in a list of his own works sent to the Belgian Royal Academy of Science, Letters, and Arts upon his nomination into this respected organization. (AMF 8902), cited in Nommick-fuego, XXXV and XLVIII. From a letter María Martínez Sierra-Falla dated 30 August 1918, María says, "All these days I am wanting to write to you, but I have not had nay a free moment, consecrated to preparing our operetta." ("Todos estos días estoy queriendo escribir a V. pero no he tenido ni un momento libre, consagrada a la confección de nuestra opereta.") AMF, 7251/7252 (quoted in Nommick, Fuego, p. XXVIII). It may be that the first idea was to write an operetta, not an opera. Both have spoken dialogues. The distinction lies in that the operetta is lighter, more frivolous, and may include songs and dances of the more popular nature as well; whereas the comic opera, especially from the 19th century onward, is more closely allied to serious opera with its dramatic style. Just a few years later, Falla would work on yet another comic opera (*opera buffa*), *Lola la comedianta*, with Federico García Lorca from 1922–1924. The Spanish *zarzuela*, which Falla composed early in his career, and the project of *Fuego fatuo* have some elements in common, such as the exaggerated dramatic aspects that are therefore ironical, paradoxical, or comical; spoken dialogue; use of popular tunes; inclusion of dances; sung theatrical work, to name a few. Pinnamonti's "provisional" conclusions may point the way, in this respect, for this work being a growing realization of a "return to order." Perhaps it was Falla's transformation of the *zarzuela* tradition in erudite language.

118. Christoforidis, *Enciclopédia*, 898.

119. Summary based on that of Nommick, Fuego, XVI.

120. Nommick, Fuego, XIX.

121. Table format as used by Nommick, Fuego, XIX.

122. José Tragó studied with George Mathias at the Paris Conservatory, where he took first prize in 1877. Mathias was a former pupil of Chopin.

123. Many of Falla's concerts programs and press releases are housed at the AMF and confirm this aspect. For some details, Yvan Nommick's article "*Fuego fatuo:* un homenaje de Falla a Chopin" in Nommick, Fuego listed above, may be consulted.

124. Perhaps the first example of "Chopin in opera" is found in Umberto Giordano's *Fedora*, produced at the Lyric Theater in Milan in 1898, but probably Falla would have been unaware of it. See Pinamonti-Chopin, 84–87.

125. Nommick, Fuego, XIX.

126. Nommick, Fuego, XIX.

127. April Fitzlyon, "Pauline (Michelle Ferdinande) Viardot" in *The New Grove* (1980), ed. Stanley Sadie, vol. XIX, 694–95. Pauline Viardot (Paris, 18 July 1821–Paris, 18 May 1910) was the daughter of the famous singer-pedagogue Manuel García, who initially trained her voice until his premature death when she was only eleven. It is known too that Viardot, a Chopin pupil, sang in the Mozart's *Requiem* at Chopin's funeral (Jean-Jacques Eigeldinger, *Chopin pianist and teacher as seen by his pupils* (1986), translated by Naomi Shohet with Krysia Osostowicz and Roy Howat, edited by Roy Howat. Cambridge: Cambridge University Press, 188).

128. OMM-Ravel, 95.

129. Nommic, Fuego, XVI, fn. 21. María de la O Lejárraga was born on 28 December 1874, at San Millán de la Cogolla in Spain. In 1880 the family became established in Madrid, where María studied to be a schoolteacher at the Normal School. She followed this profession until 1907. In the summer of 1897 she became close friends with Gregorio Martínez Sierra and began their collaborations, marrying in November of 1900, at which time they had already published five works. In 1905, with a scholarship from the Normal School to study pedagogy in other European countries, María went to Belgium, which, according to her, was very important for her personal and political development. Eventually Gregorio Martínez Sierra won critical acclaim with the work *Cación*, and was awarded the Royal Academy Prize. In 1906 he met and began an affair with the actress Catalina Bárcena, even though he didn't separate from María until 1922, the year of the birth of his and Catalina's daughter. From 1914, María began to participate in the Spanish and international feminist movements, such as Alianza Internacional del Sufragio de la Mujer. Eventually she became interested in socialism and in 1933 was elected an official deputy of the courts of Granada. In 1934 she began to dedicate her time to the National Committee of Women against Facism. At the onset of the Spanish civil war, the Republican government sent her to Switzerland in an official capacity. Soon, however, she left and settled in her house in Nice, France, until 1950. Afterwards, she lived briefly in New York, Hollywood, Mexico, and finally Argentina, where she lived until her death in 1974. She continued writing and translating works. This biographical excerpt is taken from María Martínez Sierra's *Una mujer por camino de España* (1989), introduction by Alda Blanco. Madrid: Editorial Castalia, S.A., Instituto de la Mujer.

130. Paolo Pinamonti, "Manuel de Falla, Frédéric Chopin y el enigmático *Fuego fatuo*" in *Falla-Chopin, La música más pura,* ed. de Luis Gago, Granada: Publicaciones del Archivo Manuel de Falla, Colección "Estudios," Serie "Música," no. 2, 67–121; 95–96.

1) Creo que la génesis de esta obra teatral (insisto en su carácter decididamente op-
erístico) puede leerse como una lenta toma de conciencia por parte de Falla de esa
actitud de elegancia neoclásica que caracteriza la música francesa de la últimas dé-
cadas del siglo XIX y los primeros años del siglo XX, también sus diversas declina-
ciones, una actitud a cuya maduración ne es ajena la recepción, eminentemente
francesa, de Chopin. 2) Esta ópera es también una prueba de la gran pasión por
Chopin que . . . el compositor español llevó casi hasta una identificación expresiva
con el músico polaco. . . . 3) Es quizás por todo ello por lo que creo que no se puede
hablar frente a "Fuego fatuo" de una ópera neoclásica, en primer lugar porque no existe una acepción única de neoclasicismo musical. . . . En segundo, porque falta ex-
presamente en Falla esse alejamiento desencantado, cuando no también desenfadado,
que reencontramos en otras operaciones análogas en el panorama europeo de aquellos años. 4) Quizás esta obra, que lo acompañó durante el caluroso verano de 1918,
sin que llegara nunca a representarse pero hacia la que Falla sentía un gran cariño,
favoreció la maduración de esa particular elegancia y sobriedad compositiva que en-
contraremoes en sus obras de los años veinte. En otras palabras, "Fuego fatuo" no
puede más que ser reconducido a la experiencea narrativa de la vocalidad teatral.

131. Nommick, Fuego, XVI.

Falla, gran admirador de Chopin, formó el proyecto de instrumentar unas cuantas de
sus mejores páginas—baladas, nocturnos, mazurcas y estudios com el proósito de
ensartarlas en una acción dramática representable, a su parecer y al mío, con pe-
spectivas de indudable éxito. [. . .] Imaginé un "argumento" con todo el romanti-
cismo correspondiente a la música y a la época en que se escribiera.

132. Pahissa, 119.
133. Nommick, Fuego, XVI.

No he conocido tarea más agobiante que la de insertar o incrustar palabras en una
melodía compuesta de antemano, conservándoles ritmos, acentos y hastas vocales
definidas para que puedan cantarse sin dificultad insuperable, si al mismo tiempo se
intenta decir com claridad y sentido común lo que el argumento y la lógica exigen.
A veces, en esta ingratísima tarea, estuve a punto de perder, ya que no la paciencia,
el sentido. . . . [. . .] No estaba acostumbrada a este absurdo método de trabajar.

134. Pahissa, 120.
135. María Martínez Sierra, *Gregorio y yo,* 146.
136. From the list of the main characters and their romantic entanglements, it
could be surmised the following: Leonardo (Manuel); Lisa (María), Clara
(Falla's Muse—Music), Lord Tristan (Gregorio). Although the personage of
Carlos briefly appears as one of Lisa's new lovers at the end of act II, this role
is not important.
137. Nommick, Fuego, XVIII. Letter dated 14 August 1934 (AMF 7262).
138. Nommick, Fuego, XXXV, XLVIII.

Chapter 5

Granada (1920–1939)

The trips Falla made to Granada from March of 1915 and the warmth with which he was received by guitarist Ángel Barrios led him to leave Madrid and settle there. He traveled there in September of 1920 with his sister, María del Carmen, and the English critic J. B. Trend, taking a house next to Ángel Barrios's father (Antonio Barrios, "el Polinario") in the Carmen of Santa Engracia at no. 43 Calle Real de la Alhambra.[1] The success of *El sombrero de tres picos* had made it possible for him to live modestly and to be able to dedicate his time to composition. From this time onward, he mostly appeared as a performer or conductor in his own works. He had planned to divide his time between Granada and abroad, especially Paris.[2]

HOMENAJE POUR "LE TOMBEAU DE CLAUDE DEBUSSY"

In 1918, Falla had taken part in the events in Madrid commemorating the passing of Debussy. He read his discourse "El arte profundo de Claude Debussy" (The Profound Art of Claude Debussy) and afterwards Henri Prunières asked for his contribution in a memorial issue of *La Revue Musicale*. Falla complied with a guitar work, *Homenaje pour "Le tombeau de Claude Debussy"* (Homage for the Tomb of Claude Debussy), which cites a fragment from Debussy's piano piece "La soirée dans Grenade" (Evening in Granada from the suite *Estampes)*, as well as an article entitled *Claude Debussy et l'Espagne*. Both of Falla's contributions appeared, along with those of other prominent musicians, in the second issue of the magazine in December of 1920.

Falla completed *Homenaje pour "Le tombeau de Claude Debussy"* in August of 1920, just before settling in Granada. The piece was premiered first on harp-lute by Marie-Louise Henri Casadesus on 24 January 1921, in the Salle des Agriculteurs in Paris. Most likely it was written for Miguel Llobet, who gave the first guitar performance at the Teatro de la Comedia in Madrid on 8 March 1921.[3] Other performances were given by guitarist Emilio Pujol in Barcelona in April of 1921 and in Paris at the Conservatory of Paris on 2 December 1922. Falla also considered composing two other works for guitar for Miguel Llobet. *La tertulia* (The Club) was projected for Andrés Segovia. Of these works only some sketches remain.[4]

Falla moved several times in Granada, but came to reside permanently in a *carmen* (country house with garden) in the Alhambra district at Antequeruela Alta, no. 11, now the Casa-Museo (House-Museum) open to visitors. The house was decorated according to the advice of his artist friend Ignacio Zuloaga, who suggested Spanish simplicity.[5] These early years in Granada were happy and fruitful ones, of dreams fulfilled. With a more cordial atmosphere as found in the meetings at the tavern of Antonio Barrios or in the evening parties of the Rinconcillo, or the Sunday afternoon gatherings at his home. J. B. Trend describes the nocturnal magic of Granada, as a special guest of Falla.

> . . . I realised how immensely the emotional and musical resources of guitar, lute and bandore are enchanted by the open air. . . . We felt that we were witnessing one of the best and most effectively produced operas which it was possible to imagine. Sr. De Falla, of course, has long realized what sort of music and what instruments are most suited to the gardens of Spain, as some people in England have learnt that the music most expressive for an English garden is to be found in unaccompanied madrigals.[6]

Falla initiated several projects with his new circle of friends, such as the poet Federico García Lorca, the artists Manuel Ángeles Ortiz and Hermenegildo Lanz, as well as Fernando de los Ríos and Antonio Gallego Burín. Other friends Falla received in Granada include: Miguel Llobet, Andrés Segovia, Paco García Lorca, Raúl Carazo, Miguel Cerón, Fernando Vilchez, Pedro Borrajo, E. García Gómez, Francisco González Méndez, Ismael González de la Serna, Hernando and José Viñes, Ramón Pérez Roda, and Manuel Jofré, amongst others. Even his former love, María Prieto Ledesma, visited occasionally at his residence in Antequeruela and at one point wrote to Falla's brother's daughter, María Isabel de Falla (Maribel), that she could have been her aunt.[7]

Falla's international fame gave prestige to the city. He made trips with these friends, especially Lorca, to collect folksongs. In January of 1921, Zuloaga visited Falla and his sister, at which time the *Cante jondo* Competition was apparently conceived. The objective of the competition was to attempt to return the *Cante jondo* to a purer, more noble state since its decline. Falla conceded that the microtonal divisions of the scale that naturally occurred had been reduced to something akin to "Italian decadence" rather than to the "primitive songs of the Orient," that the characteristic narrow vocal range had been "clumsily amplified," that the richness of the ancient modal scales had been impoverished by the substitution of adherence to principally the major and minor modes, and that "metric heaviness" had deprived the expression of one of its greatest beauties—that of "rhythmic flexibility."[8]

Falla's health at this time was something of a problem, but he continued with many of his professional engagements. From letters to Zuloaga, Falla indicated that he suffered some illness, which could have been serious enough to warrant surgery but fortunately was averted.[9] In May he traveled to London and Paris, where he saw his old friend Georges Jean-Aubry. *Fanfare pour une fête*, commissioned by the British journal Fanfare, was composed in August, while work continued on *El retablo de Maese Pedro*, a commission he had received in 1918 from the Princesse de Polignac in Paris. Falla completed his concert arrangements from *El sombrero de tres picos* (Suite no.1 and Suite no. 2). A player-piano version of the Suites was also made.

CANTE JONDO COMPETITION (*DEEP SONG*[10] COMPETITION)

The year 1922 saw several important events: the death of Felipe Pedrell in Barcelona, the creation of the Orquesta Bética in Seville, and the *Cante jondo* Competition in Granada. The latter was preceded on 19 February by Federico García Lorca's lecture entitled "Historical and Artistic Importance of the Primitive Andalusian Song called *Cante jondo*," with Andrés Segovia playing four concerts at the Alhambra Palace Hotel, and Falla reading a somewhat controversial text he had prepared about *Cante jondo*. Michael Christoforidis contends that Falla's lecture was not evidence of "a great labor of recompiling folklore nor of an historical synthesis. It was more of a very personal and idiosyncratic apology for the *Cante jondo* of a composer whose work had been nurtured by elements of this music and who wanted to stress its impact on universal art."[11]

The competition itself took place on 13–14 June. In an attempt to maintain the purer form of *cante jondo* and lift it out of the adulterated state into which it had fallen, professional singers were forbidden to enter the competition. The categories of the competition included: (1) *Siguiriyas gitanas*; (2) *Serranas, Polos, Cañas,* and *Soleares*; and (3) Songs without guitar accompaniment: *Martinetes-carceleras, Tonás, Livianas,* and *Saetas viejas*. Cash prizes from 250–1,000 pesetas were awarded.[12] The competition had far-reaching consequences both at home and abroad.

Falla published anonymously an article in the program book of the competition, in which he characterizes *cante jondo*.

> Three factors in Spanish history have influenced to a different degree the general life of our culture, and have an obvious relevance to our music history: the adoption by the Church of Byzantine chant, the Arab invasion, and the settlement in Spain of numerous groups of gipsies [sic].[13]

To Pedrell's explanation of "orientalism" in some Spanish popular songs, as the result of the Byzantine Church of Spain-Roman liturgy trajectory, Falla suggested that in the Andalusian song-type of the *siguiriya* are found certain elements of the ancient Byzantine chant:

> . . . the tonal modes of the primitive systems (which must not be mistaken for the modes we now call "Greek" . . .); the use of enharmonic intervals typical of primitive modes; . . . finally, the absence of a metrical rhythm in the melodic line, and its wealth of modulating inflexions.[14]

Pedrell concluded, "The Moors, therefore are those who have been influenced." Falla admitted that Pedrell must have been referring only to the Andalusian Moors, for in other forms, especially those of dance music, there exist certain melodic and rhythmic elements that cannot be possibly traced to Spanish primitive liturgical chant. Falla pointed out that the "Andalusian music of the Moors of Granada" that is found in Morocco, Algiers, and Tunis today is different from other Arab music and reveals the origin of several Andalusian dance-types, such as the *sevillana, zapateado, seguidilla,* etc.[15]

Falla believed that the *siguirilla* song form originated from the gypsies who settled in Spain in the 15th century. And that from this kind of singing developed the known style of *cante jondo*. The *cante jondo* is actually a group of Andalusian songs, according to Falla, of which the *siguiriya gitana* is the most genuine type. From this stems the *polo, martinete, soleares*. The common people put all these into a category called *flamenco*, which is known in the modern world for regional characteristics, such as *malagueñas, granadinas, rondeñas, sevillanas, peterneras*, etc. Falla deemed the *siguiriya gitana* as being perhaps "the only European song which preserves in all its purity—in structure as well as in style—the highest qualities of the primitive song of oriental people."[16]

Some of the characteristics of the *Cante jondo* are also shared with songs from India and the Orient. These are: "the use of enharmonic intervals as a modulating means"; melodic range of a sixth; "the repeated, even obsessive, use of one note, frequently accompanied by an upper or by a lower appoggiatura"; the use of ornamental features at specific moments, in order to express extreme emotion; shouts, so as to encourage the singers and instrumentalists.[17]

In addition, Falla noted the influence of primitive music on European culture, from Scarlatti to Debussy and particularly in Russia and France. Yet he maintained a contrary position to those who stressed the impact of the Arabs on the range of Iberian music.[18]

Falla underlined the historic role of the guitar, especially in the Castille region played with *rasqueado* or strumming, in *cante jondo*, saying that "our instrumentalists of the fifteenth century probably were the first who harmonically accompanied the vocal or instrumental melody."[19] The Spanish-Latin guitar was used harmonically, while the Moorish guitar, with its plucking of the strings, was more akin to the lute and *bandurria*, and was employed melodically. The open strings of the Spanish-Latin guitar, according to Falla, "are a marvellous revelation of unsuspected possibilities of sounds."[20]

OTHER PROJECTS

Falla was not only occupied with the competition but had been involved with a project with his colleagues Zuloaga and Enrique Larreta in the lyrical adaptation of Larreta's book, *La gloria de Don Ramiro*. Although this project was ill-fated, Falla and Zuloaga seriously considered in 1921 the realization of a triptych based on the romantic medieval play of *El Cid*. There remains some musical sketches from this project.

The only works completed in these two years were *Fanfare pour une fête* in 1921 and the piano arrangement of *Canto a los remeros del Volga*, collected by Balakirev, and dedicated to Russian refugees under the protection of the League of Nations. This was Falla's contribution, through his diplomatic friend, Ricardo Baeza, to help alleviate their hunger. Antonio Iglesias calls attention to the fact that Falla derives the ornaments in the piece as harmonic resonances based on concepts of Louis Lucas and such as those found in Falla's *Superposiciones*.[21] *Fanfare* was commissioned by the London magazine with the same name and appeared in its first issue in August of 1921. The letters of Arbós appear as notes in the reverse order as (S) Sol, (O) Do, (B) Sib, (R) Re, lacking only one (A) La. Falla would write another fanfare on Arbós name in 1934, including the initials of his first other names, E (Mi) and F (Fa), in probably the closest Falla came to Schönberg's system. Falla's system in the Arbós piece, as might be expected, contained seven notes.[22]

Throughout Falla's life, he was always actively involved in creating. From his conceived boyhood project, *El Conde de Villamediana*, to his final *Atlántida*, Falla's imagination fueled the spark within. However, not all projects bore fruit, as is seen in example 5.1 below. As it is not known if *El Conde de Villamediana* (1891?) ever existed or not, it is not included here.

Example 5.1 Falla's Uncompleted or Unrealized Projects

Title/Date	Genre	Collaborator
1. *Las flores,* 1909–1910	Opera	Serafín and Joaquín Álvarez Quintero
2. *La pasión,* 1914	Incidental Music	Martínez Sierras
3. *La devoción de la cruz,* 1914	Opera	Martínez Sierras
4. *Pascua florida,* c. 1915: "El jardín venenoso"; "El descanso de San Nicolás"; "El corazón que duerme bajo el agua"; "El pan de Ronda que sabe a verdad" (completed); "El sol de Gibraltar"; Ciudades orientales"; "Cádiz se echa a navegar"; possibly "Peregrinación del Abad."	Song Cycle	María Martínez Sierra

Example 5.1 Falla's Uncompleted Unrealized Projects (*continued*)

Title/Date	Genre	Collaborator
5. *Lola la comedianta*	Operetta	Federico García Lorca
6. *La muerte de Cármen,* 1914	Opera	
7. *La gloria de D. Ramiro,* 1919	Opera	
8. Untitled, c. 1921–1922	Two guitar pieces	For Miguel Lobet
9. *La Tertulia,* c. 1921–1922	Piece for guitar	For Andrés Segovia
10. *D. Juan,* c. 1921	Opera	
11. *Romancero,* c. 1921	Instrumental music	
12. *Los encantos de la culpa,* c. 1926	Based on Calderón de la Barca	
13. *Circé,* c. 1926	*Auto sacramental* based on Calderón de la Barca	
14. *Ode al Santísimo Sacramento del Altar,* c. 1929	Music based on García Lorca's poem published in *Revista de Ocidente* in homage to Falla; possible *auto sacramental?*	Federico García Lorca
15. *Atlántida,* 1929 for Exposición Universal de Sevilla	Pantomime	José María Sert
16 For other projects, see list of Falla's Musical Works in the Index.	*La celestina,* harmonization of Greek Folksong, film projects, etc.	

TEATRO DE CRISTOBICAS
(THE LITTLE MARIONETTE THEATER OF CRISTOBICAS)

Falla had shown an interest, since his childhood, in the Andalusian tradition of marionette theaters. Urged on by Lorca,[23] the two decided to explore this medium. Falla had reason to do so, as he had been commissioned by Princesse de Polignac[24] (the American heiress to the Singer fortune) to write a work for a puppet theater. Falla drew on essays by

Miguel de Unamuno, Azorín, and José Ortega y Gasset's *Meditaciones sobre el Quijote* (Meditations on Quixote), the latter of which has a part about Master Peter's Puppet Show.[25] The result was Falla's conception of the Cervantes-Quixote story, *El retablo de Maese Pedro*, featuring the legendary story of Melisendra and Don Quixote. The staging problems inherent in *Retablo* prompted Falla to experiment with Lorca in these works: *Los dos habladores* (attributed to Cervantes), *La niña que riega la albahaca* (Lorca text), and *Auto de los Reyes Magos* (13th-century text). Falla made the musical arrangements for a quartet of mixed instruments[26] and the occasional use of children's voices, taking fragments from modern works of Debussy, Stravinsky, Albéniz, and Ravel, as well as ancient Spanish music found in Pedrell's *Cancionero*. Lanz and Ortiz, with Lorca's help, fashioned the puppets and made the settings. The "Títeres de Cachiporra"[27] in Lorca's home were performed for some friends and their children on 6 January 1923, during Epiphany. Thus was born Lorca's Teatro de Cristobicas (Cristobicas Theater). The expected tour of this production was never realized.[28]

EL RETABLO DE MAESE PEDRO (MASTER PETER'S PUPPET THEATER)

On 27 July 1922, Falla presented a concert with Ursula Grenville and Kurt Schindler at the Artistic Center in Granada. Wanda Landowska also played some concerts at the Alhambra Palace Hotel during that year and studied the harpsichord part in *Retablo* with Falla.

> The idea of using a harpsichord in the orchestra of Master Peter had occurred to Falla during a trip to Toledo one Easter Week. While there he visited the house of Don Ángel Vegué y Goldoni, a Fine Arts professor, who possessed an impressive collection of antique keyboard instruments, among them various harpsichords and clavichords.[29]

Wanda Landowska's visit to Granada in November of 1922, evoked by Falla in his article "Wanda Landowska à Grenade," allowed Falla to consult about the use of the harpsichord, one of the principal instruments he was using in *Retablo*. This would be the first time the harpsichord was used in a modern orchestra. The wish to experiment with the harpsichord led to a delay in the planned staged version of the work, with Falla asking permission from its benefactress, the Princesse de Polignac to first perform the work in a concert version in Seville. Thus, the concert debut took place on 23 and 24 March, 1923, with the newly-formed Orquesta Bética de Cámara under Falla's direction and with the patronage of the Sociedad Sevillana de Conciertos. It had the following interpreters: Sr. Lledó ("Don Quixote"), Sr. Segura ("Maese Pedro"), and Francisco Redondo ("Trujamán").[30]

At the first official, but private, performance of *Retablo* on 25 June in Paris for the work's patron, the Princesse de Polignac, Hector Dufranne ("Don Quixote"), Tomás Salignac ("Master Peter"), and Amparito Peris ("Trujamán") (as well as Manuel García, according to Antonio Gallego[31]) performed with an orchestra conducted by Vladimir Golschmann with Wanda Landowska at the harpsichord and Marie-Louise Henri Casadesus on the harp-lute. Falla was the scenic director. Fellow composer Federico Mompou was also in attendance.[32]

In between the March and June performances of *Retablo* Falla found time to do a tour of several European capitals. On 13 November Falla conducted the official "public" performance at the Jean Wiener concerts in Paris.[33] Other performances followed: in New York (1926); in Europe, from San Sebastián to London, Bristol (1924), Amsterdam (scenic direction by Luis Buñuel with Mengleberg conducting on 26 April 1926), Zurich (ICSM Festival on 20 June 1926), Berlin, and Venice, among the most notable. The concert version was given its first performance in Madrid at the Teatro de la Comedia on 28 March 1924.

Falla's colleague, Francis Poulenc, remarked that *Retablo*, his favorite Falla work, was "an incredible masterpiece."[34] He claimed the work has a "secret architecture," a specialized form, and could not be classified as an oratorio, nor an opera, but rather as a "musical object, like those works of art by the Renaissance goldsmiths, in which they connect, in an uneven and wonderful way, precious stones in a rich *setting.* . . ." He also noted that a predominant form, such as is found in works by Ravel and Bartók, does not exist in works by Falla and that by comparing the bacchanal ending of Ravel's *Daphnis et Chlöe* with the ending of Falla's *The Three-Cornered Hat*, a clear difference is readily discernible. "Ravel's music advances fluidly with grandeur, whereas Falla's treads over the same spot again and again, which is the logical thing for a Spanish dance to do."[35]

ORQUESTA BÉTICA DE CÁMARA (BETIC CHAMBER ORCHESTRA)

During Easter week of 1922, shortly before the *Cante jondo* Competition, Falla traveled to Seville for the Holy Week festivities. He was accompanied by Alfonso Reyes, who quoted Falla as saying, "In Seville the *saeta* [the popular street processional performed during Holy Week] has been corrupted by Flamenco."[36] Falla must have remembered his trip there as a boy who had begged his parents to live in that Andalusian city.

Falla took advantage of this trip to contact cellist Segismundo Romero and Chapel-master at the Seville Cathedral, Eduardo Torres. He wished to form a subsidized regional chamber orchestra dedicated to modern music and whose musicians would be of solo caliber. With regard to the creation of the chamber orchestra, Sopeña refutes Orozco's premise that the OBC was a copy of Franz Joseph Haydn's orchestra used in the *Seven Last Words of Christ*, noting that it was a complete chamber orchestra.[37] This group, unique to Spain and rare in Europe, would be dedicated to the 18th-century orchestral ideal of balanced winds and strings, an observation made by Landowska in her book *Musique ancienne* (1921) and whose personal copy is annotated in this section.[38] Falla explained this aesthetic position in an article for the inaugural concert on 11 June 1924.

Falla told "Segis" that his works had not been played in Spain for the last four years and that his Spanish author's rights were not even enough to buy his breakfast.[39] Because of Torres's previous contractual obligations, Falla recommended the young and promising Ernesto Halffter (1905–1989) as conductor for the new orchestra, the Orquesta Bética de Cámara (OBC), officially formed in 1924. Ultimately, both Falla and Halffter shared this responsibility.

Ernesto Halffter, after the premières in Madrid of his String Quartet and *Un cuento* (A Tale) de Leonideas Andreief by the Quarteto Hispanía, as well as *Peacock Pie* by Andrés Segovia, gave his debut with the OBC at the Teatro Llorens of Seville on 11 June 1924.[40] He was still a teenager. He had spent a few days in Granada with Falla, obtaining counsels for the program that he was to conduct. Juan Gisbert Padró, a colleague from the Pedrell days, gave unremitting support to Falla and the problems of organization and promotion of the OBC. A successful businessman in Barcelona, Gisbert Padró was able to relieve Falla of much of the daily tedium of the project.

The Orquesta Bética de Cámara, seated in the capital of Andalusía, was now fully underway. Its constituent elements included: woodwinds, two horns, two trumpets, four (or five, when needed) first violins, three (or four, when needed) second violins, two violas, two 'cellos, bass, plus piano, harp, tympanis, and other percussion, as needed. The orchestra's official "manifesto" appeared in May of 1924.[41]

Having inspired the creation of the OBC, Falla set out to make a series of arrangements especially for it. He revised Giacomo Rossini's "Overture to the Barber of Seville" removing the trombone parts, as the OBC had none. Falla made an arrangement of Debussy's *Prélude à l'après-midi d'un faune*, which Ernesto Halffter said sounded "better than the original."[42] Falla orchestrated the first of the *Preludios* by Adolfo Salazar; Ernesto Halffter orchestrated the second; and from correspondence it is known that Oscar Esplá intended to orchestrate the third Prelude.[43]

The fate of the OBC was less than desired. According to Sopeña, it could have become a "delicious toy in the hands of Don Manuel" but instead was converted into a "wasps' nest of problems that obliged him to travel. . . ."[44]

PYSCHÉ

Falla wrote his homage to Pedrell in 1923, who had died in the previous year. Subsequently, in 1924, he worked on an arrangement of the parts of Pedrell's *La Celestina*. Another work begun but not completed, with Lorca's libretto, was a kind of operetta, *Lola la comedianta*. With Lorca's move to Madrid in 1923, their contact was less frequent. Some musical sketches remain.

Too, he was also busy at work on his orchestral versions of suite no. 1 and suite no. 2 from *El sombrero de tres picos*, which were published in 1922 and 1924 respectively, as well as an arrangement for player piano (1921). *El amor brujo* had been given its definitive form as a ballet in one act and Falla set about to make an orchestral suite from it. Deploring the noise of the Corpus Christi celebrations in Granada, Falla went to Malaga in the spring of 1924, where he spent a few days working quietly.

Falla meanwhile was busy working on *Psyché*, a chamber work for soprano and five instruments, on poetry by Jean-Aubry, director of *The Chesterian*. Falla worked sporadically on it during 1923 and 1924. The influence of Domenico Scarlatti is noted. Falla says in a letter to Madame Alvar that in composing *Psyché*, he has imagined a small court concert that takes place in the Alhambra Palace around 1730 with King Philippe V and Queen Isabelle Farnèse, in the Queen's boudoir now known as "Tocador de la Reina."[45] A final version of *Psyché* was completed during 1924 and plans got under way for a new stage version of *El retablo* (Seville, Teatro San Fernando, 30 January 1925, OBC) with Lanz and Ortiz. The debut of *Psyché* took place on 9 February 1925, at the Palau de la Música Catalana in Barcelona with soprano Josepa Regnard, harpist Raquel Martí, flutist Miguel Pérez, violinist Fermín Pérez, violist Fernando Romero, cellist Segismundo Romero, and the composer as conductor.[46] This concert was the second of the Associació de Música "Da Camera" series and was dedicated to Falla. The Paris première took place the same year with Louise Alvar and Lili Laskin.

The French text is as follows:

Psyché la lambe est morte; éveille toi.
Le jour te considère avec des yeux no-yés d'amour,
Et le désir nouveau—de te servir encore.
Le miroir, confident de ton visage en pleurs, refléte, ce matin,
lac pur parmi des fleurs, un ciel—laiteux ainsi qu'une
éternelle aurore
Nidi s'approche et danse, ivre sur ses pieds d'or.
Tends lui les bras, sèche tes pleurs; dans un essor abandonne,
Psyché, la langueur de ta couche.
L'oiseau chante au sommet de l'arbre: le soleil sourit d'aise
en voyant l'universel éveil, et le Printemps s'étire, une rose à la
bouche.

Psyché later inspired these words from Rodolfo Halffter, cited by biographer Angel Sagardía:

I don't believe that there exists today in Europe today [1932] another master, with the exception of Maurice Ravel, who writes so perfectly as Manuel de Falla. Everything is calculated and nothing is left to luck. The reading of a score by the maestro from Cádiz gives the impression that nothing is excessive and that nothing is lacking. Each of his works is a lesson in Latin clarity, in precision, discipline, and also, sensitivity.[47]

CONCERTO

Falla's health declined and was accompanied with more religious fervor and greater mysticism than was usual for him. In order to fortify his soul, he initiated an annual vow of silence. For Falla, composition was linked to inspiration and he believed that this was a divine spark. Nevertheless he was very aware of the necessity to develop a good technique for having the means of the best expression required. Thus, his trips abroad allowed him to observe contemporary trends. He was fascinated with the study of acoustics, with the concept of resonance and its relation with the broader approach to tonality, moreover with the possibility to be expressed even in microtones.[48] For him, each new work was a new level of evolution. In order to achieve it, he prepared meticulously and conscientiously. Thus, one of his greatest masterpieces, the *Concerto*, commissioned by Wanda Landowka, underwent vigorous preparation and laborious crafting. Falla began work on the piece in October of 1923.

For this new way of expression and re-creation, Falla, as his personal library will attest, read medieval ballads; Spanish literature, especially from the Golden Age; and literature linked to Granada, in particular, the Alhambra. He also studied the works of other composers, such as Stravinsky's *L'Histoire du soldat, Pulcinella*, and the *Concerto* for piano and wind instruments. Works of Ravel, Bartók, and Schoenberg received his detailed scrutiny, as did a review of Debussy's contributions. From the past, he studied scores of Purcell (afforded him by J. B. Trend) and Monteverdi in Malipiero editions. The Scarlatti sonatas, in the Longo edition, were perused, as well as other Baroque Latin composers, and Bach, now vindicated by the Parisian vanguard. The publication of the remaining volumes of Pedrell's *Cancionero* and the *Cancionero de Palacio* of Barbieri were focal points. Polyphonic vocal arrangements by Kurt Schindler, as well as Latin American folk music, principally from Cuba and Peru, interested him.[49]

The *Concerto* was premiered by Landowska on 5 November 1926, in Barcelona at the Palau under the auspices of the Associación de Música de Cámara, with Falla conducting flutist Josep Vila, oboist Cassià Carles, clarinetist Josep Novi, violinist Enric Casals, and cellist Bonaventura Dini. It was a fiftieth-birthday tribute. Pablo Casals also conducted on the program.

Landowska wrote to Falla on 21 September 1926, "My great, wonderful friend, your Concerto is a masterpiece. I am trembling with joy and happiness. I work day and night and the only thing I can think about is how to find the authentic and perfect accents to remain faithful to you. I have written you some words here to ask you to enlighten [me]. But meanwhile these words to acknowledge your music so human, so strong and so full of sunlight. Your faithful Wanda"[50] At another time, she suggested changes. Falla didn't comply.

In the Paris debut on 14 May 1927, at Salle Pleyel, Falla played his *Concerto*, not Landowska, once on harpsichord and again on piano with musicians Marcel Moyse, Georges Bonneau, Emile Godeau, Auguste Cruque, and Jean Pasquier. Falla recorded the *Concerto* in June of 1930 with flutist Moyse, oboist Bonneau, clarinetist Godeau, violinist Auguste Cruque, and cellist Marcel Darrieux.

Henry Prunières, in an article for *La Revue Musicale* dated 1 July 1927, commented about the work.

> Yet never before has Falla's art achieved such frugality. . . . The technique, with its persistent repetition and monothematicism, is extremely curious. We cannot speak of a return to past techniques; although Manuel de Falla makes use of a contrapuntal style akin to that of the great predecessors of J. S. Bach, it is in the service of a personal science of construction and of the most modern harmonic sensibility, Manuel de Falla has willingly abandoned the elements furnished by folk music, but he has used the rhythm of the guitar, the modes of the liturgy, all the musical elements that his remembrance of aristocratic and religious life of ancient Spain offered.[51]

LA GENERACIÓN DEL '27 (GENERATION OF '27)

The Gongorists—the artists, literary personages, and musicians who were devoted to the renovation and discovery of a new Spanish national language in its diverse components—glorified the ideals of Cordobese poet, Luis de Góngora (1561–1627), of Spain's golden age. Members of the illustrious alliance included Federico García Lorca, Luis Buñuel, Salvador Dalí, José María Sert, and Joan Miró, amongst others. They were also known as the Generación del '27.

The principal Madrid composers of the Generación del '27 banned together, calling themselves "Grupo de los Ocho" (Group of Eight). They were: Rodolfo and Ernesto Halffter, Julián Bautista, Gustavo Pittaluga, Fernando Remacha, Salvador Bacarisse, Juan José Mantecón, and the only female member, Rosa García Ascot, Falla's piano pupil. For them, Falla embodied the ideals of this "school." Adolfo Salazar remarked, "Albéniz had his imitators, but has left no disciples. That is natural. Disciples spring from inner principles. . . . But it is through Falla that the teaching, that vital factor which is gradually raising our 'provincial' departure point to a universal level, must continue."[52] The "Grupo de los Ocho" never considered Falla to be an Impressionistic composer. Neoclassicism as found in works of Ravel and Stravinsky, combined with "a luminosity and clarity typical of the works of Domenico Scarlatti and Antonio Soler as well as a brevity of form" characterized their contemporary musical language.[53] Falla's contribution to the Góngora tricentenary commemoration in 1927 was *Soneto a Córdoba*, a work for voice and harp based on a poem of Góngora.

Without a doubt, the two pillars of Falla's mature style, and which served as models for the composers of the Generación del '27, were *Retablo* and the *Concerto*. Stravinsky too agreed. "For me, these two works mark an indisputable progress in the development of his great talent, which has been resolutely liberated here from the folklorist tendency under which it ran the risk of becoming diminished."[54] Falla's colleague Adolfo Salazar commented along similar lines.

> The music of Master Peter . . . makes quite clear reference . . . to Spanish primitive religious, romantic and popular music, and to old Spanish court music. However the elements from which the Concerto is built are more abstract, more difficult to pinpoint than the others because they are more personal and intense. In other words, they repeat Falla's evolving process. . . .[55]

Falla was very aware of the position he held in the forefront of Spanish music and felt a responsibility towards the young generation of composers, not only the "Grupo de Ocho," but others as well, for example, Roberto Gerhard, Joaquín Rodrigo, and Joaquín Nín-Culmell. The Residencia de Estudiantes (Student Residence) in Madrid was a frequented place for new experimental music concerts. Falla gave some consideration to elaborating a curriculum for the Odero Conservatory in his native city of Cádiz.[56] He did make curriculum sketches for a composition class at the Madrid Conservatory. These documents are housed at the AMF.[57]

NEW PROJECTS

After the *Concerto*, Falla decided to make a synthesis of two works of Calderón de la Barca—*Circé* and *Los encantos de la culpa*. Without the Martínez Sierras, he decided to undertake the libretto himself, as he had done in *Retablo*. José María Sert and scenic director Max Reinhardt wished to collaborate with him in a religious play on Calderón. Of all Falla's Calderón projects, only his incidental music for Antonio Gallego Burín's production of *El gran teatro del mundo* remains. Lanz had created the decor for the celebration of Corpus Christi in 1927 in Granada. However, the music of this Falla-Calderón work is much the music of the prologue of *Atlántida*.[58]

In April of the same year, Falla organized a Beethoven memorial concert, even though he maintained an ambivalent position about the composer. He expressed his views in an article about the German composer.[59] To pay homage to one of his most admired composers, Falla played an entire piano recital devoted to the keyboard works of Domenico Scarlatti in December of that year.

HOMAGE TO FALLA

Falla's fiftieth birthday was commemorated early by the Paris Opéra Comique, which organized a season of his works, including *Retablo* with scenery by artist Ignacio Zuloaga and puppets by Maxime de Tomás. Another birthday tribute, naming Falla "an adopted son," took place in Seville on 14 December with the Orquesta Bética and singer Conchita Badía and pianist Frank Marshall, Falla's old rival from the 1905 piano competition. On 17 and 18 December Falla's native city of Cádiz paid homage to him, granting him honorary citizenship, naming him its "favorite son," and placing a plaque on the house of his birth.

Other homages were paid to him as well: in Granada, whose town council commissioned a bust from Juan Cristóbal and proclaimed Falla as honorary citizen; in Guadix, as that cave-city's (Sombrero) "adopted son" (28 February 1927); in Madrid (3 November 1927), where a reception was held in his honor by the city council and a Festival Falla was held (5 November) with the debut in that city of *Concerto* with Falla performing; in Barcelona, with a series of concerts (1927) and remembrance of Granados, by Falla and some friends, who tossed a bottle (filled with three pages of musical score from Beethoven's last quartet, Granadoss' *Goyescas,* an autograph of Falla, and words of love and admiration) into the sea; in Seville 20 March 1930; in London, where the debut of *Retablo* was part of a program dedicated to the composer, who also played in the Concerto (22 June 1927); and in Paris, at Salle Pleyel (14 May 1927) with a debut of *Soneto a Córdoba* and the *Concerto*—played twice on the same program with *Fantasía bætica, Siete canciones populares españolas*, and *Psyché*.[60] In 1926 poet Juan Ramón Jiménez painted a lyrical portrait of Falla in his *Olvidos de Granada*. Yet Falla refused membership into the Spanish Academy of Fine Arts in 1929, because of his friend's, composer Conrado del Campo, exclusion. He was inaugurated into the Orden de Alfonso XII on 13 May of that year.

Falla's name was now linked to those of international musical elite, such as Stravinsky, Ravel, and Bartók, as well as to many French and Italian composers of renown, such as Poulenc, Milhaud, Malipiero, Castelnuovo-Tedesco, and Eugène Goossens, who showed admiration for his work. His mature works were heard in England, the United States, Italy, and France, while his scenic works resounded from Moscow to Buenos Aires.[61] He was bestowed the Legion of Honor by the French government. In 1934 he followed Sir Edward Elgar as the Foreign Academician of the Académie des Beaux-Arts, the highest honor that France can bestow on an artist. In 1929 and 1930 the first monographs dedicated to his life and works appeared by J. B. Trend and Alexis Roland-Manuel respectively, which complemented other studies of various authors. The enthusiastic acclaim awarded his works in South America, especially in Argentina, Mexico (warmly supported by those composers who had been in Paris, namely Manuel M. Ponce and Carlos Chávez), and Cuba, gave rise to a Hispano-American musical nationalism.[62]

HOMAGE FROM FALLA—*ATLÁNTIDA*

It was also in Falla's fiftieth year that he began his own homage to Spain—"to Cádiz, Barcelona, Seville, Granada"—to Christopher Colombus, to the lost continent of Atlantis, to the ideology of justice, retribution, redemption, and a new moral law, when he began composing his final work, *Atlántida*. It was based on a poem by the Catalan poet-monk, Jacinto Verdaguer (1845–1902), coincidentally also celebrating its fiftieth birthday in the same year as Falla.

The subject matter deals with the mystical connection between the submerged continent and the exploration of the New World by Columbus, under the Catholic banner. Falla envisioned a one-act scenic cantata, with accompanying murals, although the initial idea became modified through time. He drew on literary and historical sources that may be classified into six categories: (1) *Atlantis* legend; (2) Christopher Columbus and the conquest of the New World; (3) Latin American civilization and culture; (4) the history of his native Cádiz; (5) the Catalan language; and (6) philosophies of the classic antiquity.[63]

Upon his return from the ISCM (International Society of Contemporary Music) festival in Zurich in June of 1926, Falla had begun his study of Verdaguer's epic work, while perfecting his knowledge of Catalan and Latin, the languages of the poem.[64] Yet two years would pass before Falla revealed his specific ideas to his proposed scenic collaborator, José

María Sert. Sert, upon his return from the Salzburg Festival, told Falla of Max Reinhardt's wish to stage Falla's next lyric work.[65] Sert also collaborated in Darius Milhaud's *Cristóbal Colón* (debut in 1928) produced by Reinhardt. In a letter to Sert from Granada dated 10 November 1928, Falla is very clear about some scenic ideas. He suggests that the scenes will be without movement, but that the main action of a scene can be divided into two or three parts, separated by a "tulle" curtain. The scenes represent the stained glass windows of a cathedral. In the prologue, Falla envisions Atlas supporting the firmament with Atlantis submerged. The lengthy letter is full of further indications and ends with Falla saying that the première cannot possibly take place before 1930. Falla had been offered *carte blanche* to first produce *Atlántida* in the United States, but he turned it down, citing loyalty to his country.[66]

When Milhaud visited Falla in Granada in 1929, he commented,

> When I had begun to compose Christopher Colombus, he (Falla) warned me that Christopher Colombus would be one of the supporting characters in his next work. I responded that I did not mind, because Christopher Colombus was the very basis of my opera. My admiration for Falla and this situation in particular spurred me to dedicate my work to him.[67]

The New World discovery continued to be an absorbing theme, for Milhaud went on to write yet two other works: *Maximilien* (1930) and *Bolivar* (1943). The Brazilian composer, Heitor Villa-Lobos, would begin work on a project about the discovery of Brazil for the film *Descobrimento do Brasil* (H. Mauro) in 1937. Falla was not alone.

By 1927 the idea of a short work had changed considerably. Falla said in an interview for the Catalan newspaper, *Ahora*, that the work would fill an entire concert program.[68] Falla affirmed loyalty to the Verdaguer's text and said that the use of soloists, choruses, and orchestra would be employed.

> Verdaguer's poem will be absolutely respected, not only because of the profound admiration the Catalan poet merits, but also because *La Atlántida* [as it was first entitled] has existed in my being since childhood. Cádiz, where I was born, offered me its Atlantic through the Pillars of Hercules and opened my imagination to the most beautiful garden of the Hesperides.[69]

Shortly before his death, upon being shown photographs of the famed Machu Picchu ruins in Peru by Sergio de Castro, Falla exclaimed, "That is Atlantis! That is Atlantis!"[70]

Falla returned to his native city in 1930 (the year Budwig refers to as the "Greek year" in which Falla made exhaustive study of Greek sources) to experience "Atlántida," to visit Santi Petri where the ancient temple of Hercules lay, and to "hear the sea!"[71]

Writer José María Pemán, a fellow citizen of Cádiz, quoted Falla as saying, "*La Atlántida* represented for him, as for the mystic, the search for the First Cause."[72] He affirmed, "In reality it was born of the religious obsession which dominated him all his life. His greatest ambition was to write a Mass, and *Atlántida* was a *rezo de prima* [first-class prayer], a matin prayer, a preparation for this ultimate Mass that he never wrote."[73] Falla's Mallorcan friend, Padre Juan María Thomas, quotes from a letter written by Falla in Granada on 26 September 1926, of his "keen desire to compose a Mass and (his) prayer to God that the time will come when he will be able to realize his project worthily, and with the necessary serenity of spirit."[74]

At the beginning of June of 1929, José María Sert visited Falla in Granada. Previous plans to present a pantomime or some part of *Atlántida* for the upcoming International Expositions in Seville[75] and Barcelona[76] were scrapped, as were at the Pedrera (Quarry) of Tarragona and the Monastery of Poblet.[77] However, work continued as Falla composed the episode "Incendio en los Pireneos" ("Fire in the Pyrenees"). From 1930–1934 he worked on the first two parts of *Atlántida*. He began to have some doubts, perhaps because of his health problems, of the appropriateness of the incorporation of pagan themes. Thus, from 1932 he began to concentrate on the use of sacred music for the third part, advancing these scenes in 1936 and 1938. He used a great variety of musical types in composing *Atlántida*. Plainsong was complemented with ancient Greek music and Byzantine liturgical melodies. For the declamatory models of the first and second parts, he studied folk music and other monodic models. Using the chorus as protagonist, Falla would remember the monumental works of Stravinsky and Milhaud, as well as the works from Spain's golden age of polyphony, and Bach, Haendel, Saint-Saëns, Haydn, Beethoven, Ravel, and Debussy, amongst others. He worried about contrapuntal writing and being able to handle large orchestral ensembles.[78]

HEALTH ISSUES

Meanwhile, health problems continued to plague Falla. In letters to Ernesto Halffter on 31 May and 28 June of 1928 he describes an attack of iritis, an inflammation of the iris, which prevented him from reading or writing.[79] It is supposed that the iritis was the manifestation of an "incipient tubercular infection" as were "hemorrhaging (with its accompanying dizzy spells) shortness of breath, and bone ailments. . . ."[80] His sensitivity to noise also increased. He also suffered from hemorrhages, breathing difficulties, and some bone problems which required surgical intervention. By 12 September of that year Falla had recovered enough to make a trip with Juan Gisbert Padró and Pedro Bauchs to Siena, where he performed his *Concerto* at the International Society of Contemporary Music with enormous success.[81] On the return trip he stopped over in Barcelona and in October he received his old friend Maurice Ravel in Granada.[82]

In 1996, during the fiftieth anniversary of Falla's death, musicologist and cataloguer Antonio Gallego questioned the myths around Falla's health problems and presented a possible answer.

> How to explain the terrible physical decadence—and thus compositionally—in his last twenty years, from, for example, 1927 to 1946? The traditional explanations are totally insufficient, and full of prejudice. One of my most emotional experiences of this Falla year has been a public "clinical session" in which two doctors from La Coruña, urged on by doctor-musicologist Xoan Manuel Carreira, analyzed—by way of still incomplete data obtained from bibliography, epistolary, and of course, iconography—the possible illness of Falla, that which practically converted him into an invalid from his fiftieth year. It could not be tuberculosis (old romantic myth, as is well known) nor the impossible syphilis of which Campodónico spoke and that investigated my professor Sopeña without results. Nor does it have anything to do with improbable homosexuality, above all not demonstrated, nor religious repression. . . . Even though we are far from the final documented diagnosis, it seems that it could be dealt with as an illness of long gestation, that in his time was not diagnosed and that today, certainly, doesn't even have a definite cure: A "spondilitis" [spondylitis, or inflammation of the spinal column]. *That would explain many things.*[83]

PRE-REPUBLICAN YEARS (1929–1931)

Falla continued to reap the fruits of his labors. On 4 August 1929, he played a concert with Nirva del Río at the Palace Hotel in Granada. Concerts dedicated to his works were given in Paris, London, and Barcelona. He made recordings, such as his *Concerto* in Paris, in 1930, as well as other vocal works with María Barrientos in 1928 and 1930. In 1931 Falla conducted his *Retablo* for the BBC in London. His old English friends, J. B. Trend and Edward Dent, had assisted him for many years. Alfredo Casella visited Falla in Granada in 1930. They would meet again during Falla's trip to Italy in 1932. Casella, a great advocate of Falla's music, deplored the fact that *Fantasía bætica* was not better known throughout the world.[84]

On a personal level, his brother, Germán, was married in Paris to María Luisa López Montalvo in 1929, the only remaining Falla sibling to marry and produce an heir.

Another potential project arose when Lorca approached Falla to collaborate with him in his *Oda al santísimo sacramento del altar*, a poem which was published in 1929 in the *Revista de Occidente*. Falla declined. In a letter from Falla to Lorca dated 9 February 1929, Granada, Falla explained his differences of approach to that of his younger friend, admitting that Federico's work always possessed beauty and expression, but that Falla would take a humble approach to the project, one in which all humanity could be deified through the blessed Sacrament.[85]

TURBULENT YEARS[86]

The formation of the Second Republic in April of 1931 was initially well received by Falla, given his inclination towards renovation and to his circle of liberal friends. He even participated as director of the first Junta Nacional de Música y Teatro (National Congress of Music and Theater). However, he changed his stance when the burning of churches began in May. The confrontation between the state and the church caused him to appeal to his political friends to put a stop to the attacks, as he called them "collective blasphemy."[87]

Fernando de los Ríos, his friend and García Lorca's former mentor, became minister of justice in the Republic. After convents and churches had been destroyed in Granada, Falla cabled Ríos on 14 May 1931, as well as the president of the Republic, Niceto Alcalá Zamora, urging their intervention. The following month he again wrote to Ríos, on 19 June, expressing his despair and desperation, saying that had Ríos been in Granada his "great moral authority" would have been enough to have prevented the destruction.[88]

A second time, Falla appealed to Ríos. Falla, as an international Spanish treasure, made very clear to Ríos that he had always protected

Spain's image and had never said or done anything that "could belittle in the least Spain's prestige in the eyes of a foreigner. . . ."[89]

Last night, in spite of the finally measure adopted, the San Nicolás church continued burning until its destruction, while someone unashamedly rang the bells. What a shame for Spain and that between one and another they continue destroying her. . . . You know perfectly well what my ideals are, that they transcend political limits, and it is my soul's desire that the needs of and the injustices suffered by the people be alleviated and put right. And now, as the senseless political-military movement that has given origin to those deeds in question has been produced, I have been one of the first to condemn it, but it is no less senseless that which has occurred in Granada, where that movement has not had the slightest repercussion. . . . I say all this to you, not only as loyal information to a dear friend, but also as to the man responsible for the government of Spain and in protest (respectfully, but nobly indignant as a Christian, as a Spaniard, and as an Artist by my occupation) before so many share with you the dreadful responsibility. My conscience and my honor propel me to do it. . . .[90]

Falla stood his ground, faithful to his principles, by his refusal of homage by the city of Seville in June of 1932. He expressed his position, "If God is 'officially' denied any sort of tribute, then how can I, his poor creature, accept. . . ."[91]

Falla showed a great interest in the reading of San Juan de la Cruz (St. John of the Cross) and other Christian mystics. He maintained a long-standing correspondence with Jacques Maritain, whose books he read and admired. However, he was not accepting of the nationalistic traditionalism of Ramiro de Maetzu, "which will finish, like any exaggerated nationalism, by opposing Christ's genuine teachings."[92]

Concerned about the lack of morality rampantly evident, he wrote his will in February of 1932. He placed restrictions on his scenic works, stipulating that the execution and scenic interpretation of his works must always, and without any exception, observe the cleanest, Christian moral standards, and always be accompanied by works of obvious dignity of moral and artistic spirit. He also requested that his cadaver be put in a sepulcher in a sacred place according to the Roman Catholic rites, to whose Holy Church he had the glory of belonging. He asked that a cross be mounted on his grave.[93]

On 3 September 1932, Falla conducted *Retablo*, as well as his expressive interpretation of works by T. L. de Victoria, at a concert in San Sebastián. He also made a trip to Venice with Pedro Segura and Andrés

Segovia where he conducted the debut of *Retablo* at the International
Festival of Music with great success. Stops were also made at Paris and
Geneva on the return trip, as well as in Barcelona, where he participated
in a Falla festival on 13 December at the Palau Theater.[94]

MALLORCA

With his nerves deteriorating, Falla decided to take temporary refuge on
the island of Mallorca. On 18 January 1933, Falla's sister, María del
Carmen wrote to Padre Juan María Thomas to ask for help.

> My brother Manuel has recently suffered a very serious attack of nervous
> illness and now has been ordered to follow a regimen of rigorous isolation,
> working exclusively on "Atlántida." The doctors allow him this extraordi-
> nary concession only on the condition that he is not to occupy himself with
> anything else. This is the reason why I am writing to you in his name . . .
> nothing could be better for him than to go to Palma. . . .[95]

Falla went to Palma from February to June of 1933 and again from
December 1933 to June 1934. On 21 May 1933, Falla's *a capella Balada de Mallorca*, based on portions of Chopin's second Ballade and a
poem of Verdaguer, was premiered at the Third Chopin Festival in
Valldemosa by the Capella Classica.

Unfortunately a tragic event also occurred during Falla's stay on the
island—the death of the daughter of Falla's friend Isaac Albéniz, forty-
two-year old Enriqueta Albéniz, and the wife of Vicente Alzamora, secretary of the Mallorcan Sociedad Filarmónica. Falla was quick to note
that her death occurred two months after his arrival in Palma, just as her
father's death had occurred two years after Falla's arrival in Paris.[96] Juan
María Thomas also substantiates Falla's nervous condition and superstitious nature in the composer's unpleasant encounter with a black chauf-
feur-driven car whose horn played Beethoven's "fate" theme from the
Fifth Symphony. Secretly, Padre Thomas had the theme modified in order to allay Falla's nerves.[97]

CRUZ Y RAYA

During all Falla's musical career his literary bent was never stilled. With
José Bergamín and others Falla founded the magazine *Cruz y Raya*,

which published his article about Richard Wagner in its first issue in September of 1933. Relations soon deteriorated and led to the breakup of the friendship with Bergamín. Falla called the direction that the magazine was taking "monstrous," but refused to say specifically what displeased him, leaving Bergamín to speculate. He expressed bitterness over Falla's reaction. Falla concluded:

> Being sincere in the friendship I profess for you, I write you with apologies for the upset I may cause you, but my conscience demands that I do so quickly and decisively. This is not a question of simple scruples: It is nothing more than upholding the second commandment of God's law in its most essential meaning, even though it is not the most commonly applied. What more need I add to one who has such a sensitive understanding? . . .
>
> Forgive me for the bad moments—I regret them I assure you—which reading this letter may cause you, and I send you my affectionate regards and my faithful friendship.[98]

OTHER EVENTS

On 19 November 1933, Falla voted for the first time in his life in the elections in Granada. At the Liceo in Barcelona he gave a concert of his compositions before returning to Palma in December. In Madrid, a homage concert was planned for Falla's friend Enrique Fernández Arbós, conductor of the Orquesta Sinfónica, whose seventieth birthday was 24 December 1933.

Falla was also approached by film director, Harry d'Abbadie d'Arrast, assistant to Charlie Chaplin, to allow him to adapt his music from *El sombrero de tres picos* for a new film, *La traviesa molinera* (The Miller's Wife's Wager), on the same Alarcón theme. Falla declined and suggested that Rodolfo Halffter compose the musical score instead. Halffter accepted with great appreciation to Falla. The film was finished in 1934 with Edgar Neville writing the screenplay.[99] The press called the film "perfect" and Rodolfo Halffter was hailed as "the author of the best Spanish music at the service of the image that we have heard" (*ABC*, 5 October 1934).[100] Outstanding reviews were also given to Halffter's music by critics from *El Sol* (14 October 1934), *El Debate* (5 October 1934), and *La Libertad* (28 October 1934, by Gerardo Diego). He himself said in a letter to Falla how difficult it had been to compose this music as there already existed a predecessor, "a model work that I admire profoundly: *El sombrero de tres picos*."[101] He went on to say that with respect to that which Falla had said about the excessive intention to un-derline the scenic action, it was an evident error, and that Falla had been correct about it.[102] Unfortunately Halffter destroyed his film scores, more than twenty. However, some of the music of *La traviesa molinera*[103] was reworked into his ballet *La Madrugada del panadero*, op. 12 (1940).

Falla, as one of fourteen composers invited to submit a work, heard his *Fanfare sobre el nombre de Arbós* in the concert on 28 March 1934, at Madrid's Teatro Calderón with Fernández Arbós conducting. The work was composed during Falla's winter stay in Palma and later would be incorporated as the first movement of his suite *Homenajes*. Another notable success followed the same year in Madrid, with "La Argentina's" production of *El amor brujo* with Vicente Escudero, Pastora Imperio, and Miguel de Molina—this, in the city which had not always received so well.

Back in Mallorca in the spring of 1934, Falla heard his *Balada* sung in the definitive version at the fourth Chopin festival. However, it was performed in a rather unusual setting. Pianist Alfred Cortot first played Chopin's Ballade in F major. As he finished, he held his hands over the keyboard in order to invoke absolute silence. Then the Capella Classica began pianissimo Falla's "a capella" version. The audience went wild at the end. Falla was called to the stage and Cortot finished by playing Chopin's Twenty-four Preludes, as only he could.[104]

In June of 1934 Falla returned to Granada, hoping to complete his *Atlántida* by the end of that year; however, problems arose with "La salve en el mar," which would become the next-to-last piece of that work. In a letter from Falla to Padre Thomas dated 11 February 1935, Falla's doubts "about the moral propriety of its text re-surfaced and again he submitted it to ecclesiastical censure as he had three years earlier."[105] Doubts about "the rectitude" of all his works arose. It was yet another moral and religious crisis in the midst of tremendous political upheaval.

Therefore, another revision of his will ensued on 9 August 1935. He forbade scenic presentations of his works unless his inheritors needed "the products of the author's rights as an indispensable means of living." He added that his will should be scrupulously observed when his works entered into public domain.[106]

Musician Walter Starkie, who had met Falla years before, saw him for the last time in 1935 in Granada.

. . . it was the first time I had seen him for years. During this time, his face had wasted away and was even more emaciated. I still remembered him just as I had found him in 1921, still full of the passion of his creations, the wild Fire Dance and The Three-cornered Hat, an intellectual levelling himself against a throng of Andalusian demons. Now he looked like an ascetic monk, whose life was spent between meditation in his cell and reverie in his garden. Now his only ambition was peace and seclusion.[107]

Falla was still uneasy about war breaking out in Europe. Yet he was able to continue composing. In December he completed *Pour le tombeau de Paul Dukas*, perfumed with *Atlántida*, in memory of his friend who had died earlier in the year. He also finished the incidental music for the auto sacramental of Lope de Vega entitled *La vuelta de Egipto*, which was presented at the 300th anniversary of Vega's death (1635–1935) at the University of Granada. A thirteen-measure invocation, *Invocatio ad individuam Trinitatem*, was also written for the occasion.

The Spanish civil war broke out in 1936. The military pronouncement had been perceived by Falla at first as a stabilizing factor, in a similar way of Primo de Rivera's regime in the 1920's. The harsh reality was soon evident when southern Spain—including Granada—fell very quickly. Falla went to the defense of his friends, often risking his own safety. On 23 May Falla appealed to Manuel Azaña, on behalf of all Spanish Christians: "Thus I beg you, not just as President of the Republic but as a man of fine literary sensibility whom I consider my friend, to help us at this difficult time by exercising your supreme authority."[108] For Falla's friend, Federico García Lorca, it was of no avail. He was tragically assassinated just three months later. In November Falla came to his friend Lanz's aid, who had been held on suspicion by the new regime.[109]

On 4 August 1936, Falla made the final revision of his will, caring for his heirs from whatever money was deposited into his national or foreign accounts from the rights of his works, whether published or performed in concerts or "representations." Other provisions were also made; among them Falla remembered his parents, grandparents, Padre Francisco de Paula Fedriani, and his teachers don Clemente Parodi, Sister Eloísa Galluzzo, Felipe Pedrell, and José Tragó.[110]

Polemical matters would arise as a result of these restrictions and the validity of the wills would be questioned. In a letter to Federico Sopeña on 1 July 1988, lawyer Eduardo García de Enterría states that under Spanish law the only will which is valid is the last one, which does not prohibit the "scenic representations" of Falla's works. Other considerations are also mentioned such as there can be no doubt that Falla's works form part of the Spanish Historical Patrimony in the terms defined by article no.1 of the law of 25 June 1985. Therefore, if it were possible to-day to oppose the "scenic representation" of Falla's works, this would be overridden by means of other legalities.[111] Hence, Falla's scenic works continue to be produced today.

After Lorca's assassination on 19 August 1936, Falla secluded himself at home in work and prayer. His health was very delicate. A blood analysis on 22 August revealed "grave mal-nutrition."[112] In a letter to José María Pemán on 18 September 1936, Falla says that the church burnings ("collective blasphemy") in Cádiz were the cause of his "severe relapse."[113]

Pemán visited Falla in 1937 with a proposal for a project, which Falla refused, but he did compose *Himno marcial* (Military Hymn) for voice, piano, and drums—an adaptation of Pedrell's "Canto de los Almogávares" from Los Pirineos, set to Pemán's lyrics.

Falla continued to isolate himself, and was surrounded only by his sister, his close friends, and some neighbors, such as Pedro Borrajo, Hermenegildo Lanz, Valentín Ruiz Aznar, Ramón Pérez de Roda, Sr. Ghys, Miguel Cerón, and Luis Jiménez. He lost yet another close friend when Maurice Ravel died in Paris that year.

Without prior knowledge, Falla was named president of the new Spanish Institute in Salamanca on 1 January 1938, by the government of the Nationalist Zone. Securing Pemán's help, he was able to resign from the position on the grounds of his poor health. With the rumblings in Europe on top of the turmoil already experienced in Spain, Falla now gave serious thought to leaving for Argentina. On 25 May he wrote to a friend there to help him realize that possibility. An invitation from the Institución Cultural Española (Spanish Cultural Institution) of Buenos Aires to conduct several concerts was forthcoming. Thereupon, Falla spent the summer of 1939 in Zubia, a village near Granada, working on his *Homenajes* that he was to premiere upon his arrival in the New World. His literary tribute to Ravel after his death—"Notas sobre Ravel"—had appeared in *La Revue Musicale* in March, dedicated to his friends Roland-Manuel and Maurice Delage.

NOTES

1. OMM, 133.
2. Christoforidis, *Enciclopédia*, 900.
3. *Poesía*, 133; Michael Christoforidis, "Manuel de Falla's homage to Debussy . . . and the guitar" in *Context 3 (Winter 1992)*, 6.
4. Christoforidis, *Enciclopédia*, 900.

5. Christoforidis, *Enciclopédia*, 900.

6. J. B. Trend, *A Picture of Modern Spain. Men & Music*. London: Constable & Co. Ltd., 241–42.

7. Sopeña, 29.

8. Demarquez, 144.

9. Sopeña, 123.

10. "Deep Song" is the literal translation but it is perhaps better understood as "Profound Song," due to the strong emotional conveyance associated with its expression.

11. Michael Christoforidis, "Un acercamiento a la postura de Manuel de Falla en el *Cante Jondo* (canto primitivo andaluz)." Granada: Archivo Manuel de Falla, commemorative edition of the seventy-fifth anniversary of the *cante jondo* competition of 1922, insert into facsimile edition of *Concurso de "Cante Jondo" canto primitivo andaluz, Granada 1922*, published by Camara Oficial de Comercio, Industria y Navegación de Granada, Ayuntamiento de Granada and Archivo Manuel de Falla. Granada: Urania, 1997, 1–2.

12. Program book of *Concurso de "Cante Jondo" (Canto Primitivo Andaluz), Granada, Corpus Christi, 1922, Que se Celebrará Las Noches de los Días 13 y 14 de Junio, en la Placeta de San Nicolás del Albayzín*. Granada: Editorial Urania, Manuel Paso, 2, 3.

13. OMM, 101.

14. OMM,101.

15. OMM, 102.

16. OMM, 103.

17. OMM, 103–6.

18. Christoforidis, *Enciclopédia*, 900.

19. OMM, 110.

20. OMM, 111.

21. Iglesías, 246.

22. See part III (Works) for an example of the cover page of the manuscript of this piece.

23. The first meeting of Falla and Federico García Lorca is thought, by Gerardo Diego, to be as early as 1917, in Granada. Gerardo Diego, "Falla, teleguía" in *Un jándalo en Cádiz* (intro. by P. Paz Pasamar). Cádiz: Caja de Ahorros de Cádiz, 1974, 15.

24. Winnaretta Eugénie Singer (b. New York, 1865) was the daughter and heiress of the inventor of the sewing machine. She eventually married Edmond de Polignac, and became one of Paris's great patrons of the arts and lent support to such artists as Debussy, Satie, Fauré, Stravinsky, Chabrier, Diaghilev, and, of course, Falla. Falla was present on 2 January 1908, when the Princesse's friend, Blanche Selva, premiered the first three books of Albéniz's *Iberia*. The American patroness was also a pianist and painter. Another American patroness of the arts, Mrs. Coolidge, had invited Falla to lunch with her and to visit Ostia during one of his visits to Italy (most likely in May 1923). According to Demarquez

(p. 150), Falla was so overwhelmed by his first visit to the Vatican and the Sistine Chapel that he arrived just in time for dessert, a fact that was not well-received by his "could-be" patroness.

25. Michael Christoforidis, http://english.uq.edu.au/conferences/interdis/abstracts/christoforidis.html, 6/24/2001.

26. For more details, see part III, Works. However, according to Antonio Gallego in the official AMF catalogue, there is uncertainty as to whether the harpsichord and lute were used, but possibly were, due to this experiment, alias "rehearsal," for *Retablo*.

27. The exact translation of this title into English is awkward, being "big-clubbed puppets." It is perhaps best understood that the word "cachiporra" could designate a "stick with a big knob used by country people" or could also be a "vulgar exclamation." However, its commonplace connotation seems clear enough. As the projects by Falla and García Lorca included children, the title is seen as a comical "spoof" or jest.

28. Christoforidis, *Enciclopédia*, 900.

29. *Poesía,* 175, 176.

30. Sopeña, 130.

31. Gallego, *Católogo*, 195.

32. Sopeña, 131.

33. Demarquez, 138.

34. *Poesía*, 265.

35. *Poesía*, 265.

36. *Poesía*, 156.

37. Sopeña, 137.

38. Wanda Landowska (1921) *Musique ancienne*. Paris: Senart, Chapter XIV, "Interprétation," 161 [AMF 1459].

39. Orozco, 134.

40. *Ernesto Halffter (1905–1989), Músico en dos tiempos*, produced by Yolanda Acker and Javier Suárez-Pajares. Madrid: Publicaciones de la Residencia de Estudiantes and AMF, 137.

41. Sopeña, 275.

42. Gallego, *Católogo*, 225.

43. Gallego, *Católogo*, 203.

44. Sopeña, 137.

45. Preface to Chester Edition of *Psyché* (1927).

46. Gallego, *Católogo*, 204. Demarquez gives the première date as December of 1924 with Conchita Badía in Barcelona (Demarquez, 155, 245).

47. Ángel Sagardia, *Vida y Obra de Manuel de Falla*. Madrid: Escelicer, S. A., 1967, 97. "Yo no creo que exista hoy en europa outro maestro, salvo Mauricio Ravel, que escriba con la perfección de Falla. Todo está calculado y nada dejado al azar. La lectura de cualquier partitura del maestro gaditano deja la impresión de que no sobra nada, y también de que no falta nada. Cada obra suya es una lección de claridad latina, de precisión y de disciplina, asimismo de sencillez."

48. Christoforidis, *Enciclopédia*, 901.

49. Christoforidis, *Enciclopédia*, 901.

50. Letter Landowska-Falla dated 21 September 1926 (from St. Leu la Forêt). AMF 7170.

Mon grande merveilleux ami,
   Votre concerto est un chef d'œuvre. J'en suis toute vibrante de joie et de bonheur. Je le travaille du matin à la nuit, et je ne pense qu'a trouver des accents *vrais* et *justes* pour vous rester fidèle. Je vous écrivait d'ici quelques mots pour vous demander des lumières. Mais en attendant ces quelques mots de reconnaissance pour votre musique si humaine, si forte et si pleine de soleil.
   Votre fidèle Wanda.

51. Demarquez, 167–68.

52. *Poesía*, 199.

53. Harper, 1985–1994.

54. Sopeña, 134.

55. *Poesía,* 184.

56. Christoforidis, *Enciclopédia*, 902.

57. Document reproduced in Nommick, Thesis, III, as Document 87, 544–555.

58. Sopeña, 212.

59. See chapter 10.

60. Orozco, 162.

61. Christoforidis, *Enciclopédia*, 902.

62. Christoforidis, *Enciclopédia*, 902.

63. Nommick, thesis, II, 295–96. For a complete listing, see *op. cit.* 296–302.

64. Demarquez, 177.

65. Demarquez, 173.

66. *Poesía*, 248–53, and Demarquez, 185–86.

67. *Poesía,* 209.

68. Demarquez, 175.

69. Demarquez, 175.

70. *Poesía,* 258.

71. Demarquez, 174.

72. Demarquez, 174–75.

73. Demarquez, 174–75.

74. Demarquez, 184.

75. Sopeña, 212.

76. *Poesía*, 150.

77. Christoforidis, *Enciclopédia*, 903.

78. Christoforidis, *Enciclopédia*, 903.

79. Chase-Budwig, 41.

80. Chase-Budwig, 27.

81. Orozco, 163–64.
82. *Poesía*, 150.
83. Antonio Gallego, "Reflexiones sobre el año Falla 1996 in *Jambou-Sorbonne*, 1999, 545. "Cómo explicar la terrible decadencia física—y por lo tanto compositiva—en sus últimos 20 años, desde, por ejemplo, 1927 a 1946?Las explicaciones tradicionales son totalmente insuficientes, y llenas de prejuicios. Una de mis experiencias más emocionantes de este año Falla ha sido una "sesión clínica" pública en la que dos médicos de La Coruña, espoleados por el médico-musicólogo Xoan Manuel Carreira, analizaron—a través de datos aún incompletos obtenidos en la bibliografía y en el epistolario, y, por supuesto, de la iconografía—la posible enfermedad de Falla, la que le convirtió prácticamente en un inválido a partir de sus 50 años. No pudo ser la tuberculosis (viejo mito romántico, como es bien notorio) ni la imposible sífilis de la que habló Campodónico y que rastreó sin resultados mi maestro Sopeña. Ni tiene nada que ver con improbables homosexualidades, en todo caso no demostradas, ni con represiones religiosas. . . . Aunque aún estamos lejos del diagnóstico final documentado, parece que pudo tratarse de una enfermedad de larga gestación, que en su época no tenía diagnóstico y que hoy, por cierto, no tiene aún curación asegurada: Una "espondiloartritis." Eso explicaría muchas cosas."
84. Demarquez, 111.
85. *Poesía*, 212.
86. *Key Events in Spanish Politics, 1874–1975*—taken from Hess, 1995, 57.

Bourbon Restoration, Alfonso XII proclaimed King.
Spanish-American War. Spain loses Cuba, Puerto Rico, the Philippines.
"Tragic Week" in Barcelona.
Maura abandons Conservative party, becomes Chief of "Maurists."
Military uprisings, new government formed under Dato (June); worker's strikes (August).
Coup d'état of General Primo de Rivera, parliamentary system overthrown.
Founding of fascist newspaper by Ramiro Ledesma Ramos (March).
Monarchy collapses, Alfonso XIII leaves Spain, founding of the Second Republic (April).
Founding of the Catholic authoritarian party, *Acción popular* (April).
Founding of the fascist party, *Juntas de Ofensiva nacional-Sindicalista (JONS)* (October).
José Primo de Rivera founds *Falange Española*.
Presidency of Manuel Azaña.
Spanish Civil War breaks out (July).
Francisco Franco unites right-wing parties (*Falange*, Carlists, Catholic authoritarian) into *Falange Española Tradicionalista y de la JONS*.
1939–1975 Dictatorship of Francisco Franco.

87. Christoforidis, *Enciclopédia*, 902.

88. *Poesía*, 220.

89. Letter Falla-Fernando de los Ríos, dated 13 August 1932, from Granada, AMF 7492. "Yo, que tan vigilante cuidado pongo en no hacer ni decir nada que pudiera en el Extranjero amenguar en los más mínimo el prestigio de España." . . .

90. Letter Falla-Fernando de los Ríos, dated 13 August 1932, from Granada, AMF 7492.

Anoche mismo, a pesar de la precauciones por fin adoptadas, la iglesia de San Nicolás seguía ardiendo hasta su destrucción, mientras alguien volteaba desvergonzadamente las campanas . . . ¡Qué pena da España, y como entre los unos y los otros la siguen destruyendo! . . .

Usted conoce perfectamente cuales son mis ideales, tan por encima de cuanto a política transciende, y que con todo el anhelo de mi alma procuro que sean aliviadas y corregidas las necesidades y las injusticias que sufra el pueblo. Y ahora, al producirse el insensato movimiento político-militar que ha dado origen a los hechos en cuestión, yo he sido uno de los primeros en condenarlo; pero no es menos insensato lo que ha ocurrido en Granada, donde aquel movimiento no ha tenido la menor repercusión. Digo a usted todo esto, no solo como leal información al amigo querido, sino también al hombre responsable del gobierno de España, y como protesta (respetuosa, pero noblemente indignada como cristiano, como español y como artista por mi oficio) ante con usted comparten aquella tremenda responsabilidad. Mi conciencia y mi honor me impulsan a hacerlo. . . .

91. Budwig, 29.

92. *Poesía*, 232.

93. Sopeña, 244.

94. Sopeña, 276.

95. Demarquez, 176–77.

96. Demarquez, 181.

97. *Poesía*, 222.

98. *Poesía*, 226.

99. Xochiquetzal Ruiz Ortiz, *Rodolfo Halffter*. Mexico, D. F.: CENIDIM, 269.

100. Ruíz Ortiz, 268.

101. Letter Halffter-Falla dated 22 February 1935, published in "Cartas inéditas de Rodolfo Halffter a Manuel de Falla" in *Pauta,* no. 35 (July 1990). Mexico City: CENIDIM, 14.

102. Letter Halffter-Falla dated 22 February 1935, *Pauta*, 14.

He tenido una gran alegría al leer los párrafos que, en su carta, dedica a mi música para *La traviesa molinera*. Era difícil salir airoso por existir un antecedente, una obra maestra que yo admiro profundamente: *El sombrero de tres picos* de Ud. En cuanto a lo que Ud. dice respecto de la excesiva intención de subrayar la acción escénica, es un error evidente. Tiene Ud. razón.

103. Ediciones Mexicanas de Musica has published a piano version of "Munué" from *La traviesa molinera*.

104. Demarquez, 183.
105. Chase-Budwig, 30.
106. Sopeña, 244.
107. *Poesía*, 231.
108. *Poesía*, 232.
109. *Poesía*, 216.
110. Sopeña, 245.
111. Sopeña, 246–47.
112. Orozco, 205.
113. Chase-Budwig, 29.

Chapter 6

Argentina (1939–1946)

On 28 September 1939, Falla and his sister María del Carmen bade farewell to his brother, Germán, his sister-in-law María Luisa, his niece Maribel (María Isabel), and his friends in Granada. Falla's close collaborator, Hermenegildo Lanz, wrote an account of the event, commenting afterwards, "Today, a day later, after sleeping badly, and very little, I count the hours since my second father Don Manuel de Falla left me—the man who had shaped my mind . . . God's will be done!"[1]

Falla and his sister sailed from Barcelona on 2 October on the *Neptunia* reaching Buenos Aires on the eighteenth of the same month. Stopovers were made in Tangiers, the Canary Islands, Brazil, and Uruguay. María del Carmen described the interesting journey in a letter to Germán.[2] The change of scenery was good for Falla. His concerts (4, 11, 18, and 23 November, Teatro Colón) went well and his health improved temporarily. His Suite, *Homenajes*, was premiered on 18 November at the Teatro Colón in Buenos Aires. He came to know the composer and conductor Juan José Castro and his wife Raquel Aguirre, who would frequently assist Falla. The Wagnerian Association honored him on 20 November.

Musicologist and friend Kurt Pahlen recalled the following event.

> The Colón Orchestra had the highest respect for him. None of the orchestra's professors expected him to be an accomplished conductor, but they all felt they were before an authentic composer, of sound training, with a clear opinion concerning musical questions, who knew exactly what he wanted and who had a well-defined concept of how both his music and music by others should be interpreted, even if his opinions were often diametrically opposed to the opinions of other interpreters.[3]

From the outset, the Spanish government tried to entice him back to Spain, with an offer of an annual pension of 25,000 pesetas. Falla, however, decided to settle definitively in Argentina. Finding the air too damp in Buenos Aires, he took a house in a suburb of Córdoba, "Villa Carlos Paz," and later "Villa del Lago." He conducted a charity concert for flood victims on 30 May 1940, of the Orquesta Sinfónica of Córdoba and subsequently concerts for the Buenos Aires *Radio El Mundo*. On 13 July he was awarded the Great Cross of the Civil Order of Alfonso X the Wise. Pianist Artur Rubinstein visited him at his new residence at Villa del Lago.

Due to World War II Falla was not able to receive his author's rights from Europe. His Argentine and exiled Spanish friends—Juan José Castro, Francisco Cambó, Guido Valcarenghi, and José María Hernández Suárez—came to his aid. Work continued on *Atlántida*, but in 1941 Falla fell ill with a fever and temporarily stopped work. From 1941–1942, he made an extensive revision of the orchestration of two of Pedrell's songs *Romance de Don Joan y Don Ramón* and *Glósa*, as well as "La morte de Giovana," "I Guinocchi," and "Canción de la estrella" from Pedrell's *Los Pirineos* for a concert planned in homage of Pedrell's centenary.[4] And he revised and prepared "expressive versions" of works of T. L. Victoria for a commemorative concert. These works may have given him respite from the arduous task of *Atlántida*.[5] The Teatro Colón realized a production of *The Three-Cornered Hat* in 1941. Proposals from the San Miguel Studios promoted Falla to consider film versions of *El retablo* and *La vida breve,* projects contemplated as early as 1936 with José Cubiles and *Fantasía bœtica*. He initially was against the idea due to poor sound quality. However, he acknowledged that parts of *Retablo* could be better realized through this media and began work on these two projects. In 1943 Metro Goldwyn Mayer proposed to stage and film a two-piano version of "Ritual Fire Dance" with pianists José and Amparo Iturbi, which Falla eventually accepted and which helped to ease his financial difficulties.

Falla's contact with his friends was paramount. Always a great conversationalist, Falla maintained friendship with Carlos Guastavino, Julián Bautista, Conchita Badía, and many others. His friends in Granada sent him books and musical scores, as well as dismantled his house in 1942 after a burglary, placing his effects in storage. The only recording of his voice (from 8 and 15 December 1940, "El Mundo" radio) heard on the CD ROM *Manuel de Falla*[6] reveals his great strength of spirit, passion, and conviction. His observations were always acute and penetrating.

Assisted by Cambó in 1942, Falla settled in his final house in Alta
Gracia, outside of Córdoba, in a house called "Los Espinillos," a place
he particularly liked because of its similarity to Granada. There he received friends and continued his work on *Atlántida*, mentioning the possibility of playing a concert version of it.

> Los Espinillos . . . stands in the oldest and highest part of the town, at the
> end of a wide street. . . . It is surrounded by a garden with a very stony soil,
> cypress trees by the gate, and pines at the back. Many orange, pomegran-
> ate, mimosa and other trees stand amidst aromatic shrubs, and large-leafed
> cacti grow against the walls of the house. The veranda, which catches the
> sun, looks out onto a nearby sierra, with its dense vegetation of evergreen
> interspersed with trees which the autumn turns to yellow or red and dotted
> here and there with black cypresses.[7]

Health problems continued to plague him and his work. He became
obsessed with it, taking huge quantities of medicines, checking and jot-
ting down his temperature several times a day. He was deathly afraid of
drafts, to the extent that he went around the house closing windows as he
walked from one room to another. He maintained his ascetic way of life.
His room was practically bare, with a simple iron bed, a chair, a table.
His workroom contained a large table covered with piles of papers and
books. Typical of his interior discipline, he maintained a strict schedule,
devoting many hours daily to his ample correspondence. He arose late,
devoted five hours a day to personal care and health, after which he tack-
led his correspondence. Then, in Spanish style, he had lunch around
three or four in the afternoon, followed by a siesta, then tea, then time
for composing. He made rough drafts of all his writings, including apparently simple letters, in the same way he did with his compositions.[8]

Falla kept quiet about his progress on *Atlántida*, always saying that it
was near completion, to the point that in 1943 he mentioned the possibility of programming a part of the work in a concert. Even though he
was enthused with the project, and the change of climate had been stimulating to him, nevertheless his progress was slow and sporadic. He
completed "La Salve en el mar" and continued to work on "Els Atlants
en el temple de Neptu."[9]

In 1944, Jaime Pahissa visited Falla and began work on his biography, which Falla proofed before its publication. In 1956, ten years after Falla's death, Pahissa released the second, amplified version, including important statements that had been originally cut by Falla,
thereby shedding more light on the personality and moral character of
the composer. Also, in 1944, Falla began to study cinematography in

anticipation of the film version of *Retablo*. He made the text for the preliminary scenes. He revised the orchestration of his *Homenajes*, preparing it for publication.

In 1945, an invitation from the Spanish government was extended to Falla to return to his homeland. He refused on the grounds of poor health. In reality he did not want to compromise his freedom, nor to allow the repressive government to use his image for their benefit. He preferred to stay in Argentina until the situation became better. He maintained correspondence with friends, such as María Barrientos, and was nominated to the Argentine National Academy of Fine Arts. In this year before Falla's own demise came the sad news of the deaths of his friends Ignacio Zuloaga and José María Sert, his scenic collaborator in *Atlántida*. Sert's death was enough to cause Falla to reconsider *Atlántida* as a purely musical work without scenic representation. In the last year of his life, Falla dedicated himself to preparing sections of the work for only a musical presentation. He made a clean copy of the prologue, as well as changes and refinements in the beginning numbers of the first part.

Falla received also such visitors as actress Margarita Zirgu, poet Rafael Alberti, guitarist Paco Aguilar, and pianists Donato Oscar Colacelli and Marisa Regules, amongst others. From another regular visitor, Sergio de Castro (then a young musician-composer who later devoted his talents to the plastic arts), one of the most comprehensive accounts of daily events in Falla's life in Argentina can be found.[10]

> I had the privilege to see Manuel de Falla in Alta Gracia (Córdoba, Argentina) and to help him in the measure of my modest means, from March 1945 until his death in November 1946.
>
> He lived with his sister María del Carmen in the village of "Los Espinillos" ("The Mimosas") situated in the residential quarter of Alta Gracia, which was originally a Jesuit colony where it sustains a beautiful church.
>
> Falla was an extremely attentive man, precise and kind. His vivacity, his humor, were the signs of a magnificent internal youth. He was interested as much in the things said of the spirits of the things of daily life, in those things he unearthed that could render them less banale; a little amused him. His memory was prodigious, as if time were only the present continued. He spoke abundantly, but also he asked a lot of his interlocutors. He was above all kindly. Kindly and enthusiastic, in spite of a delicate constitution. His health was always weak, and he never was better at the end of his life. Yet only a single time in two years, on 18 July 1946, his sister wrote to me in order that I not come to Alta Gracia because her brother was suffering.

Falla bore badly the solitude in which he lived. Not only in that which he had always investigated as a composer, but in that which the events and the geographical distance had woven. A great solitude, in spite of excellent friends, attentive to his health and to his situation, of which the majority lived in Buenos Aires or abroad. From where his joy came on the occasion of certain visits, those were in my opinion too short, just the time of a meal, or simply a coffee.

Straightaway, a very good contact was established between us. One of the first questions he asked me was: "How old are you?" I responded to him: "I will be 23 years old in September." He then said to me: "You are the same age that Federico García Lorca was when were had organized the "Cante Jondo Competition" in Granada in 1922."

Usually, I returned to "Los Espinillos" on Saturdays and Sundays. I arrived around mid-day and immediately we were occupied in practical things: some purchases to do in the capital (books, writing paper, etc.), but above all the copies that he trusted me with of his transcriptions and arrangements of composers such as those of Orazio Vecchi or Felipe Pedrell, for example, just as the revisions that he brought to his own works. All that I had to pass cleanly and in ink, for Falla nearly always used crayon for his manuscripts. When the weather was nice, we walked in the garden on the terrace that descended just to a little waterfall, "El cañito" (the little pipe), just until the moment that María del Carmen called us to come to the table.

This meal at three was very animated and the cooking very simple, excellent and copious. Contrary to the legend, Falla took few medicines at the table. His appetite was without fuss, and at dessert, he smoked cigarettes that he habitually rolled himself.

The living room, that acted as the dining room, opened to the "loggia" on the west side. From the distance, the sweetness of the curves of the hills, just as the light, reminded him of the landscape that he had gazed upon from his home at the Alhambra, the street Antequeruela Alta.

We met again at the end of the afternoon, especially in summer, following our discussions. After dinner, we settled ourselves in the "loggia" until an advanced hour; Sometimes under the moonlight, where it was protected by being in the shadow projected by the pillars under the three bay windows.

Falla was extraordinarily attentive to all that was sonorous, and above all to the silence. We passed very long moments listening to the silence. He would make pavilions with his open hands over his ears in order to better capture the sounds. For, he said, we would be able to vary the position of the pavilions of our ears as we can vary the opening of our eyelids.

In winter, my visits were less long. Falla worked always at night, very late, sometimes just until dawn, and he would arise at the end of the morning.

Mealtimes were Spanish: lunch at three o'clock in the afternoon, dinner at nine thirty p.m. He never took a nap. Towards the end of March, when the days were getting shorter (in the austral hemisphere, the autumn begins on 21 March), he wanted to take his nap before the sun went down; otherwise, he said, it was not beneficial for him.

Often, he asked me about the number of my visits to "Los Espinillos." I had not counted them, but I easily deduced that there had been fiftyish. In this number, I included the visits where I was alone with him, that is to say, the majority of the time, but equally those, many less numerous, where we found ourselves in the company of other people: friends of Falla like Pérez de Ayala, for example, or common friends, like Erich Kleiber, with whom I had been linked in friendship since 1938.

The very numerous subjects of strictly musical order broached by Falla were centered around tonality-modality, in the large sense of these words and, beginning with that which constituted in his eyes the musical phenomenon "par excellence," that is to say, the ratio of the external rhythm (figuration, range, intensity), with the internal rhythm (duration established through cadences, sequences). If the ratio was exact, there was music.

In great number also were the subjects of another order; I refer above all to the anecdotes. . . . From this group: . . .

The musicians who came back the most often in their intention.
The list of books that he counseled me to study.
An anecdote Falla-Stravinsky that was raised in 1929.
Some words about "Atlántida."

(1) Falla placed Pérotin at the summit of all those he had known of the Notre Dame school and of its influence. Less far in time, the masters of the Spanish Renaissance were for him a kind of spiritual food. This is well known for the mark that it had on his work, particularly in certain pages of "Atlántida."

He had often evoked Nicolaus Gombert, although Flemish but Chapelmaster at Madrid: Juan de la Encina, and certainly Pedro de Escobar. Equally Luis Milán; Cristóbal de Morales; Antonio de Cabezón, signaled to me that his son Hernando and his brother Juan were equally musicians; Tomás Luis de Victoria; Luis de Narvaez; Francisco Guerrero, etc.

Curiously, Falla compared Palestrina with Raphaël, because, he said, of the air that circulated amongst artists, and the treatment of the voice by the musician. But he preferred Roland de Lassus to Palestrina, giving all the same applause to Victoria.

Often, he established a kind of "pendant" between Orazio Vecchi and Claudio Monteverdi, signaling the purely auditory character of the first and, in the operas of the second, the audio-visual.

From amongst the composers born near the end of the 17th century, he did not place anyone higher than Domenico Scarlatti where the music, he rightly said, is arch-Spanish. Or, when he was in a bad mood, he would take him for an Italian musician.

Bach and Haendel, naturally. Of course he wouldn't acknowledge that they were both born in 1685, the same year as Domenico Scarlatti.

He loved Haydn, Mozart and Beethoven, the difference of which he established with finesse; but he didn't like Brahms at all, whom he considered heavy and rhetorical.

Falla had a true predilection for Frédéric Chopin.

Richard Wagner returned in this commentaries sometimes with eulogy, but also with a severity still more terrible than his text of 1933 published on the occasion of the 50th anniversary of the death of Wagner.

Amongst his contemporaries, Claude Debussy was his absolute God, and as such, he rendered him incessant homage. He was marveled that the music of Debussy was, in certain works, also absolutely and profoundly Spanish. On the other hand, he was astonished that Debussy was only fourteen years older than himself. He said to me: "Think that I myself am sixteen years older than Milhaud."

Concerning always his contemporaries, Falla spoke often to me of his friendly debt to Paul Dukas, as of his close ties of friendship with Ravel and Stravinsky, but also of his true interest in the Viennese School, a thing that at first surprised me.

Falla shared with me the eulogies of Stravinsky relative to "Pierrot Lunaire" of Schoenberg that he had heard in Berlin in December 1912. Equally of those, very warmly, of Ravel, who had attempted to play this work in Paris in 1913.

Falla possessed a large musical scores of "Pierrot Lunaire" since 1922–1923, that today is found in the Manuel de Falla Archives [AMF] in Granada. These archives posses equally a letter of Falla, dated from 1940 in Argentina, addressed to one of his friends who remained in Granada, asking him to send him his pocket score of "Pierrot Lunaire" entirely annotated in his hand.

The new concept of chamber music that this work or Schoenberg represented has without doubt influenced the vocal part of "Retablo." I can affirm it, given the indications that I have from Falla himself.

Regarding Webern, the "Cinq pièces opus 10" for orchestra, [Five Pieces for Orchestra, op. 10] of 1913, figured beside that of "Retablo" at the time of the festival organized by the S. I. M. C. (International Society for Contemporary Music) in Zurich in 1926, festival of which Falla regretted still, in Alta Gracia, of not having been able to attend. At the same festival figured the "Quintette pour instruments à vent opus 26" [Wind Quintet, op. 26] of Schoenberg.

On the other hand, two years later in Sienna, Falla attended the festival following that of S.I.M.C. during the course of which was present the "Retablo," and where he played the "Concerto pour clavecin et cinq instruments" [Concerto for Harpsichord and Five Instruments]. On the same program figured the "Trio à cordes op. 20 [String Trio, op. 20] of Webern which was to be produced in Vienna the same year. Falla was still indignant when he told me of the monstrous scandal that provoked the execution of this "Trio" that he himself considered as a masterpiece.

Later, Falla understood the "Cinq pièces pour Orchestre opus 10" of Webern of which he compared to me their brevity to the tiny size of precious pearls.

Returning to Sienna after the festival, in September 1928, Falla visited the Campo Santo de Pisa and contemplated a long time the famous frescos of the 14th century, "Le Triomphe de la Mort" [Death's Triumph], then attibuted to Orcagan. I will never forget the retrospectively intact emotion of Falla evoking this frescos as though he had seen it the previous day, to such point that he had tears in his eyes. I add a significant detail that seems to me little known, or unknown. Falla said to me that he constantly had the spirit of these frescos present when he composed the *Hommage to Dukas,* "Spes Vitae," in 1935.

(2) Here are the books that Falla advised me to study:

Études sur la modulation de Max Reger [Studies on Modulation by Max Reger].

Études sur les notes de passage de Charles Koechlin (sic) [Studies on passing notes by Charles Koechlin].

Contrepoint et Fugue de Richter [Counterpoint and Fugue by Richter].

Traité pratique de composition musicale de Lobe [Practical treatise of musical composition by Lobe].

Traité d'instrumentation de Widor [Treatise of Instrumentation by Widor].

The non-conventional spirit of Falla apparent as evidenced in this list of books that he had himself studied. Non-conventional, that is to say, never confined in that which could be considered as purely Latin or exclusively Germanic.

(3) In September 1945, on a beautiful Spring day, we lunched, Falla and I, all the time speaking about the oboe. Falla knew perfectly the construction and the mechanism of all the instruments, beginning with the piano. He loved it. His sister María del Carmen had told me that when don Manuel had bought his first typewriter the vender had left flabbergasted from their house: her brother had not stopped to compare each detail of the typewriter to that of the piano, the harpsichord, or to a wind instrument.

Briefly, we spoke then of the oboe: its sonority, its beauty of the notes emitted very rapidly by whole steps or half steps; but also, he said to me, the magnificent leaps of the fifth or the seventh in the middle range. . . . At this moment, I interrupted him: "Certainly, as for example at the beginning of the instrumental Fugue of Stravinsky's 'Symphony of Psalms'" and I began to sing it.

Upon hearing me, he nearly choked, swallowing the wrong way, becoming very red, and with desperate gestures, he said to me: "Stop! Stop! I beg you! . . ." I was frightened: "What has happened to you, don Manuel?" He then told me this:

"Often, in Paris, we lunched together, Stravinsky and I, without anyone else. This was every time that Stravinsky desired to submit to me an ethical problem; he had taken my advice beforehand. At the end of 1929, at the end of one of these meals, each one of us was worried to know what the other one was underway to compose. I spoke to him then of the first sketches of 'Atlántida' that was in risk of becoming a kind of scenic oratorio, for narrator, soloists, choir, and orchestra, etc. Stravinsky said to me that he thought also himself to write a work for choir and orchestra; a kind of Symphony based on three of the Psalms of David, etc., for he received a commission from Boston. Thus, we solemnly promised ourselves to never hear one single note of the score of the other before having finished each his own. Finally that one could never say that one of us had copied or influenced the other."

And to finish don Manuel:

"You understand, my dear Sergio, that I had a duty to interrupt you in order to keep my word."

(4) After the end of 1945, Falla said to me that he wished to be able to play the Prologue and the first part of "Atlántida" in Buenos Aires. That represented, according to him, a good half hour of music completed, orchestrated, etc.

Is it the death of his friend José-María Sert, which occurred on 27 November 1945, that caused Falla to decide—finally—that a part of his work would be heard? I don't know. Sert was occupied for such a long time with the scenery, or all at least, as don Manuel said to me, of the "visualization aspect" of "Atlántida."

Always I must copy the Prologue and the first part. We were both of us enthusiastic. His telegram of 3 January 1946, before my trip to Bolivia and to Peru, thus that his postcard of 20 February upon my return, is testimony. My visites of March and April served, in part, to prepare all: the music paper, the color of the ink, the carton of design with lace that I had expressly acquired in order to arrange everything, etc. His telegram of 17 April is thus formulated: "I wish that you can come—to be expected Thursday— 7 o'clock in the evening in order to make a plan—I embrace you—Falla." The plan in question was the copy of which I speak.

Still today, I am inconsolable when I think of this somber afternoon in wintry May, where Falla decided to suspend his project of scheduling a performance of part of "Atlántida"; and where, in spite of all my efforts, I was not successful in convincing him to stay with it. One can discuss, and in-the-field, it gives me the reason of his attitude. He differed from those that himself had to advance later; and of those that others had imagined. No, the reason that he gave to me is incredible: "If the performance is not success-ful, the strength fails me to complete 'Atlántida.'" Absurd reason, insane, for an artist that played from such renown; but also reason of such "youth". . . of such modesty and vulnerability in front of opinion and public.

Falla renounced the copy that I had made, then went to add to the suite between us the other episodes on the subject of "Atlántida" that proved that point he had taken, being occupied and preoccupied with his work. I relate some of this in my text for the catalogue of the magnificent exposition "Manuel de Falla—Sept espaces pour la scène" [Manuel de Falla—Seven Spaces to the Stage] opened last June at the Charles V Palace in Granada.

I am witness that Falla worked without slackening on "Atlántida" right up to the end, ardently desiring to have the health and the time to finish it. He said to me: "You see, Sergio, Wagner was not dead before hearing his 'Parsifal,'" . . . translated: "I will not die before hearing 'Atlántida.'"

Destiny decided otherwise. Manuel de Falla died on 14 November at dawn. "Atlántida," it, was finished at dawn, the dawn of a new world. All true work is a new world. The dawn of a splendid world, unknown, im-possible to reach, around which sometimes men are transported.

True to his superstitious nature, Falla almost lived to see his seven-tieth birthday. He always believed that his life fell into seven-year peri-ods—seven years in Paris, in Madrid, in Argentina. Victim of a cardiac attack, he died peacefully in his sleep on 14 November, less than two weeks before his next birthday. His body was found when the maid, bringing his lunch, knocked on his door and got no response. The ca-daver was later taken to Córdoba for embalming. Some say that such deaths are reserved for the just.

Innumerable tributes from around the world poured forth to remem-ber the greatest Spanish composer of the twentieth century. An impres-sive funeral was held on 19 November at the cathedral of Córdoba with civil authorities and the Ambassador of Spain in attendance.

The body was then taken to cemetery of San Jerónimo where it was left in a sepulchral vault of the Carmelites.[11] María del Carmen decided, with others, to return the corpse to Cádiz. On 22 December, she left on the ship *Cabo del Buen Esperanza* (Cape Good Hope) with her brother's remains, the unfinished score of *Atlántida*, and two nuns to accompany

her. Arriving in the Canary Islands, the cadaver was then transferred to a Spanish warship. They arrived in Cádiz on 9 January 1947, where Falla was buried in the crypt of the cathedral.

The funeral service in Cádiz was enhanced by the singing of Juan María Thomàs's Capella Classica of Mallorca, which Falla esteemed. Music performed included a Bach chorale and a requiem by Victoria—"the only drapery worthy of covering the coffin of the formost Spanish musician of our times," wrote Joaquín Rodrigo. The coffin was lowered into the crypt to the sound of *In Paradisum*, where Falla reposes under his requested inscription: "El honor y la gloria solo son de Dios" (Honor and glory belong only to God).

Above the tomb is now constructed a monument by architect José Menéndez Pidal on 8 September 1960. In Argentina, a memorial stamp was issued, depicting Falla's "Los Espinillos" home. Through recitals and concerts of his friends in Córdoba, funds for a monument were collected. The sculptor Vicente Torró Simo, of Spanish descent, won the competition and since 1956 this monument has stood in the Parque Sarmiento. Other memorials have been made, such as the naming of conservatories in Falla's name and the composition of musical works in homage to him, to mention a few. But the greatest memorial of all is undoubtedly the legacy of Manuel de Falla's music.

NOTES

1. *Poesía*, 234.
2. *Poesía*, 241–42.
3. *Poesía*, 267.
4. Jorge de Persia, *Los últimos años de Manuel de Falla*. Madrid: Sociedad General de Autores de España (Fondo de Cultura Económica, S. A. de C. V.), 1993, 141–42.
5. Sergio de Castro in Jorge de Persia, 1993, 24. ". . . estos trabajos pequeños le servían como 'refrescos' en medio de la fuerte tarea de la *Atlántida*."
6. *Manuel de Falla, Música eu los Jardines de España,* CD ROM, Madrid: Instituto Nacional de las Artes Escénicas y la Música, Ministério de Educación y Cultura, 1997.
7. Demarquez, 196.
8. Christoforidis, *Enciclopédia*, 904.
9. Christoforidis, *Enciclopédia*, 904.
10. Sergio de Castro, "Falla en 1945–1946" in Jambou, Sorbonne, 19–24, reproduced with kind permission.

J'ai eu le privilège de fréquenter Manuel de Falla à Alta Gracia (Córdoba, Argentine), et de l'aider dans la mesure de mes modestes moyens, de mars 1945 jusqu'à sa mort en novembre 1946.

Il habitait avec sa sœur María del Carmen la villa "Los Espinillos" ("Les Mimosas") située dans le quartier résidentiel de Alta Gracia, qui fut à l'origine une colonie des Jésuites dont il subsiste une belle église.

Falla était un homme extrêmement attentif, précis et aimable. Sa vivacité, son humour, étaient les signes d'une magnifique jeunesse intérieure. Il s'intéressait aussi bien aux choses dites de l'esprit qu'à celles du quotidien, dans lesquelles il dénichait ce qui pouvait les rendre moins banales; un rien l'amusait. Sa mémoire était prodigieuse, comme si le temps ne fût qu'un présent continu. Il parlait d'abondance, mais aussi il interrogeait longuement ses interlocuteurs. Il était avant tout bienveillant. Bienveillant et enthousiaste, malgré une constitution délicate. Sa santé fut toujours défaillante, et elle ne s'améliora pas à la fin de as vie. Pourtant, une seule fois en deux ans, le 18 juillet 1946, sa sœur m'écrivit pour que je ne vienne pas à Alta Gracia, car son frère était souffrant.

Falla supportait mal la solitude dans laquelle il vivait. Non pas celle qu'il avait toujours recherchée pour composer, mais celle que les événements et la distance géographique avaient tissé. Une grande solitude, malgré d'excellents amis attentifs à sa santé et à sa situation, mais dont la majorité vivait à Buenos Aires ou à l'étranger. D'où sa joie à l'occasion de certaines visites, lesquelles étaient à mon avis trop brèves, juste le temps d'un repas, ou simplement d'un café.

D'emblée, un très bon contact s'établit entre nous. Une des premières questions qu'il me posa fut: "Quel âge avez-vous?" Je lui répondis: "J'aurai 23 ans en septembre." Il me dit alors: "Vous avez le même âge qu'avait Federico García Lorca quand nous avons organisé le "Concurso de Cante Jondo à Grenade en 1922."

D'habitude, je me rendais à "Los Espinillos" les samedis et dimanches. J'arrivais vers midi et tout de suite nous nous occupions de choses pratiques: quelques achats à faire dans la capitale (livres, papier à lettre, etc.), mais surtout des copies qu'il me confiait de ses transcriptions et arrangements de compositeurs tels que Orazio Vecchi ou Felipe Pedrell, par exemple, ainsi que des révisions qu'il apportait à ses propres œuvres. Tout cela, je devais le passer au propre et à l'encre, car Falla se servait presque exclusivement de crayon pour ses manuscrits. Par beau temps, nous nous promenions dans le jardin en terrasse qui descend jusqu'à un petit cours d'eau, "El cañito" (le petit tuyau), jusqu'au moment où María del Carmen nous priait de passer à table.

Ces repas à trois étaient très animés et la cuisine était simple, excellente et copieuse. Contrairement à la légende, Falla prenait peu de médicaments à table. Son appétit était sans histoires, et au dessert, il fumait des cigarettes qu'il roulait lui-même habilement.

La salle de séjour, qui faisait office de salle à manger, ouvrait sur une "loggia" côté ouest. Au loin, la douceur des courbes des collines, ainsi que la lumière, lui rappelait le paysage qu'il avait contemplé de chez lui à l'Alhambra, calle de Antequeruela Alta.

Nous nous rencontrions à nouveau en fin d'après-midi, surtout en été, poursuivant nos entretiens. Après le dîner, nous nous installions dans la "loggia" jusqu'à une heure avancée; parfois sous la lumière de la lune, dont il se protégeait en se plaçant dans l'ombre projetée par les piliers soutenant les trois baies.

Falla était extraordiairement attentif à tout ce qui est sonore, et surtout au silence. Nous passions de très longs moments à écouter le silence. Il le faisait en dressant dans ses mains ouvertes le pavillons de ses oreilles afin de mieux capter les sons. Car, disait-il, nous devrions pouvoir varier la position des pavillons de nos oreilles comme nous pouvons varier l'ouverture de nos paupières.

En hiver, mes visites étaient moins longues. Falla travaillait toujours la nuit, très tard, parfois jusqu'à l'aube, et il se levait en fin de matinée.

L'heure des repas était à l'espagnole: déjeuner à trois heures de l'après-midi, dîner à neuf heures et demie du soir. Il ne manquait jamais la sieste. Vers la fin mars, quand les jours raccourcissent (dans l'hémsphère austral, l'automne commence le 21 mars), il veillait à faire sa sieste avant que le soleil ne se couche; autrement, disait-il, elle ne lui était pas profitable.

Très souvent, on m'interroge sur le nombre de mes visites à "Los Espinillos." Je ne les ai pas comptées, mais je déduis facilement qu'il y en eut une cinquantaine. Dans ce chiffre, j'inclus les visites où j'étais seul avec lui, c'est-à-dire, la plupart du temps, mais également celles, beaucoup moins nombreuses, où nous nous trouvions en compagnie d'autres personnes: amis de Falla comme Pérez de Ayala, par exemple, ou amis communs, comme Erich Kleiber, auquel j'étais lié d'amitié depuis 1938.

Les très nombreux sujets d'ordre strictement musical abordés par Falla étaient sur la tonalité-modalité, dans le sens large de ces mots et centres, partant, à ce qui constituait à ses yeux le pénomène musical par excellence, c'est-à-dire, le rapport du rythme extérieur (figuration, hauteur, intensité), avec le rythme intériur durées établies par les cadences, séquences). Si ce rapport était juste, il y avait musique.

En grand nombre aussi étaient les sujets d'un autre ordre; je me refère surtout aux anecdotes. Aussi bien celles qu'il me rapportait que celles que j'ai vécues.

De cet ensemble, le professeur Louis Jambou, vu le peu de temps dont nous disposons, a souhaité que je retienne:

Les musiciens qui revenaient le plus souvent dans ses propos.
La liste des livres qu'il me conseilla d'étudier.
Une anecdote Falla-Stravinsky remontant à 1929.
Quelques mots sur "Atlántida."

(1) Falla plaçait Pérotin au sommet de tout ce qu'il avait pu connaître de l'École Notre-Dame et de son rayonnement.

Moins éloignés dans le temps, les Maîtres de la Renaissance Espagnole étaient pour lui une sorte d'aliment spirituel. Ceci est bien connu, ainsi que la marque qu'ils ont laissé dans son œuvre, particulièrement dans certaines pages de "Atlántida."

Il a souvent évoqué Nicolas Gombert, bien que Flamand mais maître de chapelle à Madrid; Juan de la Encina et, bien sûr, Pedro de Escobar. Également Luis Milán; Cristóbal de Morales; Antonio de Cabezón, en me signalant que son fils Hernando et son frère Juan étaient également musiciens; Tomás Luis de Victoria; Luis de Narvaez; Francisco Guerrero, etc.

Curieusement, Falla comparait Palestrina à Raphaël, à cause, disait-il, de l'air qui circule entre les personnages du peintre, et le traitement des voix par le musicien. Mais il préférait Roland de Lassus à Palestrina, donnant tout de même la palme à Victoria.

Souvent, il établissait une sorte de "pendant" entre Orazio Vecchi et Claudio Monteverdi, signalant le caractére purement auditif du premier et, dans les opéras du deuxiéme, l'auditif-visuel.

Parmi les compositeurs nés vers la fin du dix-septième, il ne plaçait personne plus haut que Domenico Scarlatti dont la musique, disait-il avec raison, est archi-espagnole. D'où sa mauvaise humeur quand quelqu'un le prenait pour un musicien italien.

Bach et Haendel, naturellement, dont il ne revenait pas qu'ils fussent nés en 1685, la même année que Domenico Scarlatti.

Il aimait Haydn, Mozart et Beethoven, dont il établisait avec finesse les différences; mais il n'aimait pas du tout Brahms, qu'il considérait lourd et rhétorique.

Falla avait une véritable prédilection pour Frédéric Chopin.

Richard Wagner revenait dans ses commentaires parfois avec éloge, mais aussi avec une sévérité plus terrible encore que dans son texte de 1933 publié à l'occasion du cinquantenaire de la mort de Wagner.

Parmis ses contemporains, Claude Debussy était son Dieu absolu, et comme tel, il lui rendait incessament hommage. Il s'émerveillait que la musique de Debussy fut, dans certaines œuvres, aussi absolutement et profondément espagnole. D'autre part, il s'étonnait que Debussy n'eut que quatorze ans de plus que lui. Il me disait: "Pensez que j'ai moi-même seize ans de plus que Milhaud."

Concernant toujours ses contemporains, Falla m'a beaucoup parlé de sa dette amicale envers Paul Dukas, ainsi que de ses liens étroits d'amitié avec Ravel et Stravinski, mais aussi, de son véritable intérêt pour l'École de Vienne, chose que de prime abord me surprit.

Falla me fit part des éloges de Stravinski à propos de "Pierrot Lunaire" de Schoenberg qu'il avait écouté à Berlin en décembre 1912. Également de ceux, très chaleureux, de Ravel, lequel avait essayé en 1913 de faire jouer cette œuvre à Paris.

Falla possédait la grande partition de "Pierrot Lunaire" depuis 1922–1923, elle se trouve aujourd'hui aux "Archives Manuel de Falla" de Grenade. Ces archives possèdent également une lettre de Falla, datée de 1940 en Argentine, adressée à un de ses amis resté à Grenade, lui demandant l'envoi de sa partition de poche du "Pierrot Lunaire" entièrement annotée de sa main.

Le nouveau concept de musique de chambre que représente cette œuvre de Schoenberg a sans aucun doute influencé la mise en chantier du "Retablo." Je peux l'affirmer, vu les indications que je tiens de Falla lui-même.

Quant à Webern, les "Cinq pièces opus 10" pour orchestre, de 1913, figuraient à côtè du "Retablo" lors du festival organisé par la S.I.M.C. (Société Internationale de Musique Contemporaine) à Zürich en 1926. Festival auquel Falla regrettait encore à Alta Gracia de ne pas avoir pu assister. Au même festival figurait le "Quintette pour instruments à vent opus 26" de Schoenberg.

En revanche, deux ans plus tard à Sienne, Falla assistait au festival suivant de la S.I.M.C. au cours duquel fut présenté le "Retablo," et où il joua le "Concerto pour clavecin et cinq instruments." Au même programme figurait le "Trio à cordes opus 20" de Webern qui venait d'être créé à Vienne la même année. Falla était encore indigné en me racontant le scandale monstre que provoqua l'exécution de ce "Trio" qu'il considérait, lui, comme un chef-d'œuvre.

Plus tard, Falla entendit les "Cinq pièces pour Orchestre opus 10" de Webern dont il me compara leur brièveté à la taille réduite des pierres précieuses.

En revenant de Sienne après ce festival, en septembre 1928, Falla visita le Campo Santo de Pise et contempla longuement les fameuses fresques du XIVe siècle, "Le Triomphe de la Mort," alors attribuées à Orcagan. Je n'oublierai jamais l'émotion rétrospectivement intact de Falla évoquant ces fresques, comme s'il venait de les voir la veille; à tel point que j'avais les larmes aux yeux. J'ajoute un détail significatif qui me semble peu connu ou inconnu. Falla me dit de ces fresques qu'en composant l'Hommage à Dukas, "Spes Vitae," en 1935, il les avait constamment présentes à l'esprit.

(2) Voici les livres que Falla me conseilla d'étudier:

Études sur la modulation de Max Reger.
Études sur les notes de passage de Charles Koechlin.
Contrepoint et Fugue de Richter.
Traité pratique de composition musicale de Lobe.
Traíté d'Instrumentation de Widor.

L'espirt non-conventionnel de Falla apparaît avec évidence dans cette liste de livres qu'il avait lui-même étudiés. Non-conventionnel, c'est-à-dire, nullement cantonné dans ce qui pourrait être considéré comme purement latin ou exclusivement germanique.

(3) En septembre 1945, par une belle journée de printemps, nous déjeunions, Falla et moi, et nous parlions tout à coup du hautbois. Falla connaissait à la perfection la construction et la mécanique de tous les instruments, à commencer par le piano. Il adorait ça. Sa sœur María del Carmen m'avait rapporté que lorsque don Manuel avait acheté sa première machine à écrire, le démonstrateur était sorti ahuri de chez eux: son frère n'avait cessé de comparer chaque détail de la machine à écrire à ceux du piano, du clavecin, ou d'un instrument à vent.

Bref, nous parlions donc du hautbois: sa sonorité, la beauté de ses notes émises très rapidement par tons ou demi-tons; mais aussi, me dit-il, les magnifiques sauts de quinte ou de septième dans le registre moyen. . . . À ce moment, je l'interrompis: "Bien sûr, comme par exemple au début de la Fugue instrumentale de la 'Symphonie de Psaumes de Stravinsky,' et je me mis à le chanter.

En m'écoutant, il faillit s'étrangler, avala de travers, devint tout rouge, et avec des gestes désespérés, me dit: "Arrêtez! Arrêtez, je vous prie! . . ." J'étais effrayé: "Que se passe-t-il, don Manuel?" Il me raconta alors ceci:

"Souvent, à Paris, nous déjeunions ensemble, Stravinsky et moi, sans personne d'autre. C'était chaque fois que Stravinski désirait me soumettre un problème de morale; il tenait à connaître mon avis là-dessus. Fin 1929, en terminant un de ces repas, chacun de nous s'est inquiété de savoir ce que l'autre était en train de composer. Je lui parlais donc des première ébauches de 'Atlántida' qui risquait de devenir une sorte d'Oratorio scénique, pour récitant, solistes, chœur et orchestre, etc. Stravinski me dit qu'il pensait, lui aussi, écrire une œuvre pour chœur et orchestre, une sorte de Symphonie basée sur trois Psaumes de David, etc., car il venait de recevoir une commande de Boston. Alors, nous nous sommes promis—solennellement—de ne jamais écouter une seule note de la partition de l'autre avant d'avoir terminé chacun la sienne. Afin qu'on ne puisse jamais dire que l'un d'entre nous avait copié ou influencé l'autre."

Et don Manuel de conclure: "Vous comprendrez, mon cher Sergio, que j'ai dû vous interrompre pour tenir parole."

4) Depuis la fin 1945, Falla me dit qu'il souhaitait faire jouer le Prologue et la première partie de "Atlántida" à Buenos-Aires. Cela représentait, d'après lui, une bonne demi-heure de musique terminée, orchestrée,etc.

Est-ce la mort de son ami José-María Sert, survenue le 27 novembre 1945, qui amena Falla à se décider—enfin—à entendre une partie de son œuvre? Je l'ignore. Sert s'occupait depuis fort longtemps des décors, ou tout au moins, comme me disait don Manuel, de la "visualisation partielle" de "Atlántida."

Toujours est-il que je devais copier le Prologue et la première partie. Nous étions tous deux enthousiastes. Son télégramme du 3 janvier 1946, avant mon voyage en Bolivie et au Pérou, ainsi que sa carte postale du 20 février à mon retour, en témoignent.

Mes visites de mars et avril servirent, en partie, à tout préparer: le papier à musique, la couleur de l'encre, le carton à dessin avec lacets que j'avais acquis expressément pour ranger le tout, etc. Son télégramme du 17 avril est ainsi formulé: "Souhaitant que vous puissiez venir—êtes attendu jeudi—7 heures du soir pour combiner plan—je vous embrasse—Falla." Le "plan" en question était la copie dont je parle.

Encore aujourd'hui, je suis inconsolable quand je pense à ce sombre après-midi de mai annonçant l'hiver, où Falla décida de suspendre son projet de faire jouer partiellement "Atlántida"; et où malgré tous mes efforts, je ne réussis pas à le convaincre de la maintenir. On discuta, et sur-le-champ, il me donna la raison de son attitude. Elle diffère de celles que lui-même a pu avancer plus tard; et de celles que d'autres ont imaginées. Non, la raison qu'il me donna est incroyable: "Si l'exécution n'a pas de succès, les forces me manqueront pour achever 'Atlántida.' Raison absurde, insensée, pour un artiste qui jouissait d'une telle renommée; mais aussi raison d'une telle "jeunesse" . . . d'une telle pudeur et vulnérabilité vis-á-vis de l'opinion et du public.

Falla renonça à la copie que je devais faire, puis vinrent s'ajouter par la suite, entre nous, d'autres épisodes au sujet de "Atlántida" qui prouvent à quel point il était pris, occupé et préoccupé par son œuvre. J'en relate quelques-uns dans mon texte pour le catalogues de la magnifique exposition "Manuel de Falla—Sept espaces pour la scène" ouverte en juin dernier au Palais de Charles V, à Grenade.

Je suis témoin que Falla travailla sans relâche sur "Atlántida" jusqu'à la fin, souhaitant ardemment avoir la santé et le temps pour la terminer. Il me disait: "Vous voyez, Sergio, Wagner n'est pas mort avant d'entendre son 'Parsifal,'" . . . traduire: "Je ne mourrai pas avant d'entendre 'Atlántida.'"

Le destin en décida autrement. Manuel de Falla mourut le 14 novembre à l'aube. "Atlántida," elle, se termine à l'aube, à l'aube d'un nouveau monde. Toute œuvre véritable est un nouveau monde. L'aube d'un monde splendide, inconnu, impossible à atteindre, vers lequel parfois les hommes s'acheminent.

11. Demarquez, 199.

Part II

FACETS OF FALLA'S LIFE AND WORKS

Chapter 7

Falla in His Religion

"And to my religious conviction (Catholic, of course) I owe, above all, the infinite vision of life that in nothing human can we attain."[1]

To say that Falla was deeply religious in every aspect of his life and work is to state the obvious. Many are the testimonies to his ardent Catholic fervor, his preference for attending daily Mass over teaching his musical precepts. Equally important to his abundant and outward piety was Falla's practical application of his beliefs in daily life. The generosity with which he gave to the poor, the modest way he lived his life, the genuine humility manifested during the pre- and post- phases of his life of international fame, and the strong adherence to the abiding principles of Christianity during one of the world's greatest periods of turbulence—all mark Falla as a man riveted by inner convictions and staunch spirituality, tenaciously holding to his marked tenets. His belief system was intimately bound to his choice of profession.

EARLY INFLUENCES

The education afforded Falla by his affluent Catholic parents denied him little. Tutored at home by the best educators available, his religious instruction was typical of that Spanish epoch, being centered in the Marian teachings of the Virgin Mary and the Rosary. Young Manuel seemed to have been a pious but somewhat difficult child with his mother very much in the forefront of his training.[2] He was perhaps not so sickly as is said, but was perhaps somewhat unusual.[3] His father took a less active role, being involved in business and material matters.

Throughout his life, Falla was closely associated with male religious figures, from Clemente Parodi and Padre Fedriani in Cádiz (the latter also in Madrid) to Valentín Ruíz Aznar in Granada, Padre Juan María Thomas in Mallorca, Jacques Maritain in France and indirectly, the Catalan Jacinto Verdaguer, inspirational source for the *Atlántida* libreto. Of these figures, Father Fedriani dominated until Falla left for Paris. Regarding this matter, the opinion of biographer Federico Sopeña is hardly flattering.

> In Falla the adolescent and youth, already decided on his musical vocation, there suddenly appears a singular and not attractive figure that is going to dominate almost, or not almost, in a despotic manner. In Spain at the end of the century the religious and apostolic regulation of the male youth was monopolized by the Jesuits, in the form called Congregación de los Luises, [Luises Congregation] characterized by its Marian fervor posted in the manifesto of 8 December, the Immaculate Conception commemoration . . . Padre Fedriani was not Jesuit but secular clergy, free, with enough means of fortune that permitted him to travel to Madrid and to have a house in Cádiz, in Dos Hermanas, and later in Córdoba. We have in the Archives a memorandum book of letters, telegrams, and postcards addressed to Falla, but lamentably not the responses, as the Padre destroyed them.
>
> The secular priests in Spain are not called Padre, but Don. But this priest assumes this role and calls Falla "son," "son of the soul," with such insistence that it disgusts. He meddles regularly in everything, until the least detail, including the lessons with Pedrell: without a doubt some tendency towards scruples that was the basis of the neurosis throughout all Falla's life comes from here. In those years the situation with the family is in the economic tragedy, with horrible oppression.
>
> Falla never indicates any desire to be a priest, nor to be celibate; this comes later. We know the name, surname and picture, symbol of the frustrated love, [María Prieto Ledesma] which then passed and this woman later formed part of, with her husband, the Granadine circle of Falla's friends. At this time, until 1907, the dictatorship of Padre Fedriani pervaded, which decreed recitations, prayers, and acts until it suffocated.[4]

PARIS YEARS

The Paris years were fertile testing ground for some of the spiritual qualities associated with the mature Falla. His close friend, Ricardo Viñes, was undergoing a conversion to Catholicism at the time of Falla's arrival in 1907. Viñes, who had been previously attracted to theosophy and to the teachings of the Belgian philosopher Leon Bloy, indicated in his diary that they also interested Falla especially by the concepts of asceticism and poverty.[5] This adherence perhaps helped to ease the pain from the austere life that Falla passed in Madrid and in Paris. Even a trip was made in homage to the Belgium socialists organized by "L'Humanite," the socialist newspaper.

Always aware of new trends and currents of thought, Falla may have heard the words of Sir 'Abdu'l-Bahá Abbas at the Parisian Theosophical Society, which lent support to his earlier admission of reliance on the mysterious forces of INSPIRATION in his compositions and his remarkable rectitude of conduct. This talk was given on 18 November 1911, around the time of Falla's speculated religious crisis:[6]

> In the teaching of Bahá'u'lláh, it is written: "By the Power of the Holy Spirit alone is man able to progress, for the power of man is limited and the Divine Power is boundless." . . . The greatest philosophers without this Spirit are powerless, their souls lifeless, their hearts dead! Unless the Holy Spirit breathes into their souls, they can do no good work. No system of philosophy has ever been able to change the manners and customs of a people for the better. Learned philosophers, unenlightened by the divine spirit, have often been men of inferior morality; they have not proclaimed in their actions the reality of their beautiful phrases.[7]

Falla's religiosity was described by some of those who knew him in Paris. Stravinsky characterized him as "unpityingly religious," while Poulenc observed that Falla did not project his faith on others and described him as "The purest kind of mystic, limpid . . . as a lump of crystal."[8] Others still referred to him as St. John of the Cross reincarnated.

Piety and religiosity did not make Falla immune to the desires of the flesh. Earlier he wished to marry his cousin, María Prieto Ledesma, his mother's sister's daughter. Other female interests would follow. Ronald Crichton commented, "There must have been considerable inner tension between the monk-like side of his nature and the side that could so unerringly capture the essence of popular music, with its alternations of physical joy and despair."[9]

Celibacy, according to medical doctor-biographer Manuel Orozco who examined Falla's cadaver, was his choice.

> When we analyse the life of the great masters of contemporary music, we find the following: . . . the great musicians of the past century, those of our world . . . like Stravinsky, Schönberg, Bartók, Webern . . . have upheld an exterior decorum of life, an order, a certain admirable modesty that is already

> evident. In the case of Falla, that is given, and more: all the characteristics of his work of art, the fundamental of a very deep passion that is vexed by a perpetual need of work well done . . . are also in his life. . . . Don Manuel de Falla brought, first of all, something that is at the same time exigent of sacrifice and coexistence of passion sublimated to the maximum: the celibate . . .[10]

Falla's life has been characterized as a life on the edge, in which he opted for all to be purified, clean, frugal, personal, and renewed.[11]

RELIGION AND CREATIVITY

> . . . after the truth of God, the first is Art, but illumined and sustained by "this eternal and hidden fount. . . ."[12]

Falla always recognized the source of this inspiration, but was careful not to make his art become an inheritance from religion.[13] Like Stravinsky, Falla deplored the idea of using the theater as a temple for public prayer. The former's *Symphony of Psalms* and the latter's *Atlántida* testify to the need for a renewal of religion or at least for a renewal of religious musical expression. Falla's desire to renew the oratorio form, to compose religious music, and to write a large lyrical work were amongst the reasons for undertaking the *Atlántida* project. Yet, unlike his literary friend, Juan Ramón Jiménez, Falla opposed the concept of aesthetic pantheism, a fact that might explain why Falla never set any of his friend's verses to music.

Some religious practices also spill over into Falla's approach to musical composition. Economy of means, or paucity of musical material, is increasingly evident in works after *La vida breve.* This musical kind of *asceticism* may be found in such works as the *Concerto,* when Falla avoids thematic development in the first movement, choosing instead to vary the motive repeatedly.

The concept of *renewal* or *absolution* is evident in his constant striving for purity and perfection through reworkings of many pieces, such as *La vida breve, El amor brujo, El sombrero de tres picos,* amongst others; or when he creates a new version of the same work (ex. *Homages, Balada de Mallorca,* or the "expressive interpretations").

The quality of *transformation* occurs in Falla's harmonic system. Unable to leave the realm of tonality, Falla found escape through various inventions. One concrete example is the harmonic generation of chords through juxtapositions and superpositions of tonal combinations employed in various works such as *Quatro piezas españolas, Siete canciones populares españolas, El amor brujo, Fantasía bœtica, Concerto,* and *El retablo,* amongst others. Falla justifies his adherence to tonality while stretching it to the limit, like his life "on the edge," reactionary, but within stated boundaries. He closely studied Schönberg's "heretical" twelve-tone equality, Stravinsky's rhythmic savagery, and the raw barbarism of Bartók's axis system. In conservative belief systems, Falla's behavior might be called fanatic; in his art, it was termed "avant-garde." Falla's fierce loyalty to tonality, like Christianity, would not permit him to deviate, in spite of his far-reaching excursions.

As Rodolfo Halffter put it:

> If Falla were alive and could hear my dodecaphonic works, I am sure that he would be scandalized. He, who believed in the eternal law of tonality, would have refused to admit that there was a certainty of the collapse of tonality. I would have tried to explain to him that my adherence to the twelve-tone system did not represent a substantial change of aesthetic position nor of musical ideology and that I continued being one of his most faithful servants. . . .[14]

The striking dissonance of Falla's usage of canons at the interval of the second in the first movement of the *Concerto* and the eventual resolution of the harmonic "problem," as evidenced in the third movement, might be construed as the concept of *penance.* Here the Prodigal son has returned home. Homage to revered composers in the expressive versions or reworking of pieces, such as the suite *Homages,* may also be viewed as a form of penance.

Mysticism too played a pivotal role in Falla's musical and personal philosophy. Mysticism, in the higher sense of the word, is closely bound up with God and with spiritual practices. In the lower sense, it could be construed as superstition and magic. Nowhere does this dual perception manifest itself more clearly than in *Atlántida* and *El amor brujo,* respectively. Falla ends his statement about receiving INSPIRATION to become a composer by negating an alleged superstitious nature, "In truth, unfounded fear has never played a dominant part in my personality."

Charity is also seen as the motive for the composition of "Canto de los remeros de Volga," when asked by his diplomatic friend Ricardo Baeza in 1922 for a piece to benefit the Russian refugees.

RELIGION AND POLITICS

Falla did not allow religion to make him weak-willed and submissive to political motives. On the contrary, he publicly acclaimed his convictions and repeatedly expressed his horror at the brutalities evinced during the turbulent years of the coming Civil War. He was appalled at the "damaging mixture of religion with politics" (from a letter to Cardinal Vidal Barraquer, Archbishop of Tarragona, published in *Razón y Fe*, July–Aug. 1976). Several incidents during this time reflect Falla's scrupulous adherence to his principles:

1. His break with José Bergamín, liberal Catholic and one of the cofounders of the magazine *Cruz y Raya*, in which Falla's essay on Wagner appeared;
2. His denial of the homage proposed by the city of Seville and Fernández Ballesteros.[15] The Sevillian newspaper, *La Unión*, tried to create a polemical situation by taking advantage of Falla's refusal. Their motive was to attack the Republicans. Falla had other, deeper reasons for declining. On 8 June 1932, he wrote a long letter to Ballesteros, amongst which he said:

    The Christians of Spain passed through moments of bitterness and profound pain; but I understand that we must never serve ourselves from religion like a political arm, nor employ personal attack, nor any similar thing. . . . In my judgement, the true Catholic must always be recognized by his hunger and thirst for justice and his love for charity.[16]

3. His alliance with Jacques Maritain, whose complete works he treasured and possessed during his last years in Argentina;

    I have received "Art et Scolastique" and you cannot imagine my joy to have the book from you yourself, for apart from the admiration maintained for a man like you, certain coincidences of aspirations cause me to love your work in a very special way.[17]

4. His deep study of religious and mystical writings as attested to by the holdings in his personal library, such as those of the 16th century mystic, St. John of the Cross, a personal connection Falla felt for he came to live in the Carmen de los Mártires, a few feet from the Convento de los Santos Mártires de Carmelitas Descalzos, and was a "brother of Carmen."[18]
5. His differences with the right-wing sector, as seen in his rebuttal to Ramiro de Maeztu, and written on his behalf by his sister María del Carmen on 8 July 1936:

Don Manuel is very sorry that he cannot agree on many points in your letter. In his opinion, the Revolution was not fundamentally the work of writers and philosophers, but rather the result of the fact that Catholics had forgotten their principles of justice and love, which are essential to Christian belief. For this reason God permitted the revolutionary scourge, in order to teach and punish all of us, and to purify and clear the air, as Maritain puts it in one of his works. For Don Manuel de Falla, the only solution for this is not a conservative counter-revolution, which would certainly retain the execrable, but rather another deeper and more noble revolution, guided by the love of God, above all things, and of our neighbor, as you would have him love you. Until this comes about it is useless to resort to tradition . . . there is only one consistently truthful and worthwhile tradition, the eternal tradition of the word of God; any other is imperfect and impure and should be constantly corrected and purified, because every age demands new solutions and more generosity and love for our fellows. What does not conform to this represents nationalist traditionalism which will finish, like any exaggerated nationalism, by opposing Christ's genuine teachings.[19]

6. His appeals for restoration of Christian values in Spain, as expressed to his old friends Fernando de los Ríos and Manual Azaña, now prime minister and president of the new Republic respectively.

To Fernando de los Ríos, his longtime friend and collaborator with García Lorca on the *El cante jondo* pamphlet, he wrote on 23 January 1932:

. . . it is such that the bitterness of my spirit and so deep the protest that inspires me the reiterated task of de-Christianization of Spain, that I decided to write. . . . You remember our conversations about Saint Augustín, about the Christian State and about the "necessity to evangelize Spain" (these were your own words). And you ask now: "How will this evangelization be accomplished when the child is deliberately separated . . . from the idea of God and from His Law, the Crucifixion is taken out of the schools, rebellion is inculcated in the conscience of the child . . . the Holy Name of God is cut out of all manifestation of official character, permitting, in turn, that impure blasphemies will be offered publicly?". . .

"Why confuse an anticlerical position with an anti-Christian offensive?"

"Why this 'official' obligation to make the Republic antipathetic to all true Christianity, for the anti-monarchy that it is? In the name of 'Liberty,' until we are want to prohibit, with wrong ties that arrange our own cadavers, converting the Cemetery (The Holy Camp for the Christians) into a municipal depository of human plunder.

The State severely punishes rebellion against its laws, but leaves un-punished, and up to a certain point, sometimes, stimulates this rebellion, when it is manifested against God and against the Doctrine of Christ and I ask: does not the religious susceptibility of the Spanish Christians deserve at least the same respect that is given to the Moors and the Jews of Mo-rocco? Or is it that the School of the Arab States, which is projected to be established in Spain, will be prohibited to study the Koran?

I cannot believe that a correct conscience, as yours is, remains insensi-tive before the tremendous responsibility that will unite the religious school material if it wants to be established in Spain. I am certain that the proba-tion of this politic could not consume you without your conscience forcibly fighting to win the sense of responsibility. Why do we suppose . . . that someone, even though insensitive to the virtue of a medicine for the health of others, would produce, in exchange, a very efficient result: how, know-ing this strange benefit, could someone, in clear conscience, impede it, or at least, make it difficult?

Clearly this . . . represents the imposition of forces in those that so exist the feeling of responsibility; like the dramatic situation of the governed? that is seen as insipid to them, but these are political realities in which I do not pretend to get mixed up in: I simply want to mention those deeds. . . .

Then I add that Christianity represents a moral law that has not stopped being the essence of our civilization, of our legislation, and of our customs.

. . . My friendship for you is always, and the same frankness of which I speak is proof of it. Only I have pretended to deposit my most intimate bit-terness in your mind and in your heart.[20]

Months later, on 13 August 1932, Falla again appealed to him:

My dear friend:

I have always taken the utmost care not to do or say anything that could belittle in the slightest detail Spain's prestige to the eyes of a foreigner. But I am amazed to see that in a touristic city, such as Granada, foreigners have witnessed and comment on, with evident damage to the national prestige which many of us had tried so conscientiously to maintain intact, the un-punished violence which has been committed there without any military or political reason to justify it. Last night, in spite of the measure taken at last, the San Nicolás church was still burning to the ground, while someone rang the bells unashamedly . . . Spain is pitiful, and between one and an-other they are going to keep on destroying it!

I am not judging, nor am I the right person to do so, where the blame of what has happened should lie, I only wish to refer to them and the grievous impression they have had on thousands of people with clear consciences, and I am sure that yours too is deeply shaken by such abominable crimes.

You know perfectly well what my ideals are, that they go beyond political limits, and it is my heart's desire that the injustice suffered by the pop-
ulation and their needs be alleviated and put to right. I am one of the first
to condemn the senseless political-military movement which has given rise
to the events in Granada, where that movement has not the least support. It
is tragic that, to all appearances, those who should upkeep law and order
have sat back, and only at the very end have they attempted to give the impression that they exist. I tell you all this, not only to give a dear friend
trustworthy information, but also to a man responsible to the government
of Spain, and as a protest (respectfully, but with the noble indignation of a
Christian, a Spaniard and as an artist) to all of those who lie you share this
tremendous responsibility. My conscience and my honor oblige me to do
so. On the contrary I would hold myself, to a certain degree, responsible
too for the "acquiescence" which has facilitated countless irreparable and
punishable deeds. I am so sincere in what I say that, as I write to you, I feel
my conscience free itself from the weight which oppresses it, because it is
my firm belief that in the present chaotic situation, silence means com-
plicity with evil. I wish to do everything in my power to prevent the repetition of such evil. Can you believe that yesterday some people tried to in-
cite the destruction of the Alhambra Palace? . . .

I want to finish by assuring you that, as always, I have spoken to you
with "my heart on my sleeve" following your insistent requests that I
should do so. Likewise—from the bottom of our hearts—we have thought
about you and your family and the dreadful misfortune you have suffered
with the loss of your sister (who is in God's grace), endorsing once again
the deep feelings we expressed in our telegram.

Your sincere and faithful friend,

Manuel de Falla[21]

Falla reproached Manuel Azaña's anticlericalism. On 23 May 1936,
Falla appealed to Azaña, his old friend who wrote the 1920 review of the
debut of *El sombrero de tres picos*, to exercise his "supreme authority" as
president of the Republic to effect changes in Spain:

My DISTINGUISHED friend,

I take this opportunity to sincerely congratulate you on your rise to the
Presidency of the Republic and to express a heartfelt desire, shared by
many Spaniards: that these bitter times come to an end in which Spanish
Christians have suffered the destruction of temples, in which public and
collective blasphemies have gone unpunished—commencing with the
most horrendous insults against the Holy Name of God, revered up to now
over the centuries and by all the educated and ignorant people of this
land—and in which people who consecrated their lives to charity have
been martyred. Thus I beg you, not just as president of the Republic but as

a man of fine literary sensibility whom I consider my friend, to help us at this difficult time by exercising your supreme authority.

With this hope I write you this letter, the first in a long time, because of a serious illness caused by these sacrilegious events, which has endangered my life. Rest assured that I speak to you solely as a Catholic, free from any political (which I have never had) or purely humanistic interest, which I have always considered reprehensible.

Sincerely wishing you, as a good Christian and a faithful friend, every success with your presidential work. I gladly send you my respect and affection,

Manuel de Falla[22]

FALLA'S WILLS

Falla clearly repudiated totalitarianism. One of the most significant actions that Falla took during these agitated years, apart from refusing any kind of special treatment or state protection from the politically ambitious, through the use of his famous name, was to write and revise his last will and testament. This was done in February of 1932, on 9 August 1935, and on 4 August 1936. He began to sign his letters with a symbol of the cross inscribed by the Latin word for peace, *pax*. This symbol appears on his wills. In typical Falla style, it may be noted that he initiated his first will at the beginning of a new seven-year cycle, 1932. This was perhaps not by chance, even though precipitated by the violence of his surroundings. Falla strongly believed that his life fell into seven-year periods and this one would mark the beginning of the penultimate phase. The wills reaffirm his religious faith, while remembering those who helped him in this life.

Falla's Will Dated February 1932

In the Holy Name of GOD, Father, Son, and Holy Spirit, I declare my will that my cadaver be taken to a sacred place and put in a sepulchre, all according to the Roman Catholic ritual, to whose Holy Church I have the glory to belong.

I equally require, in the most formal and terminant way, that the execution and scenic interpretation of my works is always preserved—and without any possible exception—the cleanest Christian moral, as such they always are accompanied by works of evident dignity of moral and artistic spirit.

Granada, February of 1932

Signed: *Manuel de Falla*

Falla's Will Dated 9 August 1935

And it is also my firm will that if my inheritors do not need, *as indispensable living means*, the products of the author's rights that the *scenic* representations of my works provide, such representations would be prohibited. And this will of mine must be scrupulously observed when my theatrical works and moreover all the others come to be in the *public domain*.

(Equally I confirm how much I have consigned earlier with respect to the scenic interpretation of my works and to those that may accompany them in those programs of production.)

Granada, 9 August 1935

Signed: *Manuel de Falla*

Falla's Will Dated 4 August 1936

In the Holy Name of GOD, FATHER, SON, AND HOLY SPIRIT I give beginning to this Second part of my will.

It is my expressed will to designate as inheritors-executors, for the national and foreign values, as well as the sums that can be left to be deposited in my name in banks in Spain or in other countries, and of which rights that are awarded my works (editorial rights, listening rights, performance rights, production rights, etc., etc.) to my beloved brother and sister Doña María del Carmen de Falla y Matheu and don Germán de Falla y Matheu, who will reserve for themselves the amount indispensable for taking care of all their needs within a discreet and Christian modesty, giving the rest, as much as to attend, with the most possible freedom, to other needs, such as suffrages for my soul and for those of our dead in the form and the mode then determined, thus contributing, if be necessary, and in the needed proportion, to sustain the Purity in our Holy Catholic Church. Also it is to be secured the cost of a lamp, as representation of our souls, that burns constantly before the Cibary of the parochial Church.

In that which concerns the suffrages before-mentioned in my will, which independently of that which is celebrated during the Month of Animas of each year, as, according to the established custom, is celebrated for my soul at my death and continue celebrating in successive years, accompanied always by pure activities, is dedicated others in the same way to the holy memory and the eternal rest of our beloved parents (and in a very special way on the dates of their birthdays and in the festivals of San José and the Holy name of Jesus), as well as in suffrage of our grandparents and all of our dead relatives, to that which is added others for the soul of the Priest of Christ, don Francisco de Paula Fedriani, my first confessor and spiritual director and to whom I owe the most holy and clean counsels and instructions to guarantee my religion and to find to complete the obligations that it imposes with all humility, disciple of

Our Lord Jesus Christ. (In the days 2 April and 27 November of each year the said suffrages are to be celebrated in a special way.) Adding moreover others, in a general way, for the souls of those who were my other confessors, my music professors, my benefactors and my loyal friends, are special mention of those who started me or helped me perfect the duty of my office, beginning with don Clemente Parodi (my good teacher of initiation), for Sister Eloísa Galluzzo, who together with my dear Mother started me in music, as well as for don Felipe Pedrell and don José Tragó, all faithful Christians and apt, consequently, for which the mercy of God and the intercession of Our Lady makes pure the suffrages offered for the eternal rest of their souls.

And here I finish the 2nd and next-to-last part of my testamentary arrangements, in the day 4 August 1936.

Signed: *Manuel de Falla*

Handwritten: This copy faithfully conforms to the original. Manuel de Falla.[23]

NOTES

1. From the inaugural session of Federico Sopeña's induction into the Academia de Bellas Artes de San Fernando. *La música en la vida espiritual*. Madrid: Taurus Ediciones, S. A., 1958.

2. Federico Sopeña Ibañez, "La Espiritualidad de Manuel de Falla" in *Manuel de Falla tra la Spagna e l'Europa*. Edited by Paslo Pinamonti. Florence: Leo S. Olschki, 1989, 73–74.

3. Ibid.

4. Ibid.

En el Falla adolescente y joven, decidida ya su vocación de músico, aparece una singular y no atrayente figura que va a dominar casi, o sin casi, de manera despótica. En la España de final de siglo la regulación religiosa y apostólica de la juventud masculina estaba monopolizada por los Jesuitas, en forma de la llamada Congregación de los Luises, caracterizada por su fervor mariano puesto de manifiesto el día 8 de diciembre, festividad de la Inmaculada Concepción. . . . El Padre Fedriani no era jesuita sino clérico secular, libre, con bastantes medios de fortuna que le permiten viajar a Madrid y tener casa en Cádiz, en Dos Hermanas y más tarde en Córdoba. Tenemos en el Archivo un mamotreto de cartas, telegramas y postales dirigidas a Falla, pero lamentablemente no las respuestas, que el Padre destruía.

Llamo la atención sobre el siguiente detalla: en la España de entonces, a los sacerdotes seculares no se les llama Padres sino Don. Pero esto de Padre se lo asimila de inmediato el cura y no cesa de llamar a Falla hijo, hijo del alma, con tal insistencia que empalaga. Se mete a regular todo, hasta el mínimo detalle, incluso las lecciones con Pedrell: sin duda alguna de ahí viene una tendencia al escrúpulo que será fondo de neurosis para toda la vida de Falla. Pienses que en estos años la situación de la familia es de tragedia económica, de horrible agobio.

Falla no indica ningún deseo de ser sacerdote, ni siquiera célibe: eso vendrá más tarde. Conocemos el nombre, apellido y retrato, símbolo de un amor frustrado, que luego pasó y esta señora formó parte con su marido del círculo granadino de amigos de Falla. En este tiempo, hasta 1907, permanece la dictadura del Padre Fedriani, que le señala rezos, oraciones y actitudes hasta la asfixia.

5. Sopeña, Frederico (November 1976) "Fallas artista cristiano" in *Revista Arbor* CCCLXXI, November, 1976, 191–202.

6. From concert programs at the AMF there are those in Paris on 5, 7, 14, and 21 November 1911, as well as two in Madrid on 13 and 15 November. None are found for October or December. The author is in the process of checking the *Lotus Bleu* Archives in Paris.

7. "The Eleventh Principle—The Power of the Holy Spirit" in *Writings and Utterances of 'Abdu'l-Bahá Abbas*, Bahá'í Publishing Trust, New Dehli, India, 2001, 782–83. 'Abdu'l-bahá was in Paris from 3 October to 2 December 1911.

8. Crichton, *Manuel de Falla*, Chester Muisc: London, 1983, 4.

9. Crichton, 1983, 4.

10. Sopeña, 1976, 192.

Cuando analizamos la vida de los grandes maestros de la música contemporánea nos encontramos lo siguiente: frente a la cuidada antología de desvergüenzas que cosechamos en las vidas de los grandes músicos del siglo pasado, los de nuestro mundo, los grandes, como Stravinsky, Schönberg, Bartók, Webern, han afirmado un exterior decoro de vida, un orden, un cierto admirable pudor que es ya testimonio. En el caso de Falla se da eso y más: todas las características de su obra de arte, la fundamental de una hondísima pasión que se crucifica por una exigencia perpetua de obra bien hecha, lo son también de su vida. Pero más, más: durante no pocos años y precisamente por unas necesarias coordenadas de antirromanticismo, se extremaba la cercanía del artista al artesano, al funcionario casi. No: creemos que el artista necesita lleva una vida aparte, pero, por aparte, de muchísima mayor exigencia. Don Manuel de Falla aporta, en primer lugar, algo que es a la vez exigencia de sacrificio y presencia de pasión sublimada al máximo: el celibato. Sobre él, sobre su religiosidad, Falla, misteriosamente, con unos granos de sal andaluza para cada cruz, edifica una vida al margen. Enemigo de la bohemia, pero incapaz de la burocracia, de la nómina; una vida en la que todo es significativo porque todo se quiere depurado, sobrio, limpio, personal. . . .

11. Miguel Alonso, in his article "Christian Testimonies of Manuel de Falla" cites many examples of Falla's personal religious conviction in his daily life. There are frequent references of gratitude to God for his return to good health, for the fact that the concerts went well, for strength in the middle of calamities, for the "good disposition" to maintain his musical work, etc. (*Ara*, 1976).

12. Sopeña, 1958.

13. Sopeña, 1976, 193.

14. Harper, "Si Falla vivirá y escuchará mis obras dodecafónicas seguro estoy que se escandalizaría. Él, [sic] que creía en la ley eterna de la tonalidad, se hubiera negado a admitir que era un hecho cierto el derrumbamiento de la tonalidad. Yo hubiera tratado de aclararle que mi adscripción al dodecafonismo no representaba un cambio substancial de posición estética ni de ideología musical, y que continuaba siendo uno de sus más fieles discípulos. . . ." Kurt Pahlen "Rodolfo Halffter en la Música de su Tiempo" Heterofonia XV/2, April–June, 1982, 35.

15. Segura, Manuel. "Semblanza religiosa de Manuel de Falla" in *Razón y fe*, July–August, 1976, 93.

16. Sopeña, 1976, 94.

17. Sopeña, 1976, 78; letter Falla-Maritain, Granada, 26-5-1928, AMF.

18. Nommick, Granada, 51.

19. Falla-Fernando Ríos written by María del Carmen.

20. Falla-Fernando de los Ríos, AMF.

21. Ibid.

22. Falla-Manuel Azaña cited in Sopeña, *Vida y Obra de Falla*. Madrid: Turner, 1988, 85.

23. Sopeña, 1988, 244–45. (For an alternative translation, see Andrew Budwig's doctoral dissertation, "Manuel de Falla's '*Atlántida*': An Historical and Analytical Study," University of Chicago, 1984, Appendix F, 457–461.)

En el Santo Nombre de DIOS, Padre, Hijo y Espíritu Santo, declaro mí voluntad de que sean (n is crossed out) mí cadáver conducido a lugar sagrado y en él sepultado, todo ello según el rito Católico-romano, a cuya Santa Iglesia tengo la gloria de pertenecer.

Igualmente exijo, del modo más formal y terminante, que en la ejecución e interpretación escénica de mis obras se conserve siempre—y sin ninguna posible excepción—la más limpia moral cristiana, así como que sean siempre acompañadas por obras da evidente dignidad de espíritu moral y artística.

Granada, Febrero de 1932

Firmado: *Manuel de Falla*

Y es también mi firme voluntad que si mis herederos no necesitasen, *como medios indispensables de vida*, los productos de los derechos de autor que provengan de las representaciones *escénicas* de mis obras, dichas representaciones sean prohibidos. Y esta voluntad mía debe de ser escrupulosamente observada cuando mis obras teatrales y todas las demás restantes pasan a ser *de dominio público*.

(Igualmente confirmo cuanto he consignado anteriormente respecto a la interpretación escénica de mis obras y a las que puedan acompañarles en los programas de espectáculos.)

Granada, 9 de Agosto 1935

Firmado: *Manuel de Falla*

En el Santo Nombre de DIOS, PADRE, HIJO Y ESPIRITU SANTO doy comienzo a esta Segunda parte de mi testamento.

Es mi expresa voluntad designar como herederos-albaceas, tanto de los valores nacionales y extranjeros, como de las sumas que pueda dejar depositadas a mi nombre en bancos de España o de otros países, y de cuantos derechos devenguen mis obras (derechos editoriales, de audición, de ejecución, de representación, etc., etc.), a mis amados hermanos doña María del Carmen de Falla y Matheu y don Germán de Falla y Matheu, que reservarán para sí mismos las sumas indispensables para atender a todas sus necesidades dentro de una discreta y cristiana modestia, destinando el resto, tanto para atender, con la mayor liberalidad posible, a ajenas necesidades, como a sufragios por mi alma y por las de nuestros difuntos en la forma y el modo luego determinado, así como para contribuir, de ser necesario, y en la debida proporción, al sostenimiento del Culto en nuestra Santa Iglesia Católica. También se seguirá costeando una lámpara que en representación de nuestras almas, arda constantemente ante el Sagrario de la Iglesia parroquial.

En los que concierne a los sufragios antes indicados es mi voluntad, que, independientemente de los que se celebren dentro del Mes de Animas de cada año, así como, según la costumbre establecida, se celebren por mi alma a mi fallecimiento y sigan celebrándose en años sucesivos, acompañados siempre de eficaces limosnas, se dediquen otros en la misma forma a la santa memoria y al eterno descanso de nuestros amados padres (y de modo muy especial en las fechas de aniversario y en las fiestas de San José y del Santo nombre de Jesús), así como en sufragio de nuestros abuelos y de todos nuestros demás difuntos, a las que se añadirán otros por el alma del Sacerdote de Cristo don Francisco de Paula Fedriani, mi primer confesor y director espiritual y a quien debo los más santos y eficaces consejos y instrucciones para afianzar mi religión y para procurar cumplir las obligaciones que ella impone a todo humilde discípulo de Nuestro Señor Jesucristo. (En los días 2 de Abril y 27 de Noviembre de cada año se han de celebrar de modo especial dichos sufragios.) Añádanse todavía otros, de un modo general, por las almas de quienes fueron mis demás confesores, mis maestros, mis bienhechores y mis amigos fieles, son especial mención de quienes me iniciaron o procuraron perfeccionar en el cumplimiento de mi oficio, comenzando por don Clemente Parodi (mi buen maestro de primera enseñaza), por Sor Eloísa Galluzzo, que en unión de mi muy querida Madre me inició en la música, así como por don Felipe Pedrell y don José Tragó, todos fieles cristianos y aptos, por consiguiente, para que la misericordia de Dios y la intercesión de Nuestra Señora hagan eficaces los sufragios ofrecidos por el descanso eterno de sus almas.

Y aquí termino la 2ª y penúltima parte de mis disposiciones testamentarias, en el día 4 de Agosto de 1936.

Firmado: *Manuel de Falla*

Handwritten: Esta copia es verdaderamente conforma al original. Manuel de Falla

Chapter 8

Falla as Educator

While Falla has denied ever wanting to be considered as the head of a musical "school," his innate talent for educating others and his profound influence on the younger generation of composers around him, such as the those of the "Generación del '27" (Generation of '27), cannot be denied. His pedagogical talent began in childhood. During the six years of his boyhood imaginary city of Atlantis, complete with newspapers and journals, Falla instructed his fellow pupils how they could avoid the terror of examinations. This practice was serialized in his publications of *El Mês Colombino*, *El Burlón*, and *El Cascabel*. He took his own advice when he successfully completed the entrance exams for the undergraduate degree, *bachillerato*.[1]

The age-old debate of whether a child is born innately talented and knows everything that should eventually be developed or whether the child is not the product of his innate talent but rather his environment—the nature-nurture debate—is certainly a case for study in Falla's musical and stylistic evolution. In most musical lives both aspects are apparent: the child is born gifted, but is shaped by his contacts with the musical personalities who come into his world at critical, or impressionable, periods.

In Falla's case, he was not considered to be a child prodigy, but was multifaceted and multitalented. His delicate and sensitive nature left him open to considerable influences throughout most of his adult life. What was immediately obvious in Falla's musical development was his early predilection for theater, his great powers of imagination, and his ability to concentrate for long periods of time in the projects that he created and which absorbed him.

Falla's mature adult life coincided with one of the most fascinating periods of all Western musical history—the first half of the twentieth century. To be alive and active as a composer, especially in Europe and especially in Paris—as Falla was—was a great bounty and a great stimulus. Joaquin Nin-Culmell, whose father (the famous pianist-composer Joaquín Nin) Falla was well acquainted with in Paris, gives his impression of Falla as pedagogue.[2] Nin-Culmell asks: *How was Falla as a pedagogue? Initiator? Advisor? Inspirational? Sower of seeds? As a man, as a composer, as a Catholic, Falla always taught that which he was, and that which he was was always a lesson.*[3]

According to Nin-Culmell:

1. The first thing learned was not to call Falla "maestro," but to address him as "don Manuel."[4] This was because, for Falla, there was only one Maestro. Falla never taught "Falla."
2. Falla abhorred the idea of creating a school. His advice to young composers was not to do as he had done, not to emulate or imitate his technique, but to find their own way, their own answers to their own musical questions. His was his way and not transferable. He followed the voice from inside him. For him, knowledge was nothing without the inspiration of the Holy Spirit.[5]
3. Falla also advised not using the piano too often while composing, a tool he often employed. "The fingers are useful, but must not dictate the music" was good advice.[6]
4. Principles were more important than musical form. Counterpoint is very much more important than the fugue, even though the fugue is a crystallized form while counterpoint, to the contrary, is more principles than form.

As might be expected, another quality that Falla esteemed was that of truthfulness, in students and family alike. One such example of educating his niece, Maribel (María Isabel de Falla, daughter of his brother, Germán), clearly shows this characteristic.

His love of truth is one of the most vivid images that I store in my memory. When I was with him, he discovered one time that I had lied and this was the cause that he became disgusted with me for several days. I didn't forget that he seized me by the shoulders and with great energy he told me never to lie again in my life. He punished me by not letting me hear him play the piano, which was one of the things that I liked the most.[7]

Given Falla's deep religious nature, it could be construed, by some, that in his adult years he was subconsciously emulating the role of the priests by exerting influence upon young composers. In spite of all his hopes for not creating a "school" or following, the inevitable happened. For the "Grupo de los Ocho" (Group of Eight) Spanish composers, Falla became their model. The quantity of new music performed at the Madrid Student Residence, "La Residencia de Estudiantes," (the "Resi") testifies to this fact.

In an article published in the *Daily Mail* (18 July 1919) entitled "To The Young Composer. Senor Manuel de Falla and German Formalism," Falla's feelings about not creating "schools" are made very clear. "If there is a "chief" among Spanish composers it is, he would say, the veteran Felipe Pedrell."[8] Falla continued,

> But he [Pedrell] is an individualist. He will not admit the term "school of composers."
>
> Music can only be the utterance of an individual. A "school" cannot compose music. What it can most easily do is to frustrate the individuality of the young. Oh, young composer! I am middle-aged enough to exhort "do speak freely after your own heart. This freedom is the hardest thing to achieve. It is the only one worth while."
>
> To the musician's heart music is implicit in all things, in the gait of folk as in the cadence of their speech, in the colour of the river, and in the outline of the hills in the landscape.
>
> Now this is why I am at daggers drawn with German formalism. Schubert and Mendelssohn no doubt spoke after their own hearts, but I cannot have it that the art of such men (or any) is to be a fixed norm in music.
>
> Ah, we too have in Spain the academics who set their pupils to write, say, a quartet in the manner of Mendelssohn. But that manner, of course, excludes all that the young man's heart is saying—for Mendelssohn's alien manner necessarily knows nothing of the special music implicit in our Spanish scene, in the gait and speech of our folk, in the outline of our hills. Such a task is nothing but noxious.
>
> Most nineteenth-century music is to be mistrusted, and as regards the classical symphonies and concertos the teacher's one duty is to utter warnings against them. The freedom and spontaneity of the eighteenth century were only recaptured by such non-German composers as Rimsky-Korsakoff and Debussy. Friends, the grammar of music is not fixed, like Attic Greek! The one way of studying it is to follow its course of development, preferably as exemplified in one's own country.[9]

Strong words indeed, but Falla had very clear ideas and stayed with them. And interestingly enough, Falla outlined an entire curriculum for the training of orchestration for young composers. In the AMF is housed a document sketched "Memory for the Study of the Modern Orchestra in the Musical Composition Class of the National Conservatories."[10] Falla's interview "¿Cómo ven la nueva juventud española?" championed young Spanish composers. He noted their austere working conditions at home, deplored their lack of performing conditions and publishing houses, and stressed the favorable conditions abroad, especially in Paris.

Falla too was a piano teacher for many years, although he seldom gave lessons after his rise to fame. Rosa García Ascot, later married to composer-musicologist Jesús Bal y Gay, benefited from Falla's pedagogical counsels, such as in the interpretation of his *Concerto* or in *Noches*, appearing with Falla in a two-piano version of this work.

In other ways too Falla was an educator—by the model of his life, by his search for truth, and through his meticulous way of investigating and analyzing works or ideas in order to re-create something entirely new. To paraphrase his own words regarding his teacher, Pedrell: *FALLA was a TEACHER in the highest sense of the word; through his doctrine, and with his example, he led Spanish musicians towards a profoundly national and noble art. . . .*

NOTES

1. Demarquez, 2.
2. At the request of his mother, Falla gave some compositional counsels to Nin-Culmell in Granada.
3. Nin-Culmell, Joaquín, "Manuel de Falla, pedagogo" in *Revista de Occidente*, no. 188, December, 1996, 38. "¿Como era Falla como pedagogo? ¿Iniciador? ¿Consejero? ¿Inspirador? ¿Sembrador? Como hombre, como compositor, como católico, Falla siempre euseñaba lo que era, y lo que era siempre fue una lección."
4. Nin-Culmell, 41.
5. Nin-Culmell, 38, 40.
6. Nin-Culmell, 41.
7. Garrido Lopera, 28. "Su amor a la verdad es una de las imágenes que más vivamente guardo en la memoria. Mientras estuve con él, descubrió una vez que había dicho una mentira y esto fue causa de que estuviera disgustado conmigo varios días. No olvidaré que me cogió por los hombros y con gran energía me dijo que jamás había que mentir en la vida. Él me castigaba no dejándome ir a escucharle tocar el piano, que era una de las cosas que más me gustaban."
8. *Daily Mail* (18 July 1919) "To The Young Composer. Senor Manuel de Falla and German Formalism." AMF.
9. Ibid.
10. "Memoria sobre el estudio de la orquesta moderna en las clases de composición musical de los conservatorios nacionales." AMF 8937.
11. Sopena, *Escritos,* 4th ed., 127–28.

Chapter 9

Falla and the Piano

The piano, like the human voice, was central to Falla the musician. He was an excellent pianist, having won a national competition against Spain's best pianists. Although he was, at times, occupied with other "familial" instruments—the harmonium, the harpsichord, the harp-lute, the harp, the guitar, the *pianola* (player piano)—the piano played a pivotal role in Falla's life as a composer and particularly as a performing artist. Even though Debussy and Ravel had no *sostenuto* pedals on their pianos and were pianistically hindered from taking advantage of this sonorous device, Falla's aim, on the other hand, went beyond pianistic conception. His very original way of emulating aspects of *cante jondo* in *Fantasía bætica* through the use of the damper pedal and the juxtaposition of dissonances, derived from Lucas's theories, is enlightening. Too, his Pleyel piano in Granada possessed a harpsichord stop.[1] And Falla used the *una corda* pedal for special effects or for timbric contrasts. Like Stravinsky, he often used the piano to aid him in his compositional work. Wherever he went, he was always with a piano in his residence, the only luxury he permitted during his years of struggle. The piano, for Falla, was essential, even though he did not write many solo works for it. Without this instrument, Falla would have been quite another musician.

SOME OF FALLA'S PIANO-RELATED BOOKS

The early influence of Eloísa Galluzzo regarding Falla's piano formation in Cádiz has already been mentioned in chapter 1. However, a piano guide by S. Orelgamar, *El auxiliar del pianista. Modelos de ejercicios, escalas y arpegios; fragmentos de estudios y otras obras, tal como deben de estudiarse para adquirir la perfección* (The Pianist's Assistant, Models of exercises, scales and arpeggios; fragments of studies and other works, such as those must be studied in order to acquire perfection),[2] was given to Falla by his former teacher during his Paris years. Its dedicatory reads: "To my old and distinguished disciple, the eminent pianist Manuel Falla Matheu as proof of admiration and true affection. Sister Eloísa Galluzzo, Madrid, 30 November 1909." The book was published in this same year.

The author of the book himself says that the idea is not to write a method, but to assist those students, most of whom, "do not know how to study by themselves." Two main objectives are found—what to study and how to study—those of the study of the "mechanism" or technique of playing the piano, and the other of how to organize the study time.

The technical suggestions include how to choose a method and how to choose a teacher. With regard to the choice of methods, such as those foreign ones (by Adam written in 1812, Kalkbrenner, Herz, Bertini, Le Couppey, and others) or Spanish ones (by Compta, Albéniz, Miró, or Montalbán's *La unión artística* or The Artistic Union and the "excellent" work *Escuela elemental de Piano* or Elemental School of Piano), the objective is the same: to "fortify the fingers, make them equal, to make them flexible, independent, and finally apt to execute with perfection all classes of pianistic works."[3] Amongst the exercises included are found some by Bertini, Kalkbrenner, Czerny, Kullak, Cramer, Clementi, Heller, and works by Handel, Bach, Steibelt, Dussek, Mozart, Chopin, and Weber.

Orelgamar's advice includes Felix Le Couppey's classification (translated from the French) of various works in the piano repertory, as well as his own suggestions as how to divide one's practice time always keeping in mind "awareness" while practicing.[4] He counsels children to begin with only one hour daily and two sessions of half an hour each. This division of time is the guiding principle for more advanced students who must practice several hours daily. For example,[5]

1st Session	2nd Session
½ hr. exercises of fixed position and extension	½ hr. exercises of the thumb, scales and arpeggios
½ hr. Study (Étude)	½ hr. Sonata or piece

1st Session	2nd Session	3rd Session
½ hr. exercises of fixed position and extension	½ hr. exercises of the thumb, scales, and arpeggios	¼ hr. scales or thumb exercises
½ hr. Study (Étude)	½ hr. Sonata or piece	¼ hr. easy sight-reading ½ hr. review of old pieces

1st Session	2nd Session	3rd Session
½ hr. exercises of fixed position and extension	½ hr. scales and arpeggios	½ hr. review of old pieces
1 hr. of Études, one of which is technical	1 hr. Sonata or piece	½ hr. sight-reading

1st Session	2nd Session	3rd Session	4th Session
½ hr. exercises of fixed position	½ hr. of scales, preceded by thumb work	½ hr. sight-reading	½ hr. scales, arpeggios, 7ths, other exercises
1 hr. of Études	1 hr. piece	½ review of old pieces	½ hr. according to advice of teacher

From the lack of annotations and date of publication, Falla did not use this study himself. He was already a prize-winning pianist, but he may have recommended it to students or colleagues. In his childhood Falla had been exposed to *The Art of the Piano, Counsels Dedicated to the Youth*, by Robert Schumann, and indeed, one of his copies acquired in Cádiz is annotated.[6] Amongst those passages marked by Falla with *x* are the following:

1. "The education of the ear is of the most important. Procure this from the beginning, discerning each tone and tonality. Analyze every class of sounds: that which produces the bell, the glass . . . etc., etc.";[7]
2. "Play in time! The performance of many concert artists is perceived like running from a drunk. Do not follow similar models.";[8]
3. "You mustn't think who is listening to you when you play.";
4. "When they give you some composition to sight-read, don't forget to run your eyes over the entire work before beginning."[9]

Another book found in Falla's personal library is *Las formas pianísticas, orígenes y transformaciones de las formas instrumentales, estudiadas en los instrumentos de teclado moderno, tomo primero*, by Felipe

Pedrell[10] (The Pianistic Forms, Origins and Transformations of the Instrumental Forms, Studied in the Modern Keyboard Instruments, vol. 1). Pedrell gives a systematic study of the sixteenth variations through the modern forms of the sonata and various dance-forms. Falla's copy is not annotated, probably because it was published and acquired at a time beyond Falla's formational period.

JOSÉ TRAGÓ (1856–1934)[11]

Before settling in Madrid, Falla had achieved local success in Cádiz. Shortly before he left his native city, tribute was paid to him in the *Diario de Cádiz* (*Actualidades*).[12] Soon afterwards another tribute was published in the same newspaper by a certain "V.", probably Salvador Viniegra. He notes that this "son of Cádiz" and student of Odero and Tragó (whose school of piano is the most correct), who does honor to these teachers, shows a pianistic personality closer to that of Piantó than to [Anton] Rubinstein. He sums up Falla's qualities as pianist by saying, "He executes the most difficult passages without any effort, and with the same apparent naturalness as the easy ones . . . he shows true artistic sentiment and exquisite delicacy."[13] The reviewer is surprised that Falla would choose works full of difficulties, but finds it not so surprising in chamber music or when accompanying concert artists. "I am sure the concert artists whom Falla accompanies . . . will not forget him, because it is not easy to find artists who can sublimate their own personalities when accompanying others. Such is the pianist."[14]

The writer then speaks of Falla's talents as a composer, using words such as "unhoped for," "inspired," "spontaneous," etc., and mentioning the fact that the *Melodía* for violoncello and piano, although written only in first position, nevertheless introduces difficult passages into the modulatory section, and thus can be enjoyed by the beginner or the concert artist. These are qualities, according to the reviewer, which are given to genius alone. The article is summed up by referring to Falla as an "eminent pianist" and one of the "best contemporary composers."[15]

Falla's advanced studies with José Tragó at the Madrid Conservatory had a deep impact upon him. Tragó, also a composer,[16] was considered to be one of the best performers in Spain. Often he arrived before giving lessons in order to play a bit. Naturally, the students all gathered outside his door to listen. And naturally, Tragó, when sensing they were there, stopped playing.[17]

Tragó had studied with Georges Mathias, a former child prodigy under Kalkbrenner's guidance and a pupil of Chopin from the age of twelve.[18] Mathias, however, did not use Chopin's beginning position of E-F#-G#-A#-B or the B major scale, preferring instead to have students begin with the white-keyed C major scale.[19] He also required that his students transcribe his *Conseils sur l'étude du Piano* (Counsels on the Study of the Piano) before beginning their lessons. There is no reference as to whether Falla had to do this with Tragó or not, although Tragó's copy of this document is found in the *Biblioteca Musical* (Musical Library) in Madrid.[20] Through Mathias a connection to Bach could also be made, as Chopin's first piano professor (and also a violinist) was Wojciech Żywny (1756–1842), who had been a pupil of one of the disciples of Bach. Thus, the Bach-Żywny-Chopin-Mathias-Tragó-Falla is also established.[21]

The Falla-Tragó correspondence in the AMF covers a span of thirty-two years, from 1897–1929, during which time he still referred to his student as "Manolito" (little Manuel). Falla's seriousness about his piano studies is reflected in several of these documents. In a letter dated 17 December 1899, to Falla's patron, Salvador Viniegra, Tragó writes:

> Our friend Falla set (as you have undoubtedly heard) a very high standard in the last end of term exams and competitions. He is a very studious and conscientious boy, with a good artistic nature, for whom a gratifying future surely awaits in our difficult art.[22]

Falla's commitment to the piano is readily evident from the detailed questions he asked. Tragó's response of 15 July 1897, sheds light on technical matters.[23] The pieces he mentions most likely were part of the official program of the Madrid Conservatory at that time and therefore requisites to the final exams.

> With respect to the pedal, there is much to speak about and it is difficult to terminate thus by letter the use that it must and can be used.
> In Paris exists a work entitled "Les pédales du Piano" (The Pedals of the Piano) by Falkenberg [sic].[24] You could ask for it and find something interesting, that which is always is useful.
> Some general lines about the pedal.
> —It can be used with impunity in arpeggios, chords, etc.
> —In the scales it has to be used little and with much care.
> —In the chromatic scales nothing.
> —In the high register of the piano (right hand) the pedal can be used more
> —than in the middle range and the low range. . . .
> —The pedal can be used in each new chord or change of harmony.
> —It can be used in the notes that have an accent, sf, etc.

—It can be used to connect the distances that the hand cannot reach and that are necessary to sustain.

—In the cantabile phrases . . . it must be used constantly, etc., etc.

—In order to make the 10ths of the last page of the Perpetual Motion of Weber the exercises of broken octaves can be used. In one of the studies in octaves of Czerny there is one that I believe you already played. In the 1st book of those of Clementi there is another also very useful for the objective. This is in Eb major. Also you can make an exercise with the left hand in broken tenths and chromatics. That is to say for the white and black keys. All this is useful and it is that which now occurs to me about the particular.

You say to me that after having worked the right hand carefully, some notes don't sound, or that if they sound they are not with the equality that you desire.

For equality [independence of the fingers] it is necessary to give each finger (above all the first and the fifth) the strongest force possible and to acquire there is nothing like the held notes.

. . . perfection thus will come with time and effort.

When I heard you in this, I did not observe that you had such unevenness as you imagine.

The Allegro of Saint-Saëns you can leave for a little later, as it is difficult and something original is very expensive.

From Merkte's exercises you may begin looking at the following: page 53 until n° 11 inclusive of [page] 56. Afterwards page 110 and 111 inclusive. . . .

Falla was quite determined and dedicated to his piano studies. More advice from Tragó is found in a letter dated 25 November 1897, when he gives interpretative advice about Schumann's *Arabesque* and *Carnaval de Vienna*, as well as cautions Falla not to use any kind of strange apparatus, like Schumann did, in order to strengthen his fingers.[25]

Don't use any type of rings or other trifles for style. I committed atrocities when I studied a lot and today I suffer the consequences in the form of muscular pains, tiredness, etc. It is then necessary to do the work systematically in order not to be destroyed, and to suppress the rings and other instruments of torture that in the long run can bring fatal consequences.

Tragó continues in this same letter to encourage Falla to work on studies other than those of Moscheles and to continue, in order, the *Concertista* of Czerny, which are excellent (especially the last ones) for the technique. He tells Falla he can work on Bach fugues (if he hasn't already) such as no. 11, 13, 15, 17, etc., and can follow the octaves of

Czerny. After doing this, he may then proceed to Kullak studies and can continue the Mertke exercises, especially those for thumb passages.

Surprisingly, from a letter written in June 1898, we learn that Falla is considering the vocation of piano teaching. This is in contrast to the famous statement he made about confirming his true calling as a composer when he was seventeen. Tragó responds to Falla's query about the teaching of piano and about the decision to dedicate himself to this vocation in Cádiz, noting ". . . the most important point of your last letter: . . . the question of the Teaching of the Piano and of the decision that you manifested to me to dedicate yourself to it in Cádiz, asking me moreover my opinion about the matter."[26]

Tragó assures Falla that he can make a great contribution to the teaching of the difficult art of playing the piano. This is because of Falla's advanced study of the instrument, the awareness that he brings to it, and the scrupulous study of technique (the base of all good teaching and all good pianists) are guaranteed to be more than sufficient for everyone to have confidence in him. Tragó then recommends two books for Falla: *Le manual de l'elève* [The Student Manual] by Hortense Parent (Libreria Hachette, Paris)—and "Mécan" [École de Mécanisme][27] by Marmontel. These books are not contained in Falla's personal library, but he could have acquired them. Some of his personal effects were lost upon leaving Paris for Madrid.

In another letter from February 1899 we learn that Falla is preparing for the sixth-year exam. Tragó tells Falla to study no. 17 of the Kalkbrenner pieces, as well as the last ("toccatta") [sic] and in general those that work the *staccato* touch. Tragó says that Falla has enough in his repertoire for the exam and that goes for fugues. With regard to the Cramer studies, he tells Falla not to worry as they are not required for the sixth-year exam. He notes that Falla has already studied several important works and that after finishing the B minor Concerto of Hummel he should look at another and it would be good if it were the finale of Mendelssohn's F# minor Fantasy. He also includes the technical-musical realization of a series of trills found on page fifty of the Peters Edition of the Hummel Concerto. In this example—a series of first inversion chords with trills on the upper notes—he advises that the lower notes be played with the left hand, while the right hand plays a continuous thirty-second note melissma based on the trill beginning on the principal note. Another counsel is regarding a Liszt transcription, which he says Falla may work on and is an excellent study for the wrist. The fingering that Falla indicated, while Tragó says is not bad, would be better instead of 5-1-2-1 and 2-1-4-1 (Falla) to use 5-3-2-1 and 5-4-2-1 (Tragó). This is because the passage in question is arpeggiated.

There is a decided difference in tone in Tragó's correspondence after Falla's winning the Ortiz y Cussó competition. Always helpful, Tragó begins to speak with Falla as more an equal. With Falla now teaching some pupils, Tragó urges him to be "rigid and severe" with those who do not study enough (30 August 1906). The aging Tragó, eventually retired, maintains his close ties with Falla throughout his life. Especially tender is one of his last letters, dated 10 December 1928, in which he says:

> My very dear friend: I have received your interesting concerto for harpsichord or piano, strings and winds, that you have had the kindness to send me. I must tell you that it will interest me and I will study it with great feeling. . . .

The letter is lengthy and after sending regards from his wife, Tragó signs it as "your old friend and admirer who cares for you and embraces you always, José Tragó."

EARLY PROFESSIONAL CONCERTS

One advice Falla did not take from Tragó was to delay his Conservatory exams. Anxious to complete this course of study so that he could begin to earn money to go to Paris, Falla completed his course in just two years. This was due to the permission and liberal attitude of the Conservatory's director and Falla's hard work.[28] From 1897–1898 he passed first, second, and third years of solfège, plus the first through the fifth years of piano with a high grade of "very good." From 1898–1899 he passed the remaining two years of piano subsequently being unanimously awarded the first prize. (Documents reproduced in Manuel Orozco Diaz's *Falla*. Barcelona: Salvat Editores, S. A., 1985, 28.)

Falla gave concerts in order to raise money, charging in 1897–1898 in Cádiz "three pesetas (about 80 cents) for a box and one peseta for a balcony seat."[29] Some of his early repertoire during the Madrid years naturally included the pieces he studied with Tragó and probably others: Schumann's *Arabesque* and *Romance*; Chopin's *Berceuse, Étude,* op. 10/3, *Polonaise*; Godard's *Valse,* Raff's *La Fileuse;* Weber's *Rondó;* Grieg's *Sonata in e minor,* op. 7; Saint-Saëns' *Allegro appassionata*; Mendelssohn's *Fantasia,* op. 28 and *Fugue in f minor*; works of

Paderewski, Daquin, and his own works of *Vals capricho, Serenata an-daluza,* and *Nocturno.* He also played ample chamber music, such as the Schumann Quartet in Eb, op. 47; or his own *Mireya, Serenata andaluza,* or *Melodía.*[30] He also gave piano lessons, charging two pesetas per hour, and lowering the price to six reales if the student objected to his price in order not to lose the student.

ORTIZ Y CUSSÓ PIANO COMPETITION

The piano competition has been discussed in chapter 2. Here is the review of Falla's presentation. From the *Diario de Cádiz,* dated 27 April 1905, the following opinion of the competition, obviously a rivalry between Marshall and Falla, we learn:

> Marshall is completely an artist. Technique, boldness, strength, expression, all these he combines. I didn't hear him but I have spoken about him, about his art of interpretation, about the poetical feeling of the works, and his convictions are those of an artist, those that have already a fixed criteria and an orientation. He studied with Granados, with Bauer, and with Risler, and hasn't wasted his time. His major success was obtained here in the works of Chopin and Schumann, of Scarlatti and in the "Campanella," that he played in a marvelous way.
>
> Manuel de Falla played yesterday. His art is completely internal, without concessions to the effect, without external showmanship, without the brilliance and the power that so easily conquers the applause. Neither the pianissimo is unclear, nor the fortissimo of powerful sonority. His executions always move in a medium tint: but in it what poetry, what intention, and what state of the soul so beautiful and so penetrating! Bach, Beethoven, Chopin, and Schumann shown in their versions with an austere, narrative and poetical spirit. Those of Scarlatti and Saint-Saëns were inferior in grace and delicacy to those of many other competitors.
>
> All of this above, with the exception of the first lines, was written before knowing the decision of the jury. For me it was a very interesting problem. Do the judges pronounce between two artists of equal stature for the interior art, or would prefer the more refined?
>
> My artistic convictions make me applaud without reserve the judgment that awards the prize to Sr. Falla and asks an honorable mention for Sr. Marshall from the Minister of Support [patronage], even though such Minister doesn't have anything to do with a prize that a private firm has established by its own and free will. But it is mentioned to Mr. Marshall and that only just.[31]

FIRST CONTACT WITH DEBUSSY

Falla's first contact with Debussy, beyond knowing some of his music, was through his request for interpretative advice when performing Debussy's piano transcription of the harp part of Debussy's *Danses*. (Falla did own and annotate Debussy's two piano transcriptions of "Danse sacrée" and "Danse profane" (*Danses*, Paris, Durand, 1904, 22 pages, for principal piano and second piano, orchestral reduction). AMF 304. Jacques Durand also published his own transcription of the work for piano solo in 1904. Here Debussy responds in a letter dated 13 January 1907, just a few weeks before the performance on 7 February.

> . . . what you ask me is quite difficult to answer! One cannot demonstrate the exact value of a rhythm just as one cannot explain the dreamy expression of a phrase! The best thing, in my opinion, is to refer it to one's own feelings. . . . For me, the color of the two dances is clearly contrasted. You must find some way of linking the "seriousness" of the first with the "humor" of the second for a musician like yourself it should not be difficult, and I believe that I can surrender myself to your judgement with complete confidence.[32]

Also regarding Debussy's pianistic advice, Falla remembered how Debussy wanted "only the hammers to strike and that the fingers not be transformed into hammers."[33]

From the program of the referred concert of "classical and modern music" on 7 February 1907, at the *Teatro de la Comedia* (Comic Theater) with Tomás Breton conducting a string orchestra, Falla played a very big program, further showing his dedication to performing:

- Part 1 = Schumann's *Kreisleriana*, op. 16 (no. 1, 3, 4, 5)
  Beethoven's Sonata, op. 27/2 ("Moonlight");
- Part 2 = Bach's Concerto in d minor ("for piano and with accompaniment of string orchestra");
- Part 3 = Debussy's *Danses* ("for piano and with accompaniment of string orchestra") of "Danse sacrèe" and "Danse profane."
  —Chopin's Ballade, no. 4
  —D'Indy's *Laufenburg* (Vals)
  —Paganini-Liszt *La Campanella*

For this concert Falla played on an Erard piano, offered by the Dotésio Firm. The public was asked neither to enter nor to leave the hall during the playing. Prices for the concert ranged from one to twenty-one pesetas.

SOME OTHER NOTEWORTHY RECITALS

Parallel to his dedication to composition, Falla continued playing the piano for most of his life, publicly or privately, solo or in chamber works. In what was probably his last public solo recital, given in Granada on 11 December 1927, Falla performed a program of only Scarlatti sonatas, most of them with an Iberian predisposition. Too, he used the recital venue to play works of his colleagues and/or to expound his musical views.

Also interesting are notes from a lecture-recital allegedly given in 1916 on the subject of *New Music*.[34] In the recital Falla, while demonstrating "new" classical forms performed the first movement of Ravel's *Sonatine* and the "Andante" from Debussy's Quartet. He showed folk influences by playing Bartók's "Dance of the Bears." Falla then used two pieces to contrast the sacred and the profane in Russian music from a fragment of the opening of the second scene (coronation of Boris) of Mussorgsky's *Boris Godunov* (1872) (an inspiration later in *Atlántida*?) and two scenes from Stravinsky's "*Le Sacre du Printemps*" (1913).

FALLA'S COMPOSITIONS FOR/WITH PIANO[35]

Falla works that include piano comprise the majority of his output, taking also into account the piano-vocal scores of the *zarzuelas* or of *La vida breve*. The categories listed in example 9.1 below contain the solo piano works, the piano transcriptions, the chamber works (vocal and instrumental), the theatrical works with piano, one work for piano and orchestra, and the *pianola* versions.

Example 9.1   Solo Piano Works—Original or Transcription[36]

Title	Date of Composition
Nocturno	1896
Mazurca en do menor	1899
Serenata andaluza (transcription?)	1900
Canción	1900
Vals capricho	1900
Cortejo de gnomos	1901
Serenata	1901
Allegro de concierto	1903–1904
La vida breve (Two Spanish Dances)	1905–1913
	Copyright 1923 by Max Eschig,
	J. W. Chester, and Wilhelm

	Hansen Edition held the rights for the British Commonwealth and South Africa
Pièces espagnoles	1906–1909
El amor brujo (Dance of Terror, The Fisherman's Song,[37] Ritual Fire Dance,Pantomime) from ballet version	AMF LXVIII Copyright for Ritual Fire Dance and Pantomime = 1921; copyright for Dance of Terror and The Fisherman's Song = 1922 by Chester
El sombrero de tres picos (Miller's Dance, Miller's Wife's Dance, Dance of the Neighbors) Final Dance (Jota)	1917–1919 Transcriptions copyrighted 1921 by Chester
Fantasía bǽtica	1919
Homenaje, pour le tombeau de C. Debussy (transcription)	1920
Canto de los remeros del Volga (arrangement)	1922
Pour le tombeau de Paul Dukas	1935

Instrumental Chamber Works with Piano—Including Transcriptions

Title	Date of Composition
Melodía para violonchelo y piano	1897
Romanza para violonchelo y piano	1898
[Pieza para violonchelo y piano en do mayor]	1898
Cuarteto en sol (vln.,.vla.,vlc., piano)[38]	1898–1899
Serenata andaluza (violin and piano)	1899
El amor brujo (sextet for piano + 2 violins, viola, violoncello, contrabass)—transcription	1915
Concerto (harpsichord or piano)	1923–1926

Vocal Chamber Works with Piano

Title	Date of Composition
Preludios ("Madre, todas las noches")	1900
Rima ("Olas gigantes")	1900
¡Dios mio, qué solos se quedan los muertos!	1900
Tus ojillos negros	1902–1903
Con afectos de jubilo y gozo	1908
Trois mélodies	1909–1910
Siete canciones populares españolas	1914
Oración de las madres que tienen a sus hijos en brazos	1914

Vocal Chamber Works with Piano (*continued*)

Title	Date of Composition
El pan de Ronda que sabe a verdad	1915
Canto de los remeros del Volga	1922
Psyché (voice and harp or piano)	1924
Soneto a Córdoba de Luís de Góngora (soprano and harp, or piano)	1927
Himno marcial (Pedrell) (voice, piano and drums)	1937

Theatrical Works with Piano

Title	Dates of Composition
La vida breve	1905–1913
El amor brujo (all versions)	1915+
El corregidor y la molinera	1916–1917
El sombrero de tres picos	1917–1919
Fuego fatuo (piano four hands)	1918–1919
El corazón ciego?	1919
Españoleta	1922
Atlántida (two pianos)	1927–1946

Works with Piano and Orchestra

Title	Date of Composition
Noches en los jardines de España	1909–1916
Piano treated as obligatto or for orchestral color more than as a piano concerto	

Arrangements for Pianola (Player Piano). Made for Pleyela in Paris

Title	Date of Composition
"Andalouza, pièce espagnole no. 4"; roll no. 8232	1921–1926
Song Accompaniments of the *Siete canciones populares españolas*; rolls no. 9333–93396	1921–1926
El sombrero de tres picos, based on Chester's edition of the piano-vocal score; rolls no. 8401–8405	1921–1926

The interchangeability of the piano with other instruments is an interesting aspect of Falla's aesthetic and compositional conception. For example, the harpsichord (*Concerto*), the harp (*Soneto a Córdoba*), the guitar and the harp-lute (*Le tombeau de Debussy*) are interesting choices whose special characteristics should be considered when performing those specific works on piano. Sometimes the substitution of one instrument for another was purely practical. For example, when Falla and García Lorca produced the Epiphany plays the harp-lute was used for the harpsichord. Or when a harpsichord was not available, Falla told Rosa García Ascot to play the *Concerto* on the piano with the harpsichord stop, "like the one he used when he played it in Madrid."[39] Falla's own Pleyel in Granada was this type of piano with its pedal system that was capable of transforming the piano into a harpsichord.[40] The only keyboard instrument not favored by Falla is the one closely associated with the church—the organ. This is a curious matter, but no doubt purposely intended.

Falla's use of the piano acoustically speaking was often experimental, not in the sense of a "prepared" piano as John Cage and others have used it, but in an aesthetical blending or search for new expression. One such example is found in the effects of the *cante jondo* in *Fantasía bœtica*. Desirous of expressing sonorities in microtones, he undoubtedly must have felt this frustration with the semitone limits of the piano, for in an article in *The Daily Mail* entitled "To the Young Composer Manuel de Falla and German Formalism," dated 18 July 1919 (the same year as the composition of *Fantasía bœtica*), Falla says, "Musical instruments, too—particularly keyed instruments like the piano—will no longer be tolerated if they cannot distinguish between, say, C sharp and D flat." Falla's solution in the *Fantasía bœtica* is quite original, which juxtaposes appoggiaturas of C and C sharp against B, for example.

Yvan Nommick, in his article, "L'évolution des effectifs instrumentaux dans l'œuvre de Manuel de Falla" (The evolution of the instrumental effects in the works of Manuel de Falla), sums up the various ways in which Falla uses the piano in the orchestra: (1) to reinforce the unison winds (Introduction and Scene from *El amor brujo*); (2) to reinforce the wind accents ("Canción del amor dolido"—Song of Painful Love—from *El amor brujo*); (3) to help double the basses ("Dance of Terror" from *El amor brujo*); (4) to help double the harmonics of the strings ("At Midnight" from *El amor brujo*); (5) to help double the *pizzicati* ("Canción del fuego fatuo"—Song of Foolish Love—from *El amor brujo*; and (6) to play the role of the harp or to associate with that instrument ("Miller's Dance" from *El sombrero de tres picos*).[41]

FALLA AND OTHER PIANISTS

During the Ortiz y Cussó competition in Madrid, Falla had the opportunity to compete against more than thirty of Spain's best pianists, Frank

Marshall being singled out as the most outstanding. Hearing these pianists Falla would have been aware of the level of playing in his own country. From the concert programs at the AMF, there is a steady trail of impressive pianists that Falla most likely heard at home or abroad. For example, from 1902–1911 he heard pianists Ignacy Jan Paderewski, Gabriel Fauré, Alfred Cortot, Joaquín Nin, Ricardo Viñes, Gabriel Pierné, Marguerite Long, Camille Saint-Saëns, Emil Sauer, Florent Schmitt, Lazar Lévy, Alfred Casella, Harold Bauer, Nadia Boulanger, Wanda Landowska, and Mark Hambourg.[42] Other musicians he probably heard during this period were Fritz Kreisler, W. Mengelberg, Richard Strauss, Gustav Mahler, Vincent d'Indy, Georges Enesco, Pablo Casals, Jacques Thibaud, Pierre Monteux, Fritz Kreisler, Eugène Ysaye, Miguel Llobet, Lilli Lehmann, Maggie Teyte, and others. And of course he would have heard Artur Rubinstein, Maurice Ravel, and others.

Other pianists of his day also played or recorded his music, such as Rubinstein, Leopoldo Querol, Manuel Navarro, José Cubiles, Frank Marshall, Ricardo Viñes, J. Sabater, O. Colacelli, and George Copeland, the latter of which described his meeting with Falla in Switzerland in the 1930's.

> He was a kind and delightfully amusing human being. He seemed as unlike a composer as anybody could be. And it was always amazing to realize that all the torrential fire and color and blazing music could come out of this wizened little hypochondriac. His music was entirely of his own creation—naturally you know it is Spanish, but it is much more than just that. He was ardent about his country and proud of his race, and he never wanted to leave Spain. . . .[43]

Another eyewitness account testifies to Falla's powers as a pianist in middle age. José Mora Guarnido visited Falla during the "Retablo years" and gives this impression.

> When Falla—a magnificent pianist—sat down to play, he was never selfish but generous. He liked to search for scores . . . on hand and choose fragments that evoked the previous conversations. But he had a special preference for harpsichord music and of French and Italian harpsichordists—Couperin Le Grand, Scarlatti, Rameau, etc.—later he would introduce . . . Bach and Mozart, or the Russian group "The Five" and, if it had some bearing on his work, he did not disdain the use of fragments by contemporary composers. Only very rarely and, when we insisted, did he accede to play his own works, but never, the ones he was composing, of which he only spoke. I was part of the small group for which he played fragments from "Master Peter's Puppet Show," which he was

then composing, and for which we listened to because he wanted our advice about which phrases that could be cut without appreciably mutilating the text, in order to find a precise adhesion between word and rhythm to avoid making the recitatives drag. After playing all our requests and when it was time to leave—we always left late because time went without realizing it—he played us a kind of inframusical ablution, to relieve us, he said, from the load received throughout the session, interpreting with funny displays of virtuosity, amidst loud laughter and a truly raucous gabble of improvised tremolos and arpeggios, the "Habanera" of [Sebastian] Iradier or the "Carnaval of Venice."[44]

Falla's "disciple," Ernesto Halffter, commented on Falla's approach to tone, insisting on a deep tone. Falla reportedly said, "It seems that some pianists play like the keyboard is on fire, raising their hands and not making the sound at the bottom of the key."[45]

The complexity of Falla's personality is once again revealed by carefully following his piano pursuits throughout his career. At one time he considered the teaching of piano to be his principal profession. And although composition would be where he would make his mark in the world, he never gave up playing the piano. Like so many other passions in his life—history, literature, writing, art, teaching—the piano was incorporated into his musical career in a unique and very personal way, whether as an instrument for performance, for composition, or for instruction. And like his pen, the piano was a love that endured until the end.

NOTES

1. Nin-Culmell—pedagogo, 41.

2. AMF 1227; The book also reads: *Propriedad* and possibly stamped *Moergs* (Property of Moergs) and has printed an inscription on the front cover: "En cualquier carrera que abraceis, proponeos un fin elevado y poned à su servicio una constancia inquebrantable" ("In whatever career that you embrace, propose an elevated end and put at your service an unbreakable constancy").

3. Orelgamar, S. *El auxiliar del pianista. Modelos de ejercicios, escalas, arpegios; fragmentos de estudios y otras obras, tal como deben de estudiarse para adquirir la perfección.* (Madrid) s. ed., 1909, AMF, 227, 1.

4. Orelgamar, 126.

5. Orelgamar, 125–26.

6. In the AMF are found two copies of this book: (1) AMF, no. 1358, *El Arte del Piano, Consejos dedicados a la Juventud*, by Robert Schumann: Spanish version by Juan Salvat y Crespí, published by Iberia Musical, Fabregat, Plantada

y Alegret, Casa Editorial de Música, Canuda, 45—Barclona (n.d.) and bears the stamp of the publisher, and contains no annotations; (2) AMF, no. 1359, *El Arte del Piano, Consejos dedicados a la Juventud*, by Robert Schumann: Spanish version by Juan Salvat y Crespí, published by Rafael Guardia of Barcelona (n.d.) and bears the stamp of Manuel Quirell, Rosario, 17, Cádiz. On the inside front cover is the inscription *Estos consejos fueron escritos por SCHUMANN para servir de prefacio á* [sic] *su Álbum dedicado á la juventud op. 68, colección de 13 piezas en forma de estudios* (These counsels are written by SCHUMANN to serve as the preface to his Album for the Young, op. 68, collection of thirteen pieces in the form of studies).

7. Schumann, 3. "La educación del oído es lo más importante. Procurad ya desde el principio discernir cada tono y cada tonalidad. Analizad toda clase de sonidos: el que produce la campana, el cristal . . . etc., etc."

8. Schumann, 4. "¡Tocad a compás! La ejecución de muchos concertistas se parece bastante al andar de un beodo. No sigáis jamás semejantes modelos."

9. Schumann, 4. "Cuando os presenten alguna composición para hacérla tocar a primera vista, no dejéis de recorrerla con los ojos en toda su extensión antes de empezarla."

10. *Las formas pianísticas, orígenes y transformaciones de las formas instrumentales, estudiadas en los instrumentos de teclado moderno, tomo primero*, by Felipe Pedrell (1918), Manuel Villar, publisher, 15, Paz, 15, Valencia, M. 107 V.

11. Tragó studied with Georges Mathias in Paris; other pupils of Matias included Teresa Carreño, Isidore Philipp, Erik Satie and Paul Dukas (see Nommick, Fuego, p. XII, fn. 3).

12. Cited in *Poesía*, 30; reference is made to a previous article on 29 March, but no year is given. It is surmised to be 1897.

13. "Ejecuta los pasos más difíciles sin esfuerzo alguno, y con la misma aparente naturalidad que los fáciles . . . demuestra verdadero sentimiento artístico y delicadez exquisita." *Actualidades* from *Diario de Cádiz,* 29 March, 1897(?), newspaper clipping cited in *Poesía*, 30.

14. ". . . seguro . . . que el concertista á quien Falla acompañe . . . no lo olvidará, porque no es fácil encontrar artistas que se despojen de su propia personalidad cuando acompañan á otros. Tal es el pianista." *Actualidades* from *Diario de Cádiz*, 29 March 1897(?), newspaper clipping cited in *Poesía*, 30.

15. *Actualidades* from *Diario de Cádiz*, 29 March 1897(?), newspaper clipping cited in *Poesía*, 30.

16. Nommick, Thesis, I, 26, fn. 11.

17. LC, 9.

18. LC, 436–37.

19. LC, 437.

20. LC, 437.

21. Nommick-Bach, p. 15 and Zofia Chechlinska, "Wojciech Żywny," *The New Grove*, vol. 20, 1980, 727.

22. Letter Tragó-Falla, 7 December 1899, AMF, 7694.
23. Letter Tragó-Falla, 15 July 1897, AMF, 7694.

. . . Respecto del pedal habria mucho que hablar y es dificil de terminar asi por carta el uso que de él debe y puede hacer-se.

En Paris existe una obra titulada "Les pédales du Piano par Falkenberg.[sic] Podría pedirla y enterase algo, lo cual siempre es útil.

Algunas líneas generales sobre el pedal.

—Se puede usar impunemente en los arpegios, acordes, etc.

—En las escalas hay que usarle poco y con mucho cuidado.

—En las cromáticas nada.

—En las parte alta del Piano (mano dcha) [mano derecha] se puede usar el pedal mas que en la parte media y los bajos. . . .

—Se puede usar el pedal en cada acorde nuevo ó cambio de harmonía.

—Se puede usar en las notas que tienen un acento, sf, etc.

—Se puede usar para ligar estas distancias que no alcanzan las manos y que es preciso sostener.

—En las frases cantabiles . . . se debe usar casi constantemente, etc., etc.

—Para hacer iguales las décimas de la última página del Mov.to [Movimiento] perpetuo de Weber se pueden utilizar los ejercicios de 8as [octavas] hay uno que creo yá tocaba V. En el 1er cuaderno de los de Clementi hay otro también muy útil para el objeto. Está en mi bemol mayor. También puede V. hacer con la izquierda un ejercicio de décimas partidas y cromáticas. Es decir para las teclas blancas y negras. Todo esto es útil y es lo que ahora se me ocurre sobre el particular.

Me dice V. que después de haber trabajado con cuidado la mano derecha, dejar de dar algunas notas, ó que si las da no lo hace con la igualdad que desea.

Para la igualdad es preciso dar en cada dedo (sobre todo el 1º y 5º) la mayor fuerza posible y para que adquieran esta no tengo como las notas tenidas.

. . . la perfección, pues esta yá vendrá con el tiempo y el trabajo.

Cuando yo le oí en esta no observé que tuviera tanta desigualdad con V. supone.

El allegro de St Saëns puede dejarle para un poco mas tarde, pues es difícil y algo original deme carísimo.

De los ejercicios de Merkte, puede ir mirando los siguientes. Página 53 hasta el nº 11 inclusive de la 56. Después página 110 á la 11 inclusive. . . .

24. Georges Falckenberg, see LC, 436.
25. Letter Tragó-Falla, 25 November 1897, AMF, 7694.

No use V. ninguna clase de anillos ni otras zarandajas por el estilo. Yo hice atrocidades con mis manos cuando estudiaba mucho y hoy sufro las consecuencias en forma de dolores musculares, cansancio, etc. Es pues necesario hacer el trabajo ordenadamente para no aniquilarse y suprimir anillos y demás instrumentos de tortura que à la larga pueden traer fatales consecuencias.

26. ". . . para contestar al punto más importante de su última carta: el que se refería à la cuestión de la Enseñanza del Piano y á la decisión que V. me manifestaba de dedicarse á ella en Cádiz, preguntándome además mi opinión sobre el asunto." Letter Tragó-Falla, June 1898, AMF, 7694.

27. LC, 436.

28. Campodónico, 9.

29. Budwig, 8.

30. Repertoire taken from various notices in the *Diario de Cádiz*, AMF, 6408.

31. *Diario de Cádiz*, 27 April 1905, AMF, 6408.

Marshall es todo un artista. Mecanismo, desenvoltura, fuerza, expresión, todo lo reune. No le oí; pero he hablado son él sobre el arte de interpretar, sobre el sentido poético de las obras, y sus convicciones son las de un artista, de las que tiene ya un criterio y una orientación fija. Ha estudiado con Granados, con Bauer y con Risler, y no ha desperdiciado el tiempo. Su éxito mayor lo obtuvo aquí en las obras de Chopin, de Schumann, de Scarlatti y en la "Campanella," que tocó de un modo maravilloso.

Manuel Falla actuó ayer. Su arte es completamente interior, sin concesiones al efecto, sin exterioridades deslumbradoras, sin la brillantez y la fuerza que tan fácilmente conquistan el aplauso. Ni llega al pianísimo esfumado, ni trata siquiera de abordar el fortísimo de sonoridad poderosa. Sus ejecuciones se mueven siempre en una media tinta; pero en ella, ¡cuánta poesía, cuánta intención, y qué estado de alma tan hermoso y tan penetrante! Bach, Beethoven, Chopin y Schumann desfilaron en sus versiones con un espíritu austero, narrativo y poético. Las de Scarlatti y Saint-Saëns fueron inferiores en gracia y finura á las de otros muchos opositores.

Todo lo que precede, exceptuando las primera líneas, lo tenía escrito antes de conocer el fallo del Tribunal. ¿Se pronunciarían los juíces, entre dos artistas de igual talla, por el arte más interior, ó preferirian el de más refinamiento?

Mis convicciones artísticas me hacen aplaudir sin reservas al fallo que adjudica el premio al señor Falla, y pide una mención honorifica para el Sr. Marshall al ministro de Fomento, aunque el tal ministerio no tenga nada que ver en un premio que ha establecido un particular por su voluntad propia y libérrima. Pare se menciona al Sr. Marshall, y esto es lo justo.

32. Debussy's letter to Falla, 7 February 1907, AMF, 6898.

33. Demarquez, 198.

34. Unclassified papers in the AMF; cited in and translated by Michael Christoforidis's Ph.D. thesis, *Aspects of the Creative Process in Manuel de Falla's "El retablo de Maese Pedro" and "Concerto,"* The University of Melbourne, Faculty of Music, 1997, Appendix 1.5, 1–3.

35. Only completed works are included with data based on the official AMF catalogue of works by Antonio Gallego (1987). Works that have not been found or the *zarzuelas,* about which there is little information, are not included.

36. *Mireya* is the earliest piano transcription (1899), but unfortunately it is lost.

37. The transcription of The Fisherman's Song was published with Falla's "Polo" from *Siete canciones populares españolas* in a musical supplement to *La revue musicale*, no. 8, 1 June 1921.

38. Only fragments of this work exist, but at least two movements are known to have been premiered. Early biographers Roland-Manuel and Pahissa make reference to it.

39. Undated letter written by Maria Carmen de Falla, on her brother's behalf, to Rosa García Ascot, cited in *Poesía*, 225.

40. Nin-Culmell-pedagogo, 41.

41. Nommick, "L'évolution des effectifs instrumentaux dans le'oeuvre de Manuel de Falla" in *Manuel de Falla, Latinité et Universalité*, ed. Louis Jambeu Paris: Presses de l'Université de Paris—Sorbonne, 1999, 330.

42. Taken from concert programs held at the AMF.

43. Unpublished autobiography of George Copeland from the Dubal collection, used with kind permission from David Dubal, professor of piano literature at the Juilliard School in New York.

44. "Cuando Falla—magnifico pianista—se sentaba a tocar, no era avaro ni mucho menos, sino generoso. Le gustaba rebuscar en el anaquel de partituras que tenía al alcance de la mano e ir seleccionando fragmentos evocados a lo largo de la conversación. Pero tenía especial preferencia por la música en el clavicordio y por los clavecinistas franceses e italianos—Couperin Le Grand, Scarlatti, Rameau . . .—; luego se introducía . . . de Bach y de Mozart, o en el grupo de 'Los Cinco' rusos, y, si se traía a colación su obra no desdeñaba los fragmentos de compositores contemporáneos. Sólo muy raramente y cuando se le pedía con insistencia, accedía a tocar cosas suyas, nunca, sin embargo de lo que estaba componiendo y de lo que apenas hablaba. Sólo a un grupo reducido entre el que me conté, nos tocó fragmentos del 'Retablo de Maese Pedro' que entonces estaba haciendo, y esto para escuchar nuestro consejo sobre las frases que se podían suprimir, sin mutilar sensiblemente el texto, para buscar una exacta adhesión de la palabra el ritmo y no hacer moroso el recitado. Después de tocar todo lo que se le pedía y llegada la hora de marcharse, siempre retrasada porque el tiempo pasaba sin darse cuenta, nos ofrecía una especie de ablución inframusical, para aliviarnos—decía—de la carga recibida a lo largo de la sesión, interpretando con graciosos alardes de virtuoso, entre carcajadas y una verdadera algarabía improvisada de trémolos y arpegios, la 'Habanera' de Iradier o el 'Carnaval de Venecia.'" Cited in José Mora Guarnido in *Federico García Lorca y su mundo*, Buenos Aires: Losada, 1958, 157–158. The author also mentions a letter from Falla dated 1 February 1924, in which he remembers these Sunday meetings.

45. Cited in Helena Sá e Costa, *Memórias. Uma vida em Concerto*. Co-edition: Porto: Casa da Música, Porto 2001. Capital Europeia da Cultura e Campo das Letras, 2001. ". . . parece que alguns pianistas tocam como se o teclado estivesse a arder, levantam as mãos e não nos dão o som do fundo das teclas."

Chapter 10

Bach-Scarlatti-Chopin-Beethoven-Romanticism

This short chapter contains some brief quotations of Falla that apply to specific composers or subjects not treated independently in his collected (incomplete) writings, *On Music and Musicians*.

J. S. Bach

The huge musical heritage before Johann Sebastian Bach is systematically and voluntarily ignored or rejected, although the art of sounds had not had an existence deserving consideration before the great Cantor.[1]

Domenico Scarlatti and Frederic Chopin[2]

You make me "say" (and with the aggravation of a category and underlined affirmation) that my "idols" in music are Scarlatti and Chopin. This—that without a doubt you understood—is not in any way that which I "wanted" to say to you, and even more when I didn't understand that I was to formulate the question that now I see in your article. That affirmation becomes more serious because only a few months ago, on the occasion of an international inquest, I affirmed—as I have always affirmed—the impossibility, for my way of feeling, that in art exists an absolute conviction with far-away ideals and aesthetic forms, even if it be the beauty and the magnitude of the model. As you see, nothing further than "idolatry" !...That which indeed I remember to have said to you is that in the music of Domenico Scarlatti and of Chopin there is a force of musical substance, very superior at times to the other great musicians, who, however, enjoy the more elevated prestige, and that this perhaps was due to (as you already indicate) the limited instrumental means to which they were subjected, as much Chopin as "our" Scarlatti.[3]

Ludwig van Beethoven[4]

Independently of the admiration owed to Beethoven and the greater or lesser coincidence of my sentiments and aspirations with his works, these offer three powerful examples which I have always made an effort to follow.

1. The nobility and lack of self-interest with which he served music, convinced of its elevated social mission.
2. His desire for rhythmic-melodic-tonal purity.
3. Beethoven's resolute undertaking to Germanise his music; an undertaking which should serve us as a luminous example so as to make sure that the Latin character, in its diverse forms, is reflected with the greatest possible intensity in the artistic production of our race.

I believe that this sincere, simple and faithful declaration (—made with love, good will and with the vehement desire that it be received with the same sentiments—) is the best homage that I can offer to the genius whose centenary is celebrated universally by the Art of Music.

Frederic Chopin[5]

Chopin is for me one of the rare composers whose work offers us a pure musical substratum [substance] in a nearly continuous manner.

Romanticism[6]

How colossal is the subject matter that forms the notion of Romanticism! Whole worlds of antagonistic feelings and ideas, a multitude of formal problems! Our generation knows the romantic period well: from the historical perspective, the proximity of this great epoch is too close, and the bonds between the experiences and creations of that era and our times are too strong, to forget about. Not only do we marvel at the achievements of the masters of those days, or deeply admire their works, but we view many issues relating to the Romantic style with a critical perspective which cannot overlook the serious impediments in the Romantic trend.

It seems to me that the influence of romanticism upon the Spanish School is often overstated. In Romanticism, insofar as the artwork is concerned, the genuine and potent emotional tension must not be identified with the improvisational freedom of form, which was surrounded by so much uncertainty during the romantic Period in music.

As far as my work is concerned, it seems to me that it is only in my symphonic impressions *Noches en los jardines de España*, and some theatrical works that one could find certain resonances of romanticism. My recent works (e.g., Concerto for harpsichord) are totally free of such influences; they rather approach the pre-classical style.

NOTES

1. OMM, 19. According to Yvan Nommick, there are only two references to Bach in Falla's writings. The one given above and another taken from his unpublished "Reminiscence on the Creation of an Auxiliary Class of Musical Technique at the National Conservatory of Music and Declamation" [Madrid]. In the latter, Falla suggests: "[the student] will execute a fugue of three or more voices of Johann Sebastian Bach at the piano, in order to demonstrate his technical knowledge of the instrument which will serve him in the class as the practical examples." (AMF 8937) quoted in Yvan Nommick "La 'vuelta a Bach' en Manuel de Falla y sus contemporáneos" in *Bach Homenaje de Chillida, Bach en el pensamiento, las artes y la música* (2000) Granada: AMF, 19. "Ejecutará al piano una fuga a tres o más partes, de Juan Sebastián Bach, para demostrar sus conocimientos técnicos del instrumento que há de servirle en la clase para los ejemplos prácticos."

2. Extract from a letter Falla-Raffaele Calzini dated 20 October 1929 (AMF 6812).

"Me hace usted 'decir' (y con la agravante de una categórica y subrayada afirmación) que mis 'ídolos' en música son Scarlatti y Chopin. Esto—que sin duda entendió usted—no es en manera alguna lo que yo 'quise' decirle, y tanto más cuanto que yo no comprendí que me formulase la pregunta que ahora veo en su artículo. Esa afirmación resulta más grave porque hace pocos meses, con ocasión de una 'enquête' internacional, afirmé—como siempre he afirmado—la imposibilidad que, a mi modo de sentir, existe en arte de una absoluta compenetración con ajenos ideales y formas estéticas, sea cual fuere la belleza y magnitud del modelo. Como ve que en la música de Domenico Scarlatti y de Chopin hay una fuerza de substancia musical muy superior, a veces, a la de otros grandes músicos que, sin embargo, gozan de más elevado prestigio, y que esto tal vez fuese debido (como usted ya indica) a los limitados medios instrumentales de que se sirvieron, tanto Chopin como 'nuestro' Scarlatti."

3. The Scarlattian influence was present throughout Falla's career as a composer (*La casa de tócame Roque, El sombrero de tres picos*—"Danza del Corregidor," *Psyché*, and *Concerto*) and as a performer (one of his last recitals on 11 December 1927, in Granada featured only Scarlatti sonatas). See Elena Torres's article "La presencia de Scarlatti en la trayectoria musical de Manuel de Falla" in *Manuel de Falla e Italia, estudios de Montserrat Bergadà, Elena Torres, Stefano Russomanno,* edición y prólogo de Yvan Nommick, Colección "Estudios," Serie "Música," no. 3. Publicaciones del Archivo Manuel de Falla, Granada, 2000, 63–122.

4. Cited in Michael Christoforidis's "Manuel de Falla on Romanticism: Insights into an Uncited Text" in *Context 6 (Summer 1993–1994)*, 28–29. Falla's final draft of a text on Beethoven which was published in the *Vossische Zeitung* and reproduced in Barcelona's *La Noche* on 26 March 1927, for the 100th anniversary of the death of Beethoven. This translation by Michael Christoforidis is used with kind permission of the translator. Falla also mentions Beethoven and em-

phasis on the religious character in his *Canzona in modo lidico* (see "Back from Paris," OMM, 19): "Beethoven was more or less a practising Catholic, and the Lydian is the fifth ecclesiastical mode in the series named 'authentic,' and the third in the primitive series which preceded the Gregorian reform."

5. "Chopin es para mí uno de los raros compositores cuya obra nos ofrece de manera casi continua un puro sustrato musical." Quote in the Paris magazine, *Bravo*, June 1932, 25. Correspondence between Falla and Georges R. Manue, the magazine's director, may be found with Falla's sketches of this quote in AMF 7236. See Nommick, Fuego, XI, for more details.

6. This text is subject of Michael Christoforidis's article "Manuel de Falla on Romanticism: Insights into an Uncited Text" in *Context 6 (Summer 1993–1994)*, 26–31, and appears on p. 26. Falla's text on Romanticism was published in the Polish magazine *Muzyka*, in a special issue entitled *Romantyzm w Muzyce* at the end of 1928 with commentaries by other composers on the subject, such as Dukas, Elgar, Honegger, Delius, Korngold, Krenek, Prokofiev, and Ravel. Falla's Polish text was translated into English by Alan Lem.

Chapter 11

Louis Lucas[1]

In most biographies—with the exception of Federico Sopeña (1988)[2]—credence is given to Falla's harmonic reliance upon his "chance encounter" of Louis Lucas's (1816–1863) *L'Acoustique nouvelle, ou Essai d'application d'une méthode philosophique aux questions élevées de l'Acoustique, de la Musique et de la Composition musicale* (*The New Acoustics—A Revolution in Music—An Attempt to Apply a Philosophical Theory to Music—Preceded by a Preface by Théodore de Banville and Followed by a Treatise by Euclid and by Plutarch's Dialogue on Music*). This second Parisian edition, which Falla acquired while strolling through the outdoor Rastro market in Madrid,[3] dates from 1854.[4] It differs from the first edition only by a change of cover, title, and different paper for the title pages.[5]

The exact date of Falla's acquisition of the book is not known. Speculation in various biographies ranges anywhere from 1901–1906.[6] However, Falla himself, in correcting Roland-Manuel's manuscript of his biography, *Manuel de Falla*, says: "I came across this book when I was starting to compose *La vida breve*, . . . when Debussy and his music were still unknown to me."[7] The earliest AMF sketches of the opera are dated 4 November 1904.[8]

Falla had been deeply impressed by his studies with Felipe Pedrell (1901–1904). Pedrell's return to Barcelona in 1904, for health reasons, left a void in Falla's still formative years as a composer. Falla's subsequent championing of the Lucas theories allowed him to develop further, and not in disagreement with the essence of Pedrell's teachings. Falla's personal annotated copy of the Lucas book is found in the AMF.[9] Heavily worn and amply annotated, it is certain proof of Falla's perusal, especially as far as chapter XV.

To sum up the basic premise, Lucas gives support to "the abandonment of the artificial rules of contemporary Western music in favour of a much more natural art-form."[10] Alternatives, he offers, may be found in:

1. the ancient Greek modes;
2. or the Indian Sriraga scale (in which "there are four mobile notes, G, B, C, F, which may vary at the whim of the artist by a quarter-tone either way," implying that the "different degrees of the scale . . . function as leaning-notes");
3. or perhaps other "popular, exotic and ancient forms of music."[11]

Many of the ideas contained in the book must have intrigued Falla and paved the way for future developments, such as those found in his folksong, or Andalusian, period of *nationalism* (*Siete canciones populares españolas, Noches en los jardines de España, Fantasía bætica, El sombrero de tres picos,* amongst others) and in his subsequent search beyond nationalism, for *universality* (*Concerto, Pour le tombeau de Paul Dukas, Atlántida,* for example). Certainly, two things may have resonated in Falla. First, the concept of the division of the scale into microtones as found in nature and in folk music, would support Falla's interest in Andalusian folk music and the *Cante jondo*. Secondly, Falla's harmonic experiments would have been justified by the idea that by adhering only to the major and minor modes (i.e., remaining within the bonds of tonality), we create "impassable" barriers to those of other cultures, such as in the Orient.[12] Falla's interest in non-Western modes may be seen in various items in his personal library.

In categorizing music as a science, Lucas upholds:

1. perfect consonance, "which exists only in the major triad, since this chord is implicit in (the first few terms of) the overtone series, the only naturally occurring musical phenomenon."[13];
2. "the function of small intervals," such as what he calls *enharmony*; this is the law of attraction based upon the division of the scale *not* into regular semitones, but instead in irregular intervals, including quarter-tones, for the purpose of resolution. Ideally, Lucas suggests that the scale be divided into two four-note series (similar to tetrachords in the equal-temperament system), one towards F, the other

towards C (ascending "tetrachord" of C-F; and ascending "tetra-chord" G-C). Within these divisions, numerous types of scales are possible when permitting the inclusion of microtonal functions of resolution.[14]

For Lucas, there are three basic laws of *attraction* that govern the two elements (the major chord and microtones). These are: the law of *consonance* (an absolute law); the law of *succession* (an absolute law); and the law of *comparison* (a contingent law, in order to "satisfy the needs of the . . . moment"). Some fifteen years later, Falla writes in the sketch material for *El retablo de Maese Pedro*, reminding himself to refer to the introduction of Lucas's book: "It should not be forgotten that the law of attraction is the origin of the other laws. . . ."[15]

Falla's adherence to the first element as a closing technique—the major chord ("The one and only chord whose form is unchangeable. . . ."[16])— is remarkable. According to Chris Collins, only one of Falla's works, act II of *La vida breve*, ends in the minor.[17] As stated, Falla was composing this opera when he came upon Lucas's book.

While Falla never employed microtones in his music, *per se*, they do exist naturally in the *cante jondo* singing such as is found in *El amor brujo* or *Siete canciones populares españolas*. In an interview in the *Daily Mail*, Falla spoke about this topic on 18 July 1919: ". . . the folk-songs of my native Andalusia derive from a much subtler scale than can be found in an octave of twelve notes. All I can do in my day is to give an illusion of these quarter-tones by superimposing chords of one key on another."[18] For Falla, the purist, adherence to equal temperament and to the division of the scale into twelve equivalent semitones would be the ideal to be followed, religiously, but with freedom. For example, (1) in compositions using the piano, this technique would be apparent when the pedals would be employed, for the rich harmonics would give the "illusion" of microtones; (2) implied microtones would also result in appoggiaturas being pitted against their accompanying chords, such as found in the piano pieces *Canto de los remeros del Volga* and *Le tombeau de Paul Dukas*; or (3) the original way Falla uses the appoggiaturas against each other to give the illusion of microtones as in the *cante jondo* sections in the *Fantasía bætica*, as has been mentioned in chapter 9.

The close link of the earthy *cante jondo* with earlier primitive elements, to which Lucas refers, is undeniable. According to Falla,

. . . in "cante jondo," just as much as in the primitive songs of the East, the musical scale is a direct consequence of what we could call the oral scale. Some even suppose that speech and song were originally the same thing. . . .[19]

Lucas, discussing the virtues of *enharmony*, with its natural division of the scale into irregular intervals, says that it is "the first which appears in the natural order, through the imitation of birdsong, of animals' cries and of the infinite rumblings of matter." [20]

In 1922, when Falla and Federico García Lorca produced the *Cante jondo* Ccompetition, Falla, in an anonymous essay, commented upon three factors that contributed to Spanish culture: "the adoption by the church of Byzantine chant, the Arab invasion, and the settlement in Spain of numerous groups of gipsies [sic]." [21] Quoting Pedrell, in his *Cancionero Musical Popular Español*, he acclaimed: "The persistence of musical orientalism in various Spanish popular songs is the deep-rooted result of the influence exerted by the most ancient Byzantine civilization. . . ."[22] For Falla (who seems to be quoting Lucas), the elements of Byzantine chant are best preserved in the Andalusian song-type of the *siguiriya* and may be summarized as: ". . . the tonal modes of the primitive systems (which must not be confused with the modes which we now call Greek, although they sometimes partly share the same structure); the *enharmony* inherent in primordial modes (in other words, the division and subdivision of the leading-notes in respect of their tonal attractive functions); and finally, the absence of metrical rhythm and the wealth of modulatory inflections in the melodic line."[23]

More light may be shed upon Falla's creative processes and the resulting application of Lucas's theories. Two collections of sketches— one unpublished and known as the *Retablo notebook* and the other one published as the *Superposiciones*—reveal important information needed to understand Falla's application of Lucas's principles. The first probably dates from 1919–1923, the years when Falla was working on *El retablo*.[24] Speculation of the dating of the second document might include the same years, as there is no example present from the *Concerto*, but Falla does refer to the printed edition of *Siete canciones populares españolas* when he indicates some of their page numbers in the examples on page 4. This work was published in 1922. Another theory is that the document is merely a pedagogical tool to explain to some of Falla's students and was written in haste, which is evident because of some errors. This theory could date the document much later.

The fact of the document's publication as a set does not preclude the existence of other such similar papers, which may be still outside of the AMF, in private collections.

The *Retablo notebook* consists of fifty-four pages of a small note-book, in which Falla kept his thoughts, observations, and ideas related to the composition he was then creating. The only direct reference to Lucas's *L'Acoustique nouvelle* in the *Retablo notebook* (in ff. 19–20) reveals his fascination with certain modulatory techniques, such as obtaining consonance from dissonance. Falla writes,

> The links [between chords] must be made either by maintaining equal distances in the intervals which separate the chords (although exceptionally some of these intervals may change) or by following the laws of attraction in the notes which possess this quality [i.e., the leaning-notes]. This latter procedure should particularly be employed at modulations. It should not be forgotten that the law of attraction is the origin of the other laws, namely those of succession, consonance and comparison. (See the Introduction to Lucas's book.)[25]

The *Superposiciones* deals with chord generation rather than modulation techniques. The *Superposiciones*, published in 1975–1976 for the centenary of Falla's birth, consists of four pages of sketches in Falla's hand. Antonio Iglesias reproduces a similar version, with pages out of order, in the first edition of his book, *Manuel de Falla (su obra para piano)* and corrected in the second edition.[26]

Rodolfo Halffter[27] (1900–1987), who received some compositional counsels from Falla, told of the origin and his connection to the *Superposiciones*.[28]

> It was some day during the month of June in 1971. Gerardo Gombau, musician of great stature and my inseparable friend, and I were walking close to the Puerta del Vino.
>
> "Gerardo, I don't know where I read that," that the contemplation of the picture postcard in vivid colors of this celebrated monument of the Alhambra started Debussy in one of his most Andalusian preludes.
>
> "It is," I remember it well, "that which Falla proclaimed in his *Escritos* about Debussy. How could I have forgotten it?" I exclaimed astonished. "I who was the first to know perfectly the *Escritos* of Don Manuel."
>
> We spoke then of happenings of years gone by. Of course, we remembered those concerts of new music, during the decade of the thirties, which we organized in the Students' Residence in Madrid, causing a big commotion.
>
> "Rodolfo, then we were young. We, our souls, were restless. Both of us

were motivated by the same illusion, to present ourselves as artists partic-
ipating in ambitious musical enterprises. But the damned Spanish Civil
War dashed all of our hopes."

Nightime fell upon us. Gerardo and I began our descent from the Alhambra to the city. The path was dimly lit by the dying light of a pair of
old lanterns.

"Be careful, Gerardo, you are going to trip." Suddenly, we encountered
Don Valentín Ruíz Aznar, priest, chapelmeister, and intimate friend of
Falla. In the dark, we recognized him by the familiar sound and kindness
of his voice.

"I was looking for you. Someone told me that you were up here. I am
glad to have found you. I am going to give you a very valuable gift. You
will appreciate it very much because you are musicians."

There were four pages of manuscript paper that contained notes, numbers, and scribblings drawn in Falla's own hand. And without more commentary, Don Valentín gave us each a set of these papers.

"Thank you, Don Valentín." With rapid and affectionate hugs we left him.

We stayed in the hotel, Gerardo and I, in the center of Granada, where
other teachers of the second Manuel de Falla Course, part of the 20th Festival of Music and Dance, also resided.

In my room, while my wife Emilia was looking at a magazine, I examined with growing curiosity the pleasure that Don Valentín had just given
me. In its material aspect it constituted a set of four photostatic copies of
four pages of manuscript paper with quotations and annotations of Falla.

Did Don Valentín give to Gerardo the original manuscript? Or did he
give him photostatic copies the same as mine? I don't know.

Granada, 2 March 1972

Afterward I examined those papers of Falla and their importance is very
great. Thus is treated the only written testimony that Falla has left about his
technique.

The first two of the four pages that comprise the *Superposiciones* reveal
a rich assortment of various harmonic possibilities from simply adding or
subtracting the intervals of the perfect, augmented, or diminished fifth to
the root, third, or fifth of a major or minor chord. Falla uses a plus sign ($+$)
to add an indicated interval above the note and/or to indicate an augmented interval. He also uses a minus sign ($-$) to indicate the subtraction
an interval (an interval below the note) and a slash through a number to
indicate its diminished form. In the chart below the slash is substituted
with the symbol, °; for example, 5° is the symbol for a diminished fifth.

Halffter, who was acquainted with Falla's working processes, describes
the *Superposiciones* in his unpublished document "Notas." After speaking
of the content, he describes the concept of a "sonorous conglomerate."

A sonorous conglomerate is composed [formed as a whole entity] of the addition of the notes of a major or minor triad plus the notes added or stacked in conformity with the numerous possibilities of superpositions that the method thought of by Falla offers.

A sonorous conglomerate can be composed [formed as a whole entity] also by virtue of the sum of a fragment of diatonic scales, whose tonic is the fundamental note of a triad, plus the added or superimposed notes.[29]

The following is a summary of the content of Falla's *Superposiciones*. The shaded headings are a translation of Falla's own. This writer has categorized them according to page and number; for example P1, N1 refers to page 1, example number 1. As Halffter has pointed out in his "Conjunto de Series Dodecafonicas . . . ,"[30] in some cases there is a similarity between serial technique and the technique of the *Superposiciones*.[31] The prime form of each conglomerate is given in order to point out one aspect of this type of similarity. By doing so, it become obvious that the example P1, N4 possesses characteristics of both the pentatonic scale and the tunings resultant from the strings of the guitar. It is doubtful that this observation would have escaped Falla's close scrutiny, although the author is unaware of any documentation in support of this fact.

Example 11.1a   Page 1—*Superposiciones*

Example	Generator/ Resonance	Derivative	Prime Form	Bitonal or other possibilities
On a minor chord				
P1, N1	CE♭G/A♭D	5+5, 3-5	(0,1,3,7,8)	A♭ lydian/ c minor
P1, N2	CE♭G/AD	5+5, 3-5...	(0,2,3,6,8)	D major/ c minor
P1, N3	CE♭G/FA	3-5..., 1-5	(0,2,4,6,9)	*F major/ c minor
P1, N4	CE♭G/FB♭	3+5, 1-5	(0,2, 4, 7, 9)	B♭ major/ c minor; pentatonic; same interval content as guitar tuning

Example	Generator/ Resonance	Derivative	Prime Form	Bitonal or other possibilites
		On a minor chord (continued)		
P1, N5	CE♭G/FB	3+5+, 1-5	(0,1,4,6,8)	B locrian/ c minor
P1, N6	CE♭G/F#B	3+5+, 1-5...	(0,1,4,7,8)	B major/ c minor
P1, N7	CE♭G/F#B♭	3+5, 1-5...	(0,1,4,6,9)	F# major/ c minor
P1, N8	CE♭G/F#D	5+5, 1-5...	(0,1,4,5,7)	G major/ c minor
P1, N9	CE♭G/A♭B	3+5+, 3-5	= P1, N1	*
P1, N10	CE♭G/AB	3+5+, 3-5...	(0,2,4,5,8)	*
		Major chords		
P1, N11 (A)	CEG/B♭F#	3+5..., 1-5...	(0,2,3,6,8)	B major/ C major¨
P1, N12 (B)	CEG/AC#	5+5..., 3-5	= P1, N7	A major/ C major¨
P1, N13 (N . . . 2 of 6 sounds)	CEG/A♭B♭ D	5+5, 3+5..., 3-5+	(0,1,3,5,7,9)	
P1, N14	CEG/B♭G#	3+5..., 1+5+	(0,1,3,5,9)	
P1, N15 (super-positions)	CEG/FA♭	3-5+, 1-5	(0,1,3,4,8)	F minor/ C major
P1, N16 (super-positions)	CEG/FA	3-5, 1-5	(0,1,3,7,8)	F lydian/ C major
P1, N17	CEG/FB	ƒ 1-5, 3+5		B locrian/ C major
		New forms of these chords (as examples)		
5 versions called A	P1, N11			
2 versions called B	P1, N12			
		Minor chords		
P1, N18 (a)	C E♭ G/AC#	5+5..., 3-5...	= P1, N2	= P1, N12
P1, N19 (b)	C E♭ G/FA	3-5..., 1-5	(0,2,4,6,9)	= P1, N3
P1, N20 (c)	Inversion of P1, N19			
P1, N21 (d)	C E♭ G/FA♭	3-5, 1-5	= P1, N3	= P1, N15

Example 11.1a   Page 1—*Superposiciones* (continued)

Example	Generator/ Resonance	Derivative	Prime Form	Bitonal or other possibilites
	New forms of these chords (as examples)			
	4 versions of a (P1, N18); 2 versions of b (P1, N19); 1 version of c (P1, N20); 1 version of d (P1, N21)			
	Chords of 6 sounds [notes]			
P1, N22 (minor)	GB♭D/AEF 4 versions	5+5, 3+5, 3-5...	(0,1,2,5,6,8)	G minor/ a minor
P1, N23 (major)	AEC#/FBG 3 versions	5+5, 3+5..., 3-5+	= P1, N13	A major/G mixolydian
P1, N24 (major)	GBD/FC# A 2 versions	5+5, 3+5..., 1-5...	= P1, N131	G major/ d minor (melodic. ascending)

" = idea of Rodolfo Halffter presented to the author in 1984.
f = Falla writes incorrectly 3-5, 1+5.

- Example 3 bis with its derivative notes of A and F yield the possibility of Bb major over c minor. Falla notes a 4+ chord (V of Bb chord).
- Example 6 bis has the same result as P1, N6. Falla notes a first inversion for B major and its enharmonic, Cb major.
- Example 7 bis has the same result as P1, N7. Falla notes the root of the chord, Eb.
- Example 9 bis with its derivative notes of Cb and Ab yield the possibility of ab minor over c minor. Falla notes a second inversion chord over Ab.
- Example 10 bis with its derivative notes of B and A yield the possibility of E major over c minor. Falla notes a V of E as 6.

- Example 10-3 has the possibility of V7-i (G7-c minor). Falla writes V of C, as 7.

Example 11.1b P1, N1—*Superposiciones*

The document intitled *Superposiciones (Superpositions)* was published in 1975 and gives a representation of de Falla's system. For example, from a minor chord C–Eb-G, (on *Page 1, Number 1* from now on referred to as P1, N1), de Falla generates the resonances of Ab and D by using the formula 5+5, 3–5. This means that to the fifth of the chord, the note G, is added another perfect fifth, thereby resulting in D; and to the third of the chord, the note Eb, is subtracted a perfect fifth, thereby resulting in the note Ab.

Example 11.2 P2—N1, N2, N3, N4, N5, N6, N7—*Superposiciones*

Example	Generator/ Resonance	Derivative	Prime Form	Bitonal possibilites
For the minor 7th or its inversion of major 9th				
1. P2, N1 (2 versions)	C E G/ F# Ab (G#)	3-5+, 1+5...	(0,1,2,4,8)	F# major/ C major
2. P2, N2 (6 versions)	Bb D F/ Gb Ab	3+5..., 3-5+	P1, N10	Gb major/ Bb major
3. P2, N3	A C E/ G G# F#	3+5+5+, 3-5...	(0,2,3,4,5,8)	
4. P2, N4	G Bb D/ F Gb Ab	5+5..., 5-5..., 3+5	P2, N3	Db major/ G minor
5. 2 P2, N5	Eb Gb Bb/ Db Ab	3+5, 1-5	(0,2,4,7,9) P1, N4	Db major/ Eb minor
Distinct planes–[5 note chords]				

Example 11.2   P2—N1, N2, N3, N4, N5, N6, N7—*Superposiciones* (*cont.*)

Example	Generator/ Resonance	Derivative	Prime Form	Bitonal possibilites
	Distinct planes–[5 note chords] (continued)			
1. P2, N6 (4 versions)	= P2, N1 (transposed) F#AC#/BE	3-5+, 1+5...	P2, N1	
2. P2, N7 (3 versions)	= P2, N2 (transposed) CE♭G/B♭F = P1, N4	3+5..., 3-5+	P2, N2	
3. P2, N8 (3 versions)	GEA/F# G# (+ trans- positions)	3+5?5+, 3-5...	(0,1,2,3,5)	
	BDF#/EA = P1, N4 (transposed)		(0,2,4,7,9) P1, N4	B minor/ A major; pentatonic
4. P2, N9 (3 versions)	FDG/ F# G# (+ trans- postions)	5+5..., 5-5+, 3+5	(0,1,2,3,6)	
	ACE/GD = P1, N4 (transposed)		(0,2,4,7,9) P1, N4	A minor/ G major; pentatonic
5-2. P2, N10 (3 versions)	G♭B♭E♭/ D♭ A♭ (+ trans- postions) = P1, N4		(0,2,4,7,9) P1, N4	E♭ minor/ D♭ major; pentatonic
5. P2, N11 2 chords (major + relative minor) generate the resonances (5 versions)	A major/ F# minor = (F#) BE; Eb major/ C minor = F, C, (B♭), (F); D major/ B minor = E, (B), A, (E); A minor = D, (E); E♭ minor = A♭, D♭			

Falla indicates an example, no. 5, at the end of each section under "Distinct Planes."

The last two pages show practical applications of these chord generations in Falla's own works.[32]

Example 11.3   Page 3—*Superposiciones*

Example	Title	Location[33]
Example 1		
C major = 5+5...+5+, 3+5...	Ritual Fire Dance ("Danza ritual del fuego") from *El amor brujo*	Ms. 21–26
Example 2		
A major = 5+5, 3-5	Ritual Fire Dance from *El amor brujo*	No. 27, ms. 1–3
Example 2 bis		
E minor = 3+5, 1-5	Ritual Fire Dance from *El amor brujo*	No. 26, ms. 9–11
Example 3		
D major = 3+5, A major = 3+5	Midnight[34] ("Medianoche")— The Magic Spell (Los sortilegios) from *El amor brujo*	Ms. 1–2
Example 4		
C major = 5+5, 3+5...-5, 1-5	The Magic Circle ("El círculo mágico") from *El amor brujo*	No. 23, ms. 9–11
Example 4 bis		
Bb major = 3+5-5 E minor = 1-5	The Miller's Dance ("Danza del Molinero") (Farruca) from *El sombrero de tres picos*	No. 9, ms. 9–10
Example 5		
A major = 5+5..., 1-5	Dance of the Play of Love ("Danza del juego de amor") from *El amor brujo*	No. 55, ms. 3–8
Example 6		
E minor = 3+5, 1-5	Finale—The Bells at Dawn ("Las Campanas del Amanecer") from *El amor brujo*	No. 64, ms.1

Example 11.3   Page 3—*Superposiciones* (continued)

Example	Title	Location
Example 7		
G minor = 1-5	Afternoon	Ms. 15 before no. 1
C minor = 5..., 3+5	("Atardecer") from	
	El sombrero de tres	
	picos	
Example 8		
Db major = 5+5, 1+5	By night the cuckoo sings	No. 19, ms. 3–7
C minor = 3 + 5..., 1-5	("Por la noche canta	
	el cuco") from *El*	
	sombrero de tres picos	
Example 9		
E minor = 3+5, 1-5	*Fantasía bætica*	Ms. 29
Example 10		
E minor = 3+5, 1-5	*El retablo de Maese*	Ms. 30; source:
A minor = 3-5	*Pedro*, Cuadro II	Pedrell's *Cancionero*,
	(Melisendra)	I, p. 22, 23, 25
Example 11		
G major = 5+5, 3-5	*El retablo de Maese*	No. 32, ms. 1 and
	Pedro, Cuadro III—	Finale, no. 96,
		ms. 4
The Moor's	Supplication ("El	
	suplico del Moro")	
Example 12		
B minor 3+5..., 1-5	*El retablo de Maese*	No. 41, ms. 4–9
	Pedro, Cuadro III	

Page 11.4   Page 4—*Superposiciones*

Example	Title	Location
Example 1		
B major = 5+5+,	*El retablo de Maese*	No. 75, ms. 1–4
3+5..., 1-5 = 1-5-5,	*Pedro*, Cuadro IV	
1-5-5-5	(Fuga)	
Example 2		
	"El paño moruno" from	Ms. 1–4
	Siete canciones	
	populares españolas	
Example 3		
	"El paño moruno" from	Ms. 65–67
	Siete canciones	
	populares españolas	

Example	Title	Location[33]
Example 3 bis		
	"El paño moruno" from *Siete canciones populares españolas*	Ms. 58–60
Example 4		
	"Jota" from *Siete canciones populares españolas*	Falla writes p. 15 (22) referring to the published version; F clef; and other jottings
Example 5		
	"Jota" from *Siete canciones populares españolas*	Ms. 59 (A) and 60 (B). Continuation of Ex. 4, with melody broken down into two parts, "A" and "B"
Example 6		
	"Asturiana" from *Siete canciones populares españolas*	Ms. 10–12 in left hand; Falla also writes ("last page")

It is also presumed that Falla was concretely developing these ideas as early as his work on *Piezas españolas* (1906–1909). There appears a reference to the "resolution of the notes of attraction" in the sketch material for "Aragonesa," as well as indications "to make a harmonic design over a chord, give the melody notes foreign to it."[35]

Musicologist Chris Collins says that Falla's application of using the perfect fifths superposed upon major and minor triads may be related to Lucas, but no justification is found for using augmented or diminished fifths, or the overtone series, for that matter.

So Falla may have found in "L'Acoustique nouvelle" the inspiration for a method of generating chords involving the superimposition of perfect fifths above notes of a base triad. By contrast, his methods involving the overtone series (used only to achieve a special effect) and superimposed augmented and diminished fifths (perhaps not used at all) owe little or nothing to Lucas's ideas. The blame for the prevailing misunderstanding must seem to lie with Roland-Manuel and Pahissa, both of whom sought to link these methods with "L'Acoustique nouvelle."[36]

A similar lack of justification would also seem to be the case for chords generated from the strings of the guitar—EADGBE (prime form = 0,2,4,7,9 and similar to the P1, N4 conglomerate of the *Superposiciones* and also found in the *Sriraga* mode). The prevalent interval found in this tuning, the perfect fourth, is not given priority by Lucas. However, Falla could have rationalized its usage by considering it as the inversion of the perfect fifth. In the *Retablo notebook* on page 31 he writes:

> Other harmonic procedures [:] or to a melodic note or a perfect fifth, or its inversion (a perfect fourth) add a perfect major or minor chord which results from the harmonic resonance of the fundamental, the fifth or of a simple melodic note (1st case). 2. In the cases of appoggiaturas already observed, study the use of appoggiaturas of the appoggiaturas or neighbouring notes themselves.[37]

The only other interval present in the guitar strings is the major third between G and B and this interval has been discussed within the context of the major triad.

A theory of natural resonance (or a system of harmonic generation derived from the laws of natural resonance), whose basis is found in the overtone series, could explain some aspects but not all. However, Lucas's book barely mentions this concept.

Rodolfo Halffter views Falla's application of the superposition technique in a different way. In the notes to his unpublished document, "Conjunto de Series Dodecafonica . . ." (Dodecaphonic Series Aggregate Projected and Utilized by Me), he claims that *melody* is the generator of the harmony, not the other way around. "The melodic line—tonal or modal—always firmly designed, is the element that regulates the connection of the sonorous conglomerates amongst themselves."[38]

Falla must first have been influenced in this direction by his teacher Pedrell.

> The mere comparison of some of the songs transcribed and harmonized by Pedrell with the transcription and the harmonization of the same songs appearing in preceding collections, will show us how a song that we hardly noticed before becomes singularly significant in his hands. The reason is that the very peculiar modal character of some of those songs is reduced in the older collections to the invariable tonal sentiment of the major and minor scales, whereas Pedrell extracted from them their true modal and harmonic essence.[39]

If melody is indeed the basis (and the justification) for harmony, then Falla's fascination with folksong, with chant, and with different modes is seen in a different light. Indeed, on page 15 of the *Retablo notebook*, Falla affirms this concept.

> The tonality resides in the melodic line. IMPORTANT 1/Considering what I have done—generally speaking—up to now, I propose in the future that

Manuel de Falla's Birthplace in Cádiz, Spain, Plaza de Espoz y Mina, no. 3

"La Morilla," Moorish nanny, and Manuel de Falla

*Manuel de Falla in "bullfighter"
Carnival costume*

*Falla family: Manuel de Falla,
with his father, mother, sister
and two aunts*

Eloísa Galluzzo, Falla's second piano teacher, after his mother

Piano method by Orelgamar, presented to Falla in Paris by Eloísa Galluzzo

Musical evenings at the Viniegra salon

Claude Debussy: "To Manuel de Falla with profound admiration from Emma and Claude Debussy"

LA CLASSE DIÉMER EN 1895

Photo du Monde Musical

L. AUBERT, BERNARDEL, GROVLEZ, IMBERTI, GALLON, CORTOT, BOUCHERLE, ESTYLE, BÉRIA, ROUSSEL
Devant le piano : Louis DIÉMER, Lazare LÉVY, Victor STAUB

LA CLASSE CH. DE BÉRIOT EN 1905

Photo du Monde Musical

RAVEL, DECREUS, LHÉRIÉ, BERNARD, LEMAIRE, SCHIDENHELM, ROBICHON, CHADEIGNE, R. VIÑÈS, CORTÈS
SALOMON, MOTTE-LACROIX
Assis devant le piano : CH. DE BÉRIOT, MALATS

Piano students at the Paris Conservatoire, classes of Diémer (1895) and Beriót (1905)

Igor Stravinsky as child: "To Manuel de Falla, to whom this child adores with all his heart," Igor Stravinsky, Paris, 17-V-1930

Oil painting by Georges D'Espagnat depicting Ricardo Viñes at the piano surrounded by Maurice Ravel, Déodat de Sèverac, Albert Roussel, Florent Schmitt, Cyprien Godebski, and his son, M. P. Calcocoressi

Manuel de Falla y una escena de "La vida breve".

La vida breve *at the Teatro de la Zarzuela in Madrid, November of 1914,
with the composer.*

Manuel de Falla, Gregório and Maria Martínez Sierra, and María's sister

EN EL TEATRO LARA
PASTORA IMPERIO EN LA GITANADA "EL AMOR BRUJO", DE MARTINEZ SIERRA Y FALLA. (CARICATURA POR FRESNO)

Caricature of Pastora Imperio

Leonid Massine in
The Three-Cornered
Hat, *1919*

One of Picasso's scenery depictions for The Three-Cornered Hat, *1919*

Pianist Artur Rubinstein, who commissioned and premiered Fantasía Bætica

Manuel de Falla with Don Quixote of El retablo de Maese Pedro, *Venice, 1932*

Ernesto Halffter conducting the Orquesta Bética de Cámara with Falla in rehearsal

*Francisco García Lorca, Antonio Luna, María del Carmen de Falla, Federico
García Lorca, Wanda Landowska, Manuel de Falla, and José Segura in Granada*

Falla and musicians recording Falla's Concerto *in Paris in 1927*

Daniel Vazquez Diaz's depiction of Manuel de Falla (who never composed for the organ), composing The Three-Cornered Hat, *Teatro Real, Madrid*

Scene from Calderón de la Barca's El gran teatro del mundo

Machu Picchu, Falla's "Atlántida"

Falla's disembarking at Sancti Petri Island, Cádiz, accompanied by José María Pemán

Manuel de Falla upon departure for Argentina pictured with Germán, sister-in-law María Luisa López, and their daughter, María Isabel (Maribel)

Falla's last house in Argentina, "Los Espinillos" in Alta Gracia

Manuel de Falla and María del Carmen in the garden at "Los Espinillos"

The last photo of Manuel de Falla

The ship Buen Esperanza *(Good Hope) bringing Falla's cadaver back to Cádiz for burial.*

each chord or group of harmonic sounds be a direct consequence of the note or melodic turn they accompany or complete without taking into account the *tonal* value of that note or melodic figure apart from the cases in which it acts in a *cadential* manner. But even in these cases, it is the bass, more than the chord, which must correspond to the tonal value of the melody. The harmonic resonances (χ) (simple or double) that this bass produces will, therefore, be free.[40]

Through Lucas, Falla found justification for some of his ideas in the search for a renewal of a Spanish musical idiom: reliance upon *cante jondo*, rationalization of the law of consonance, absolute law of the major triad (i.e., tonality), etc. Through Lucas, Falla could also find justification for foreign application of "hispanizing" music, for example, in Debussy and others. Falla's profound respect for Debussy's music and Debussy's understanding of Spanish music are well documented. For example, jottings from Debussy's *Quartet* are found in the sketch material for "Montañesa" of the *Piezas españolas*.[41]

. . . [Debussy's] music is not written in the Spanish style, but rather in Spanish, or better still, in Andalusian, since our "cante jondo" in its most authentic form is the origin not only of those of his works with an intentionally Spanish character but also of certain musical values found in other works of his which were not composed with that intention. We refer to his frequent use of certain modes, cadences, links between chords, rhythms and even melodic shouts which reveal a clear relationship with our natural music.[42]

Through Lucas, too, Falla could find a way to experiment beyond the bonds of tonality without leaving tonality—a concept completely acceptable to him. As was mentioned in chapter 7, tonality was for him tantamount to his faith in God. His quasi-atonal writing in such works as *Le tombeau de Paul Dukas* (1935) and parts of *Atlántida* (1927–1946) or his assignment of pitches to the name of E. F. Arbós in his work *Fanfare sobre el nombre de Arbós* (1934)—as in the Schönberg twelve-tone system or via Bartók through his Axis system[43]—would have been liberal applications of the Lucas concepts. Indeed Rodolfo Halffter pointed out the similarities of the *Superposiciones* with some twelve-tone applications in his explanation *Conjunto de series*.[44]

The concepts of internal rhythm ("the relation of symmetry between periods and cadences"[45] that Falla so admired in some of the works of Domenico Scarlatti[46]), natural resonance (based on the overtone system), and "apparent poly-tonality" have been frequently written about when referring to the Lucas influence upon Falla. Falla's early biographers, Pahissa and Roland-Manuel, too elaborated on them, with Falla's approval.

However, Chris Collins comes to the conclusion that Falla's role in perpetuating the myth—that he learned the system of chord generation based on the harmonic series from Lucas—may have been for aesthetic reasons. His direct references to the book, according to Collins, mostly occurred during the decade of the 1920's.[47] By that time, he had already assimilated the ideas of Lucas. He was looking to escape the bonds of nationalism with its ready folk-identity. Falla's categorizing of the qualities of the *cante jondo* as "primitive," "natural," and "pure" were thus "defined through reference to Lucas's theories."[48]

> "L'Acoustique nouvelle" offered a theoretical rational of music's "purest" principles: perfect consonance, free subdivision of the octave, and so on. With the full superimposition technique, Falla had discovered a way of demonstrating the purity of his harmonic language; by associating it with Lucas's primitivist theories, he was able to demonstrate the purity of the technique itself.[49]

Taken in this light, Sopeña's statement—"The importance that Falla gives to the casual encounter and the impassioned study of *L'Acoustique nouvelle* of Louis Lucas can seem to be exaggerated"[50]—is clearly understood.

NOTES

1. The author is indebted for much of the content of the first part of this article to Chris Collins in his article "Manuel de Falla, *L'Acoustique Nouvelle* and Natural Resonance: a Myth Exposed," published in the *Journal of the Royal Musical Association*, no. 128/22 (May 2003), and used with kind permission; and in the second part to Rodolfo Halffter, who, before his demise in 1987, graciously gave me valuable, unpublished information regarding his own, and Falla's, music.

2. Sopeña's text appears with his misspellings. "Puede parecer exagerada la importancia que Falla da al encuentro casual y al estudio apasionado de 'L'acustique nouvelle' de Luis Lucas. La verdad que ni en España ni en la misma Francia aparecen el autor y el libro como trascendentales: para Roland Manuel que pudo investigar más a fondo se trata de un libro 'olvidado,' incluso com el prólogo del importante Bainville" (Sopeña, 26).

"The importance of Falla's casual encounter and passionate study of 'L'acustique nouvelle' of Luis Lucas can seem exaggerated. The truth that neither in Spain nor in France itself do the author nor the book appear transcendental: for Roland Manuel, who could investigate more deeply, it is treated as 'forgotten,' including the prologue of the important Bainville" (Sopeña, 26).

3. The Rastro is given by biographer Roland-Manuel and near the Botanical Gardens is given by biographer Pahissa. Both biographers were read and approved by Falla.

4. The first edition, *Une revolution dans la musique*, was published in 1849, and being a poor seller was revised and reedited by the author. (*The New Acoustics—A Revolution in Music—An Attempt to Apply a Philosophical Theory to Music—Preceded by a Preface by Théodore de Bainville and Followed by a Treatise by Euclid and by Plutarch's Dialogue on Music*, Paris, published by the Author, 1854. Scanty biographical details about Lucas may be found in *Biographie universelle des musiciens et bibliographie générale de la musique*, 2nd ed. Paris, 1878 by F.-J.Fétis, who complains that Lucas plagarizes his theories.)
  5. Collins, 4.
  6. Collins, 47, fn. 23. "All authorities agree that he came across the book in Madrid, though the precise location is disputed. The accounts given in the three Falla biographies written with the composer's assistance are inconsistent: according to Adolfo Salazar and Jaime Pahissa, he acquired it from one of the bookstalls outside the Madrid Botanical Gardens (Salazar, *La música contemporánea en España* (Madrid, 1930), 161; Pahissa (transl. Jean Wagstaff), *Manuel de Falla: His Life and Works* (London, 1954), 29–30), while Roland-Manuel claims he bought it in the Rastro street-market (*Manuel de Falla* (Paris, 1930), 28). These three writers are even more vague on the date of the book's purchase. Though dates are suggested by most modern Falla biographers, few agree and none cite supporting evidence. Suggestions range from 1901 (Manuel Orozco Díaz, *Falla* (Barcelona, 1985), 32–33) to 1906 (Enrique Franco, *Manuel de Falla y su obra* (Madrid, 1976), 14; Ronald Crichton, *Falla*, 13; José Luis García del Busto, *Falla* (Madrid, 1995), 13). The evidence in support of a date around 1904 is Falla's statement that he acquired his copy of the book around the time that he began to compose *La vida breve* (sketch for letter to Roland-Manuel, undated [30 December 1928]: Archivo Manuel de Falla, correspondence folder 7520. The earliest date found in the sketches for this opera is 4 November 1904 (AMF, MS XXXV A1)."
  7. Collins, 40 (AMF, 7520).
  8. Collins, 47 (AMF, MS XXXV A1).
  9. AMF, 11502. "The majority of his annotations serve to emphasise sections of the text: passages are underlined, bracketed and summarised in the margins. But there are some annotations which correct errors in the text, and others which define or translate difficult concepts (sometimes through the use of musical notation), or cross-refer to other sections of the book. The range of these marginalia reveal that Falla took great pains to read Lucas's book and to come to terms with his ideas. In places, Falla emphasised sections by writing the word 'importante'—or even 'importantísimo' [very important]—in the margin; this implies much more than a passing curiosity. There is evidence that Falla's study of the book extended over a long period: several different writing instruments are used, and there are a range of handwriting styles" (Collins, 8).
  10. Collins, 3.
  11. Collins, 5.
  12. Demarquez, 20.
  13. Collins, 4.
  14. Collins, 4–5.

15. These are Falla's words in *Retablo notebook* to see the introduction of Lucas's book in Collins, 15, fn. 32).

16. Collins, 10.

17. Collins, 49, fn. 30. "This work is *La vida breve* (Act Two). Apart from this, the only other principal works which conclude with a chord other than a plain major triad are: *Andaluza* and *Les Colombes* (which are bare fifths), the *Homage to Debussy* (bare octave), *Seguidilla murciana, Canción* and *Fantasía bœtica* (major triads with added notes), the *Homage to Dukas* (minor triad with an added sixth), and *Asturiana* and *Psyché* (dissonance)."

18. Collins, 25–26, fn. 47. The interview appeared on 18 July 1919, in the *Daily Mail* and is entitled "To the young composer: Senor Manuel de Falla and German formalism." It also appears in Adolfo Salazar's *Sinfonia y ballet,* Madrid: Mundo Latino, 1929 as well as in OMM, 68.

19. Collins, 28, fn. 51.

20. Ibid.

21. OMM, 101.

22. OMM, 101.

23. OMM, 101.

24. Chris Collins puts the date around 1920, see Collins, 9. Michael Christoforidis discovered the *Retablo notebook* and named it during his research at the AMF.

25. Collins, 14–15, fn. 32.

26. Madrid: Alpuerto, 1983 (1st ed.) and 2nd ed. Titled *Manuel de Falla (su obra para piano) y Noches en los jardines de España*, coedition Manuel de Falla Ediciones + Alpuerto, Madrid, 2001.

27. As a member of the Grupo de Ocho "Group of Eight" (the group of eight young composers who strove to create a new Spanish nationalist language and who had Falla as their ideal), Halffter later continued to be influenced by Falla after his exile to Mexico by applying the superposition technique to dodecaphony.

He is one of few composers who was able to ingeniously incorporate the concept of "apparent poly-tonality" into the twelve-tone system. He says, "Observe, in some cases, the existing relation between serial technique and the technique of the *Superposiciones*" (Conjunto de Series—RH).

28. Nancy Lee Harper, *ex tempore,* . . . *Retiro Atardecer Granadine*

Es un día cualquiera del mes de junio de 1971. Cerca de la Puerta del Vino deambulamos Gerardo Gombau, músico de gran talla y amigo mío entrañable y yo.

"Gerardo, no sé en donde he leido," que la contemplación de una tarjeta postal que ofrecia en vivos colores una vista de este celebre monumento de la Alhambra inició a Debussy uno de sus Preludios mas andaluces.

"Eso es," lo recuerdo bién, "lo que asegurá Falla en sus *Escritos* sobre Debussy. ¿Comó he podido olvidarlo?" exclama asombrado. "Yo que primero de saber y conocer al dedillo los *Escritos* de Don Manuel."

Hablamos luego de acontecimientos de años difuntos. Por supuesto, evocamos aquellos conciertos de música nueva, que en las decada de los treinta, organizamos en la madrileña residencia de estudiantes, armando un sonado alboroto.

"Rodolfo, entonces eramos jóvenes. Nosotros, nuestras almas, estaban colmadas de inquietudes. Nosotros nos animaba una idéntica ilusión de realizarnos como artistas, de participar en empresas musicales ambiciosas. Pero la maldita guerra civil española truncó todas nuestras esperanzas." La noche se nos hechó encima. Gerardo y yo, inciamos el descenso de la Alhambra a la ciudad. Debilmente alumbra el camiño la luz mortecina de un par de vetustas farolas.

"Cuidado, Gerardo, vas a tropezar." De repente, nos sale al encuentro Don Valentín Ruíz Aznar, sacerdote, maestro de capilla, y amigo íntimo de Falla. En la oscuridad, le reconocemos por el timbre familiar y bondadosa de su voz. "Os estoy buscando. Alguien me dijo que estabais ahí arriba. Me felicitó de haberlos encontrado. Yo voy hacerlos un regalo muy valioso. Lo sabreis apreciar porque son músicos."

Se trata de cuatro hojas de papel pautado que contiene notas, cifras y garabatos trazados con la própria mano de Falla. Y sin añadir más comentario Don Valentín nos entraga sendos juegos de esos papeles.

"Muchas gracias, Don Valentín." Con apretados y afectuosos abrazos nos despidimos de él.

El hotel, en el que nos hospedamos, Gerardo y yo, está ubicado en el centro de Granada. Ahí residen también otros profesores del segundo curso Manuel de Falla, curso este organizado dentro del marco del veinte Festival de Música y Danza.

En mi habitación, mientras Emilia, mi esposa, ojea una revista, yo examiné con curiosidad cresciente el obsequio que acaba de hacerme Don Valentín. En su aspecto material lo constituye un juego de cuatro copias fotostáticas que reproducen los cuatros hojas de papel pautado con las cotaciones y anotaciones de Falla.

¿Entregó Don Valentín a Gerardo el manuscrito original de Don Manuel, o al igual que hizo consigo, conmigo le dió solo copias fotostáticas, lo ignoro?

Como Gerardo falleció repetinamente algunos meses más tarde quien me lo iba a decir no he podido averiguar.

Granada, 2 de Marzo de 1972

Después he examinado estos papeles de Falla y su importancia es muy grande. Pues que se trata del único testimonio por escrito que Falla ha dejado acerca de su técnica.

29. "Un conglomerado sonoro está integrado por la suma de las notas de una tríada mayor o menor más los sonidos añadidos o agregados, de conformidad con las numerosas posibilidades de superposiciones que ofrece el método ideado por Falla."

"Un conglomerado sonoro puede integrarse también mediante la suma de un fragmento de escala diatónica, cuya tónica es la nota fundamental de una tríada, más los sonidos añadidos o superpuestos." From "Notas," unpublished document by Rodolfo Halffter presented to the author by Halffter in 1984 during the course of her doctoral studies related to his piano sonatas.

30. "Conjunto de Series Dodecafonicas Proyectadas y Utilizadas por Mi" (Dodecaphonic Agregate Series Projected and Utilized by Me), parts of which were published in my *ex tempore* article. In Halffter's document, he deciphers Falla's shorthand used in the *Superposiciones*, as well as points out similarities to the twelve-tone serial technique, amongst other things.

31. Harper, *ex tempore*, 65. Some of the bitonal combinations come from unpublished papers of Halffter presented to the author during her doctoral studies, while others belong to the author.

32. See Harper, *ex tempore* 88, for a complete identification of Falla's examples from his own works.

33. No. refers to rehearsal numbers and ms. refers to measures.

34. Antonio Gallego surmises that Falla wrote the *Superposiciones* document from memory, due to the error in the chord in Example 3, page 3, ms. 2 of "Medianoche," whose inner note should be a D and not an E. See Antonio Gallego, *Manuel de Falla y El amor brujo.* Madrid: Alianza, 1990, 156–57 (fn. 325).

35. Antonio Gallego, *Catálogo*, 67.

36. Collins, 38–39.

37. Falla, "Retablo notebook 31. "Otros procedimientos harmónicos a una nota melódica o a una Quinta justa, interval o invertida (una 4ª justa) añadir el acorde perfecto mayor o menor que resulta de la resonancia harmónica de la fundamental de la 5ª o de la simple nota melódica (1er caso). 2. En los casos de apoyaturas ya estudiados estudiar el uso de apoyatura(s) de aquellas mismas apoyaturas o notas vecinas." Cited in MC diss., 484.

38. "La línea melódica—tonal o modal—siempre firmemente dibujada, es elemento que ajusta el enlace de los conglomerados sonoros entre sí." From "Notas," unpublished document by Rodolfo Halffter, given to the author in May, 1983.

39. OMM, 60.

40. "Es en la linea melódica donde reside la tonalidad. IMPORTANTE 1/Entre lo que he hecho—generalmente—hasta aquí, me propongo en adelante considerar cada acorde o conjunto de sonidos harmónicos como consecuencias directas de la nota o giro melódico que acompañan o completan, sin tener en cuenta el valor *tonal* de dicha nota o giro más que en aquellos casos en que supongan un valor *cadencial*. Pero aun en estos casos, el bajo, más bien que el acorde, es el que ha de corresponder al valor tonal melódico. Las resonancias harmónicas (X) (simples o dobles) que dicho bajo produzca, serán, por lo tanto, libres." Cited in MC diss. appendix 1.6: 15, 468.

41. ACG, p. 68 (XXXVII A 7).

42. Collins, 29, fn. 54; also cited in OMM, 108–9.

43. Bartók Axis System, see Yvan, Nommick, *Manuel de Falla: Oeuvre et Évolution du Langage Musical*, Ph.D. dissertation, Université de Paris-Sorbonne (Paris IV), II, 1998–1999, 408.

44. For a more detailed explanation, see my article in *ex tempore*, 65.

45. Otto Mayer Serra, "Falla's Musical Nationalism," *The Musical Quarterly*, vol. XXIX, no. 1, January 1943, 10.

46. Two of the Scarlatti sonatas analyzed by Halffter with Falla were Longo 15 (d minor) and Longo 58 (a minor). See Harper, *ex tempore*, 58.

47. Collins, 41.

48. Collins, 41.

49. Collins, 41.

50. "Puede parecer exagerada la importancia que Falla da al encuentro casual y al estudio apasionado de *L'acustique nouvelle* de Luis Lucas." cited in *Vida y Obra de Falla* by Federico Sopeña, Madrid: Turner, 1988, 26.

Chapter 12

From Folksong to Plainchant: Musical Borrowings and the Transformation of Manuel de Falla's Musical Nationalism in the 1920s[1]

Michael Christoforidis

You will hear in [Manuel de Falla's] Concerto that the regional influences play a lesser role than in his preceding works. This music is a composite of Hispano-Castilian elements rather than an echo of impressions of Andalusia or another Spanish province. It is extremely important to stress this point because naturally every concert-goer, and even a musician, expects and rejoices in advance at the thought of hearing in the new [de] Falla Concerto some languishing motifs of the Alhambra accompanied by arpeggios imitating the guitar.[2]

These remarks were transmitted by Wanda Landowska to the American critic Lawrence Gilman in December 1926 with Manuel de Falla's knowledge, in an attempt to shape the critical reception of the composer's new style. In his music of the 1920s Falla progressively shifted from evoking Spanish folklore, and especially that of Andalusia, to exploring Spain's musical past. *El retablo de Maese Pedro* (1918–1923), the puppet opera based on passages from Miguel de Cervantes' *Don Quijote*, and the *Concerto* for harpsichord (1923–1926) constitute Falla's principal works from this period and mark his conscious reinterpretation of nationalism in the light of emerging neoclassical trends. This paper explores some of the factors behind the transformation of Falla's nationalism and the impact of this change upon his integration of Hispanic musical sources.

CASTILE, EUROPE, AND HISPANIC NATIONALISM

From their initial performances, both *El retablo de Maese Pedro* and the *Concerto* have been described as "Castilian" or "Hispano-Castilian" and

Falla himself encouraged this denomination, in part to counter preconceived expectations both of his own style and of what constituted "Spanish" music at home and abroad. Falla's output to the end of World War I had been indebted to Romantic and Impressionistic imagery of Spain and it was during his Paris years (1907–1914) that he came under the full influence of Alhambrism and the Romantic perceptions of Granada as the nearest manifestation of the Orient. From 1908 he began to read the seminal French texts by François René Chateaubriand, Victor Hugo, and Théophile Gautier which disseminated the nostalgic vision of Granada, and by extension Spain, as the last European refuge of Arab culture and presented its gypsy dwellers as their progeny or exotic substitutes.[3] These perspectives were not restricted to European (and particularly French) constructions of Spain as exotic Other but were also adopted as legitimate expressions of nationalism by Spanish artists themselves.[4] Much of Falla's early salon music and his first opera, *La vida breve* of 1905, recreate these topics and are even indebted to the means employed by Romantic composers to denote Spanishness in numerous *espagnolades*, while *Noches en los jardines de España* (1909–1916) draws on various impressionistic evocations of Spain in its poetic conception and style. In *El amor brujo* (1914–1915), the *Fantasía Bætica* (1919), and passages of *El sombrero de tres picos* (1917–1919) Falla redefined imitations of flamenco and the guitar and reinterpreted visions of the gypsy in the light of the primitivist aesthetic which had pervaded Paris.[5]

Falla expressed his stylistic transformation in the 1920s by espousing a Castilian identity. This effectively reinforced his nationalist credentials and served to counter accusations from some of his colleagues that he had forsaken the creation of a Spanish musical language.[6] Unlike some of his European contemporaries Falla continued to foreground the nationalist ethos of his creations and did not view nationalism and modernism as necessarily antithetical trends. In February 1923, Falla wrote:

> I console myself by thinking that everything that is alive in European music is a result of a well-understood musical Nationalism. As Ravel says: Whatever is said or done, in the end we nationalists are the only ones who are correct. . . . And how are we to consider our musical nationalism exhausted when we have hardly done anything more than demonstrate the odd laudable intention?[7]

In a statement from 1925 Falla insisted that "the essential elements of music, the sources of inspiration are nations and people."[8] However, by

1929, this position was less pronounced, although he listed as one of his "Centres of aversion" a "mean-spirited nationalism,"[9] thus differentiating his own works from those of traditional nationalist composers, which included many of his more conservative compatriots.

Igor Stravinsky's disavowal of nationalism as the aesthetic driving force of his work in the 1920s and the directions explored by the postwar Parisian milieu also influenced the reorientation of Falla's musical nationalism. His shift from folklore to historical sources was in part conditioned by his desire to create a Spanish music that was relevant to the prevailing aesthetic and musical currents. This transformation gained the general approbation of his peers and especially that of his most esteemed colleague, Stravinsky:

> Falla was always very attentive to me and my work. When, after the premiere of his Tricorne, I told him that the best music in his score was not necessarily the most Spanish, I knew my remark would impress him.[10]

In his autobiography Stravinsky concluded that

> In my opinion [*El retablo* and the *Concerto*] give proof of incontestable progress in the development of his great talent. He has, in them, deliberately emancipated himself from the folklorist influence under which he was in danger of stultifying himself.[11]

Falla's "emancipation" from folklore is reflected in his conscious adoption of the term "Castilian" as a metaphor for a more universal Spain. In doing so he redefined Spain's racial characteristics, historical ties, and cultural legacy to achieve a construction of greater contemporary relevance. Falla's concept of nationalism evolved after his return to Madrid from Paris at the outset of World War I and was inextricably linked to broader questions of Spanish identity. He gravitated toward the progressive Spanish liberals who espoused a pro-French position, and who encouraged the involvement of musicians within a more wide-ranging cultural debate. In 1915 Falla was one of the signatories to a document issued by the intelligentsia of Madrid to make their pro-allied views public. It comprised a cross section of figures ideologically aligned with the *generaciones* (Spanish denominations of cultural generations) of 1898 and 1914, and included some of their principal members.[12] Falla assumed the ideals of Spanish renewal held by the cultural elites of the generation of 1898 who "extolled the power and glory of Castile and were not Castilians" and simultaneously "argued for the Europeanization

of Spain, [although] one finds tradition omnipresent in their works."[13]
Such views caused Falla to question the validity of a musical nationalism steeped solely in the idioms of his native region of Andalusia. In an
attempt to apply these ideas to music he did not, however, primarily embrace the folksong of Castile, which had been a source of local color in
the turn-of-the-century *zarzuela* and provided the basis of the musical
language of several of his contemporaries.[14] Rather, he searched for the
more universal aspects of its culture and history, and sought to project
the austerity and idealism of the Castilian spirit as it was encountered in
the great figures of her golden age (which for Falla included El Greco,
Miguel de Cervantes, and St. John of the Cross). In his reading of contemporary Spanish authors Falla underlined numerous passages which
conveyed these notions, such as the following by Azorín:

> Is there anything more romantic, more exalted, more generous than the
> spirit of Castile? There you have the work of our mystics; there would be
> few souls in history with such a great and pure idealism.[15]

Falla's idea of creating a work based on *El ingenioso Hidalgo Don
Quijote de la Mancha* was closely tied to these tendencies, and not
only because of its setting in Castile during Spain's golden age. Several key authors of the generations of 1898 and 1914, including
Miguel de Unamuno, Azorín, and José Ortega y Gasset, were fascinated by the figure of Don Quijote and employed Cervantes's novel
as a medium through which Spain's current situation could be analyzed.[16] This movement brought *Don Quijote* back into the main-
stream of Spanish cultural debate in the first decades of the twentieth
century, and the subject prompted Falla's creative impulses on numerous occasions prior to embarking on *El retablo de Maese Pedro*.[17]
An important catalyst for Falla's interest had been his attendance in
1905 at a conference marking the third centenary of the publication of
the first volume of *Don Quijote*. This seminal event held at Madrid's
Ateneo, a prominent institution in the movement for cultural renewal,
gave further impetus to interpretations of *Don Quijote* which related
the work to contemporary questions of Spanish identity. Falla referred
to the published conference proceedings upon commencing work on
El retablo de Maese Pedro and based several of his musical ideas on
works that Cecilio de Roda had employed to illustrate his lectures on
"Las canciones del Quijote" and "Los instrumentos, músicos y danzas
en el Quijote."[18] It is also interesting to note that the conference ended

with a reading of the Maese Pedro episode which Falla later employed.[19] Perhaps of greatest importance to the genesis of *El retablo de Maese Pedro*, however, was Falla's awareness of José Ortega y Gasset's *Meditaciones sobre el Quijote* of 1914.[20] This work by the influential Spanish philosopher includes a two-page commentary on Master Peter's puppet show which probably conditioned Falla's dramatic conception of the work. It may have also prompted his use of two sets of puppets and the incorporation of several musico-dramatic structures to intimate the levels of reality perceived by Ortega y Gasset in his interpretation of the episode.

In *El retablo de Maese Pedro*, Falla most clearly aligned himself with the ideals of post-1898 Spanish nationalism. This work was inspired by "the growing cult of Don Quijote as a symbol of national identity, which surfaced in 1905 . . . [and] culminated in the royal decree of 1920 that mandated daily reading of a passage of *Don Quijote* in all primary schools." [21] It also reflects the preoccupations with Castile, Spanish history and traditions, and the quest for modernity and contemporary European relevance, which formed part of the discourse of the generations of 1898 and 1914.

EARLY MUSIC, SOBRIETY, AND NEOCLASSICISM

Falla's stylistic redirection and the changing sources of his musical borrowings in the 1920s were clearly influenced by emerging neoclassical ideals in France and in the milieu of the Ballets russes. Yet Falla's transformation was also indebted to ideas of renewal or *regeneración* in the domain of Spanish music.[22] His contact with Felipe Pedrell, one of the principal ideologues of Spanish musical nationalism, exposed Falla to these currents and was crucial to his appreciation of pre-nineteenth-century Spanish music. An important element of *regeneración* in the second half of the nineteenth century had been the rediscovery of Spain's "glorious musical past," and with it the identification of national traits. Following in the steps of Hilarion Eslava, Mariano Soriano Fuertes, Baltasar Saldoni, and Carmena y Millán, Francisco Asenjo Barbieri undertook his musicological research in the second half of the nineteenth century partly to demonstrate to Europe the worth of Spain's past and present music. Pedrell had furthered Barbieri's musicological research on similar grounds. In his nationalist manifesto, *Por nuestra música* (1891), Pedrell outlined his thesis on the nexus between folk music and early music and created a framework for the employment of Spanish music of the past within contemporary operatic composition.[23]

The interrelation and interaction of folk and early music, and their role in stimulating contemporary musical production, was a theme developed by several Spanish musical commentators in the first two decades of the twentieth century. During his period of study with Pedrell between 1901 and 1904, Falla was encouraged to explore Spain's musical past, in particular the polyphony and instrumental music of the sixteenth and seventeenth centuries, in line with Pedrell's current interests and his work on the music of Tomás Luis de Victoria and Antonio de Cabezón. Falla also became familiar with Pedrell's *Hispania Schola Musica Sacra* and other publications of liturgical and organ music. Following Barbieri and Pedrell's examples, Rogelio Villar, Rafael Mitjana, Luis Villalba, Cecilio de Roda, and other musicians undertook research into early Spanish music and commented on its relevance to contemporary music. Both prior to his departure from Madrid in 1907 and after his return in 1914, Falla was very much part of this milieu and maintained close contacts with Roda and Villar.

This historical viewpoint also had practical repercussions in the performances promoted by the progressive nationalists who formed the Sociedad Nacional de Música in 1915. The presentation of new Spanish and European music (especially works by French composers) by this society was complemented by performances of early music and of transcriptions or arrangements of folksongs from published anthologies. For example, at the society's concert of 27 April 1915, the second half of the program was dedicated to the performance of works taken from Dámaso Ledesma's folksong collection, the *Cancionero Salmantino*. Even in its first season, the Sociedad Nacional de Música promoted performances of the thirteenth-century *Cantigas de Santa Maria*, in transcriptions and adaptations by Pedrell, as well as string quartet arrangements by P. Villalba of sixteenth-century vihuela compositions.

Pedrell refined his thesis on the relationship between folk music and early music in the prologue to the first volume of the *Cancionero musical popular español* published in 1917.[24] In the four volumes of this work which appeared by 1922, he presented an anthology of Spanish folk music alongside a range of Spanish music dating from the thirteenth to the eighteenth centuries. In an essay written during the composition of *El retablo de Maese Pedro* Falla commented that "one of the main achievements of the *Cancionero* is to unfold before our eyes the evolution of folk song, and its technico-musical treatment in our primitive and classical art."[25] Falla agreed with Pedrell that "the character of really national music is to be found not only in folk song and in the instinctive expression of primitive ages, but also in the great masterpieces," [26] but had reservations about Pedrell's "inclusion of musical passages taken from classical composers in some of his works, as well as the frequent use he made of folk music in its authentic form." [27] Pedrell's practice was indebted to nineteenth-century ideas on the employment of folk music, and he also incorporated fragments of early music in certain dramatic passages of his historical operas. Falla's application of Pedrell's theories involved a greater degree of conceptual and stylistic abstraction and was mediated by the aesthetic precepts of neoclassicism.

Pedrell's theories led Falla to conclude that "Excessive ornateness and useless complication have no affinity with the severely sober though expressive character of our best classical works." [28] This reinterpretation of the essential characteristics of Spain's music to focus on the sobriety of its early music formed the theoretical framework for Falla's composition of *El retablo de Maese Pedro* and had far-reaching stylistic repercussions in his music. It also paralleled in musical terms some of the issues raised by contemporary Spanish authors. Discussions of simplicity and sobriety were repeatedly annotated by Falla in his reading, and he was particularly taken by Azorín's discussion of simplification and the search for the "essence" of an object (which Falla paraphrased to describe his own creative process):

> When one has written much, when one has lived somewhat, then we disdain a multiplicity of details. We want just one detail to give the sensation of something. But the supreme thing in art is to remove the accessory, what is useless, the profuse, so as to conserve and fix what is characteristic.[29]

Azorín also perceived traits of concision and clarity in Spanish Medieval *Romances*, a genre that Falla was exploring in the 1920s and which informed passages of *El retablo de Maese Pedro*.

> Are these Romances the work of a true artist, that is to say, a man who has come to know that the supreme art is that of sobriety, simplicity and clarity?[30]

Several authors also framed the ideals of clarity and simplicity in terms of Latin traits. Although José Ortega y Gasset rejected such notions of Latin clarity in *Meditaciones del Quijote*,[31] Falla noted Azorín's remarks on concision, clarity and the Mediterranean in the works of Cervantes.[32] By focusing on such characteristics Falla also reflected the aesthetic concerns prevalent in Paris. From the prewar works of Satie and Ravel to the wartime production of Stravinsky and culminating in Cocteau's manifesto of 1918, *Le Coq et le Harlequin*, a greater directness and simplicity of musical language were espoused. Combined with notions of Latin clarity, transparency, and classicism they were presented as antidotes to German complexity.[33]

The nexus between early music and nationalism had also been reinforced during Falla's Paris years, when he was exposed to much pre-19th-century music. Through his close association with Claude Debussy, Maurice Ravel, and Paul Dukas, Falla was conscious of the fact that French artists "were drawn to their pre-romantic past which was construed to embody a purity inherent in their race."[34] The affinities in aesthetics and style between Debussy and the eighteenth-century composers Couperin and Rameau were noted by Falla, as was Ravel's fascination with the music of Couperin. This period also coincided with the incipient authentic instrument revival and Falla befriended many of its protagonists, including Henri Casadesus and Wanda Landowska, who would later play seminal roles in the performance of Falla's neoclassical works. Falla frequently attended concerts and lectures at the Schola Cantorum, which enabled him to hear operas by Rameau and Monteverdi, and the polyphonic sacred music of Palestrina, Morales, and Guerrero.[35]

The contemporary interest in Spanish music in Paris also extended to the rediscovery of Spain's musical past, as is evident in the influential monograph by Falla's friend, Henri Collet, on Spanish musical mysticism.[36] Collet lauded the austerity and idealism of the Castilian spirit and its manifestation in the works of Antonio de Cabezón and Tomás Luis de Victoria. Falla's contacts in Paris with the Spanish-Cuban pianist Joaquín Nin also exposed him to much early keyboard music, and to claims that the music of Domenico Scarlatti was indebted to Spanish popular styles imbibed during decades of residence in the Iberian peninsula.[37] French interest in Scarlatti's music was well known to Falla, both through the efforts of Georges Jean-Aubry and the preparation of a volume of the sonatas by Falla's mentor Paul Dukas. Falla offered to assist Dukas by looking for previously unknown Scarlatti sonatas in Spanish archives in 1917 and 1918.[38] Although this search did not prove fruitful it furthered Falla's knowledge of the music and manuscript sources of Scarlatti and of Antonio Soler, a composer whose works he played through in El Escorial and was even considering editing.[39]

While *El retablo de Maese Pedro* reflects many of the contemporary concerns of French and Spanish musical nationalism, the immediate impetus for Falla's employment of early music probably came from his close association with Serge Diaghilev and the Ballets Russes during World War I. Influenced by the company's production of ballets based on earlier works, such as Respighi's arrangement of pieces by Rossini for the ballet *Le boutique fantastique* and Tommasini's orchestration of Scarlatti sonatas in *Les femmes de bonne humeur*, in 1918 Falla embarked on a project of constructing a comic opera from works by Chopin. In mid-1919 Diaghilev actually suggested to Falla that he orchestrate some Italian baroque pieces which were to form the basis of Stravinsky's *Pulcinella*. Falla rejected the offer because of prior commitments, but witnessed Stravinsky's treatment of this material before undertaking the bulk of his work on *El retablo de Maese Pedro*.[40]

EARLIER USE OF FOLK AND FLAMENCO SOURCES

In his neoclassical works of the 1920s Falla did not abandon folk music altogether, but often used it in tandem with pre-Romantic Spanish music. The extent of Falla's musical borrowings varies throughout his output, and even within a work, depending on the work's conceptual dictates. The processes by which he studied, quoted, and integrated both folk and early music within his compositions are remarkably similar. In the works preceding *El retablo de Maese Pedro* Falla's exploration of folk music was mainly undertaken through published collections. An overview of Falla's incorporation of folk music in his scores to the end of World War I precedes the discussion of his use of musical borrowings in the 1920s.

Falla's most explicit statement on the use of folk music in contemporary composition was made in an essay from 1917 entitled "Nuestra música":

> Let us now turn to folksong. Some consider that one of the means to "nationalize" our own music is the strict use of popular material in a melodic way. In a general sense, I am afraid I do not agree, although in particular cases I think that procedure cannot be bettered. In popular song I think the spirit is more important than the letter. Rhythm, tonality and melodic intervals, which determine undulations and cadences, are the essential constituents of these songs. The people prove it themselves by infinitely varying the purely melodic lines of their songs. The rhythmic or melodic accompaniment is as important as the song itself. Inspiration, therefore, is to be found directly in the people, and those who do not see it so will only achieve a more or less ingenious imitation of what they originally set out to do.[41]

The position espoused by Falla has often been interpreted too literally, and taken to imply that he mainly relied on by live performances
of folk music and eschewed the strict use of melodies he derived from
this practice.[42] Despite his claims to be inspired "directly in the people"
for the most part Falla did not take an active role in folksong collection, the true situation being rather closer to Béla Bartók's assessment
of Falla's procedures.

> It may be that the Russian Stravinsky and the Spaniard Falla did not go on
> journeys of [folksong] collection, and mainly drew on the collections of
> others, but they too, I feel sure, must have studied not only books and mu-
> seums but the living music of their countries.[43]

This observation by Bartók on the sources of the folk material employed by Stravinsky in his Russian works has been supported by a body
of research demonstrating Stravinsky's use of folksong collections.[44]
The extent to which Falla may have utilized such collections was initially considered in two articles by the eminent Spanish folklorist
Manuel García Matos, and these have provided the basis for much of the
later discussion surrounding Falla's use of folk material.[45] Greater access to Falla's personal library and compositional sketch materials over
the past decade has led to the identification of the collections handled by
the composer and provided further insights into his assimilation of folk
and other musics.[46]

Falla's activity as a folksong collector was not extensive prior to his
return from Paris to Spain in 1914. Despite being raised in Andalusia—
the region which provided the characteristics for much of what was seen
to be "Spanish" in nineteenth-century Europe—Falla lived in the cosmopolitan city of Cádiz, where his contact with folk music was not as
extensive as may first be thought. As a child and youth Falla led a relatively isolated existence, mainly socializing with the children of the
bourgeois merchant class, although he must have been exposed to numerous folk, popular, and flamenco forms. In an attempt by the mature
composer to demonstrate his early imbibing of folk music, Falla stressed
his exposure to the folklore of Andalusia as an infant through the songs
and stories of his nursemaid, "La morilla."[47] From this setting, Falla
moved to Madrid in his early twenties to further his studies at the Con-
servatorium. Several of Falla's early works, such as the *Serenata andaluza*, display the impact of Andalusian folk music and guitar techniques as they occur within the context of nineteenth-century salon
songs and instrumental pieces in the Andalusian style.[48] The *zarzuelas*

he composed in the subsequent years, and later suppressed, are littered with melodies taken from published folksong collections.[49] It was not until he came to study with Pedrell that Falla was actively encouraged to study folksong directly from the people. Pedrell's labors as a folksong collector were a source of profound inspiration for Falla,[50] and Antonio Gallego has argued that Falla's only extant collection of folksongs, a set of Christmas carols entitled *Cantares de Nochebuena*, was gathered in 1903 under the influence of Pedrell's teachings.[51]

Despite this experience in folksong collection, Falla continued to make use of published folksong anthologies as a compositional aid, even after ceasing his studies with Pedrell in 1904. In that year, he embarked on his first opera, *La vida breve*, which is set in the Albaicín quarter of Granada. Given that he had never been to Granada, Falla relied heavily on postcards of the town, printed anthologies of folksongs, and guitar scores containing songs and dances of the province to evoke the atmosphere of the Carlos Fernández Shaw's libretto.[52] This practice led to some awkward moments at the work's first production in Nice where Falla was obliged by the French cast and crew to relate his "first-hand" descriptions of the town.[53]

Falla's move to Paris in 1907 estranged him from the living source of Spanish folk music and prolonged his reliance on printed collections, although his contact with Spanish performers like the guitarist Angel Barrios did much to nurture his knowledge of flamenco forms.[54] *Cuatro piezas españolas* (1906–1908) and *Noches en los jardines de España* incorporate folk melodies taken from printed sources. Following his experiences with Pedrell, Falla's use of such material was informed by a greater understanding of the context, sonority, and performance practices of the musics employed, and a growing awareness of contemporary theoretical constructions of folk music and the ways that it was employed by European nationalist composers, especially his French colleagues. While melodic quotations from folk sources are employed in *Noches en los jardines de España*, and to a greater extent in *La vida breve* and *Cuatro piezas españolas*, the thematic material in these works is often based on the scales, rhythms, modes, cadences, and ornamental figures that characterize Andalusian folk music.

In his mature works preceding *El retablo de Maese Pedro* Falla brought elements of folk music into his scores in a number of ways. *Siete canciones populares españolas* is the composition which makes most extensive and literal use of folksongs and is indebted to the methods employed in contemporary settings by his Parisian colleagues, especially by Ravel in *Cinq Mélodies populaires grec-ques*, *Chants populaires* and *Deux Mélodies hébraiques*.[55] All seven songs ("El paño moruno," "Seguidilla murciana," "Asturiana," "Jota," "Nana," "Canción," and "Polo") are inspired by models taken from published collections. The fact that they were composed in 1914, towards the end of Falla's seven-year Paris sojourn,[56] may have contributed to his dependence on such sources. The extent to which the melodic lines and accompaniment figures are adapted by Falla dif-fers from song to song, from the precise melodic reproduction in "Canción" to the extensive elaboration and development of an ac-companiment figure and transformation of the melodic contour in "Jota." A brief examination of Falla's compositional process in three of the songs from this set will demonstrate his reliance on and ma-nipulation of printed sources of folk music.

"El paño moruno" is based on "El paño" from José Inzenga's *Ecos de España*,[57] and in this instance it is clear that Falla constructed his initial draft of "El paño moruno" over the printed model (see example 12.1). Falla faithfully reproduces the lyrics and the two-strophe struc-ture. The melodic alterations introduced are minimal, the main differ-ence being the repetition of the consequent phrase, and the initial ideas for his piano accompaniment are also borrowed from this source. The early ideas for the bass line and harmonic accompaniment of the melody are adaptations of Inzenga's piano part, although Falla's subsequent reworkings explore further the triple/duple and major/minor dichotomies. Another printed source which Falla had in his possession in Paris provided the model for the sixth song, "Nana."[58] Falla clearly based his "Nana" on a melody of the same name which was reproduced at the end of the play *Las flores* by Ser-afín and Joaquín Alvarez Quintero.[59] The "Nana" therein is also marked by Falla in line with his initial ideas for the rhythmic trans-formation of its opening (see example 12.2). A binary structure would eventually be employed, and the text is based on variants of the third stanza of the version in *Las flores*. The cadential resolution of each re-frain was substantially reworked by Falla. The model for the final song, "Polo," is the "Polo gitano o flamenco" from Eduardo Ocón's *Colección de aires nacionales y populares*.[60] Falla edited and thor-oughly reordered the melodic material, often changing its rhythmic outline while maintaining the original pitch (see example 12.3). The idea for Falla's piano introduction in the "Polo" is also derived from one of the guitar figures in the Ocón model (see example 12.4).

Example 12.1 José Inzenga, *Ecos de España*, "El paño moruno," pp. 65–66, with autograph annotations by Manuel de Falla, AMF.

Example 12.1   José Inzenga, *Ecos de España*, "El paño moruno," pp. 65–66, with autograph annotations by Manuel de Falla, AMF (*continued*).

Example 12.2a "Nana" from *Las flores* with autograph annotations by Manuel de Falla, AMF.

Example 12.2b   Manuel de Falla, *Siete canciones populares españolas,* "Nana," vocal line, ms. 3–10.

Example 12.3a   Eduardo Ocón, *Colección de aires nacionales y populares,* "Polo gitano o flamenco," vocal line, ms. 71–107.

Example 12.3b   Manuel de Falla, *Siete canciones populares españolas,* "Polo," vocal line, ms. 32–52.

Example 12.4a   Eduardo Ocón, *Colección de aires nacionales y popu-lares,* "Polo gitano o flamenco," guitar part, ms. 60–63.

Example 12.4b   Manuel de Falla, *Siete canciones populares es-pañolas,* "Polo," piano part, ms. 1–4.

The evocation of Andalusian and flamenco elements in *El amor brujo*, *El sombrero de tres picos*, and the *Fantasía bœtica* was far less literal. Falla relied more heavily on his direct experience with flamenco music, primarily through Pastora Imperio and her family and then in his extensive travels throughout Andalusia during World War I. In these works the rhythms and forms of flamenco and other Spanish music were internalized by Falla and translated into a contemporary musical idiom. Instead of direct melodic quotation, Falla studied the modal scales and ornamental procedures of this music, along with its cadential formulas, and used these to generate his own thematic material. However, Falla also relied on printed sources to further his understanding of Andalusian music. In addition to the aforementioned collections by Inzenga and Ocón, Falla's main source of knowledge of this genre was provided by flamenco guitar scores by Julián Arcas and Rafael Marín.[61] These were studied by Falla not only for guitaristic effects, but to gain a greater understanding of distinct forms. To this end, his annotations make reference to formal structure, harmonic progressions, cadential formulae, and rhythmic features (see example 12.5). He also paid attention to melodic lines and motives, several of which are stylised in the *Fantasía bœtica*, as are the flamenco guitar's figurations and the idiosyncratic harmonic formations emanating from its chordal strumming patterns and tuning.

Melodic quotation of Spanish folk music was used more extensively in *El sombrero de tres picos*, chiefly as a dramatic device in order to characterise the protagonists and denote their places of origin. There was also a sustained attempt by Falla in these scores to translate the instrumental color of the music he was evoking. To this end, in 1917, he advised composers wanting to create strictly national music to

listen to what we would call popular orchestras (formed by guitars, castanets and tambourines in my part of the world); only in them will they find that tradition that they long for so much and which is impossible to discover elsewhere.[62]

In the *Fantasía bœtica* and in passages from *El sombrero de tres picos*, especially in the final "Jota," Falla tended to repeat, develop, and juxtapose short melodic fragments, many of which are taken directly or adapted from folk and flamenco sources. This practice can be seen in sections from Falla's earlier works, including the second dance from *La vida breve* and the "Aragonesa" from the *Cuatro piezas españolas*. Falla continued to make arrangements of folk music even while composing *El*

Example 12.5   Rafael Marín, *Aires andaluces,* **extract from "Granadinas,"** **with autograph annotations by Manuel de Falla, AMF.**

retablo de Maese Pedro composition. The most notable examples comprise a chamber setting of the Catalan song *El Desembre congelat* and a stylised piano version of the *Canto de los remeros del Volga* [Song of the Volga Boatmen] in 1922, both of which were taken from printed sources.

MUSICAL BORROWINGS AND NEOCLASSICISM

Adolfo Salazar first hinted at the character of the music employed in the score of in *El retablo de Maese Pedro* in his 1921 interview with Falla, in which he commented on the "pure Castilian character of the music, based in part on the folk song of Castile and on the concerted music of her classic composers—in a manner which closely follows Pedrell's doctrine." [63] Falla gave more details of the types of music he had consulted in an interview with his longstanding friend Georges Jean-Aubry, which preceded the first staged performance of *El retablo* in June 1923. Upon being asked if he had used any themes from the Cervantes period, Falla replied:

> No, before writing, I saturated myself in the music of the Cervantes period and I also studied the scales used in the music which, in Spain, preceded Cervantes; because you must remember that when Cervantes wrote Don Quixote, knight-errantry had already become a thing of the past, and, therefore it is to previous centuries that the great composer is referring in his immortal masterpiece. [64]

In an anonymous program note Falla echoed Pedrell's ideas by drawing both folk and early music into the category of "*natural* Spanish music." He claimed that "in [*El retablo de Maese Pedro*] as in all the works of its author there is a very restricted use of the authentic folk document [melody]. The essence of the old noble and popular Spanish music is . . . the solid base upon which this composition has been organised," and he concluded with the statement that "the rhythms, melodies and instrumental fabric are based on the essential elements of *natural* Spanish music." [65] Falla borrowed mainly from pre-18th-century sources to evoke the action of the Medieval legend or *Romance* portrayed in the puppet play. For the most part folk sources are employed to characterize the rustic setting of the inn, and in the narrator's part Falla attempted to conflate the street cries of Andalusian vendors with aspects of liturgical plainchant. [66]

At the outset of *El retablo de Maese Pedro*'s composition Falla wrote to Pedrell about sources he could study for the music of the *Romance* and specifically the legend of Gayferos and Melisendra. In reply to these queries Pedrell wrote on 25 January 1919:

> Dearest Manuel, I hasten to satisfy your questions. Of all the Romances I know, I have never come across any which have referred to Gaiferos or the Princess Melisendra. But you yourself can make use of the Tonada most applicable to your project. You will find various characteristic ones in Volume I of my Cancionero. . . . In the said volume, check section V (Romance Tonadas), page 21 of the musical text, and page 61 of the corresponding literary text. [67]

Falla embraced Pedrell's suggestion of using his transcriptions of the *Tonadas,* examples of early popular songs included by Francisco de Salinas in his sixteenth-century treatise. These *Tonadas* are quoted literally, as in the melodic outline of Melisendra's scene, or transformed, as is the case in one of the melodies intoned by the Trujaman (see example 12.6).

Some of the pieces suggested by Cecilio de Roda in his 1905 lectures as being evocative of the music of Cervantes's time were also employed by Falla. These included the popular seventeenth-century guitar pieces of Gaspar Sanz, used both within the *Romance* and the rustic scenes, and a sixteenth-century polyphonic song, "O prado verde y florido" by Francisco Guerrero, as the basis for Don Quijote's ode to Dulcinea.[68] In his transformation of a "Gallarda" by Sanz, Falla recalls Pedrell's orchestrations of some seventeenth-century guitar pieces in volume 3 of the *Cancionero* (see example 12.7). Like several of the sources employed in *El retablo de Maese Pedro*, these are reproduced with minor changes or are successively transformed in various sketches, much like Falla's handling of folk sources in *Siete canciones populares españolas.*

Example 12.6a   Felipe Pedrell, *Cancionero popular musical español,* vol. 1, p. 23, with autograph annotations by Manuel de Falla, AMF.

Example 12.6b   Manuel de Falla's transformation of this line in LXV A6, AMF.

Example 12.6c   Manuel de Falla's reworking of this line in sketch LXV A2, AMF.

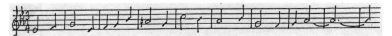

Example 12.6d   Manuel de Falla, *El retablo de Maese Pedro,* vocal line, definitive version no. 59.

1

Gaspar Sanz.

Indicaciones.

⌒ = arrastre   ⌢ = sin herir.

♪ = trémolo (vibrado)

Instrucción de Música sobre
la Guitarra española. 1674.

GALLARDA.

Example 12.7a Opening of Gaspar Sanz's *Gallarda*, transcribed by Cecilio de Roda.

Example 12.7b Manuel de Falla, *El retablo de Maese Pedro*, No. 19, with kind permission of Chester Music editions.

226

88)

Españoleta y Paso y medio

*Transcripción para peque-
ña orquesta de distintos temas
de tratados de tañido.*

F. Pedrell.

Example 12.7c   Opening of "Españoleta y Paso y medio" by Felipe Pedrell, *Cancionero popular musical español,* vol. 3, p. 226.

In 1923 Falla stated to Jean-Aubry that "except in one or two themes, I have not made exact use of anything."[69] In his own early sketches it seemed as if Falla were going to identify at least two of the models employed, conspicuously providing, in French, the following labels: "D'après un thème de Sáenz" and "D'après une chanson de l'époque (Francisco Guerrero)."[70] Falla's own further development of these models in subsequent drafts may have prompted him to drop the attributions in the final score. The mixed reception surrounding the hybrid authorship in Stravinsky's *Pulcinella* may have also influenced Falla in suppressing the titles of the pieces used.

Falla also made use of fragmentary motives taken from early Spanish instrumental sources, and this is especially so in the "Sinfonia" and the "Final." These motives are combined, developed, and juxtaposed in a manner which obscures their origins but informs the soundscape of a given passage. Several motives from Cecilio de Roda's transcriptions of Sanz were noted among the sketch material.[71] The "Sinfonia" presented Falla with the opportunity of constructing a whole movement through the continued interpolation of such motivic material (see example 12.8). Falla's employment of these fragments present similarities to the motivic juxtapositions that he outlined in the Sinfonias from Monteverdi's *L'Orfeo*. Many of the melodic cells noted by Falla are either taken directly, paraphrased from or inspired by his study of scores by Gaspar Sanz, Antonio de Cabezón, and the repertories of other sixteenth- and seventeenth-century composers. Falla was not only interested in the melody and surface rhythm of his sources, but observed other parameters such as harmonic and cadential progressions, and was eager to immerse himself in the totality of the music he was studying. The new harmonic language of *El retablo de Maese Pedro* was in part conditioned by the sources employed by Falla. This harmonic reorientation was complemented by his contemporary deliberations on the harmonic series and the exploration of extended tonal frameworks through the use of superpositioned resonances. It may also have been prompted by Stravinsky's harmonic treatment of the baroque fragments in *Pulcinella*.[72]

Example 12.8   Motives copied by Manuel de Falla for the "Sinfonia" (here labeled "Preludio"), *El retablo de Maese Pedro,* **LXV A5, AMF.**

Folk sources were also explored by Falla, principally through the transcriptions in Dámaso Ledesma's *Cancionero Salmantino*. This collection, of which Falla had been aware since his Paris years, became one of his principal guides to the music of greater Castile. Of special interest to Falla were the *Charradas*, although he also noted the sections documenting the music of the *dulzaina* and *gaita* [Spanish oboe and bagpipe]. The wind repertory of *Folklore de Castilla* by Olmeda and Inzenga's *Cantos y bailes populares de España* may have also been consulted at this time.[73] The early sketch material for *El retablo de Maese Pedro* also includes references to *Cangas* for *gaita* as well as a sketch of a *Seguidilla manchega*.[74] The opening "Toccata" of the work is created through the juxtaposition of phrasal units, and rhythmic and melodic cells gleaned from wind pieces from Castile, León, and Galicia. Other musical borrowings incorporated by Falla in *El retablo de Maese Pedro* included the Catalan Christmas carol *El Desembre congelat*, the Spanish Royal March, and even Arab sources for the depiction of the Moors in the *Romance*. Falla also indulged in a degree of self-quotation through his allusions to a theme from *El amor brujo*.

In his next work, the *Concerto*, Falla employed an even greater diversity of sources and for each of its three movements he adapted different conceptual, harmonic, structural, and timbral ideas from the materials borrowed. Despite certain instances of literal quotation, on the whole there is a greater degree of abstraction and conflation of the sources. Falla wrote to Adolfo Salazar in mid-1927 and stated that seventeenth-century music "provides the basis of the greater part of the *Concerto*, to which is added the primitive-religious element,"[75] although this only represents part of the key to the amalgam that is the *Concerto*.

The first movement is driven by a contrapuntal and thematic deconstruction of Juan Vazquez's sixteenth-century imitative polyphonic setting of the popular song *De los álamos vengo, madre*.[76] While not Castilian in the modern geographical sense, this presents an example of an old folk melody treated imitatively by a Spanish composer at the height of old Castile's power. *De los álamos vengo, madre* was in part chosen for the imitative nature of its setting, and even in the early sketch material for the first movement Falla explored the possibilities arising from the polyphonic writing and not just the principal melodic shape. Falla considered constructing complex imitative textures derived from variants of this source, as well as presenting the theme in combination with strands of its original polyphonic accompaniment, a practice reminiscent of Renaissance parody techniques. His observation of canonic entries, thematic diminution, and fracturing in Vazquez' setting also prompted the development of these techniques in his own presentation[77] (see example 12.9).

The religious element referred to by Falla is predominant in the second movement. Numerous commentators have tried to demonstrate the similarity between this movement's theme and the *Pange Lingua* plainchant,[78] and there is little doubt that Falla was trying to evoke a liturgical melody, perhaps modeled on the *Pange Lingua*. In this process he studied and annotated various religious, and even secular, models which display similar contours.[79] Falla searched for the appropriate technical means for the presentation of his chantlike theme. In an attempt to recreate the medieval atmosphere of the procession and to create a more austere harmonic language, Falla adapted early polyphonic practices, including specific allusions to organum and the assimilation of the medieval technique of the *caccia* or *caza* from Pedrell's transcriptions from the fourteenth-century Catalan manuscript, the *Llibre Vermell*. In his introduction to the transcriptions Pedrell stressed the importance of canonic songs to every aspect of the life of pilgrims to Montserrat,[80] and Falla noted the following passage in the Pedrell's *Cancionero*:

Example 12.9 Manuel de Falla, sketch material for first movement of *Concerto*, AMF, incorporating passages taken from Juan Vázquez's setting of *De los álamos vengo, madreo*, AMF.

The unison gregorian melody was converted into harmony of two or three voices. . . . The resulting harmony of the canon is, as one can guess, a little primitive and rudimentary, but in its very simplicity captivated the good pilgrims.[81]

Informed by Falla, Roland-Manuel claimed that these *cazas* "offered the composer of the *Concerto* the example for his abrupt polyphony: closed, crammed imitations, impatient canons in which the voices follow so closely that they threaten to stumble over each other." [82] Falla employs a variety of canonic presentations of the theme, often making use of perfect intervals (unisons, octaves, fourths, and fifths) and even stark polytonal passages. On occasion these procedures were meant to evoke the sonorities of organum, whereas in the third movement tertial harmonies predominate in line with the sources evoked.

According to Falla's own propaganda: "The greater one's understanding of the Spanish influence on Domenico Scarlatti, the more one comprehends the final movement of the *Concerto.*" [83] Falla's analyses of several parameters of Scarlatti's sonatas inform this movement in its thematic contours, monothematic structure, keyboard writing, differentiated two-part textures, and angular melodic writing.[84] Other parameters of the sonatas which relate to Falla's conception of the *Concerto* include the exploration of thematic areas based on the juxtaposition of short or irregular contrasting motives, or the tenacious repetition of such motives, and the examination of abrupt modulations and irregular harmonic-phrase lengths.[85] These informed his concept of *ritmo interno* which was underpinned by harmonic and rhythmic logic, and stimulated his desire for less regularity in the phrase lengths of the *Concerto.* Scarlatti's imitation of Spanish folk forms and of the guitar also led Falla to annotate the scores on numerous occasions.

Of particular relevance to the third movement of the *Concerto* was Falla's study of rhythmic effects in the Scarlatti sonatas, including the use of hemiola, syncopation, and the alternation of double and triple rhythms within the same metric framework. Falla saw rhythmic similarities with Spanish baroque works transcribed in volumes 3 and 4 of Pedrell's *Cancionero*, particularly in the *tonos humanos* and popular instrumental pieces associated with the theater of Spain's golden age. Following on from Pedrell's theories, Falla sought parallels of these rhythmic practices in the folk music of Castile and other regions, including the Hispano-Cuban *Zapateado del Monte*. In the context of these studies and contemporary debates on neoclassicism in music, Falla noted what he perceived to be "the melodic character of rhythm [in] eighteenth-century objective music," which he classified as "*Monotonal and Polyrhythmic music*"[86] (see example 12.10).

The difficulties involved in creating a unified construct from the assimilation of a plethora of materials in the *Concerto* led Falla to rationalize the work in purely musical terms which he considered to be of contemporary relevance. In February 1926, towards the end of the work's composition, Falla noted the following: "*Concerto*—Unwritten sounds—Reflecting distinct contemporary values—1st part Harmonic-contrapuntal—2nd Harmonic—3rd Contrapuntal."[87] However, in an anonymous program note for the *Concerto*, Falla stressed the symbiosis of historical, folk, and modern elements, thus reflecting contemporary discussions on the definition and creation of Spanish identity.

> [B]oth in its rhythmic-tonal-melodic character, and in its style of writing, [the Concerto] has its origin in general Hispanic music, religious, noble and popular, and the procedures employed by the composer, in many cases, follow those of earlier works . . . although they are subjected to current practices and possibilities of expression.[88]

Falla's stylistic evolution in the 1920s resulted in a more eclectic and abstracted form of nationalism through the assimilation of neoclassical ideals, although these were interpreted within the framework of contemporary theories of Spanish identity. The progressive integration and conflation of folk and preclassical sources in Falla's work of this period complemented his reinterpretation of Spanishness in terms of "Castilian" or "general Hispanic" values, through which he consciously sought to redefine Spain and its music, not as a manifestation of the exotic Other on the European periphery, but as a culture linked to the continent's historical and artistic traditions. In doing so, Falla forged one of the most powerful and coherent syntheses of nationalist and neoclassical ideals, and attempted to reconcile tradition with modernity.

Example 12.10   José Inzenga, *Ecos de España,* "Zapateo del monte," p. 77.

NOTES

1. This essay is based on a paper given at the 1998 conference of the American Musicological Society in Boston. For a detailed discussion of the ideas outlined in this chapter see Michael Christoforidis, *Aspects of the Creative Process in Manuel de Falla's* El retablo de Maese Pedro *and* Concerto, Ph.D. diss., University of Melbourne, 1997. My sincere thanks to Doña Isabel de Falla and the Archivo Manuel de Falla for all their assistance and for permission to reproduce the examples. Special thanks to Concha Chinchilla, magnificent archivist and wonderful friend.

2. Wanda Landowska's letter to Lawrence Gilman, 24 December 1926. Copy sent by Landowska to Falla held at Archivo Manuel de Falla [hereafter, AMF]. Unless otherwise indicated, all sources referred to are held at AMF.

3. Falla's reading lists include references to Chateaubriand's *Le dernier Abencerrage*, Hugo's *Les orientales*, and Gautier's *Voyage en Espagne* from this period. Falla's extant personal library at the AMF includes his annotated copies of Alhambrist texts like Chateaubriand, *Le dernier Abencerrage* [in French and Spanish translation], Inventory Number AMF [I.N.] 2598 and 3401, Washington Irving, *Cuentos de la Alhambra*, I.N. 2014, and Théophile Gautier, *Loin de Paris*, I.N. 3866.

4. Alhambrist notions had inspired works by two of the composers who reorientated Falla's musical nationalism in Paris: Isaac Albéniz and Claude Debussy.

5. For a discussion of the impact of primitivism on Falla see Michael Christoforidis, "Un acercamiento a la postura de Manuel de Falla en El '*Cante Jondo*' (*canto primitivo andaluz*)," in Manuel de Falla, *El "Cante Jondo" (canto primitivo andaluz)*, facsimile edition, Granada: Ayuntamiento, Archivo Manuel de Falla, Imprenta Urania, 1997.

6. The critical reception of *El retablo de Maese Pedro* was mixed, with several more traditional nationalist composers, such as Federico Moreno Torroba and Joaquín Turina expressing their misgivings about Falla's new stylistic direction. Many observers have commented on the apparent contradiction that, as Falla moved to Andalusian Granada from Castilian Madrid in 1920, his music became more Castilian. The most recent repetition of this cliché can be found in Manuel Orozco, *Manuel de Falla y Granada,* Granada: Ayuntamiento, 1996, 57.

7. "Pero me consuelo pensando que todo cuanto vive en la música europea procede de un nacionalismo bien entendido. Ya lo dice Ravel: Dígase y hágase cuanto se quiera, pero a la postre los nacionalistas somos los únicos que llevamos razón. . . . Y ¿cómo vamos a considerar agotado nuestro nacionalismo musical cuando apenas hemos hecho otra cosa en ese sentido que demostrar alguna que otra laudable intención?" Letter Falla-Adolfo Salazar, 3 February 1923,

AMF. Falla wrote this letter in reply to an extended letter from Salazar which explored the question of nationalism in Spain.

8. Manuel de Falla, in *Excelsior, On Music and Musicians,* ed. F. Sopeña, trans. D. Urman, J. M. Thomson (London: Marion Boyars, 1979) 71.

9. Falla, in *Musique, On Music* 73.

10. Igor Stravinsky and Robert Craft, *Memories and Commentaries,* London: Faber, 1960, 81.

11. Igor Stravinsky, *An Autobiography,* London: Calder and Boyars, 1975, 133. Originally published in French as *Chroniques de ma vie,* Paris, 1935.

12. Published on 9 July 1915, in *España,* its signatories included Azcárate, Buylla, Américo Castro, Cejador, Cossío, Goyanes, Lafora, Madinaveitia, Marañón, Menéndez Pidal, Ortega y Gasset, Pittaluga, Posada, F. de los Ríos, Simarro, Turró, Unamuno, Zulueta, Falla, Turina, Vives, Ramón Casas, Romero de Torres, Zuloaga, Rusiñol, Julio Antonio, Clará, Alomar, Araquistaín, Azaña, "Azorín," Carner, Ciges Aparicio, Grandmontagne, Amadeo Hurtado, Antonio Machado, R. de Maeztu, Martínez Sierra, Enrique de Mesa, Palacio Valdés, Pérez Galdós, Pérez de Ayala, and Valle-Inclán. See Manuel Tuñon de Lara, *Medio siglo de cultura española* (Madrid: Tecnos, 1984) 153. Falla became acquainted with most of these men and some, like Manuel Azaña and Fernando de los Rios, were to become prominent figures in the Republican governments of the 1930s. Much of the associated intellectual activity was centered around institutions like Madrid's Ateneo, and new publications were founded for the diffusion of liberal ideas, principally the newspaper *El Sol,* the journal *España,* and, later, *La Revista del Occidente.* In the sphere of music the Sociedad Nacional de Música, established in 1915 with Falla as one of its founding members, most clearly reflects this group's aspirations.

13. John A. Crow, *Spain: the Root and the Flower,* 3rd ed., Berkeley: University of California Press, 1985, 263. This at times contradictory espousal of a Castilian identity and Europeanisation as models for national regeneration is possibly best represented in the poetry of Falla's Andalusian contemporary Antonio Machado and in the essays and philosophical writings of Miguel de Unamuno and Azorín.

14. Much of the other Castilian nationalist music of this period tended towards a greater use of folksong and was marked by a more localised nationalism, in the works of Rogelio Villar and Antonio José, for example.

15. "¿Hay algo más romántico, más exaltado, más generoso que el espíritu de Castilla? Ahí teneis la obra de nuestros místicos; pocos almas habrá en la historia de un tan grande y puro idealismo." Passage annotated by Falla [*PAF*], Azorín, *Lecturas españolas* (Madrid: Rafael Caro Raggio, 1920) 145, vol. 10 of *Obras Completas*; I.N. 3222, AMF.

16. Examples of these works include *Vida de Don Quijote y Sancho* (1905) by Miguel de Unamuno, *La ruta del Quijote* (1905) by Azorín, and José Ortega y Gasset's *Meditaciones del Quijote* (1914). Falla also read Azorín's *El alma*

Castellana 1600–1800 (Madrid: Renacimiento, 1900) I.N. 3780, AMF, which includes sections on Castilian literature and mysticism and marked Azorín's comments on *Don Quijote* in *Los valores literarios,* Madrid: Renacimiento, 1900, 9–10 I.N. 3780, *AMF,* which refer to the work's modernity.

17. The most developed project was related to *Las figuras del Quijote* by Carlos Fernández Shaw, which Falla considered setting in 1910. For a full list see Christoforidis, "Aspects of the Creative Process," chapter 4.2.

18. *El Ateneo de Madrid en el III centenario de la publicación de* El ingenioso Hidalgo Don Quijote de la Mancha, Madrid: n.p., 1905.

19. On this occasion the parts of Don Quijote and Maese Pedro were delivered by two librettists Falla had worked with, Carlos Fernández Shaw and Serafín Alvarez Quintero, respectively.

20. This work is not preserved in Falla's library, but it was one of numerous *Don Quijote* commentaries known to Falla, as can be surmised from notes among his working papers.

21. Royal decree of 6 March 1920, signed by Natalio Rivas. Quoted in Carolyn P. Boyd, *Historia Patria: Politics, History and Identity in Spain, 1875–1975,* Princeton: Princeton UP, 1997: 182–183.

22. For an overview of these issues see Emilio Casares, "La música española hasta 1939, o la restauración musical," *España en la Música de Occidente*, Proc. of International Conference, vol. 2, Madrid: Ministerio de Cultura, 1987; Beatriz Martínez del Fresno, "El pensamiento nacionalista en el ámbito madrileño (1900–1936): Fundamentos y paradojas," *De musica hispana et aliis*, ed. Emilio Casares and Carlos Villanueca, vol. 2, Santiago de Compostela: Universidad, 1990, 351–397; and Adolfo Salazar, *La música contemporánea en España,* Madrid: La Nave, 1930.

23. Felipe Pedrell, *Por nuestra música,* Barcelona: Henrich y Cia., 1891.

24. Felipe Pedrell, *Cancionero musical popular español,* Barcelona: Valls, 1917.

25. Falla, "Felipe Pedrell," *La Revue musicale* 4.4, February 1923, 1–11, *On Music*, 60.

26. Falla, "Felipe Pedrell," *On Music*, 55.

27. Falla, "Felipe Pedrell," *On Music*, 55.

28. Falla, "Felipe Pedrell," *On Music*, 56. Falla qualified these remarks by stating that he was referring to "polyphonic texture" and not the superficial ornamental richness of some Spanish folk music.

29. "Cuando se ha escrito mucho, cuando se ha vivido algo, entonces desdeñamos ya la multiplicidad de detalles. Queremos ya que un solo detalle de la sensación de la cosa. Pero es lo supremo en el arte: el descatar lo accesorio, lo inútil, lo profuso para conservar y fijar solo lo característico." *PAF*, Azorín, *Páginas escogidas*, Madrid: Calleja, 1917, 19; I.N. 3424, AMF.

30. "¿Son estos romances la obra de un verdadero artista, es decir, un hombre

que ha llegado a saber que el arte supremo es la sobriedad, la simplicidad y la claridad?" *PAF*, Azorín, *Al márgen de los clasicos*, 28, I.N. 3335, AMF.

31. See *Meditations on Quijote*, trans. Evelyn Rugg and Diego Marín, New York: Norton, 1961.

32. Azorín, *Al margen de los clásicos*, Madrid: Residencia de Estudiantes, 1915; I.N. 3335, AMF.

33. Falla's annotations to his library include various references to Latin values. In musical terms one of the most important references is found in Jean-Aubry, *La musique française d'aujourd'hui*, Paris: Perrin, 1916, especially 34; I.N. 1453, AMF. Falla underlined Gabrielle d'Annunzio's *La hija del lorio*, Madrid: Minerva, 1917, xvii [I.N. 2475, AMF] at the point where the author expresses his desire to celebrate the definitive triumph of the Latin brotherhood. Falla also questioned Felix Clement's comments on the genius of the North as opposed to those of the Mediterranean in *Músicos Célebres*, Barcelona: Daniel Cortezo, 1884; I.N. 3809, AMF.

34. Scott Messing summarizes the contemporary French situation: "In seeking compelling alternative models [to the legacy of Wagner and Brahms], many French artists, fortified by a milieu of increasingly vociferous nationalism, were drawn to their pre-romantic past which was construed to embody a purity inherent in their race." Messing, *Neoclassicism in Music: From the Genesis of the Concept through the Schoenberg/Stravinsky Polemic*, Ann Arbor: UMI Research Press, 1988, 24.

35. Falla's library preserves several scores published by the Schola Cantorum, including masses by Guerrero and Morales; I.N. 160, 167, AMF.

36. Henri Collet, *Le mysticisme musical espagnol au XVI siècle*, Paris: Librairie Felix Alcan, 1913; I.N. 1469, AMF.

37. Numerous publications in this area appeared in Paris, including important contributions by the Spanish musicologist Rafael Mitjana. Joaquín Nin was actively involved in the rediscovery and performance of early keyboard music, especially the works of Antonio Soler and Scarlatti. Falla marked a copy of a text by Joaquín Nin expressing these ideas, which was reproduced in a program organised by the pianist in Brussels at the Salle de la Grande Harmonie on 31 January 1912, AMF.

38. For further information see correspondence between Falla and Dukas, Durand, and Pedrell during this period, AMF. Extracts from this correspondence are reproduced in Elena Torres "La presencia de Scarlatti en la trayectoria musical de Falla," in Yvan Nommick ed., *Manuel de Falla e Italia*, Granada: Archivo Manuel de Falla, 2000, 73–75.

39. See correspondence with Isidro Cortázar (Monasterio El Escorial). On 5 April 1919, Cortázar wrote to Falla: "Do you have any plans to publish something by P.[Padre] Soler, or from this Archive?" [Tiene V. algún plan para publicar algo de P. Soler, ó de este Archivo?].

40. Falla saw *Pulcinella* on 20 May 1920. For an outline of the compositional process of *El retablo de Maese Pedro* see Christoforidis, "Aspects of the Creative Process."

41. Falla, *On Music* 31–32.

42. Gilbert Chase, *The Music of Spain,* New York: Dover, 1941, 188; Burnett James, *Manuel de Falla and the Spanish Musical Renaissance,* London: Victor Gollancz, 1979, 73.

43. Béla Bartók, "The Influence of Peasant Music on Modern Music" (1931) in Benjamin Suchoff, ed. *Béla Bartók Essays,* New York: St. Martin's Press, 1979, 341.

44. An important article in this respect is Richard Taruskin's "'Russian Folk Melodies in *The Rite of Spring*," *JAMS* 33.3 (1980) 501–43. Taruskin's fn. 19 provides details of previous studies of folk music in Stravinsky's works. For a detailed discussion of Stravinsky's debt to folk music see Richard Taruskin, *Stravinsky and the Russian Traditions: A Biography of the Works Through* Mavra (Berkeley: University of California Press, 1996).

45. Manuel García Matos, "Folklore en Falla," *Música* 3–4, January–June 1953, 69–83, and "Folklore en Falla," *Música* 6, October–December 1953, 41–68. A later article by García Matos, "El folklore en *La vida breve* de Manuel de Falla," *Anuario Musical* 26, 1972, 173–97, discusses folk music in Falla's first opera.

46. For a discussion of the literature relating to Falla's use of folk music see Michael Christoforidis, "Manuel de Falla's *Siete canciones populares españolas*: The Composer's Library and the Creative Process," *Anuario Musical* 55, 2000, 213–235.

47. Falla made reference to this in a letter, dated 30 December 1928, which included his corrections to Roland Manuel's first draft of his biography, copy held at AMF. This must have been a preconscious exposure to this repertoire as he claimed that "La morilla" was only his nursemaid during early infancy.

48. See Michael Christoforidis, "La guitarra en la obra de Manuel de Falla," *La guitarra en la historia* 9, Córdoba: Ayuntamiento, 1998, 29–57.

49. Inmaculada Quintal Sánchez, *Manuel de Falla y Asturias,* Oviedo: Instituto de Estudios Asturianos, 1989, 12–25.

50. For an outline of Pedrell's ideas on the use of folksong prior to the years that Falla studied with him see Felipe Pedrell, *Por nuestra música*, especially chapter 5. In his 1923 article "Felipe Pedrel," *La Revue musicale* 4.4, February 1923, 1–11, Falla outlined the importance of Pedrell's example.

51. See Antonio Gallego's prologue to the edition of Manuel de Falla, *Cantares de Nochebuena,* Madrid: Ediciones Manuel de Falla, 1992. I am currently in the process of gathering Falla's jottings of folk melodies he heard, some of which have appeared in the course of my research.

52. See Michael Christoforidis, "Manuel de Falla, Debussy and *La vida breve,*" *Musicology Australia* 18, 1995, 3–12; "De *La vida breve* a *Atlántida*: al-

gunos aspectos del magisterio de Claude Debussy sobre Manuel de Falla," *Cuadernos de la música iberoamericana* 4, 1997, 15–32; and Yvan Nommick, "Manuel de Falla: *La vida breve* de 1905 à *La vie brève* de 1913. Genèse et évolution d'une œuvre," *Mélanges de la Casa de Velázquez* 30.3, 1994, 71–94.

53. Jaime Pahissa, *Manuel de Falla: His life and works,* trans. Jean Wagstaff, London: Museum, 1954, 32.

54. Pedro Morales, "Angel Barrios," in A. Eaglefield Hull ed., *A Dictionary of Modern Music and Musicians,* London: J.M. Dent & Sons, 1924, 29. Falla provided Morales with some information for his entry on Barrios.

55. For a detailed study of the *Siete canciones populares españolas* see Christoforidis, "Manuel de Falla's *Siete canciones.*"

56. During this period, Falla is known to have returned to Spain on only one occasion: in early 1908.

57. José Inzenga, *Ecos de España,* Barcelona: n.p., [1874], I.N. 1007, AMF.

58. Previous scholars have been unable to identify clear precedents for this song, although some allude to its similarities with the contours of Andalusian and even foreign lullabies. García Matos, "Folklore [I]," and Crivillé y Bargalló, "Las *Siete canciones.*"

59. In the course of 1909 and 1910, Falla had commenced work on an opera based on this play, which was never completed. The second edition of *Las flores* (1906), preserved in the Falla library, displays the composer's marking of the text and includes a signed dedication from the authors. Serafín y Joaquín Alvarez Quintero, *Las flores*, 2nd ed., Madrid: Sociedad de Autores Españoles, 1906; I.N. 3262, AMF. Crivillé y Bargalló, in "Las *Siete canciones populares españolas* y e folklore" *Manuel de Falla tra la Spagna e l'Europa,* Firenze: Olschki, 1989, 148, noted the similarity of this "Nana" from *Las flores* to that of Falla but mistakenly dated the play as 1911 and only knew of the 1923 publication in Serafín y Joaquín Alvarez Quintero, *Teatro Completo*, vol. 3, Madrid: Sociedad General Española, 1923. He thus precluded it from being a possible model for Falla.

60. Eduardo Ocón, *Cantos españoles. Colección de aires nacionales y populares,* Málaga, 1876. Four editions of this work were published to 1906. "Polo gitano o flamenco" begins on p. 92 in at least the second edition (1888). Of all the volumes consulted by Falla in the course of composing *Siete canciones populares españolas*, this is the only one no longer present at the Archivo Manuel de Falla.

61. These included *Los tientos* [I.N. 38 AMF], *Malagueñas* [38], *Granadinas* [39], *Tangos* [40], *Soleares* [41], and *Siguirillas gitanas* [42] from the "Aires Andaluces" series by Rafael Marín, Madrid: Sociedad de Autores Españoles, 1902, and *Rondeña* [I.N. 136 AMF], *Soléa* [137], and *Murcianas* [138] by Julián Arcas, Barcelona: Dotesio, n.d. For a more complete account of Falla's interaction with the flamenco guitar see Michael Christoforidis, "Manuel de Falla y la

guitarra flamenca," *La Caña* 4, 1993, 40–44, and "La guitarra en la obra de Manuel de Falla."

62. Falla, "Nuestra música," 1917, *On Music,* 82.

63. "carácter puramente castellano de la música concertada de sus grandes clásicos—siguiendo así estrechamente la doctrina pedrelliana," Adolfo Salazar, "Manuel de Falla, En Granada." *El Sol* [Madrid], 25 October 1921.

64. Georges Jean-Aubry, "De Falla Talks of his New Work Based on a Don Quixote Theme," *Christian Science Monitor,* 1 September 1923.

65. "tanto en esta obra, como en todas las de su autor se hace un uso muy restringido del documento popular auténtico. La sustancia de la vieja música, noble o popular española es, repetimos, la sólida base. . . ." "Los ritmos, las melodías, así como el tejido instrumental, están basados sobre los elementos esenciales de la música natural española, . . ." Manuel de Falla, unsigned program note for Orquesta Bética de Camara, Seville, 30 January 1925.

66. For further information on the sources employed by Falla see Christoforidis, "Aspects of the Creative Process," and "Forging a Spanish Declamatory Style: Manuel de Falla's *El retablo de maese Pedro,*" *Aflame with Music,* Melbourne: Centre for Studies in Australian Music, 1996, 69–78.

67. "Querido Manuel: Me apresuro a satisfacer sus demandas. En tantos romances como conozco no he tropezado jamás con algunos que tratan de Gaiferos ni la Princesa Melisendra. Pero puede V. mismo aplicar la tonada más a propósito de su intento. Hallará varias a cual más característica en el Tomo I de mi *Cancionero.* . . . Registra en dicho tomo desde la sección V (Tonadas de romances) en el texto musical pag. 21, y la parte de texto literario correspondiente, desde la pag. 61." Letter Pedrell-Falla, 25 January 1919, AMF.

68. For a discussion of Falla's transformation of Guerrero's music see Antonio Gallego, "Dulcinea en el prado (verde y florido)," *Revista de Musicología* X, ii, 1987, 685–699.

69. Jean-Aubry, "De Falla Talks."

70. Sketch material XLA 5 and XLA 9, respectively, AMF. The numbering used at AMF is based upon Antonio Gallego, *Catálogo de obras de Manuel de Falla* (Madrid: Ministerio de Cultura, 1987).

71. Among these is a two-bar passage from a "zarabanda" by Sanz, which was reiterated and developed by Falla in the passage beginning at no. 97 which precedes the final cadence of *El retablo de Maese Pedro.*

72. See Michael Christoforidis, "Hacia el mundo sonoro de *El retablo de maese Pedro,*" Louis Jambou ed., *Manuel de Falla: Latinité et Universalité,* Paris: Presses de l'Université Paris-Sorbonne, 1999, 219–235.

73. Federico Olmeda, *Folklore de Castilla o Cancionero popular de Burgos,* Sevilla: María Auxiliadora, 1903; I.N. 989, *AMF*; José Inzenga, *Cantos y bailes populares de España: Cantos y bailes de Galicia,* Madrid: A. Romero,

1888; I.N. 988, AMF. Falla may have earlier consulted these sources when writing the incidental music for Gregorio Martínez Sierra's *Amanecer* in 1915, although the music is no longer extant.

74. See sketch material XLV A6. Amongst Falla's working papers for *El retablo de Maese Pedro* there are also references to Castilian elements which reinforce the above sources and suggest others. Included in the listing are *"Romances* (alone), Liturgical chant, Chords of the *realejo* [chamber organ], Archaic Castilian song and Archaic dances."

75. "procede el Concerto en su mayor parte, uniendo esto al elemento religioso-primitivo"; draft of letter Falla-Salazar, 18 July 1927, AMF.

76. Falla's source was Pedrell's transcription in vol. 3 of the *Cancionero* of Miguel de Fuenllana's sixteenth-century vihuela intabulation of Juan Vázquez's polyphonic setting of the popular song.

77. These techniques were signaled by Falla in the copies that he made of sections of the piece, including LXXI A1, AMF.

78. Juan Alfonso García, *Falla y Granada*, Granada 1991, 79; Gianfranco Vinay, "La lezione di Scarlatti e di Stravinsky nel *Concerto* di Falla," in Paolo Pinamonti ed., *Manuel de Falla tra la Spagna e L'Europa,* Florence: Olschki, 1989, 186.

79. Similar melodic shapes were marked in quasi-liturgical classical and folk music. Falla's belief that liturgical chant had influenced the development of folksong may have also led him to mark some folksongs with religious associations. (See especially Pedrell's setting of a Galician Alalá, no. 210, in Pedrell, *Cancionero,* vol. II) Christoforidis, *Aspects of the Creative Process,* vol. I, 196–197.

80. Pedrell, *Cancionero*, vol. 3, 5; I.N. 1482, AMF.

81. Pedrell, *Cancionero*, vol. 3, 5–6; I.N. 1482, AMF.

82. Roland-Manuel, *Manuel de Falla*, trans. Vicente Salas Viu, Buenos Aires: Losada, 1945, 80.

83. For a more extended discussion of the impact of Scarlatti's music on Falla's neoclassical works see Christoforidis, *Aspects of the Creative Process.* For a thorough exploration of Falla's contact with Scarlatti's music and its impact on his creative process see Elena Torres's meticulous study "La presencia de Scarlatti en la trayectoria musical de Falla."

84. Melodic leaps of sevenths or ninths are often indicated by Falla. Scarlatti's imitation of Spanish folk forms and the figurations of the guitar also led Falla to annotate the scores on numerous occasions, especially Falla's annotations, accompanied by the word "guitarra," to Sonata L 422, Domenico Scarlatti, *48 nouvelles sonatas*, Benjamín Cesi ed., Paris: Ricordi, n.d., I.N. 1029, AMF.

85. An example of this can be seen in Falla's analysis of Sonata L475. The ideas he gained in this respect were integral to the formulation of his concept of internal rhythm (*ritmo interno*).

86. Unclassified papers, AMF.

87. Amongst miscellaneous papers relating to the *Concerto* in the *Carpeta Concerto*, AMF.

88. Draft of unsigned program note for the *Concerto* in the *Carpeta Concerto*, AMF.

Chapter 13

Falla in Europe:
Relations with His Contemporaries

Chris Collins[1]

There is a tendency for music historians to confine their discussion of Falla's work under the heading "Spain."[2] To some extent this is understandable: he was intensely proud of his nationality, and almost all of his music is clothed in the colors of his country and its culture. On this surface level, affinities between Falla's work and that of his older compatriots—Pedrell, Albéniz, and Granados—are obvious. But under that surface flow deeper currents for which there are few precedents in Spanish music: the carefully filtered use of genuine folk material; a fascination with the music of distant cultures; a proclivity towards small ensembles in unusual configurations; polyrhythm, polytonality, primitivism, and neoclassicism.

It will not have escaped notice that these are all more commonly associated with an illustrious Russian-born contemporary of Falla. This is no coincidence. Falla and Stravinsky knew one another well, and each paid close attention to the other's stylistic development.

And, of course, it is not only with Stravinsky that parallels may be drawn. Falla shared aesthetic and technical concerns with all his fellow modernists across the Pyrenees, most of whom he knew personally.

During his lifetime, the universal relevance of his art was unquestioned throughout western Europe and the Americas. Just as many of his major works were given their world premières outside Spain as within it; moreover, all of them were published by firms in France, Britain, or Italy. In all these countries, the general public held his work in the highest esteem. Writing about the reception of *Noches en los jardines de España* in London during the 1920s, J. B. Trend notes: "Falla's Nocturnes

stood out as serious, genuine music, and the audience at the Queen's
Hall . . . does not often break into cheers, as it did on this occasion."[3]
    His music was especially popular in France. The following observa-
tion was made by Louis Aubert in a review written in 1930: "the people
of Paris were delighted to demonstrate to the great visiting musician
their pleasure at having him present amongst them, and to assure him,
once again, of their fond admiration."[4] It is significant that Aubert was a
composer too, for the public's admiration for Falla was matched by that
of a number of his most eminent European contemporaries, among them
Ravel, Poulenc, and even Messiaen.[5]
    This international regard for Falla mirrors his own affection for the Eu-
ropean countries that he visited, especially France, Italy, Switzerland,
Belgium, and the United Kingdom. The periods he spent outside Spain
were frequent and prolonged (see appendix 1, p. 268). France occupied a
special place in his affections: he lived there for seven years from 1907,
and would have settled permanently had it not been for the outbreak of
the First World War.[6] After the Armistice, he went to France nearly every
year, and, at the time of his last visit in 1931, he was again contemplat-
ing a permanent move there (this time to Provence).[7] On more than one
occasion, he declared France to be his "second homeland."[8]
    In the context of this cosmopolitanism, it is hardly surprising that
Falla was fascinated by the music of his European contemporaries (especially his French ones). He worked tirelessly to promote it, both in
Spain and abroad. Before the war, he was involved in the Parisian Société Musicale Indépendante. When he returned to Madrid, he helped to
found the Sociedad Nacional de Música, whose programs during the
course of the war alone included works by Debussy, Ravel, Szymanowski, Skryabin, Schmitt, Sévérac, Stravinsky, Roussel, Roger-
Ducasse, Satie, Prokofiev, Goossens, Roland-Manuel, Poulenc, and
Casella;[9] he even played works by some of these composers himself. He
continued to promote contemporary European music into the 1920s,
through his involvement with the Orquesta Bética de Cámara. In the
1930s, he was elected an honorary officer of the International Society
for Contemporary Music and became an honorary committee member of
the Triton concert society in Paris.[10]
    His published writings also attest to his interest in his contempo-
raries and their work: over half of his articles are devoted to them.
Among the articles he wrote in the 1920s and 1930s, two concern
French composers (Debussy and Ravel)[11] and another the Polish harp-
sichordist Wanda Landowska,[12] while only one is dedicated to a

Spanish composer (Pedrell).[13] He even included in his fairly lengthy booklet on *cante jondo* a section entitled "Influence of these songs on modern European music," in which are mentioned Rimsky-Korsakov, Borodin, Balakirev, Stravinsky, Debussy, and Ravel.[14]

The specific purpose of most of the articles he wrote during the First World War was to promote the work of his contemporaries, among them Borodin, Balakirev, Mussorgsky, Rimsky-Korsakov, Fauré, Debussy, Richard Strauss, Dukas, Satie, Roussel, Schmitt, Skryabin, Sévérac, Schoenberg, Ravel, Bartók, and Kodály.[15] He devoted an entire one thousand-word article to Stravinsky.[16] In contrast, only five Spanish composers are mentioned (Granados, Pedrell, Albéniz, Francisco Barbieri, and Conrado del Campo).

He was very knowledgeable about the music of his European contemporaries: it accounts for a sizable proportion of his personal library of over a thousand musical scores (see appendix 2, p. 268–269). French composers are particularly well represented: he owned twenty or more scores each by Ravel, Poulenc, Milhaud, and Koechlin, and almost double that number by Debussy. The ten Dukas scores in his collection amount to almost all of that composer's published output. Russia is represented by Stravinsky (almost thirty scores), Prokofiev, and Rakhmaninov; Britain by Vaughan Williams, Holst, Walton, Lord Berners, and Eugène Goossens; Italy by Casella, Malipiero, and Castelnuovo-Tedesco; Hungary by Kodály, Bartók, and Dohnányi; and Poland by Szymanowski. Many of these scores he purchased himself (a number bear the stamps of music retailers, usually in Madrid or Paris), while others were given to him by their composers (many contain handwritten dedications).

In addition to his library of scores, he also built up a collection of music periodicals, which enabled him to keep abreast of his contemporaries' work not only via critical and analytical articles but also through excerpts from their latest works published in musical supplements.[17] Young composers were especially well represented in these supplements, and thus it was that Falla was able to sample works by Messiaen, Jolivet, Manuel Rosenthal, and others.

The extent to which he perused each of the scores in his collection is hinted at by their physical condition; in some cases, evidence of his detailed study of them survives as handwritten marginalia. Some of these annotations relate to interpretation: the piano pieces that he practised most diligently are identified by penciled-in fingerings. A particularly revealing annotation of this variety is found in his copy of the solo harp part of Debussy's *Danses sacrée et profane*,[18] which he played—on the piano—in Madrid in 1907.[19] He had written to Debussy to ask his advice on their interpretation, and had received a reply in which his future mentor observed: "There is something to be found in the progression from the 'solemnity' of the first to the 'grace' of the second; for a musician such as you this should not be a problem, and I believe that I can in all confidence rely on your taste."[20] Falla's solution was to maintain exactly the same tempo; after the printed instruction "Enchaînez," he wrote: "y siguiendo con el mismo valor de [dotted minim]" ("and carrying on with [dotted minim] at the same value").

Another type of annotation corrects engravers' errors. While some of these errors are obvious (missing mid-stave clefs, for instance), many others are not, and Falla can have been aware of them only through hearing performances of the works in question or by having them pointed out to him by the composers themselves.

A very few scores contain annotations which set out formal, rhythmic, melodic, or harmonic analyses. A larger number have marginalia drawing attention to matters of orchestration, with the brass and percussion parts receiving the greatest scrutiny. But the majority of Falla's annotations are cryptic, consisting of crosses in margins, rings around notes, and square brackets above and below the staves. It would be reckless to read too much into these; Joaquín Nin-Culmell, one of Falla's few pupils, remembered that

> When he decided to look at a score, he would study it and take notes which sometimes one would find tucked away in some obscure corner of the score. The latter would always be in light pencil in order that—as he would say—one might erase them more easily. And he would be in dead earnest when he would say this.[21]

There is also much to be gleaned about Falla's experience of contemporary music from his collection of concert programs, representing well over a thousand events. A significant number of these took place in Paris, where much more new music could be heard than in Spain. This resource, however, cannot be taken at face value: the date and location of each concert must be checked against the documented facts of Falla's whereabouts and activities. He certainly did not attend every one: many of the programs are from performances of his own works in locations as distant as California and Tokyo. In addition, he must have attended other concerts not represented in his collection of programs, as well as a multitude of private performances; this much is clear from references to his concert-going in various contemporary sources of evidence (not least the surviving correspondence). It is probable, for instance, that he attended most concerts of the Société Musicale Indépendante between 1910–1914, and most of those given by the Sociedad Nacional de Música between 1915–1920.

Falla's interest in the work of his European contemporaries has to be considered in relation to the ways in which he interacted with them. Remarkably, there is scarcely one well-known European composer of his own generation with whom he did not come into some manner of personal contact. It was through these associations that he was able to hear much of their work; by the same token, it was his interest in and admiration of their work which fanned his desire to get to know them and to be counted as one of their number.

The enormous value he attached to these relationships is discernible in his published writings (not least the articles on Stravinsky, Debussy, and Ravel), and in the biographical works on which he collaborated.[22] This is especially true of Jaime Pahissa's biography, which furnishes his encounters with composers as diverse as Camille Saint-Saëns and Vittorio Rieti with rich anecdotal detail.[23]

But it is in Falla's extensive correspondence that the strength of these friendships is most vividly manifested. The tally of extant letters between Falla and his most important contemporaries is shown in appendix 3, page 269. That so many have survived is largely due to Falla's own meticulousness: not only did he keep most of those that he received, but he also preserved sketches and carbon copies of many of his own letters.

His correspondence with some composers was brief, and concerned with very specific matters. His only known correspondence with Prokofiev, for instance, deals exclusively with his Russian colleague's request that he donate copies of some of his works to the library of the Moscow Composers' Union.[24] Most of the letters he exchanged with his contemporaries, however, document warm friendships with them.

Save for a childhood encounter with Saint-Saëns,[25] and the correspondence with Debussy mentioned above, Falla did not come into contact with any foreign composers until his arrival in Paris in 1907. It was during the next seven years, however, that most of his lifelong friendships with other European composers were initiated. This was furthermore the period of their most intense fraternization.

He socialized particularly frequently with composers belonging to the private circle of artists known as "Les Apaches." These included Ravel, Roussel, Florent Schmitt, Déodat de Sévérac, and Maurice Delage, at whose home in Auteuil their meetings were held.[26] Falla was introduced to their number around the beginning of October 1907, by his compatriot Ricardo Viñes.[27] At that first meeting he played through *La vida breve*, ensuring himself a place in their elite ranks. Ravel and Delage were both present on this occasion;[28] within a matter of weeks, Falla had got to know Florent Schmitt,[29] and before long he was attending what he later recalled as "those weekly meetings at . . . dear Maurice Delage's house."[30]

There can be little doubt that Falla's nationality was a contributory factor in his admittance to this circle; the "Apaches" boasted other Spaniards among its members (not least Viñes). Ravel's Spanish sympathies were at their height in 1907, the year in which both *L'Heure espagnole* and the *Rapsodie espagnole* were composed.[31] That Falla was fully accepted into their midst is implicit in a remark of Ravel's in his published review of the Paris première of *La vida breve*: "Among his compatriots, M. Falla offers the closest affinity with present-day French musicians."[32]

The same fraternity frequented regular soirées at the home of Cipa and Ida Godebski, and continued to do so long after they ceased to meet at Delage's home.[33] Here, the group was augmented by a wider cross-section of musicians, writers, and artists;[34] Stravinsky recalled that it was at the Godebskis' that he first met Falla,[35] and other visitors included Casella, Satie, Vaughan Williams, and Gabriel Grovlez.[36]

One aspect of Falla's relationships with his fellow "Apaches" was social, even altruistic. Stravinsky recalled that Falla was one of his most frequent visitors when he was ill with typhoid in Paris in 1913.[37] Viñes's diary records his attempts to procure paid work for Falla as an accompanist,[38] while the good word that Ravel put in for him at the house of Durand led to the publication of the *Piezas españolas*.[39] The well-known tale of Falla's presence on the occasion of the death of Ravel's father suggests that these two composers were often to be found in one another's company.[40]

But it was the artistic experiences he shared with his colleagues, rather than their camaraderie, which was to have the deepest effect on his work. Music was discussed and performed extensively at their meetings; a contemporary painting depicts Ravel, Roussel, Schmitt, Sévérac, M.-D. Calvocoressi, and Cipa Godebski and his young son Jean gathered around Viñes at the piano.[41]

Their musical interests centered on the new and the exotic. One of the things which had brought them together in the first place was their admiration for Debussy's *Pelléas et Mélisande*;[42] this enthusiasm must have been passed on to Falla, who attended three performances of the opera in one week in June 1908.[43] Recent Russian music also met with their approval; Viñes's diary specifically records Falla's enthusiasm for Rimsky-Korsakov's *Antar* when it was played—presumably in a piano duet version—at one of their meetings.[44] The music of more distant cultures was represented through the medium of Delage, who visited India and Japan in 1912,[45] bringing back recordings of traditional music;[46] the impression that these made on Falla was so great that, over thirty years later, he was able to recall it in detail for Pahissa's benefit.[47]

But it must have been the works of the very composers who assembled for these meetings that were heard most often. According to Casella, "It was not rare that some composer would reserve for the Godebski house the first hearing of some important work which he had just finished."[48] Thus Falla found himself at the cutting edge of Parisian musical developments; the only work by any of the "Apaches" that he had known before leaving Spain was Ravel's *Sonatine*.[49] It is extremely probable that one of the first performances of the *Cuatro piezas españolas* took place on such an occasion, given either by Falla himself or by Viñes.[50] They probably also discussed works in progress; it was at Delage's house that Ravel told Falla of his plans to compose pieces entitled *La Cloche engloutie* and *Saint François d'Assise*.[51]

But Falla's membership of the "Apaches" was not his only means of widening his musical horizons at this time. Scores of contemporary music were more freely available in Paris than in Spain, and he obtained lots of them. He took full advantage of the many opportunities presented for ballet-, opera- and concert-going. In 1908 alone, he went to hear Richard Strauss conducting the Berlin Philharmonic in performances of *Don Juan* and *Till Eulenspiegel*, a concert of modern Czech choral music (including Janáček's *Maryčka Magdónova*), and Diaghilev's renowned production of *Boris Godunov* at the Paris Opéra.[52] We may safely surmise that he was a devotee of the Ballets Russes, whose first five Paris seasons—including the premieres of *Jeux*, *Daphnis et Chloé*, *The Firebird*, *Petrushka*, and *The Rite of Spring*—coincided with his sojourn in the city.[53]

An important outlet for new music with which Falla was particularly closely associated was the Société Musicale Indépendante (SMI), founded in 1910 by members of the "Apaches," along with Fauré, Aubert, Roger-Ducasse, Jean Huré, Koechlin, and others.[54] His involvement dates from the society's very inception: he and Ravel were the pianists at the unsuccessful audition of Delage's *Conté par la mer* for the Société Nationale de Musique, the incident which sparked the creation of the SMI.[55] Falla was the first non-French composer to perform his own work in its concerts,[56] and by 1914 he was serving on its committee.[57]

In the years leading up to the First World War, the SMI programmed works by all major living French composers and a good selection of foreign ones, including Casella, Turina, Vaughan Williams, Schoenberg Kodály, and Glier.[58] The repertoire extended to early music, and even to transcriptions of Far Eastern music for Western instruments.[59] Involvement in the society was undoubtedly social too, and must have facilitated encounters with composers and performers from across Europe. When Falla, back in Spain in 1914, asked Casella for news of their friends in Paris, it was as "our SMI comrades" that he described them.[60]

Falla's use of the term "comrade" here is significant. "Colleague" and "friend" were other words he used for composers of his own generation. He addressed his musical seniors, however, with a very different word: "master" ("maître").[61]

Among those he encountered in Paris were Saint-Saëns, Fauré, Messager, D'Indy, and Widor.[62] Of these, Messager was the only one to have any direct influence on Falla, recommending that he compose the second dance of act II of *La vida breve*.[63]

The other two French composers whom Falla addressed as "master" were rather more deserving of the title. The homes of Paul Dukas and Claude Debussy were his first ports of call when he arrived in Paris in 1907:[64] a clear indication of his admiration for their music. As far as Dukas is concerned, that admiration was founded on a single work: *The Sorcerer's Apprentice*, a performance of which he had heard in Madrid shortly before his departure,[65] and which had so impressed him that he purchased the score.[66] His knowledge of Debussy's music was much wider (understandably so, given the paucity of Dukas's published output): by the time he left Spain, he owned scores of the *Deux Arabesques*, *Estampes*, *Cinq Poèmes de Baudelaire*, the String Quartet, *Danses sacrée et profane*, and perhaps other works too.[67] As we have seen, it was his performance of the latter piece which had led him to establish contact with Debussy, by mail.

Falla's relations with these composers were very cordial indeed; this is evident from New Year greetings sent by Debussy in 1910 and 1911 and by Dukas in 1911 and 1914.[68] But Falla did not socialize with them in the same way that he did with the "Apaches"; instead, their meetings took the form of consultations on specific matters.[69] These meetings were nearly always prearranged, probably by letter: Pahissa records that there was only one occasion on which Falla visited Debussy without warning him in advance,[70] and several letters survive which refer to dates and times of meetings.[71]

One matter on which Falla sought his mentors' advice was the publication of his work. Pahissa records that Dukas and Debussy joined Ravel in recommending the *Piezas españolas* to Durand;[72] an undated letter from Dukas to Falla reveals that he had also spoken to Rouart et Lerolle about them.[73] A few months later, Debussy sought to overturn Durand's decision to refuse the *Tres melodías*; he also offered to recommend them to Rouart, their eventual publisher.[74]

But there can be no doubt that most of the advice for which he asked was about compositional technique. He invited comment on works in progress, and even on his plans for future compositions (including a new *Barber of Seville*).[75] It was at one of these meetings, on 10 October 1908, that Debussy recommended certain specific revisions to *La vida breve*, including the truncation of the final scene and the conjoining of the two scenes of the first act.[76] On another occasion, Debussy expressed his dissatisfaction with the introduction to "Chinoiserie" (the second of the *Tres melodías*), the piano part of which he felt to be incongruous with the rest of the song.[77] Falla responded by cutting the piano accompaniment from the introduction almost entirely; he also trimmed the song's conclusion, which uses the same material.[78]

The aspect of Falla's compositional technique into which Debussy and Dukas had most input was orchestration. Pahissa records that "Dukas advised him to study the methods of each instrument, this being the best way of learning its possibilities, scope and resources," and goes on to note that by 1913 Falla "had acquired a complete mastery of instrumentation by following the method advised by Dukas."[79] He owned several French-language instrumental methods, no doubt acquired during his years in Paris;[80] his annotations in their pages attest to the course of study advocated by Dukas, as do marginalia in scores by a number of composers (not least Dukas and Debussy themselves). Further evidence survives in the form of Falla's copious handwritten notes on the capabilities of various instruments; his notes on the trombone record Debussy's advocacy of writing *pianissimo* passages for the instrument.[81] As Yvan Nommick has demonstrated, such advice came in very useful when Falla came to touch up the orchestration of *La vida breve* around 1913.[82]

It would be difficult to overstate the import of Falla's seven years in Paris. The influences exerted on him during this period led to the transformation of his musical language and intentions. This may be illustrated by a plethora of examples from the time in question. The influence of his French colleagues' work is manifest in the shimmering orchestration of *Noches en los jardines de España*, and—even more so—in the first two of the *Tres melodías*, which demonstrate Falla's proficiency at pastiche and his keen sensibility towards contemporary fashions (not least orientalism).[83]

The *Piezas españolas* furnish us with a particularly neat illustration of the evolution of his style during this period. Falla told Pahissa that he composed the first two ("Aragonesa" and "Cubana") before he left for Paris.[84] He also claimed to have begun the third ("Montañesa") at this time, but this assertion is contradicted by earlier (and more reliable) evidence: a letter to the French composer and musicologist Henri Collet dated 15 April 1909, in which he explains that this piece was inspired by the scenery he encountered during his concert tour in northern Spain in January 1908 (i.e., after his arrival in Paris).[85] That the fourth piece ("Andaluza") was composed in Paris is not in doubt.[86]

The first two pieces in the set were the most original and demanding works for piano that Falla had written so far; they contain many idiomatic touches, such as the parallel minor thirds descending chromatically in bars 4 to 9 of the "Aragonesa," and the little mordentlike figures which decorate the melodies of both pieces. However, the harmonic and pianistic language represents little advance on the style of, say, Liszt.

With "Montañesa," however, comes a perceptible shift in style; it is as though Falla had suddenly discovered Debussy (which, as we have seen, was quite literally the case). At the visible level, the greater use of the French language draws attention to itself. "Aragonesa" contains no French at all, "Cubana" just three short words ("court," "cédez," and "expressif"), probably added at a later date.[87] The French expressions in the last two pieces are longer, however: "Montañesa" has "le chant bien en dehors" and "comme un écho" ("Cubana" had used "come un eco"), while "Andaluza" has "lointain," "très rythmé et avec un sentiment sauvage," and "bien chantant[,] très expressif et la mélodie toujours bien en dehors." These directions all relate to the aesthetic interpretation of the music rather than its technical execution, and their precision recalls similar instructions in contemporary French piano music: "en dehors" was a particular favourite of both Debussy and Ravel.

The effects of Falla's Parisian sojourn are also betrayed in the notes themselves. Both "La Cathédrale engloutie" (*Préludes*, Book 1) and "Montañesa" (published in the same year: 1910) employ the interval of a perfect fifth to evoke the sound of bells. Distancing devices, separating melodies from accompaniments, also recall impressionist techniques: there is a distinct similarity, for instance, between the unfurling of the opening arabesque over a static harmony in "La Soirée dans Grenade" (from *Estampes*, which Falla knew at this time) and the treatment of the melody at the "Più animato" of "Montañesa" and of that at the "Doppio più lento ma sempre mosso" of "Andaluza." (The opening of "Les Colombes," the first of the *Tres melodías*, presents a further parallel.) The influence of impressionism is evident also in the harmonic language of the *Piezas españolas*; the essentially triadic style of the first two gives way in "Montañesa" to a sea of added sixths, unresolved sevenths, and quartal harmonies.

Paris showered Falla with a wealth of new experiences and stimuli. It was not until he had returned to Spain, however, that these bore their full fruit. The four years of the First World War were the most productive years of his entire career, during which he completed no fewer than four major works: the *Siete canciones*, *El amor brujo*, *Noches en los jardines de España*, and *El corregidor y la molinera*.

*   *   *

Though Falla remained in Spain throughout the war, he did not entirely sever links with his foreign colleagues. He sent out two sets of letters to his friends in France: one shortly after his return to Paris, in which he expressed his full confidence in France's eventual victory, and another, congratulatory in nature, on the occasion of the Armistice. He maintained occasional correspondence with Debussy, Ravel, and Dukas, and assisted the latter in his research for a new edition of Scarlatti keyboard sonatas.[88] He exchanged a number of letters with Alfredo Casella, who had returned to Italy and who, in a display of Latin unity in the face of Teutonic oppression, sought to establish an alliance among societies promoting the performance of new music in Spain, France, and Italy.[89]

The only foreign composer whom he encountered personally during this period was Stravinsky, who visited Spain in June 1916.[90] (It was on this occasion that Falla wrote the aforementioned article on Stravinsky.) The occasion enabled the two men to keep abreast of one another's latest work. Falla must have introduced Stravinsky to *Noches en los jardines de España* and to his sketches for *El corregidor y la molinera*; Stravinsky expressed his dislike of some of the music for the character of the Miller's Wife, and Falla promptly rewrote it.[91] Meanwhile, Stravinsky deeply impressed Falla with what he had written of

Les Noces (still entitled *Noces villageois* at the time). Their friendship also yielded practical benefits: in 1918, Falla and Ernest Ansermet were the go-betweens when Rubinstein commissioned Stravinsky to compose what turned out to be *Piano-Rag-Music*.[92] (*Fantasía bœtica* was commissioned at the same time.)

Falla resumed his foreign travels in 1919, when he traveled to London to attend rehearsals for the first production of *El sombrero de tres picos* (though the trip was cut short as a result of his mother's illness and death).[93] His passage through France *en route* seems not to included a stay in Paris, but he made his first full return visit to that city a few months later, in December. That stay lasted until February 1920, and he returned again in May for the first of a series of springtime visits to the French capital, each one of which lasted several weeks. The only circumstances which prevented him from undertaking these visits were overwork (in 1922) and ill health (in 1924, 1926, and 1929). He made his last trip to Paris in 1931, and remained in France throughout the summer, spending several weeks on holiday in the Haute-Savoie and in Provence.

Italy was another country which he toured extensively; over the course of three visits, in 1923, 1928, and 1932, he visited most of the major cities on the west coast. His 1928 visit was to Siena, where he attended the sixth festival of the International Society for Contemporary Music and took part in a performance of the *Concerto*. He also attended the fourth ISCM festival in Zurich in 1926, which included two staged performances of *El retablo de Maese Pedro*.

In 1923, he traveled to Brussels to attend a production of *La vida breve* at the Théâtre de la Monnaie. He also made three more visits to London (1921, 1927, and 1931), where he took part in performances of his own works.[94] (He never visited any other part of the United Kingdom.)

His resumed European travels led to many reunions with his old friends. His letter writing also reached its apex during this period, bridging the gaps between social calls. These two means of communication complemented one another; it is significant that his isolation in Spain from 1932 onwards coincides with the beginning of the decline in the volume of his correspondence.

Among the friendships which blossomed anew between 1919 and the mid-1930s were those with Ravel, Stravinsky, Schmitt, and Dukas. Just as the latter had been the first composer whom Falla had met after arriving in Paris in 1907,[95] he was also the first with whom he was reunited after the Armistice: both happened to be in London in July 1919.[96] Further encounters took place in Paris in 1920, 1928, and 1931,[97] and their letter writing continued until just a few months before Dukas's death in 1935.[98]

In 1931, Falla sought associate membership of the French Society of Authors, and he asked Dukas and Florent Schmitt to propose his application.[99] That Falla's choice should have fallen on Schmitt may be taken as an indication that they saw much of one another in Paris; though there is little surviving correspondence between the two men, what there is reveals that they were on first-name terms (an extremely rare circumstance in Falla's friendships).[100] Falla probably saw a great deal of Ravel too (certainly more than Arbie Orenstein implies in the article accompanying his edition of the Falla-Ravel correspondence).[101] We know that they met during Falla's 1927 stay in Paris;[102] they probably met also during his visits in 1919–20, 1923 (perhaps both times he was there that year) and 1925, and maybe also in 1930 and 1931.[103] Ravel was one of the few who visited Falla in Granada; he gave a concert of his own works there on 21 November 1928, with the singer Madeleine Grey and the violinist Claude Lévy.[104] In between these meetings, their correspondence was warm, chatty, and frequent. Even more extensive and demonstrative, however, is Falla's postwar correspondence with Stravinsky. These two were reunited fairly frequently too: five times in Paris (1920, 1927, 1930, and twice in 1923),[105] twice in Madrid (1921 and 1924)[106] and once in London (1927).[107]

Other composers who visited Falla in Granada included Koechlin, Casella, and Delage. The latter's trip, undertaken with Roland-Manuel in September 1929,[108] led to the resumption of a friendship that had been in abeyance since the First World War. This eventually bore fruit in "Rêves," the second of Delage's *Contrerimes*, inspired by the trip and dedicated to Falla.[109] Koechlin was one of the last visitors Falla received in Granada: his visit took place in April 1932. Though they had known one another in Paris before the war (Koechlin published a review of *La vida breve* in 1914 which Falla considered to be particularly perceptive),[110] their friendship did not bloom until the 1920s. After the war, they met in Paris at least five times (twice in 1923 and once in 1925, 1928, and 1931).[111] As we have seen, Casella was one of the few prewar Parisian associates with whom Falla maintained contact throughout the First World War, and their correspondence continued right through to the outbreak of the Second. They met in Paris in 1923 and 1931,[112] and on each of Falla's last three visits to Italy.[113] On 18 January 1930, Casella took part in a concert at the Casa de los Tiros,[114] and probably stayed in Granada for several days.[115]

One composer whose planned trip to that city was cancelled at the eleventh hour was Bartók. It would have taken place in February 1931 had it not been for the poor state of Falla's health; Bartók noted in a letter that "your Granada engagement was one of the main reasons why I took the decision (at the last moment) to accept this tour . . .: it would have given me so much pleasure to see you."[116] Falla's reply reveals that they had met before;[117] this was probably in Barcelona in March 1927.[118]

Falla also made a number of new acquaintances in the course of his travels from 1919 onwards, including Szymanowski (Paris, 1923), Kodály (Zurich, 1926), and possibly even Webern (Zurich, 1926).[119] Malipiero, whom he met in 1923,[120] became a particularly close friend, and his wife Anna (a conscientious Roman Catholic and fellow caffeine addict) even more so.[121] Falla and Malipiero corresponded until the very last year of Falla's life.

Prominent amongst the new friends he made after the First World War are a host of younger composers. He met Arthur Honegger and William Walton at ISCM festivals in Zurich (1926) and Siena (1928), respectively.[122] In Paris, he befriended Francis Poulenc, Darius Milhaud, Georges Auric, Henri Sauguet, and Pierre-Octave Ferroud, and also consolidated his friendship with Roland-Manuel.[123] Of the Italian younger generation, he was well acquainted with Mario Castelnuovo-Tedesco and Vittorio Rieti,[124] and he counted Eugène Goossens among his friends in England.[125]

Falla interacted differently with these men than he did with composers of his own generation. They looked up to him as a model, perhaps recognizing in him a Latin alternative to Stravinsky; they sent him their latest scores and several of them dedicated compositions to him. In return, Falla offered unconditional moral support; he always praised their work (albeit usually in the most general terms), and even occasionally furnished them with specific compositional advice (notably in the case of Castelnuovo-Tedesco's *Dos romances viejos*).[126]

Milhaud and Poulenc were two of his closest friends among his juniors; their correspondence was regular, they met frequently during Falla's trips abroad (mainly in Paris, but also in Venice in Poulenc's case, and Aix-en-Provence in Milhaud's),[127] and both also visited Falla in Granada. Milhaud's visit took place in April 1929;[128] at the time, both men were composing works in which Christopher Columbus featured as a character (*Christophe Colomb* and *Atlántida*).[129] Milhaud ultimately dedicated his opera to Falla, who acknowledged it as "magnificent."[130] Poulenc also dedicated a work to Falla: the *Trio for piano, oboe and bassoon* (1926). His five-week stay in Granada took place in April and May 1930.[131] Ironically, Falla was in Paris for much of this period,[132] but the two men did meet up to hear some *cante jondo*.[133] An important link between these two composers is the fact that both composed harpsichord concertos for Wanda Landowska. The *Concert champêtre* is a very different work to Falla's *Concerto*—it is scored for full orchestra, and cast in much more traditional form; nevertheless, Poulenc delayed its completion until he had an opportunity to hear Falla's work.[134] Indeed, he was well aware of its indebtedness: his handwritten dedication in Falla's copy of the miniature score reads: "For you, my dear Falla, this very little brother to your magnificent *Concerto*."[135]

The interest which Falla and many of his contemporaries maintained in one another's work is evident in their occasional discussion of musical matters. Ravel and Koechlin were particularly fond of discussing their latest projects. The latter, for instance, sent Falla a copy of almost everything he had published between 1921 and 1936 (including pedagogical treatises as well as musical compositions), and he provided a commentary on many of them in his letters. His respect for Falla's work led him to include excerpts from it in his *Traité de l'harmonie*.[136]

But Falla's interest in his contemporaries' music at this time was eclipsed by his concern for the welfare of the composers themselves—a phenomenon mirrored by an obsession with his own health and well-being, which had a detrimental effect on his productivity. The Stravinsky correspondence typifies this tendency: discussion of musical topics is heavily outweighed by expressions of personal affection.

This change of attitude is manifested also in his acquisition, experience, and promotion of his contemporaries' music. In the 1920s and early 1930s, while he was continuing to travel abroad, he seized every opportunity to hear performances of his colleagues' work, and he continued to promote it when he returned home. In January 1923, for instance, he performed Ravel's *Berceuse sur le nom de Fauré* and excerpts from Debussy's *Children's Corner* and Stravinsky's *The Soldier's Tale*, as incidental music to the Epiphany puppet shows staged at the Lorca family home.[137] Over the next few years he sought to include in the repertoire of the Orquesta Bética de Cámara works by Auric, Malipiero, Milhaud, Poulenc, Ravel, Roland-Manuel, and Stravinsky.[138] In later years, however, he was prevented from continuing this work by adverse political circumstances, his poor health, and his isolation in provincial Spain and Argentina.

The 1920s also saw a decline in his purchasing of scores, though he continued to receive complimentary copies of his admirers' works. There is no doubt that his knowledge of the work of some of his contemporaries suffered as a result of this reliance on gifts: not least Ravel, of whose post-1918 compositions he possessed only two (*Chansons madécasses* and *L'Enfant et les sortilèges*).[139] He never obtained scores of *Boléro*,[140] *Don Quichotte à Dulcinée*, or the two piano concertos, for instance, and this would seem to demonstrate a waning of interest.

Not only did he buy fewer scores from the mid-1920s on, but he also subjected those he did obtain to less intense analysis. There are many fewer annotations in these later scores: marginalia relating to aspects of a work's orchestration, for instance, are found almost exclusively in scores published before 1914. Works by younger composers are particularly lacking in pencil marks: there is only one annotation in all of his Milhaud scores,[141] and none in anything by Poulenc. Furthermore, many of the musical supplements he received as a subscriber to *Le Monde musical* and *La Revue musicale* remain uncut.[142]

While annotations in his scores clearly reveal his study of his contemporaries' work in prewar Paris, such evidence is denied us about the later period. Similarly, there is no indication that his contemporaries continued to influence him personally. Stravinsky's comments on *El corregidor y la molinera* in 1916 were probably one of the last pieces of direct compositional advice upon which he acted.

Nevertheless, the development of his work from 1914 onwards follows a trajectory which closely parallels that of the European modernist movement in general. Given his awareness of his contemporaries' work, this was no coincidence; some cross-fertilization must have taken place.

Something of the way in which his contemporaries' work is interrelated with his own may be observed in the specific example of one composer whom he held in particularly high regard: Stravinsky. Falla's respect for his Russian colleague was so overt and loyal that he could freely joke about it without fear of misapprehension. In 1929, he dedicated a score of the *Concerto* with the words: "to Igor Stravinsky, whom I love so much, in spite of my profound antipathy for his music. . . ."[143] Stravinsky's reply continues the jest.[144] The same wit is found without the sarcasm in the inscription Falla wrote a couple of months later on a copy of his portrait: "To Igor Stravinsky, *the Chosen One*, with all my old and deep affection."[145] This is a clear allusion to the sacrificial victim in *The Rite of Spring*—but it also indicates his definite awareness of its composer's unique gifts.

Stravinsky was perhaps the only composer whom Falla kept under close observation after the First World War. He continued to purchase scores of his Russian friend's works long after he had ceased to buy those of his other contemporaries: an extreme case is his piano score of *Jeu de Cartes*, published as late as 1937, but nevertheless containing several handwritten corrections and other annotations.[146] Stravinsky also kept an eye on developments in Falla's art. He was present at the Paris premiere of *El retablo de Maese Pedro* in 1923, and at the London premiere of the *Concerto* in 1928,[147] a work which he conducted in America the year after Falla's death.[148]

It is in Stravinsky's work, perhaps, that the evolution of Falla's style is most closely mirrored. It will be recalled that a number of their shared techniques were listed at the very beginning of this chapter; the parallels are strengthened by the fact that several of them appeared in both composers' music simultaneously. Around 1923, for instance, each began to compose a work entitled *Concerto*, scored for keyboard with predominantly woodwind accompaniment. Stravinsky mentioned that he was composing his *Concerto* in a letter to Falla dated 27 February 1924,[149] and he may even have showed him some of it when they met in Paris in November 1923. Falla probably obtained his copy of the two-piano reduction of this work while he was still working on his own *Concerto*.[150] But, though Falla's work was not completed until 1927, it seems that its conception predates that of the Stravinsky, albeit only by a matter of days. It is apparent from his correspondence with Wanda and Eve Landowska that the work was already projected at the time of the *Retablo* premiere in June 1923.[151] As we have seen, Stravinsky was present on this occasion—and the first sketches for his *Concerto* date from July of that year.[152]

The chronology and hierarchy of this relationship, therefore, is not always clear. Did one composer imitate the other's innovation? Were there common external influences? Or did the parallels in their art come about in isolation, occurring simultaneously by pure coincidence?

The actual relationship is probably an abstruse combination of all three of these hypotheses. It is true, for instance, that the unusual scorings of *El retablo de Maese Pedro* and the *Concerto* came about after Falla's exposure to *Renard* and *The Soldier's Tale*. But he had already begun to experiment with reduced orchestral forces during the war, with the first version of *El amor brujo*; at this time he knew nothing of

Stravinsky's orchestral work after *The Rite of Spring* and *The Nightin-gale*. Moreover, unusual scorings had been explored even earlier by Schoenberg (whose *Pierrot lunaire* made a deep impression on Stravinsky in Berlin in 1912),[153] and even by Ravel (whose *Introduction and allegro for flute, clarinet, harp and string quartet* was written as early as 1906).

Paradigmatic of the shared vision of these two composers is their concern with primitivism, an aesthetic concept brought to the fore by the infamous première of *The Rite of Spring*. Falla nailed his primitivist colors to the mast on a number of occasions. Notably, the word "primitive" appears several times in the *cante jondo* essay—not least in the full title of the pamphlet itself: *El "cante jondo" (canto primitivo andaluz)*—and in 1916 he made the observation that "music's primitive spirit . . . is very much of the here-and-now" (a more extended version of this quotation is given below).[154] Stravinsky was notoriously reticent on the question of his early aesthetic standpoints; nevertheless, Richard Taruskin has revealed in his compositional method—as in Falla's—the "abstraction of stylistic elements from folk music,"[155] and the composer himself gave away the fact that he was aware of a primitivist ideal inherent in this technique: "If any of these pieces *sounds* like aboriginal folk music, it may be because my powers of fabrication were able to tap some unconscious 'folk' memory."[156]

The ways in which the primitivist ideal is manifested in the work of these two composers are remarkably similar. *El amor brujo*, first performed just two years after *The Rite of Spring*, shares with that work its central themes of spells, rituals, and superstitions. Both works make use of obsessive rhythmic figures (as at figure 13 of *The Rite* and in the "Canción del amor dolido" of *El amor brujo*). Static and repeated harmonies play a significant role too (compare figure 62 of the Stravinsky with the opening of the second scene of the 1915 version of the Falla), as do folklike melodies, heard alone or over a static accompaniment (*The Rite of Spring*, figure 48; *El amor brujo* [1915], "Interludio," bars 5 to 11). Given the enormous stylistic disparity between these two works, however, it is unlikely that Falla was consciously imitating his younger colleague. Both works are products of the same modernist tendencies.

One contemporary tendency which bypassed Falla entirely, and which made itself felt in Stravinsky's music only after the Second World War, was the wholesale rejection of the principles of tonality. The strength of Falla's convictions on this subject is evident in J. B. Trend's biography of the composer, a uniquely dependable source thanks to its having been written by a close friend, but without Falla's own biased direct input:

> [Falla] would resent an accusation of atonality as he would resent an accusation of atheism, and regards any weakening of tonal feeling—such, for instance, as even Haydn shows in some of his quartets, by the use of "anticipations"—as a weakening of faith.[157]

The Haydn comment is bizarre—though Trend makes it clear that this is his own opinion rather than Falla's. In relation to the *Concerto*, he goes on to indicate that Falla's interpretation of the tonal principle freely embraced polytonality: "The tonality may be modal, or there be two or three different tonalities in evidence at the same time; but they are always strongly individualized, contrasted, and distinguished."[158]

Falla's appreciation of polytonal music is implicit in his affection for certain of Milhaud's works, notably the distinctly bitonal "Ipanema" from *Saudades do Brazil*. "I'll end up playing *Ipanema* off by heart I like it so much," he told its composer.[159]

Nevertheless, Pahissa claims that "Falla did not want any part of his work to be regarded as polytonal. He maintained that the aggregation of notes within his chords resulted from his system of natural harmonics of the perfect chord."[160]

Elsewhere, Pahissa links this system with the teachings of Louis Lucas,[161] though in fact those theories can have been no more than the point of departure for the development of a system which Falla used only occasionally.[162] In any case, the difference resides in the ear of the listener, and even Pahissa was impelled to admit that "it cannot be denied that some passages . . . are apparently polytonal."[163] There are no passages in Falla's oeuvre, however, that are apparently atonal.

His dislike of atonality is at the heart of his rejection of contemporary German and Austrian music. Though he professed admiration for Richard Strauss and Arnold Schoenberg,[164] he wrote that "it would be difficult, if not impossible, for us to find another composer from either country whose works demonstrate, in form and technique, the slightest progress over the musical conquests of Richard Wagner."[165] And he was keen to point out that "Schoenberg's music, particularly, is atonal, and the displeasure which many of his compositions produce in us is undoubtedly due to this very serious mistake."[166]

Yet he tried to have it both ways, and sought to associate himself with all of his European contemporaries, even where he dissented from their methods. In the same article, he included Schoenberg's name in a list of composers whose work evinced tendencies of which he approved.[167] In 1928, in response to a request from the French periodical *Musique* for a definition of the "poles of attraction" in his art, he noted his inclination towards "Music in which the eternal laws of rhythm and tonality— closely unified—are consciously observed," but then added the following provision:

> This statement, however, should not be taken to imply a rebuke to those who—nobly—act in an opposing manner. On the contrary: I think that progress in an art's technique, and the discovery of real possibilities which contribute to its greater blossoming, are often due to the use of apparently arbitrary procedures, subjected later to eternal and unchanging laws.[168]

The composers whom he identified as sharing Schoenberg's aspiration were Debussy, Stravinsky, Dukas, Schmitt, Satie, Ravel, Albéniz, Kodály, Bartók, and Skryabin; he did not include his own name in the list, but it is clear that he subscribed to the same tenets. And his description of that aspiration is one of the finest manifestos of early modernism ever written:

> that of producing the most intense emotion by means of new melodic and modal forms; of new harmonic and contrapuntal sound combinations; of obsessive rhythms emanating from the music's primitive spirit, which is very much of the here-and-now, and ought always to have been preserved; a magical art of evoking feelings, essences and even places by means of rhythm and sonority.[169]

*   *   *

Given that it is the innate Spanishness of Falla's music which today obscures its universality, it is paradoxical that it was this very factor which was largely responsible for its popularity outside Spain during his lifetime. According to Trend,

> Falla's music . . . gave everyone the chance of becoming acquainted with the tendencies of serious contemporary composers. His methods sometimes reminded the audience of Stravinsky, Bartók, or Vaughan Williams; but they seemed to be more immediately accessible. . . .[170]

Thus it was that Falla's voice held particular significance in the development and dissemination of modern European music.

His success outside his own country was unprecedented, and remains unique among modern Spanish composers. He was neither the first nor the last to cross the Pyrenees—but he was the only one who participated fully in the global development of the art. At the same time, he achieved the rare distinction of attaining both public popularity and the respect of his most illustrious contemporaries, and even of exercising a minor influence upon his juniors. By the 1930s, he was publicly acclaimed by his fellow artists as one of the world's greatest composers. In 1931, the International Society for Contemporary Music boasted only five honorary members: Maurice Ravel, Jean Sibelius, Richard Strauss, Igor Stravinsky, and Manuel de Falla.[171]

Stravinsky told Robert Craft: "When, after the *première* of his *Tricorne*, I told him that the best music in his score was not necessarily the most 'Spanish,' I knew my remark would impress him."[172] As they were such good friends, he was in an excellent position to judge.

Appendix 1   Falla's European travels

BELGIUM	Brussels	July 1908
		April 1923
	Spa	Summer 1907
	[unknown location(s)]	Summer 1907
FRANCE	Aix-en-Provence	September 1931
	Amboise	May 1927
	Arles	September 1932
	Evian and environs	September 1912
		August to September 1931
	Dieppe	*c.* September/October 1908
	Le Havre	October/November 1910
	Nice	January to April 1913
	Paris	Summer 1907 to January 1913 (with occasional absences)
		April 1913 to August/September 1914
		December 1919 to February 1920
		May to June 1920
		May 1921
		June 1921
		April 1923
		May to July 1923
		November 1923
		May to June 1925

Appendix 1   Falla's European travels (*continued*)

FRANCE		May to June 1927
(*continued*)		February to April 1928
		May to June 1930
		June to July/August 1931
	Tours	March 1928
	[unknown location(s)]	Summer 1907
GERMANY	[unknown location(s)]	Summer 1907
ITALY	Florence	May 1923
	Frascati	May 1923
	Milan	September 1912
		September 1932
	Padua	September 1932
	Rome	May 1923
	San Remo	September 1932
	Siena	September 1928
	Tivoli	May 1923
	Venice	September 1932
	Verona	September 1932
	Vicenza	September 1932
LUXEMBOURG	[unknown location(s)]	Summer 1907
		December 1907
SWITZERLAND	Geneva	Summer 1907
		June 1926
		September 1932
	Kulm (Rigi)	June 1926
	Winterthur	June 1926
	Zurich	June 1926
	[unknown location(s)]	Summer 1907
UNITED KINGDOM	London	May 1911
		June to July 1919
		May to June 1921
		June 1927
		June 1931

Appendix 2   Number of scores of works by selected composers in Falla's library (not including periodical supplements)

Louis Aubert	1	Vincent D'Indy	2
Georges Auric	5	Claude Debussy	37
Béla Bartók	1	Maurice Delage	10
Lord Berners	5	Ernö Dohnányi	1
Alfredo Casella	1	Paul Dukas	10
Mario Castelnuovo-Tedesco	5	Gabriel Fauré	2
Gustave Charpentier	2	Pierre-Octave Ferroud	7

Reyngol'd Glier 1
Gustav Mahler 1
Gian Francesco Malipiero 4
Georges Migot 12
Darius Milhaud 21
Gabriel Pierné 1
Francis Poulenc 24
Sergey Prokofiev 2
Sergey Rakhmaninov 2
Eugène Goossens 4
Gustav Holst 1
Zoltan Kodály 4
Charles Koechlin 20

Stan Golestan 1
Maurice Ravel 22
Ottorino Respighi 2
Gustave Samazeuilh 1
Camille Saint-Saëns 7
Henri Sauguet 4
Florent Schmitt 7
Arnold Schoenberg 1
Richard Strauss 2
Igor Stravinsky 28
Karol Szymanowski 1
Ralph Vaughan Williams 5
William Walton 3

Appendix 3   Number and location of extant items of correspondence (including sketches) between Falla and selected European contemporaries

	To Falla	From Falla	Total
Aubert	3 (AMF)	3 (AMF)	6
Auric	2 (AMF)	11 (AMF)	13
Bartók	1 (AMF)	2 (not known; AMF)	3
Boulanger, Nadia	5 (AMF)	0	5
Canteloube	1 (AMF)	1 (Séverac Archives)	2
Casadesus, Francis	4 (AMF)	1 (AMF)	5
Casella	34 (AMF)	22 (*I-Vgc*)	56
Castelnuovo-Tedesco	7 (AMF)	5 (AMF)	12
Charpentier	2 (AMF)	0	2
Collaer	5 (AMF)	2 (AMF)	7
Collet	15 (AMF)	13 (priv. coll.; AMF)	28
Debussy	9 (AMF)	2 (AMF)	11
Delage	3 (AMF)	4 (AMF)	7
Duboscq	6 (AMF)	5 (AMF)	11
Dukas	22 (AMF)	16 (AMF)	38
Ferroud	7 (AMF)	5 (AMF)	12
Goossens	4 (AMF)	3 (AMF)	7
Grovlez	11 (AMF)	4 (AMF)	15
Inghelbrecht	2 (AMF)	1 (AMF)	3
Knosp	26 (AMF)	11 (AMF)	37
Kodály	1 (AMF)	0	1
Koechlin	30 (AMF)	23 (priv. coll.; AMF)	53
Laparra	4 (AMF)	2 (AMF)	6
Malipiero	14 (AMF)	15 (*I-Vgc*)	29
Messager	3 (AMF)	1 (AMF)	4
Migot	3 (AMF)	1 (AMF)	4
Milhaud	23 (AMF)	19 (priv. coll.; AMF)	42

Appendix 3   Number and location of extant items of correspondence (including sketches) between Falla and selected European contemporaries (*continued*)

	To Falla	From Falla	Total
Pierné	4 (AMF)	6 (AMF)	10
Poulenc	6 (AMF)	18 (priv. coll.; AMF)	24
Prokofiev	2 (AMF)	0	2
Ravel	14 (AMF)	9 (*F-Pn*; AMF)	23
Rieti	2 (AMF)	0	2
Roland-Manuel	39 (AMF)	65 (priv. coll.; AMF)	104
Roussel	5 (AMF)	1 (AMF)	6
Samazeuilh	19 (AMF)	6 (AMF; private coll.)	25
Sauguet	1 (AMF)	4 (AMF)	5
Schindler	9 (AMF)	6 (AMF)	15
Schmitt	6 (AMF)	6 (*F-Pn*; AMF)	12
Sévérac	0	1 (private coll.)	1
Stravinsky	17 (AMF)	28 (*CH-Bps*; AMF)	45
Wellesz	1 (AMF)	0	1
Widor	4 (AMF)	2 (AMF)	6

Library sigla:
   CH-Bps   Paul Sacher Stiftung, Basel, Switzerland.
   AMF   Archivo Manuel de Falla, Granada, Spain.
   F-Pn   Bibliothèque Nationale de France, Paris, France.
   I-Vgc   Fondazione Giorgio Cini, Venice, Italy.

NOTES

1. With thanks to Bruce Wood, Nigel Simeone, Joaquín Nin-Culmell, Robert Orledge, Elena Torres, Elena García de Paredes de Falla, Yvan Nommick, Concha Chinchilla, and all the staff of the Archivo Manuel de Falla, Granada. Unless otherwise indicated, translations from French and Spanish are by the present author. A fuller discussion of Falla's relationships with non-Spanish composers of his own generation may be found in Chris Collins, *Manuel de Falla and his European contemporaries: Encounters, relationships and influences*, Ph.D. dissertation, University of Wales, Bangor, 2002.

2. See, for instance, Donald Jay Grout and Claude V. Palisca, *A History of Western Music*, 5th ed., New York: Norton, 1996, 676–77.

3. J. B. Trend, *Manuel de Falla and Spanish Music*, New York: Alfred A. Knopf, 1929, 65–66.

4. Article in *Le Journal* (Paris), 14 June 1930; the article is preserved as a cutting at the Archivo Manuel de Falla, Granada (hereinafter AMF). The review was of a gala performance of Falla's works which took place at the Grande Salle Pleyel on 14 May 1930.

5. Ravel expressed his admiration for Falla's work in two newspaper reviews: *ABC* (Madrid), 1 May 1924, and *De Telegraaf* (Amsterdam), 6 April 1932 (translations of both are given in Arbie Orenstein, *A Ravel Reader*, New York: Columbia University Press, 1990, 432 and 493 respectively); in addition, he told Roland-Manuel that he considered Falla's *Concerto* to be "the masterpiece of contemporary chamber music" (Roland-Manuel, *Manuel de Falla* [Paris: Cahiers d'Art, 1930], 59; letter Roland-Manuel-Falla, 3 January 1938 [AMF, folder 7520]). Poulenc recorded his admiration for Falla in the first of his *A Bâtons rompus* radio broadcasts about Spain (transcribed in Francis Poulenc [ed. Lucie Kayas], *A Bâtons rompus: écrits radiophoniques*, Paris: Actes Sud, 1999, 90), and in conversation with Stéphane Audel (Francis Poulenc, *My Friends and Myself*, London: Dennis Dobson, 1978, 87–96). Messaien did the same during an interview with José Bruyr (José Bruyr, *L'Écran des musiciens*, ii, Paris: José Corti, 1933, 130).

6. Jaime Pahissa, *Vida y obra de Manuel de Falla*, Buenos Aires: Ricordi Americana, 1947, 85; abridged English translation: *Manuel de Falla: His Life and Works*, London: Museum Press, 1954, 79–80.

7. Pahissa, *Vida y obra*, 51 and 166–67; *His Life and Works*, 44 and 154. He also considered emigrating to Switzerland around this time.

8. Letters from Falla to: Henri Collet, 23 October 1914 (photocopy at AMF, folder 6854); Florent Schmitt, 6 November 1914 (Bibliothèque nationale de France, Paris [hereinafter *F-Pn*], Département de Musique, L. a. Falla 9); Charles-Marie Widor, undated [shortly after 26 January 1935] (sketch at *AMF*, folder 7781); Gabriel Grovlez, 29 January 1936 (sketch at AMF, folder 7085).

9. These names are taken from Sociedad Nacional de Música programs preserved at AMF.

10. Falla is named in the former capacity in the program of the ninth ISCM Festival, held in Oxford and London in July 1931; a copy is preserved at *AMF* (NFE 1931-013). The latter office is mentioned in Michel Duchesneau, *L'Avant-garde musicale et ses sociétés à Paris de 1871 à 1939*, Sprimont: Mardaga, 1997, 135.

11. Manuel de Falla, "Claude Debussy et l'Espagne," *La Revue musicale*, i, 2, December 1920, 206–10; *Id.*, "Notes sur Ravel," *La Revue musicale*, xx, 189, March 1939, 81–6. Except where otherwise indicated, all of Falla's writings discussed in this chapter are collected (in Spanish) in Manuel de Falla (ed. Federico Sopeña), *Escritos sobre música y músicos*, 4th ed.; Madrid: Espasa Calpe, 1988. An inaccurate English translation of this volume exists as *On Music and Musicians*, London: Marian Boyars, 1979; translations in this chapter are by the present author.

12. Manuel de Falla, "Wanda Landowska à Grenade," *La Revue musicale*, iii (identified on the cover as volume iv), 4, February 1923, 73–74. This article is not reproduced in *Escritos sobre música y músicos* or *On Music and Musicians*.

13. Manuel de Falla, "Felipe Pedrell, 1841–1922," *La Revue musicale*, iii, 4, February 1923, 1–11.

14. [Manuel de Falla], *El "cante jondo" (canto primitivo andaluz)*, Granada: Urania, 1922, 13–18.

15. Manuel de Falla, "Enrique Granados: evocación de su obra," *Revista musical hispanoamericana*, April 1916, 11–12; *Id.*, "Prólogo a *La música francesa contemporanea* de G. Jean-Aubry," *Revista musical hispanoamericana*, July 1916, 7–13; *Ibid.*, "Introducción a la música nueva," *Revista musical hispanoamericana*, December 1916, 4–6; "Nuestra música," *Música* 11, June 1917, 1–5.

16. Manuel de Falla, "El gran músico de nuestro tiempo: Igor Stravinsky," *La Tribuna*, 5 June 1916, 4.

17. Notable among such periodicals are *La Revue musicale* and *Le Monde musical*. Falla possessed a complete run of the former, from its inception in 1920 until its temporary cessation in 1940 (AMF, 5875). His collection of the latter extends almost complete from 1919 to 1939 (including musical supplements from 1926 onwards) (AMF, 7861); in addition, he owned a number of issues from between 1909 and 1914, without musical supplements.

18. AMF, 304.

19. Pahissa, *Vida y obra*, 42; *His Life and Works*, 37.

20. Letter from Debussy to Falla, 13 January 1907 (AMF, folder 6898; transcribed in François Lesure [ed.] *Claude Debussy: Lettres 1884–1918*, Paris: Hermann, 1980, 157; English translation in François Lesure and Roger Nichols [eds.], *Debussy Letters*, London: Faber, 1987, 176; this translation by the present author).

21. Unpublished notes made (in English) by Joaquín Nin-Culmell around 1989, preserved at AMF. Quoted by kind permission of the author.

22. In addition to the books by Pahissa and Roland-Manuel, the following sources may be considered as "authorized" biographies: Georges Jean-Aubry, *La Musique et les nations*, Paris: La Sirène, 1922, 73–5 and 127–43; Adolfo Salazar, *La música contemporánea en España*, Madrid: La Nave, 1930, 155–86.

23. Pahissa, *Vida y obra*, 21 and 129–30; *His Life and Works*, 18 and 118–19.

24. Letters Prokofiev-Falla, 15 February and 1 April 1934 (AMF, folder 7449).

25. Roland-Manuel, *Manuel de Falla*, 17.

26. Other musicians in the group included Michel-Dmitri Calvocoressi, André Caplet, Désiré-Émile Inghelbrecht, Tristan Klingsor, Paul Ladmirault, Roland-Manuel and Ricardo Viñes. Firsthand accounts of their meetings are given in the following sources: M.-D. Calvocoressi, *Musicians Gallery: Music and Ballet in Paris and London*, London: Faber, 1933, 55–66; Roland-Manuel, *Maurice Ravel*, London: Dennis Dobson, 1947, 33–37.

27. Viñes's first encounter with Falla is recorded in his diary (see Nina Gubisch, *Ricardo Viñès à travers son journal et sa correspondance*, Ph.D. dissertation, Université de Paris-Sorbonne, 1977, 152). Pahissa records that Falla had been given a letter of introduction to Viñes's brother Pepe (an aircraft engineer working in Paris) by a mutual friend (*Vida y obra de Manuel de Falla*, 47; *Manuel de Falla: His Life and Works*, 40). The intricacy of this story gives it

weight over Roland-Manuel's assertion that Falla and Viñes were introduced by Albéniz (*Manuel de Falla*, 32).

28. Slightly differing accounts of this first meeting are found in Gubisch, *Ricardo Viñès à travers son journal et sa correspondance*, 155–156, and in Falla, "Notes sur Ravel," 82.

29. This is confirmed in a letter to Salvador Viniegra, undated but clearly written in late 1907, transcribed in Juan J. Viniegra, *Vida íntima de Manuel de Falla y Matheu*, Cádiz, 1966, 76.

30. Letter Falla-Roland-Manuel, 1 January 1938 (AMF, folder 7521). See also Pahissa, *Vida y obra*, 80; *His Life and Works*, 74.

31. Roger Nichols, *Ravel* (London: Dent, 1977), 55.

32. *Comœdia illustré*, v, 8 (20 January 1914), 390–1; translation from Orenstein, *A Ravel Reader*, 373–74.

33. It is not clear precisely when the final move to the Godebskis' house took place. Calvocoressi mentions that they were meeting there by 1910, but also indicates that there was a period when meetings were taking place at both locations (*Musicians Gallery*, 64). Roland-Manuel states that the last meeting of "Les Apaches" proper took place in 1909 (*Maurice Ravel*, 34), but this date may be wrong, for he also indicates that the group had by this time admitted Stravinsky as a member (an assertion backed up in Victor Seroff, *Ravel*, New York: Holt, 1953, 161), an impossibility given that Stravinsky did not visit Paris until June 1910 (see Stephen Walsh, *Stravinsky: A Creative Spring: Russia and France 1882–1934*, London: Jonathan Cape, 2000, 140 and 584, fn. 1).

34. Calvocoressi, *Musicians Gallery*, 64.

35. Igor Stravinsky and Robert Craft, *Memories and Commentaries*, London: Faber, 1960, 80.

36. The first two are mentioned as habitués of the Godebskis' soirées in a letter from Georges Jean-Aubry to Falla, 4 April 1915 (AMF, folder 7131/1). The other two are identified as visitors in Alfredo Casella, *Music in My Time*, Norman: University of Oklahoma Press, 1955, 108. Falla is known to have been acquainted with all of these. He corresponded with both Grovlez and Casella from 1914 onwards (AMF, folders 7085 and 6830 respectively; Falla's letters to Casella are preserved at the Fondazione Giorgio Cini, Venice [hereinafter *I-Vgc*]). A brief encounter with Satie is mentioned in Pahissa, *Vida y obra*, 54; *His Life and Works*, 47. His acquaintance with Vaughan Williams is noted in a letter from Falla to J. B. Trend, 4 July 1928 (carbon copy at AMF, folder 7697).

37. Igor Stravinsky, *An Autobioigraphy*, London: Calder and Boyars, 1975, 50.

38. Gubisch, *Ricardo Viñès à travers son journal et sa correspondance*, 160–3.

39. Pahissa, *Vida y obra de Manuel de Falla*, 55; *Manuel de Falla: His Life and Works*, 48.

40. Falla, "Notes sur Ravel," 84. Falla wrote a more impassioned account of the same events in a letter to Roland-Manuel, 17 April 1938 (carbon copy at AMF, folder 7520), part of which is quoted (in French translation) in Jean Roy,

"Correspondance adressé par Maurice Ravel à Manuel de Falla," *Cahiers Maurice Ravel*, iii, 1987, 24.

41. This is "Réunion de musiciens chez Monsieur Godebski," by Georges d'Espagnat. The work is reproduced in numerous sources, including Luis Campodonico, *Falla*, Paris: Seuil, 1959, 79; Gonzalo Armero and Jorge de Persia (eds.), *Manuel de Falla: His Life and Works*, London: Omnibus Press, 1999, 56; Gerald Larner, *Maurice Ravel*, London: Phaidon, 1996, 83.

42. Roland-Manuel, *Maurice Ravel*, 35.

43. This is recorded in Falla's 1908 diary, preserved at the Museo-Arxiu, Montblanc; see Michael Christoforidis, "Manuel de Falla, Debussy and *La vida breve*," *Musicology Australia*, xviii, 1995, 4.

44. Gubisch, *Ricardo Viñès à travers son journal et sa correspondance*, 157.

45. Takashi Funayama, *"Three Japanese Lyrics* and Japonisme," in Jann Pasler (ed.), *Confronting Stravinsky: Man, Musician and Modernist*, Berkeley: University of California Press, 1986, 278; Jann Pasler, "Reinterpreting Indian Music: Albert Roussel and Maurice Delage," in Margaret J. Kartomi and Stephen Blum (eds.), *Music-Cultures in Contact: Convergences and Collisions*, Basel: Gordon and Breach, 1994, 132–133. Roussel also visited India during Falla's stay in Paris, in 1909 (ibid., 124–125).

46. Pasler has attempted to identify some of the Indian recordings ("Reinterpreting Indian Music," 135).

47. Pahissa, *Vida y obra*, 96–97; the English translation of this section (*His Life and Works*, 88–9) is curtailed.

48. Casella, *Music in My Time*, 108. The poet Léon-Paul Fargue (one of the "Apaches") made a similar observation with regard to the meetings at Delage's house ("Maurice Ravel," *Plaisir de France*, August 1936; quoted in Roland-Manuel, *Ravel*, 33).

49. Falla, "Notes sur Ravel," 82.

50. Viñes's diary entry for 25 August 1908 records that he had begun to practise these pieces (Gubisch, *Ricardo Viñès à travers son journal et sa correspondance*, 159).

51. Pahissa, *Vida y obra*, 117; *His Life and Works*, 108. See also Falla, "Notes sur Ravel," 85.

52. Programs preserved at AMF (NFE 1908-001, -002, and -012).

53. Only one prewar Ballets Russes program survives at AMF; this is for the performance at the Théâtre des Champs-Élysées on 23 June 1913, which included *Daphnis et Chloé*, the Polovtsian Danses from *Prince Igor*, *Prélude à l'Après-Midi d'un Faune*, and *Le Spectre de la Rose* (NFE 1913-001). However, it is unlikely that Falla missed out on other productions, and his failure to acquire further programs is probably attributable to their high price. In "El gran músico de nuestro tiempo," he discusses the Paris premières of *The Firebird*, *Petrushka*, *The Rite of Spring*, and *Le Rossignol* in such a way as to imply that he was present.

54. Duchesneau, *L'Avant-garde musicale et ses sociétés à Paris*, 66.

55. Pahissa, *Vida y obra*, 80–1; *His Life and Works*, 74–5.

56. The first complete performance of the *Tres melodías* took place at the second concert of the SMI, on 4 May 1910; a copy of the program is preserved at AMF (FE 1910-002).

57. He is identified as such in a letter from Koechlin to Falla, undated [shortly before 31 January 1914] (AMF, folder 7153; transcribed in Madeleine Li-Koechlin, "Charles Koechlin 1867–1950: Correspondance," *La Revue musicale* 348–350, 1982, 19–21). Both Pahissa and Casella identify Falla as a founder member of the SMI (*Vida y obra*, 80; *His Life and Works*, 74; *Music in My Time*, 91), though he does not seem to have been a committee member from the outset (Duchesneau, *L'Avant-garde musicale et ses sociétés à Paris*, 66).

58. These names are taken from the lists of works performed in SMI concerts published in Michel Duchesneau, *L'Avant-garde musicale et ses sociétés à Paris*, 305–38.

59. Two of the movements of Koechlin's *Suite javanaise* (Op. 44bis) were given during the same concert as the première of Falla's *Tres melodías*.

60. Sketch for letter from Falla to Casella, 30 October 1914, written on the back of a letter from Casella dated 19 October 1914 (AMF, folder 6830).

61. A clear distinction between masters and colleagues is evident in three published letters written by Falla in the early 1910s: to Carlos Fernández Shaw, 31 March 1910 (transcribed in Yvan Nommick, "Manuel de Falla: De *La vida breve* de 1905 à *La Vie brève* de 1913: genèse et évolution d'une œuvre," *Mélanges de la Casa de Velázquez*, xxx, 3, 1994, 91); to Georges Jean-Aubry, 28 August 1910 (Yvan Nommick, "*La vida breve* entre 1905 y 1914: evolución formal y orquestal," in Nommick, ed., *Manuel de Falla: La vida breve*, Granada: Publicaciones del Archivo Manuel de Falla, 1997, 33–34); to Jules Ecorcheville, 15 November 1912 (Arbie Orenstein, "Ravel and Falla: an unpublished correspondence, 1914–1933," in Edmond Strainchamps and Maria Rika Maniates, eds., *Music and Civilization: Essays in Honor of Paul Henry Lang*, New York: Norton, 1984, 335).

62. Falla's Parisian encounters with Saint-Saëns, Fauré, Messager, and D'Indy are mentioned in Pahissa, *Vida y obra*, 21, 50, 62–65, and 81, respectively (*His Life and Works*, 18, 43–44, 56–58, and 75). Pahissa is incorrect in stating that this was the only time that Falla met Saint-Saëns; Roland-Manuel reveals that they first met in Cádiz when Falla was only eleven (*Manuel de Falla*, 16–17). His acquaintance with Widor is implicit in the fact that Falla sent him a message of goodwill on the occasion of the Armistice; this letter is lost, but Widor's reply survives, dated 21 November 1918 (AMF, folder 7781).

63. Pahissa, *Vida y obra*, 65 and 78; *His Life and Works*, 58 and 72.

64. Pahissa, *Vida y obra*, 49; *His Life and Works*, 42; letter from Falla to Carlos Fernández Shaw, 31 March 1910 (transcribed in Nommick, "Manuel de Falla: De *La vida breve* de 1905 à *La Vie brève* de 1913," 91).

65. 13 April 1907 (program preserved at AMF: NFN 1907-002).

66. One of Falla's copies of the miniature score of *The Sorcerer's Appren-*

tice (AMF) is stamped by the retailer Casa Dotesio, Madrid; such stamps do not appear in any scores in his library that were published after 1907.

67. AMF, 307 (*Arabesques*), 293 (*Estampes*), 312 (*Baudelaire*), 1143 (quartet), 303 and 304 (*Danses*). All of these scores are stamped by Casa Dotesio. He owned other Debussy scores published before 1907 which do not bear the Dotesio stamp, but which he still may have acquired in Spain.

68. AMF, folders 6898 (Debussy) and 6930 (Dukas).

69. In Falla's 31 March 1910, letter to Fernández Shaw, he observed that Dukas offered "as many consultations as I should like to take" (transcribed in Nommick, "Manuel de Falla: De *La vida breve* de 1905 à *La Vie brève* de 1913," 91).

70. Pahissa, *Vida y obra*, 53. The English translation of this passage (*His Life and Works*, 47) is inaccurate: "as usual without letting him know" should read "without letting him know, which he usually did."

71. Letters from Debussy to Falla, 6 December 1908, 13 April 1910, 3 January 1911, "Dimanche soir" [8 October 1911], "27 septembre 1913" [probably 28 or 29 September 1913] and 23 October 1913 (AMF, folder 6898); letter from Dukas to Falla, 21 June 1909 (AMF, folder 6930). Also surviving (folder 6898) is an undated sketch for a letter from Falla to Debussy (written shortly before 21 October 1909), in which he seeks to arrange a meeting. Presumably many more such letters were sent.

72. Pahissa, *Vida y obra*, 55; *His Life and Works*, 48.

73. AMF, folder 6930. This letter must have been written between *c.* July and 16 October 1908.

74. Sketch for letter from Falla to Debussy, undated [shortly before 21 October 1909]; letter Debussy-Falla, 23 October 1909. AMF, folder 6898.

75. Pahissa, *Vida y obra*, 118–19; *His Life and Works*, 109–10.

76. Falla recorded the advice that Debussy furnished on this occasion; his notes are preserved at AMF (folder 9001; transcribed and translated in Christoforidis, "Manuel de Falla, Debussy and *La vida breve*," 5; see also Pahissa, *Vida y obra*, 78; *His Life and Works*, 71–72). The original version of both passages may be seen in an early piano score of the opera preserved at AMF (ms. number XXXV A1), of which a facsimile has been published: Antonio Gallego, ed., *La vida breve: facsímil del manuscrito XXXV A1 del Archivo Manuel de Falla*, Granada: Publicaciones del Archivo Manuel de Falla, 1997; see especially pages 62–9 and 155–67.

77. Pahissa, *Vida y obra*, 78–79; *His Life and Works*, 72–3.

78. The original version is preserved at AMF (ms. number XXXVIII A4; the first page of this manuscript is reproduced in Antonio Gallego, *Catalogo de obras de Manuel de Falla*, Madrid: Ministerio de Cultura, 1987, 75). A remnant of the lost material persists at bars 80–81 of the published song.

79. Pahissa, *Vida y obra*, 49 and 62; translation (by Wagstaff) from *His Life and Works*, 42 and 55.

80. The instruments represented are the flute, the oboe (and cor anglais), the

clarinet, the bassoon (and sarrussophone), the violin, and the cello. These methods are listed, with full references and AMF inventory numbers, in Nommick, "*La vida breve* entre 1905 y 1914," 36–37.

81. AMF, folder 7915. The page in question in reproduced in Nommick, "*La vida breve* entre 1905 y 1914," 107.

82. Nommick, "Manuel de Falla: De *La vida breve* de 1905 à *La vie brève* de 1913," 83–85.

83. The similarity between the first of these songs ("Les Colombes") and "En Sourdine" from Debussy's *Fêtes Galantes* is discussed in Chris Collins, "Manuel de Falla, *L'Acoustique nouvelle* and natural resonance: a myth exposed," *Journal of the Royal Musical Association*, cxxviii, 1, May 2003.

84. Pahissa, *Vida y obra*, 55. The English translation of this passage (*His Life and Works*, 48) is inaccurate; for "When Falla arrived in Paris he had with him the first and second parts of the *Four Spanish Pieces* for piano, along with the greater part of the third," read "When Falla arrived in Paris, he had with him—in a very advanced state—the first and second of the *Four Spanish Pieces* for piano, and part of the third."

85. Photocopy at AMF, folder 6854; translated in Armero and Persia, eds., *Manuel de Falla: his Life and Works*, 65.

86. Pahissa, *Vida y obra*, 55; *His Life and Works*, 48.

87. This hypothesis is supported by the fact that the abbreviated Italian word "espress." is used elsewhere in this movement.

88. Letters from Dukas to Falla, 12 July 1917, 14 January 1918, 27 June 1918, and 28 November 1918 (AMF, folder 6930).

89. The societies he sought to bind were the Sociedad Nacional de Música in Spain, the Société Musicale Indépendante in France, and the Società Nazionale di Musica (later the Società Italiana di Musica Moderna) in Italy. Letters from Casella to Falla, 1 December 1915, 17 December 1916, and 16 January 1918 (AMF, folder 6830; transcribed in Fiamma Nicolodi, "Falla e l'Italia," in Paolo Pinamonti [ed.], *Manuel de Falla tra la Spagna e l'Europa*, Florence: Leo S. Olschki, 1989, 241–43).

90. Walsh, *Stravinsky: A Creative Spring*, 265.

91. Letter from Falla to Stravinsky, 7 July 1916 (Paul Sacher Stiftung, Basel [hereinafter *CH-Bps*]); an incomplete translation is published in Robert Craft (ed.), *Stravinsky: Selected Correspondence*, ii, London: Faber, 1984, 160–161.

92. Letters from Ansermet to Falla, 10 March 1918, and 19 July [1918] (AMF, folder 6706; transcribed in Claude Tappolet [ed.], *Ernest Ansermet: Correspondances avec des compositeurs européens (1916–1966)*, i, Geneva: Georg, 1994, 167 and 169); letter from Falla to Ansermet, 1 May 1918 (transcribed in ibid., 168); letter from Falla to Stravinsky, 1 May 1918 (*CH-Bps*; translated in Craft, ed., *Stravinsky: Selected Correspondence*, ii, 162); Pahissa, *Vida y obra*, 114–15; *His Life and Works*, 106.

93. Pahissa, *Vida y obra*, 112–13; *His Life and Works*, 104–5.

94. In London, Falla took part in a performance of *Noches en los jardines de España* on 20 May 1921, and of *El amor brujo*, *El retablo de Maese Pedro*, the *Concerto* and *Soneto a Córdoba* on 22 June 1927. He conducted *El retablo* for the BBC's London regional service on 24 June 1931.

95. Pahissa, *Vida y obra*, 49; *His Life and Works*, 42; letter from Falla to Carlos Fernández Shaw, 31 March 1910 (transcribed in Nommick, "Manuel de Falla: De *La vida breve* de 1905 à *La Vie brève* de 1913," 91).

96. In a letter to Durand written in London on 18 July 1919, Dukas noted, "today I'm to see good old Falla." Letter transcribed in Georges Favre, ed., *Correspondance de Paul Dukas*, Paris: Durand, 1971, 126–127.

97. The 1920 meeting is hinted at in letters from Dukas to Falla, postmarked 24 January and 24 February 1920 (AMF, folder 6930). The 1928 encounter is mentioned by Joaquín Rodrigo in "Los músicos que conocí a través de mis recuerdos: Manuel de Falla," in Antonio Iglesias, ed., *Escritos de Joaquín Rodrigo* (Madrid: Editorial Alpuerto, 1999), 100. It is also alluded to in a letter from Falla to Adolfo Salazar, 23 August 1929 (carbon copy at AMF, folder 7573). Their meeting in 1931 is described in Pahissa, *Vida y obra*, 51; *His Life and Works*, 44.

98. Dukas's last letter to Falla was written on 26 January 1935 (AMF, folder 6930). He died on 17 May.

99. Sketches for letters from Falla to Dukas, 26 March and 6 April 1931, and from Falla to Schmitt, 26 March 1931 (*AMF*, folders 6930 and 7608 respectively).

100. AMF, folder 7608.

101. Orenstein, "Ravel and Falla: an unpublished correspondence," 335–43.

102. Both Falla and Ravel were guests at a dinner party at the home of Henry Prunières on 2 June (letters and telegrams from Prunières to Falla, 27 May 1927, and undated [28 May 1927], and letter from Falla to Prunières, 28 May 1927, sketched on the back of Prunières's letter of 27 May [AMF, folder 7453]). They probably also met at Falla's concert at the Salle Pleyel on 14 May; Ravel was certainly present on this occasion (letter from Roland-Manuel to Falla, 3 January 1938 [AMF, folder 7520]).

103. 1919–1920: Meeting implied in two letters from Abbé Léonce Petit to Falla, undated [before 23 May 1920] and 29 May 1920 (AMF, folder 7410). 1923: It was probably in November 1923 that Falla told Ravel about the newly founded Orquesta Bética de Cámara, with a view to having it perform some of his works (letter from Falla to Ravel, 7 July 1924 [*F-Pn*, Musique, L. a. Falla 30; transcribed in Orenstein, "Ravel and Falla: an unpublished correspondence," 335–43]). We cannot be certain that they met during Falla's earlier visit that year, though Ravel's documented inability to attend the premiere of *El retablo de Maese Pedro* and Falla's subsequent failure to visit Ravel in Montfort-l'Amaury does not discount an earlier meeting (letter from Ravel to Falla, 26 June 1923 [AMF, folder 7476]; letter from Falla to Ravel, 1 July 1923 [*F-Pn*, Musique, L. a. Falla 18; both are transcribed in Orenstein,

op. cit., 345–6]). 1925: Falla was almost certainly present at the first performance of the second of Ravel's *Chansons madécasses*, given on May 24 by Jane Bathori accompanied by Ravel himself (program at AMF [NFE 1925-003]; letter from Elizabeth Sprague Coolidge to Falla, 25 October 1926 [AMF, folder 7650]). 1930: Falla was invited to visit Ravel on two separate occasions (letter from Madeleine Grey to Falla, 4 May [1930] [AMF, folder 7084]; letter from Suzanne Roland-Manuel to Falla, undated [shortly before 29 May 1930] [AMF, folder 7520]). 1931: Falla expressed his desire to see Ravel, either in Paris or Montfort, in his letter of 14 July 1931 (*F-Pn*, Musique, L. a. Falla 13).

104. Letter from Ravel and Madeleine Grey to Falla, 13 November 1928 (*AMF*, folder 7476). Precise date of concert given in letter from César Figuerido to Fernando de los Ríos, 12 November 1928 (*AMF*, folder 6894). Identities of the performers confirmed in sketch for telegram from Falla to Count Chigi Saracini, 22 November 1928 (AMF, folder 6887).

105. 1920: Stravinsky dedicated a copy of the full score of *Pribaoutki* on 4 February, "in Ernest [Ansermet]'s presence, room number 311 with 2 beds" (AMF, 775). June 1923: Stravinsky was present at the première of *El retablo de Maese Pedro* at the Princesse de Polignac's salon on 25 June (Corpus Barga, "Reflejos de París," *El Sol*, 30 June 1923, 1); Falla probably attended the performance of *Les Noces* at the same location on 10 June (letter from Polignac to Falla, 7 June [1923] [AMF, folder 7432]). November 1923: Falla and Stravinsky met to discuss hiring orchestral material for *Pulcinella*, for the Orquesta Bética de Cámara (letter from Falla to Romero, 28 November 1923 [transcribed in Manuel de Falla (ed. Pascual Pascual Romero), *Cartas a Segismundo Romero*, Granada: Ayuntamiento, 1976, 160–61]). They probably met also at the concert of Stravinsky's works (including the *Octet* and the suite from *The Soldier's Tale*) given under the composer's direction at the Salle des Agriculteurs on 7 November; six days later, Falla took part in a concert in the same series (programs for both are preserved at AMF [FE 1923-030, -031, and -032]). (Incidentally, Pahissa mistakenly conflates the contents of these two concerts [*Vida y obra*, 133; *His Life and Works*, 121].) 1927: Stravinsky dedicated a vocal score of *Oedipus Rex* to Falla on 9 June (AMF, 772); Falla may have attended the Paris première of this work, under Stravinsky's direction, on 30 May at the Théâtre Sarah-Bernhardt. 1930: Stravinsky dedicated a childhood photograph of himself to Falla in Paris on 17 May (AMF, photograph number 8/51).

106. The handwritten dedication in Falla's full score of the Suite from *The Soldier's Tale* is dated 5 April 1921 (AMF, 765). Stravinsky and Falla each took part in concerts in Madrid on 25 and 28 March 1924, respectively; in his letter to Stravinsky of 1 March 1924 (*CH-Bps*), Falla seems certain that they will meet.

107. Stravinsky's presence at the concert of Falla's works (including the *Concerto*) given at the Aeolian Hall on 22 June 1927, is confirmed in an anonymous review of this concert in the next day's *The Scotsman*.

108. Letter from Roland-Manuel to Falla, undated [shortly before 27 July

1929] (AMF, folder 7520); letter from Delage to Falla, 29 October 1929 (AMF, folder 6899).

109. The work was published by Durand in 1933; Falla's copy is preserved at AMF (322).

110. ". . . nothing more *acute* has ever been said about this work" (letter from Falla to Koechlin, 25 April 1933 [photocopy at AMF, folder 7153]). The article itself was published in *La Chronique des arts, c.* January 1914; it is transcribed in Li-Koechlin, "Charles Koechlin 1867–1950," 19–21.

111. Letters from Koechlin to Falla, undated [shortly before 25 June 1923], 16 July [1931] and 19 July [1931]; sketch for letter from Falla to Koechlin, undated [19 December 1923] (*AMF*, folder 7153); further information from Koechlin's diaries (details kindly communicated by Robert Orledge). The man standing with Falla in the photograph reproduced in Javier Suárez-Pajares, *Iconografía/Iconography, Manuel de Falla 1876–1946: La imagen de un músico/the image of a musician*, Madrid SGAE, 1995, 102, is not Koechlin, but Emil Hertzka, managing director of Universal-Edition.

112. Falla dedicated a copy of *Noches en los jardines de España* to Casella in Paris on 3 July 1923 (*I-Vgc*). Their 1931 meeting is implied in a letter from Falla to Casella, undated [June–July 1931] (*I-Vgc*; transcribed in Nicolodi, "Falla e l'Italia," 252).

113. Falla and Casella were photographed together at all of these meetings (*AMF*, photograph numbers 7/44 [1923], 7/27 [1932]; Teatro de La Fenice Historical Archive [1928]; reproduced in Suárez-Pajares, *Iconografía/Iconography*, 128, 141, and 147, respectively).

114. The location is mentioned in a letter from Falla to Casella, 14 November 1934 (*I-Vgc*; transcribed in Nicolodi, "Falla e l'Italia," 254); the date may be inferred from a cutting from an unspecified newspaper, 19 January 1930 (AMF, folder 6417).

115. Casella left Valencia for Granada on 14 January (letter from Salazar to Falla, 14 January 1930 [AMF, folder 7572]). Several photographs survive that were taken during Falla and Casella's visit to the Alhambra on this occasion (AMF, photograph numbers 7/142 to 146 inclusive; reproduced in Suárez-Pajares, *Iconografía/Iconography*, 115–18), and Casella later wrote a lengthy account of his stay in the city (Alfredo Casella, "Visita a Manuel de Falla," *L'Italia letteraria*, 2 February 1930, 5; reprinted in *Id.*, *21 + 26*, Rome: Augustea, 1931, 195–202).

116. Letter from Bartók to Falla, 8 February 1931 (AMF, folder 6752).

117. Letter from Falla to Bartók, 22 February 1931 (carbon copy at AMF, folder 6752; transcribed in D. Dille [ed.], *Documenta Bartókiana*, iii, Budapest: Akadémiai Kiadó, 1968, 158).

118. Falla was in Barcelona on the occasion of Bartók's concert there on 24 March (János Demény [ed.], *Béla Bartók Letters*, London, 1971, 405; press reports in *El Sol*, 24 March 1927, and *El Día Gráfico*, 25 March 1927). D. Dille

claims that the two men met at Bartók's concert in Paris on 8 April 1922 (*Documenta Bartókiana*, iii, 160, n. 5); this was not possible, for Falla was in Spain at the time.

119. Falla and Szymanowski took part in the same concert at the Vieux Colombier on 13 June 1923. Kodály was in Zurich to attend a performance of *Psalmus hungaricus* on 17 and 18 June 1926, as part of that year's ISCM Festival; he dedicated a copy of the first volume of *Magyar népzene* to Falla on this occasion (AMF, 827). Webern conducted a performance of his *Five Pieces*, op. 10, four days later.

120. Pahissa, *Vida y obra*, 129; *His Life and Works*, 118; handwritten dedication in Falla's vocal score of Malipiero's *San Francisco d'Assisi* (AMF, 1136); letter from Falla to Malipiero, 11 August 1923 (*I-Vgc*; transcribed in Nicolodi, "Falla e l'Italia," 257).

121. Anna herself wrote a description of her relationship with Falla in an open letter to the composer, published (in Spanish translation) in Gian Francesco Malipiero, *Manuel de Falla: Evocación y correspondencia*, Granada: Universidad de Granada, 1983, 31–34. Malipiero's last letter to Falla is dated 12 September 1946 (AMF, 7232; transcribed in Nicolodi, "Falla e l'Italia," 266–67).

122. Honegger was in Zurich to attend a performance of *King David*. He and Falla were photographed standing together (AMF, photograph 7/40bis). Walton was in Siena to conduct a performance of *Façade*. There is a copy of the piano-duet version of this work in Falla's library (AMF, 663), along with similar scores of *Portsmouth Point* and *Siesta* (664 and 665, respectively). All three bear the stamp "Complimentary copy," and were probably presented to Falla by Walton himself.

123. Falla had met Roland-Manuel in Paris before the outbreak of the First World War (letter from Falla to Roland-Manuel, 23 January 1914; *AMF*, folder 7521). Poulenc claimed that he first met Falla at Viñes's Paris home in 1918 (*My Friends and Myself*, 91), but since Falla did not visit Paris that year, this first meeting must have taken place in 1919 or 1920. It is not clear exactly when he came to know Milhaud, Auric, Sauguet, and Ferroud, but they had become acquainted by 1922, 1924, 1927, and 1928 respectively (dates of items of correspondence and dedications in scores sent as gifts).

124. He first encountered both men in May 1923 (letter from Castelnuovo-Tedesco to Falla, 15 May 1923 [*AMF*, 6382]; Pahissa, *Vida y obra*, 129–30; *His Life and Works*, 118–19).

125. He must have met Goossens for the first time during his stay in London in 1919; Falla possessed a signed photograph of the composer bearing this date (AMF, photograph number 8/116).

126. Letter from Castelnuovo-Tedesco to Falla, 15 March 1934; sketch for letter from Falla to Castelnuovo-Tedesco, 27 March 1934 (AMF, folder 6382).

127. Falla and Poulenc were both in Venice in September 1932, for the Second International Music Festival (Poulenc, *My Friends and Myself*, 88). Falla

and his sister visited Milhaud in Aix in September 1931 (letter from Falla to Milhaud, 10 September 1931; photocopy at AMF, folder 7282).

128. Sketch for telegram from Falla to Milhaud, 27 April 1929 (AMF, folder 7282). An account of this visit is found in Darius Milhaud, *Notes sans musique*, Paris: René Julliard, 1949, 243–247.

129. Milhaud, *Notes sans musique*, 246.

130. Letter from Falla to Milhaud, 8 February 1930 (photocopy at AMF, folder 7282).

131. Letter from Poulenc to Falla, undated [before 13 March 1930] (AMF, folder 7441; translated in Francis Poulenc, ed. Sidney Buckland, *"Echo and Source": Selected Correspondence 1915–1963*, London: Gollancz, 1991, 88–89).

132. Letter from Falla to Poulenc, 13 March 1930 (photocopy at AMF, folder 7441; translated in Poulenc, *"Echo and Source,"* 89).

133. Assuming, that is, that this event was not a figment of Poulenc's imagination (Poulenc, *A bâtons rompus*, 90).

134. Poulenc began to work on the *Concert champêtre* around 1926 (Poulenc, *"Echo and Source,"* 345 n. 5); the work is mentioned in a letter from Landowska to Poulenc dated 19 January 1927 (translated in ibid., 82–83). The first time that he heard Falla's *Concerto* was almost certainly on the occasion of its Paris premiere, at the Salle Pleyel on 14 May 1927. It was not until July or August 1928, however, that Landowska received the first installment of Poulenc's concerto (letter from Landowska to Poulenc, 2 August 1928; ibid., 84).

135. AMF, 1166.

136. Charles Koechlin, *Traité de l'harmonie*, ii, Paris: Max Eschig, 1930, 227, 238, 244, and 249–50. The excerpts are taken from *Siete canciones populares españolas*, *Noches en los jardines de España* and *El retablo de Maese Pedro*.

137. Programs for this event are preserved at AMF (FN 1923-001 et seq.).

138. Evidence for this is found in the following items of correspondence: Auric to Falla, 7 May [1924] (AMF, 6725); Falla to Malipiero, 20 August and 20 December 1924 (preserved at *I-Vgc*; transcribed in Nicolodi, "Falla e l'Italia," 259–60); Falla to Milhaud, 10 July 1924, and 28 January 1926 (photocopies at AMF, 7282); Falla to Poulenc, 28 April 1924 (photocopy at AMF, 7441); Falla to Roland-Manuel, 7 February 1924, and 3 August 1927 (sketches at AMF, 7520); Falla to Segismundo Romero, 28 November 1923 (transcribed in Falla, *Cartas a Segismundo Romero*, 160–61).

139. AMF, 396 and 1146 respectively. Ravel sent the *Chansons madécasses* shortly after 2 February 1927 (letter of that date [AMF, folder 7476; transcribed in Orenstein, "Ravel and Falla: an unpublished correspondence," 348]). The score of *L'Enfant et les sortilèges* contains a typed note from Madeleine Grey, and may have been presented to Falla on the occasion of the concert she gave with Ravel in Granada in November 1928.

140. It should be noted in passing that he did own a recording of *Boléro* (AMF, 8638), one of a very small number of works by foreign contemporaries in his collection of discs.

141. This is a note on the last page of his copy of the vocal score of *La Délivrance de Thésée* (AMF, 365), drawing attention to the section of the score at rehearsal figure 145.

142. His collections of these two periodicals are preserved at AMF (7861 and 5785, respectively).

143. A sketch of this dedication is preserved at AMF (folder 7658).

144. Letter from Stravinsky to Falla, 12 February 1929 (AMF, folder 7657; translated in Craft, ed., *Stravinsky: Selected Correspondence*, ii, 168).

145. This item is preserved at *CH-Bps*; it was enclosed with Falla's letter of 18 March 1929.

146. AMF, 769. These annotations suggest not only that he studied the work in detail, but also that he either heard a performance or had access to an orchestral score.

147. See notes 105 and 107 above.

148. Craft, ed., *Stravinsky: Selected Correspondence*, ii, 168, fn. 16.

149. AMF, folder 7657; transcribed in Craft, ed., *Stravinsky: Selected Correspondence*, ii, 164–5.

150. AMF, 1185.

151. Letter from Eve Landowska to Falla, 25 August 1923 (AMF, folder 7170).

152. Walsh, *Stravinsky: A Creative Spring*, 372.

153. Igor Stravinsky, *An Autobiography (1903–1934)*, London: Marion Boyars, 1975, 43–44; Walsh, *Stravinsky: A Creative Spring*, 189–90.

154. Falla, "Introducción a la música nueva."

155. Richard Taruskin, "From *Firebird* to *The Rite*: Folk Elements in Stravinsky's Scores," *Ballet Review*, x, 2, Summer 1982, 80.

156. Stravinsky and Craft, *Memories and Commentaries*, 98. The pieces about which he was referring were *The Rite of Spring*, *Pribaoutki*, *Four Russian Peasant Choruses*, *Four Russian Songs*, and *Berceuses du Chat*.

157. Trend, *Manuel de Falla and Spanish Music*, 153.

158. Ibid.

159. Letter from Falla to Milhaud, 30 May 1922 (photocopy at AMF, folder 7282). In a letter dated 5 January 1927 (AMF, 7282), Falla also expressed his particular predilection for the *Serenade*, op. 62.

160. Pahissa, *Vida y obra*, 145–46; translation (by Wagstaff) from *His Life and Works*, 132.

161. Pahissa, *Vida y obra*, 83; *His Life and Works*, 77.

162. See Collins, "Manuel de Falla, *L'Acoustique nouvelle* and natural resonance."

163. Pahissa, *Vida y obra*, 146; translation (by Wagstaff) from *His Life and Works*, 132–33.

164. Falla analyzed at least two of Strauss's orchestral works during his prewar studies in orchestration; a heavily annotated miniature score of *Don Juan* is preserved at AMF (580), as are handwritten notes on aspects of the scoring of

Till Eulenspiegel (folder 7915). He possessed only one score by Schoenberg; this is *Pierrot lunaire* (819), and it contains no annotations. In addition, it is probable that he heard a performance of the Wind Quintet, op. 26, at the 1926 ISCM Festival in Zurich.

165. Falla, "Introducción a la música nueva." Mention should be also be made here of Kurt Schindler, German composer, editor, arranger, and folksong collector. Schindler was largely responsible for introducing Falla to the work of Russian composers of his own and younger generations (not least Rakhmaninov). By the time they met, he had already been resident in the United States of America for a number of years.

166. Ibid. Falla had a second, darker reason for his response to German and Austrian music. His feelings towards these nations were colored by his intense abhorrence of the German offensive against France in 1914, his views of which he clearly expressed in a number of contemporary letters (not least that he wrote to Henri Collet on 23 October 1914, an excerpt from which is printed in Collet, "Le mort de Manuel de Falla," *La Revue musicale*, xxiii, 204, January 1947, 27). The personal nature of his revulsion is hinted at in his later comments on Wagner. No doubt paraphrasing Falla, Roland-Manuel noted his early "enthusiasm for the musician[,] mixed with a secret antipathy for the man" (*Manuel de Falla*, 19). In 1933, he found himself observing that ". . . whenever I am faced by Wagner's music, I try to forget about its author" ("Notas sobre Wagner en su cincuentenario," *Cruz y raya*, 6 [September 1933]).

167. Falla, "Introducción a la música nueva."
168. *Musique*, ii, 8 (15 May 1929), 897.
169. Falla, "Introducción a la música nueva."
170. Trend, *Manuel de Falla and Spanish Music*, 175.
171. See note 10 above.
172. Stravinsky and Craft, *Memories and Commentaries*, 81.

Chapter 14

Alexandre Tansman
Remembers Manuel de Falla

Louis Jambou

The relationship of the Polish composer Alexandre Tansman with Spain
while resident in France is made through three distinct pathways. In reality, beyond the fertile land that permeates European music after the second third of the 19th century, there are three personalities that have allowed Tansman to become enmeshed in Spanish culture in general and in
its music in particular. Andrés Segovia is the inevitable ambassador of the
classical and contemporary guitar that entices the composer in his numerous compositions for that instrument.[1] Salvador Madariaga—a political
man of the beginning of the 20th century, essayist, and a renowned man
of the humanities—is a direct collaborator with Tansman in the elaboration of certain libretti, being, at the same time, the inspirer of a few poems
set to music by the composer.[2] And last, Manuel de Falla, his elder, seems
to have been his protective angel who, together with Bartók, accompanies
his composer's trajectory linked to folk sources, even if imaginary, and to
tradition in musical composition. Doesn't he declare, at the twilight of his
life, in 1980: "I can say it spontaneously. I have made a similar trajectory
as Bartók or Falla, for example, in the imagined folklore. I have not used
popular themes, but I used this type of melodic line."[3]

   In this declaration, late in his itinerary, the composer feels eminently
in debt to the two great composers of the final musical "nationalism" that
precedes him by one generation. However, even from the first studies on
Tansman's work, in the thirties, the critics primarily compared him to
Ravel, Stravinski, Milhaud . . . Bartók and their influence over his work.
The name of the Spanish composer does not seem to appear beneath
these pens. Elsewhere there is no documentary element that allows us to

affirm that there has been a meeting between the two composers—Falla and Tansman—nor contact, nor even epistolary exchange. None of the archives—of Falla, in Granada, or of Tansman, in Paris—has a trace of a letter. Nor even the music department of the French National Library in Paris; moreover, in the abundant correspondence between Segovia and Tansman, we have only found two references to the work *Hommage à Falla*, second of the two pieces that Tansman dedicates to the memory of or in homage to Falla. In a first letter, dated from Geneva on 5 August 1954,[4] Segovia asks the composer not to forget to superimpose the guitar part over that of the piano for a more facilitated reading. This is a common recommendation from the guitarist to the composer so that the soloist himself can prepare the performance of the work. In the second [letter], written in Siena on 21 August 1954,[5] the guitarist is happy with the "reconstruction of the piece in *Hommage à Falla*," that it gives him "a great pleasure," and that he promises to work with him at the Summer Academy in the Italian city.

THE WORKS

There are two works that Tansman offers to the memory or in homage of the Spanish master. Both are in manuscript and conserved at the Association Alexandre Tansman in Paris. The first—*à la mémoire de*—dates from the year of the death of Manuel de Falla, 1946. The second—*en hommage à*—is composed eight years later, in 1954, and is dedicated to the guitarist Andrés Segovia. Another work,[6] without alluding to Falla, would be close to it in its style and date of composition. We mean *Spanish Mood* belonging to *Ten Diversions for The Young Pianist*; its edition dates from the year of death of the Spanish, 1946, and in its music, especially its rhythm, homage is paid to him.[7]

I. Introdusione e/Danza Gitana for piano or Danse Gitane for band
    The first work is presented in two manuscript versions. One, for piano (I), is titled *A la mémoire de Manuel de Falla, Introdusione e/Danza Gitana for piano*. It is written on three sheets of manuscript paper, front and back, with six systems of two staves each. It does not seem to be an autograph copy: only the agogics, the dynamics, and perhaps the fingerings could be made by the composer's hand. The lower part of the first page indicates *(small notes: ossia)* and *Tous droits reservés* (All rights reserved).

The second version (II), for wind ensemble, is titled *In memory of Manuel de Falla, Danse Gitane for band*. It is written on five pages of a paper with twenty-four staves. It is a guide for the conductor, in a clear state, prepared for future edition, at the bottom of the first page of which is written: *Tous droits reservés* (All rights reserved), *Leeds Music Corporation, New York*.[8] The indications for instrumentation use abbreviations at times that are difficult to read. Castanets, the first references to hispanism that Falla uses after his first works, are introduced in the movement *Vivace*. The agogic indications differ in the writing, but not necessarily in the intention, to those of the piano version, and have sometimes additional metronomical markings:

I-Lento = II-Andante sostenuto, un poco rubato (quarter-note = 84)
I-Molto lento = II-lento cantabile (quarter-note = 70)
I-Vivace = II-Vivace (quarter-note = 176)
I-Cantabile con anima = II-Cantabile

II. Hommage à Manuel de Falla

The composition of the second work dates, according to Segovia's letters, from 1954. Dedicated to him—"*à Andrés Segovia*"—it has nevertheless remained unfinished. Titled *Hommage à Manuel de Falla, pour guitare et orchestre de chambre* (Homage to Manuel de Falla, for guitar and orchestra), it consists of four movements:

I-Notturno (Lento tranquilo)
II-Vivo (quarter-note = 144)
III-Lent (quarter-note = 72)
IV-(placed after V) Naña (= Nana) (Lent, quarter-note = aprox. 56)
V-unreadable (quarter-note = 112)

The work occupies three sheets of paper, each page containing twenty-four staves. The part of the guitar is written on one staff, the orchestra being but a rough draft written on two staves, with no indications of instrumentation. The Tansman archives have a second version of the first movement, *I-Notturno*, that presents some modifications towards the first draft. In fact, it introduces a virtuoso element into the body of the piece and finishes with another passage of guitaristic brilliance. However, the duration, calculated by the composer for the movement, remains the same: 4'. In addition, if the orchestral intentions are not clearly stated in this version, the guitar part is reinforced in a part of the movement written on a double staff. This version superimposes the guitar part over that of the orchestral reduction for piano: is this the one, "re-made" version according to the terms of Segovia, that is sent by Tansman to Segovia and to which he alludes on his second letter referred to above?

The work of Tansman is full of real, or imagined,[9] popular motives, particularly the ones from his native Poland. In the same way, his connections with the music of the previous centuries form another constant in his compositions in the 1920s and 1930s[10] and contribute to the affirmation of his style, a tendency that continues beyond his early mature years in Paris.[11] His historical belonging—the vast current and nebulous mass of the neoclassicism—invites all composers, more than in any other epoch except, no doubt, the 15th and 16th centuries, to feed on the techniques and materials of the past and to apply them in their own compositional path. Tansman finds there a setting, an absolute paradigm of the "immutable laws" that define music at his eyes.[12] In the Parisian 1920s, Tansman is filled with this movement and he will not neglect—withstanding the assimilation of the formal settings—the citations or the "quasi-citations,"[13] in a way of practicing a sort of "musical polyglot"[14] so that in his works he better masters even the most insignificant details, the traits of the composers of the past centuries or those contemporary with him. This attitude and connection of Tansman with the works of the past—by himself or by other composers—does not impede him and will be one of his concerns later in his life: he will clearly refuse to use imitation, as some late correspondence testifies. In 1975, Segovia invited him to write a piece for guitar and harp on one of his early works. Tansman, in a letter dated 22 March 1975, resists doing it ("I don't like to constantly change the works already composed" is his reply) and finally yields twice: in his previous works, Tansman superimposes another timbric color, the harp, in both cases. In the same letter of 22 March 1975, Tansman alludes to yet another intervention in works other than his own, taking into consideration another proposal by Segovia: "I could later re-harmonize the pieces by Paganini, but I don't know them."[15]

Yvan Nommick has made a catalogue of the "Homages" to Falla: overall, about a hundred works have been written, from 1922 to 1996, by composers from all horizons but especially Spanish. He proceeds with a judicious study distinguishing three main techniques of the "Hommages" writing: the invocation of the places or images belonging to the life of Falla; the citation of fragments or motives from one or another of the master's work; the variations, the work of Falla becoming the substance of the newly written work.[16]

This brief note will not go to the point of thoroughly searching for rhythms or motives that in these works could be close or inspired directly by Falla, considering that certain traits belong to an epoch as much as to a particular composer. We can inclusively discern characteristics appropriately "Tansmanian" that are found equally in the work of Falla: obsessive rhythm; bitonality, polytonality, or tonal superimposing; or also the "Tansmanian" chord,[17] present, without doubt, in the present works, there where we could search and would too quickly find perhaps the principles of superimposition, a characteristic of the native of Cádiz.

However, it is easy to discern in these works by Tansman some stylistic traits that belong to the world of Hispanic sounds and that are genially present in the work of Falla. We can notice some that first form the musical lexicon and then touch afterwards the syntax. It is readily the *acciacatura*, which the composers of the 1920s have regained, as Falla did in a number of his pieces. The use of the dotted eighth-note + thirty-second-notes and eighth-note + triplet of sixteenth-notes, is equally a constant in the two works. The first rhythm and the creation of the bands of *ostinati* naturally characterizes the *Danse Gitane* and equally the *Notturno* of the *Hommage*. It is furthermore the use of a deliberate expansion of the first cell: Tansman does not neglect the very ornamented melismatic motive. If the *Danse Gitane* ignores it, the *Hommage*, notably in its 3rd and 4th movements, takes pleasure in delving into, through consecutive notes, the curled up and circular impetus of the first sound above itself. At last, Tansman's modal sensitivity is omnipresent in these two pieces, a modality that would be interesting to explore in other works by the composer. It could be that the composer has a particular purpose in these works about Falla: the phrygian mode, the mode of "E," still called "Andalusian mode," is exploited in both works.

These works, homage to a genius admired by Tansman and whose interpreters ignore the ties that unite the two composers, are proof of the Polish master's ductility and knowledge in the exploitation and adaptation of a Spanish musical lexicon that, as is known, pertains to a wave of musical nationalism more than to the whole of music of this century.

Alexandre Tansman se souvient de
Manuel de Falla
par Louis Jambou

Les rapports du compositeur polonais Alexandre Tansman, résidant en
France, avec l'Espagne reposent sur trois passerelles ou voies d'introduction distinctes. En réalité, outre le terreau fertilisant qui irrigue la
musique européen depuis le second tiers du XIXe siècle, ce sont trois
personnalités qui lui ont permis de tisser des liens avec sa culture d'une
façon plus particulière. Andrés Segovia est l'ambassadeur incoutourn-
able de la guitare classique et contemporaine qui entraîne le compositeur
dans ses nombreuses compositions guitaristiques.[1] Salvador Madariaga,
homme politique du début du Xxe siècle, essayiste et homme de lettres
renommé est un collaborateur direct de Tansman dans l'élaboration de
certains de ses livrets à la fois que l'inspirateur de quelques poèmes mis
en musique par le compositeur.[2] Enfin Manuel de Falla, son aîné, semble avoir été l'ange tutélaire qui, avec Bartók, accompagne son parcours
de compositeur attaché aux sources populaires, fussent-elles imagi-
naires, et aux traditions dans la composition musicale. Ne déclare-t-il
pas, au soir de son existence, en 1980: "Je peux le dire spontanément.
J'ai fait le même parcours à peu près que Bartók ou de Falla, par exemple le folklore imaginé. Je ne me suis pas servi des thèmes populaires,
mais enfin, j'ai utilisé ce genre de ligne mélodique."[3]

Dans cette déclaration, tardive dans son itinéraire, le compositeur
se sent éminemment redevable envers deux immenses compositeurs
du "nationalisme" musical finissant qui le précèdent d'une généra-
tion. Cependant alors même que dès les premières études sur l'œuvre
de Tansman, dans les années trente, les critiques mettent en avant les
rapports du jeune compositeur avec Ravel, Stravinski, Milhaud . . .
Bartók et leur influence sur son œuvre, le nom du compositeur espagnol ne semble pas apparaître sous ces plumes. Par ailleurs aucun
élément documentaire ne permet d'affirmer qu'il y eut rencontre entre les deux compositeurs—Falla et Tansman—ni entretien, ni même
échange épistolaire. Aucune des archives—de Falla, à Grenade, ou de
Tansman, à Paris—ne conserve trace de lettre ni non plus le département de musique de la bibliothèqu nationale de France à Paris; par
ailleurs dans l'abondante correspondance entre Segovia et Tansman
nous n'avons relevé que deux allusions à l'œuvre "Hommage à
Falla," seconde des deux pièces que Tansman consacre à la mémoire

de ou en hommage à Falla. Dans une première lettre, datée à Genève le 5/VIII/1954,[4] Segovia prie le compositeur de ne pas oublier de superposer la partie de guitare à celle du piano afin que sa lecture soit plus aisée. C'est là une recommandation assez habituelle du guitariste au compositeur afin que le soliste qu'il est puisse préparer la mise en place de l'œuvre. Dans la seconde, écrite de Sienne le 21/VIII/1954,[5] le guitariste se réjouit de "la reco[n]struction de la pièce en *Hommage à Falla*" qui lui *"fait un grand plaisir"* et qu'il promet de travailler avec lui lors de l'Académie d'été de la cité italienne.

LES ŒUVRES

Ce sont deux œuvres que Tansman offre à la mémoire de ou en hommage au maître gaditan. Toutes deux sont manuscrites et conservées à l'association Alexandre Tansman à Paris. La première—*à la mémoire de*—date de l'année même du décès de Manuel de Falla, 1946. La seconde—*en hommage à*—est composée huit ans plus tard, en 1954, et dédiée au guitariste Andrés Segovia. Une autre œuvre[6] sans allusion à Falla en serait cependant proche par son style et date de composition. Il s'agit de "Spanish Mood" contenu dans *Ten Diversions for the Young Pianist*: son édition date de l'année même de la mort du gaditan, 1946, et en sa musique, notamment en son rythme, lui rend hommage.[7]

I. Introdusione e / Dansa Gitana for piano ou Danse Gitane for band
    La première œuvre se présente sous deux versions manuscrites. L'une, pour piano (I), est intitulée *A la mémoire de Manuel de Falla Introdusione e/Danza Gitana for piano*. Elle est écrite sur trois feuillets, recto et verso, d'un papier à six systèmes de double portée. Elle ne semble pas être une copie autographe: les indications agogiques et dynamiques et, peut-être, les doigtés pourraient être de la main du compositeur. Le bas de la première page indique (*small notes: ossia*) et *Tous droits réservés*.
    La seconde version (II), pour formation à vent, est intitulée *"In memory of Manuel de Falla, Danse gitane for band"*: Elle est écrite sur cinq pages d'un papier à 24 portées. C'est un conducteur pour le chef, un état préparé pour a mise au net et future impression, la première page étant souscrite: *"Tous droits réservés, Leeds Music Corporation, New York."*[8] Les indications d'instrumentation usent d'abréviations parfois peu lisibles. Des castagnettes, références premières à l'hispanisme auxquelles

Falla a renoncé après ses premières œuvres, sont introduites dans le mouvement "Vivace." Les indications d'agogique diffèrent, dans la lettre mais non forcément dans l'intention, de celles de la version pour piano et y ajoutent parfois des précisions métronomiques:

I-Lento = II-Andante sostenuto, un poco rubato (noire = 84)
I-Molto lento = II lento cantabile (noire = 70)
I-Vivace = II Vivace (noire = 176)
I-Cantabile com anima = II Cantabile

II. *Hommage à Manuel de Falla*

La composition de la seconde œuvre date, selon les lettres de Segovia, de 1954. Dédiée *à Andrés Segovia*, elle est restée inachevée. Intitulée *Hommage à Manuel de Falla, pour guitare et orchestre de chambre,* elle est formée de quatre mouvements:

 I-Notturno (Lento tranquilo)
 II-Vivo (noire = 144)
III-Lent (noire = 72)
IV-(placé après le V) Naña [= Nana] (Lent, noire = env. 56)
 V-Illisible (noire = 112)

L'œuvre occupe trois feuillets d'un papier à 24 portées par page. La partie de guitare est écrite sur une portée, l'orchestre ne présentant qu'une ébauche avancée du travail d'élaboration présentée sur deux portées, sans indication d'instrumentation. Les archives Tansman possèdent une seconde version du premier mouvement I-*Notturno* qui présente quelques modifications par rapport à l'ébauche première. En effet elle introduit un élément virtuose dans le corps de la pièce et s'achève par un autre passage de déploiement guitaristique. Cependant la durée prévue par le compositeur du mouvement reste la même: 4'. Par ailleurs, si les intentions orchestrales ne sont pas davantage manifestes dans cette version, la partie de guitare est renforcée dans une partie du mouvement écrite sur une double portée. Cette version superpose bien la partie pour guitare à celle de la réduction de l'orchestre pour piano: est-elle celle qui, "reconstruite" selon les termes de Segovia, est envoyée par Tansman à Segovia et à laquelle il fait allusion dans la seconde des lettres citées plus haut?

L'œuvre de Tansman est imprégnée de motifs populaires réels, notamment ceux de sa terre polonaise, ou imaginés.[9] De même ses rapports avec la musique des siècles antérieurs forment une autre constante de ses compositions des années vingt-trente[10] et contribuent à l'affermissement de son style, tendance qu'il prolongera au-delà de ces années de première maturité parisienne.[11] Son appartenance historique, le vaste courant et nébuleuse du néo-classicisme, invite tout compositeur plus qu'à tout autre époque—à l'exception sans doute des XVème-XVIéme siècles—à se nourrir de techniques et matériaux du passé et à les impliquer dans la propre démarche compositionnelle. Tansman y trouve un cadre, un paradigme absolu des "'lois immuables" definissant la musique à ses yeux.[12] Dans les années 20, Tansman, parisien, est imprégné de cette mouvance et il ne négligerait donc pas—en-deça de l'assimilation de cadres formels—les citations ou les "quasi-citations"[13] en sorte que pratiquant une sorte de "polyglotisme musical"[14] afin de mieux maîtriser, dans ses œuvres mêmes les plus "infimes," les linéaments des compositeurs des siècles passés ou contemporains. Il n'empêche que cette attitude et ce rapport de Tansman à l'œuvre antérieure—celle de lui-même ou celle d'autres compositeurs—seront, plus avant dans sa vie, l'une de ses préoccupations: il se refuserait clairement à l'emprunt comme en témoigne une correspondance tardive. En 1975 Segovia l'a invité à écrire une œuvre pour guitare et harpe sur une de ses œuvres anciennes. Tansman, par lettre du 22 mars 1975, y résiste ("Je n'aime pas tripoter dans les œuvres composées déjà" lui répond-il) et finalement y succombe et y succombera à deux reprises: à des œuvres antérieures, Tansman superpose une autre couleur timbrique, la harpe dans les deux cas. Dans le même courrier du 22 mars 1975, Tansman fait allusion à une autre intervention dans des œuvres extérieures à lui-même en envisageant une autre proposition de Segovia: "je pourrais plus tard reharmoniser les morceaux de Paganini, mais je ne les connais pas."[15]

Yvan Nommick a dressé un catalogue des "Hommages" à Falla: en tout une centaine d'œuvres ont été écrites, de 1922 à 1996, par des compositeurs de tous horizons mais surtout espagnols. Il procède également à une approche judicieuse de leur étude en distinguant trois techniques principales d'écriture des "hommages": l'évocation de lieux ou d'images proches de la vie de Falla; la citation de fragments ou motifs de l'une ou l'autre œuvre du maître; les variations, l'œuvre de Falla devenant la substance de la nouvelle œuvre écrite.[16]

Cette brève note n'ira pas jusqu'à débusquer rythmes ou motifs qui en ces œuvres pourraient être proches de Falla ou s'en inspireraient directement d'autant que certains traits appartiennent tant à l'époque qu'à un compositeur particulier. Ne discerne-t-on pas par ailleurs des traits proprement tansmaniens qui sont également en l'œuvre de Falla: rythmique obsessionnelle, bitonalisme, polytonalité ou superpositions tonales ou encore accord "tansmanien"[17] présent sans doute en les présentes œuvres là où l'on chercherait et verrait trop rapidement peut-être les principes de superpositions propres au gaditan.

Cependant il est facile de discerner en ces œuvres de Tansman quelques traits stylistiques propres au monde sonore hispanique et présents génialement en l'œuvre de Falla. On en notera quelques-uns qui forment le lexique musical premier puis touchent ensuite à la syntaxe proprement dite. C'est tout d'abord l'*acciacatura* que se sont réappropriés les compositeurs des années 20 et Falla en nombre de ses pièces. L'emploi de la croche pointée + triples croches et de la croche + triolet de doubles croches est également une constante des deux œuvres. Le rythme premier et obsessionnel et la création de plages d'*ostinati* caractérise naturellement la "Danse Gitane" mais également le "Notturno" de l'"Hommage." C'est ensuite l'usage d'une volonté expansive de la cellule première: Tansman ne néglige pas le motif mélismatique très orné. Si la "Danse gitane" l'ignore l'"Hommage," notamment en ses mouvements III et V, se plait à sonder, en degrés conjoints, l'enroulement et la circularité du son premier sur lui-même. Enfin la sensibilité modale de Tansman est omniprésente en ces deux pièces, modalisme qu'il serait intéressant d'explorer en d'autres œuvres du compositeur. Il semblerait que ces œuvres autour de Falla aient une volonté signalisatrice de la part du musicien: le mode phrygien, le mode de mi, dit encore mode andalou, est exploité dans l'une et l'autre œuvre.

Hommages à un génie admiré par Tansman dont les exégètes ignorent les liens qui unissent les deux compositeurs, ces œuvres témoignent de la ductilité et du savoir du maître polonais dans l'exploitation et l'adaptation d'un lexique musical espagnol dont on sait qu'il appartient à un courant de 'nationalisme' musical plus qu'à la totalité de la musique de ce pays.

NOTES

1. Jambou, Louis, "Alexandre Tansman—compositeur—et Andrés Segovia—interprète—ou un en-deçà de l'œuvre musicale" *Hommage au compositeur Alexandre Tansman (1897–1986),* éd. Pierre Guillot, Paris PUPS, 2000, 231–54.

2. *Alexandre Tansman (1898–1986). Catalogue de l'œuvre, établi par Gérald Hugon, Paris,* éditions Max Eschig, 1995, 1, *"La toison d'or" (1938),*

opéra bouffe en 3 actes et 4 tableaux, livret de Salvador Madariaga; pp. 86–87
"*Deux mélodies 'Mad(a)ri(a)gaux.*" 1ère version (1952 [créé en 1959] et "*Deux mélodies 'Mad(a)ri(a)gaux de* 1972 dédiés à "mes chers amis Salvador et Mimi." L'incipit littéraire en est 1—"*El sol es de oro*" et 2—"*El sol quería bañarse*" dont le mouvement musical est distinctement indiqué; p. 31: après le décès de Madariaga (1978), Tansman lui dédie ses "*Dix commandemnets*": *à la memoire de mon ami Salvador de Madariaga* (1978–1979).

3. Hugon, Gérald, "Présentation du compositeur et de son," *Hommage au compositeur Alexandre Tansman (1897–1986)*, éd. Pierre Guillot, Paris, PUPS, 2000, 20, fn. 12.

4. Archives de l'Association Alexandre Tansman, Paris, lettre de Segovia à Tansman. Nous remercions les héritières de Tansman, notamment Mme. Zanuttini, de nous avoir accordé toute facilité pour la consultation de la correspondance ainsi que des deux manuscrits qui font l'objet de ce court essai.

5. Archives de l'Assocation Alexandre Tansman, lettre de Segovia à Tansman.

6. De nombreuses autres œuvres renvoient, dans leur titre, au monde sonore hispanique mais non, semble-t-il, plus précisément à Falla.

7. Nous remercions le prof. Pierre Guillot de nous avoir signalé cette œuvre citée dans son art. "Alexandre Tansman et sa musique pour enfants: petits ou grands? Dans l'ouvrage cité *Alexandre Tansman*, 219.

8. Le catalogue cité, édité par Max Eschig, indique p. 23, le titre "Introduction et danse gitane." Il aurait été édité par Leeds Music Corporation. L'éditeur fait porter une orchestration précise qui n'existe pas sur les mss consultés: Picc/10/1/1-saxo-1/1/1/0-timb., perc (trg. cast.). Nous n'avons vu aucun exemplaire de cette hypothétique édition.

9. Voir Gérald Hugo, dans *Alexandre Tansman*, 20, note 20 qui mentionne quelques-unes des œuvres influencées par la musique polonaise.

10. Granat-Janki, Anna "Les changements de style d'Alexandre Tansman dans sa musique instrumentale," *Hommage à Alexandre Tansman*, éd. Pierre Guillot, Paris, PUPS, 2001, 71.

11. Revelons dans son catalogue, Paris, Max Eschig, 1995, les titres suivants qu'il serait intéressant d'étudier dans les rapports intertextuels qu'ils entretiennent avec le passé: ses transcriptions et orchestrations de pièces de J. S. Bach "Toccata et fugue en ré mineur" de 1937, "Deux chorals" de 1939, "Suite dans le goût espagnol," de 1949, "Ricercari," de 1941–1949, "Suite baroque," de 1958.

12. Voir les art. de Marco Urvietta et Louis Jambou dans l'ouvrage cité *Alexandre Tansman*, respectivement p. 134, fn. 44, et. 253–54.

13. Voir art. cité de Anna Granat-Janki, 71.

14. Voir l'art. de Pierre Guillot, "Alexandre Tansman et sa musique pour enfants: petits ou grands?" dans l'ouvrage cité *Hommage à Alexandre Tansman*, 218.

15. À la fin des années 30, Tansman avait abordé le problème de la transcription et orchestration de deux œuvres de J. S. Bach (voir fn. 11).

16. Nommick, Yvan, "Des *Hommages* de Falla aux 'Hommages' à Falla," *Manuel de Falla,* Paris, PUPS, 1999, 515–41.

17. Voir l'art. cité de Granat-Janki ainsi que celui de Marco Urvietta "Alexandre Tansman et les équivoques de la critique," *Hommage à Alexandre Tansman*, Paris, PUPS, 2001, 113–48.

Chapter 15

Manuel de Falla's Personal Library and Insights into the Composer's Annotations[1]

Michael Christoforidis

Manuel de Falla's personal library provides a unique resource for the study of a composer's assimilation of ideas. The integrity of the surviving collection, when studied in conjunction with his voluminous correspondence, compositional sketch material, and working papers, permits a multifaceted study of Falla's creative process and unique insights into the life of this very private artist. While he was largely self-taught and had always acquired knowledge through private study, Falla's residence in Granada from 1919 made him more reliant on printed media to gain information on musical and cultural developments in Spain and abroad. The composer's lifelong habit of annotating his reading material and scores also heightens the library's usefulness to an understanding of his creative process. The extended period of gestation for most of Falla's works meant that he explored an ever increasing range of contemporary, historical, and folk musical models, literary and historical sources, and religious, philosophical, and aesthetic ideas, in an attempt to realize his aims. Some aspects of this process can be traced through Falla's annotations to his library.[2]

Unlike the collections of some of his musical contemporaries,[3] Falla's library remains largely intact and contains volumes from the period of his childhood in Cádiz in the 1880s right through to his final years in Argentina during World War II. The material was reassembled and stored first by his brother, Germán de Falla, and then his niece, Isabel de Falla, who further ordered the collection and presented it to the Archivo Manuel de Falla in Granada in 1991. The library comprises more than four thousand titles, which range from literary, historical, and reference works to books relating to music and over a thousand printed musical scores of great stylistic diversity.[4] The collection is supplemented by a large body of journals, concert programs, and newspaper cuttings, not solely his own press, but also articles he collected of a more general nature.[5] Many of the scores and books consulted by Falla contain his pencil markings. It was common for Falla to provide a page index of his annotations, combined with the odd word or brief reference which alludes to the text marked up, underlined and/or asterisked by the composer (see example 15.1).[6]

An indication of Falla's personal thoughts and aesthetic leanings can be gained from some of the ideas which are repeatedly underlined or indexed in the books he possessed. Several themes recur and one that is prominent in his later years is the question of regionalism. Falla marked the following passages outlining the relationship between regionalism and universality while reading José María de Cossío's commentaries on one of his favorite Spanish authors, José María de Pereda:

> Make yourself more "local" by the day, so that you can become more universal.[7]

> This [universality] resides in the human depth of conflicts and characters, be they of any class or race. Fortunately, Pereda was able to tap this human depth in rural characters, whereas many authors could not find it in the most cosmopolitan of atmospheres.[8]

Falla also marked a passage which conveyed Menéndez Pelayo's ideas on the question of regionalism and patriotism in the Spanish context.

> One cannot love his country if he does not love his region and use this love as the basis for a broader patriotism. A selfish form of regionalism is both odious and sterile, but a benevolent and fraternal regionalism can be an important element for progress and perhaps the only salvation for Spain.[9]

It is possible that these ideas relate to some of Falla's contemporary thoughts on regionalism and the political situation in Spain in the aftermath of the Civil War, and even to some of his aesthetic deliberations during the composition of his unfinished scenic cantata *Atlántida* (1927–1946).

Although music was his principal creative outlet, Falla initially displayed a strong interest in art and literature. The numerous drafts of his published writings and much of his extensive correspondence demonstrate a sustained interest in precise and elegant modes of expression. Art

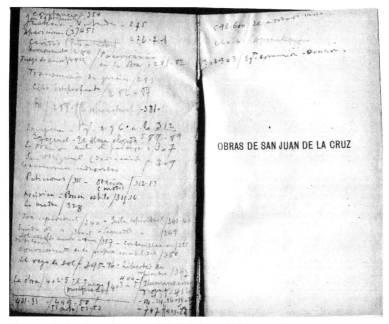

Example 15.1   Part of Manuel de Falla's index (title page and annotated opposite page) of St. John of the Cross, *Obras de San Juan de la Cruz* (Madrid, 1926), AMF.

and literature also inspired the poetic conception of some of his purely musical works. Through an examination of the composer's library it is possible to shed light on the nexus between his evocative orchestral score *Noches en los jardines de España* and numerous sources, which include the writings of his favorite poet, Rubén Darío, verses by the French poet Paul Drouot,[10] the travel essays of Gregorio Martínez Sierra and Salvador Rueda, and *Jardines*, a book of illustrations by Santiago Rusiñol.[11]

Falla's annotations to his library also encourage speculation on the sources of literary inspiration for projected works. One such case is the piece that Falla had contemplated composing for the guitarist Miguel Llobet after completing the *Homenaje pour "Le tombeau de Claude Debussy"* in late 1920. Falla claimed to his last contemporaneous biographer, Jaime Pahissa, that he had wanted to write a piece for the guitar entitled *La tertulia*, which evoked the atmosphere of the nineteenth-century salon.[12] The text that follows is taken from a passage that Falla had indexed with the words "La tertulia" in Benito Pérez Galdós's *Los apostólicos*, one of that author's *Episodios nacionales* which Falla is known to have read in the early 1920s.

> The Lady of the house appeared to be satisfied in sustaining the perfect equilibrium between the apostolic and political elements, each of whom had a leader at her tertulias. But not everything revolved around politics. Almost three quarters of the time was spent in reading verses and talking of plays, and music did not occupy the least important position. After an afficionado played a Haydn sonata on the harpsichord or any Italian of the opera company twittered an aria from Zelmira, the lady of the house would take the guitar and then. . . . There is no other way of expressing the grace of her person and of her voice than to say that it was as if Euterpe herself had descended from Parnassus to discredit the plectrum and to convert our grave national instrument into the lyre of the gods.[13]

Falla also marked references to other 19th-century *tertulias* in Pérez Galdós's *El audaz* and *Los cien mil hijos de San Luis*.

Pérez Galdós too was one of Falla's favourite authors, and this is reflected in the number of the *Episodios nacionales* that he read and annotated over the last three decades of his life. The contents of the library serve as a guide to Falla's literary tastes and interests, and provide insights into his character. While Spanish is the the predominant language of the collection it is closely followed by books in French, Falla's other reading language. From an overview of the books he annotated it is evident that his literary tastes lie with the Spanish authors of the "Generation of 1898," despite his relations with and decisive impact upon the "Generation of '27." Apart from the *Episodios nacionales* of Pérez Galdós, there is a preference for the works of José María de Pereda and the essays of Azorín. Falla's growing asceticism and religious inclinations from the 1920s are attested to by a large collection of material in this area, ranging from the poetry of St. John of the Cross to various works dealing with Catholic devotional practice. Also of interest in this regard is Falla's study of texts by contemporary French authors dealing with spiritual matters, especially the writings of Jacques Maritain. By the 1930s Falla's rejection of the immoral tone of some of the works he had read led him to scribble "Rómpese" (tear this up) and "Reservado" (reserved for reading with the permission of his confessor) at the outset of numerous books such as Ramón del Valle Inclán's *Ligazón*, and on José Zorrilla's *Don Juan Tenorio*, a work he had earlier been interested in setting. This practice also extended to books by European authors such as Lord Byron and Honoré de Balzac.[14]

A more direct link between Falla's library and his output is evident through the books which inspired the librettos or scenarios for his works. Falla's possession of a marked up copy of Pedro Antonio de Alarcón's *El sombrero de tres picos* suggests he collaborated with the Martínez Sierras in the adaptation of this text.[15] Despite owning several editions of Miguel de Cervantes's *El ingenioso Hidalgo Don Quixote de la Mancha*, none of these seems to have served as the copy Falla employed in the fabrication of the libretto for *El retablo de Maese Pedro*, and some of the pre-nineteenth-century editions in his library were in fact gifts bestowed on the composer after the completion of his opera. The often laborious process of drafting a libretto can be surmised from the numerous annotated copies of Jacinto Verdaguer's *La Atlántida*, which formed the basis for Falla's own adaptation in the scenic cantata *Atlántida*. Other books marked in this fashion provide concrete details about works which were never realized, such as the projected opera based on Joaquín and Serafín Alvarez Quintero's *Las flores* (1909–1910). From Falla's annotations to two anthologies of theatrical works by Pedro Calderón de la Barca, there are some indications of the libretto that Falla envisaged creating from an adaptation of passages of *El mayor encanto amor* (otherwise known as *La Circe*) and *Los encantos de la culpa* during 1926 and 1927 (see example 15.2).[16] The *Comedia* and the *Auto sacramental* by Calderón de la Barca share the same protagonist, the Homeric "Ulises" (Ulysses/Odysseus), and revolve around his sojourn on Circe's island. Some of Falla's notes make reference to musical ideas he intended to explore: "Slow declamation, marking the accents," "Textless vocal music," "over distant songs of victory."[17] Falla also underlined allusions to music in the text of the plays and in the critical notes to the editions he consulted, which include references to "the deafening sound of barbarous bugles and trumpets" and "sad music and song."[18] In 1927 Falla wrote the incidental music for a production of Calderón de la Barca's *El gran teatro del Mundo*, and some of the musical ideas encountered among his notes on the "Ulises" plays are present both in *El gran teatro del Mundo* and in the early sketches for *Atlántida* (1927–1946).

Falla's practice of collecting a great deal of background literature and information pertaining to the projects he was undertaking in part accounts for the extended gestation period for many of his works. Such attention to detail meant that his library often served as a source of documentation for his projects. In the case of *Atlántida* the literary material consulted by Falla ranged from biographies of Christopher Columbus to numerous texts on the Atlantis legend, which includes those of Plato and

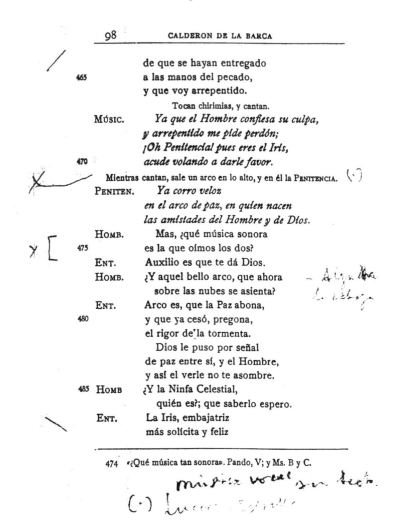

de que se hayan entregado
465   a las manos del pecado,
y que voy arrepentido.

Tocan chirimías, y cantan.

MÚSIC.   *Ya que el Hombre confiesa su culpa,*
y arrepentido me pide perdón;
¡Oh Penitencia! pues eres el Iris,
470   *acude volando a darle favor.*

Mientras cantan, sale un arco en lo alto, y en él la PENITENCIA.

PENITEN.   *Ya corro veloz*
en el arco de paz, en quien nacen
las amistades del Hombre y de Dios.

HOMB.   Mas, ¿qué música sonora
475   es la que oímos los dos?

ENT.   Auxilio es que te dá Dios.

HOMB.   ¿Y aquel bello arco, que ahora
sobre las nubes se asienta?

ENT.   Arco es, que la Paz abona,
480   y que ya cesó, pregona,
el rigor de la tormenta.

Dios le puso por señal
de paz entre sí, y el Hombre,
y así el verle no te asombre.

485 HOMB   ¿Y la Ninfa Celestial,
quién es?; que saberlo espero.

ENT.   La Iris, embajatriz
más solícita y feliz

474   «¿Qué música tan sonora». Pando, V; y Ms. B y C.

Example 15.2   Pedro Calderón de la Barca, *Autos sacramentales* (Madrid, 1926), annotations by Manuel de Falla, AMF.

Herodotus. Falla also referred to texts which outlined classical Greek musical and dramatic practice, and even descriptions of ships and clothing, which were meant to inform aspects of the music, vocal production, and staging of *Atlántida*.[19] A single page of notes with the heading "Grecia" illustrates Falla's practice of taking notes from different volumes in his library which relate to aspects of the work he was composing.[20] Here he made notes on Ancient Greek music and its employment in a dramatic context, and drew from Curt Sachs's *La música en la antigüedad* and Théodore Reinach's *La musique grecque*, books which Falla read in the early 1930s, and the ideas outlined relate closely to some of Falla's compositional deliberations on *Atlántida* at that time.[21] Not only are there cross references to the books by Reinach and Sachs in this document, but Falla also alludes to his experimentation with North African Arab melodies which can be traced to his annotations to scores in the *Collection Yafil* and the journal *Hespéris* in his library.[22]

In several instances the ideas espoused by Falla in his writings on music can be traced to his annotations. Falla's knowledge of flamenco forms and the evolution of this genre was shaped by a variety of sources, some of which are in his library. In the case of his 1922 essay *El "cante jondo" (Canto primitivo andaluz)*, the principal volumes which informed his arguments on flamenco and its origins are F. M. Pabanó, *Historia y costumbres de los gitanos* (1915), which outlines the geographical and cultural origins of the gypsies and made Falla emphasize their ties with India; Felipe Pedrell, *Cancionero musical popular español*, vol. 2 (1918), in which the possible precursors of flamenco forms are discussed and greater emphasis is given to their connections with Byzantine and liturgical music than the music of the Arabs; Felipe Pedrell, *Emporio científico e histórico de organografía musical antigua española* (1901) on which Falla based his discussion of the differences between the "castellana" and "morisca" styles of guitar playing; and the monograph by Louis Lucas, *L'Acoustique nouvelle* (1854), which provided some information on Indian and Arab scale formations and other musical practices. Falla also relied on passages from his copies of D. S. Estébanez Calderón, *Escenas andaluzas* (1883), Pedro Antonio de Alarcón, *La Alpujarra*, (1882), Juan Ruiz, Arcipreste de Hita, *Libro de Buen Amor* (1913), Ginés Pérez de Hita, *Guerras civiles de Granada* (1900), and André Suarès, *Don Quijote en Francia*, trans. Ricardo Baeza (1916). His annotations to transcriptions of North African music (Algiers: MNE Yafil) and notated pieces of flamenco music, especially the *Aires andaluces* for guitar by Rafael Marín (1902), also coincide with many of his speculations in this essay and informed Falla's assimilation of aspects of this genre in his scores.[23]

Some of the books on music in the Falla library had a decisive impact on his musical thought and style. Principal among these is the aforementioned monograph by Louis Lucas, *L'Acoustique nouvelle*, which shaped some aspects of Falla's harmonic language and helped redefine his construction of tonality after World War I. The refinement of Falla's style of orchestration can also be traced through an examination of the treatises which he studied, many of which preserve his markings on the subject. He followed the advice of Paul Dukas and Claude Debussy and made a thorough study of the techniques of individual instruments, as can be surmised from his annotations to G. Koecrert's *Les principes rationnels de la technique du violon* (1904) and the *Nouveau traïté d'instrumentation* by F. A. Gevaert. Falla also studied and annotated numerous orchestration treatises at different times, the principal ones being F. A. Gevaert, *Cours méthodique d'orchestration* (1885), Charles Marie Widor, *Technique de l'Orchestre moderne* (1904), Richard Strauss, *Le Traïté d'orchestration d'Hector Berlioz* (1909), and Nicolai Rimsky-Korsakov, *Principes d'orchestration* (1914). In the case of many of these treatises extra pages had to be inserted into the volumes to carry Falla's extensive annotations.

The evolution of Falla's musical language can also be related to his examination of scores by other composers. Of his contemporaries, Claude Debussy was perhaps the composer most closely studied by Falla, and this is particularly evident in the annotations which make reference to Debussy's orchestration. Scores such as *Pelléas et Mélisande, La Mer,* and *Ibéria* were repeatedly reviewed in this regard and influenced Falla's orchestral conception in works ranging from *La vida breve* and *Noches en los jardines de España* to *Homenajes, Suite,* and *Atlántida.* Particularly significant is Falla's assimilation of Debussy's orchestral image of Spain in *Ibéria,* and especially its second movement "Parfums de la nuit," which shaped the timbral and evocative parameters of passages of *Noches en los jardines de España* and informed the scoring of Falla's own orchestral homage to Debussy in the second movement of *Homenajes, Suite.*[24] Falla also applied his knowledge of Debussy's orchestral style to his arrangements of the French composer's music. Inside the score of Debussy's *Prélude à l'après-midi d'un faune,* five pages of manuscript notes were found which outline the transformations made by Falla in reducing this work for chamber orchestra, a task which he undertook for the Orquesta Bética de Cámara in 1924.[25]

Various models provided the stylistic impetus and framework for Falla's *Concerto* for harpsichord and chamber ensemble. These include the contrapuntal idiom and instrumentation of several works by Igor Stravinsky and Arnold Schoenberg's *Pierrot Lunaire*. Unfortunately, only the full score of *Pierrot Lunaire* remains at the Archivo Manuel de Falla; the miniature score which Falla probably annotated was forwarded to him in Argentina in 1940 and has subsequently been lost.[26] However, Falla copied passages from *Pierrot Lunaire*, with specific page references to the score, which elucidate his interest in the instrumental textures and contrapuntal techniques employed in the work.[27]

Falla's reliance on musical borrowings in his compositions means that a study of the printed scores in his possession often gives the provenance of his musical ideas. His limited fieldwork in the realm of folk music meant that much of this material which was incorporated into his output was derived from published sources. In *Manuel de Falla y Asturias,*[28] Inmaculada Quintanal Sánchez outlined Falla's debt over an extended period to one such collection, José Hurtado's *100 cantos populares asturianos.*[29] Falla used themes from this publication in his *zarzuela Limosna de amor*, the "Montañesa" from *Cuatro piezas españolas*, and in "La asturiana" from *Siete canciones populares españolas*. On occasion, rudimentary harmonisations of Hispanic and oriental folk melodies were jotted by Falla next to the published sources. One example of this practice can be found in some of the Moroccan melodies transcribed in the journal *Hespéris*, which is referred to in the previously mentioned document marked "Grecia" (see example 15.3).[30]

Falla's activities as a performer of his own and other composers' music are also reflected in the library. The interpretative indications present in his scores act as a useful guide both to his own style and to the performance practice of his time. Among the pieces annotated by Falla are several movements from *Iberia* by Isaac Albéniz, which Falla heard performed by the ailing composer and his principal interpreter Blanche Selva. Though fewer in number, there are also expressive markings in scores which Falla conducted, such as those in Beethoven's Septet, op. 20, which was performed for the centenary of that composer's death in 1927. The initial impetus for Falla's "versiones expresivas" of Renaissance polyphony, which he conducted, can also be found among his markings to the transcriptions in Pedrell's *Cancionero musical popular español* and Francisco Asenjo Barbieri's edition of the *Cancionero de Palacio*.

As well as being one of his chief mentors, Debussy was also the composer that Falla most performed and several of his Debussy scores

Example 15.3   Transcription of Moroccan melody in *Hespéris* (1924), p. 231, with harmonic annotations by Manuel de Falla, AMF.

include fingerings and expressive markings. The harp parts to Debussy's *Danse sacré et Danse profane* and the sonata for flute, viola, and harp had been performed on the piano by Falla, and his copies of these indicate the adjustments he made. Of even greater interest are Falla's performance indications for Debussy's original piano music, as is the case of "La Soirée dans Grenade . . ." from *Estampes* (see example 15.4). Falla heard Ricardo Viñes perform the work and may have heard a rendition from the composer himself, given Debussy's fixation with Granada, an interest which Falla helped foster.[31] The markings to the score include fingerings, the underlining of printed indications, some reference to voice leadings, and the addition of pedaling, expressive, dynamic, and tempo markings, all of which provide fascinating insights into Falla's performance strategies for this influential evocation of Spain.

Other material found in the library includes a multitude of musical sketches. Although Falla was sometimes musically inspired by the book he was reading, at other times it merely served as a surface for notating or transcribing a musical idea.[32] Musical annotations therefore include transcriptions of folksongs that Falla heard, the copying out and development of other composers' motifs, and occasionally even musical ideas inspired

Example 15.4   Final page of "La Soirée dans Grenade" from *Estampes* by Claude Debussy, with expressive marking by Manuel de Falla, AMF.

by the literary texts he was reading. One such example includes Falla's annotations to a volume of poetry by Lord Byron in which a musical sketch outlines the rhythm for a galloping horse which is alluded to in the text.[33] There is also some sketch material proper, relating to Falla's own completed works, which to date is not catalogued amongst the manuscripts.[34]

To facilitate research on the composer and the collection, an alphabetical listing of scores, as well as books and treatises on music in the Falla library that were annotated by the composer, have been included in the appendixes.[35] Ongoing research will assist in the dating of volume acquisitions and periods of consultation,[36] as well as identifying the music and books read by Falla which do not form part of the collection at the Archivo Manuel de Falla. The foregoing discussion has outlined some of the ways in which Falla employed his library and the traces he left in the process. A systematic study of the library and the composer's annotations will undoubtedly provide further insights into Falla's compositional process, creative concerns, and facets of his private world.

APPENDIXES: Published Scores, treatises, and monographs on music in Manuel de Falla's personal library which were annotated by the composer.

This list does not include Falla's own works, and is based on current holdings at the *AMF*. The numbers in square brackets are the inventory number assigned by the *AMF*.

APPENDIX 1   Scores

ALBÉNIZ, Isaac. *Iberia (1ᵉʳ Cahier)*. Paris: Edition Mutuelle, 1906. [1]
ALBÉNIZ, Isaac. *Iberia (2ᵉᵐᵉ Cahier)*. Paris: Edition Mutuelle, 1906. [2]
ALBÉNIZ, Isaac. *Iberia (3ᵉᵐᵉ Cahier)*. Paris: Edition Mutuelle, 1907. [3]
ALBÉNIZ, Isaac. *Iberia (4ᵉᵐᵉ Cahier)*. Paris: Edition Mutuelle, 1906. [4]
ALBÉNIZ, Isaac. *Suite Espagnole: Alhambra*. Madrid: Zozaya-A. Diaz y Cia. [5]
ANON. *Ballet album*. Leipzig: Peters, n.d. [584]
ANON. *Bane cheraff*. Algeria: M.M.E. Yafil, n.d. [925]
ANON. *Cançoner popular*. Barcelona: Imprenta "La Renaixensa," 1913. [1478]
ANON. *Corpus de musique marocaine*. Paris: Heugel, 1933. [1005]
ANON. *El canto popular: Documentos para el estudio del folk-lore argentino*. Buenos Aires: "Coni," 1923. [1006]
ANON. *Kadriat Senaa*. Algeria: M.M.E. Yafil, n.d. [928]
ANON. *Les feuvilles musicales*. Paris: L'Art Catholique, 1920. [876]
ANON. *Les vendredis. Cahier 1*. Leipzig: Belaieff, 1899. [712]
ANON. *Mahma iekhter fel moudelel*. Algeria: M.M.E. Yafil., n.d. [929]
ANON. *Recueil de Zendani (Deuxiéme serie)*. Algeria: M.N. Yafil, n.d. [933]
ANON. *Recueil de Zendani (Troisiéme serie)*. Algeria: M.N Yafil, n.d. [936]

ANON. *Te Deum laudamus asperges me, vidi aquam.* London: Chester, n.d. [692]

ANON. *Touchiat ghrib.* Algeria: M.M.E. Yafil, n.d. [932]

ANON. *Touchiat ghribt H'assine.* Algeria: M.M.E. Yafil, n.d. [930]

ANON. *Touchiat maia.* Algeria: M.N. Yafil, n.d. [934]

ANON. *Touchiat remel.* Algeria: M.M.E. Yafil, n.d. [927]

ANON. *Touchiat sika.* Algeria: M.N. Yafil, n.d. [937]

ANON. *Touchiat zidane.* Algeria: M.N.E. Yafil, n.d. [926]

ARCAS, Julián. *Murcianas.* Barcelona: Sindicato Musical Barcelonés, n.d. [138]

ARCAS, Julián. *Rondeña.* Barcelona: Sindicato Musical Barcelonés Dotesio, n.d. [136]

ARCAS, Julián. *Soleá.* Barcelona: Sindicato Musical Barcelonés Dotesio, n.d. [137]

AURIC, Georges. *Cinq poèmes de Gérard de Nerval.* Paris: Heugel, 1925. [283]

BACH, J. S. *30 Variationen.* Leipzig: Peters, n.d. [482]

BACH, J. S. *Brandenburgisches Koncert no 2.* Leipzig: Eulenburg, n.d. [473]

BACH, J. S. *Brandenburgisches Koncert no 3.* Leipzig: Eulenburg, n.d. [474]

BACH, J. S. *Brandenburgisches Koncert no 4.* Leipzig: Eulenburg, n.d. [475]

BACH, J. S. *Brandenburgisches Koncert no 5.* Leipzig: Eulenburg, n.d. [476]

BACH, J. S. *Concert für klavier in D moll.* Leipzig: Breitkopf & Härtel, n.d. [1042]

BACH, J. S. *Concert für Klavier, Flöte und Violine in D dur.* Leipzig: Breitkopf & Härtel, n.d. [1043]

BACH, J. S. *Concert Italien.* Paris: Maurice Senart, 1915. [487]

BACH, J. S. *Das Wohltemperierte Klavier: Band I.* Leipzig: Peters, n.d. [470]

BACH, J. S. *Das Wohltemperierte Klavier: Band II.* Leipzig: Peters, n.d. [471]

BACH, J. S. Koncert für drei Klaviere in D moll. Leipzig: Breitkopf & Härtel, n.d. [1045]

BACH, J. S. *Koncert für klavier und zwei flöten in F Dur.* Leipzig: Breitkopf & Härtel, n.d. [489]

BACH, J. S. *La Passion selon Saint Matthieu.* Braunschweig: Henry Litolff, n.d. [1041]

BACH, J. S. *La Passion selon Saint Matthieu*. Paris: Enoch, n.d. [1040]
BACH, J. S. *Matthäus-Passion*. Leipzig: Eulenburg, n.d. [478]
BACH, J. S. *Orgel-compositionen für piano, übertragen von F. Liszt*. Leipzig: Peters, n.d. [485]
BACH, J. S. *Partitas no 1–3*. Leipzig: Peters, n.d. [481]
BACH, J. S. *Passacaglia C Moll*. Leipzig: Breitkopf & Härtel, n.d. [483]
BACH, J. S. *Zum letzen Satze des Concertes D moll*. (Cadenza by Carl Reinaska). Leipzig: Breitkopf & Härtel, n.d. [490]
BACHELET, Alfred. *Scemo*. Paris: Max Eschig, 1914. [1157]
BARBIERI, Francisco Asenjo. *Cancionero musical de los siglos XV y XVI*. Madrid: Real Academia de Bellas Artes de San Fernando, 1890. [981]
BARTA, Luis. *La Peinadora*. Madrid: Unión Musical Española, 1916. [139]
BARTÓK, Béla. *10 leichte Klavierstücke*. Budapest: Karl Rozsnyai, n.d. [821]
BEETHOVEN, L. van. *Complete Collection of Beethoven's Symphonies, Arranged for the Pianoforte*. London: Cocks, n.d. [1067]
BEETHOVEN, L. van. *Quartett Op. 18 no 1 F Dur*. Leipzig: Paine, n.d. [493]
BEETHOVEN, L. van. *Septett Op. 20*. Leipzig: Eulenburg, n.d. [510]
BEETHOVEN, L. van. *Sonaten*. Leipzig: Peters, n.d. [1068]
BEETHOVEN, L. van. *Trios für Pianoforte, Violine und Violoncello: Pianoforte*. Leipzig: Peters, n.d. [605]
BERLIOZ, Hector. *Fantastic Symphony Op. 14*. New York: Kalmus, n.d. [1152]
BERLIOZ, Hector. *La damnation de Faust*. Paris: Costallat, n.d. [1150]
BIZET, Georges. *Carmen*. Paris: Chouldens-Peters, n.d. [285]
BIZET, Georges. *L'Arlesianne: Suite no 1*. Leipzig: Eulenburg, n.d. [286]
BOURGAULT-DUCOUDRAY, Louis. *Trente mélodies populaires de Grèce & d'Orient*. Paris: Henry Lemoine, 1897. [1001]
BRAHMS, Johannes. *Variationen für Orchester über ein Thema von J. Haydn Op. 56a*. Leipzig: Eulenburg, n.d. [568]
CARISSIMI, Giacomo. *Oratorii Jonas (Giona)*. Milan: Instituto Editorale Italiano, 1919. [938]
CHOPIN, Frédéric. *Recueil complet des Mélodies Polonaises de F. Chopin*. Paris: J. Hamelle, n.d. [841]
CHOTTIN, A. *Airs populaires recueillis a Fès, Hespéris: Archives Berbères*. 1924, 2nd term. Paris: Émile Larose, 1924. [1082]

COLLET, Henri. *Un tratado de canto de órgano (Siglo XVI): Manuscrito en la Biblioteca de Paris*. Madrid: Gutenberg, 1913. [1253]

D'INDY, Vincent. *Helvetia: Trois valses pour piano*. Paris: Hamelle, n.d. [434]

DEBUSSY, Claude. *Children's Corner*. Paris: Durand, 1908. [301]

DEBUSSY, Claude. *Danses pour Harpe*. Paris: Durand, 1904. [304]

DEBUSSY, Claude. *Danses*. Paris: Durand, 1904. [303]

DEBUSSY, Claude. *Deux Arabesques*. Paris: Durand, 1904. [307]

DEBUSSY, Claude. *Deux Arabesques*. Paris: Durand, 1904. [308]

DEBUSSY, Claude. *Fantasie pour piano et orchestre*. Paris: Fromont, n.d. [315]

DEBUSSY, Claude. *Ibéria: "Imagenes pour orchestre 2."* Paris: Durand, 1910. [1141]

DEBUSSY, Claude. *La Mer*. Paris: Durand, 1905. [1141]

DEBUSSY, Claude. *Nocturnes*. Paris: Jean Jobert, 1930. [1144]

DEBUSSY, Claude. *Nocturnes: II Fêtes pour piano*. Paris: Durand, 1914. [306]

DEBUSSY, Claude. *Pelléas et Mélisande*. Paris: Durand, 1902. [1142]

DEBUSSY, Claude. *Pour le piano*. Paris: Jean Jobert, 1901. [297]

DEBUSSY, Claude. *Prélude à l'apres-midi d'un faune*. Paris: Jean Jobert, 1922. [1143]

DEBUSSY, Claude. *Préludes pour piano. 1° & 2° livre*. Paris: Durand, 1910. [317]

DEBUSSY, Claude. *Sonate pour flûte, alto et harpe*. Paris: Durand, 1916. [310]

DEBUSSY, Claude. *Trois chansons de Charles D'Orleans*. Paris: Durand, 1908. [298]

DELAGE, Maurice. *Contrerimes, piano à deux mains: Rêves*. Paris: Durand, 1933. [322]

DUKAS, Paul. *Ariane et Barbe-bleue*. Paris: Durand, 1906. [1153]

DUKAS, Paul. *L'Apprenti sorcier*. Paris: Durand, n.d. [340]

DUKAS, Paul. *Symphonie en ut majeur*. Paris: Rouart Lerolle, n.d. [1155]

DUKAS, Paul. *Variations, interlude et finale pour piano*. Paris: Durand, n.d. [344]

FONTBONNE, L. *Méthode complète (Flûte)*. Paris: Costallat, 1907. [1230]

GAUTIER, Judith. *Les musiques bizarres a l'Exposition de 1900*. Paris: Librairie Ollendorff, 1901. [1455]

GLINKA, Mikhail. *Kamarinskaïa*. Leipzig: Belaieff, 1902. [717]

GOOSSENS, Eugene. *Judith*. London: Chester, 1929. [1194]

GOUNOD, Charles. *Fausto*. n.d. [1126]

GRAU, Agustí. *Hores Intimes*. Barcelona: Unión Musical Española, n.d. [156]

GRIEG, Edvard. *Albumblätter für pianoforte*. Leipzig: Peters, n.d. [851]

GRIEG, Edvard. *Aus Holbergs Zeit: Suite für pianoforte Op. 40*. Leipzig: Peters, n.d. [851]

GRIEG, Edvard. *Ave, Maris Stella*. Copenhagen: Wilhelm Hansen, n.d. [843]

GRIEG, Edvard. *Lyrische Stücke*. Leipzig: Peters, n.d. [851]

GRIEG, Edvard. *Melodien für harmonium Op. 6 no 2*. Leipzig: Peters, n.d. [851]

GRIEG, Edvard. *Norwegische Tänze Op. 35*. Leipzig: Peters, n.d. [845]

GRIEG, Edvard. *Psalmen Op. 74*. Leipzig: Peters, n.d. [847]

GRIEG, Edvard. *Slatter: Norwegische Bauerntänze Op. 72*. Leipzig: Peters, n.d. [850]

GRIEG, Edvard. *Sonate E moll für das pianoforte Op. 7*. Leipzig: Peters, n.d. [851]

GRIEG, Edvard. *Vor der Klosterpforte Op. 20*. Leipzig: Peters, n.d. [854]

GUERRERO, Francisco. *Messe "Puer qui natus est nobis."* Paris: Schola Cantorum, n.d. [160]

HAYDN, Joseph. *Die Jahreszeiten*. Leipzig: Breiktopf & Härtel, n.d. [1057]

HOLST, Gustav. *Matthew, Mark, Luke and John*. London: Curwen, 1917. [357]

HUMPERDINCK, Engelbert. *Hansel und Gretel (Nino e Rita)*. Mainz: Schott's Söhne, n.d. [1107]

HURTADO, José. *Cien cantos populares asturianos*. Madrid: Antonio Romero, n.d. [985]

INZENGA, José. *Ecos de España*. Barcelona: n.p., n.d. [1007]

KODÁLY, Zoltán. *Zongora muzika: 10 pièces pour le piano Op. 3*. Budapest: Rozsavolgyi, 1910. [826]

KOECHLIN, Charles. *Chansons bretonnes pour violoncelle et piano*. Paris: Maurice Senart, 1934. [739]

KOECHLIN, Charles. *Chansons bretonnes pour violoncelle et piano*. Paris: Maurice Senart, 1934. [740]

KORGANOV, G. O. *Bajati: Fantaisie sur des thèmes caucasiens*. Moscow: Gutheil, n.d. [810]

LAZAR, Filip. *Concerto grosso no 1 Op. 17*. Paris: Durand, 1930. [828]

LEDESMA, Dámaso. *Cancionero salmantino.* Madrid: Imprenta alemana, 1907. [986]

LISZT, Franz. *Etüden in aufsteigender Schwierigkeit.* Leipzig: Breitkopf & Härtel, n.d. [1073]

LISZT, Franz. *Héroïde funébre: Symphonische Dichtung Nr. 8.* Leipzig: Eulenburg, n.d. [833]

LISZT, Franz. *Rhapsodie hongroise no 12.* Berlin: Schlesinger, n.d. [831]

LISZT, Franz. *Totentanz.* Leipzig: Eulenburg, n.d. [834]

LISZT-PAGANINI. *La Campanella.* Leipzig: Breitkopf & Härtel, n.d. [830]

MAHLER, Gustav. *Das Lied von der Erde.* Vienna: Universal, 1910. [1190]

MARÍN, Rafael. *Granadinas.* Madrid: Sociedad de Autores Españoles, 1902. [39]

MARÍN, Rafael. *Los Tientos, Malagueñas.* Madrid: Sociedad de Autores Españoles, 1902. [38]

MARÍN, Rafael. *Siguirillas Gitanas.* Madrid; Sociedad de Autores Españoles, n.d. [42]

MARÍN, Rafael. *Soleares.* Madrid: Sociedad de Autores Españoles, n.d. [41]

MARÍN, Rafael. *Tangos.* Madrid: Sociedad de Autores Españoles, n.d. [40]

MENDELSSOHN, Felix. *Compositionen für Pianoforte Solo.* Leipzig: Peters, n.d. [1102]

MENDELSSOHN, Felix. *Concerte für Pianoforte Solo.* Leipzig: Peters, n.d. [1101]

MENDELSSOHN, Felix. *Trios Op. 49, 66.* Leipzig: Peters, n.d. [520]

MENDELSSOHN, Felix. *Vierstimmige lieder Opp. 41, 48, 59, 88 and 100.* Leipzig: Breitkopf & Härtel, n.d. [519]

MESTRES, Apeles. *Amoroses: Dotze Cansons.* Barcelona: Boileau, n.d. [56]

MONTEVERDI, Claudio. *L'Orfeo.* London: Chester, 1923. [1017]

MONTEVERDI, Claudio. *Madrigale.* Leipzig: Peters, n.d. [867]

MONTEVERDI, Claudio. *Madrigale.* Leipzig: Peters, n.d. [868]

MONTEVERDI, Claudio. *Tutte le opere.*(vols. V, VI, X, XIII) Bologna: G. Francesco Malipero. [1018]

MORALES, Christophorus. *Messe "Quaeramus cum pastoribus."* Paris: Schola Cantorum, n.d. [167]

MOSZOWSKI, Maurice. *Trois morceaux pour piano.* Oeuvre 34. New York: Schirmer, n.d. [571]

MOZART, W. A. *Don Giovanni*. Leipzig: Breitkopf & Härtel, n.d. [1063]
MOZART, W. A. *Pianoforte-Quintett. Es-dur. K.V. 452*. Leipzig: Eulenburg, n.d. [624]
MOZART, W. A. *Serenade B-dur. K.V. 361*. Leipzig: Eulenburg, n.d. [626]
MOZART, W. A. *Symphonie 40 G. Moll. K.V. no 550*. Vienna: Wiener Philharmonischer, n.d. [628]
MOZART, W. A. *Symphonie no 40. K.V. 550*. Leipzig: Breitkopf & Härtel, n.d. [629]
MUSSORGSKY, Modest. *Boris Godounow*. St Petersburg: Bessel, 1908. [1183]
MUSSORGSKY-RAVEL. *Tableaux d'une exposition*. London: Boosey & Hawkes, 1929. [1181]
NAPIER MILES, P. *Ode on a Grecian Urn*. London: OUP, 1931. [685]
OFFENBACH, Jacques. *Les contes d'Hoffmann*. Paris: Choudens, 1907. [1074]
OLMEDA, Federico. *Folklore de Castilla o Cancionero popular de Burgos*. Sevilla: Maria Auxiliadora, 1903. [989]
PAGANINI, Niccolò. *24 Capricen für violine solo Op. 1*. Leipzig: Peters, n.d. [874]
PALESTRINA, Giovanni Pierluigi da. *Messe "Papae Marcelli."* Paris: Schola Cantorum, n.d. [877]
PALESTRINA, Giovanni Pierluigi da. *Stabat Mater*. Vienna: Wiener Philharmonischer, n.d. [876]
PARGA, J. *Reminiscencias árabes: Idilio andaluz Op.13*. Málaga: López y Griffo, n.d. [171]
PASQUINI, Bernardo. *Arie ed ariette*. Rome: "Musica," 1923. [882]
PEDRELL, Felipe. *Antología de organistas clasicos españoles*. Madrid: Ildefonso Alier, n.d. [1177]
PEDRELL, Felipe. *Cancionero musical popular español*. Valls: Eduardo Castells, n.d. [1482]
PEDRELL, Felipe. *Cancionero musical popular español*. Valls: Eduardo Castells, n.d. [1483]
PELAY BRIZ, Francesch. *Cansons de la terra*. Barcelona: Alvar Verdaguer, 1874. [1474]
PROKOFIEV, Serge. *Ala et Lolly. Suite Scythe Op. 20*. Leipzig: Breitkopf & Härtel, 1923. [725]
PUCCINI, Giacomo. *La Bohème*. Milan: Ricordi, 1896. [1123]
PUCCINI, Giacomo. *Manon Lescaut*. Milan: Ricordi, 1893. [1124]
PURCELL, Henry. *Dido y Aeneas*. London: OUP, n.d. [1049]

RACHMANINOFF, Sergei. *Bless the Lord, O my Soul.* New York: Schola Cantorum, 1919. [727]

RACHMANINOFF, Sergei. *Blessed is the Man.* New York: Schola Cantorum, 1919. [728]

RAVEL, Maurice. *Chansons Madécasses.* Paris: Durand, 1926. [396]

RAVEL, Maurice. *Daphnis et Chloé.* Paris: Durand, 1910. [1145]

RAVEL, Maurice. *Introduction et Allegro.* Paris: Durand, 1906. [399]

RAVEL, Maurice. *Introduction et Allegro.* Paris: Durand, 1906. [400]

RAVEL, Maurice. *L'Heure espagnole.* Paris: Durand, 1908. [1147]

RAVEL, Maurice. *Miroirs IV: Alborada del gracioso.* Paris: Demets, 1906. [404]

RAVEL, Maurice. *Rapsodie Espagnole.* Paris: Durand, 1908. [405]

RAVEL, Maurice. *Sonatine.* Paris: Durand, 1905. [407]

RIMSKY-KORSAKOV, Nikolay. *Le Coq d'or.* Leipzig: Jurgenson, n.d. [1187]

ROBERTON, Hugh S. *The Banks o'Doon?* London: Curwen, n.d. [675]

ROLAND-MANUEL. *L'Ecran des Jeunes filles.* Paris: Heugel, 1929. [413]

ROLAND-MANUEL. *Le Tournoi singulier.* Paris: Heugel, 1924. [414]

ROSSINI, Gioacchino. *Der Barbier von Sevilla: ouverture.* Vienna: Wiener Philharmonischer, n.d. [921]

ROSSINI, Gioacchino. *Il barbiere di Siviglia.* Milan: Lucca, n.d. [1085]

SADERO, Geni. *Amuri, Amuri.* Milan: Societa degli autore Italiani, 1923. [958]

SADERO, Geni. *Come quando tira vento.* Milan: Societa degli autore Italiani, 1923. [966]

SADERO, Geni. *Curi Curuzzu.* Milan: Societa degli autore Italiani, 1923. [960]

SADERO, Geni. *Serenata siciliana.* New York: Schirmer, 1925. [883]

SADERO, Geni. *Stornellata Romanesca.* New York: Schirmer, 1925. [886]

SAINT-SAËNS, C. *2ª Symphonie en la mineur Op. 55.* Paris: Durand, n.d. [1090]

SAINT-SAËNS, C. *Etienne Marcel "Valse."* Paris: Durand & Schoenewerk, n.d. [456]

SAINT-SAËNS, C. *Le Rouet d'Omphale Op. 31.* Paris: Durand, n.d. [1091]

SAINT-SAËNS, C. *Samson et Dalila.* Paris: Durand, n.d. [1094]

SCARLATTI, Domenico. *48 nouvelles sonates.* Paris: Ricordi, n.d. [1028]

SCARLATTI, Domenico. *Allemande en Ut#, Sonate No 45*. Paris: Maurice Senart, n.d. [904]
SCARLATTI, Domenico. *Opere complete per clavicembalo*. 10 vols. Milan: Ricordi, n.d. [1029]
SCARLATTI, Domenico. *Sonate per pianoforte I–IX*. Milan: Instituto Editorale Italiano, 1919. [946]
SCARLATTI, Domenico. *Sonaten für pianoforte*. Leipzig: Peters, n.d. [902]
SCARLATTI, Domenico.*Veinticinco sonatas para clave*. Buenos Aires: Ricordi, 1940. [1027]
SCHINDLER, Kurt, ed. *The Birds Praise the Advent of the Saviour*. Boston: Oliver Ditson, 1918. [524]
SCHMITT, Florent. *Demande (Sur le lac du Bourget) Op.20*. Paris: Hamelle, n.d. [424]
SCHUBERT, Franz. *Lieder Gesänge u. Balladen*. Braunschweig: Henry Litolff, n.d. [1071]
SCHUBERT, Franz. *Symphonie VIII H-moll Unvollendete*. Vienna: Wiener Philharmonischer, n.d. [634]
SCHUBERT, Franz. *Trios Opus 99 und 100*. Leipzig: Peters, n.d. [635]
SCHUMANN, R. *Pianoforte-werke. Band II*. Leipzig: Peters, n.d. [542]
STRAUSS, Richard. *Don Juan. Op. 20*. Munich: Jos. Aibl., 1904. [580]
STRAVINSKY, Igor. *Cinq pièces faciles*. Geneva: Ad. Henn, 1917. [774]
STRAVINSKY, Igor. *Concerto (Pour piano suivi d'orchestre d'harmonie)*. Berlin: Edition Russe de Musique, 1924. [1185]
STRAVINSKY, Igor. *Jeu de cartes*. Mainz: Schott's Söhne, 1937. [769]
STRAVINSKY, Igor. *L'Oiseau de feu*. London: Chester, 1920. [770]
STRAVINSKY, Igor. *Le sacre du printemps*. Berlin: Edition Russe de Musique, 1913. [1183]
STRAVINSKY, Igor. *Le sacre du printemps*. Berlin: Russischer Musik, 1921. [1560]
STRAVINSKY, Igor. *Les Noces*. London: Chester, 1922. [1560]
STRAVINSKY, Igor. *Octuor pour instruments à vent*. Berlin: Edition Russe de Musique, 1924. [771]
STRAVINSKY, Igor. *Oedipus Rex*. Berlin: Edition Russe de Musique, 1927. [772]
STRAVINSKY, Igor. *Rossignol*. Berlin: Edition Russe de Musique, 1914. [1184]
STRAVINSKY, Igor. *Suite de l'histoire du soldat*. London: Chester, 1920. [764]

STRAVINSKY, Igor. *Suite de Pulcinella*. Berlin: Edition Russe de Musique, 1924. [778]

STRAVINSKY, Igor. *Trois pièces pour quatuor à cordes*. Berlin: Russischer Musik, 1921. [1560]

TCHAIKOVSKY, P. *Concerto for the pianoforte Op. 23*. London: Donajowsky, n.d. [787]

TORCHI, Luigi. *L'Arte musicale in Italia. Secolo XVII*. Milan: Ricordi, n.d. [1012]

TURINA, Joaquín. *Quatuor*. Paris: Demets, 1912. [111]

TURINA, Joaquín. *Sevilla: Suite pittoresque pour piano*. Paris: E. Demets, 1909. [112]

VERDI, Giuseppe. *Falstaff*. Milan: Ricordi, 1893. [1095]

VERDI, Giuseppe. *Il Trovatore*. Leon Escudier, n.d. [1099]

WAGNER, Richard. *Das Liebesmahl der Apostel*. Leipzig: Breitkopf & Härtel, 1892. [553]

WAGNER, Richard. *Die Meistersinger von Nürnberg*. Mainz: Schott's Söhne, n.d. [1105]

WAGNER, Richard. *Die Meistersinger von Nürnberg: Vorspiel*. n.p.: n.p., n.d. [1119]

WAGNER, Richard. *Eine Faust-Overture*. Leipzig: Eulenburg, n.d. [551]

WAGNER, Richard. *Il Vascello Fantasma*. Milan: Lucca, n.d. [1108]

WAGNER, Richard. *L'Or du Rhin*. New York: Breitkopf & Härtel, 1914. [1109]

WAGNER, Richard. *Les Maîtres Chanteurs de Nuremberg*. Paris: Schott, n.d. [1104]

WAGNER, Richard. *Lohengrin*. Milan: Barion, 1927. [1117]

WAGNER, Richard. *Parsifal*. Leipzig: Breitkopf & Härtel, n.d. [1103]

WAGNER, Richard. *Parsifal*. Leipzig: Eulenburg, n.d. [548]

WAGNER, Richard. *Tannhäuser: Bacchanale*. Leipzig: Eulenburg, n.d. [556]

WAGNER, Richard. *Tannhäuser: Oberture*. London: Donajowski, n.d. [555]

WEBER, C.M. von. *Der Freischütz*. Leipzig; Peters, n.d. [1121]

WHITTAKER, W.G. *The Keel Row*. London: Curwen, 1918. [666]

APPENDIX 2   Treatises and Other Theoretical Writings

AGUSTÍN FLORENCIO, Francisco. *Crotalogía o ciencia de las castañuelas*. Valencia: Salvador Faulí, 1792. [1237]

BEKKER, Paul. *La musique*. Paris: Payot, 1929. [1424]

CERONE DE BERGAMO, R.D. Pedro. *De la Musica theorica y prac-tica . . . Libro onzeno.* n.p.: n.p., n.d. [1200]

D'INDY, Vincent. *Cours de composition musicale: premier livre.* Paris: Durand, 1902.

GEVAERT, F. A. *Cours méthodique d'orchestration.* Paris: Lemoine, n.d. [1239]

GEVAERT, F. A. *Nouveau traité d'instrumentation.* Paris: Lemoine, 1885. [1238]

GEVAERT, F. A. *La mélopée antique dans le chant de l'Eglise latine.* Gand: Librairie Générale de Ad. Hoste, 1895. [1447]

HULL, A. EAGLEFIELD. *La harmonía moderna.* Madrid: J. Fernández Arias, n.d. [1215]

JADASSOHN, S. *Les formes musicales dans les chefs d'oeuvre de l'art.* Leipzig: Breitkopf & Härtel, 1900. [1259]

KOECHLIN, Charles. *Étude sur l'écriture de la figure d'école.* Paris: Max Eschig, 1933. [1208]

KOECHLIN, Charles. *Étude sur le choral d'école.* Paris: Heugel, 1929. [1211]

KOECHLIN, Charles. *Étude sur les notes de passage.* Paris: Le monde musical, 1922. [1212]

KOECHLIN, Charles. *Précis des règles du Contrepoint.* Paris: Heugel, 1926. [1209]

KOECRERT, G. *Les principes rationnels de la technique du violon.* Leipzig: Breitkopf & Härtel, 1904. [1259]

KREHL, Stephan. *Fuga.* Barcelona: Labor, 1930. [4137]

KREHL, Stephan. *Contrapunto.* Barcelona: Labor, 1930. [4138]

LEMOINE, Enrique and GARULLI, G. *Solfeo de los solfeos, 4° cuaderno.* Paris: Henry Lemoine, n.d. [1354]

LENORDMAND, René. *Étude sur l'harmonie moderne.* Paris: Monde Musical, 1913. [1218]

LOBE, J. C. *Traité practique de composition musicale.* Leipzig: Breitkopf & Härtel, 1897. [1220]

LUCAS, Louis. *L'acoustique nouvelle.* Paris: n.p., 1854. [11502]

RAMEAU, Jean-Philippe. *Elementos de música, theorica y practica por los principios de Mr. Rameau.* ms. [1203]

RICHTER, Frederich E. *Traité complet de contrepoint.* Leipzig: Breitkopf & Härtel, 1892. [1219]

RICHTER, Frederich E. *Tratado de armonía.* Barcelona: Juan B. Pujol, 1892. [1216]

RIEMANN, Hugo. *Composición Musical*. Barcelona: Labor, 1929. [2782, 4135]

RIEMANN, Hugo. *Manual del organista*. Barcelona: Labor, 1928. [4134]

RIMSKY-KORSAKOV, Nikolay. *Principes d'orchestration*. Berlin: Edition Russe de Musique, 1914. [1241]

RIMSKY-KORSAKOV, Nikolay. *Principes d'orchestration*. Berlin: Edition Russe de Musique, 1914. [1242]

RIMSKY-KORSAKOV, Nikolay. *Traité d'harmonie théorique et pratique*. Paris: Leduc, 1910. [1213]

SCHUMANN, Robert. *El arte del piano: Consejos dedicados a la juventud*. Barcelona: Rafael Guardia, n.d. [1359]

SCHERCHEN, Hermann. *El arte de dirigir la orquesta*. Barcelona: Labor, S.A., 1933. [1244]

STRAUSS, Richard. *Le Traité d'orchestration d'Hector Berlioz*. Leipzig: Peters, 1909. [1243]

SUÑOL, Gregorio, OSB. *Méthode complète de chant grégorien*. Paris: Société Saint Jean l'Evangeliste, 1927. [1260]

SUÑOL, Gregorio, OSB. *Método completo para tres cursos de canto gregoriano, según la escuela de Solesmes*. Tournai: Sociedad de San Juan Evangelista, n.d. [1258]

WIDOR, Charles-Marie. *Technique de l'Orchestre moderne*. Paris: Henry Lemoine, 1904. [1240]

ZAMACOIS SOLER, Joaquín. *Teoría perteneciente a la asignatura: Teoría-solfeo. . . . Curso 6º*. Barcelona: Conservatorio del Liceo Barcelonés, n.d. [1352]

APPENDIX 3   Monographs on Music

ANGLÉS, Higinio. *La música a Catalunya fins al segle XIII*. Barcelona: Institut D'Estudis Catalans, 1935. [1479]

ANON. *Escritos heortásticos: al maestro Pedrell*. Tortosa: Casa Social del "Orfeó Tortesí," 1911. [1480]

AYESTARÁN, Lauro. *Domenico Zipoli*. Montevideo: Impresora Urugualla S.A., 1941. [1277]

BECK, Jean. *La musique des troubadours*. Paris: Henri Laurens, n.d. [1378]

BEKKER, Paul. *La musique*. Paris: Payot, 1929. [1424]

BELLAIGUE, Camille. *Psychologie musicale*. Paris; Ch. Delagrave, 1893. [1413]

BELLAIGUE, Camille. *Verdi*. Paris: Henri Laurens, 1927. [1380]

BONNIER, Pierre. *La voix: Sa culture physiologique*. Paris: Felix Alcan, 1910. [1255]

CASELLA, Alfredo. *21 + 26*. Rome: Augustea, 1931. [1397]

CHASE, Gilbert. *La música en España*. Buenos Aires: Hachette S. A., 1943. [1408]

COLLET, Henri. *Albéniz et Granados*. Paris: Felix Alcan, 1926. [1386]

COLLET, Henri. *Le mysticisme musical espagnol au XVI siècle*. Paris: Librairie Felix Alcan, 1913. [1469]

CONSTANTIN, Léon. *Berlioz*. Paris: Émile-Paul Frères, 1934. [1524]

DEBUSSY, Claude. *Monsieur Croche, Antidilettante*. Paris: Editions de la nouvelle revue française, 1927. [1552]

DESTRANGES, Etienne. *L'évolution musicale chez Verdi*. Paris: Fischbacher, 1895. [1536]

DUNSTAN, Ralph. *A Cyclopaedic Dictionary of Music*. London, 1919. [2657]

ERNST, Alfred. *Richard Wagner et le drame contemporain*. Paris: Librairie moderne, 1887. [1544]

FARINELLI, Arturo. *Beethoven e Schubert*. Turin: Paravia, 1929. [1529]

GARCÍA MORILLO, Roberto. *Rimsky-Korsakov*. Buenos Aires: Ricordi Americana, 1945. [1391]

GASTOUÉ, Amédée. *La vie musicale de l'Eglise*. n.p.: Librairie Bloud et Gay, 1929. [1445]

GATARD, Agustin. *La Musique Grégorienne*. Paris: Henri Laurens, 1913. [1382]

GAUTHIER-VILLARS, Henry. *Bizet*. Paris: Henri Laurens, 1928. [1383]

GHÉON, Henri. *Promenades avec Mozart*. Paris, 1932. [3343]

GIANI, Romualdo. *Gli spiriti della musica nella tragedia greca*. Milan: Bottega di poesia, 1924. [1461]

HARCOURT, Raoul d' and HARCOURT, M. d'. *La musique des Incas, et ses survivances*. Paris: Librairie orientaliste Paul Geuthner, 1925. [1500]

HURÉ, Jean. *Saint Augustin: musicien*. Paris: Maurice Senart, 1924. [1441]

JEAN-AUBRY, Georges. *La musique française d'aujourd'hui*. Paris: Perrin, 1916. [1453]

LACHMANN, Robert. *Música de Oriente*. Barcelona: Labor, 1931. [4141/2]

LALO, Pierre. *La Musique, 1898–1899*. Paris: Rouart Lerolle, [1899]. [1420]

LALOY, Louis. *La musique chinoise.* Paris: Henri Laurens, n.d. [1379]
LANDOWSKA, Wanda. *Musique ancienne.* Paris: Maurice Senart, 1921. [1459]
LLONGUERES, Joan. *Els cants de la Passió.* Barcelona, 1928. [2742]
LLONGUERES, Joan. *Les cançons de Nadal.* Barcelona, 1917. [2740]
MAUCLAIR, Camille. *La religion de la musique.* Paris, 1928. [1421]
MOYANO LÓPEZ, Rafael. *La cultura musical cordobesa.* Córdoba: Imprenta de la Universidad, 1941. [1498]
PAHLEN, Kurt. *Historia gráfica universal de la música.* Buenos Aires: Centurión, 1944. [1273]
PEDRELL, Felipe. *Organografía antigua española.* Barcelona: Juan Gili, 1901. [1488]
PEDRELL, Felipe. *Por nuestra música.* Barcelona: Imprenta de Henrich y Cía., 1891. [1491]
POURTALES, Guy de. *La vie de Franz Liszt.* Paris, 1928. [3724]
POURTALES, Guy de. *Wagner: Historia de un artista.* Buenos Aires: Losada S. A., n.d. [1541]
PRUNIÈRES, Henri. *La musique du Moyen-Age.* Paris: Les Editions Rieder, 1934. [1435]
PRUNIÈRES, Henri. *La vie ilustre et libertine de Jean-Baptiste Lully.* Paris: Plon, 1929. [1547]
PRUNIÈRES, Henri. *Monteverdi.* Paris: Felix Alcan, 1924. [1389]
REINACH, Théodore. *La musique grecque.* Paris: Payot, 1926. [1454]
ROLAND-MANUEL. *Manuel de Falla.* Buenos Aires: Losada, 1945. [977]
SACHS, Curt. *La música en la antigüedad.* Barcelona: Labor, 1927. [4122]
SAKHAROFF, A. *Réflexions sur la danse et la musique.* Buenos Aires: Viau, 1943. [1370]
SALAZAR, Adolfo. *Sinfonía y ballet. Idea y gesto en la música contemporánea.* Madrid: Mundo Latino, 1929. [1407]
SCHAEFFNER, André. *Strawinsky.* Paris: Rieder, 1931. [1551]
SCHIANCA, Arturo C. *Historia de la música argentina.* Buenos Aires: Establecimiento Gráfico Argentino, [1935?]. [1496]
SCHWERKE, Irving. *Kings Jazz and David.* Paris: n.p., 1927. [1462]
STOECKLIN, Paul de. *Grieg.* Paris: Felix Alcan, 1926. [1387]
TREND, J. B. *Manuel de Falla and Spanish Music.* New York: Alfred A. Knopf, 1929. [1401]
TURINA, Joaquín. *Enciclopedia abreviada de música.* 2 vols. Madrid: Renacimiento, 1917. [3745]

TYNDALL, John. *Le son*. Paris, Gauthier-Villars, 1869. [1249]
VOLBACH, Fritz. *La orquesta moderna*. Barcelona: Labor, 1928. [4127]
WELLESZ, Egon. *Música bizantina*. Barcelona: Labor, 1930. [4139]

NOTES

1. My initial survey of Manuel de Falla's library was undertaken in 1989 and extended in 1991 with the help of a grant for Hispanicists of Spain's Ministry of Foreign Affairs. Further work on this collection, the classification of the Falla's annotations and a study of their impact on his creative process has been made possible through the financial assistance of the Archivo Manuel de Falla [AMF] and a grant from the Australian Research Council.

2. Until recently, studies have largely ignored Falla's library. For an overview of the literature that refers to this source see Michael Christoforidis, "A Composer's Annotations to his Personal Library: An Introduction to the Manuel de Falla Collection," *Context* 17, 1999, 33–68.

3. Claude Debussy's library was auctioned after his death and some of Igor Stravinsky's pre-1939 collection was lost, although a large proportion of Maurice Ravel's personal library remains intact. Of Falla's immediate Spanish contemporaries, the Joaquín Turina Archive preserves the bulk of that composer's literary monographs and musical treatises, although most of the scores are missing, and some of Conrado del Campo's library ended up in lending libraries at public institutions. Prior to the establishment of the Archivo Manuel de Falla there had been a proposal to incorporate Falla's scores and books on music as part of the general collection of the Catedra Manuel de Falla of the University of Granada.

4. Some of the books also contain drafts of Falla's correspondence and assorted papers, including visiting cards, newspaper cuttings, and other items such as entrance tickets to the Alhambra used as bookmarks. Copies of these documents have been made by the AMF to help with cross-referencing.

5. At present there are plans to produce a complete listing of all this material, which will be issued over several years in a series of catalogues to be published jointly by the Archivo Manuel de Falla and the Universidad de Granada, and edited by Yvan Nommick and Antonio Ruiz. Among the more complete sets of journals and magazines kept by Falla were *Les Beaux Arts* (1935–1937), *Cahiers d'Art* (1926–1933), *The Chesterian* (1919–1939), *Le courrier musical* (1907–1909, 1919–1936), *Cruz y Raya* (1933–1936), *La guide du concert* (1910–1911, 1930–1934), *The League of Composers Review/Modern Music* (1924–1940), *Lyrica* (1923–1939), *Litoral* (1926–1929), *Le monde artiste* (1911–1914), *Le monde musical* (1909–1914, 1919–1939), *Musicalia* (1928–1932), *Musique* (1927–1930), *Pro-Música* (1925–1929), *Revista musical catalana* (1914–1915, 1925–1936), *Revista musical hispanoamericana*

(1915–1917), *La Revue Musicale* (1920–1940), *La semaine musicale* (1920–1926), and *S.I.M.* (1909–1914). While some of these journals were annotated by Falla, many of the markings found in this collection are in a later hand (at times employing ballpoint pen).

6. This was normally included on one of the last pages or the back cover of the volume, although it can be located elsewhere and even on loose pages placed within the volume. On occasion he even marked the index to the contents of the volume. For a listing of the books not related to music which are indexed by Falla in this fashion see Christoforidis, "A Composer's Annotations to His Personal Library," 57–68.

7. "Hazle cada día más 'local,' para ser cada día más universal," José María de Cossío, *La obra literaria de Pereda,* Santander: J. Martínez, 1934, 218 [3135]. Numbers in square brackets refer to AMF inventory numbers.

8. "Esta resida en la profundidad humana de conflictos y caracteres, sean de la casta que quieran, y por dicha Pereda supo encontrar esa precisa profundidad en tipos rurales, y no supieron encontrarle muchos en los ambientes más cosmopolitas." Cossío, *La obra literaria* 405. Falla's annotated index which refers to this passage indicates: "p.405/Universalidad."

9. "No puede amar a su nación quien no ama su pais nativo y comenzar por afirmar este amor como base para un patriotismo más amplio. El regionalismo egoísta es odioso y estéril, pero el regionalismo benévolo y fraternal puede ser un gran elemento de progreso y quizá la única salvación de España." Alvaro de las Casas, *Horas de España,* Buenos Aires: Rueda, 1940, 134 [2060]. Falla's annotated index which refers to this passage indicates: "134/Regionalismo (Mz-Pelayo)."

10. Falla actually copied the complete text to Paul Drouot's *Promenade sur l'Alhambre* in one of his notebooks.

11. Many of the sources which inspired Falla in this work are outlined by Yvan Nommick in "*Noches en los Jardines de España*: Génesis y composición de una obra," *Jardines de España: de Santiago Rusiñol a Manuel de Falla,* Granada: Archivo Manuel de Falla, 1996, 5–25.

12. Jaime Pahissa, *Vida y obra de Manuel de Falla*, 2nd ed, Buenos Aires: Ricordi, 1956, 119. Some sketch material among the unclassified sketches for the *Homenaje* seems to relate to this project. See Michael Christoforidis, "La guitarra en la obra de Manuel de Falla," *La guitarra en la historia* 9, Córdoba: Ayuntamiento, 1998, 29–57.

13. "La dueña de la casa parecía complacerse en sostener equilibrio perfecto entre el elemento apostólico y el reformista, pues ambos tenían algún corifeo en sus tertulias. Pero no todo era política. Casi, casi las tres cuartas partes del tiempo se invertían en leer versos y hablar de comedias, y la música no ocupaba el último lugar. Después que algún aficionado tocaba a clave una sonatina de Haydn ó gorjeaba un aria de la *Zelmira* cualquier italiano de la compañía de ópera, solía el ama de la casa tomar la guitarra, y entonces. . . . No hay otra

manera de expresar la gracia de su persona y de su canto sino diciendo que era
la misma Euterpe bajada del Parnaso para proclamar el descrédito del plectro y
hacer de nuestro grave instrumento nacional la verdadera lira de los dioses."
Benito Pérez Galdós, *Los apostólicos,* Madrid, Sucesores de Hernando, 1917,
[3188].

14. For a listing of the volumes marked in this fashion see Christoforidis, "A
Composer's Annotations to His Personal Library" 38.

15. See Yvan Nommick, '*El sombrero de tres picos* de Manuel de Falla: una
visión a partir de los documentos de su archivo', concert program Teatro Real
Madrid (11 October 1997), 42–57.

16. Serafín y Joaquín Alvarez Quintero, *Las flores,* Madrid: Sociedad de Autores Españoles, 1906; Pedro Calderón de la Barca, *Comedias*, ed. J. E. Hatzen-
busch, Madrid: Hernando, 1925, and *Autos sacramentales I,* Madrid, 1926.

17. "declaman lentamente y marcando los acentos" (p. 79), "música vocal,
sin texto" (p. 98), "sobre cantos lejanos de victoria" (p. 131), Calderón de la
Barca, *Autos sacramentales I.*

18. "estrepitoso son de clarines y trompetas bárbaras," "triste música y canción," Calderón de la Barca, *Comedias*, 38.

19. See especially Falla's extensive annotations to Curt Sachs, *La música en
la antigüedad,* Barcelona: Labor, 1927, Théodore Reinach, *La musique grecque,*
Paris: Collection Payot, 1926, Romualdo Gianni, *Gli spiriti della musica nella
tragedia greca,* Milano: Bottega di poesia 1924, and Christián Grachede, *El
Teatro desde la antigüedad hasta el presente,* Barcelona: Labor, 1930.

20. A reproduction and transcription of this page is presented in Christoforidis, "A Composer's Annotations," 40–41.

21. Andrew Budwig claims that much of 1930 was devoted to the study of
Greek music and denotes it as Falla's "Greek" year. See Andrew Budwig,
"Manuel de Falla's *Atlántida*: An Historical and Analytical Study," Ph.D. dis-
sertation, University of Chicago, 1984, 143–145.

22. The series *Collection Yafil,* Algiers: MNE Yafil, n.d., A. Chottin, *Airs populaires recueillis a Fès*, *Hespéris: Archives Berbères* (1924, 2nd term) Paris:
Émile Larose, 1924.

23. For a more extended discussion of the sources employed by Falla in this
essay see Michael Christoforidis, "Un acercamiento a la postura de Manuel de
Falla en *El "Cante Jondo" (canto primitivo andaluz)*," in Manuel de Falla, *El
"Cante Jondo" (canto primitivo andaluz)*, facsimile edition, Granada: Ayun-
tamiento, Archivo Manuel de Falla, Imprenta Urania, 1997, and Jorge de Persia,
I Concurso de Cante Jondo, Granada: Archivo Manuel de Falla, 1992.

24. Direct evidence for Falla's reliance on Debussy's *La Mer* and *Ibéria* for
the orchestration of his homage to Debussy in the second movement of *Homenajes, Suite* can be found in his annotations to the piano score of the *Homenaje,*
among sketch material LVII B2, AMF. For further information on the influence
of Debussy's orchestration see Michael Christoforidis, "Manuel de Falla, De-

bussy and *La vida breve*," *Musicology Australia* 18, 1995, 3–12, "De *La vida breve* a *Atlántida*: algunos aspectos del magisterio de Claude Debussy sobre Manuel de Falla," *Cuadernos de la música iberoamericana* 4, 1997, 15–32, and Yvan Nommick "*La vida breve* entre 1905 y 1914: evolución formal y orquestal," *Manuel de Falla:* La vida breve, Granada: Archivo Manuel de Falla, 1997, 9–118.

25. This work is currently being published by Ediciones Manuel de Falla (Madrid), based on the full score of the arrangement which was found in the archive of the Orquesta Bética de Cámara.

26. See letter from Falla to Valentín Ruiz Aznar, 24 June 1940; AMF.

27. Michael Christoforidis, "El peso de la vanguardia en el proceso creativo del *Concerto* de Manuel de Falla," *Revista de musicología* 20, 1997, 677–90.

28. Inmaculada Quintanal Sánchez, *Manuel de Falla y Asturias* (Oviedo: Instituto de Estudios Asturianos, 1989).

29. José Hurtado, *100 cantos populares asturianos,* Bilbao, 1890, [985] AMF.

30. Falla does not seem to have developed these harmonizations further or to have incorporated the melody into a work.

31. See Christoforidis, "De *La vida breve* a *Atlántida*."

32. For a listing of the books not related to music the that contain musical sketches see Christoforidis, "A Composer's Annotations," 54.

33. Lord Byron, *Poesies*, Benjamin Laroche, tr., Paris: Louis Michaud, n.d., [2448].

34. See late sketch of the *Concerto* in Alfonso Danvila, *Almansa.* Madrid, 1926, [2291].

35. Items which obviously contain markings only by persons other than Falla have been omitted from the list, as have books which only contain dedications to Falla (even if they include an acknowledgment of receipt/reply by Falla). For the purposes of this list all volumes which contain notes which are not related to the book/score in question (for example, jottings which list addresses, shopping lists, and the like) have also been omitted. The numbers indicated in square brackets correspond to the inventory numbers of the Archivo Manuel de Falla. The inventory numbers and information in this article were last checked by this author at the AMF in 1997. The computer catalogue of Falla's personal library at AMF was prepared by their archivist Concha Chinchilla.

36. To this end useful information can be gained from book catalogues, dedications, bookshop stamps, and cross-referencing with other titles, as well as information derived from reading lists, correspondence, and sketch material for the compositions and essays. Falla's changing style of writing and his use of different types of pencils can also serve as rough indicators of when the volumes were consulted. For example, the annotations in pink pencil date mainly from the 1930s and 1940s. The present author has already undertaken substantial work on dating Falla's acquisition and annotation of the most consulted volumes in the collection.

Part III

WORKS[1]

Chapter 16

Youthful Period (1896–1904)

INTRODUCTION

Falla's creative, compositional process in his adult years was often painfully slow. Consciously, each new work became a new beginning. As María Martínez Sierra commented, Falla was incapable of writing the necessary waltz or salon piece for the young girls to play, in order to earn a much-needed wage. He was always faithful to his inspirational Muse. As such, Falla has been criticized for producing a small output. On the other hand, if Beethoven had relegated himself to the same procedural challenge in each of his piano sonatas as Falla did in general, posterity would have been left perhaps with only three sonatas. Put in this perspective, the importance of Falla's landmark works such as *El sombrero de tres picos, Noches en los jardines de Espãna, Siete canciones populares españolas, El amor brujo, Fantasía bœtica, El retablo de Maese Pedro, Concerto*, and *Atlántida* take on a different dimension. As Jean-Michel Nectoux has said, there are "few examples in the history of music of an evolution as radical as that which Manuel de Falla guides from "La Vie brève" to the "Concerto for harpsichord."[2]

This evolution, described by Yvan Nommick, may be partially seen through the various musical styles, languages, and idioms he traversed.

In effect, in thirty years Falla passed from neo-Romantic music influenced by Bellini opera, Chopin, Schumann, and Grieg, to the amalgam of modernity, from popular music and polyphonic techniques; and from the golden age that impregnated to the most beautiful pages of *Atlántida*.

During that span, he absorbed the multiple aesthetics, materials, and techniques, such as Romanticism, the *zarzuela*, Italian *verismo*, Wagnerian procedures, the noise and chants of the forge, the cries of the ambulant merchants, folklore from the different Spanish regions, Impressionism, "cante jondo," Russian folklore, neo-classicism, pre-Baroque, *Cancionero Musical* of Palacio, *De Música libri septem* of Salinas, the Cantigas of Santa Maria of Alfonso X the Wise, Mozarbe liturgy, the "Llibre Vermell," polyphony of the golden age, Medieval "organum," and the melodies of Ancient Greece.[3]

Other indications of Falla's working processes may be found in the literary works of his vast personal library. This subject has been treated more in depth in chapter 15.

Through the study of the creative processes and analysis of several works, Yvan Nommick has categorized the stages of Falla's systematic compositional process accordingly: (1) birth of the idea of a work from an exterior stimulus; (2) cumulative research followed by selection of the musical material to be used; (3) first sketches; (4) a long series of drafts present in varying degrees of elaboration; (5) outline of a provisional manuscript of which numerous variations will follow where the author transforms, corrects, enriches, purifies, adds, and retracts; and (6) striving towards a definitive manuscript that several times will be modified through the corrections of the proofs.[4]

Falla's search for the essence of an aesthetic ideal required ardous work in order to distill and then express its simplicity. Falla's colleague and collaborator, Amadeu Vives, summed it up: "There is in your works a brilliant sense of perfection of the [musical] form that is, to my understanding, the essence itself of artistic beauty."[5]

Youthful Period (1896–1904)
El conde de Villamediana
Gavotte et Musette
Nocturno
Melodia para violonchelo y piano
Scherzo (en do menor)
Romanza para violonchelo y piano
(Pieza para violonchelo y piano en do mayor)
Cuarteto en sol
Mireya (chamber version; piano transcription)
Mazurca en do menor
Serenata andaluza (violin and piano; piano transcription)

Canción
Vals capricho
Preludios ("Madre, todas las noches")
La Juana y la Petra, o La casa de Tócame Roque
Pasacalle torero
Rima ("Ola gigantes")
¡Dios mío, qué solos se quedan los muertos!
Cortejo de gnomos
Serenata
Segunda serenata andaluza
Suite fantástica
[Pieza para piano en mi mayor]
Los amores de la Inés
Limosna de amor
Tus ojillos negros, Canción andaluza
Allegro de concierto
(Movimiento para cuarteto de cuerda)
El cornetín de ordenes
La cruz de Malta
Prisionero de guerra
Cantares de Nochebuena

The compositions of Falla's youth are somewhat inspired by a spirit of discovery through his musical environment, such as the chamber concerts in Cádiz at the Viniegra home and Salón Quirell, or by the cultural life in the Spanish capital and the Conservatory of Madrid, including his studies with Pedrell and Tragó. From the dubious four-act opera *El conde de Villamediana* to the several *zarzuelas* written for commercial purposes, Falla's output show a growing maturity. A few works received some initial success either at home or abroad, especially the song *Tus ojillos negros,* the piano work *Allegro de concierto*, and the *zarzuela Los amores de la Inés.*

Falla's predilection for dramatic or scenic works may be seen not only in the idea of *El conde de Villamediana* but through his *zarzuelas.* Program music is also attempted, for example in *Mireya* or the lost *Suite fantástica.* Chamber music is mostly directed towards performance in the intimate Viniegra-Quirell settings. Of these works, pieces for cello and piano dominate—*Melodía para violonchelo y piano, Romanza para violoncelo y piano, [Pieza para violonchelo y piano en do mayor]*—and show the inexperienced composer's preoccupation with melody. Other string writing is found in the excerpt from the *Cuarteto en sol* (G major String Quartet), the lost *Serenata andaluza* for violin and piano, and the chamber work *Mireya* for flute, string trio, and piano.

Falla's later propensity for transcribing his own works is seen early on in the piano transcription of *Mireya* and *Serenata andaluza*. The solo piano pieces—*Gavotte et Musette, Nocturno, Scherzo (en do mayor), Mazurca en do menor, Canción, Pasacalle torero, Cortejo de gnomos, Serenata, Segunda serenata andaluza, Suite fantástica, [Pieza para piano en mi mayor]*, and *Allegro de concierto*, not all of which are complete or have been found—reveal a growing technical command and maturity with strong Romantic tendencies such as those found in salon pieces of the day or by Chopin, amongst other composers. Manuel's vocal compositions, excluding the *zarzuelas*, include *Preludios, Rima,¡Dios mío, qué solos se quedan los muertos!, Tus ojillos negros,* and *Cantares de Nochebuena*. The last work is written for soprano with accompaniment of guitar and percussion. It is based on folksongs from various published folksong books. The other songs are written for voice and piano on texts by Antonio de Trueba, G. Adolfo Bécquer, and Cristóbal de Castro. Of all the *zarzuelas*, only one was staged, *Los amores de la Inés*. This must have been a disappointment to Falla, as his main objective in composing them was to raise money to go to Paris and to help with the support of his family. *El cornetín de órdenes, La cruz de Malta,* and *Prisionero de guerra*, while the librettist is unknown, had the musical assistance of his colleague and neighbor, Amadeu Vives. *La Juana y la Petra, o La casa de Tócame Roque, Los amores de la Inés,* and *Limosna de amor* are of the small form, with one act, on librettos by Javier Santero, Emilio Dugi, and José Jackson Veyán, respectively.

I. *El conde de Villamediana*

While there is doubt as to whether the work actually existed or not, or was perhaps just a figment of the young Falla's overactive imagination, biographers Jaime Pahissa and Roland-Manuel agree that this youthful work was conceived for Manuel's invented theater in the imaginary city of Colón at his home in Cádiz. Its origins are estimated to be from around 1891. It is possible that the work could have been destroyed by the composer due to his reluctance to reveal the very early works.

Supposedly a serious opera in four acts, *El conde de Villamediana* is based on a ballad by Duque de Rivas (Duke of Rivas). No manuscript has been found.

However, examples of some text do exist in the Archivo Manuel de Falla. From the complete works of the Duke of Rivas (*Obras completas,*

Barcelona, 1884), Falla included two sonnets in his journal *El Cascabel*, year two, nos. 14 and 17, 1891.

II. GAVOTTE ET MUSETTE

The manuscript for this solo piano piece has not been found, although biographer Pahissa alludes to it. Antonio Gallego speculates that it dates from around 1892.

Both titles of "Gavotte" and "March" appear amongst the sketch material housed for *Cortejo de gnomos* (1901). The short imitative work in the style of Bach was written after observing from a piece published in a musical supplement of a Paris fashion magazine to which his mother subscribed. It was written in secret by the young Manuel and hidden amongst his things in fear of being found. Because only one work exists, not two, the correct title might instead be "Gavotte or Musette."

III. NOCTURNO

Manuel's affinity for Chopin is reflected in this piano piece, as might be surmised from the title. His studies with José Tragó in Madrid, a pupil of George Mathias, himself a pupil of Chopin, left a deep impression on young Manuel. Other Chopinesque evidence is found in later works, such as *Allegro de concierto, Fuego fatuo*, and *Balada a Mallorca*.

In a letter to G. Jean-Aubry dated 3 September 1910, Paris, Falla says he composed the piece "when I was 17 to 20 years old . . . when I was still a child." However, the more mature style of this work coupled with the fact that the première was not given until 1899 leave room for a possible later date of composition, as speculated by Antonio Gallego to be between 1896–1899. First performed by the composer on 16 August 1899, at Salón Quirell in Cádiz, other performances were given by him on 10 September 1899, at the Teatro Cómico in Cádiz and on 6 May 1900, at the Ateneo in Madrid.

Written in f minor in a rondolike form, Falla uses the descending "Spanish" or phygrian cadence for the opening melody, and continues to hispanisize the melody in its ending ornamental motif. Even the harmonic devices of Neopolitan and German augmented sixth chords are used to reflect the Spanish predilection for half-tone cadences. It may be seen as an A-B-A form.

Although the autograph of this piano work has not been found, it has been again republished from the 1903 Sociedad de Autores Españoles (SAE) edition by Manuel de Falla Ediciones, S. L.-Unión Musical Ediciones, S. L., and by Chester for the Falla 1996 anniversary celebrations.

From Falla's notebook "Apuntes de harmonia" ("Harmonic annotations," p. 98) housed at the AMF, two copies were sold in 1903, giving his royalties of 0.88 pesetas. It popularity gained when in 1904 it sold ten copies at a profit of 4.18 pesetas and in 1905 sixteen copies sold for a profit of 6.99 pesetas. By 1906 its popularity had declined and its price had increased to 2 pesetas per copy, with it profitable yield being only 2 pesetas.[6]

IV. *Melodia para Violonchelo y Piano*

This short, four-minute work for cello and piano is dated 19 June 1897. The work is dedicated to "my dear and respectable friend Don Salvador Viniegra" and was written for one of the Viniegra family musical soirées, at Plaza de la Candelaria, no. 4, in Cádiz, a salon which also received other musical notables such as the violin virtuoso Sarasate and bass player Botessini. Salvador Viniegra gave the première with the composer at the piano on 16 August 1899. The 118-measure manuscript is owned by the Javier Martín Artajo family. The piece is an A-B-A form.

Many years later, in a letter dated 19 March 1926, to Viniegra, Falla fondly remembers having played this piece as well as the Grieg Sonata with him. Viniegra replied (6 April) that perhaps they could play it again, for he found the melody to be very beautiful. On 30 April, Falla responded that he was thinking of the same thing, but unfortunately had not kept a copy. He indicated that perhaps upon his return from his upcoming trip, Viniegra could send him a copy to be revised so that they could play it once again. This never happened.

The work is published by MFE editions in 1994 as *Tres obras para violonchelo y piano.*

V. *Scherzo (en do menor)*

Only an eighteen-measure fragment remains of this piano piece, dated 9 November 1898. Perhaps intended to be an A-B-A form, the c minor work is not mentioned by any of Falla's early biographers. On the reverse side of the fragment is found some solfeggio exercises. The piece may well have only been a study in imitation.

Example 16.1 *Scherzo en do mayor,* AMF V A1.

VI. *ROMANZA PARA VIOLONCHELO Y PIANO*

A romance for cello and piano reflects the young Falla's interest in the Romantic idiom, as well as his inexperience in writing for the instrument. From measure fifty-three until the end, there exists an alternative ending, which is much more interesting than the first one.

This piece joins those other youthful cello-piano pieces written for concerts at the Viniegra house in Cádiz. This four-minute piece was written in
1898 and was premiered by Salvador Viniegra and Falla in Viniegra's
house concerts on 14 July 1899. Sixty-four measures in length, it begins
in g minor but ends in the parallel major. The musical form is A-B-A.

This work was not mentioned by the early biographers, but was cited by
Enrique Franco in the introduction to the 1983 Unión Musical Ediciones.
Manuel de Falla Editions has published a more recent edition in 1994.

VII. *(Pieza para violonchelo y piano en do mayor)*

Another youthful work for cello and piano, probably one of the first
composed by Falla for the Viniegra house concert setting, perhaps in
1898 or earlier. The enigma of the date of its composition has yet to be
solved, which is the date of the composition. From the manuscript in the
AMF, the immature handwriting shows an inexperienced young composer. The staff placements are awkward, the tessiture of the cello too
high, and the overall character of the piece seem to place this work as
one of Manuel's first experiments in writing for this combination.

The piece is ninety-six measures in length and approximately three
minutes in duration. Excursions from the original tonality of C major
into D-flat major and e minor culminate in the return to the home key.
The cello figures predominantly, while the piano accompaniment reveals no individual personality in this A-B-A coda form. The work is
published by Manuel de Falla Editions in 1994 as *Tres obras para
violonchelo y piano*.

VIII. *Cuarteto en sol*

Unfortunately only eleven measures of this multimovement work in
G major for piano quartet (violin, viola, violoncello, and piano) are
found in the AMF. Antonio Gallego surmises that they may belong to
the third movement, for this movement "L'andante sonne à merveille"
is mentioned by biographers Roland-Manuel and Pahissa. Its approximate date of composition is 1898–1899.

It is known that the 2nd movement—Andante tranquilo—and the 3rd
movement—Bailable ("danceable") (or *Scherzo* as Pahissa refers to it)[7]
were played by Salvador Tello de Meneses (violin), Antonio Rivas

Example 16.2 *Cuarteto en sol,* AMF VIII A1.

(viola), Salvador Viniegra ('cello), and Manuel de Falla (piano) in
the Salón Quirell in Cádiz on 16 August 1899. Other performances
were given by Antonio Rivas (violin), Francisco Rives (viola), Salvador Viniegra (cello), and Falla at the Teatro Cómico in Cádiz on
10 September 1899.

IX. *Mireya (Poema) "Canto V" (Chamber Version)*
X. *Mireya (Poema) "Canto V" (Piano Transcription)*

Written around 1899, this programmatic work for string trio, flute, and piano subtitled "El Ródano" has not been found, nor has the piano transcription. At least two movements are known to exist: "Muerte de Elzear" (Elzear's death) and "Danza fantástica" (Fantastic dance). According to biographer Jaime Pahissa, the action of this work takes place in the Ródano during the night of San Medardo. It is a fantastic tale of sinking ships and ghosts appearing on the old wooden bridge Tinquetalla, which Pahissa says Falla could have known from a trip to Italy, a bridge now replaced by a modern steel one.[8]

What is significant about this account is found in the copious notes Falla left regarding the eventual orchestration of the work. His study of the orchestration book by François Auguste Gevaert is reflected in the very specific instructions in Falla's 1902–1904 notebook "Apuntes de Harmonia" as to instrumental characteristics for this piece—such as, "Clarinets, use them for the low, held notes at the beginning, accompanying the strings in the Ródano"; or other indications for the trombones, English horn, oboe, bassoons, French horn, etc.; or in reference to specific page numbers, for example, "See in the Gevaert p. 125, example 158 and 158bis."[9]

The music must have been so vivid that it caused at least one woman, who sat in the first row of the first performance, to comment: "It seems that we are at the opera."

The first performance was given at the Teatro Cómico in Cádiz on 10 September 1899, with Antonio Rivas (violin), Francisco Rives (viola), Salvador Viniegra (cello), Anselmo Apolo (flute), and Falla (piano). Falla also made a piano arrangement of the work, playing it at the beginning of the second half of a concert given at the Ateneo in Madrid on 6 May 1900.

XI. *Mazurca en do menor*

Inspired by Falla's love for Chopin and for Grieg, this work dates from around 1899–1900, even though the manuscript found in the AMF has no date. In c minor, it contains 140 measures in form of a mazurka-rondo with regular eight-bar phrases. It is in a rondo form. The five-minute work received its first performance, according to Antonio Gallego, by

Spanish pianist Guillermo González at the Juan March Foundation in Madrid on 13 January 1989.[10]

Antonio Iglesias reproduced an old cover from this piece in his 1983 book *Manuel de Falla (Su obra para piano).*[11] This fact reveals that Falla, perhaps for the first time, was interested in publishing a work of his own. In 1992, the work was published by Ediciones Manuel de Falla.

XII. SERENATA ANDALUZA (VIOLIN AND PIANO)

Although the manuscript for this violin and piano salon piece has not been found, it is known that its première was given at Salón Quirell in Cádiz on 16 August 1899, by Salvador Tello de Meneses and the composer. It was played the following month at Cadiz's Teatro Cómico by Antonio Rivas and the composer on 10 September 1899.

The may well be the Serenata Española that Pahissa refers to in his biography and which he says "is better than the other *Serenata española* published by the Sociedad de Autores Españoles in Madrid."[12]

The work is characterized by dotted figures and is in A-B-A form.

XIII. SERENATA ANDALUZA (PIANO TRANSCRIPTION)

Composed around 1900, this was a popular salon piece in its time as well as some decades later. It may well be a piano transcription of the *Serenata andaluza* for violin and piano. The first performance was given by Falla at the Ateneo in Madrid on 6 May 1900, followed by his playing of the work at the Real Academia de Santa Cecilia in Cádiz on 16 September 1900, and again at the Teatro Cómico in Cádiz on 27 July 1902. Falla refers to the work in letters to Padre Fedriani (1902).

The work lasts approximately four minutes, contains two hundred six measures, and is in an A-B-A form.

From Falla's notebook "Apuntes de harmonia" in an entry dated 26 June 1902, seventeen copies were sold in 1902 for returns of 13.60 ptas.; thirty-two copies (1903), Falla's profit = 25.60 ptas.; ten examples (1904) = 8 ptas. return; and four copies (1905) = 3.20 ptas. profit.[13]

The first edition was published by Fuentes y Asenjo in Madrid. The 1902 edition, published by Sociedad de Autores Españoles, forms the basis for the 1996 AMF/UME and Chester editions. The work was also

published by Edward B. Marks Music Corporation in 1935 in New York
with revisions made by Luis Sucra without Falla's permission. According to Falla (letter dated 24 October 1946, to J. M. Hernández Suárez),
Sucra whimsically both added and cut measures, disfiguring a good part
of the music. The lutenist, Paco Aguilar, was responsible for bringing
this fact to Falla's attention, as he used this version in his recital programs believing it to be entirely original.

XIV. CANCIÓN

Dated 2 April 1900, this piano piece in c minor contains sixty-seven
measures and lasts approximately 2'40". Its musical form is A-B-A.

Its debut was given by Gerardo Diego, in a conference-concerto of
uncertain date.

It has been published by MFE/UME, 1996; Chester, 1996; UME,
1980, *Obras desconocidas* with *Cortejo Danza de gnomos* and *Canto de
los remeros del Volga (del Cancionero musical ruso)* with a design by
Picasso on the cover; introduction by Enrique Franco.

XV. VALS CAPRICHO

This piano work of approximately 2'44" was first performed by the
composer at the Ateneo in Madrid on 6 May 1900. Its musical form is
A-B-A.

Apparently successful in an early published version by Sociedad de
Autores Españoles in 1902, Falla noted eagerly noted the 40 percent roy-
alty payments as follows: in 1902, six copies = 4.80 ptas.; in 1903, nine
copies = 7.40 ptas.; in 1904, one copy = .80 ptas.; and in 1905 two
copies = 1.60 ptas. He refers to this work in letters to Padre Fedriani in
1902.[14] The piece has been published for the Falla fiftieth anniversary of
his death by Chester and Ediciones Manuel de Falla.

XVI. PRELUDIOS ("MADRE, TODAS LAS NOCHES")

This song for voice and piano on a text by Antonio de Trueba was written around 1900. The poem is taken from Trueba's book *Arte de
hacer versos, al alcance de todo el que sepa leer* (The Art of Making

Verses, within reach of all who know how to read), published by Librería de Juan y Antonio Bastinos, Barcelona, in 1881. It is found in the AMF in Falla's personal library.

The song's duration is approximately 3'45". The first performance was given possibly with soprano Eloísa Minoves, who married Viniegra's son, and unknown pianist. The song was later performed by Ángeles Chamorro and pianist Enrique Franco at the Festival de Barcelona in 1967.

The song is published jointly by Ediciones Manuel de Falla and Unión Musical Ediciones (UME) in 1996 with other songs: "Olas gigantes"; "¡Dios mío, qué solos se quedan los muertos!"; "Oración de las madres que tienen a sus hijos en brazos"; and "Canción andaluza: El pan de Ronda." An earlier edition by UME is exists from 1980.

XVII. *LA JUANA Y LA PETRA, O LA CASA DE TÓCAME ROQUE*

This *zarzuela* of one act and two scenes dates from 1902 and uses the libretto by Javier Santero, based on a farce of the same title by Ramón de la Cruz. It uses spoken dialogues interspersed with singing, fifteen characters including ten singers, chorus, guitar, tambourine, and other instruments unidentified.

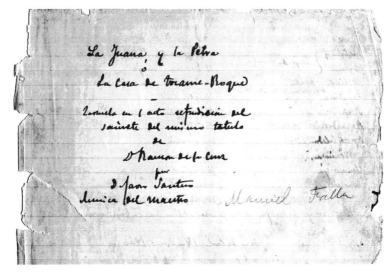

Example 16.3   *La Juana y la Petra, o la casa de tócame Roque*, AMF XVII.

From the libretto housed at the AMF, it appears that Falla wrote five musical numbers, part of which became interpolated into the "Danza del Corregidor" of the *El sombrero de tres picos.*

Although it was not performed, Falla wrote to Padre Fedriani in the autumn of 1902 of being asked to revise the work in order to make it ready for production.[15]

XVIII. *Pasacalle torero*

Only twenty-eight measures of this piano fragment, plus another sixteen measures on the reverse side of the sketch material, survive from this piece written around 1900.

It is doubtful that any performance of the work was ever done, given its incomplete state found at the AMF. Speculation is made that the work was composed to be included in a *zarzuela* with librettist José Jackson Veyán, for, in a letter dated 2 December (1899?) from the librettist to Falla, which says that although he has no libretto at the moment he still advises Falla to continue composing light music, such as "polkas, waltzes, etc., etc. that we can use later."[16]

The composer's title is found on the reverse side of a fragment of another unrelated work, *Cortejo de gnomos* for piano.

Example 16.4   *Pasacalle torero*, AMF XVIII.

XIX. *Rima* ("*Ola gigantes*")

This song for voice and piano on a poem by Adolfo Bécquer was not cited during the lifetime of the composer. It was probably composed around 1900 and is approximately 2'30" in length.

The debut of the work was given by soprano Ángeles Chamorro and pianist Enrique Franco at the Festival de Barcelona in 1967.

It is edited by MFE/UME, 1996; UME, 1980.

XX. *¡Dios mío, qué solos se quedan los muertos!*

Another song for voice and piano on a text by G. A. Bécquer belongs to the same group above and written around 1900. Approximately four minutes in length, it was given its first performance by soprano Ángeles Chamorro and pianist Enrique Franco at the Festival de Barcelona in 1967, along with *Rima*. It is yet another work not cited by Falla's biographers during his lifetime.

It is edited by MFE/UME in 1996 and UME in 1980.

XXI. *Cortejo de gnomos*

This piano piece is dated 4 March 1901. Approximately three minutes in duration, it is speculated that this work may actually precede *Gavotte et Musette*. It could be related to the *Suite fantástica*. Its musical form is A-B-A.

It has been published by MFE/UME and Chester in 1996, as well as earlier by UME in 1980.

XXII. *Serenata*

In the popular vein is the waltzlike salon piano piece of 2 April 1901. Approximately 3'50" long, the work received its first performance by Spanish pianist Guillermo González at the Fundación Juan March, Madrid, 13 January 1989. It is an A-B-A form.

The work is yet another not mentioned during Falla's lifetime, but according to Antonio Iglesias, who first described the piece, it is one of the most important of Falla's youth. It possibly bears some relation to *Segunda serenata andaluza.*

It is published by MFE, 1996; Chester, 1996.

Example 16.5   *Serenata,* AMF XXII A1.

XXIII. *Segunda serenata andaluza*

Dated 1901, the manuscript of this piano work has not been found. However, it received its first performance by the composer on 22 September 1901, at the Teatro del Parque Genovés in Cádiz. It is not cited by any biographer during Falla's lifetime, nor does it appear on subsequent programs.

Three pages of sketch material is housed in the AMF, in which the last page contains a *Chansonette* plus several chordal progressions. It may be related to the unpublished *Serenata*.[17]

Example 16.6 *Segunda serenata andaluza,* AMF XXIII A1.

XXIV. *Suite fantástica*

In this lost suite for piano, two movements, "En la rueca" and "Hadas," are known to have been performed by Falla at the Teatro del Parque Genovés in Cádiz on 22 September 1901, with the *Segunda serenata andaluza*.

Sketch material of thirty measures is housed in the AMF. In the last stave, with a later handwriting, three measures develop one of the motives of the work. It is the same handwriting and motive that appears on the reverse side of the untitled piano work, [*Pieza para piano en mi mayor*].[18]

Example 16.7 *Suite fantástica,* AMF XXIV A1.

XXV. *[Pieza para piano en mi mayor]*

Little is known about this piano piece in E major from around 1901.

A one-page sketch exists in AMF, which contains a pasted piece of paper on the fourth stave. As mentioned, on the reverse side, three measures of one of the motives of the *Suite fantástica* are found. As the work is untitled, Antonio Gallego gives it the obvious name, Piano Piece in E major.

XXVI. *Los amores de la Inés*

This *zarzuela* in one act and two scenes is based on a libretto by Emilio Dugi, alias Manuel Osorio y Bertrand, as correctly identified by Enrique Franco. The work is composed around 1901–1902. It is the only one of Falla's *zarzuelas* to be performed.

Only sketch material exists in the AMF of the Preludio, the Allegretto tranquilo movement, and the Intermedio, however the original score may be found in the Sociedad General de Autores Españoles archives in Madrid. This score contains some instrumentation with a general guide as to the instruments to be used when a piano reduction is present. A piano-vocal score published by UME in 1965 reveals five numbers.

The characters and instrumentation are as follows: Inés (soprano),

Juan (tenor), Lucas (tenor), chorus (STB) instrumentation: 2.1.2.1–2.2.3.0-tympani-perc.-st.

The musical numbers are: "Preludio" (Andante-Allegro), 1. "Seguidillas de la corrida" (song and chorus) 2. "Carcelera" (Juan and chorus) 3. "Duo" (Inés and Juan) 4. "Intermedio instrumental" 5. "Couplet" (Lucas).

The debut was given at the Teatro Cómico, Madrid on 12 April 1902. The cast included the following: Loreto Prado (Inés), Srta. Castellanos (Felipa), Srta. Fuentes (La Blasa), Sr. Redondo (Juan), Enrique Chicote (Sr. Lucas), Sr. Nart (Fatigas), Sr. León (Moreno), Sr. Ponzano (Rata Sabia), Sr. Delgado (Araña), Sr. Borda (Pesqui), and N. N. (Mozos no. 1 and 2).

With Falla's urgent need to support his family, the sale of his music was vital. However, Falla did not become rich from these sales. In 1903, one copy of no. 1 and two copies of no. 2 were sold for 50 percent of author's rights to Falla (1.50 ptas. and 2.50 ptas., respectively).[19]

A new edition of the piano-vocal score plus a reconstruction of the full score is in progress by Yvan Nommick. Other editions include: MFE/UME, 1996, UME (voice and piano), 1903; libretto, SAE, 1902.

Example 16.8 *Los amores de la Inés,* AMF XXVI A3, p. 4.

XXVII. *Limosna de amor*

Another *zarzuela* with librettist José Jackson Veyán, this one-act work from around 1901–1902 was never performed, although in a letter to José J. Rodríguez Fernández dated 22 May 1902, Falla indicated that it was about to be performed "in the coming week."[20]

It contains five numbers: "Pablo," "Romanza de Elena," "Dúo de Elena & Pablo," "Canciones y danzas de Asturias," and the final "Chorus."

It is scored for the following singers-instrumentation: Pablo (tenor), Elena (soprano), chorus (STB); instrumentation: 1+1.1.2.1–2.2.3.0-tympani-perc.-st. The AMF houses several sketches, while the archives of the Sociedad General de Autores Españoles contains a photocopy of manuscript 696 of the complete score.

Example 16.9   *Limosna de amor,* AMF XXVII A2, p. 1—Allegretto.

XXVIII. *Tus ojillos negros, Canción andaluza*

This song for voice and piano on a text by Cristóbal de Castro was written around 1902–1903. It is dedicated to the Marqueses of Alta Villa.

The song, written during Falla's studies with musicologist Felipe Pedrell, had an unexpected success both in Europe and in North America. It was sung by Lucrecia Bori in New York and by Hipólito Lázaro who also recorded it.

Leopoldo Matos (letters to Falla on 29 September 1929 and 29 October 1929) recounts that he heard an arrangement form violin and piano, but later said that he had not been able confirm if that arrangement had been published.[21]

From Falla's notebook, "Apuntes de Harmonía," we see that he received 25 percent of royalties (four ptas. in 1903 from the sale of eight copies; 9 ptas. in 1904 from the sale of eighteen copies; and 2 ptas. in 1905 from the sale of four copies).

Although the manuscript has not been found, several editions of the work have been published based on the 1903 SAE version, such as the UME edition of 1940 and the MFE/UME of 1993.

XXIX. *Allegro de concierto*

This virtuoso piano piece dates from around 1903–1904. This work was composed for the 1904 competition organized by Tomás Bretón, sponsored by the Conservatorio de Música y Declamación in Madrid, and judged amongst twenty-four works by professors Emilio Serrano and Tomás Fernández Grajal (composition) and José Tragó, Pilar Fernández de la Mora, and Manuel Fernández Grajal (piano). The first prize of 500 pesetas was won by Enrique Granados, with the works of José Guervós and Vicente Zurrón also being given distinction. Falla with Luis Leandro Maríani, Javier Giménez Delgado, Cleto Zavala, and Jacinto Ruiz Manzanares received honorable mentions.

A single movement work in sonata-rondo form, its approximate duration is 8'. Its first performance was given by the composer at the Ateneo in Madrid on 15 May 1905, just after winning the piano competition of Ortiz y Cussó that year.

Brilliant writing and stylistic borrowings from Grieg, Schumann, and Mendelssohn make this g minor Romantic work gratifying to play. Two editions in 1996 are found by MFE/CH by Chester with an introduction by biographer Ronald Crichton.

XXX. *(Movimiento para cuarteto de cuerda)*

This untitled work is given the name "Movement for String Quartet" by cataloger Antonio Gallego. The manuscript is housed in the AMF. Its first performance is unknown. It takes the form of Scherzo-Trio-DaCapo (A-B-A) and is seventy-six measures in length (24+28+24). To date, it is unpublished.

Example 16.10　　*[Movimiento para cuarteto de cuerda]*, AMF XXX A1.

XXXI. *El cornetín de órdenes*

In a rare musical collaboration with his friend-neighbor Amadeo Vives, Falla's *zarzuela grande* contains three acts. It was composed around 1903 and is based on a book by an unknown librettist. It was never performed.

The manuscript has not been found.

XXXII. *La cruz de Malta*

Another *zarzuela grande* in three acts, with musical collaboration with Amadeo Vives and an unknown librettist, this work dates from around the same time as the above—1903. No manuscript has been found.

During his Granada years, it was suggested to Falla that he recompose this work. He agreed that it was a good idea, but never did so.

XXXIII. *Prisionero de guerra*

Yet another *zarzuela* in musical collaboration with Amadeo Vives and an unknown librettist that dates from around 1903–1904, this work was found

Example 16.11 *Prisionero de guerra,* AMF XXXIII A1, no. 3, p. 1.

by Jorge de Persia in the archives of the SGAE. A copy of the piano-vocal score in AMF of nos. 1, 2, 3, 5.

The characters include: Esperanza (soprano), Juan (tenor), Julio (tenor), and a chorus (STB). The orchestration is missing.

Although the length is unknown, the following numbers may be ascertained: 1. "Introducción y número 1" 2. "Julio, Esperanza y Juan" 3. "Julio y Juan (la lección de esgrima)" 4. missing 5. "Una voz dentro y coro de marineros."

XXXIV. *Cantares de Nochebuena*

These nine popular songs for Christmas eve are scored for voice, guitar, and percussion instruments. They date from around 1903–1904 and reflect Pedrell's influence.

Approximately 7' in duration, they contain: "Pastores venir," "Maravilla nunca vista," "Esta noche ha de nacer," "Un pastor lleva un pavo," "Venga la bota," "En el portal de Belén," "Por la calle abajito," "La leche de viejas," and "Un zapatero aburrío" from *Cancioneros* (Songbooks) of Inzenga, Hurtado, Olmeda, and Ledesma.

The debut was planned for the Venetian Festival in 1987 by Crivillé i

1

PASTORES VENIR

— 10 —

Example 16.12   *Cantares de Nochebuena,* **AMF XXXIV, MFE, p. 10.**

Bargalló. However, programs at AMF do not verify the work's performance at that time. The performance by Jeannie Marsh (soprano), Michael
Christoforidis (guitar and percussion), and Ken Murray (guitar and percussion) at Trinity College Chapel, Melbourne, Australia, on 18 September 1992, is, according to Christoforidis, the world première.

    The work has been published by MFE in 1992.

NOTES

1. The dating and numbering of Falla's works are based on Antonio Gallego's official *Catalogo de Obras de Manuel de Falla*, Ministerio de Cultura, Dirección General de Bellas Artes y Archivos, Madrid, 1987. Exceptions to this rule occur when subsequent musicological research proves otherwise. The categorization of the periods of composition respond to those Yvan Nommick as cited in his doctoral thesis, *Manuel de Falla Œuvre et Évolution du Language Musical*, vol. 1, p. 19, Ph.D. dissertation, Université de Paris-Sorbonne (Paris IV), 1998–1999.

2. Nectoux, "Manuel de Falla. Un itinéraire spirituel" in *Manuel de Falla. Ses amis et ses interprètes*. EMI, 2C 153-16241/2, 1979, liner notes, p. 5. This article first appeared in *Schweizerische Musikzeitung Revue musicale suisse*. CXVII, no. 3, mai-juin 1977, p. 137. "Il est peu d'exemples dans l'histoire de la musique d'une évolution aussi radicale que celle qui conduisit Manuel de Falla de *La vie brève* au *Concerto pour clavecin*."

3. Nommick, Thesis, I, p. 12. "En effect, en trente ans Falla passe d'une mauique néo-romantique influencée par l'opéra bellinien, Chopin, Schumann, et Grieg à l'amalgame de modernité, de musique populaire et de techniques polyphonique, du Siècle d'Or qui imprègne les plus belles pages de 'l'Atlantide.' Dans l'intervalle, il a absorbé de multiples esthétiques, matériaux et apports, tels que: le romantisme, la *zarzuela,* le vérisme italien, les procèdès wagnériens, les bruits et les chants de forge, les cris des marchands ambulants, le folklore des différentes régions espagnoles, l'impressionnime, le 'cante jondo,' le folklore russe, le néo-classicism, le pré-baroque, le 'Cancionero Musical' de Palacio, le 'De Musica libri septem' de Salinas, les Cantigas de Santa Maria d'Alphonse X le Sage, la liturgie mozarabe, le 'Llibre Vermell,' la polyphonie du Siècle d'Or, l'organum médiéval, les mélodies de l'antiquité grecque."

4. Nommick, Thesis, II, p. 349–50.

5. Letter from Amadeo Vives to Falla dated 14 July 1931, from San Pol de mar (AMF 7764). ". . . un sentido genial de percepción en la forma que es a mi juicio la esencia misma de la belleza artistica."

6. Gallego, Antonio. (1987). Catalogo de Obras de Manuel de Falla. Madrid: Ministerio de Cultura, Dirección General de Bellas Artes y Archivos, 13. Hereafter abbreviated as AGC.

7. Pahissa, 28.

8. Pahissa, 28.

9. AG, 21–22.

10. Gallego, p. 5. *Manuel de Falla Mazurka para Piano*, Edición al cuidado de António Gallego, Manuel de Falla Ediciones, Madrid, 1992.

11. Antonio Iglesias, *Manuel de Falla (Su obra para piano)*, p. 30. Madrid: Alpuerto, 1983.

12. Pahissa, 41–42.

13. AGC, 25, who refers to page 95 of Falla's notebook.
14. AGC, 30.
15. AGC, 33–34.
16. AGC, 36.
17. AGC, 43.
18. AGC, 44.
19. AGC, 46–49.
20. AGC, 51.
21. AGC, 53.

Chapter 17

Period of Consolidation
of Musical Language (1905–1914)

La vida breve (La vie brève)
Con afectos de jubilo y gozo
Pièces espagnoles, Cuatro piezas españolas
Trois mélodies
Siete canciones populares españolas

This category chronologically contains more then the works listed above, which are *Soleá*, and *Oración de las madres que tienen a sus hijos en brazos*, both works closely associated with the Martínez Sierra couple, whom Falla met towards the end of his Paris years. As the pieces are directly associated with the second Madrid stay and with the characteristics of the Andaluz period therein, they are presented later. *Noches en los jardines de España* must not be overlooked either, which was begun during the Paris years but completed later in Madrid. The great influence during this period was that of the French composers, principally, but not uniquely, Debussy. Other international figures, such as Stravinsky, Diaghilev, and the *Ballets Russes*, played integral roles in this consolidation period. The Spaniards in Paris at this time were viewed in a favorable artistic light.

Falla was occupied with the assimilation of ideas gained from Pedrell and mostly Parisian composers. The absorption of a new milieu would give impetus to works and opportunities beyond this period, while the exchange between Falla and many other artists was mutually beneficial. Too, the task of revising *La vida breve* for its French version and for the world première in Nice, in 1913, played a central role at this time. This period represents a musical coming of age.

XXXV AND XXXIX. *LA VIDA BREVE (LA VIE BRÈVE)*

A lyric drama in one act on a libretto by Carlos Fernández-Shaw, this work was composed from 1904–1905. It underwent many revisions, in 1908 and again in 1913 in Paris. The French adaptation was made by Paul Milliet. See chapter 2 for a synopsis of the drama.

The original version won the first prize in a competition announced by the Real Academia de Bellas Artes de San Fernando and awarded in 1905.

The cast of characters includes: Salud, 2ª, 3ª, 4ª vendedoras (sopranos); la Abuela, Carmela, 1ª vendedora (mezzo-sopranos); Paco, una voz en la fragua, una voz lejana, vendedor (tenors); Manuel (baritone); el tío Sarvaor (bass); un cantaor; chorus; contains: first tableau (six scenes), second tableau (Intermedio), third tableau (two scenes), and fourth tableau (two scenes).

The piano-vocal score and some orchestral sketches are in AMF and have been reproduced in a facsimile edition of XXXV A1, AMF, co-produced with MFE and the Centro de Documentación Musical de Andalucía, 1997, piano-vocal score, edited by A. Gallego.

A debut of this version never took place in Falla's lifetime. However, the debut of the corrected version was given by the Orquesta Cuidad de Granada with Josep Pons conducting at the Centro Cultural Manuel de Falla in Granada, on 28 and 29 November 1997.

Revised version:
    Upon advice from Debussy and Dukas, Falla's serious opera took on dimensions of 2 acts and 4 scenes. Its instrumentation was also somewhat altered to: 2+1.2+1.2+1.2-4.2.3.1 tympani-perc.-2 harps-guitar-st. The musical numbers were changed to: Act I—1ˢᵗ Tableau + 6 scenes; 2ⁿᵈ Tableau; Intermezzo; Act II—1ˢᵗ Tableau, 1 scene, Dance, 2 scenes, 2ⁿᵈ Tableau, 2ⁿᵈ Dance, Finale. The cast of singers remained the same. The duration increased to approximately 65'.

The debut finally took place at the Casino Municipal, Niza, France, on 1 April 1913. The singers were: Lilian Grenville (Salud), Mlle. Fanty (La abuela), Mlle. Gerday (Carmela & 1ˢᵗ seller), Mlle. Daurelly (second seller), Mlle. Bernard (third seller) David Devriés (Paco) Mr. Cotreuil (Uncle Sarvaor), Mr. Raynal (the town crier), Mr. Termany (Manuel), and Mr. Rouziery (a voice of intrigue, the voice of the seller, and a distant voice). Also included were J. Miranne (orchestral conductor), Mr. Strelesky (scenic director), and R. Lassalle (scenic painter).

Other performances were given at the Opéra Comique in Paris on

30 December 1913. However, the "official debut" at the Parisian Opéra Comique was realized on 7 January 1914.

This work is dedicated to Mme. A. Adiny-Milliet, the great Wagnerian soprano, and to the memory of Falla's librettist, Carlos Fernández-Shaw. The Spanish première took place at the Teatro de la Zarzuela, in Madrid on 14 November 1914, and was sung in Spanish. The cast included: Immaculada Egido (Salud), Antonio Ordóñez (Paco), Mabel Perelstein (La Abuela), Enrique Baquerizo (Tio Sarvaor), Víctor Torres (Manuel), Mariola Cantarero (Carmela), Octavio Arévalo (Voz de fragua), "El polaco" (Cantaor), Miguel Ochando (Guitar), and Coro de Valencia (F. Perales, director).

Max Eschig published the work in 1913, 1914, and 1915, as well as the French libretto in 1914. The Spanish libretto was published by Renacimiento in Madrid in 1914. An Italian translation was also published by Otello Andolfi-Eschig and a German translation by Ludwig Andersen of Schott-Eschig. A new revised edition by J.-D. Krynen, of the piano-vocal score was published by Ediciones Manuel de Falla in 1997. The piano transcriptions of the two dances from the piano-vocal score are published by ME, MFE/CH, and MFE, 1996.

XXXVI. *Con afectos de júbilo y gozo*

A hymn for soprano, women's choir, and piano, set to a text of an unknown author, was written by Falla probably on an occasion to sing

Example 17.1   *Con afectos de júbilo y gozo,* AMF XXXVI A1, p. 1.

the praises of a Mother Superior at a girls school. The work is dated 23 March 1908.

On the reverse sides of the manuscript housed at the AMF are found notes for "Aragonesa" and "Andaluza" from *Pièces espagnoles.*

XXXVII. *PIÈCES ESPAGNOLES, CUATRO PIEZAS ESPAÑOLAS*

Falla's presence in France reflects the French title of the Four Spanish Pieces for piano. He had begun composing the work in Madrid and took them with him to Paris, whereupon he completed the last two. The four pieces, "Aragonesa," "Cubana," "Montañesa," and "Andaluza," date from 1906–1909. The musical forms may be seen as: "Aragonesa" = Introduction-A-B-A-B-Coda; "Cubana" = Introduction-A-B-A-Coda; "Montañesa" = A-B-A-Coda; and "Andaluza" = A-B-C-B-Coda.

Dedicated to Isaac Albéniz, Falla very much had Albéniz's *Iberia* in mind in composing these pieces. The approximate duration is 16'. Ricardo Viñes gave the first performance at Salle Erard (concert series of the Societé Nationale de Musique) in Paris on 27 March 1909.

Some sketches for "Aragonesa" appear on the back of the unedited hymn *Con afectos de júbilo y gozo.* Other sketches appear on the back of sketches for "Cubana." Some sketches of "Cubana" have sketches of "Andaluza" on the reverse, with one page of sketches of "Cubana" found among the manuscripts for *La vida breve.* Falla's 1908 diary indicates that he finished "Cubana" on 24 April 1908.[1]

From a recently discovered manuscript given by Eunice E. Suárez de Chirino de Sala of Coral Gables, Florida, to the city of Granada and the AMF, it appears that this manuscript (10 June 1908) shows yet a further development of the piece "Montañesa," thereby supplanting the version thought to be the final one of 25 April 1908 (AG in facsimile ed., 1). "Audaluza" is also contained in this manuscript.

In other sketches for "Montañesa" are found quotes from Debussy's Quartet, which Falla was analyzing along with *Pelleas et Melisande* during this time. And on the reverse of yet another sketch for "Andaluza" is found sketch material for the "Danza primera" of *La vida breve.*

Falla's compositional processes are now being fully developed, thereby showing *Cuatro piezas españolas* to be no mere salon music. The influence of Debussy and Lucas is evident. For example, in one of the sketches of "Aragonesa" detailed indications, such as: "(1) Move immediately from the modulations of the 5th; (2) Prepare the modulation one step in order to then begin another; (3) Take the dominant as bass pedal with the melody that is composed in the tonic; (4) Anticipations in the progressions; (5) In making a harmonic design over the chord, give notes foreign to the melody to it (the chord). This can also produce a great effect in the progressions; and (6) Resolution of the notes of attraction."[2] Falla's objective was to musically "expose the soul and the atmosphere of each of the regions indicated by their respective titles.[3]

The work was first published by Durand in 1909. Later editions include: MFE, 1996, and in revised edition by Guillermo González in 2001, and a facsimile of a new manuscript of "Montañesa" and "Andaluza" by the Ayuntamiento de Granada, 1991.

Example 17.2   "Montañesa" from *Pièces espagnoles, Cuatro piezas españolas,* MFE, p. 20.

XXXVIII. *Trois mélodies*

These three songs for voice and piano on a text by Théophile Gautier were composed between 1909–1910. The songs are "Les colombes," "Chinoiserie," and "Séguidille" and have an approximate duration of 7'.

The first performance of "Séguidille" took place at the Schola Cantorum in Paris on 14 March 1910, with Claire Hugon and the composer. The complete cycle was premiered by Mme. Ada Adiny-Milliet and Falla, at Salle Gaveau in Paris (concert series of the Societé Nationale Indépendante) on 4 May 1910. The Spanish première was given by Genevieve Vix and Falla, at a Sociedad Nacional de Música concert in Madrid on 23 May 1916.

The first song is dedicated to Mme. Ada Adiny-Milliet, the second to Mme. R. Brooks, and the third to Mme. Debussy. According to Demarquez, Debussy's "Ariettes oubliées," "Proses lyriques," "Poèmes de Baudelaire," and "Il pleure dans mon coeur" influenced "Les colombes."[4] She also says that the "Chinoiserie" is the result of Falla's being acquainted with an Oriental museum, the Musée Guimet, which was near his home at the time. Debussy's influence is perceptible too in

Example 17.3   *Trois mélodies,* "Chinoiserie," AMF XXXVIII A4.

the piece, when he advised Falla "to try to find something else" instead of the heavy opening recitative.[5]

The original manuscript was given as a gift to G. Jean-Aubry by the composer. Sketch material for the revision of *La vida breve*, plus notes for *Las flores* and *Noches en las jardines de España* are also found amongst the papers of *Trois mélodies*. The work was first published by Rouart et Lerolle in Paris in 1910.

"Seguidille" also appeared as a supplement to the Spanish magazine *Por essos mundos* in September 1916 and can be found in the Biblioteca nacional, Sección de Publicaciones Periódicas (Ref. D-1411) in Madrid. Salabert also published the work, as did International Music Company of New York in 1954 and Ediciones Manuel de Falla in 1996.

XL. *Siete canciones populares españolas*

This song cycle for voice and piano dates from 1914. Its approximate duration is 12'. It contains seven popular Spanish songs: "El paño moruno," "Seguidilla murciana," "Canción," "Jota," "Asturiana," "Nana," and "Polo."

One of the most popular of all of Falla's works, the première was given by Luisa Vela and Falla at the Ateneo (concert in homage to Falla and Turina) in Madrid on 14 January 1915.

These seven popular Spanish songs are is dedicated to Mme. Ida Godebski. The inception of the work came when a Spanish singer from Málaga who was in the cast of the first performance of *La vida breve* asked the composer which Spanish songs would be most suitable for her to sing at a concert in Paris. The composer replied that he would try to arrange some for her. As Falla had just arranged a Greek melody according to the ideas of harmonic generation of Louis Lucas, he used this as a basis for the Spanish songs. In a letter dated 4 June 1914, to Leopoldo Matos, Falla says that he must finish the songs before the next Sunday as they would be sung at the Odeón on the 10th; and on 20 July he said that he was sending the engraver the collection, of which he had made three or four versions of each song before choosing the definitive one.[6]

For a long time the exact source of each song was speculated upon. Michael Christoforidis has identified the published source for each. They are as follows: "El paño moruno" (p. 65) from José Inzenga's anthology *Ecos de España*, published in Barcelona in 1874; "Seguidilla murciana" from "Las Torras," Inzenga (p. 68); "Canción" from "Canto de Granada," Inzenga (p. 116), which is also similar to "Un pastor lleva un pavo" from

Falla's *Cantares de Nochebuena*; "La jota aragonesa," Inzenga (p. 81); "Arriméme a un pino verde" from José Hurtado's *100 cantos populares asturianos*, p. 96; "Nana" from *Las Flores*, a play by Serafín and Joaquín Alvarez Quintero (the second edition of 1906 was owned by the composer and is preserved at AMF); and "Polo gitano o flamenco" from Eduard Ocón's *Colección de aires nacionales y populares.*[7] The work was first published by Max Eschig in 1922 with a cover by Falla's brother, Germán. It included texts in French and Spanish. Later editions followed by MFE/CH in Madrid in 1994 and MFE in 1996, as well as numerous arrangements.

NOTES

1. Michael Christoforidis, "Manuel de Falla, Debussy and *La vida breve*" in *Musicology Australia* XVIII, 1995, 3–12, fn 20.
2. AGC, 67.
3. Nextoux-Suisse.
4. Demarquez, 50.
5. Christoforidis, op cit., 4.
6. AGC, 91.
7. Michael Christoforidis, "Folksong models and their sources in Manuel de Falla's *Siete cauciones populares españolas* in *Context* 9, 1995, 12–21.

Chapter 18

Andalusian Period (1915–1919)

Soleá
Oración de las madres que tienen a sus hijos en brazos
Amanecer
El amor brujo
Otelo (tragedia de una noche de verano)
El pan de Ronda que sabe a verdad, canción andaluza
Noches en los jardines de España
El corregidor y la molinera
El sombrero de tres picos
Fuego fatuo
El corazón ciego
Fantasía bætica

Falla's return to the Spanish capital in the fall of 1914 was due to the beginning of the First World War. Madrid, which had been mostly hostile to him, would receive him in a different light after his international successes in Paris. This Andalusian period reflected a mature technique and synthesis of many elements into a stylized nationalistic language, even though some critics felt Falla had become too French ("afrancesado") in his approach. Moreover, this second Madrid period has been rightly characterized as the period of collaboration with the Martínez Sierra couple, so intense was Falla's involvement with them.[1]

XLI. *SOLEÁ*

Incidental music for G. Martínez Sierra's *La pasión* for voice and guitar was composed in 1914 as a Flamenco *copla*. Although the manuscript has not been found, the debut was given by the Martínez Sierras' Company at Teatro Lara in Madrid on 30 September 1914. Parts of the work were thought to have been improvised.

According to the actress who premiered the work, Catalina Bárcena,

> . . . I had to sing a Flamenco copla, but not all of it, because I had to interrupt the copla with a sob; in reality, the copla was a pretext because I neither could nor knew how to sing Flamenco. However, Falla composed a soleá in which I was to sing at that moment, and I rehearsed every day, with he himself playing the guitar. I was ashamed, because I sang very badly and even more ashamed because I had mutilated that soleá, which was [a] very good [work]. I didn't want to sing it. But Falla insisted so much, that I had no other recourse but to humor him. "Look, maestro, I can't do it"— I said to him. And he, in order to convince me, answered me: "You don't have to be worried. It's like this: in the moment that you can't (sing) anymore, interrupt the copla and burst into tears."[2]

Example 18.1   *Soleá,* AMF XLI A1.

XLII. *ORACIÓN DE LAS MADRES QUE TIENEN A SUS HIJOS EN BRAZOS*

This song for voice and piano on a text by G. Martínez Sierra dates from December, 1914. Its approximate duration is 2'15".

Its debut was given by Josefina Revillo and Falla at the Hotel Ritz, at the inaugural concert of the Sociedad Nacional de Música in Madrid on 8 February 1915.

It was published by UME in 1980 and MFE/UME in 1996.

XLIII. *AMANECER*

Another piece of incidental music for G. Martínez Sierra's comedy of the same name was composed by Falla in 1915. Although the manuscript has not been found, it is presumed to be played in the first act. The action took place in an imaginary provincial capital in the north of Spain, which was known for its university and maritime industry.

The debut took place at the Martínez Sierras' Company, Teatro Lara, in Madrid on 7 April 1915, just one week before *El amor brujo* with Pastora Imperio.

In the very detailed correspondence between María Martínez Sierra and the composer about the last rehearsals and the première there is no mention of Falla's musical collaboration. The comedy needed music in the first act: band music, guitars, bagpipes with drums, and other instruments typical of the north of Spain.[3]

XLIV, XLV, XLVII, LI, LXVIII, LXIX. *EL AMOR BRUJO*

The first version of this work was conceived as a gypsy-ballet, a gitanería, in one act and two scenes (XLIV). It was written for the gypsy dancer Pastora Imperio on a text by G. and M. Martínez Sierra, 1915. The approximate duration of this version is 36'. For a synopsis of the plot, see chapter 4.

It is comprised of the following instrumentation: singer, recitar, and accessories, as well as 1(1).1.0.0.-1.1.0.0.-perc-p-st.quintet.

The musical numbers are:

1st Tableau: (1) "Introducción y Escena" (2) "Canción del amor dolido" (3) "Sortilegio" (4) "Danza del fin del día" (the future "Ritual Fire Dance" in the ballet version) (5) "Escena," omitted later) (6) "Romance del pescador" (7) "Intermedio" (the future "Pantomine"); 2nd Tableau: (8)

"Introducción—El fuego fatuo" (later omitted) (9) "Escena— El terror" (almost completely omitted) (10) "Danza del fuego fatuo" (later to become the "Dance of Terror") (11) "Interludio—Alucinaciones" (12) "Canción del fuego fatuo" (13) "Conjuro para reconquistar el amor perdido" (omitted) (14) "Escena—El amor popular" (15) "Danza y canción de la bruja fingida" (later the "Dance and Song of the Game of Love") (16) "Finale— Las campanas del amanecer."

The debut was given on 15 April 1915, at the Lara Theater in Madrid to mixed acclaim—enthusiastic amongst the Carmelo community and unsure amongst the erudite listeners. The following characters performed: Candelas (Pastora Imperio), the old gypsy woman (Rosa Canto), little gypsy girl (María Imperio), other little gypsy girl (Perlita Negra), and gypsy (Victor Rojas). The conductor was José Moreno Ballesteros. Néstor Martín Fernández de la Torre was the director of scenery

Example 18.2   *El amor brujo (gitanería),* **AMF XLIV A1, p. 3.**

and costumes. The musical score was thought to be lost, as Falla destroyed the materials from the orchestra of the SGAE as a result of obtaining a contract with Chester. Andrew Budwig, however, noted there is a copy in the Library of Congress in Washington, D.C. A rare copy of the libretto is housed in the Library of the Spanish Contemporary Theater at the Juan March Foundation in Madrid.

The work has been published by MFE/CH, 1996, reconstructed by A. Gallego, and edited by J.-D. Krynen. No. 12 was published by Música, Madrid in 1917, while the piano-vocal score of nos. 2 and 4 were published by Renacimiento in Madrid in 1915.

A chamber version for sextet (string quintet and piano) was also made in 1915 and revised in 1926 (XLV). Both versions are housed at the AMF and contain the approximate duration of 16'.

This version includes the movements of "Pantomima" (originally titled "Danza del fin del día") and "Danza ritual del fuego" (originally titled "Intermedio"). Antonio Gallego lists its debut as being given by the José Media Villa at the Casino Espagnol in Portugal, possibly in Lisbon, in September of 1915. However, Artur Rubinstein tells of having heard it in a theater in Madrid with Pastora Imperio late at night after some play and performed by "five or six players, the usual ensemble one hears at nightclubs; the pianist played on an upright piano."[4] Rubinstein then begged Falla for the score of the Ritual Fire Dance, asking to make an arrangement of it. According to him, Falla agreed but added that he thought that it would not have any effect on the audience.[5] Rubinstein had great success with this transcription, having to play it as an encore four times at one concert. As Rubinstein does not give the date of this incident, and as Falla's sextet version and piano transcription of the dance are both dated 1915, it is not known if the debut of the sextet version of *El amor brujo* actually occurred earlier in Madrid and to what extent Rubinstein played a role in the origin of the idea of the transcription.

In the 1926 revision, Falla changes the order of the pieces and gives them their definitive titles. This debut was played by Antonio de Rivas and Manuel Martínez, violins; José Ortega, viola; Emilio Paz, 'cello; Pedro Areán, bass; José Ma Gálvez Ruiz, piano and conductor, in an homage concert, Real Academia Filarmónia de Santa Cecilia in Cádiz on 1 May 1926.

Editions: Chester, 1995.

Example 18.3   *El amor brujo* (sextet version), AMF XLV A1, p. 1.

In the concert version for orchestra (XLVIII), dated 1915–1916, with an approximate duration of 25', Falla changes the instrumentation to: 2(1).1.2.1-2.2.0.0.-tympani-percussion-p-st. In this version the musical numbers are reduced to: 1st Tableau: (1) "Introducción y Escena, Medianoche" (2) "Danza del fin del día" (3) "Escena y Romance del Pescador—Intermedio"; 2nd Tableau: (1) La cueva de la bruja, "Introducción y Escena" (2) "Danza del fuego fatuo" (3) "Alucinaciones"; "Conjuro para reconquistar el amor perdido"—"Escena" (4) "Danza de la bruja fingida—Finale."

The debut of this version took place on 28 March 1916, at the Hotel Ritz (concert series of the Sociedad Nacional de Música), by the Orquesta Sinfónica de Madrid with Enrique Fernández Arbós conducting.

Falla had destroyed this score as a result of his contract with Chester. A performance of the reconstructed version by Antonio Gallego took place at the Teatro La Fenice in Venice on 15 May 1987, in a program intitled "Progretto Falla."

The unpublished version is reconstructed by A. Gallego from sketches and from A. Salazar's program notes, published by MFE in 1996.

Yet another concert version for small orchestra was made in 1917. This version contains:

"Introducción y Danza del fuego fatuo" (later "Danza del terror"), "Romance del pescador," "Danza del fin del día" (later the "Ritual Fire Dance"), "Intermedio" (later "Pantomima"), "Danza de la bruja fingida" (later "Danza del juego de amor"), and "Finale." The orchestration is identical to the 1916 version, of 2(1).1.2.1-2.2.0.0.-tympani-percussion-p-st.

This version is important because it marks the clear path towards the definitive ballet version and its corresponding orchestral suite by the order of its numbers and in the deletion of others.

The debut was given on 29 April 1917, by the Orquesta Sinfónica de Madrid with Enrique Fernández Arbós conducting at the Teatro Royal in Madrid. Other performances followed: Orquesta Sinfónica de Madrid, with conductor E. Fernández Arbós at the Teatro San Fernando in Sevilla (IV Congreso Internacional de Carreteras) on 8 May 1923; Same interpreters as in "ballet-pantomime" at the Royal Theater in Madrid, 9 January 1924; Orquesta Bética de Cámara with Ernesto Halffter, conducting the Suite (without songs), Llorens Theater, Seville, 11 June 1924; Soprano Mercedes Melo and Orquesta Bética de Cámara, Ernesto Halffter, conducting at Theater San Fernando, Seville, 10 December 1924.

The one-act ballet version (XLVIII) was composed over a period of years, from 1915–1925. Its approximate duration is 23'. It is scored for mezzo-soprano and orchestra with instrumentation of: voice (mezzo) + 2(1).1.2.1.-2.2.0.0.-tympani-perc-piano-st.
The musical numbers are as follows:

"Introducción y Escena (En la cueva, La noche)"; "Canción del amor dolido"; "El aparecido"; "Danza del terror"; "El círculo mágico (Romance del pescador)"; "A medianoche (Los sortilegios)"; "Danza ritual del fuego"; "Escena"; "Canción del fuego fatuo"; "Pantomima"; "Danza del juego de amor"; "Finale (Las campanas del amanecer)."

Falla consolidated the scenery of the ballet and transformed the text from the gitanería, while conserving the instrumentation of the 1916 and 1917 versions of the numbers not deleted.
The debut of this version took place at the Trianon Lyrique in Paris on 22 May 1925, with Falla conducting. It was a tremendous success and

featured: Antonia Mercé "La Argentina" (Candelas), Vicente Escudero (Carmelo), and George Wague, (El espectro). The manuscript is in the AMF. A new revised and corrected edition is in preparation by Yvan Nommick for CH. Piano versions of "Danza del terror," "Romance del pescador/El círculo mágico," "Danza ritual del fuego," and "Pantomima," were published by Eschig and Chester in 1996; CH, 1995, coedition MFE/CH; "Canción del amor dolido," "Canción del fuego fatuo," for voice-piano, CH and ME; orchestral score, CH, 1924; piano-vocal score, CH, 1921.

In the orchestral suite (XLIX) from the ballet version (1915–1925) the following instrumentation may be found: 2(1).1.2.1-2.2.0.0.
This version deletes:
"Canción del amor dolido"; six of the twelve gong strokes in "Medianoche"; "Los sortilegios"; and "La canción del fuego fatuo." It substitutes instrumental passages for vocal ones in "Danza del juego de amor" and in the "Finale"—"Las campanas del amanecer."

This version was published by Chester in 1925, taken from the same edition as the ballet. Details about its debut remain obscure.

XLVI. *Otelo (tragedia de una noche de verano)*

This incidental music based on Gregorio Martínez Sierra's translation of Shakespeare's play was composed between September–October of 1915. Although neither the manuscript nor the literary text used by Gregorio has been found, it is known that the debut of the work occurred at the Teatro Novedades in Barcelona during October of 1915, during the time that Falla lived with the Martínez Sierras in Barcelona and was also working on *Noches en los jardines de España.* Pahissa termed Falla's contribution as "the shortest but most beautiful musical illustrations of Falla," referring to the "expressive and delicate Canción del sauce of Desdémona" and the "sounds of the trumpets, noble and original."[6]

XLVII. *El pan de Ronda que sabe a verdad, canción andaluza*

This song for voice and piano is based on a text by María Martínez Sierra. It was the only completed part of a projected song cycle Pascua florida: "El jardín venenoso," "El descanso de San Nicolás," "El corazón que duerme bajo el agua," "El barrio gitano," "El salón de Carlos V," "Tinieblas en el convento," "El pan de Ronda que sabe a verdad," "El sol de Gibraltar," "Ciudades orientales," "Cádiz se echa a navegar," and perhaps, "Peregrinación del Abad."

Inspired during a trip Falla made with María during the last part of March and the first part of April of 1915 to Granada, Ronda, Algeciras, and Cádiz. According to her, Falla tore up the original version in an attack of jealousy when María entered into a similar project (*Album de viaje,* op.15) with Joaquín Turina.

It was composed shortly before Christmas, on 18 December 1915, in Barcelona. Its debut is uncertain. Its duration is approximately 1'07".

The song was published first by UME in 1980 and then in 1996 under the title *Canciones de María de O. Lejárraga* (Songs of María de O. Lejárraga, which was María's maiden name).

XLIX. *Noches en los jardines de España*

Falla began Nights in the Gardens of Spain in Paris around 1909, completing it in Madrid in 1916. Considered by some to be a piano concerto, it is perhaps considered as a piano fantasy with orchestra, in which the piano is a prominent orchestral instrument. Its duration is around 23'. In his text on Romanticism, Falla refers to this work as his "symphonic impressions" (see chapter 10).

Three movements in length, the orchestration is scored as: piano solo+ 2+1.2+1.2.2-4.2.3.1-tympani-perc-cel-harp-st. The movements or nocturnes are: "En el Generalife," "Danza lejana," and "En los jardines de la sierra de Córdoba," The musical form of each of these movements may be seen as a combination of A-B-A and variation form.[7]

According to Falla, there was a fourth movement planned—a Nocturne of Cádiz. However, this theme was ultimately used in the "Intermedio" ("Pantomina") of *El amor brujo.* Rough drafts of another Nocturne of Seville also exist.

This work is dedicated to the Catalan pianist, Ricardo Viñes. However, several possible extramusical inspirations might be María Martínez Sierra's book *Granada (Guía emocional),* the work of José Pla (*Rusiñol y su tiempo*); and a poem by Francis Jammes, "Ce sont de grandes lignes paisibles." Among Falla's sketches for Noches are found examples of Debussy's *Pelleas et Melisande.*

While dedicated to Ricardo Viñes, the debut of the work was given by

José Cubiles and the Orquesta Sinfónica de Madrid, directed by Enrique Fernández Arbós at the Teatro Real in Madrid on 9 April 1916.

Falla's colleague of the Orquesta Bética de Cámara (OBC), Eduardo Torres, made a version in 1926 of the three movements for chamber orchestra, which features solo piano + 2.2.2.2.–2.2.3.1-tympani-perc-cel-harp-st.quintet. The debut of this version was given by pianist Frank Marshall with the OBC, conducted by Falla at the Teatro de San Fernando in Sevilla on 14 December 1926.

Various editions may be found, such as by MFE, 1996; MFE/Chester, and Eschig. The work was published by coedition MFE/Eschig of full score and piano solo part; MFE, 1996; a version for the Orquesta Bética de Cámara, Eschig, 1926, omitting the harp part; two-piano score, Eschig, 1922; four-hand version of orchestral part, Eschig, 1922, by Gustave Samazeuilh with corrections by Falla.

L. *EL CORREGIDOR Y LA MOLINERA*

The Magistrate and the Miller's Wife was conceived as a mimed farce on text by G. Martínez Sierra, based on Pedro Antonio de Alarcón's novel *The Three-Cornered Hat*. It was composed between 1916–1917. Its two scenes last approximately 43' with the following instrumentation: 1(1).1.1.1-1.1.0.0.-p-st.

The musical numbers include:

1st Tableau: (1) "Los molineros y el mirlo" (2) "Los celos" (3) "Danza (fandango)" (4) "El corregidor y la molinera" (5) "Las uvas"; 2nd Tableau: (1) "La cena—Seguidilla" (2) "La espera galante" (3) "Los Alguaciles: La despedida" (4) "La copla del cuco" (5) "¡En guardia, caballero!" (6) "Garduña se multiplica" (7) "También la corregidora es guapa."

Dedicated to Leopold Matos, this work was a great success with the public. The critics lauded the music but found fault with the libretto.

The debut of the work was given by the Orquesta Filarmónica de Madrid with Joaquín Turina conducting at the Teatro Eslava in Madrid on 7 April 1917. The cast included Luisa Puchol (La molinera), Pilar Lobo (La corregidora), Julia Cerdá (Una moza), Ricardo de la Vega (El corregidor), Pedro Sepúlveda (El molinero), Jesús Tordesillas (Alguacil no. 1), Pablo Hidalgo and Juan M. Román (otros alguaciles), and Juan Beringola (*Un petimetre*). Scenery was done by Amorós y Blancas; period costumes by Juana del Molino; figurines by Rafael Penago; and the production was directed by Gregorio Martínez Sierra.

The work has been published by MFE/Chester, 1996, new edition by J.-D. Krynen and by Chester in 1983.

Example 18.4 *El corregidor y la molinera,* AMF L A1 no. 31.

LIII, LVIII, LIX, LX. *EL SOMBRERO DE TRES PICOS*

Between 1917–1919, Falla revised and adapted *El corregidor y la molinera* into a ballet in two parts under the title of The Three-Cornered Hat (LIII). Instrumentation of this version includes: 2+1.2+1.2.2-4.3.3.1-tympani-perc-cel-harp-piano-st. The approximate duration is 35'. See chapter 4 for a synopsis of the plot.

The musical numbers are:

1st Part: "Introducción," "La tarde," "Danza de la molinera," "Las uvas";

2nd Part: "Los vecinos," Danza del molinero," Danza del corregidor," plus "Danza final."

The debut of the ballet was given by Serge Diaghilev's Ballets Russes, choreographer Léonide Massine; sets and costumes designer Pablo Picasso; conductor, Ernest Ansermet; vocal soloist, Zoia Rosovsky; and a cast of: Léonide Massine (El molinero), Tamara Karsavina (La molinera), Leon Woisikovsky (El corregidor), Stanislas Idzikovsky (El petimetre), and Ballets Russes (Alguaciles, Vecinos) at the Alhambra Theater in London on 22 July 1919.

A few days prior, on 17 June 1919, the debut of the concert version took place in Madrid in a concert of the Sociedad Nacional de Música at the Teatro Eslava in Madrid, by the Orquesta Filarmónica de Madrid with Bartolomé Pérez Casas, conducting.

Published versions include a new revised and corrected version of the full score by Yvan Nommick, Chester, 1997, coedition MFE/Chester, piano versions of five dances; Chester, 1996, and also by Schott and Real Musical; CH, piano reduction, 1921; Falla made a version for Le Pleyela for player piano, Chester 1921 (LX). The original manuscript of the orchestral suites (no. 1 and no. 2) are in the British Library in London.

Around 1921, in Granada, Falla made two orchestral suites (LVIII, LIX) on *El sombrero de tres picos—Escenas y danzas de la primera parte* (Suite no. 1) [Scenes and Dances from the First Part—Suite no. 1] and *Tres danzas de la segunda parte* (Suite no. 2) [Three Dances from the Second Part—Suite no. 2]. The subtitles appeared after Falla's death.

Suite no. 1 has the following instrumentation: 2.2+1.2.2-2.2.0.0.-Tympani-perc-harp-piano-st. The four movements are: "Mediodia"; "Danza de la molinera (Fandango)"; "El corregidor"; and "Las uvas." Falla added the introductory Toccata (without the vocal part) at the last minute. The approximate duration is 14'. The manuscript is housed at the AMF, while the corrected proofs for the Chester edition of 1921 are found in the British Library in London. The debut date is uncertain.

Suite no. 2 has the following instrumentation: 2+1.2+1.2.2.-4.3.3.1-tympani-perc.-celeste-harp-piano-st. The three movements are:

"Los vecinos (Seguidillas)"; "Danza del molinero (Farruca)"; and "Danza final." The thirty-six-page manuscript is found in the AMF. The work was published by Chester in 1924. The debut is uncertain.

Between 1921–1926 Falla made a player-piano version based on the piano-vocal score, complete in five rolls. It was commercially available from Saturday, 14 May 1927, as known from a program given by Falla with Madeleine Greslé and soloists of the Orquesta de Conciertos Straram, Salle Pleyel, Paris. The arrangement is listed in Le Pleyela's catalogues of Paris. From the same catalogue Falla's "Andalouza, *Pièce espagnole*, no. 4" is included, as well as accompaniment to *Siete canciones populares españolas.* It seems clear the popularity of these works with the general public.

The example given below clearly shows the definite changes from *El corregidor y la molinera* to *El sombrero de tres picos.*

Example 18.5 *El sombrero de tres picos,* **AMF LIII A8, no. 34.**

LII. *FUEGO FATUO*

More than one person has asked what prompted Falla to embark on such a project as this comic operetta in three acts on themes by Chopin with libretto by María Martínez Sierra. The work was composed between 1918–1919, and as a result, Falla refused a valuable commission from Diaghilev for *Pulcinella*, which went to Stravinsky. Paulo Pinamonti theorizes that this Chopin exercise might well have been Falla's search for a neoclassic expression and a way out of the folksong typeset, which threatened to become a noose around his neck.

Instrumentation and characters include the following: 2.1+1.2.2-2.2.3.0-perc-piano (four hands)-harp-st.; Clara (soprano), Leonardo (baritone), Lord Tristán (bass), Lisa (soprano), Marionetta (mezzo-soprano), and chorus.

The musical form is structured as follows:

Act I: 1. Duo-Clara and Leonardo, Waltz, op. 64/3 and Scherzo no. 2, op. 31; 2. Leonardo's aria, Scherzo, no. 4, op. 54 (middle part); 3. Lord Tristán's aria, Mazurka, no. 15, op. 24/2; 4. Lisa's aria with chorus, Bolero, op. 19; 5. Trio with Lisa, Leonardo, and Lord Tristán, Mazurka no. 25, op. 33/4; 6. Clara's aria, Scherzo no. 2, op. 31;

Act II: 1. Lisa's aria, Polish songs, op. 74/2 (Sopeña indicates the "Berceuse, original in the manner of. . . ."); 2. Leonardo's aria, Étude, no. 3, op. 10/3; No. 3 duo between Lord Tristán and Marionetta, Mazurka no. 8, op. 7/4; 4. Duo between Leonardo and Lisa, first Ballade, op. 23; 5. Lisa and chorus (quintet), Waltz, no. 5, op. 42 and Mazurka no. 51 (Gailliard); 6. Leonardo's aria, Étude, no. 12, op. 10/12;

Act III: 1. Chorus, Tarantela, op. 43; 2. Lisa and chorus, Polish songs, op. 74/1; 3. Clara's song, Berceuse, op. 57; 4. Duo between Clara and Leonardo, fourth Ballade, op. 52; 5. Lisa, Clara, Leonardo, and chorus, Barcarolle, op. 60.

The work was never premiered in its original form. However, A. Ros Marbá made an instrumental version of acts I and III without voices in 1976. This first performance was given on 1 July 1976, by Orquesta Nacional de España, with A. Ros Marbá conducting at the Festival de Granada.

The manuscript of the complete vocal-piano is found in the AMF, as well as the manuscript of the orchestral score, acts I and III, and sketches of nos. 1 and 3 from act II of the orchestral suite. Also housed there is

Example 18.6   *Fuego fatuo,* AMF LII A4, Act I, no. 3, p. 1.

the libretto of act II. A facsimile edition was published in 1999 by Yvan Nommick and AMF.[8]

MFE/CH have published the Ros Marbá version in 1996, while Chester copyrighted it in 1983.

LIV. *EL CORAZÓN CIEGO*

The two men's songs for act IV of G. Martínez Sierra's comedy of the same name were composed by Falla in 1919. Although the manuscript is not found, a photocopy of "letanía mora" with vocal sketches for *Psyché* on the inverse front side and *Fanfare pour une fête* on the reverse exists in the AMF.

In a letter to Falla (13 August 1919),[9] María Martínez urgently requested Falla to write two Moorish melodies for two men's voices, one with a "happy rhythm and almost shameless" and the other of "melancholic character," for the the characters Mustafá and Alí. In a subsequent undated postcard, María sends her gratitude to Falla for the songs, saying they are for the fourth act and she doesn't know who will sing them. This work was the last of the collaboration before Falla broke with the Martínez Sierras.

The debut was given by Martínez Sierras' Company in November of 1919 at San Sebastián with the cast of: Jesús Tordesillas (Mustafá) and Juan Martínez Román (Alí). Other performances took place in Madrid by the Martínez Sierra's Company.

The text of the work may be found in G. Martínez Sierra's *Obras completas.* "El Corazón ciego" by Editora Estrella, Madrid, 1922.

Example 18.7   *El corazón ciego,* AMF LIV A1.

The original manuscript of the example below is found in AMF LXI (*Fanfare pour une fête*).

LV. *FANTASÍA BÆTICA*

This large work for solo piano was written in 1919 and is approximately 12' long. It is Falla's last virtuoso piece for piano. Although a single movement, it does contain three sections in a kind of A-B-A form. However, Yvan Nommick analyzes the piece as [A-B-C-D-]-E-[A'-B'-C'-D'-F]-Coda, but as the Intermezzo is so short (E), he discounts this section as constituting a B section in an A-B-A form.[10]

Commissioned by and dedicated to Artur Rubinstein, according to Falla, "(It is) the only work written by me with purely pianistic intentions to which its instrumental technique is referred. Another thing: the title of *Bætica* has no special Sevillan significance. With it (the title) I have tried to render homage to our Latin-Andalusian race."[11] Correspondence to Harry Kling reveals the story behind the correct spelling of "baetica," to use the diphthong "æ."

Sketch material at AMF of *Fantasía bætica* shows nineteen pages of the near-definitive version. On pages 20 and 21 (reverse) are contained sketches of a lento episode of the *Fantasía* and *Fanfare pour une fête* with dates of August 1921 and 26 December 1921. Other sketches are also found at AMF and the British Library.

Artur Rubinstein gave the debut in New York on 20 February 1920. Some biographers state that Rubinstein never played the work, but documents at the AMF show otherwise.[12] Rubinstein apparently played it also in London (1922), Madrid, Málaga, Barcelona (1923), and Cádiz (1926). He later abandoned the work, saying that he didn't understand it and that it was too long. Falla's friend Gerardo Diego was one of the next pianists to promote the piece.

The work was published by Chester in 1922 and again in 1996. See chapter 9 for a more detailed commentary of this work.

NOTES

1. Nommick, Thesis, I, 166.
2. AGC, 111–112, citing Valentín de Pedro, "Catalina Bárcena y Martínez Sierra recuerdan al Maestro Falla" in *¡Aqui esta!*, XI, n° 1098, Buenos Aires, 1946, p. 3.

3. AGC, 115.

4. Artur Rubinstein, *My Young Years*. New York: Alfred A. Knopf, 1975, 115.

5. Ibid.

6. Pahissa, 99–100. ". . . como la tan sentida y fina *Canción del sauce*, de Desdémona.—¿Y aquellos sones de trompetas, nobles y originales? . . ."

7. Nommick, Thesis, II, 389.

8. Manuel de Falla, *Fuego Fatuo*, Edición facsímil de los manuscritos 9017-I, LII A2, A6, A9, A10 del Archivo Manuel de Falla, Edición y estudio de Yvan Nommick. Granada: Archivo Manuel de Falla, 1999.

9. AGC, 168.

10. Nommick, Thesis, II, 389.

11. AGC, 170.

12. Sopeña, 115.

Chapter 19

Period beyond Nationalism (1920–1926)

Homenaje, Pièce de guitare écrite pour "Le tombeau de Claude Debussy"
Fanfare pour une fête
Canto de los remeros del Volga (del cancionero musical ruso)
Españoleta
Misterio de los reyes magos
El retablo de Maese Pedro
Dos Preludios (Adolfo Salazar)
Prélude à l'après-midi d'un faune (Claude Debussy)
Psyché
Obertura de "El barbero de Sevilla" (Rossini)
Concerto per clavicembalo (o pianoforte), flauto, oboe, clarinetto, violino e violoncello

Although fulfilling a lifelong dream to live in Granada, Paris is still close to Falla's heart in many of the works of this period, written after his split with the Martínez Sierra couple. The "period beyond nationalism" begins with Falla's formal eulogy to Debussy, which simultaneously becomes the first contemporary piece written for solo guitar. *Fanfare pour une fête* and *Psyché* also reflect the French influence, while *Canto de los remeros del Volga* uniquely incorporates some of theories of Lucas.

Falla's two masterpieces—*El retablo* and the *Concerto*—are also created during this period. To prepare for the technical and logistical problems of *El retablo*, Falla experiments in *Españoleta* and *Misterio de los reyes magos*. His fascination with the harpsichord becomes evident through his correspondence with Wanda Landowska and eventual composition of the *Concerto*.

Too, Falla's preoccupation with the creation and nurturing of the Orquesta Bética de Cámara is reflected in the arrangements for the chamber ensemble—*Dos Preludios, Homenaje, Pièce de guitare écrite pour "Le tombeau de Claude Debussy," Prelúde a l'après-midi d'une faune (Claude Debussy), Obertura de "El barbero de Sevilla"(Rossini)*.

Yvan Nommick characterizes this period as a progressive detachment from folkloric material, which he had already brought to his preceding works to a very high degree of stylization.[1] In this period Falla employs the resources that the Spanish erudite and religious musical tradition offer him. This is seen through (1) his writing becomes clearer and his style more objective; (2) his taste for perfection and concision of form is affirmed through formal structures of the past, which he treats with great freedom; (3) his orchestral conception is refined and reduced to that of a chamber orchestra; and (4) complementing the latter, Falla's writing becomes more linear, while his use of counterpoint assumes a great importance.

LVI, LVII. *Homenaje, Pièce de guitare écrite pour "Le tombeau de Claude Debussy"*

Written after the death of Claude Debussy, Falla chose the guitar to eulogize Debussy. After being asked for a piece by guitarist Miguel Llobet, Falla was able to complete both requests by composing this work. It is the first modern work for guitar and appeared, along with works of other composers, in a supplement, no. 2, of the *Revue Musicale,* edited by Henri Prunières, on 1 December 1920. Seventy measures in length, the work recalls a citation in the penultimate phrase from Debussy's "La soirée dans Granade" from his suite *Estampes*. Its date of completion is given as August 1920. Its musical form may be seen as a combination of a rondo and bipartite form.[2] Its approximate duration is 3'10" (LVI).

The debut of the work was not given on guitar but on harp-lute by Marie-Louise Henri Casadesus at the Salle des Agriculteurs in Paris on 24 January 1921. The guitar debut was given by Miguel Llobet at the Teatro de la Comedia in Madrid on 8 March 1921. Guitarist Emilio Pujol performed it in Barcelona in April of 1921. The French guitar debut was played by Emilio Pujol at the Paris Conservatory on 2 December 1922.

The piece is published by MFE/Chester in 1996 and in 1921 by Chester with fingerings by Llobet.

On 8 September 1920, Falla completed his piano transcription (LVII) of the work entitled *Homenaje, Pièce de guitare écrite pour "Le tombeau de Claude Debussy."* Knowing Falla's working processes at the piano, like those of Stravinsky, it is possible that the piece really was written first at the piano and then transcribed for guitar and then back to piano again. It is approximately 3' in duration. Chester published the piano version in 1921 and again in 1996.

LXI. *FANFARE POUR UNE FÊTE*

This through-composed fanfare for two trumpets, tympani, and snare drum was written in August of 1921. Although the manuscript has not been found, the work was published in Fanfare magazine in London in 1922. It was also used in *Atlántida*. Approximately 3' long, the première was given by Eugene Goossens in London on 22 October 1921.

It begins with the notes G (sol = S), C (do = O), Bb (sib = B), and D (re = R), the reverse order of the name of Enrique Fernández Arbós, (A)RBOS, whose last name was also inspiration for another fanfare in 1934.

In the sketch material is found some popular songs from Granada such as the *villancico* "Que entre usté, mozo . . ."; "Ya viene Don Pedro/de la

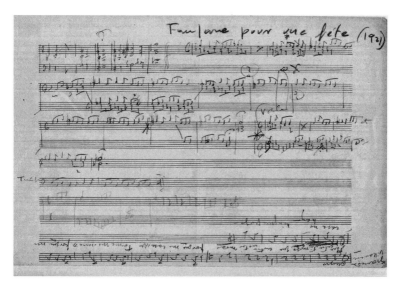

Example 19.1   *Fanfare pour une fête,* AMF LXI A1.

guerra huido" (Sierra de Parafranda); "Hacia Roma caminan/dos peregri-
nos" (Fuente Vaqueros); "Por la calle abajito/del 'tere-bol, teretarabell,
cara-col' " (Fuente Vaqueros); and "Ya viene la vieja/por las escaleras."

In other sketch material is found a version for three trumpets with the
Falla's indications "This one decidedly" and with vocal notes for *Psyché*
on the reverse, as well as notes with the title "Letania mora," perhaps related to two melodies that Falla made in 1919 for the Martínez Sierras'
El corazón ciego.

And yet on another page of sketch material are found notes for the
march "Mosqueteros del Rey de España. Desjardins (1702)" and on the
reverse "Louis XVI (Margery pére [?]. Haut-Fifres" possibly related to
the *Fanfare.*[3]

LXII. *Canto de los remeros del Volga*
(del cancionero musical ruso)

This piano piece based on a popular Russian song was petitioned by
Falla's diplomatic friend Ricardo Baeza to help relieve the hunger of
Russian refugees. It was written in March of 1922. From letters it is
known that Falla sent two original manuscripts: one for sale or auction
for the Russians' benefit and the other for Baeza's son, diplomat Fernando Baeza, to keep at his home Vera de Bidasoa. Falla apparently incorporates Lucas's theory into this piece, as seen in the accompanying
grace note figures. Its musical form may be seen as A-B-A-B-.A-Coda.
The work is aproximately 3'30".

It was published by UME in 1980. This edition contains many errors.
Later editions include: MFE/UME, 1996; and Chester, 1996. Sketches
are housed in AMF.

The debut probably took place in 1922, but definitely in 1971 in
Granada by pianist Manuel Carra.

LXIII. *Españoleta*

Falla was busy composing *El retablo de Maese Pedro,* which presented some logistical problems for him. Hence he collaborated with
García Lorca in two works—*Españoleta* and *Misterio de los reyes
magos*—that were performed in García Lorca's home puppet theater.
The incidental music for García Lorca's *La niña que riega la alba-*

Example 18.2 Programs of *Españoleta,* AMF LXIII, and *Misterio de los reyes magos,* AMF LXIV.

haca e el príncipe preguntón—*Españoleta*—was written in 1922. The manuscript housed in the AMF is complete, thus the duration is unknown. The work does include several pieces for harpsichord (possibly, according to Antonio Gallego), violin, clarinet, and lute (possibly, according to Antonio Gallego):[4]

1. An adaptation of Felipe Pedrell's *Españoleta y Paso y medio* from *Cancionero,* III, no. 88, as well as fragments of works by Debussy, Albéniz, and Ravel;
2. *Serenade of the Doll* (Debussy);
3. *La Vega de Granada* (Albéniz),
4. *Berceuse for piano and violin* (Ravel).
5. an arrangement of Stravinsky's *L'histoire du soldat* for clarinet, violin, and piano set to Cervantes's *Los dos habladores*;
6. an arrangement of Falla's setting of a thirteenth mystery, *Misterio de los reyes magos.*

The debut took place at García Lorca's house in Granada during Epiphany, on 6 January 1923, in a performance, "Títeres de Cachiporra

(Cristobita)" with Falla (harpsichord), José Gómez (violin), Alfredo Baldrés (clarinet), and José Molina (lute). Marionettes were fashioned by Hermenegildo Lanz and sets by F. García Lorca.

LXIV. *MISTERIO DE LOS REYES MAGOS*

Coupled with *Españoleta* is the incidental music of the same instrumentation as *Misterio de los reyes magos*. Several sketches are found in the AMF.

This work contains the following pieces:

1) an arrangement of *Cantiga "Ave et Eva"* (Pedrell's *Cancionero*, I, 147);
2) *Cantiga LXV (*Pedrell, *Cancionero,* III, 5);
3) Two selections from the *Llivre Vermell* (Pedrell, *Cancionero*, III, 8 and 8 bis); and
4) *Cançó de Nadal* ("Christmas Song"), an old *villancico* of the Three Kings from the East, harmonized by P. Luis Romeu.

The same musicians performed as in *Españoleta,* with the additional children singers, Isabel García Lorca and Laura de los Ríos Giner.

This work has been published as a first edition of "Cançó de Nadal" with an introduction by Yvan Nommick) by MFE in 1998.

LXV. *EL RETABLO DE MAESE PEDRO*

One of Falla's masterpieces, Master Peter's Puppet Show constitutes a unique musical adaptation and scenic presentation from an episode of Miguel de Cervantes's *El Ingenioso Cavallero Don Quixote de la Mancha* with the libretto by Falla. Falla dedicated the work to the glory of Miguel de Cervantes and to the Princesse de Polignac, who commissioned the piece for her home theater in Paris.

Falla worked on the piece from 1919–1923. It has an approximate duration of 27'. The manuscript and sketch material are housed in the AMF. It contains six scenes with the musical numbers:

Scene I—"El pregón," "La sinfonía de Maese Pedro," "Historia de la libertad de Melisendra";
Scene II—"La corte de Carlo Magno," "Melisendra";

Scene III—"El suplicio del Moro";
Cuadro IV—"Los Pirineos";
Cuadro V—"La fuga";
Cuadro VI—"La persecución"; Final.

The characters are: Trujamán (boy soprano), Maese Pedro (tenor), and Don Quijote (bass or baritone). Instrumentation includes: 1(1).2+1.1.1.-2.1.0.0.-tympani-perc-harpsichord-harp-lute-(or harp)-st (2.2.2.1.1). The concert version was given first, by the Orquesta Bética with Falla conducting at the Teatro San Fernando in Seville on 23 March 1923. In this performance were: Sr. Lledó (Don Quijote), Sr. Segura (Maese Pedro), and Francisco Redondo (Trujamán).

The debut of the scenic version took place at the Palace of the Princesse de Polignac in Paris on 25 June 1923. Cast and production crew included: Hector Dufranne (Don Quijote), Thomas Salignac (Maese Pedro), Manuel García y Amparito Peris (Trujamán), Wanda Landowska (harpsichord), Marie-Louise Casadesus (harp-lute), Concert Orchestra Golschamnn, Dr. Wladimir Golschmann, cond.; Manuel Angeles Ortiz and Marcel Guérin (frontpiece, curtain decor, and portable scenery), Hermenegildo Lanz (puppets with sculptured heads), M. Ángeles Ortiz; (figurines), Falla (scenic direction), and José Viñes Roda and Hernando Viñes (other scenery).

The work enjoyed an immediate success and was published in various languages. Chester published librettos in Spanish, French (G. Jean-Aubry), English (J. B. Trend), and German (Hans Jelmdi) from 1924–1926. The firm also published the full score and the piano-vocal score in 1924. MFE/CH republished the work in 1996.

LXVI. *DOS PRELUDIOS (ADOLFO SALAZAR)*

Falla's work in the creation of the Orquesta Bética de Cámara, with a vision to perform Spanish modern music in Spanish cities, necessitated the creation of sufficient works. Hence, transcriptions of two piano preludes by Adolfo Salazar were made by Falla (no. 1) and by Ernesto Halffter (no. 2) in 1924. The manuscript is in the AMF. The pieces are scored for: 2.1.1.1.-2.0.0.0-harp-st. In the SGAE catalogue this work is listed as *Preludio*. There was also a third prelude, which Oscar Esplá intended to orchestrate.

The debut was given by the Orquesta Bética de Cámara with Ernesto Halffter conducting at the Teatro Llorens in Seville on 11 June 1924.

PRÉLUDE À L'APRÈS-MIDI D'UN FAUNE (CLAUDE DEBUSSY)

Falla's transcription for chamber orchestra of Debussy's work dates from 1924 and was made for the OBC. The manuscript is in the AMF. Instrumentation is: 2.2.2.2-2.2.0.0.-perc-harp-st. This is the third prelude that belongs to the set of *Dos preludios* [LXVI], but is not catalogued by Antonio Gallego.

The debut probably took place on 20 November 1925, by the Orquesta Bética de Cámara, Ernesto Halffter conducting at the Teatro de San Fernando, Seville. Ernesto Halffter confessed to Eduardo Torres that this version sounded "better than the original."[5]

However, various pieces of correspondence between Falla and Segismundo Romero and others reveal Falla's attempt to make the arrangement ready for the OBC debut on 11 June 1924, at the Teatro Llorens in Seville, programs of the inaugural concert do not show that the Debussy-Falla work was played at that time.

The work is being published by MFE (date of 1996, revised by Mercedes Padilla).

LXVII. PSYCHÉ

This chamber song on a text by Jean-Aubry was composed in 1924. It is scored for voice, flute, violin, viola, cello, and harp, and is a single movement. Its approximate duration is 4'30".

As early as 1910 (correspondence on 30 December 1910) interest was shown in a joint collaboration between Falla and Jean-Aubry. Compared to *Trois mélodies* this work is much more advanced harmonically. Debussy's influence is still present.

The debut was given by M. Josepa Regnard, mezzo-soprano, and members of Orquesta Bética de Cámara: Raquel Martí, harp; Miguel Pérez, flute; Fermin Pérez, violin; Fernando Romero, viola; Segismundo Romero, cello, with Falla, conducting. The performance took place at the Palau de la Música Catalana (Associació de Música "Da Camera") in Barcelona on 9 February 1925.

It was first published by Chester in 1927 and later by MFE/CH in 1996.

LXX. *Obertura de "El barbero de Sevilla" (Rossini)*

This overture for chamber orchestra is yet another work transcribed for the OBC by Falla around 1924–1925. Based on Rossini's overture, it is a single movement with instrumentation of 1+1.2.2.2-2.2.0.0.-tympani-st. The trombone part was omitted, as no trombones were used in the OBC. The manuscript was located in the OBC archives by Luis Izquiedro, director de la Bética Filarmónica, Madrid, November 1980.

The first performance ot the overture was given by the OBC, conducted by Ernesto Halffter at the Teatro San Fernando in Seville on 20 November 1925.

The work has been published by MFE in 1996, revised by Mercedes Padilla. It has nothing to do with Falla's project for an opera on the same theme.

LXXI. *Concerto per clavicembalo (o pianoforte), Flauto, Oboe, Clarinetto, Violino e Violoncello*

Falla's innovative chamber Concerto for Harpsichord (or Piano), Flute, Oboe, Clarinet, Violin, and Violoncello was composed from 1923–1926. It is his last long work. Three movements in length, its approximate duration is 15'. Its musical form may be seen as: *Allegro* (monothematic late Baroque concerto movement); *Lento* (combination of A-B-A and variation form); and *Vivace* (monothematic sonata form).[6]

Sketch material and the manuscript are housed at the AMF. Written in response to Wanda Landowska's request for new works for the harpsichord from various composers, the *Concerto* is considered by many to be Falla's greatest achievement. In the sketch material are found three workings of the folksong "De los alamos vengo" used in the first movement. Two models of inspiration for the *Concerto* may be found in Schönberg's *Pierrot lunaire* and Stravinsky's *L'Histoire du soldat*.

The debut was given by Wanda Landowska on harpsichord with Falla, conducting at an Asociación de Música de Cámara concert in Barcelona on 5 November 1926.

The French debut was played by Falla on both harpsichord and piano at Salle Pleyel in Paris on 14 May 1927. This was followed by the British debut at Aeolian Hall in London on 22 June 1927. A Falla festival at the Palacio de la Música in Madrid on 5 November 1927 also presented the work.

Example 19.3   *Concerto per clavicembalo (o pianoforte), flauto, oboe, clarinetto, violino e violoncello,* **AMF LXXI, first movement, MFE, p. 3.**

Max Eschig published the score, as well as the keyboard part alone, in 1927. In 1996, MFE/CH and Eschig published the work for the fiftieth anniversary of Falla's death.

Noteworthy is Falla's own performance, which can be heard from the 1930 Columbia LX 1366–67, 1418 recording, reproduced in Manuel de

Falla (1876–1946), *Grabaciones históricas* on Almaviva DS 0121. The musicians performing with Falla are Marcel Moyse, Georges Bonneau, Emile Godeau, Marcel Darrieux, and Auguste Cruque.

NOTES

1. Nommick, Thesis, II, 208–209.
2. Nommick, Thesis, II, 389.
3. AGC, 188.
4. AGC, 192.
5. AGC, 225. Ernesto Halffter-Eduardo Torres letter (2 May 1924).
6. Nommick, Thesis, II, 389.

Chapter 20

Period of Research for a Universal Synthesis (1927–1946)

Soneto a Córdoba de Luís de Góngora
El gran teatro del mundo
Duo seraphim clamabant (in festo S. S. Trinitatis) de Tomás Luis de Victoria
Sanctus (T. L. de Victoria)
Ave María (T. L. de Victoria)
Jesus ait
Balada de Mallorca
L'Amfiparnaso (Horatio Vecchi)
Fanfare sobre el nombre de Arbós
La vuelta de Egipto
Comedia famosa de la Moça de Cántaro
Invocatio ad individuam Trinitatem
Pour le tombeau de Paul Dukas
Officium hebdomadae sanctae (T. L. de Victoria)
Himno marcial (Pedrell)
Homenajes, Suite
Emendemus in melius (C. de Morales)
Madrigal: Prado verde y florido (F. Guerrero)
Romance de Granada (Qué es ti desconsolado) (J. del Encina)
Tan buen ganadico (J. del Encina)
¡Ora, sus! (Escobar)
O magnum mysterium (In Circuncisione Domine) (T. L. de Victoria)
Tenebrae factae sunt (Responsorium V) (T. L. de Victoria)

Miserere mei Deus, Salmo 50 (T. L. de Victoria)
Vexilla regis (T. L. de Victoria)
In festo Sancti Jacobi (O lux et decus hispaniae) (T. L. de Victoria)
Benedictus (de la Misa Vidi Speciosam de T. L. de Victoria)
Gloria (de la Misa Vidi Speciosam de T. L. de Victoria)
Glorya al Senyor
Romance de Don Joan y Don Ramón (de F. Pedrell)
Canción de la estrella (Los Pirineos de F. Pedrell)
Atlántida

Falla's search for a universality, beyond national borders, is apparent in this period, of which many works are grounded in the historical past. It may be termed a period of homage. It is also a period fraught with turmoil and illness, political upheaval, and a voluntary departure to Argentina. Given the former successes of many of Falla's works, this period is frustratingly incomplete.

Falla's absorption with the music of Spain's golden age of polyphony is reflected in his many expressive choral arrangements of works by Victoria, Vecchi, Morales, Guerrero, Encina, and Escobar. Other historical tributes are paid to Luis de Góngora, Gaspar Sanz, Calderón de la Barca, and Lope de Vega. Chopin, too, is remembered in the *Balada a Mallorca*, as is Pedrell in several works: *Himno marcial, Pedrelliana* from the suite *Homenajes*, *Romance de Don Joan y Don Ramón, Canción de la estrella*, as well as arrangements of several songs from the *Cancionero* used in *El gran teatro del mundo*. Falla also eulogizes Paul Dukas, E. F. Arbós, and Debussy (*Homenajes*). And last, but not least, he pays tribute to Cádiz, Barcelona, Sevilla, and Granada in *Atlántida*.

LXXII. *Soneto a Córdoba de Luís de Góngora*

Falla's song for voice and harp (or piano) on the text "Canción de Cuna" of the Virgen Mary by Luis de Góngora was composed for the tricentenary of Góngora's death in 1927. It is dedicated to Sra.Eugenia de Errazuriz. Its approximate duration is 3'.

In a dedicatory issue of the magazine *Litoral* (no. 5, 6, and 7 in Malaga, 1927) eight measures of the piece appear with the explanation: "By indication of Don Manuel de Falla we must make evident that the brevity of this collaboration in this homage only depends on the impossibility to "give extensively" much of this work before being published by Oxford University Press."[1]

The debut was given by Soprano Madeleine Greslé and Mme. Wurmser-Delcourt (harp) at Salle Pleyel in Paris on 14 May 1927.

On some of the sketch material (LXXIIA7, AMF) are found notes for the 3rd movement of the *Concerto* and *El gran teatro del mundo*.

The manuscript is found in the AMF. The work was first published by Oxford University Press, London, 1930, in versions in Spanish and English adapted by J. B. Trend. Chester published it in 1956 and MFE/Chester published the work in 1996.

LXXIII. *EL GRAN TEATRO DEL MUNDO*

From May–June of 1927, Falla wrote incidental music for the *auto sacramental* by Calderón de la Barca to be produced during the Corpus Christi celebration at the University of Granada that year. He used the

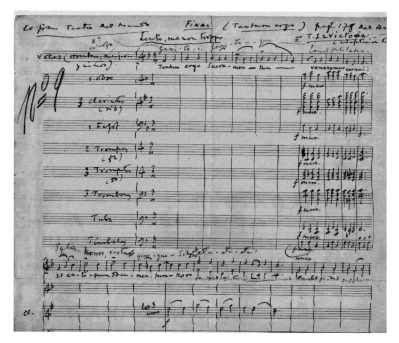

Example 20.1   *El gran teatro del mundo,* AMF LXXIII A1.

edition *Claderón de la Barca Autos Sacramentales* from the Collection "Clásicos Castellanos," published by Ediciones de la "Lectura," Madrid, 1926, which is preserved in the AMF.

The work is scored for mezzo-soprano, chorus, two guitars, oboe, four clarinets, bassoon, two trumpets, two trombones, tuba, timpani, and two guitars. Its approximate duration is 8'. It contains eight musical numbers:

1. "Toccata" (Gaspar Sanz/Cecilio de Roda;
2. "Toccata on the Amen of Dresden";
3. "Alaben al Señor" (on a Cantiga from Pedrell's *Cancionero*);
4. "Alma al otro/Que en el alma" (from Pedrell's *Cancionero*);
5. "Obrar bien" ("Amen of Dresden");
6. "Rey de este caduco imperio/Labrador a tu trabajo/Número tiene la dicha";
7. "Toda la hermosura humana" ("Amen de Dresden");
8. "Tantum ergo" (Tomás Luis Victoria).

The debut was given in June of 1927 at the Universidad de Granada, during the Corpus Christi festivities with conductor Ángel Barrios and scenic director Antonio Gallego Burín.

The musical manuscript is found in the AMF. A partially reconstructed version by Antonio Gallego was published by MFE in 1996.

LXXIV. *Duo seraphim clamabant (in festo S. S. Trinitatis) de Tomás Luis de Victoria*

Falla speaks of "two admirable pieces," the Sanctus and Ave María of T. L. de Victoria, which he was to conduct with the Orfeón Donostiarra. There is some confusion as to whether Falla made an expressive interpretation of Victoria's work or whether he merely conducted them. Antonio Gallego suggests that it is possible the idea of an expressive interpretation was a mere desire on the part of Falla and was never realized or possibly occurred in error in the printed program.[2]

It is speculated that if Falla made the work it was an expressive interpretation of the unaccompanied choral work for four-voice female choir of sopranos and contraltos (SSAA). The manuscript has not been found.

The debut thus is uncertain, although the piece is included in a printed program of the inaugural concert of the restored Antigua Abadía de San Telmo de San Sebastián on 3 September 1932, with

Falla conducting the Orfeón Donostiarra. Falla also refers to it letters to Adolfo Salazar on 15 August 1932, and to Juan Viniegra on 24 October 1932. The date is also corroborated in a program of the Orfeón Donostiarra, directed by J. Gorostidi, given in Granada at the Palacio de Carlos V on 14 May 1939.[3]

LXXV. *Sanctus (T. L. de Victoria)*

An "expressive interpretation" of Victoria's work for four-voice mixed choir dates from 1932 and was prepared for the same inaugural concert of the Orfeón Donostiarra with Falla conducting at the Antigua Abadía de San Telmo in San Sebastián on 3 September 1932.

Gallego speculates that the "Sanctus" probably belongs to the *Misa salve*, which was later included in the 1940 Argentine concerts, instead of the "Vidi Speciosam" from a 1592 edition of which Falla set the "Gloria and Benedictus" years later. The manuscript has not been found.

In a letter to José Ma Hernández Suárez in preparation for the Argentine concerts, Falla gives specific instructions for the "Sanctus" of the *Misa salve*.

LXXVI. *Ave María (T. L. de Victoria)*

Falla made yet another "expressive interpretation" of a Victoria work for four-voiced *a capella* choir in 1932. The curious mixture of seven voices each perhaps shows Falla's growing superstitious nature. For him, the number seven was symbolic, as he believed that his life fell into periods of seven years each.

It was performed at the same concert of the Orfeón Donostiarra as the two preceding pieces above. Another performance was given shortly after Falla's arrival in Argentina at the Teatro Colón in Buenos Aires on 11 November 1939.

The manuscript is found in the Teatro Colón Archives in Buenos Aires, Argentina, with some sketches located in the AMF.

LXXVII. *Jesus ait*

A short ten-measure work was written for the three-voiced children's choir of the "Cantinas escolares de Cádiz" and is dated November 1932, Granada.

Although the original manuscript is not found in the AMF, a copy of the piece was located amongst the papers of *Atlántida*. The Latin words "Jesus ait: sinite parvulos et nolite eos prohibere ad me venire" appear on the last stave of the piece.

LXXVIII. *BALADA DE MALLORCA*

This *a cappella* choral work for four-voiced mixed choir, on text by Jacinto Verdaguer, was composed in 1933 at Palma de Mallorca, a place intimately connected to Chopin, and during Falla's sojourn there to restore his health. He revised the work in 1945. The manuscript is found in the AMF. The approximate duration is 4'. The form may be seen as A-B-A'-B'-Coda.

Dedicated to Juan Ma Thomas, this work is based on the lyrical sections of Chopin's second Ballade, op. 38. Falla used two editions at least: one, a facsimile of the manscript contained in the library of the Paris National Conservatory (Paul Catin, Editor, Paris, 1930, ex. no. 14); and the other by Herrmann Scholtz entitled *Balladen und Impromptus von Fr. Chopin* of C. F. Peters, Leipzig, no date, with the stamp of "Establecimientos Musicales Casa Baña, San Martín 80, U.T. 9095."[4]

The debut was given by Capella Clásica de Mallorca with Juán Mª Thomas conducting, at the Third Chopin Festival held at the Cartuja de Valldemosa in Mallorca on 21 May 1933. Another memorable performance occurred with the same performance of the "definitive" version on 13 May 1934. The French pianist, Alfred Cortot, played the second Ballade of Chopin, then held his hands suspended over the keyboard until the choir entered with Falla's version. The performance was met with enormous applause.[5]

The work was published by Ricordi in 1975.

LXXIX. *L'AMFIPARNASO (HORATIO VECCHI)*

An "expressive interpretation" for five-voice mixed choir of Vecchi's madrigal was composed in 1934 at Palma de Mallorca. The manuscript is housed at the AMF.

Written for the Capella Clásica de Mallorca conducted by J. Ma Thomas, this work is based on the first madrigal of the Comedia Harmónica of Orazio Vecchi, act I, scene I: "O Pierulin dou'estu?" Falla used the edition of Luigi Torchi published in "L'Arte Musicale in Italia" (XIV° Secolo al SVIII°), Volume Quarto, Composicioni a più voci,

Secolo XVII°," published by Ricordi. Demarquez says Falla dedicated the work to the Capella Clásica shortly after the concert of 13 May 1934.[6]

LXXX. *Fanfare sobre el nombre de Arbós*

Another work composed on the island of Mallorca is the fanfare for brass and percussion dated February of 1934. It is a single movement with instrumentation of three trumpets, four French horns, tympani, and drums. Falla later incorporated it as the first movement of the suite *Homenajes*. Its musical form may be seen as A-B-C-D-E-A.[7]

The debut was given by Orquesta Sinfónica de Madrid with Enrique Fernández Arbós, conducting. The concert took place at the Teatro Calderón in Madrid on 28 March 1934, in celebration of the conductor's seventieth birthday.

A facsimile of the manuscript appeared in the magazine *Isla, Hojas de Arte y Letras*, no. 7–8 in Cádiz in 1935.

Example 20.2   *Fanfare sobre el nombre de Arbós,* **AMF LXXX A1.**

LXXXI. *La vuelta de Egipto*

Falla composed the incidental music for the for the 300th anniversary of the death of Lope de Vega (1635–1935) and a performance at the Universidad de Granada of a scenic representation of his *auto sacramental*. Falla's work is for four-voice mixed choir, two trumpets, and tympani. In 1935 in Granada.

It includes the musical numbers:

1. "Toccata" for two trumpets and timpani on the same theme of Gaspar Sanz, 17th c., in *El gran Teatro del Mundo*;
2. "Invocatio ad individuam Trinitatem" (original, T. L. de Victoria);
3. "Chorus," (Wagner's Parsifal/ "Amen of Dresden" used in *El gran teatro del Mundo*;
4. "Angelus Domini apparuit in somnis Joseph" for contralto and quartet of singers (16th c., F. A. Barbieri's *Cancionero de Palacio*);
5. "Cantiga LXI" "A creer devemos" harmonized by Pedrell (*Cancionero*, III/5) for chorus of four voices. Falla apparently chose some of the same pieces for the incidental music to Lope de Vega's *La moza de Cántaro*, produced by the same group in June of 1935 in Granada.

The debut was given at the Universidad de Granada in 1935 with Ángel Barrios conducting and Valentín Ruiz Aznar as musical director. Hermenegildo Lanz sculpted the figurines, while Antonio Gallego y Burín was the artistic director.

Real Musical published the work as "Invocación" in Marcos Vega's *Pequeña antología coral* in Madrid in 1987.

Example 20.3 *La vuelta de Egipto,* AMF LXXXI A1.

Comedia famosa de la Moça de Cántaro

The "Famous Comedy of the Girl from Cántaro" is mentioned but not catalogued by Antonio Gallego. This work was also produced at the Universidad de Granada under the artistic direction of Antonio Gallego y Burín, with costumes and sets by Hermenegildo Lanz, choral direction by V. Ruíz Aznar, and orchestral conductor Ángel Barrios. Ruíz Aznar referred to Falla's musical collaboration, perhaps confusing the *auto* with the comedy.[8]

LXXXII. *Invocatio ad individuam Trinitatem*

Falla wrote this short composition of thirteen measures for four-voice mixed choir for the scenic representation of the *auto sacramental* of Lope de Vega in 1935 in Granada as with the work above. The manuscript is located in the AMF.

Falla says the "Invocatio" is his, while the "Amen" is from T. L. de Victoria.[9]

LXXXIII. *Pour le tombeau de Paul Dukas*

This austere piano work written in memory of Falla's great friend in Paris, Paul Dukas, was completed in December 1935, in Granada, and contains a reference to D'Indy's sonata.[10] Its musical form may be seen as a set of monothematic variations:A-A'-A"-Coda. Its approximate duration is 3'45".

According to Sergio de Castro, who visited Falla in Argentina regularly during the last year and a half of the composer's life, Falla was influenced by the famous 14th century frescos at Campo Santo de Pisa, *Le Triomphe de la Mort* (attributed to Orcagan), when he composed this work. He had seen the frescos in 1928 when he went to Sienna for the Festival of the Société Internationale de Musique Contemporaine, where his *Retablo* was performed. However, this writer also observes some similarities to "Catacombae" of Mussorgsky's *Pictures at an Exhibition*.

The debut was given by pianist Joaquín Nin-Culmell in 1936. The work was later orchestrated, with the subtitle *Spes Vitae*, as the third piece in the suite *Homanajes*. On the reverse side of the sketch material is found the *Himno marcial*.[11]

Ricordi published the work in 1974. It first appeared in a commemorative issue of *La Revue Musicale* (May/June 1936) dedicated to the memory of Dukas (d. 17 May 1935), with pieces from Aubin, Barraine, Krein, Messiaen, Gabriel Pierné, Joaquín Rodrigo, Ropartz, and Schmitt.

LXXXIV. *OFFICIUM HEBDOMADAE SANCTAE* (*T. L. DE VICTORIA*)

Falla's "expressive interpretation" of Victoria's work is for four-voice choir. It was composed in February–March of 1937 and uses fragments from "Popule meus," "Sanctus inmortalis," "Herth," and "Destruxit quidam." It was written for the Cycle of the Holy Week of Victoria during the Spanish civil war. A two-page fragment lies in the AMF.[12]

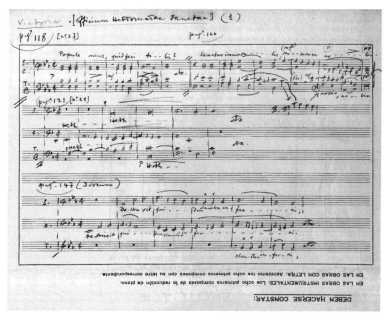

Example 20.4   *Officium hebdomadae sanctae* (T. L. de Victoria), AMF LXXXIV, A1.

LXXXV. *HIMNO MARCIAL* (**PEDRELL**)

This anthem for voice, piano, and drums was composed in Granada in 1937. It is an arrangement and adaptation of the "Canto de los Almogávares" from Pedrell's opera *Los Pirineos*, with a new text by José María

Pemán, that begins by hailing the national flag, a call to peaceful arms during Spain's turbulent war years.

Asked by government officials during the Spanish civil war to compose an anthem for them, this work is the result of Falla's efforts, then in poor health.

Sketches found at AMF include those for *Pour le tombeau de Paul Dukas* in the first version for piano, as well as a band arrangement for the band of Ricardo Dorado Janeiro, director of music of the regiment. Inf-ª San Marcial no. 22 with date of 15 January 1938, in Burgos, Spain. The Estado Mayor school was supposed to have sung it in Burgos.

LXXXVI. *HOMENAJES, SUITE*

Falla composed this four-movement suite for large orchestra between 1938–1939. He corrected it in July of 1941 in Argentina for subsequent publication. Its approximate duration is 18'. The instrumentation is: 2+1. 2+1.2+1.2+1.-4.3.3.1-tympani-perc-cel-harp-st.

The work contains the following movements:

1. "Fanfare sobre el nombre de Arbós";
2. "A Claude Debussy (Elegía de la guitarra")";
3. "A Paul Dukas (Spes Vitae)";
4. "Pedrelliana."

Only the last movement was new, the other three being orchestrations from previous works. "Pedrelliana" incorporates themes from Pedrell's *La Celestina* as a tribute to Falla's former mentor.

The debut was given on 18 November 1939, by the Orquesta del Teatro Colón in Buenos Aires, Argentina, with Falla conducting. The Spanish première was given in Barcelona on 26 February 1947.

The work was published by Ricordi in 1953.

LXXXVII. *EMENDEMUS IN MELIUS (C. DE MORALES)*

An "expressive interpretation" of Morales's work, Falla composed this work in 1939 in Granada for *a capella* five-voice mixed choir, featuring seven sopranos, seven contraltos, seven tenors (unison), seven tenors, and seven basses.

Falla said in a letter from Granada on 28 July 1939, to Dr. Rafael Vehils, president of the Institución Cultural Española of Buenos Aires, that he sent some choral works of the old Spanish masters for a concert to be held on 11 November 1939.

The debut was given by Falla and Coro del Teatro Colón, Buenos Aires, on 11 November 1939. Other works on the program were the *Sinfonietta* of Ernesto Halffter and *Noches en los jardines de España*. Juan José Castro conducted the Halffter work, while Falla conducted the remainder: *Emendemus in melius*, *Prado verde y florido* (Guerrero), *Qué es de ti desconsolado* and *Tan buen ganadico* (Juan del Encina), the *villancico ¡Ora, sus!* of Escobar, and *Ave María* of Victoria.

The manuscript lies in the AMF. The work was published by the Oliver Ditson Company of Boston in Latin and English with piano accompaniment for rehearsals (ed. Kurt Schindler) around 1939.

LXXXVIII. *Madrigal: Prado verde y florido (F. Guerrero)*

Falla's "expressive interpretation" of Guerrero's madrigal for four-voice mixed acapella choir (seven sopranos, seven contraltos, seven tenors, seven basses) was composed in Granada in 1939.

In the letter to Dr. Vehils, mentioned above, Falla says that he used the version from the third volume of Pedrell's *Cancionero*. However, Antonio Gallego contends that Falla used ideas from this madrigal in "Dulcinea's Song" (*El retablo de Maese Pedro*) taken from the vihuela version by Esteban Daza, published by Cecilio de Roda in Cervantes conferences, *Ilustraciones del Quijote*, in Madrid in 1905.

The manuscript is preserved in the AMF.

The debut is the same as the preceding work.

LXXXIX. *Romance de Granada (Qué es de ti desconsolado) (J. del Encina)*

An "expressive interpretation" of Encina's work for three-voice mixed choir, for seven contraltos, seven tenors, seven basses, was composed in Granada in 1939. The source is found in Barbieri's *Cancionero de los siglos XV y XVI*, no. 315; also Pedrell's *Cancionero*, III/19. The manuscript lies in the AMF.

The debut was the same as the preceding work.

XC. *TAN BUEN GANADICO (J. DEL ENCINA)*

Falla's "expressive interpretation" of Encina's *villancico* for four-voiced mixed choir (SATB)—seven sopranos, seven contraltos, seven tenors, seven basses—was also composed in Granada in 1939. It is taken from Palacio's *Cancionero*, no. 393.

The debut is the same as the preceding work.

XCI. *¡ORA, SUS!* (*ESCOBAR*)

Another "expressive interpretation" of Escobar's *villancico* for 4-voice mixed acapella choir (SATB)—seven sopranos, seven contraltos, seven tenors, seven basses—was also composed in Granada in 1939.

The source is found in Palacio's *Cancionero*, no.347 and Pedrell's *Cancionero*, III, no.36. The manuscript lies in the Archivo Teatro Colón. The debut is the same as the preceding work.

XCII. *O MAGNUM MYSTERIUM* (*IN CIRCUNCISIONE DOMINE*) (*T. L. DE VICTORIA*)

Falla's "expressive interpretation" of Victoria's work for SATB *a capella* choir was made between 1940–1942 in Villa del Lago, Argentina. Length: single movement; revision and "expressive interpretation" for *a capella* four-voiced mixed choir (SATB). Falla considered the possibility of instrumental accompaniment, including organ, harp, brass, strings, winds, percussion, harpsichord, and guitars.

This work was arranged for the 400th anniversary of the birth of Victoria. In July of 1940 Rafael Vehils sent Falla volumes I, V, and VII of the *Opera Omnia* of Victoria, published by Pedrell, acknowledging that Victoria had been born in 1548, not in 1540 as was generally thought.[13]

Falla chose several works to set: "O magnum misteryum (Alleluia)," I/14; "Beata Virgine," I/140; "Gloria," V/66; "Sit laus Deo," V/102; "Improperia," V/174; "In Nativitate (Alleluia)," I/142; and "In festo Sancti Jacobi," I/85. Falla also considered "Victimae Paschali," VII/147, and "Veni Sancte Spiritu," VII/141.

Reference is also made to Purcell, as can be seen when considering instrumental accompaniment of the two choruses.

As late as 1942, from correspondence with José M. Hernández Suárez, the "definitive" version was still being discussed.

The debut is uncertain, however the project resulted from a projected concert "Homage to Victoria" on the fourth centenary of his birth, sponsored by Spanish Cultural Institute. In the end it was decided to dedicate half of the concert to Victoria, half to Pedrell. According to Jorge de Persia, this concert was never realized

A photocopy of the original is found in the Archivo Teatro Colón, discovered by Jorge de Persia.

XCIII. *Tenebrae factae sunt (Responsorium V)* *(T. L. de Victoria)*

Falla's revision and "expressive interpretation" for four-voiced mixed choir (SSAT) was made for same concert as mentioned in the above work, with source being identical. It was paired with the *Miserere mei Deus,* which appreared first. It was composed from 1940–1942 in Villa del Lago, Argentina.

A photocopy of the original, with Falla's corrections plus the psalm *Miserere mei Deus* (on p. 6 and 7) was found by Jorge de Persia in the Teatro Colón Archivo, Buenos Aires.

XCIV. *Miserere mei Deus,* *Salmo 50 (T. L. de Victoria)*

Falla's revised and "expressively interpreted" choral work for double choir (SATB + SSAT), based on Victoria's work, was made from 1940–1942 in Villa del Lago, Argentina. The source is Psalm 50. It is paired with the work above to be given at the same concert.

The manuscript lies in the Archivo Teatro Colón in Buenos Aires, Argentina.

XCV. *Vexilla regis (T. L. de Victoria)*

Falla's revised and "expressively interpreted" work for four-voice *a capella* mixed choir, based on Victoria's work, was made from 1940–1942, in Villa del Lago, Argentina, for the same concert as the above work. The manuscript has not been found.

XCVI. *IN FESTO SANCTI JACOBI (O LUX ET DECUS HISPANIAE) (T. L. DE VICTORIA)*

Falla's "revised and expressive interpretation" for *a capella* mixed choir (including children), SSATB, is based on Victoria's work. It was made from 1940–1942 in Villa del Lago, Argentina.

The manuscript lies in the AMF. Photocopies of the original were found by Jorge de Persia at the Archivo Musical del Teatro Colón, with the composer's corrections; another copy also was found which is written one step higher.

The work was written for the same concert as the above work.

XCVII. *BENEDICTUS (DE LA MISA VIDI SPECIOSAM) DE T. L. DE VICTORIA*

Falla's revision and "expressive interpretation" for four-voiced mixed choir (SA (children) TT or SAAT) is placed after the "Sanctus" of the *Salve Mass*. It was made under the same conditions and sources the above works from 1940–1942, in Villa del Lago, Argentina.

Manuscript lies in the AMF. Jorge de Persia found photocopies of the original as described in the work above, as well as another copy written a step lower.

XCVIII. *GLORIA (DE LA MISA VIDI SPECIOSAM) DE T. L. DE VICTORIA*

Falla's revision and "expressive interpretation" for SSATTB was written for the same circumstances as above, using the same sources, and is based on Victoria's work. It was made from 1940–1942, in Villa del Lago, Argentina.

Falla noted on the border of the program, "Credo or Gloria of a Mass yet to be chosen." It is known that this "Gloria" closed the program.

The manuscript lies in the AMF. Jorge de Persia found photocopies as described in the work above with one being written a step lower than the other.

XCIX. *GLORYA AL SENYOR*

Falla's "expressive version" of Pedrell's "admirable motet" from Pedrell's opera, *Los Pirineos*, for four-voiced mixed choir (SSTB) was made around 1942 in Villa del Lago, Argentina, for the same concert as the above work.

This work was written for the homage concert and also to commemorate Pedrell's birth centenary (19 February 1841). In Falla's words, "Admirable motet used by Pedrell (with adapted text—'Coro de monjes cantado por seres invisibles, en el fondo de la escena') in *Los Pirineos*," this "expressive version" eulogized Falla's former mentor.

The works on the second half of the concert, dedicated to Pedrell, were to include: "Pedrelliana" (from the suite *Homenajes*), the "Romance de Don Joan y Don Ramón," the "Canción de la estrella," and the "Finale of Glossa" (*Sinfonía de las Montañas*).

The manuscript lies in the AMF.

C. *Romance de Don Joan y Don Ramón* (*F. Pedrell*)

Falla's revision and an "expressive interpretation" of Pedrell's 1902 ballad for SATTBB was made from 1941–1942, in Villa del Lago, Argentina for the same concert listed above. The work contains 100 measures.

From the original printed version by Oliver Ditson Company of New York (no date given), translated into English by Kurt Schindler with many pencil markings reconstructing the Catalan text, it is possible to reconstruct Falla's version.

J. M. Thomas says Falla may have heard Pedrell's work in Mallorca.[14] Pedrell wrote the ballad for the Capella de Manacor, includes it in his *Cancionero*, I/46, saying the song was collected by Noguera in Manacor (Palma de Mallorca).

The manuscript lies in the AMF in Folder 7920/2. The work was published by Oliver Ditson Company, 1968.

CI. *Canción de la estrella* (*Los Pirineos de F. Pedrell*)

Falla's revision of Pedrell's orquestración of this aria for soprano and orchestra was made between 1941–1942, in Villa de Lago, Argentina.

Falla said in a letter from Villa del Lago to Conchita Badía on 8 August 1942, that he had sent her a copy of the score (not known if it was a piano-vocal or orchestral score).[15]

Falla revised the orchestration to include: soprano, 2.1.1.2.2-2.0.0.0-tympani-harp-st

CANÇÓ DE L'ESTRELLA

CANCIÓN DE LA ESTRELLA

Felipe Pedrell (1841-1922)
Versión de Manuel de Falla (1876-1946)

1

Example 20.5 *Canción de la estrella* from Pedrell's *Los Pirineos,* AMF CI ("Canción de la Estrella"), MFE (ed. Yvan Nommick), p. 1.

The manuscript is housed in the AMF. Antonio Gallego expresses doubt that the example contained in the AMF (*C1A1*) is the definitive orchestration, or if the orchestration was ever finished.

The debut was given by María Orán, soprano; and the Orquesta Ciudad de Granada with Josep Pons, conducting at the Festival de Granada, in Granada on 5 July 1996.

The work was published by MFE in 1998 with a prologue (text) and orchestral score edited by Yvan Nommick; piano-vocal edition is by Miguel Zanetti.

CII. *ATLÁNTIDA*

Falla's last work occupied him for almost the final twenty years of his life and was never completed by the composer. His great escape from the potential noose of stereotyped folk usage found a new expression in the search for a universal synthesis of materials and form. His choice of a scenic cantata resulted from at least three motives:[16] (1) the desire to renew the oratorio form in the 20th century; (2) the fervent desire to compose religious music; and (3) the boyhood dream of writing a great lyrical work.[17]

With regard to the first motive, two recent, significant models in Handelian oratorio style, by Honneger in the four-part *Le Roi David* of 1921 and by Stravinsky in his two-part opera-oratorio *Œdipus Rex* of 1926–1927, would not have escaped Falla's notice.[18]

Regarding the second motive, Yvan Nommick refers to Falla's letter dated 20 August 1926, to the priest-musician Juan María Thomas (1896–1966) in Palma de Mallorca, as the first hint of the *Atlántida* project.[19]

> For some time I dedicate myself to collaborations with professional journals, and, amongst the themes that I have in project, I am extremely fond of one that seems to me would be of great usefulness to no less than my ecclesiastical colleagues whose music is found, as you know, in a state generally worthy of pity.[20]

The Catholic "Motu Próprio" of Pío X prohibited whatever type of secular music in the church and limited the use of instruments, giving primacy to the organ. It supported the composition model of the polyphony of the 16th century.[21] Given all these restrictions, it is no wonder that Falla did not compose strict religious music.

The third motive is deeply entwined with Falla's love for the human voice. It is present throughout the entire tractory of his output, even in genres where it is not normally present—from his first work, *El conde de Villamediana*, through many others, such as all of his song settings (Christmas Eve songs, chamber songs, and songs with simple accompaniment), the Gypsy ballet, the pantomime, the ballet, the scenic works, the expressive versions of the Spanish polyphonic Renaissance, and the lyrical works (opera and *zarzuela*).[22] Almost as many of the unrealized projects, most of which are operas, must be included: *Le Jardinier de la Pompadour, Las flores, La muerte de Carmen, Le Barbero de Sevilla, Don Juan de España, Fuego fatuo, La gloria de don Ramiro, Romancero, Lola la Comedianta,* and *Les charmes de la faute, La tertulia* (piece for guitar).

The *Atlántida* project is based on a text of Jacinto Verdaguer's *L'Atlántida*, arranged by Falla, in Latin and Catalan. He worked on it from 1927–1946. The definitive version of the "Aria of Pirene" is the last music that Falla completed. After his death, *Atlántida* was revised and completed by his pupil, Ernesto Halffter. Falla inscribes the work: "To Cádiz, my native city, and to Barcelona, Seville, and Granada, to whom I am also bound by the debt of profound gratitude."[24] The work was conceived as an *auto sacramental*, a religious dramatization in which the people (in Falla's case, the chorus) join in with their songs.

Falla drew on vast and varied musical sources, such as the Carillon of St. Francis; music of the Incas; Japanese, Chinese, and Indochinese music; music from Sicily, Sarinia, Naples, and Puglia; music from ancient Greece; Catalan music; 16th century Spanish music; self-quotes (*El amor brujo, Fantasía bœtica, El retablo de Maese Pedro*); music from other composers (Verdi, Monteverdi, Handel); music of the Greek tragedies; popular Greek, Italian, and Indian music; Oriental music; 13th- and 14th-century music (*Huelgas Codex*); and Wagner (*Parsifal*), amongst others.[25]

The program of *Atlántida* is as follows:

A Genovese ship sinks near the shores of Spain and only a child, the young Christopher Columbus, is saved from the shipwreck and can reach the shore where he is rescued by a solitary Old Man who from now on watches over him. The Old Man begins to explain to the child the origin of the earth and the distant seas that are present on the horizon and tells him of the sunken Atlantis. He leaves at the moment where Alcide (Hercules), who came from Greece with the aim of attacking the Atlantis people, arrives at the Spanish side of the Pyrenees that he finds ablaze, ignited by a three-headed African monster, Geryon. In the course of the blaze, the King of the Pyrenees, Tubal, dies. Alcide finds his daughter, Pyrene, dying. Before dying, Pyrene gives Alcide the sceptre of his father and supplicates him to go kill the monster that wants to dominate Spain. Having to prepare a sepulture for Pyrene, Alcide turns toward the sea and sees a white ship that arrives at an appointed spot. Thrilled by this omen, he decides to draw along the side of the ship, a port that in-memory of her (Barcina) will take her name to Barcelona. Proceeding to Cadix, Alcide stops to attack Géryon but goes first to the garden of Hes-pérides, Atlantic port, where he finds a tree of golden apples and oranges and Hesperis, widow of Atlas with her seven children. Alcide goes to kill the dragon that winds up around the tree, defends the entrance to the con-tinent, consequently thickening out the tree. The Hesperides, welcomed by singing, felt that the death of the dragon, according to an old prophecy, foretold the end of Atlantis. They die and are rejoined in Heaven where they become the Pleiades. The Atlantis people raise the alarm wanting to attack Alcide; but Alcide, following the Mediterranean coast, returns to Cadix, carrying Hesperis and the orange tree that he will present to Spanish soil. In Cadix, he kills Géryon, then Antée, who came from Africa in order to defend with the Gotgones and the Harpies. Hav-ing thus chased the monsters, he leaves the water breaking off Mount Calpé, rushes towards the Atlandtide, and engulfs its inhabitants. At Cádix, Alcide marks with his sword these words on the Rock of Gibral-tar: "Non plus ultra," marking thus that which will be from now on the limit of the continent. He made Hesperis his wife but she cried for her lost land, died, and rejoined the Heaven where she became the star Ves-per that the poets call Venus.

The child Columbus became a man, always accompanied by the Old Man dream—to pierce the mystery of the Atlantic sea. He addressed Queen Isabel of Spain. She had a dream that a Columbian would come to steal her ring and she would let it fall into the sea where flowered islands would surge. "This Columbian," she says, "is that of whom we speak. He takes away my jewels." Colombus buys the ship's wings, recruits sailors, and embarks, going to another hemisphere with the Spanish empire. The tree of the Cross multiplies, the world reflects its image. The Old Man re-mains on earth, saying, "Fly Colombus, now I can die."[23]

The three parts and prologue last approximately 80'. Instrumentation is 2(1).2(1).2(1).2(1)-4.4.3.1-tympani-perc.-cel.-2 harp-2 pianos-st; The characters include: Corifeo (baritone); El niño (child); Pirene (con-tralto); Gerión (two tenors and one baritone); seven Pleiades: Maya, Aretusa, and Caieno (sopranos), Eriteia and Electra (mezzo-sopranos), Esperetusa and Alción (contraltos); a court lady (contralto); a page (child); Queen Isabel (soprano); and mixed choir.

In 1976 the Halffter version is found: "Prólogo," "L'Atlántida sub-mergida," and "Hymnus hispanicus;" first part: "L'incendi dels Pirineus,"

"Ária de Pirene," and "Càntic a Barcelona"; second part: "Hércules I Gerió Tricèfal," "Càntic a l'Atlántida," "Els jocs de les Plèiades," "Arribada d'Alcides a Gades," "Veus missatgeres," and "La Veu Divina;" third part: "El Pelegrí, El somni d'Isabel," "Les caravel-les," "La salve en el mar," and "La nit suprema."

The debut of the concert version was given at the Teatro del Liceo, in Barcelona on 24 November 1961, with Eduardo Toldrà, conducting.

The scenic version was given on 18 June 1962; 9 September 1976, for the centenary of Falla's birth with the orchestra and chorus of La Scala, Milan, and Thomas Schippers, conducting. The definitive" version, Lucerne Festival, Jesús López Cobos, conductor.

Falla's manuscript lies in the AMF. Ricordi published the piano-vocal score of Halffter's 1976 version in 1993. The orchestral version of Halffter and Italian version by Eugenio Montale were published in 1976, Ricordi also published the piano-vocal score in 1962.

Critics praised the work in the 1962 debut, calling parts of it "the most beautiful things of all the music of our century"; another said that the choral treatment represented "the noblest, loftiest, and most inspired work modern music has produced"; while yet another found parts to demonstrated "a powerful and ingenuous capacity to create in music."[26]

Clearly, *Atlántida* is Falla's most ambitious work.

NOTES

1. AGC, 233.
2. AGC, 241.
3. AGC, 241.
4. AGC, 245.
5. Demarquez, 183.
6. Ibid.
7. Nommick, Thesis, II, 389.
8. AGC, 249.
9. AGC, 251.
10. Iglesias-Piano, 262.
11. Sergio de Castro – Jambou, 22.
12. AGC, 253.
13. AGC, 263–265. Rafael Vehils-Falla letter dated 24 July 1940.
14. AGC, 273.
15. AGC, 275.
16. Nommick, Thesis, II, 274–277.

17. Nommick, Thesis, II, 275.

18. Nommick, Thesis, II, 227.

19. Thomas, XIII. "Desde hace algún tiempo me dedico a colaboraciones a revistas profesionales, y, entre los temas que tengo en proyecto, estoy sumamente encariñado con uno que me parece sería degran utilidade a no pocos de mis colegas eclesiásticos cuya música se halla, como Vd. sabe, en un estado generalmente digno de lástima."

20. Sopeña, 213.

21. Nommick, Thesis, II, 277.

22. Summarized and translated from Ernest Ansermet program notes 3 April 1963 in Victoria Hall of Geneva, cited in Nommick, Thesis, II, 292–293.

23. For a complete list, see Nommick, Thesis II, 303–309.

24. Demarquez, 236–237.

25. Demarquez, 237.

Genealogical Record
of Manuel de Falla

Birth and death dates are indicated by *b.* and *d.* respectively, in the order of day, month, and year.

FALLA'S PARENTS AND HEIRS

José María de Falla Franco (b. Cádiz, 21-8-1849; d. Madrid, 12-2-1919)

married (6-11-1848)

María Jesús Matheu Zabala (b. Cádiz, 1850; d. Madrid, 22-7-1919)

parents of

Manuel de Falla Matheu (b. Cádiz, 23-11-1876; d. Alta Gracia, Argentina, 14-11-1946)

and

José María "Pepito" de Falla Matheu, (b. Cádiz, 7-7-1878; d. Cádiz, ca. 1885)

and

María del Carmen de Falla Matheu (b. Cádiz, 21-6-1882; d. Jerez de la Frontera, Cádiz, 1-10-1971)

and

Servando de Falla Matheu (b. Cádiz, 15-7-1889; d. Cádiz, ca. 1889)

and

Germán de Falla Matheu (b. Cádiz, 15-7-1889; d. San Fernando, Cádiz, 29-7-1959)

married 20-8-1929

María Luisa López Montalvo (b. 25-4-1892; d. 3-11-1967)

parents of

Isabel de Falla López (b. Santa Ana, El Salvador, 20-2-1932)

and

Germán de Falla López (b. El Salvador, 5-7-1935; d. El Salvador 13-7-1935)

FALLA'S PATERNAL GRANDPARENTS

Francisco de Paula de Falla Álvarez (b. Cádiz, 3-9-1818; d. Cádiz, 10-1-1890)

married (6-11-1848)

María Dolores Franco Noche (b. 23-3-1818; d. 9-1-1869)

FALLA'S PATERNAL GREAT-GRANDPARENTS

Manuel José Franco y Franco (b. Cádiz, 26-2-1781)

married (1812)

Josefa Nuche de Borja (b. Cádiz, 12-7-1789)

(parents of María Dolores Franco Noche)
and

José María de Falla Conde (b. Sevilla, 22-6-1790; d. 22-9-1867) married (17-8-1817)

Blanca María Álvarez Méndez (b. Sevilla, 10-12-1788; d. 7-10-1854), first cousin of Juan de Dios Álvarez Méndez Mendizábal

(parents of Francisco de Paula de Falla Álvarez)

FALLA'S PATERNAL GREAT-GREAT GRANDPARENTS

Mateo Franco Jiménez (b. 31-12-1750)

married (8-6-1775)

María Franco Ledesma (b. 29-3-1755)

(parents of Manuel José Franco y Franco)
and

Pedro Nuche Morora

married (22-3-1791)

Ramona de Borja

(parents of Josefa Nuche de Borja)
and

Joaquín Hilario de Falla (b. Villarosa; d. Sevilla 17-10-1800)

married

Gabriela Conde (b. Villarosa)

(parents of José María de Falla Conde)
and

José Álvarez Montáñez (b. Sanlucar la Mayor)

married

Clara Méndez Montáñez (b. Cádiz, 5-7-1746)

(parents of Blanca María Álvarez Méndez)

FALLA'S MATERNAL GRANDPARENTS

María Jesús Zabala Córdoba (b. Guatemala, 1820)

married (17-I2-1844)

Manuel Matheu Parodi (b. Cádiz, 1819)

FALLA'S MATERNAL GREAT-GRANDPARENTS

Victor Zabala Ábalos (b. Valle de la Hermida, Guatemala, 1776)

married (1811)

María Ignacia Córdoba González

(parents of María Jesús Zabala Córdoba)
and

Manuel Matheu Batallini (b. Cádiz, 13-4-1793)

married (22-3-1818)

María Magdalena Parodi Quaglia (b. Cádiz, 22-7-1781)

(parents of Manuel Matheu Parodi)

FALLA'S MATERNAL GREAT-GREAT-GRANDPARENTS

Agustín Zabala

married

María Ábalos

(parents of Victor Zabala Ábalos)
and

José Córdoba

married

María Luisa González

>> (parents of María Ignacia Córdoba González)
>> and

Miguel Matheu (b. Mataró, 1757; d. Cádiz, 1816)

>> married (26-7-1784)

Manuela Batallini Copa (b. Cádiz, 1765)

>> (parents of Manuel Matheu Batallini)
>> and

Bartolomé Parodi Parodi (b.Villa San Cipriano)

>> married (1-4-1780)

Ana Quaglia Copa (b. Vélez-Málaga)

>> (parents of María Magdalena Parodi Quaglia)

For more details see *Iconografía/Iconography Manuel de Falla*, Madrid: SGAE, p. 68–69.

Bibliography

MONOGRAPHS (INCLUDING WRITINGS AND FACSIMILE EDITIONS)

Abad, Juan José. *Manuel de Falla*. Madrid: Ediciones Urbión, S.A., "Biblioteca Historica Grandes Personajes," 251 pp. Buenos Aires: Hyspamerica Ediciones Argentina, S.A., 1984.

Anonymous [Eric Blom]. *Manuel de Falla* "Miniature Essays," no. 4. London: J. &.W. Chester, 1922.

Arizaga, Rodolfo. *Manuel de Falla*. Buenos Aires: Goyanarte. 166 pp., 1961.

Aviñoa, Xosé. *Falla*. Barcelona: Daimon-Manuel Tamayo, 101 pp., 1985.

Benedetto, Alessio di. *Manuel de Falla. Homenaje pour "Le tombeau de Claude Debussy."* Milan: Carisch, 1996.

Campoamor González, Antonio. *Manuel de Falla, 1876–1946*. Madrid: Sedmay, 1976.

Campodónico, Luis. *Falla* (trans. F. Ávila), 2nd ed. Barcelona: Edicions 62, 1991; 1st ed. Paris: Editions du Seuil from "Collections Microcosme, Solfèges, no. 13," 188 pp., 1959.

Casanovas, José. *Manuel de Falla, Cien años*. Barcelona: Nuevo Arte Thor, 94 pp., 1976.

Costas, Carlos José. *Falla: cincuenta años después del "Retablo."* Cádiz: Ed. de la Caja de Ahorros de Cádiz, 48 pp., 1973.

Crichton, Ronald. *Falla* "BBC Music Guides" London: British Broadcasting Corporation, 104 pp., 1982.

Cúllar, José María de. *Falla: otro español universal*. Madrid: Ed. PPC, 48 pp., 1968.

Demarquez, Suzanne. *Manuel de Falla* (with introduction by B. Gavoty). Paris: Flammarión, 252 pp., 1963; English trans. by Salvator Attanasio, Philadelphia: Chilton Books (1968 and 1983), (Da Capo Press reprint, 1983 of Chilton 1st ed.

in 1968), 253 pp.; in Spanish, trans. by Juan-Eduardo Cirlot, Barcelona: Nueva Colección Labor (1968), 271 pp.

Falla Matheu, Manuel de. *El "cante jondo" (canto primitivo andaluz)*, facsimile ed. Granada: AMF, 1997.

――――. *Hymnus Hispanicus*, Facsimile ed. Granada: Ayuntamiento, 1993.

――――. *On Music and Musicians*, trans. by David Urman and J. M. Thorson. London: Marion Boyards, 1979.

――――. *Piezas españolas: Montañesa (Paisaje) y Andaluza.* Facsimile ed.Granada: Ayuntamiento, 1991.

――――. *Superposiciones.* Facsimile ed. Madrid: Carlos Lecea, 1975–1976.

――――. *La vida breve*, Facsimile ed. Antonio Gallego, dir. Granada: Publicaciones del AMF, 1997.

Fernández-Shaw, Guillermo. *Larga Historia de "La vida breve"* 2nd ed. Madrid: Ediciones de la *Revista de Occidente*, S.A., 1972. *Larga historia de "La vida breve:" Años de lucha de Manuel de Falla*, 1st ed. Madrid: Talleres Gráficos de la Sociedad de Autores Españoles, 1962.

Franco, Enrique. *Manuel de Falla y su obra.* Madrid: Publicaciones Españolas, 1976.

Gallego Gallego, Antonio. *Manuel de Falla y el amor brujo.* Madrid: Alianza Música, 1990.

García, Juan Alfonso. *Falla y Granada y otros escritos musicales.* Granada: Centro de Documentación Musical de Andalucía, 1991.

García del Busto, José Luis. *Falla.* Madrid: Alianza Cien, 1995.

Garrido Lopera, J. M. and E. D. de la Higuera. *Biografia de Manuel de Falla* (with introduction by Dámaso García Alonso). Granada: Juventudes Musicales Españolas-Comisión Pro-Centenario Manuel de Falla, 1977.

Gauthier, André. *Manuel de Falla. L'homme et son oeuvre.* Paris: Seghers, 1996.

Harper, Nancy Lee. *Manuel de Falla: A Bio-Bibliography.* Westport, Conn. and London: Greenwood Press.

Hess, Carol A. *Manuel de Falla and Modernism in Spain, 1898–1936.* Chicago and London: The University of Chicago Press, 2001.

Hoffelé, Jean-Charles. *Manuel de Falla.* Paris: Librairie Arthème Fayard, 1992.

Iglesias, Antonio. *Manuel de Falla (su obra para piano) y "Noches en Los Jardines de España"* (intro. by A. Gallego Morell), 2nd ed. Madrid: Coedition with Manuel de Falla Ediciones and Alpuerto, 2001.

Jaenisch, Julio. *Manuel de Falla und die spanische Musik.* Zurich: Atlantis Verlag, 1952.

James, Burnett. *Manuel de Falla & the Spanish Musical Renaissance.* London: Victor Gollancz, 1979.

Jiménez, Luis. *Mi recuerdo humano de Manuel de Falla* (intro. by Juan Alfonso García). Granada: Universidad de Granada-Comisión Pro-Centenario Manuel de Falla, 1980.

Kastiyo, José Luis. *Casa-Museo "Manuel de Falla"* Obra cultural, no. 7. Granada: Caja de Ahorros de Granada, 1971.

Manuel de Falla-Fuego Fatuo, edición facsímil de los manuscritos 9017-1, LII A2, A4, A6, A9, A10 del Archivo Manuel de Falla, edición y estudio de Yvan Nommick. Colección "Facsimiles." Serie "Manuscritos," no. 2. Granada: Publicaciones del Archivo Manuel de Falla, 1999.

Manuel de Falla, Piezas españolas, montañesa (Paisaje) y Andaluza, Paris 1908, edición facsímil, Introducción y Descripción de Antonio Gallego Gallego. Granada: Cuidad de Granada, 1991.

Masciopinto, F. Adolfo. *El nacionalismo musical en Manuel de Falla.* Santa Fe: Universidad Nacional del Litoral-Instituto Social ("Extensión Universitaria" no. 75), 1952.

Molina Fajardo, Eduardo. *Manuel de Falla y el "cante jondo."* Granada: *Universidad de Granada (Catedra "Manuel de Falla"),* 1962; facsimile edition with preface by Andrés Soria, Granada, 1990.

Orozco Díaz, Manuel. *Falla. Biografía ilustrada.* Barcelona: Salvat Editores, 2nd ed., 1985; 1st ed., Barcelona: Destino, 1968.

———. *Manuel de Falla. Historia de una derrota.* Barcelona: Destino, 1985.

Pahissa, Jaime. *Vida y obra de Manuel de Falla,* 2nd rev. and enlarged ed. Buenos Aires: Ricordi Americana, 1956; 1st ed., 1947.

Pahlen, Kurt. *Manuel de Falla und die Musik in Spanien.* Olten: Otto Walter, 1953. *Manuel de Falla y la música en España,* 1960.

Pedrell, Felipe. *Por nuestra música. Algunas observaciones sobre la magna cuestión de una Escuela lírica nacional motivadas por la Trilogía (tres cuadros y un prólogo) Los Pirineos, poema de D. Victor Balaguer, música del que suscribe y expuestas por.* Barcelona: Imp. de Henrich y Cia, 1981; facsimile edition by A. Gallego. Madrid: Ed. Música Mundana, Colección "Una cosa rara," no. 6, 1985.

Persia, Jorge de. *50 aniversario del viaje de Manuel de Falla de Granada a Argentina, 1939–1989.* Granada: Ayuntamiento de Granada, 1989.

———. *Los últimos años de Manuel de Falla.* Madrid: Sociedad General de Autores de España (Fondo de Cultura Económica, S. A. de C.V.), 1993.

Porras Soriano, Francisco. *Los títeres de Falla y García Lorca.* Madrid: Francisco Porras Soriano. 1995.

Roland-Manuel, Alexis. *Manuel de Falla.* Paris: Éd. d'aujourd'hui, reprint of 1st (1930) version, Paris: Cahiers d'art, 1977; Spanish translation by Vicente Salas Viu, Buenos Aires: Editorial Losada, 1945.

Sá e Costa, Henena. *Memórias. Uma vida em Concerto.* Coedition: Porto: Casa da Música, Porto 2001. Capital Europeia da Cultura and Campo das Letras, 2001.

Sagardía, Angel. *Vida y obra de Manuel de Falla,* 2nd ed. Madrid: Escelicer, S.A., 1967; *Manuel de Falla,* 1st ed. Madrid: Unión Musical Española, 1946.

Sopeña, Federico. *Vida y Obra de Falla.* Madrid: Turner Libros, S.A., 1988.

Thomas, Juan María. *Manuel de Falla en la isla.* Palma de Mallorca: Capella Classica, 1947.

Trend, John Brande. *Manuel de Falla and Spanish Music.* New York: Alfred A. Knopf, 1929; reprinted by Scholarly, St. Clair Shores, Michigan: 1977.

Viniegra y Lasso de la Vega, Juan J. *Vida íntima de Manuel de Falla y Matheu* (in collaboration with Carmen & Carlos Martel Viniegra), Cádiz: Diputación Provincial y Ayuntamiento-Caja de Ahorros y Monte de Piedad-Cámara Oficial de Comercio, Industria y Navegación, 1966.

ARTICLES AND OTHER REFERENCES TO FALLA IN MONOGRAPHS

Acker, Yolanda (Summer 1992–1993) "Manuel de Falla and Ernesto Halffter : a view from their correspondence" *Context*, no. 4, 35–41.

Adessi, Anna Rita (1999) "Aspects de l'influence stylistique de Debussy sur Manuel de Falla" in *Manuel de Falla, Latinité et Universalité, Actes du Colloque International tenu en Sorbonne 18–21 novembre 1996,* ed. Louis Jambou. Paris: Presses de l'Université de Paris-Sorbonne, 179–204.

Ager, Laurence (November 1967) "Fanfare" *Musical Times*, no. 108, 1001–1002.

Aguilar, Paco (1944) "Un día de Manuel de Falla" *A orillas de la música.* Buenos Aires: Losada (Biblioteca Contemporánea, no. 137), 9–17.

Alarcón Montero, Orlando (1985) "Manuel de Falla (1876–1946)" *Amor y neurosis en los genios de la música.* Madrid: Talleres Tipográficos AF, 76–79.

Alavedra, Joan (1975) "La intérprete ideal" C*onxita Badía, Una vida d'artista.* Barcelona: Pòrtic (Colleció Memòries, no. 18), 135–161.

Alcaraz, José. Antonio (1987) *Rodolfo Halffter.* Madrid: Asociación de compositores Sinfónicos Españoles ("El Compositor y su obra," no. 1), 11–18.

Alfaya, Javier (December 1996) "Manuel de Falla en su Cincuentenario" *Scherzo*, no. 110, 123.

Alonso, Miguel Manzano (January-March 1977) "Testimonios cristianos de Manuel de Falla" *Ara*, LI, 15–19.

———. (1993) "Fuentes populares en la música de *El sombrero de tres picos* de Manuel de Falla" *Nassarre, Revista Aragonesa de Musicología,* IX, no. 1. Zaragoza: Institución Fernando el Católico, 119–144.

Altermann, Jean-Pierre (June 1921) "Manuel de Falla" *La Revue Musicale*, VIII, 202–216.

d'Amico, Fedele (1989) "Un genio fra parentesi" *Manuel de Falla tra la Espagna e l'Europa.* Firenze: Leo S. Olschki Editore, 1–6.

Anderson, Walter V. (1 November 1931) "Manuel de Falla" *Ritmo*, 4.

Andrade da Silva, Tomás (January–June 1953) "El piano de Manuel de Falla." *Música*, III-IV, 69–83.

Ansermet, Ernest (29 September 1962) "Falla's *Atlántida*" *Opera News*, 8–13.

Ara, Pedro (1951) *El espíritu de Manuel de Falla.* Buenos Aires: Imprenta Balmes.

Aracil, Alfredo (October 1996) "El mundo musical de Manuel de Falla" Sevilla: *El siglo que viene*, no. 28, special commemorative edition. 26–34.

Arizaga, Rodolfo (1965) "La Atlántida" *Ars, Revista de Arte*, no. 100. Buenos Aires.

———. (1969) "Manuel de Falla y Juan José Castro" Buenos Aires: *Ars, Revista de Arte*.

———. (January–April 1982) "Crónicas americanas en la vida y la muerte de Manuel de Falla" *Revista Musical de Venezuela*, 49–71.

Arozamena, José María de (1970) "Falla y Zuloaga en un concurso de *cante jondo*." *I. Zuloaga, el pintor, el hombre*. San Sebastián: Sociedad Guipuzcoana de Ediciones y Publicaciones, 219–234.

Arrebola, Alfredo (1986) *El sentir flamenco en Falla y Picasso*. Málaga: Universidad de Málaga.

Auric, Georges (15 April 1928) "Manuel de Falla à l'Opéra Comique" *Les annales*, 366.

Bal y Gay, Jesús (January 1947) "Manuel de Falla" *Nuestra Música*, V, 19–24.

———. (n.d.) "Manuel de Falla visto en sus escritos." AMF: Folder 9094.

———. (Fall–Winter 1983) "La música en la Residencia" in *Poesía*, XVIII-XIX (monograph issue dedicated to the Residencia de Estudiantes), 156–158.

Barce, Ramón (February 1963) "Atlántida, el problema formal" *La estafeta literaria*, no. 258, 14–15.

———. (October 1996) "Falla visto por un compositor de nuestros días" *Manuel de Falla y su entorno*. Madrid: *Boletín de la Fundación Juan March*, no. 263 35.

———. (December 1996) "El rechazo de una generación." *Scherzo*, no. 110, 132–133.

Beardsley, Theodore S. (1969) "Manuel de Falla's Score for Calderon's *Gran teatro del mundo*: The Autograph Manuscript" in *Kentucky Romance Quarterly*, XVI, 63–74.

Bergamín, José (1985) "El canto y el santo: Manuel de Falla, maestro en la música y en la fe" *Prólogos epilogales*, (ed. "Epílogo prologal" by N. Dennis). Valencia: Pre-Textos, no. 62, 107–110.

Blas Vega, José (Winter 1993) "Manolo de Huelva (1892–1976), el guitarrista que inspiró a Falla" *La Caña*, no. 4, 4–8.

Blom, Eric (March 1947) "Manuel de Falla" *Tempo*, XVIII, 1–3.

Brody, Elaine (1977) "Viñes in Paris: New Light on Twentieth-Century Performance Practice." *Bernstein Festschrift*, 45–62.

Brownscombe, Peter (1973) "Spanish Nationalism and Impressionism as represented in Manuel de Falla's *Homenaje: pour le tombeau de Debussy*." *Dissonance* V, 1–10.

Budwig, Andrew (January-June 1982) "Una metodología para el estudio de la *Atlántida* de Manuel de Falla" *Revista de Musicología*, I, 155–159.

———. (Spring 1984) "The Evolution of Manuel de Falla's *The Three-Cornered Hat* (1916–1920)." *Journal of Musicological Research*, V, 191–212.

————. (1989) "The Rebirth of *Atlántida:* Preparing the Way for a new Edition" *Manuel de Falla tra la Spagna e l'Europa.* Firenze: Leo S. Olschki Editore, 189–207.

Campo, Conrado del (1984) "Manuel de Falla, músico español" *Escritos de Conrado del Campo* (recompiled, with comments by A. Iglesias). Madrid: Alpuerto, 111–134.

Campodónico, Luis (July 1968) "Manuel de Falla y José Bergamín" *Nuevo,* no. 25, 15–24.

Carpentier, Alejo (1980) *Ese músico que llevo dentro,* I, II (ed. and intro. by Z. Gómez). La Habana: Letras Cubanas ("Música") vol. I: " Monument to Falla," 231–232; vol. II: "El retablo de don Manuel," (86–88) "La vida breve," (109–111) "La Atlántida" (118–120) and "El estreno de El retablo" (372–374).

Casares Rodicio, Emilio (September–October 1982) "La música en España en las década de los veinte y treinta" *Hilo Musical,* CIIVI, 6–10.

————. ed. (1984) "Música y músicos de la Generación del 27" *La Música en la Generación de la República, Homenaje a Lorca 1915–1939.* Madrid: Ministerio de Cultura, 20–34.

————. (29 October 5–November 1987) "Falla y la gravitación de su magisterio" *España en la música de Occidente (Actas del congreso internacional celebrado en Salamanca),* II. Madrid: Minsterio de Cultura, 296–303.

————. (1989) "Manuel de Falla y los músicos de la Generación del 27" *Manuel de Falla tra la Spagna e l'Europa.* Firenze: Leo S. Olschki Editore, 49–63.

Castelnuovo Tedesco, M. (January 1923) " Musicisti contemporanei: Manuel de Falla" *Il Pianoforte,* I, 8–10.

Castro, Sergio de (1996) "Falla y sus trabajos 'atlantes,' 1945–46" *Manuel de Falla: Siete espacios para la escena.* Madrid: SGAE, 61–64.

Chase, Gilbert (January-March 1940) "Manuel de Falla's Music for Piano Solo" *The Chesterian,* CXLVIII, 41–46.

————. *The Music of Spain,* 2nd. rev. ed. New York: Dover, 1955; 1st ed., W.W. Norton & Co. and as *La música de España.* Buenos Aires: Hachette, 1943.

————. (Autumn 1967) "Manuel de Falla y 'La Gloria de don Ramiro'" (text in English and Spanish, trans. by M. Davies) *Artes Hispánicas-Hispanic Arts,* II, 4–26.

————. "Manuel de Falla" *The International Cyclopedia of Music and Musicians,* 10th ed., ed. Bruce Bohle, 1975. New York: Dodd, Mead, & Co., 666–669.

Chávez, Carlos (23 July 1970) *Falla en México.* México: Colegio Nacional; reprinted in *Pauta,* VII, no. 26–28, 61–68.

Chinchilla, Concha (July-December 1996) "Manuel de Falla, una bibliographía" *ÆDOM, Boletín de la Asociación Española de Documentación Musical,* III/2, 34–72.

Christoforidis, Michael (Winter 1992) "Manuel de Falla's homage to Debussy . . . and the guitar" *Context 3,* 3–8.

———. (Summer 1993–1994) "Manuel de Falla on Romanticism: Insights into an Uncited Text" *Context* 6, 26–31.

———. (Winter 1993) "Manuel de Falla y la guitarra flamenca" *La Caña*, no. 4, 40–44.

———. (1995) "De la composition d'un opéra: les conseils de Claude Debussy à Manuel de Falla" *Cahiers Debussy*, no. 19, 69–76. French translations by Odile Hirsch; Falla facsmilies translated by Sarah Hirsch.

———. (1995) "Manuel de Falla, Debussy and *La vida breve*" *Musicology Australia*, XVIII, 3–10.

———. (1995) "Folksong models and their sources in Manuel de Falla's *Siete canciones populares españolas.*" *Context 9*, 12–21.

———. (Feb.–March 1995) "Manuel de Falla y la guitarra flamenca" *Concerto* 5, 19–26.

———. (1996) "La chitarra flamenca nell'opera e nel pensiero di Manuel de Falla" *Guitart*, I, (special edition on Manuel de Falla) 35–40.

———. (1996) "*El retablo de Maese Pedro*: Manuel de Falla's Attempt at Forging a New Declamatory Style in Spanish" *Aflame with Music: 100 Years of Music at the University of Melbourne*, 69–78.

———. (1997) "Un acercamiento a la postura de Manuel de Falla en el *cante jondo* (canto primitivo andaluz)." *Concurso de "Cante Jondo" Canto Primitivo Andaluz, Granada 1922*, facsimile edition. Granada: Archivo Manuel de Falla, Imprenta Urania.

———. (January 1997) "The *Life* of Falla" *24 Hours* (A.B.C. Radio), 36–38.

———. (1999) "Hacia un nuevo sonoro en *El retablo de maese Pedro*" in *Manuel de Falla, Latinité et Universalité, Actes du Colloque International tenu en Sorbonne 18–21 novembre 1996,* ed. Louis Jambou. Paris: Presses de l'Université de Paris-Sorbonne, 219–235.

Christoforidis, Michael and Juan Ruiz Jiménez (1996) "Content and Context of Manuscript 975 of the Manuel de Falla Library" *Aflame with Music*, 499–504.

Coeuroy, André (1928) "Pedrell, Falla et l'ibérisme" *Panorama de la Musique Contemporaine*. Paris: Simon Kra ("Les Documentaires"), 37–45.

Collet, Henri (1929) "Le realisme d'Albéniz, et de Falla." *L'Essor de la musique espagnole au XXe Siècle*. Paris: Max Eschig, 67–81.

———. (January 1947) "La mort de Manuel de Falla" *La Revue Musicale*, CCIV, 27–28.

Crichton, Ronald (17 March 1978) "Falla-Berio" *Financial Times*, 8.

———. (1982) "Manuel de Falla" *Encyclopedia Salvat de los grandes compositores*, IV. Pamplona: Salvat, 259–289.

———. (1989) "The final version of *El amor brujo*" *Manuel de Falla tra la Spagna e l'Europa*, 153–157.

Crivillé i Bargalló, Josep (January-February 1973) "De Cádiz a Granada, homenaje a Manuel de Falla" no. monograph of *Litoral* XXXV–XXXVI (III año literario). Reprinted as *Versión literaria de Manuel de Falla.*

——. (1988) "El folklore musical" *Historia de la música española*, vol. 7, Pablo López de Osaba, dir., reprinted from 1983. Madrid: Alianza Editorial, 272–275.

——. (1989) "Las *Siete canciones populares españolas* y el folklore" *Manuel de Falla tra la Spagna e l'Europa*. Firenze: Leo S. Olschki Editore, 141–152.

Cubiles, José Antonio (December 1996) "Mi recuerdo personal" *Scherzo*, no. 110, 142–143.

Demarquez, Suzanne (February 1962) "La Atlántida de Manuel de Falla." *Música*, XCV, 55–57.

Dent, Edward J. (28 Mayo 1921) "Manuel de Falla" *The National & The Atheneum*, 335–336.

Diego, Gerardo (9 June 1938) "Manuel de Falla" Conference text given at the Teatro Robleado de Gijón.

——. (1 June 1945) "Las canciones de Falla" *Música*, 12, 14–15.

——. (January 1947) "Falla y la Literatura" *Insula*, XIII, 2.

——. (14 November 1947) "Los *Homenajes* de Falla" *A.B.C.*, Madrid, 6–7.

——. (26 May 1977) "Crónica del Centenario de Góngora (1627–1927)" *Informaciones*, Madrid, Artes y Pensamientos, 5–7.

Diego, Gerardo, Joaquín Rodrigo, and Federico Sopeña (1949) "Manuel de Falla" *Diez años de música en España: musicología, intérpretes, compositores*. Madrid: Espasa-Calpe, 192 pp. 147–149.

Esplá, Oscar (1986) "*La Atlántida* y la religiosidad de Falla" *Escritos de Oscar Esplá*, III (translation, compilation, and commentary by A. Iglesias). Madrid: Alpuerto, 287–292.

Evans, Edwin (28 May 1921) "The Day of the Don" *Musical News and Herald*, MDXXII, 679–680.

——. (May 1921) "*The Three Cornered Hat*" *The Chesterian*, XV, 453–456.

——. (November 1924) "Master Peter's Puppet-Show" *The Chesterian*, XLII, 53–55.

Falla, María Isabel de (October 1984) "El Manuel de Falla americano" *Cádiz-Iberoamérica*, II, 50–52.

——. (November 1997) "El Archivo Manuel de Falla" *Tutti Música*, III/6, 5–7.

Franco, Enrique (July 1962) "La grande avventura di Atlántida" *Muisca d'oggi*, 4–5.

——. (1962) "Spain" *Musical Quarterly*, no. 48, 248–251.

——. (April–June 1966) "Manuel de Falla, cima y síntesis de la música española" *Tercer programa*, I, 141–164.

——. (January–March 1972) "Amadeo Vives y Manuel de Falla" *Boletín de la Sociedad General de Autores de España*, 15–19.

——. (24 December 1977) "La niña que riega la albahaca" *El País*, Madrid, Arte y Pensamiento, v.

——. (7 May 1978) "Dos proyectos goyescos de Manuel de Falla" *El País*, Madrid, 12.

——. (1980) "Falla (y Matheu), Manuel de" *The New Grove Dictionary of Music and Musicians* (ed. S. Sadie), VI. London: Macmillan, 371–374.

———. (December 1980) "En torno a *La vida breve*." *Música en España*, VII, 21–23.

———. (1986) "Manuel de Falla y sus mundos" and "Historia musical de *El amor brujo*." *El amor brujo*. Madrid: Círculo de Lectores, 11–63.

———. (March-April 1996) "*La vida breve*, noventa años después." Madrid: Teatro de la Zarzuela.

———. (1996) "*La vida breve*" *Manuel de Falla: Siete espacios para la escena* (Exposition catalogue) Madrid: SGAE.

———. (1996) "Falla en Fuendetodos" *Revista Atlántica. poesía*, no. 11, XXI–XXV.

———. (December 1996) "Los Testamentos de la Antequeruela." *Scherzo*, no. 110, 124–125.

Gallego Gallego, Antonio (May–August 1987) "Dulcinea en el prado (verde y florido)" *Revista de Musicología*, X/2, 685–699.

———. (1988) "Manuel de Falla folclorista: *Cantares de Nochebuena*" *Ritmo*, IX, no. 593 (special sixtieth anniversary supplement), 229–231.

———. (1988) "Manuel de Falla: Música per *El gran teatro del mundo* di Calderón" Pedro Calderón de la Barca, Manuel de Falla: *El gran teatro del mundo*, org. by Paolo Pinamonti for the Olimpico Vicenza Festival 1988 in Vicenza. Venice: Marsilio Ed., 195–217.

———. (1989) "De la pantomima *El corregidor y la molinera* al ballet *El sombrero de tres picos*" *Actas del Congreso "España y los Ballets Russes."* Granada: Festival de Granada.

———. (1989) "Los inéditos de Manuel de Falla. (Notas para el Catálogo completo de su obra musical" *Manuel de Falla tra la Spagna e l'Europa*. Firenze: Leo S. Olschki Editore, 87–106.

———. (1989) "Manuel de Falla y Felipe Pedrell : crónica de una amistad" *Anales de la Universidad a Distancia*. Tortosa: Centro Asociado de Tortosa, 181–218.

———. (December 1990) "Manuel de Falla y el Conservatorio" *Cuatro Lecciones magistrales* (pub. in 1992), 37–48.

———. (Spring-Summer, 1991) "Nueva obras de Falla en América: 'El canto a la estrella,' de *Los Pirineos* de Pedrell," *Inter-American Music Review, (Festchriften)* XI/2. Los Angeles: U. of California, 85–97.

———. (11 May 1993) *La España de Manuel de Falla*, Madrid: Fundación Juan March.

———. (October 1996) "Falla: una nueva imagen" "Manuel de Falla y su Entorno." Madrid: *Boletín de la Fundación Juan March*, No. 263, 31. (Issues no. 259 and 260 announce the concerts and conferences in Madrid of the fiftieth anniversary of the composer's death).

———. (1996) "Gerardo Diego, Cinco poemas a Falla" *Revista Atlántica, poesía*, IX-XI.

———. (1996) "*Pascua florida*, un proyecto poético de María O. de Lejárraga para Manuel de Falla" *Revista Atlántica, poesía*, XXXIII-LIV.

——. (1997) *"La vida breve" El sombrero de tres picos/La vida breve*. Madrid: Teatro Real-Fundación del Teatro Lírico, 58–69.

——. (1999) "Reflexiones sobre El año Falla 1996" in *Manuel de Falla, Latinité et Universalité, Actes du Colloque International tenu en Sorbonne 18–21 novembre 1996*, ed. Louis Jambou. Paris: Presses de l'Université de Paris-Sorbonne, 543–547.

Gallego Morell, Antonio (1996) "Falla, ante Calderón y Lope" *Manuel de Falla: Siete espacios para la escena*. Madrid: SGAE, 55–58.

Gallego y Burin, Antonio (18 October 1925) "Un gran músico español, el maestro Manuel de Falla." *La Razón*.

García, Juan Alfonso (October-December 1973) "Stravinsky-Falla, convergencias y divergencias" *Tesoro Sacro-Musical*, DCXXVI, 99–103.

——. (October-December 1976) "Manuel de Falla y la música eclesiástica" *Tesoro Sacro-Musical*, IV, 99–106.

——. (July-Sept. 1977) "Manuel de Falla y la música eclesiástica," II. *Tesoro Sacro-Musical*, III, 80–84.

——. (October-December 1977) "Manuel de Falla y la música eclesiástica," III. *Tesoro Sacro-Musical*, IV, 99–104.

García de Paredes, Elena (1989) "Nota bibliografica" *Manuel de Falla tra la Spagna e l'Europa*, 269–288.

García del Busto, José Luis (November 1976) "La Música de Falla, entre el antes y el después" *Reseña*, no. 99, 44–45.

——. (April-December 1988) "Entre Falla y hoy" *Pauta*, VII, no. 26–28, 70–76.

——. (1996) "Una mirada literaria sobre *El retablo de Maese Pedro* de Manuel de Falla" *Revista Atlántica. poesía*, no. 11, XXVII-XXXII.

García Lorca, Federico (1981) *Lola la comedianta* (critical ed. by P. Menarini with intro. by G. Diego). Madrid: Alianza Editorial ("Alianza Tres" no. 74).

García Lorca, Francisco (1980) "Manuel de Falla" *Federico y su mundo*. Madrid: Alianza Editorial ("Alianza Tres" no. 58), 148–157.

García Matos, Manuel (January-June 1953) "Folklore en Falla" *Música, Revista trimestral de los Conservatorios españoles y de la Sección de Musicología contemporânea del Instituto Español de Musicología del C.S.I.C.*, III-IV, 41–68.

——. (October-December 1953) "Folklore en Falla. II" *Música, Revista trimestral de los Conservatorios españoles y de la Sección de Musicología contemporañea del Instituto Español de Musicologia del C.S.I.C.*, VI, 33–52.

——. (1972) "El folklore en *La vida breve* de Manuel de Falla" *Anuario Musical*, XXVI, 173–197.

García Montero, Luis (1997) "Entre la nostalgia y la realidad" *El sombrero de tres picos/La vida breve*. Madrid: Teatro Real-Fundación del Teatro Lírico, 106–111.

García Morillo, Roberto (October 1941) "Manuel de Falla y la Fantasía Bética" *Boletín Latino-Americano de Música*, V, 585–599.

García Poliz, Susana (March-April 1996) "Nacionalismo y vanquardia en el lenguaje de Falla: su plasmación en la *Fantasía Bética*" *Concerto*, 8, 18–28.

———. (1999) "*Cante jondo y vanguardia europea en la Fantasía bœtica* in *Manuel de Falla, Latinité et Universalité, Actes du Colloque International tenu en Sorbonne 18–21 novembre 1996*, ed. Louis Jambou. Paris: Presses de l'Université de Paris-Sorbonne, 237–250.

Garms, Thomas. *Einflusse der spanischen Volksmusik in Manuel de Falla Werken*. Wiesbaden: Breitkopf & Haertel, 1990.

Gauthier, André. (February 1980). "Manuel de Falla: un itinéraire spirituel" and "Manuel de Falla, discographie critique." *Harmonie*, CLV, 44–51; 52–61.

Gibert, Rafael (February-March 1997) "El último tributo de Eugenio d'Ors a Manuel de Falla" *Nueva*, Revista de Política, Cultura y Arte, no. 49, 148–153.

Gibson, Ian (1985) "Manuel de Falla en Granada y Falla, Lorca y el *cante jondo*." *Federico García Lorca*. Barcelona: Grijalbo ("Colección/80"), 266–283 and 303–328.

Gómez Amat, Carlos (1976) "Falla, Arbitro" *La estafeta literaria*, no. 592–593, 5–7.

———. (6 March 1993) "Música en la Residencia" *La Esfera*.

———. (1997) "Falla y el Real" *El sombrero de tres picos/La vida breve*. Madrid: Teatro Real-Fundación del Teatro Lírico, 74–81.

González Barrón, R. (1984) *Religiosidad y polifonía en la obra de Manuel de Falla*. Series "Colección Musicalia" no. 5. Madrid: Conservatorio Superior de Música de Sevilla, Alpuerto.

Gubisch, Nina (1980) "Le journal inédit de Ricardo Viñes." *Revue Internationale de Musique Française*, I, no. 2, 154–248.

Gullón, Ricardo. (1961) *Relaciones amistosa y literarias entre Juan Ramón Jiménez y los Martínez Sierras*. San Juan de Puerto Rico: Ediciones de la Torr.

Halffter, Cristóbal (February 1963) "*Atlántida*, el problema formal" and "*Atlántida:* el tratamiento coral" *La estafeta literaria*, no. 258, 14–15; 30–31.

Halffter, Ernesto (February 1970) "Inolvidable Manuel de Falla" *Selecciones del Reader's Digest*, CCCLI, 11–17.

———. (12 June 1973) *El magisterio permanente de Manuel de Falla*. Madrid: Real Academia de Bellas Artes de San Fernando, 7–17.

———. (1977) *Falla en su Centenario. Homenaje en el Centenario de su nacimiento*. Madrid: Ministerio de Educación y Ciencia.

———. (October 1983) "La música de Falla en Iberoamérica." *Cádiz-Iberoamérica*, I.

———. (23 November 1984) "Palabras de Don Ernesto Halffter Escriche." AMF 9095.

Halffter, Rodolfo (February 1942) "El sistema armónico disonante de Falla." *Revista Musical Mexicana*, III, 53–56.

———. (1976) "Manuel de Falla y los compositores del grupo de Madrid de la Generación del 27," 43–59, *Rodolfo Halffter (su obra para piano)* by Antonio Iglesias (1979) Madrid: Editorial Alpuerto

Harper, Nancy Lee (Summer 1996) "Rodolfo Halffter and the *Superposiciones* of Manuel de Falla." *Ex Tempore*, 58–94.

Henry, Leigh (July-August 1921) "Contemporaries: Manuel de Falla." *Musical Opinion*, DXXVI, 847–848.

Hernández, Mario (24 December 1977) "García Lorca y Manuel de Falla: una carta y una obra inédita" *El País*, Arte y Pensamiento, iv.

Hess, Carol A. (1995) "Manuel de Falla's *The Three-Cornered Hat* and the Right-Wing Press in Pre-Civil War Spain" *Journal of Musicological Research*, vol. 15, 55–84.

———. (2001) "Falla (y Matheu), Manuel de." *The Revised New Grove Dictionary of Music and Musicians*, ed. Stanley Sadie and John Tyrrell, 8: 529–35. London: Macmillan.

Hontañón, Leopoldo (January 1997) "Falla, Gerhardt y los estrenos musicales españoles de 1996" *Cuadernos Hispanoamericanos*, no. 559, 95–100.

Howat, Roy (1999) "La influencia de Chopin en el París del cambio de siglo" in *Falla-Chopin, La múisca más pura*, ed. de Luis Gago, dir. Y. Nommick, Colección "Estudios," Serie "Música," no. 2. Granada: Publicaciones del Archivo Manuel de Falla, 33–66.

Istel, Edgar (October 1926) "Manuel de Falla, a Study." *The Musical Quarterly*, IV, 497–525.

Jambou, Louis (October 1996) "Manuel de Falla y París" in "Manuel de Falla y su Entorno." Madrid: *Boletín de la Fundación Juan March*, no. 263, 32.

Jankélévitch, Vladimir (1994) *Écrits sur la musique* Paris: Seuil.

Jean-Aubry, Georges (1 April 1917) "Manuel de Falla" *Musical Times*, DCC-CXC, 151–154, reprinted in *Revista Musical Hispano-americana* (30 April 1917), 1–5.

———. (5 July 1919) "Manuel de Falla" *Arts Gazette*, 364–365.

———. (June 1928) "The Glory of Manuel de Falla" *The Chesterian*, LXXI, 214–218.

Jiménez, Juan Ramón (1960). "Manuel de Falla " *Olvidos de Granada*, 1924–1928, illustrated by Angel Ferrant, San Juan de Puerto Rico: La Torre-Universidad de Puerto Rico ("Publicaciones de la Sala Zenobia-Juan Ramón" no. 1), 37–38.

———. (July-December 1993) "Retratos de Falla, Granados, y Casals" *Pauta*, XII, 65–69.

Jover Flix, Mariano (1972) *Felipe Pedrell (1841–1922), Vida y obra*. Tortosa: Patrinato Municipal de Música.

Karsavina, Tamara. (1953) *Los Ballets Russes (Mis memorias)*, Spanish translation by Helen Ferro. Buenos Aires: Ed. Shapiro.

Kochino, Boris (1970) *Diaghilev and the Ballets Russes*. New York: Harper and Row.

Koechlin, Charles (January 1914) "Chronique Musicale, *La vie brève*." *La Chronique des Arts*, 26; reprinted in *La Revue Musical,* no. 348–350, (1982) 18–21.

———. (n.d.) *Traité de l'Harmonie*, 3 vols. Paris: Max Eschig, III, 244.

Koppers, Mario H.A. (1986) "Tonal elements of Andalusian folk music in Manuel de Falla's *Fantasía baetica* (1919)" *South African Journal of Musicology*, VI/1–2, 41–48.

Krynen, Jean Dominique (1997) "*La vida breve*: un purgatorio editorial," "Estudios," series *Música*, no. 1. Granada: Publicaciones del Archivo Manuel de Falla, 149–167.

Lamillar, Juan (October 1996) "Manuel de Falla y la Literatura" *El siglo que viene*, no. 28, 39–45.

Landowska, Wanda (1964) "Manuel de Falla" *Landowska on Music* ed. and trans. by D. Restout, collaboration with R. Hawkins). New York: Stein & Day, 18–19.

Le Bordays, Christiane (1977) "Manuel de Falla" *La musique espagnole*. Vendôme: Presses Universitaires de France, 115–118.

Legendre, M. (July 1922) "La Fête-Dieu à Granade en 1922, *Le cante jondo*" *Le Correspondant*, MCDXXXV, 148–155.

Lesure, François (1989) "Manuel de Falla, Paris et Claude Debussy." *Manuel de Falla tra la Spagna e l'Europa*. Firenze: Leo S. Olschki Editore, 15–22.

Livermore, Ann (1972) *A Short History of Spanish Music* London: Duckworth.

Lliurat, Federico (September-October 1929) "El *Concerto* para clavicémbalo y cinco instrumentos, de Manuel de Falla." *Musicalia*, VIII, 48–53.

Lolo, Begoña (1997) "*Las relaciones Falla-Pedrell a través de La vida breve*," "Estudios," series *Música*, no. 1. Granada: Publicaciones del Archivo Manuel de Falla, 121–138.

López García, Pedro Ignacio (December 1996) "Azorín y Manuel de Falla." *Revista de Occidente,* 63–82.

Lores, Juan Carlos (1997) "Breve paseo por el amor, pasión y la muerte" *El sombrero de tres picos/La vida breve*. Madrid: Teatro Real-Fundación del Teatro Lírico, 112–117.

Madariaga, Salvador de (1974) "Manuel de Falla." *Españoles de mi tiempo*. Barcelona: Planeta ("Espejo de España" no. 9), 169–180.

Malipiero, Gian Francesco (1955) *Manuel de Falla* (trans. H. Siccardi). Buenos Aires: Ed. Argentina de Música.

Manso, Carlos (1990) *Conchita Badía en Argentina*. Buenos Aires: Tres Tiempos.

Manso, Carlos. (1993) *La Argentina, fué Antonia Mercé*. Buenos Aires: Ediciones Devenir.

Manzano Alonso, Miguel (1993) "Fuentes populares en la música de *El sombrero de tres picos* de Manuel de Falla." Zaragoza: *Nassarre*, (Revista Aragonesa de Musicología) IX, no. 1, 119–144.

———. (October 1996) "La música popular de tradición oral en la obra de Falla" *Manuel de Falla y su entorno* Madrid: *Boletín de la Fundación Juan March*, no. 263, 34.

Marco, Tomás (September-October 1976) "Algunos aspectos progresistas en la obra de Falla" *Bellas Artes 76*, LIII, 8–10.

———. (November 1976) "La frustrada influencia de Manuel de Falla" *Reseña*, no. 99, 42–43.

———. (July-August 1976). "Convención y progreso en la obra de Falla" *La estafeta literaria*, no. 592–593, 8–10.

———. (1983). *Historia de la música española, 6, Siglo XX*. Madrid: Alianza, 25–37.

———. (1997) "La influencia de Falla en la composión musical" *El sombrero de tres picos/La vida breve*. Madrid: Teatro Real-Fundación del Teatro Lírico, 126–139.

Martínez Sierra, María (1953) "Manuel de Falla" *Gregorio y yo, Medio siglo de colaboración*. Mexico: Exportadora de Pulicaciones Mexcianas ("Biografías Gandesa"), 118–148.

———. (1965) "Manuel de Falla" Buenos Aires: *Ars, Revista de Arte*, no. 100.

Massine, Leonide. (1968) *My Life in Ballet*, ed. Phyliss Hartrell and Robt Rubens. London: Macmillan.

Mayer-Serra, Otto (January 1943). "Falla's Musical Nationalism" *The Musical Quarterly*, XXIX, 1–17.

Menarini, Piero, ed. *Lola la comedianta* by Federico García Lorca, preface by Gerardo Diego.Madrid: Alianza Editorial, 1981.

Mila, Massimo, ed. (1962) *Manuel de Falla*. Milan: G. Ricordi & Co. ("Symposium" no. 3).

Milhaud, Darius (July 1923) "A propos d'une œuvre de Manuel de Falla." *Le courrier musical et théâtral*, XIII, 226.

———. (1953) *Notes without Music*. New York: Knopf.

Millán, Tony (March-April 1996) "El *Concierto* para clave y cinco instrumentos, de Manuel de Falla" *Concerto*, 8, 29–39.

Molina Fajardo, Eduardo (1970) "Soneto de homenaje a Manuel de Falla" *La estafeta literaria*, no. 15, 5.

———. (1979) "Manuel de Falla en su intimidad (Retablo granadino de maese Falla)" *Cuadernos de la Asociación Cultural Hispano- alemana*, III, 1–40.

Mora Guarnido, José (1958) "Don Fernando y Falla" *Federico y su mundo, Testimonio para una biografía*. Buenos Aires: Losada, 148–165.

Murray, Ken (Winter 1992) "Manuel de Falla's *Homenajes* for orchestra" *Context 3*, 9–13.

———. (Winter 1996) " 'From an Andalusian point of view': Manuel de Falla's compositional advice to Angel Barrios" *Context 11*, 33–39.

Navarro Mota, Diego (1976) "Falla y el Conservatorio" *La historia del conservatorio de Cádiz en sus documentos*, Homenaje a Manuel de Falla (intro. by José María Pemán) Cádiz: Instituto de Estudios Gaditanos-Excma. Diputación Provincial, 101 pp., 52–54.

Nectoux, Jean-Michel (May-June 1977) "Manuel de Falla, Un itinéraire spirituel" *Schweizersche Musik Zeitung-Revue Musicale Suisse*, III, 137–142.

———. "Lorsque Falla analyse ses *Quatre Pièces espagnoles*" in *Revue musciale suisse*, Mai-Juin, 1977 (117th year), no. 3, 14.

———. trans. (May-June 1977). "Dokuments. Lorsque Falla analyse ses *Quatre pièces espanoles" Schweizersche Musik Zeitung-Revue Musicale Suisse, III*, 154.

Nichols, Roger, ed (1987). *Remembered*. London-Boston: Faber & Faber.

Nicolodi, Fiamma (1989) "Falla e l'Italia" *Manuel de Falla tra la Spagna e l'Europa*. Firenze: Leo S. Olschki Editore, 215–267.

Nieva, Francisco (1997) "Examen y propósitos para un montaje de *La vida breve" El sombrero de tres picos/La vida breve*. Madrid: Teatro Real-Fundación del Teatro Lírico, 70–73.

Nin, Joaquín (30 April 1917) "Música Moderna" *Revista Musical Hispano-americana*, 5–8.

Nin-Culmell, Joaquín (December 1996) "Manuel de Falla, pedagogo" *Revista de Occidente*, no. 188, 37–46.

Nogales Bello, Jaime (September-October 1982) "*Atlántida* de Manuel de Falla y Ernesto Halffter." *Hilo Musical*, CXXVI, 64–68.

Nommick, Yvan (1994) "Manuel de Falla: de *La vida breve* de 1905 à *La vie brève* de 1913, Genèse et évolution d'une œuvre." Madrid: *Mélanges de la Casa de Velázquez,* XXX-3, 71–94.

———. (1996) "De Premanuel de Antefalla à Manuel de Falla: bilan de la première période créatrice du compositeur (1891–1904)" *Mélanges de la Casa de Velázquez,* XXXII-3.

———. (1996) "La interpretación de las *Noches:* Una carta de Falla a Ansermet" *Jardines de España. De Santiago Rusiñol a Manuel de Falla*. Granada: AMF, 27–46.

———. (1996) "*Noches en los jardines de España:* génesis y composición de una obra" *Jardines de España. De Santiago Rusiñol a Manuel de Falla*. Granada: AMF, 5–25.

———. (November 1997) "El Archivo Manuel de Falla: un centro de estudios y un instrumento fundamental al servicio de la investigación" *Tutti Música*, III/6, 8–13.

———. (1997) "*El sombrero de tres picos* de Manuel de Falla: una visión a través de los documentos de su Archivo" *El sombrero de tres picos/La vida breve*. Madrid: Teatro Real-Fundación del Teatro Lírico, 42–57.

———. (1997) "*La vida breve* entre 1905 y 1914: evolución formal y orquestal," "Estudios," series *Música*, no. 1. Granada: Publicaciones del Archivo Manuel de Falla, 11–118.

———. (1999) "L'évolution des effectifs instrumentaux dans l'œuvre de Manuel de Falla: continuité ou discontinuité" in *Manuel de Falla, Latinité et Universalité, Actes du Colloque International tenu en Sorbonne 18–21 novembre 1996,* ed. Louis Jambou. Paris: Presses de l'Université de Paris-Sorbonne, 323–338.

———. (1999) "Des Hommages de Falla aux "Hommages" à Falla in *Manuel de Falla, Latinité et Universalité, Actes du Colloque International tenu en Sorbonne 18–21 novembre 1996,* ed. Louis Jambou. Paris: Presses de l'Université de Paris-Sorbonne, 515–547.

———. "Andalucía en la obra para piano de Manuel de Falla" *Cuadernos Manuel de Falla*, no. 1. Granada: AMF, 1998.

———. "L'évolution des effectifs instrumentaux dans l'œuvre de Manuel de Falla: continuité ou discontinuité?" in Jambou, Louis, ed. (1999) *Manuel de Falla. Latinité et universalité*. Paris: Presses de l'Université de Paris-Sorbonne, coll. "Musiques/Écritures," 1999.

———. "Des *Hommages* de Falla aux 'Hommages' à Falla" in Jambou, Louis, ed. (1999) *Manuel de Falla. Latinité et universalité*. Paris: Presses de l'Université de Paris-Sorbonne, coll. "Musiques/Écritures," 1999.

Orozco Díaz, Manuel (1980) "La Casa de Manuel de Falla" *Casa-Museo de Manuel de Falla*, Granada: Casa-Museo Manuel de Falla, 7–31.

———. (1996) *Falla y Granada*. Granada: Caja de Ahorros de Granada ("Temas de nuestra andalucía" no. 42).

Ortiz Nuevo, José Luis (October 1996) "La relación de Falla con el Flamenco" *El siglo que viene*, special commemorative edition, no. 28, 46–49.

Pahissa, Jaime (10 December 1946) "La vida de Falla en sus últimos tiempos." Buenos Aires: *Cabalgata 16.*

———. (1955) "Manuel de Falla, El hombre y el músico." *Sendas y cumbres de la música española*. Buenos Aires: Hachette ("Colección El Mirador" no. 23), 81–100.

Pahlen, Kurt (1985) "Manuel de Falla, mi amigo gaditano" *Cádiz Iberoamérica*, no. 3, 80–82.

———. (1989) "Recuerdos personales" *Manuel de Falla tra la Espagna*. Firenze: Leo S. Olschki, 7–13.

Parker, Robert (January-December 1996) "A Falla Champion in Mexico: Carlos Chávez." *Sociedad española de musicología, Revista de musicología*, vol. XIX, no. 1–2, 227–237.

Pemán, José María (1957) "Mis encuentros con Manuel de Falla" *Cien artículos*. Madrid: Escelicer ("Colección 21" no. 15), 165–179.

Pérez de Arteaga, José Luis (December 1976) "Religiosidad y ascetismo en Manuel de Falla." Madrid: *Ritmo.*

Pérez Gutiérrez, Mariano (October-December 1976) "El binomío Falla- Ravel o la confluencia enigmática de dos genios paralelos e independientes" *Tesoro Sacro-Musical*, IV, 107–119.

———. (1982) "Falla y Turina hermanos en el Paris de sus sueños. La amistad de Falla y Turina en la etapa parisina, documentada a través de sus escritos." Barcelona: *Anuario musical,* XXXVII, 129–148.

———. (1987) *La temática popular en la etapa parisiana de Manuel de Falla*. Sevilla: Real Maestranza de Caballería de Sevilla; reprinted in 1996.

———. (1987) "Las amistades y el ambiente hispánico de Ravel en Paris: Viñes y Falla" *La estética musical de Ravel*, Madrid: Alpuerto, 332–342.

———. (1987) "Les voyages de Ravel en Espagne" *Revue International de Musique Française* XXIX, 38–49.

Pérez Zalduondo, Gemma (1995) "El nacionalismo como eje de la política musical del primer gobierno regular de Franco (30 de enero de 1938–8 de agosto de 1939) *Revista de Musicología* XVIII, 1–2, 1–27.

Persia, Jorge de (1986) "La música en la Residencia de Estudiantes" *La Música en la Generación del 27: homenaje a Lorca, 1915–1939*. Madrid: INAEM (Ministerio de Cultura), 41–63 and appendixes.

———. (1989) "Falla en Argentina, en torno a *Homenajes.*" *Manuel de Falla tra la Spagna e l'Europa.* Firenze: Leo S. Olschki Editore, 65–72.

———. (October 1992) "Sobre Atlántida de Manuel de Falla." *Montsalvat*, no. 208, 12–15.

———. (April-June 1993) "Archivo Manuel de Falla at Granada" *Fontes artis musicae,* XL/2, 115–119.

———. (May 1994) "Falla, Ortega y la renovación musical" *Revista de Occidente*, no. 156, 102–116.

———. (1996) "El entorno guitarristico de Manuel de Falla" *Guitarra en la historia*, vol. VII. Córdoba: Junta de Andalucía, 57–72.

———. (December 1996) "El Alejamiento" *Scherzo*, no. 100, 126–128.

———. (December 1996). "Imágenes e imaginaciones" *Revista de Occidente,* no. 187, 47–62.

———. (1996) "Entre lo efímero y lo trascendente." *Manuel de Falla: Siete espacios para la escena.* Madrid: SGAE, 49–52.

———. (April 1996) "Falla i Catalunya, una relació d'afecte sentit" *Revista Musical Catalana*, no. 133, 36–39.

———. (1997) "París, desde el tipismo al 'vrai espagnol'" *El sombrero de tres picos/La vida breve.* Madrid: Teatro Real-Fundación del Teatro Lírico, 82–93.

Pinamonti, Paolo, ed. (1988) *Pedro Calderón de la Barca-Manuel de Falla: El gran teatro del mundo*, Venezia: Marsilio.

———. (1989) "*L'acoustique nouvelle* interprete 'inattuale' del linguaggio armonico di Falla" *Manuel de Falla tra la Spagna e l'Europa.* Firenze: Leo S. Olschki Editore.

———. (1999) "Manuel de Falla, Frédéric Chopin y el enigmático *Fuego Fatuo*" in *Falla-Chopin, La música más pura*, ed. de Luis Gago, dir. Y. Nommick, Colección "Estudios," Serie "Música," no. 2. Granada: Publicaciones del Archivo Manuel de Falla, 69–121.

Polignac, Princesse Edmond de (August 1945) "Memoirs of the Late Princesse Edmond de Polignac" *Horizon* XII, 110–141.

Poulenc, Francis (1963) "Manuel de Falla" *Moi et mes amis, Confidences recueillies par Stéphane Audel.* Paris: La Palatine, 113–127.

Powell, Linton E. Jr. (Winter 1975–76) "Guitar Effects in Spanish Piano Music" *Piano Quarterly* 101, 40–43.

Prieto Marugan, José (November 1976) "Preguntas a Manuel de Falla" *Hilo Musical*, LXVIII, 12–15.

Proust, Christine (February 1992). "Manuel de Falla: *Concerto pour clavecin*" *Analyse Musical,* no. 26, 55–58.

Puente, Juan Manuel (November 1976) "En torno a *La vida breve,* Falla y la Ópera" *Reseña,* no. 99, 45–46.

Quintanal Sánchez, Inmadulada (1989) *Manuel de Falla y Asturias, Consideraciones sobre el nacionalismo musical.* Oviedo: Gráficas Summa, S.A.

Ramos, Francisco (October 1996) "Falla en el contexto musical de su época" *El siglo que viene,* no. 28, 35–38.

Ramos Rodríguez, Prudencio (December 1996) "Perfil humano de un músico" *Scherzo, XII,* 110, 134–140.

Rattalino, Piero (1989). "Dal pianoforte al clavicembalo: Note sul pianismo di Falla" *Manuel de Falla tra Spagna e l'Europa.* Firenze: Leo S. Olschki, Editore, 173–177.

Rigoni, Michel (January 1990) "Nuits dans les jardins d'Espagne de Manuel de Falla: de la couleur locale au classicisme." *Analyse Musicale,* no. 18, 49–53.

———. (November 1990) "De Falla: *Le Concerto pour clavecin*" *Analyse musicale,* no. 21, 55–64; also in "Analyse musicale et sciences cognitives: Contributions au 1er colloque de l'ESCOM," *Trieste,* 27–29 Octobre 1991, Issue 26 (February 1992), no. 5472.

———. (February 1992) "De Falla: *Le Concerto pour clavecin*" *Analyse musicale,* no. 26, 55–58.

Ripoll, José Ramón (1996) "Manuel de Falla 50 años después" *Revista Atlántica. poesía,* no. III-VIII.

———. (1997) "El *cante jondo* como fuente y espejo de la obra de Falla" *El sombrero de tres picos/La vida breve.* Madrid: Teatro Real-Fundación del Teatro Lírico, 94–105.

Rivas Cherif, Cipriano de (28 February 1920) "*El Tricornio,* Crónica rimada del baile del Tricornio, representado triunfalmente en París, el 23 de enero de 1920" *España,* CCLII, 12–13.

Roales–Nieto, Amalia (June 1988) "Manuel de Falla et Paris (1907–1914)" *R.I.M.F. (Revue Internationale de Musique Française)* no. 26, 85–92.

Roda, Cecilio de (1905) *Ilustraciones del Quijote, Los instrumentos, músicos y las danzas, Las canciones.* Madrid: Bernardo Rodríquez.

Rodrigo, Antonina (1984) "Manuel de Falla en El polinario" and "El concurso de *cante jondo.*" *Memoria de Granada: Manuel Angeles Ortiz y Federico García Lorca.* Barcelona: Plaza & Janés, 310 pp., 181–192.

———. (1996) "Falla-Lorca, una amistat productiva" *Revista musical catalunya,* no. 133, 40–43.

Rodrigo, Joaquín (several dates) "Recuerdos y consideraciones sobre Manuel de Falla." Compilation of various texts, AMF 9095.

Roland-Manuel, Alexis (October 1925) "Visite a Falla" *Revue Pleyel,* XXV, 16–19.

———. (15 April 1928) "Manuel de Falla" *Musique,* VII, 293–297.

————. (15 September 1928) "Les débuts de Manuel de Falla, part I" *Musique*, X-XI, 488–490.

————. (15 October 1928) "Les débuts de Manuel de Falla, part II" *Musique*, I, 575–583.

————. (September 1929) "Manuel de Falla et ses derniers ouvrages" *Musique*, XI-XII, 1044–1051.

Rubinstein, Artur (1976) *Les jours de ma jeunesse (Memorias, vol. I). Mes longues années: grande est la vie (Memorias, vol. II,* 1980) *Mes longues années: ma jeune vieillesse (Memorias, vol. III,* 1980). Paris: Robert Laffont.

Ruggenini, Mario (1989) "L'incanto della terra e della notte nella musica di Falla" *Manuel de Falla tra la Spagna e l'Europa.* Firenze: Leo S. Olschki Editore, 165–172.

Sainz de la Maza, Regino (November 1939) "Manuel de Falla en Buenos Aires" *Hispania*, CXXXVII, 20–22.

Sala, Emilio (1989) "In Margine alla 'Première' della Vie Brève, Spagna e spagnolismi nella 'Couleur locale,'" *Manuel de Falla tra la Spagna e l'Europa.* Firenze: Leo S. Olschki Editore, 121–130.

Salas, Roger (1996) "Manuel de Falla y el ballet español" *Manuel de Falla: Siete espacios para la escena.* Madrid: SGAE, 43–45.

Salas Viu, Vicente (January 1963) "The Mystery of Manuel de Falla's *La Atlantida.* Washington, D.C., Pan American Union: *Inter-American Music Bulletin*, no. 33, 1–6.

Salazar, Adolfo (May 1924) "Polichinela y Maese Pedro" *Revista de Occidente*, II, 229–237.

————. (March 1927) "Manuel de Falla" Havana: *Social*, 23, 80.

————. (1929) "Una pantomima-ballet española: De *El corregidor y la molinera* a *El sombrero de tres picos*" *Sinfonía y ballet.* Madrid: Mundo Latino, 343–352.

————. (1930) *La música contemporánea en España, Monografías y manuales historicos.* Madrid: Ediciones La Nave, 155–186.

————. (1947) *Manuel de Falla o el mar de por medio.* Mexico: Ultramar, 1.

Salvetti, Guido (1989) "*La vida breve*: Specchio deformante di naturalismo e folclore" *Manuel de Falla tra la Spagna e l'Europa.* Firenze: Leo S. Olschki Editore, 131–140.

Samazeuilh, R. C. (December 1939) "A Day in Granada" *Chesterian*, 108–111.

Saportes, José (1989) "Balletto e spagnolismo: Il tricorno" *Manuel de Falla tra la Spagna e l'Europa.* Firenze: Leo S. Olschki Editore, 159–164.

Segura, Florencio (November 1976) "Un viaje con don Manuel" *Reseña*, no. 99, 38–40

————. (1996) "Manuel de Falla, primer centenario de su nacimiento" *Música*, XXXVIII, 99.

Segura, Manuel (July-August 1976) "Semblanza religiosa de Manuel de Falla" *Razón y Fe*, no. 942–943, 87–99.

Sierra, José (October 1996) "Falla y la música culta" in "Manuel de Falla y su entorno" Madrid: *Boletín de la Fundación Juan March*, no. 263, 33.

Sobrino, Ramón (1996) "Manuel de Falla y la música teatral de principios de siglo" *Siete espacios para la escena*. Madrid: SGAE, 17–23.

Sopeña, Federico (1942) "Manuel de Falla y *El retablo de Maese Pedro*" *Dos años de música en Europa (Mozart-Bayreuth-Strawinsky)*. Madrid: Espasa-Calpe, 117–126.

———. (January 1947) "Manuel de Falla, Escritor" *Insula*, XIII, 3.

———. (1958) *Historia de la música española contemporánea*. Madrid: Rialp ("Biblioteca del Pensamiento Actual" no. 89), 41–194.

———. (1962) *Atlántida, Introducción a Manuel de Falla*. Madrid: Taurus, 1962.

———. (July-August 1976) "Dos centenarios juntos: Falla y Cambó" *Bellas Artes 76*, LII, 3–5.

———. (1976) *Manuel de Falla y el mundo de la cultura española, Siete lecciones en el Instituto de España*. Madrid: Instituto de España.

———. (November 1976) "Falla, artista cristiano" *Revista Arbor*, CCCLXXI, 191–202.

———. (November-December 1981) "Juan Ramón Jiménez y Manuel de Falla" *Los Cuadernos del norte*, II/10, 54–57.

———. (1982) "Picasso-Falla y Picasso sin Falla" *Picasso y la música*. Madrid: Ministerio de Cultura, 70–78.

———. (1989) "La espiritualidad de Manuel de Falla" *Manuel de Falla tra la Spagna e l'Europa*. Firenze: Leo S. Olschki Editore, 73–86.

Starkie, Walter (1958) *Spain: A Musician's Journey through Time and Space*. Geneva: EDLISI. French version: "Manuel de Falla (1876–1946)." *Espagne, Voyage musical dans le temps et l'espace*, II. Paris-Geneva: René Kister ("Histoire universelle de la musique"), 149–154.

———. (11 November 1961) "Atlántida" *Saturday Review*, 64–65.

Stolanova, Ivanka (1989) "Manuel de Falla et le groupe des cinq" *Manuel de Falla tra la Espagna e l'Europa*. Firenze: Leo S. Olschki Editore, 23–48.

Stravinsky, Vera and Robert Craft (1978) *Stravinsky in Pictures and Documents*, New York: Simon and Schuster.

Testa, Alberto (1989) "Falla e il suo Teatro di Danza in Italia." *Manuel de Falla tra la Spagna e l'Europa*. Firenze: Leo S. Olschki Editore, 209–214.

Thomas, Juan María (December 1926). "Manuel de Falla's *Concerto*" *The Chesterian*, LIX, 92–93.

Torres, Elena (2000) "La presencia de Scarlatti en la trayectoria musical de Manuel de Falla" in *Manuel de Falla e Italia*, ed. y prologue de Yvan Nommick, Colección "Estudios," Serie "Música," no. 3. Granada: Publicaciones del Archivo Manuel de Falla.

Trend, John Brande (April 1922) "Falla in Arabia" *Music & Letters*, II, 133–149.

———. (May 1928) "Falla's Puppet-show in Paris" *The Dominant*, VII, 11–14.

———. (July 1928) "Falla and the Harpsichord" *The Music Bulletin*, ed. Basil Maine, X, no. 7, 190–192.

———. (January, 1947) "Recollections of Falla" *Musical Times*, 15–16.

———. (July 1948) "Two Books on Falla" *Chesterian*, no. 22, 8–10.

Turina, Joaquín (May 1920) "Manuel de Falla" *The Chesterian*, VII, 193–196.

Verdaguer, Mario (1957) *Medio siglo de vida barcelonesa*. Barcelona: Editorial Barnasa, 180–189.

Vilardebó, Inmaculada (June 1997) "Manuel de Falla-Ernesto Halffter , Historia de una amistad" *Tutti música*, II/5.

Villar, Rogelio (August 1916) "Músicos ilustres españoles, Manuel de Falla" *Por esos mundos*, CCLVII, 161–167.

———. (October 1927) "Manuel de Falla" *La Revista de Música*, IV, 222–225; reprinted in *Ritmo* (28 February 1930), 5–6.

———. (1932) "Falla y su *Concierto de cámara*" Madrid: *Ritmo*.

Vinay, Gianfranco (1989) "La Lezione di Scarlatti e di Stravinsky nel *Concerto per Clavicembalo* di Falla" *Manuel de Falla tra Spagna e l'Europa*. Firenze: Leo S. Olschki Editore, 179–188.

Vlad, Roman (1982) "Le avanguardie musicali e la S.I.M.C." *Chigana, Rassegna annuale di studi musicologici*.

Zubialde, I. (September 1913) "*La vida breve*" *Revista Musical*, IX, 201–204.

COLLECTIONS OR SPECIAL EDITIONS

Ars, Revista de Arte, no. 100 (1965) Buenos Aires.

Atlántida, Madrid: Ministerio de Educación Nacional, (1961).

Los Ballets Russes de Diaghilev y España, ed. Yvan Nommick and Antonio Álvarez Cañibano. Granada: Archivo Manuel de Falla and Madrid: Centro de Documentación de Música y Danza INAEM (Instituto Nacional de las Artes Escénicas y la Música), 2000. Articles by Antonio Gallego, Yvan Nommick, Carol A. Hess, Joan Acocella, Miguel Manzano Alonso, Yolanda F. Acker, Marilyn McCully, et al.

Conciertos de inauguración del Archivo Manuel de Falla, A. Gallego, ed. Granada, 1991: AMF.

I Concurso de Cante jondo, commemorative edition (1922–1992), Granada: AMF, 1992.

Cuatro Lecciones Magistrales. Madrid: Real Conservatorio Superior de Música de Madrid, 1992.

Destino, no. 1771 (2 October 1971) "Rostros del siglo XX: Manuel de Falla" Barcelona.

La estafeta literaria, no. 233 (22 February 1962) "Manuel de Falla desde *Atlántida*." Madrid.

La estafeta literaria, no. 258 (2 February 1963), Madrid.

La estafeta literaria, no. 592–593 (July-August 1976) "Centenario de Falla," Madrid.

Falla-Chopin. La música más pura, ed. Luis Gago; Director: Yvan Nommick. Colección "Estudios." Serie "Música," no. 2. Granada: Publicaciones del

Archivo Manuel de Falla, 1999. Estudios de Jim Samson, Roy Howat, Paolo Pinamonti, Víctor Estapé.

Falla y Lorca, Entre la tradición y la vanguardia, ed. Susana Zapke. Kassel: Edition Reichenberger, 1999. Articles by C. Wentzlaff-Eggebert, K. Wolfgang Niemöller, S. Zapke, Jorge de Persia, Eckhard Weber, José Luis Abellán.

Guías del Festival, ed. Rafael del Pino. Granada: Festival Internacional de Música y Danza, 1996.

Guitart I (Feb.-April 1996), AMF.

Historia y vida, XXIX, no. 343 (October 1996).

El homenaje de Córdoba a Manuel de Falla. Córdoba, Argentina: Comisión Pro Monumento a Manuel de Falla, 1956.

"Hommage à Manuel de Falla" (13 December 1946) *Bulletin des bibliothèques de L'Institute Français en Espagne*, Paris.

Jambou, Louis, ed. *Manuel de Falla. Latinité et universalité*. Actas from the international colloquial, 18–21 Nov. 1996, organized by the Doctoral School of the Department of Music and Musicology of the Sorbonne, Paris: Presses de l'Université de Paris-Sorbonne, coll. "Musiques/Écritures"; 1999.

El jardín de Melisendra. Colección "Catálogos," Serie "Exposiciones," no. 2. Granada: Publicaciones del Archivo Manuel de Falla, 1999. Articles by Yvan Nommick, Antonio García Bascón, Nicolás Torices Abarca, Antonio Sánchez Trigueros.

Insula, no. 13 (January 1947), Spain.

Litoral, no. 35–36 (January-February 1973) "De Cádiz a Granada, homenaje a Manuel de Falla" Malaga.

Los domingos de "A.B.C." (29 August 1976) "Número dedicado al centenario de Falla", Madrid.

Manuel de Falla en Argentina, 1939–1946. Madrid: SGAE, 1989.

Manuel de Falla a través de su música (1876–1946). A Coruña: Fundación Pedro Barrié de la Maza, Conde de Fenosa, 1996.

Manuel de Falla e Italia. Colección "Estudios." Serie "Música," no. 3. Granada: Publicaciones del archivo Manuel de Falla, 2000. Articles by Montserrat Bergadà, Elena Torres, Stefano Russomanno.

Manuel de Falla en Granada. Granada: Publicaciones del Archivo Manuel de Falla, 2001. Articles by Isabel de Falla, José García Román, Yvan Nommick, Eduardo Quesada Dorador, Concha Chinchilla.

Manuel de Falla: Su vida y obra, Poesía, 36 & 37. Jorge de Persia, dir. Madrid: Ministerio de Cultura, 1991. French version, Paris: Instituto Cervantes, 1993; English version, Madrid: Ministerio de Asuntos Exteriores, 1996.

Manuel de Falla, La vie brève, L'amour sorcier, Les Tréteaux de Maître Pierre. Paris: L'Avant Scène Opera, no. 177, 1997.

Manuel de Falla: La vida breve. Colección "Estudios." Serie "Música," no. 1. Granada: Publicaciones del Archivo Manuel de Falla, 1997. Articles by Yvan Nommick, Begoña Lolo, Jean-Dominique Krynen, José Miguel Castillo.

Manuel de Falla y Asturias: consideraciones sobre el nacionalismo musical: discurso, ed. I. Quintanal Sánchez. Oviedo: Instituto de Estudios Asturianos, 1989.

Manuel de Falla, Symposium, 3 (July-October 1962) *Musica d'oggi*, IV-V, Mila Massimo, ed. Milan: Ricordi.

Manuel de Falla tra la Spagna e l'Europa, Atti del Convegno Internazionale di Studi (1989), Paolo Pinamonti, ed. (Venezia, 15–17 maggio 1987) Quaderno della Rivista Italiana di Musicologia, no. 21. Firenze: Leo S. Oslchki, ed.

Música, XII (June 1945). "Número especial dedicado a Falla" Spain.

Ese múisco que llevo dentro I, II (1980) La Habana: Letras Cubanas.

Poesía, La música en la Residencia (Autumn-Winter 1983) Madrid: Ministerio de Cultura.

Reseña, no. 99 (November 1976) "Manuel de Falla (1876–1976)" Madrid.

Revista atlantica. Poesía, 11 (1996) Cádiz: Servicio de Publicaciones de la Diputación Provincial de Cádiz.

Revista de Occidente, 187 (December 1996) Fundación Ortega y Gasset.

Ritmo, no. 323 (December 1961) Spain.

Ritmo, no. 467 (1976) "Falla, 1876–1976".

Ritmo, IX, no. 593 (1988). "Special 60th Anniversary Supplement."

Scherzo, XII, no. 110 (December 1996) Madrid.

El siglo que viene, no. 28 (October 1996).

La vida breve. "Estudios," series *Música*, no. 1, Granada: Publicaciones del AMF. Articles by A. Gallego, Y. Nommick, Begoña Lolo, José Miguel Castillo Higueras, and Jean-Dominique Krynen, 1997.

La vida breve/El sombrero de tres picos (1997). Madrid: Fundación Teatro Real.

PRESS CLIPPINGS—PREVIEWS, REVIEWS, AND INTERVIEWS

(17 August 1899) *Diario de Cádiz.*

(11 September 1899) "El concierto de anoche." *Diario de Cádiz.*

(22 September 1901) "El concierto de hoy" *Diario de Cádiz.*

(17 April 1902) *Diario de Cádiz.*

(14 April 1905) "Actualidades" *Diario de Cádiz.*

(2 December 1905) *Diario de Cádiz.*

(13 February 1907) *Diario de Cádiz.*

(27 February 1907) *Diario de Cádiz.*

(April 1909) *Revista musical.*

(12 May 1913) "Nuestro arte en el extranjero." Madrid: *La Correspondencia de España.*

(29 May 1913) "Quincenas musicales" "La vida breve" Barcelona: *La Vanguardia.*

(5 January 1914) "Triunfo de un músico español en Paris." Madrid: *El País.*

(January 1914). "La Vida Breve." *Revista Musical Hispano-americana,* año VI, I, 4–6.

(11 January 1914). *"La vie brève* par Manuel de Falla." *L'art moderne,* II, 12–13.

(15 May 1914). "Manuel de Falla y *La vida breve.*" *Revista Musical Catalana,* CXXV, 4–6.

(14 November 1914) "Hablando con el Maestro Falla." *La Mañana.*

(15 January 1915) "Falla y Turina." Madrid: *La Mañana.*

(February 1915) "En honor a Falla y Turina, Un discurso" *Lira española, XXII,* 3–5.

(9 February 1915) "La Sociedad Nacional de Música." Madrid: *El Imparcial.*

(March 1915) "Los músicos nuevos, El Maestro Manuel de Falla." *Por essos mundos,* 269–270.

(6 April 1915) "Manuel de Falla, en Cádiz." *Diario de Cádiz.*

(15 April 1915) "Hablando con Manuel de Falla" *La Patria,* Madrid, 3.

(16 April 1915) *"El amor brujo" La Tribuna,* Madrid.

(16 April 1915) *La Patria,* Madrid.

(11 May 1916) *Diario de Cádiz.*

(15 April 1917) *"El corregidor y la molinera" Música,* Madrid, 2–3.

(30 April 1917) "El corregidor y la molinera" *Revista Musical Hispano-americana,* 8–13.

(1 May 1917) *A.B.C.,* Madrid.

(28 April 1918) "Homenaje a Debussy." Madrid: *El Universal.*

(2 August 1919) "The Diaghilief Season at the Alambra" *The Musical Standard,* 31–32.

(2 August 1919). "New Operas and Ballets, A Spanish composer: Manuel de Falla." *The Ladies' Field,* 292.

(November 1919). "The Three-Cornered Hat." *Musical Opinion,* DVI, 122–123.

(24 January 1920) "Un Baile Ruso español." Madrid: *El Sol.*

(1 February 1920) "Crónicas Musicales." Madrid: *El Sol.*

(5 February 1920) "Nota sobre un baile español." Madrid: *El Imparcial.*

(28 February 1920) "El tricorno" *España,* Paris, 2.

(21 April 1920) "Las Conferencias del Instituto Francés. Final." Madrid: *El Sol.*

(9 May 1920) "La vida musical." Madrid: *El Sol.*

(4 June 1920) *"El sombrero de tres picos,* de Manuel de Falla, y la critica francesa." Madrid: *El Sol.*

(25 October 1921) "Crónicas musicales." Madrid: *El Sol.*

(14 June 1922) "Alrededor de un concurso de c*ante jondo."* Granada: *La Voz.*

(1922) "Manuel de Falla" *La musique et les nations.* London: Chester, 127–143.

(23 March 1923) "Estreno de *El retablo de Maese Pedro* de Manuel de Falla" *El sol,* Madrid, 6.

(29 March 1923) "La vida musical." Madrid: *El Sol.*

(30 March 1923)"Un triunfo de Manuel de Falla." Granada: *Noticiero granadino.*

(17 April 1923) "Apuntes del momento." Valencia: *Las provincias.*

(July 1923) "Une première: El Retablo de Maese Pedro." *Lyrica*, XVII, 105.

(1 September 1923) "De Falla Talks of His New Work Based on a Don Quixote Theme." *Christian Science Monitor*, 17.

(October 1923) "*El Retablo* by Manuel de Falla." *The Chesterian*, XXXIV, 37–46.

(19 September 1925) "Manuel de Falla's *Psyché.*" *Christian Science Monitor*, 19.

(10 December 1925)"Introducing Ueber-Marionettes" *New York Sun,* sec. 2, 1.

(21 June 1926) "Vida musical" *La noche*, Barcelona, 8.

(March 1927) "Manuel de Falla" *Social*, Havana, 23, 80.

(16 May 1927) "Hommage à Falla" *Excelsior*, Paris, 4–5.

(1927) "Le *Concerto* de Manuel de Falla, langage et style, Classicisme et modernisme." *Cahiers d'art*, X, 352–355; reprint from "Folletones de *El Sol*" (8 November 1927).

(8 April 1928) "De Falla Festival in Paris" *New York Times*, sec. 8, 9.

(May–June 1928) "Manuel de Falla en París." Havana: *Musicalia*, 12–14.

(4 August 1928) "Las obras de Falla en la Opéra-Comique y la crítica francesa" *El sol*, Madrid, 5.

(1 February 1929) Interview with Falla: "¿son la nueva juventud española?" *La gaceta literaria*, Madrid, 1.

(23 November 1930) "An Interview with Manuel de Falla" *New York Times*, sec.8, 8.

(21 November 1931) "Carta de Falla" *El sol*, Madrid, 4.

(10 June 1932) "Una carta de don Manuel de Falla" *La unión*, Seville, 5; reprinted in *Ideal*, Granada, 14 June 1932.

(3 July 1932) "Una carta" *Diario de Cádiz*, 2.

(21 August 1934) "Una carta de Falla" *Diario de Cádiz*, 1.

(February 1935) "El *Concerto de clavicembalo* de Manuel de Falla." Havana: *Grafos.*

(5 November 1937) "Una carta de Falla" *Ideal, 1.*

(22 October 1939) "La interviú que no quiso dar el maestro Falla" *Radio Nacional*, Madrid, 1.

(23 October 1939) "Corrientes" *Nueva época*, Buenos Aires, 7.

PUBLISHED COLLECTIONS OF LETTERS

José Bergamín — Campodónico, Luis (25 July 1968) "Manuel de Falla y Bergamín. El contexto de una correspondencia." *Mundo Nuevo*, XXV, 15–24.

José Bergamín, — Nigel Dennis, ed. *El Epistolario José Bergamín-Manuel de Falla* (1924–1935). Valencia: Pre-Textos, 1995.

Francisco Cambó — Buqueras, Ignacio. *Cambó*. Barcelona: Plaza & Janes, 1987.

Claude Debussy — Lesure, François. *Claude Debussy. Lettres 1884–1918.* Paris: Hermann, 157, 1980.

Gerardo Diego — Sopeña, Federico. *Correspondencia Gerardo Diego-Manuel de Falla.* Santander: Fundación Marcelino Botín-Sanz de Sautuola y López, 1988.

Paul Dukas — Dukas, Paul. *Correspondance de Paul Dukas.* Ed. Georges Fairie. Paris: Durand, 1971.

Carlos Fernández-Shaw — Lozano Guirao, Pilar (July-December 1962) "Archivo epistolar de Carlos Fernández-Shaw" in *Revista de Literatura,* XXII, 43–44.

Carlos Fernández-Shaw — Lozano Guirao, Pilar (July-December 1967) "Segunda parte del archivo epistolar de Carlos Fernández-Shaw" in *Revista de literatura,* XXVIII, 63–64, and 265–321.

Carlos Fernández-Shaw — Fernández-Shaw, Guillermo. *Larga historia de "La vida breve",* 1972.

Federico García Lorca — García Lorca, Federico. *Cartas, postales, poemas y dibujos.* Ed. A.Gallego Morell. Madrid: Ed. Moneda y Crédito, 1968.

Federico García Lorca — Hernández, Mario (24 December 1977) "García Lorca y Manuel de Falla: una carta y una obra inédita" *El País,* Madrid, iv.

Federico García Lorca — Menarini, Piero, ed. *Lola la comedianta,* 1981.

Federico García Lorca — Maurer, Christopher Maurer, ed. *Federico García Lorca, Epistolario I.* Madrid: Alianza Editorial, 55–56, 67–68, 71, 83, 86, 91, 107, 119, 153, 156, 1983.

Federcio García Lorca — Maurer, Christopher. *Federico García Lorca, Epistolario II.* Madrid: Alianza Editorial, 63, 71, 88, 153, 157, 162, 1983.

Federico García Lorca — Porras Soriano, Francisco. *Los títeres de Falla y García Lorca,* 1995.

Ernesto Halffter — *Homenaje a Ernesto* Halffter. Madrid: Fundación Juan March, 1983.

Rodolfo Halffter — Halffter, Rodolfo (July-September 1990) "Cartas inéditas de Rodolfo Halffter a Manuel de Falla." *Pauta,* IX, no. 35. Mexico City: CENI-DIM, 8–14.

Rodolfo Halffter — Halffter, Rodolfo (January-March 1992) "Cartas inéditas de Manuel de Falla y Rodolfo Halffter." *Pauta,* XI, no. 41. Mexico City: CENI-DIM, 5 -10.

Juan Ramón Jiménez — Jiménez, Juan Ramón. *Cartas, primera selección.* Ed. Francisco Garfias. Madrid: Aguilar, 1962.

Juan Ramón Jiménez — Jiménez, J. R. *Selección de cartas, 1899–1958.* Ed. Antonio Beneyto. Barcelona: Ed. Picazo. 1973.

Juan Ramón Jiménez — Sopeña, Federico (November-December 1981). "Juan Ramón Jiménez y Manuel de Falla." *Los Cuadernos del Norte,* X, 54–57.

Charles Koechlin — "Charles Koechlin 1867–1950, Correspondance."*La revue musicale,* 348–350, 17, 55–56, 68–70, 98, 1982.

Charles Koechlin — Koechlin, Charles. *Correspondance 1867–1950*, Madeleine Li-Koechlin ed. Paris: *La Revue Musicale*, 1983.

Gian Francesco Malipiero — Malipiero, G. F. *Manuel de Falla Evocación y correspondencia*. Ed. & trans. by A. Soria with intro. by F. Sopeña. Granada: Universidad de Granada, 1983.

María Martínez Sierra — Gallego, Antonio. "Pascua florida: un proyecto poético de María O. de Lejárraga para Manuel de Falla" *Revista atlántica, poesía*, no. 11, 33–55, 1996.

Felipe Pedrell — *Spanien und die neue Musik*, ed. Jacoba Grunfeld, 1968.

José María Pemán — Sánchez García, Fernando, ed. (1991) *La correspondencia inédita entre Manuel de Falla y José María Pemán (1929–1941)*, 2nd. ed. Sevilla: Alfar, 1991. 1st ed. Jerez de la Frontera: Caja de Ahorros de Jerez, 1988.

Francis Poulenc, — Wendel, Hélène de, ed. *Francis Poulenc, Correspondance 1915–1963*. Paris: Editions du Seuil, 32, 48, 78, 93, 1967.

Maurice Ravel — Orenstein, Arbie. "Ravel and Falla: an unpublished Correspondence, 1914–1933" *Music and Civilization: Essays in Honor of Paul Henry*. New York: W. W. Norton, 1984.

Maurice Ravel — Roy, Jean (September 1987) "Correspondance adressée par Maurice Ravel a Manuel de Falla" *Cahiers Maurice Ravel*, III, 7–25.

Maurice Ravel — Orenstein, A., ed. *Lettres, écrits, entreiens*, trans. D. C. Collins, Paris: Flammarion, 1989.

Joaquín Rodrigo — *Epistolario Falla-Rodrigo* in *Homenaje a Joaquín Rodrigo*. Madrid: Fundación Juan March, 24–53, 1981.

Joaquín Rodrigo — Bustos, Juan (7 January 1982) "La correspondencia entre Manuel de Falla y Joaquín Rodrigo" *Patria*, Granada, 8.

Segismundo Romero — Recuero, Pascual. ed. *Cartas a Segismundo Romero*. Granada: Ayuntamiento de Granada-Patronato "Casa-Museo Manuel de Falla," 1976.

Valentín Ruiz Aznar — García, Juan Alfonso. *Valentín Ruiz Aznar (1902–1972): Semblanza biográfica, Esudio estético y Catálogo cronológico*. Granada: Real Academia de Bellas Artes Nuestra Señora de las Angustias, 1982.

Igor Stravinsky — Stravinsky, Igor and Robert Craft. *Memories and Commentaries*. London: Faber and Faber, 1960.

Igor Stravinsky — Stravinsky, Igor. *Selected Correspondence* vol. II, ed. and commentaries by Robert Craft. New York: Alfred A. Knopf; London: Faber and Faber Limited. Translated from the French, 160–176, 1984.

Juan María Thomas — Thomas, Juan María. *Manuel de Falla en la isla*. Palma de Mallorca: Capella Classica, 1947.

Joaquín Turina — Pérez Gutiérrez, Mariano**.** *Falla y Turina a través de su epistolario*. Madrid: Ed. Alpuerto ("Colección Musicalia," 2), 1982.

Ricardo Viñes — *Spanien und die neue Musik,* Jacoba Grunfeld, ed., 1968.

Ignacio Zuloaga — Sopeña, Federico, ed. *Correspondencia entre Falla y Zuloaga, 1915–1942*. Granada: Ayuntamiento de Granada, 1982.

Selected References to Other Correspondence

Bufano, Remo (4 March 1926) Boston Public Library.

Chase, Gilbert "Collection of Manuel de Falla Correspondence (1931–1945)" New York Public Library, Lincoln Center.

Copeland, George. Unpublished Autobiography, held in the private collection of David Dubal, New York City.

Dille, D. ed. *Documenta Bartokiana*, 4. vols. Mainz: B. Schotts Sohne, III/158–160, 1968.

Franco, Enrique. "Falla en Fuentetodos" *Revista Atlántica, poesía*, no. 11, XXI-XXV, 1996.

García Montero, L. "Manuel de Falla y Rafael Alberti" in *Revista atlántica. poesía*, 1991.

Junyent, Eduardo and Martín de Riquer, ed. "Preface" to *L'Atlàntida*, Jacint Verdaguer. Barcelona: Ayntamiento, 1946.

League of Composers Collection of Letters (1925–1930) New York Public Library, Lincoln Center.

Mary Flagler Cary Music Collection, Pierpont Morgan Library.

"Manuel de Falla, el gran maestro español, dirigirá un concierto en nuestra ciudad" (17 May 1942) *Hoy*, Buenos Aires.

Ruiz Tarazona, Andrés (December 1976) "La correspondencia Falla-Olallo Morales" *Ritmo*, no. 467, 40–41.

Bibliographic and Works Catalogues

Catálogo de la obra de Manuel de Falla. Madrid: Manuel de Falla Ediciones, 1996.

Chase, Gilbert and Andrew Budwig. *Manuel de Falla, A Bibliography and Research Guide*, New York: Garland Publishing, 1986.

Christoforidis, Michael. *Catálogo de compositores: Manuel de Falla*. Madrid: SGAE. 1999.

Crichton, Ronald. *Manuel de Falla: Descriptive Catalogue of his Works*, 2nd ed. London: Chester Music, 1983; 1st ed., 1974; Spanish ed., Madrid: Fundación Banco Exterior, 1990.

Gallego Gallego, Antonio. *Catálogo de obras de Manuel de Falla*, Madrid: Ministerio de Cultura, Dirección General de Bellas Artes y Archivos, 1987

Ruiz-Pipó, Antonio. *Catalogue de l'œuvre de Manuel de Falla*. Paris: Max Eschig, 1993.

Expositions

Exposición Manuel de Falla. Granada: Monasterio de San Jerónimo. Granada XI Festival Internacional de Música y Danza-Ayuntamiento de Granada, 1962.

Manuel de Falla y Granada. Homage edition ed. by Centro Artístico, Literario y Científico, and patronized by the Excmo. Ayuntamiento de Granada, under the direction of Rafael Jofré García. Granada, 1963.

Museo Manuel de Falla. Altagracia (Córdoba-Argentina): Ministerio de Educación y Cultura, 1970.

Casa-Museo Manuel de Falla. Granada: Obra Cultural de la Caja de Ahorros, 1971.

Manuel de Falla en el centenario de su nacimiento (1876–1946), E. Franco,ed. Granada: Banco de Granada. Granada: Fundación Rodríguez-Acosta, 41 pp., and *Manuel de Falla*, E. Franco, ed. Granada: Hospital de Santa Cruz. Madrid: Ministerio de Educación y Ciencia, 1976.

La Música en la Generación del 27, Homenaje a Lorca 1915/1939, Emilio Casares Rodicio, dir. Madrid: Ministerio de Cultura, 1984.

Artur Rubinstein (1887–1982), Recuerdos de España. Santander: Fundación Isaac Albéniz, 1987.

España y los ballets rusos. Granada: Ministerio de Cultura, 1989.

50º Aniversario del viaje de Manuel de Falla de Granada a Argentina 1939–1989. Granada, 1989.

Manuel de Falla. Diálogos con la cultura del S. XX. Granada: AMF, 1991.

Manuel de Falla, Imagenes de su Tiempo. Granada: Archivo Manuel de Falla, 1992.

Hermenegildo Lanz, escenógrafo: las experiencias teatrales en los años veinte granadinos (1922–1936). Granada: Ayuntamiento de Granada, Ministerio de Cultura, AMF, Imprenta Urania, 1993.

Hermenegildo Lanz. Granada y las vanguardias culturales (1917–1936). Granada: Caja General de Ahorros de Granada, 1994.

Un Retablo para Maese Pedro: En el centenario de Manuel Angeles Ortiz. Granada: Ministerio de Cultura and AMF, Imprenta Urania, 1995.

Cinco años del Archivo Manuel de Falla en Granada. Granada: Ayuntamiento de Granada, 1996.

José María Rodríguez-Acosta, un pintor en la Granada de Falla. Granada: Fundación Rodríguez-Acosta, 1996.

La guitarra, visiones en la vanguardia. Granada: Casa-Museo García Lorca, Laura García Lorca de los Ríos, dir., 1996

Las músicas de Manuel de Falla. Granada: Ministerio de Cúltura, 1996.

Manuel de Falla y Granada. Granada: Ministerio de Cultura, 1996.

Manuel de Falla. Siete espacios para la escena. Madrid: SGAE, 1996.

Cinco escenografías para Manuel de Falla 1919–1996. Granada: Diputación Provincial de Granada, 1996.

(27 February/ 23 March 1997) *Generación del 27: Artistas de Preguerra.* Sevilla: Caja San Fernando.

Ernesto Halffter (1905–1989), Músico en dos tiempos. Madrid: Publicaciones de la Residencia de Estudiantes and AMF, produced by Yolanda Acker and Javier Suárez-Pajares, 1997, 1997.

Jardines de España, de Santiago Rusiñol a Manuel de Falla. Granada: AMF, 1997.

Conchita Badía, Canción del arte, 1897–1975. Granada: AMF, 24 March- 24 May, 1997.

(24 November 1997–24 January 1998) *La vida breve*, Granada: AMF.

(November 2001–January 2002) *La Europa de los nacionalismos musicales*, ed. Yvan Nommick, VII Encuentros Manuel de Falla, Granada: Archivo Manuel de Falla, Orquesta Cuidad de Granada.

Val de Oscuro. Julio Juste. coll. "Catálogos," series "Exposiciones," no. 1. Granada: Publicaciones del Archivo Manuel de Falla, 1998.

ICONOGRAPHY, ILLUSTRATIONS, AND PLASTIC ARTS

Iconografía/Iconography Manuel de Falla 1876–1946, La imagen de un músico/The image of a musician, 2nd ed. J. Suárez Pajares, ed., 1996; 1st ed. Madrid: Sociedad General de Autores y Editores, 1995.

THESES AND DISSERTATIONS

Adessi, Anna Rita. *Per una definizione del concetto di "influenza stilistica" con uno studio applicativo su Manuel de Falla e Claude Debussy*, Dottorato di Ricerca in Musicologia, Universita' di Bologna, academic year, 1995–1996, 1997.

Allan, Diana Gail. *Cante jondo: An Aesthetic Force as Reflected in Manuel de Falla's "Siete canciones populares espanolas."* D.M.A., the University of Texas at Austin, 1995.

Budwig, Andrew. *Manuel de Falla's "Atlántida": An Historical and Analytical Study.* Ph.D., University of Chicago, 1984.

Bukaczewski, Carole. *Manuel de Falla et le nationalisme musical en Espagne.* Mémoire de Maîtrise, Paris: Université de Paris III, La Sorbonne Nouvelle, 1987–1988.

Chinchilla Marín, Isabel. *Las artes plásticas en la vida y obra de Manuel de Falla.* Licentiate, Granada: Universidad de Granada, 1985.

Christoforidis, Michael. *Aspects of the Creative Process in Manuel de Falla's "El retablo de Maese Pedro" and "Concerto."* Ph.D. dissertation, University of Melbourne, 2 vol., 1997.

Collins, Chris. *Manuel de Falla and his European contemporaries: Encounters, relationships and influences.* PhD diss., U. of Wales, Bangor, 2002.

———.. *Manuel de Falla and "L'acoustique nouvelle."* M. Phil., University of Wales, Bangor, 1997.

Cooper, David Cornish. *A Survey of the Solo Piano Works of Manuel de Falla.* D.M.A., University of Kentucky, 1991.

Douglas-Brown, Deborah Jean. *Nationalism in the Song Sets of Manuel de Falla and Enrique Granados.* D.M.A., University of Alabama, 1993.

Ernst, G. *Manuel de Falla (1876–1947): El retablo de Maese Pedro (Meister Pedros Puppenspiel).* Tesina, Universitat von Erlangen, Nürnberg, 1994.

Foltz, Roger Ernest. *Pitch organization in Spanish music and selected late works of Manuel de Falla,* Ph.D. dissertation, University of Texas, Austin, 1997.

Garms, Thomas. *Der Flamenco und die spanische Folklore in Manuel de Fallas Werken,* U. Frankfurt am Main, Wiesbaden: Breitkopf & Haertel: 1990, 305 pp. Ph.D. dissertation. Reviewed by Klaus-Peter Koch in *Die Musikforschung* XLV/3 (1992), 1990.

Glück, Marliese *Manuel de Fallas "El Sombrero de tres picos," Musik, Pantomime, Tanz.* Magister, University of Munich, 1993.

Gubisch, Nina. *Ricardo Viñes a travers son journal et sa correspondance.* Ph.D. Paris: Université Sorbonne, 2 vol., 1977.

Harper, Nancy Lee. *The Piano Sonatas of Rodolfo Halffter: Transformation or New Techniques?* D.M.A. University of North Texas, 1985.

Hess, Carol Ann. *Manuel de Falla's "The Three-Cornered Hat" and the Advent of Modernism in Spain.* Ph.D. dissertation, University of California at Davis, 1994.

Koppers, Marinus Hendrikus Abraham *A Stylistic Study of the Compositions of Manuel de Falla (1876–1946) with special reference to his solo and chamber music.* Master of Music, University of South Africa, 1985.

Minor, Martha Danielson. *Hispanic Influences on the Works of French Composers of the Nineteenth and Twentieth Centuries.* D.M.A., University of Kansas, 1983.

Morrison, Donald N. "Influences of Impressionist Tonality on Selected Works of Delius, Griffes, Falla and Respighi," 80–117. *Dissertations Abstracts,* XXI, 641–642, 1960.

Murray, Kenneth James. *Angel Barrios: The Guitar, Granada and Manuel de Falla,* Master's thesis, University of Melbourne, 1994.

———. *Manuel de Falla's "Homenajes."* Bach. Mus. Honors' Degree, University of Melbourne, 1990.

Nommick, Yvan. *Manuel de Falla: œuvre et évolution du langage musical,* Ph.D. Université de Paris-Sorbonne (Paris IV), 3 vol., 1998–1999.

Ragsdale, Dana. *The revival of the harpsichord in the twentieth century with particular attention to the harpsichord concerti of Manuel de Falla and Francis Poulenc.* D.M.A., U. of Cincinnati, 1990.

Seitz, Elizabeth Ann. *Manuel de Falla's years in Paris, 1907–1914.* Ph.D. dissertation, University of Boston, 1995.

Tosi, Daniel. *Etude Analytique de la Musique contemporaine espagnola après 1939: aspects sociales et politiques, historiques et esthetiques, et compositionnel* Ph.D., Université de Sorbonne-Paris, 1980.

———. *Retour aux sources et ouverture sur le monde contemporain dans les dernieres oeuvres de Manuel de Falla.* Maitrise d'Education Musicale, Université de Sorbonne-Paris, 1977.

Urchueguía Scholzel, María Cristina. *Lieder Manuel de Fallas.* Magister, Universitat-Würzburg, 1995.

Vázquez de Castro, Isabel. *Le théatre de marionnettes populaire et son influence sur le renouveau scénique au cours du XXème siècle en Espagne,* Université de Paris IV, Sorbonne, 1996.

Weber, Eckhard. *Studien zu den buhnen Werken der mittleren Schaffensperiode von Manuel de Falla.* Magister, University of Köln, 1992.

Index

Abbas, 'Abdu'l-Bahá, 147
Adam, Jean Louis, 165
Adiny-Milliet, Ada, 46–47, 357, 360
Aeolian Hall (London), 389
Aguilar, Paco, 130, 340
Aguirre, Raquel, 127
Agustín Florencio, Francisco, 317
Alarcón, Pedro Antonio de, 66, 117, 301, 303, 372
Albéniz, Enriqueta, 116
Albéniz, Isaac, xxxvi, l, 25, 28, 42–47, 64, 76, 81, 101, 116, 121n24, 247, 249, 266, 305, 308, 358, 385
Alberti, Rafael, 130
Alcalá Zamora, Niceto, 114
Alfonso X (The Wise), 5, 128, 330
Alfonso XII, 109, 124n86
Alfonso XIII, 13, 124n86
Alhambra Theatre. *See* Teatro Alhambra
Almagro de San Martín, Melchor, 50
Altermann, Jean-Pierre, 49–50
Alvar, Louise, 104–5
Álvarez Quintero, Serafin and Joaquín, 48, 60–61, 220

Alzamora, Vicente, 116
Amorós y Blancas, 372
Andersen, Ludwig, 357
Andolfi-Eschig, Otello, 357
Ángeles Ortiz, Manuel, 95, 101, 105, 387
Anglés, Higinio, 319
Anonimous, 308, 319
Ansermet, Ernest, 78, 277n92, 374
Antigua Abadía de San Telmo (San Sebastián), 396
Apolo, Anselmo, 338
Arcas, Julián, 225, 309
Archivo Manuel de Falla (AMF), xxvii, 10, 133, 269–70, 306–7, 339, 341, 348, 350–52, 364, 366–68, 373, 375–76, 379, 384–85, 390, 394–95, 397–99, 403, 406–9
Areán, Pedro, 367
Arévalo, Octavio, 357
"La Argentina" (Antonia Mercé), 63, 118, 370
Associació de Música "Da Camera." *See* Palau de la Música Catalana
Ateneo (Madrid), 361

453

Cabezón, Juan de, 132
Cadadesus, Francis, 269
Cage, John, 177
Calderón de la Barca, Pedro, 22, 49,
  108, 301–2, 393–95
Calderón, D. S. Estébanez, 303
Calvocoressi, Michel-Dimitri, 43,
  48, 252, 272n26
Cambó, Francisco, 128–29
Campo, Conrado del, 109, 249
Campodónico, Luis, 49, 74, 113
Cantarero, Mariola, 357
Cante jondo Competition, 96–98,
  102, 189. *See also* Falla y
  Matheu, Manuel de, Albéniz and,
  Cante jondo Competition
Canteloube, Josef, 269
Canto, Rosa, 62
Capella Clásica de Mallorca, 397
Caplet, André, 272n26
Carazo, Raúl, 96
Carissimi, Giacomo, 310
Carles, Vassià, 106
Carra, Manuel, 384
Carré, Albert, 48, 52
Carré, Marguerite, 52
Carreira, Xoan Manuel, 113
Carreño, Teresa, 180
Casadesus family, 51
Casadesus, Henri, 216
Casadesus, Marie-Louise, 95, 102,
  382, 387
Casals, Enric, 106
Casals, Pablo, 21, 44, 106, 178
Casa-Museo, 13, 95
Casella, Alfredo, 51, 178, 249, 254,
  257, 259–60, 268–69,
  280n112–15, 320
Castelnuovo-Tedesco, Mario, 110,
  249, 252, 260, 268–69, 281n126
Castro, Cristóbal de, 30, 332, 348
Castro, Juan José, 127–28, 403
Castro, Sergio de, 111, 130–36, 400
Cerdá, Julia, 372

Cerón, Miguel, 120
Cerone de Bergamo, R. D. Pedro,
  318
Cervantes, María, 34
Cervantes, Miguel de, 53, 101, 209,
  212, 215, 227–28, 301, 386
Chabrier, Emmanuel, 121n24
Chamorro, Ángeles, 341, 343
Chapí y Lorente, Ruperto, 20, 23
Chaplin, Charlie, 117
Charpentier, Gustave, 268–69
Chase, Gilbert, 66, 320
Chateaubriand, François René, 210
Chávez, Carlos, 110
Chester, J. W. (Chester publishers),
  67, 77, 334, 339–40, 343, 344,
  349, 362, 367–68, 370, 372–74,
  377, 379, 382–83, 387–88, 390,
  394
Chinchilla Puertas, Concepción
  ("Concha"), xxx, 238n1, 325n35
Chopin, Frédéric, 7, 20–21, 34, 41,
  80–84, 118, 133, 165, 168,
  171–73, 184–85, 217, 310, 329,
  332–33, 338, 376, 393, 397
Chottin, A., 310
Christ, Jesus, 151–52, 155–56
Christoforidis, Michael, xxix, xxx,
  xxxi, 96, 209, 298, 352, 361
Chueca, Ruperto, 25
Clementi, Muzio, 165, 169–70
Club des Apaches, 43, 50–51,
  251–52, 254, 272n26, 273n33
Cobos, Jesús López, 412
Cocteau, Jean, 216
Colacelli, Donato Oscar, 130, 178
Collaer, Paul, 269
Collet, Henri, 49, 65, 81, 216, 256,
  269, 271n8, 311, 320
Columbus, Christopher (Colón), 3,
  110–11, 190, 260–61, 301,
  410–11
Collins, Christopher Guy, xxix, xxx,
  xxxi, 201, 204, 204n1, 247–84

About the Author and Contributors

Nancy Lee Harper is associate professor of piano with aggregation at the Universidade de Aveiro, Portugal. Her interest in Manuel de Falla grew from her doctoral studies of the piano sonatas of Rodolfo Halffter. Her first book, *Manuel de Falla: A Bio-Bibliography,* was published by Greenwood Press in 1998 and documents the holdings of the Archivo Manuel de Falla in Granada, Spain.

Michael Christoforidis, lecturer in musicology at the University of Melbourne, completed his Ph.D. on aspects of Manuel de Falla's neoclassical music. He has published extensively on Falla and Spanish music and is currently writing a monograph on Hispanic music in belle-époque Paris. Other research interests range from 16th-century polyphonic instrumental music to Romantic ballet and the music of Igor Stravinsky.

Chris Collins lectures in music at the University of Wales, Bangor. His research interests focus on early twentieth-century music in general, and the life and work of Manuel de Falla in particular. His current projects include a new English-language study of Falla and a collected edition of that composer's correspondence with his European contemporaries.

Louis Jambou, musicologist and professor emeritus at the Sorbonne in Paris, is a specialist in hispanic studies of the 16th century. His important work in the area of Manuel de Falla has resulted in several publications, most noteworthy of which is *Manuel de Falla, Latinité et Universalité* (Sorbonne, 1999).